WITHDRAWN

FOUNDATIONS OF EDUCATION
Social and Cultural Perspectives

Maurice P. Hunt
California State University, Fresno

HOLT, RINEHART AND WINSTON
New York Chicago San Francisco Atlanta
Dallas Montreal Toronto London Sydney

Library of Congress Cataloging in Publication Data

Hunt, Maurice P.
    Foundations of education

    Includes bibliographical references and indexes.
    1. Educational sociology—United States. 2. Edu-
cation—United States—1965-   I. Title.
LC191.H76   370.19'3'0973   74-30091
ISBN: 0-03-085246-3

5 6 7 8   038   9 8 7 6 5 4 3 2 1

To FRANCES ANN GUERARD

friend and partner

CONTENTS

PREFACE

This book is intended as a basic textbook for college and university upperclassmen and graduate students in courses in Cultural Foundations of Education, Social Foundations of Education, Sociological Foundations of Education, Educational Sociology, School and Society, and the like. Although the author expects this book to be most useful in these required courses, he also hopes that it will present enough challenges and include enough fundamental background materials to be useful to students in graduate degree programs and to in-service teachers.

How does one justify a new textbook in a field where books already reflect a rather wide range of philosophical premises and content emphases? The author believes that the present volume differs significantly in many ways from others now in print and fundamentally in several ways from any texts in cultural/social foundations of education. This Preface will suggest some of these differences; the Prologue will elaborate on what the author is trying to achieve.

The writer feels that most books in cultural/social foundations published during the past decade or so tend to focus on the "sociology of the school" and its immediate community, with little attention given to analysis of our national culture in its international setting. In contrast, the present volume focuses on certain educational problems which the writer sees as so closely linked to broad national and international problems that they cannot be understood unless one takes into consideration the total cultural milieu. Hence, we have drawn heavily from scholarly interpretations of a number of critical national social issues which—unless resolved in a rational manner—could lead to the destruction of a viable human culture and conceivably even to the end of life on earth. Such an approach necessarily involves including considerable content from the various social sciences, social and clinical psychology, human biology, and other disciplines regarded by some as outside the domain of professional education. *From the writer's view, this interdisciplinary approach seems inescapable if one is even to begin to understand the problems of education.*

This leads us into the distinction between macro- and microanalysis. We interpret macroanalysis as an attempt to see situations in their totality —a way of viewing things for which we have used such terms as "field," "system," "Gestalt," and "homeostasis." Microanalysis, in contrast, concentrates on studying parts, elements, small units. Although there is a tendency to see macro- and microanalysis as incompatible—or at least leading to different ends—the author does not regard the two as dichotomous. Through macroanalysis one moves to a consideration of smaller units which can be understood only in conjunction with the larger picture. The most significant datum for study, as this author sees it, is usually the interaction of single units with the whole (or the linkages beween the whole and its parts). For example, the overall functioning of the economy is an important macroconcept. The economy of a school district is a microconcept which we need to understand; but we cannot understand the school district economy unless we see how it links with the national— and international—economy. The same may be said for power systems, systems of jurisprudence, systems for resolving racial and ethnic tensions, ecological systems, and other systems.

The content of the present book will work back and forth, in reciprocal fashion, between broad aspects of the international, national, and regional scenes, and local community scenes, with the focal point being, of course, the role and functioning of the schools. If readers of this Preface wonder whether this is too formidable a task, the only answer we can give is that it certainly is not easy, is susceptible to error, but *needs desperately to be done.*

What we have said so far makes this volume sound as if it would be impossibly complex, at least for student reading. However, the author has organized content around a limited number of themes which will be stated as clearly as possible at the outset and repeated on occasion for emphasis. When readers understand these themes, the content of the book should be easy to grasp.

The foremost theme of the book is a consideration of how education, particularly schooling (but also other educational agencies), could play a decisive role in keeping democracy as it now exists alive in an advanced industrial culture. It is the author's studied opinion that since World War II, and especially in the 1970s, the democratic strands in American civilization are under the most severe threat since the founding of the nation; and that what occurs during the next decade or two is likely to determine decisively whether the United States will edge toward cultural chaos lasting for an indeterminate period, toward a Fascist or para-Fascist dictatorship, or toward a fuller democracy.

In view of education's tendency to mirror the status quo (or even some earlier status quo), to hope that changes in education could have a crucial effect on which way our culture moves may seem like foolishly blind optimism. Nevertheless, the writer sees no other arena which offers as much potential for instigating democratic cultural change. Suggesting how that potential might be put to work in the 1970s is the major purpose of the book. This is, of course, a "social reconstructionist" view of education, but one of more sophistication and contemporary practicality than earlier books with a reconstructionist theme.

Secondary themes, all of which are related directly or indirectly to the survival of democracy, include:

1. *The cultural revolution* (which virtually all students of culture agree exists but the precise nature of which few cultural analysts agree on). Symptoms of a profound change in patterns of belief can be seen throughout the culture, but perhaps most clearly among the culture's most revealing microcosms—the colleges and universities and to a somewhat lesser degree the public schools.

2. *Cultural change, particularly as related to the cultural revolution.* Change in the United States has been largely directionless, a matter of drift and accident. It occurs at accelerating speed and generates deeply problematic conflict. A complex industrial civilization, spinning out of orbit, leads to cognitive dissonance, alienation, anomie, and, for many, irreversible psychological breakdown. The idea of "culture shock" fits here, but we are highly skeptical that the psychological impact of change can be eased through measures as simple as Alvin Toffler suggests.*

3. *Conflicting ideological patterns, particularly as related to cultural revolution and uncontrolled change.* Although it may be assumed that all cultures are fundamentally ideological, it is not necessarily assumed that the ideology of a culture may often be unrelated to or contradict the hard

---

*Alvin Toffler, *Future Shock*. New York, Random House (Bantam Book ed.), 1970.

facts of unfolding events. It seems that in the United States the ideology which individuals and institutions proclaim as true is, more often than not, either unrelated to the nitty-gritty of life as it is lived, or, even worse, often almost wholly inconsistent with the existential state of affairs. Such a situation, if carried on for long, can only produce madness and cultural dissolution.

4. *Changes in both the methodology and structure of the scholarly disciplines which nurture education.* Such areas of inquiry as sociology, social and clinical psychology, and philosophy appear to show increased internal polarization each year. This polarization can be variously described as liberal versus conservative, humanistic versus mechanistic, democratic versus authoritarian, dynamic versus static, modern versus old-fashioned. When the experts cannot agree among themselves, those who depend on the authority of supposedly expert knowledge find themselves adrift in confusion.

5. *Polarization in education itself, in such areas as governance, curriculum, and teaching strategy.* As of the 1970s, at least a large part of this polarization appears to stem from the clash between educators committed to some version of humanism (who are themselves split between the romantic humanism of a John Holt and the scientific humanism of a Jerome Bruner) and educators who are committed to mechanistic/totalitarian values (for example, B. F. Skinner's environmentally determined totalitarian utopia).

Readers may understand the book better if they know the evolution of the author's present viewpoint—reared a Christian idealist; as a late teenager converted to a stubborn Comtist positivism; as a university student veered sharply toward a Deweyian scientific-humanism; as an adult, developed a major commitment to a liberal-democratic mode of human relations and a relativistic world view reflecting the convergence of the Peirce-James-Dewey philosophical tradition and a Lewinian cognitive-field psychology, upon which is superimposed a certain warmth toward existentialism.

Perhaps of more consequence to readers is the author's commitment to candor. This book will be as honest as the author can make it. It is a book intended to stimulate fresh thinking, to encourage the making and testing of challenging hypotheses which will carry students far beyond this beginning. As such, it is bound to be controversial—as probably all textbooks should be. As what one needs to know increases at an exponential rate, while what one learns can hardly keep pace with that rate, the book raises many more questions than it answers.

The book begins with a fairly extensive Prologue which we feel is necessary to help students understand the book's rationale, its themes, and some of its more frequently used concepts. Part I is designed to help students see how the cultural foundations of education, and their supportive scholarly disciplines, can shed light on matters of prime importance to teachers. Chapter 1 tries to demonstrate how the culture concept can be used in the analysis of cultural change; its primary emphasis is on understanding the morphology of cultural revolution. Chapter 2 addresses itself to the conservative-liberal polarization of our culture and the kinds of educational problems that result from such polarization. Chapter 3 reviews a number of the more critical dissonances in American culture and discusses the alienation and anomie that stem from them. Chapter 4 is about the youth movement of the 1960s and its implications for the 1970s and beyond.

Part II contains eight chapters on cultural areas of special concern to teachers. In each chapter ideological patterns, both old and new, are described; this is followed by the testing with factual data of a selected controversial hypothesis suggested by the ideological complex. This marshaling of evidence around hypotheses provides readers with in-depth cultural analyses in areas of major conflict and also suggests how teachers might best pursue cultural studies in the classroom. The final section of each of these chapters develops the implications of the prior cultural analysis for education at the classroom level. These chapters combine macro- and microanalysis—they first look at the cultural Gestalt, then try to interpret as part of the Gestalt a number of educational situations and problems which in the past have too often been approached atomistically as if they were primarily of local origin.

Part III is less a matter of investigating what *is* than deducing what *should be*—provided the analyses of Parts I and II are essentially correct. The first chapter of this section, Chapter 13, discusses what the long-range goals of education should be, given our present cultural trends and dilemmas, if schools are to serve democratic purposes. The following chapter questions how education would need to be controlled if it were to serve the proposed long-range goals. The Epilogue suggests changes in curriculum and teaching strategies that must occur if we are to have any hope that the postulated goals are to be met.

There is nothing sacred about the organization of the book, except that to a considerable degree each chapter builds on what has come before. For example, the concepts in the later chapters might be unclear without having read what precedes them, particularly the Prologue and Chapter 1. With the Prologue and Chapter 1 firmly in mind, other chapters can be read out of order if readers so wish; if, in so doing, they encounter new concepts it should be simple to turn back to where they are first introduced by using the index.

The writer would never have attempted this project had it not been for the full-time assistance of Frances Ann Guerard, whose skills in research, writing, editing, assisting others to think straight, and simple moral encouragement made the book possible. Ms. Guerard, in addition, wrote one of the key chapters—Chapter 11 on "Sexism and Education." In a very real sense, Ms. Guerard must be considered a co-author.

We are greatly indebted to the several hundred California State University students enrolled in my course, "Cultural Foundations of Education," who wrote helpful critical reviews of the manuscript's mimeographed version over its three-year period of classroom testing. Several graduate students gave major help in researching specific materials: Jackie Estes, Marilyn Osganian, Franca Read, and Kathy Christensen.

I am most grateful for the secretarial assistance of Linda Smith.

The writer will always be grateful to John Tugman, Education Editor of Holt, Rinehart and Winston, whose moral support and patient urging kept the writing moving. Nor can we neglect Mr. Tugman's assistant, Heidi Leibowitz, whose friendly notes of encouragement added to the warm relationship that evolved between author and publisher.

Dr. R. Freeman Butts, William F. Russell Professor in the Foundations of Education at Teachers College, Columbia University, was in on the project from the beginning; his reactions to early specimen chapters were of immeasurable help in suggesting a way to organize the book. Dr. Butts read the final overly long manuscript with great care, and his detailed critique and suggestions for cutting made this a much better book than would otherwise have been written. In addition to Professor Butts, Professors W. Eugene Hedley, John M. Rich, Gerald Unks, and Kalil Gezi read parts or all of the manuscript and also made perceptive suggestions for improving and cutting.

A book of this complexity and magnitude is bound to contain errors of fact and interpretation, and the author invites readers to call his attention to any they find. The author takes full responsibility for weaknesses that remain, and reiterates that, however the book is judged, it is much the better for the help given by the persons noted above.

M.P.H.

Fresno, California
December 1974

Schools are no better than the social, philosophical, and psychological foundations upon which they rest. *(Copyright ©
George Ballis, all rights reserved)*

Prologue

WHY COURSES IN CULTURAL FOUNDATIONS OF EDUCATION?

The purpose of this Prologue is to elaborate the rationale of courses in cultural/social foundations of education as the author sees their purpose in the 1970s; and, in addition, to explain the particular approach of this book. The Prologue is intended for professors considering this book for use in their classes and for students.

Students should give careful attention to the entire Prologue. Otherwise they are likely to find some novel aspects of the book confusing. The Prologue makes a start in defining some of the more abstract concepts used regularly in the book—concepts which may have familiar labels but which are used in a special sense in this volume.

THE NEED FOR CULTURAL UNDERSTANDING

Teacher education curriculums across the country usually include at least one required course that draws heavily from

1

interdisciplinary social science and supporting subjects and relates subject matter to problems of education. Whether a course is called Cultural Foundations of Education, Social Foundations of Education, Educational Sociology, Educational Anthropology, School and Society, or some similar name, the underlying purpose is the same: to acquaint prospective teachers with the culture and/or society in which they live (the words "culture" and "society" usually do not carry the same meaning, but to avoid stylistic monotony writers sometimes use the words interchangeably); and further, to help students see how cultural or societal understanding bears on educational matters. Some commonly stated reasons for such courses are discussed in the following sections.

Cultural Understanding versus Fragmented Knowledge

Freshmen and sophomore college and university students are virtually always required to take a specified number of units of "general education" (also known as liberal arts education). These programs include courses in the natural and social sciences, literature, psychology, and philosophy, among others. In some colleges and universities the general education requirements form a more-or-less cohesive pattern; the courses are linked together to provide students with a broad but unified picture of the total culture. Students attending such schools are lucky. A majority of schools, in spite of good intentions, do not integrate their general education requirements so that students emerge with some unified understanding of the culture. Rather, students reach their junior or senior years with their knowledge of the culture being fragmented, atomistic, and not of practical use.

This suggests one important purpose of including in the sequence of education courses one or more offerings which review previous learning about the culture, fill in gaps, and pull it all into a sensible pattern. When viewed this way, courses in cultural/social foundations of education are an extension of the freshman and sophomore general education programs. It can be argued that all college and university students should be required to take some kind of "capstone" course or sequence to help them make sense out of their fragmented knowledge of culture. But, unfortunately, capstone courses are not commonly required. Schools of Education try to compensate for this curriculum lack by offering such courses for prospective teachers.

Cultural Understanding and Long-Range Goals of Education

Another reason for requiring education majors to take capstone courses in cultural understanding, even though majors in other fields may not have such a requirement, is the general belief that teachers, more than any others, need to understand the central issues and problems of their culture. It may not always be true that prospective teachers need this kind of terminal education more than other students, but, because of the way we define the roles that teachers play, we cannot afford to let teachers remain confused about the world in which they live.

One commonly accepted role for teachers is to transmit to students that part of our cultural heritage pertinent to the present. We designate schools with the task of perpetuating that which is useful in the ongoing stream of culture. This conservator role of teachers is quite necessary if culture is to have continuity from one generation to the next.

Another role commonly regarded as essential for teachers is to help their students see how the culture can be improved—what its more crucial inadequacies are and what proposals have been made for remedying them. To perform this role teachers need to be intelligent social critics; but in addition to being critics, they need to know the most promising ideas students of culture have developed for social change. This progressive role of teachers is at least as important, if not more so, as the conservator role. To play either role a teacher must be sophisticated about the culture.

Cultural Understanding and Specific Objectives of Education

Teachers should all be social philosophers and in the final analysis be even more concerned with broad, long-range goals of education than with specific course objectives. (We will defend this assertion later in the book.) But teachers do teach in delineated subject matter areas and need the guidance of more specific, shorter-range objectives to make decisions about course content and appropriate teaching strategies. Mathematics teachers have in mind concrete achievements in math for their students, just as physical education teachers have in mind concrete achievements in their field.

Influenced by the movement known at the public school level as Performance Based Education (PBE) and at the college/university school of education level as Performance (or Competency) Based Teacher Education (PBTE), many teachers are under the illusion that they can make lists of objectives in their specialties without concern for basic cultural tendencies and issues. They are, in fact, often compelled by state law or by school district policy to develop lists of specific "behavioral" objectives which do not necessarily bear any relation to a broader cultural context.

Specific objectives developed without relation to the whole cultural context are self-defeating. Specific subject matter objectives are either means for achieving long-range and more philosophical goals, or they are busy work. Specific objectives are either *instrumental* to some larger achievement, or they are not worth bothering with. Otherwise, how do teachers determine if their specific goals have any value to individual students or to the cultural good?

The writer submits that specific subject-oriented objectives are meaningless unless developed within the framework of a long-range, pervasive social philosophy. Unless a mathematics teacher understands the function of mathematics as instrumental to some important goal of the total culture he has lost sight of achievement in mathematics as a means to a larger end. What kind of mathematics makes sense, given the social and technical demands of the culture? How does a teacher justify teaching Euclidean geometry if such knowledge has a bearing on neither the health of the culture nor the technical know-how needed for personal functioning in the culture of today and tomorrow?

Likewise, how can a history teacher justify using content about our nation's wars unless such information is clearly instrumental to understanding war as a social phenomenon, as an activity which would rarely occur unless it performed a positive function for those who lead—or rule—the nation? In the case of either mathematics or war a teacher can select the kinds of knowledge he wants to confront students with, or expects them to think about, only if he sees where such knowledge fits within the cultural whole.

As we will show later, much education in this country is no longer acceptable to students because they find it *not relevant* to anything in their perceived world. We have produced a new generation of writers who tell us that our schools are failures. They offer as evidence for their arguments that curriculums have little bearing on the deeper problems of the culture. The thousands of behavioral objectives and lesson plans give students few clues as to how the nation will resolve its major issues. Schooling in specific subject matters can be made relevant, but only by teachers who know the culture far better than most teachers do.

Cultural Understanding and Self-Identity (Identity Crisis)

Although we plan to treat the subject of the "identity crisis" of the present era much more fully later, it must be sketched in at this point. A person has a sense of self-identity, or awareness of self, if he has comparatively stable guiding values and understands what these values are. A person who is valueless, that is, lacking in goals, is a person adrift. He is incapable of evaluating his thoughts and actions in relation to any guiding principle and therefore lacks "selfhood." Psychologists and social scientists refer to this mental state as *anomie*, and a person so afflicted as *anomic*. An anomic person is incapable of behaving rationally; in fact, anomie is but another name for a serious kind of psychosis.

It appears that some amount of anomie is common in most, if not all, advanced industrialized cultures, and as such is an inherent part of such cultures. Such an assertion should be qualified, however, because urban industrial civilization may be possible in forms other than those we now have.

It also seems clear that there is a close relationship between how a person sees his culture and whether he is likely to be anomic. If a person can see only fragments of culture—fragments that he cannot put together in sensible fashion—he tends to become fragmented inside himself. The chief candidates for anomie are those persons who cannot perceive any meaningful pattern in their own or any other culture.

A culture might be so fragmented, so disintegrated, that a sane person would not be able to perceive it as a meaningful totality; but a sane person living in such a culture is capable of conceptualizing cultural models which are at least theoretically viable. Simply having in mind a cultural model that makes sense gives a person something to strive for and hence a basis for valuing. It may be—as some social observers now think—that American culture is too fragmented, contradictory, and directionless to be regarded a "sane culture."

Cultural states can also be referred to as anomic; and anomic cultures produce anomic people. People can save themselves from personal anomie in such a culture only by rejecting the culture and tying their own values to some cultural alternative. A person may have to become a revolutionary to save his sanity.

Although we do not suggest that simply knowing more about American culture will help keep teachers and their charges in good mental health, we do suggest that cultural study *which includes the study of cultural alternatives* may be very helpful both in preserving the sanity of teachers and in helping them build sanity into their students. An understanding of alternatives gives an individual a greater feeling of personal power, a greater feeling that he can do something constructive with his life, than a lack of such understanding. We presume that many persons who feel an identity crisis would be helped if they had clear-cut goals which, if not achievable in the culture in which they feel trapped, might be achievable in an alternative culture.

Many contemporary critics of public education charge that our schools now promote identity crises among their students. Schools do this, they claim, because their curriculums do not provide students with more than a glimpse at a few fragments of culture. If this is the case, and there is pretty substantial evidence that it is, then such a curriculum defect seems traceable largely to teachers who themselves lack any integrated picture of culture. So we have here a very cogent reason for requiring teachers to be versed in cultural knowledge.

Cultural Knowledge and Intelligent Citizenship

During the past decade, social scientists, psychologists, practiced social observers, and social philosophers have produced a massive "literature of pessimism." Although this viewpoint has been expressed since man's earliest writings, it appears that only in this century—primarily since World War II—have writers other than theologians, artists, and philosophers produced such a torrent of gloom. Our most eminent scholars more often than not take a generally pessimistic stance concerning man's future. This pessimism in contemporary social science, psychology, and philosophy points to a great variety of social problems, with opinions ranging from the conviction that man has already passed the "point of no return" in humanity's struggle for survival to the milder conviction that the human situation is likely to get much worse before it gets better.

What concerns us here is only one idea in this broad picture of Homo sapiens having created problems he has not yet determined how to solve—*the idea of maintaining democratic means of decision making.* Where democracy has been seriously practiced in the literate world, from the period of Athenian democracy to the present, it has always come under attack. In the United States we have had our dedicated anti-democrats— authoritarians of various shades of belief—who have maintained a steady attack against the ideas and practice of democracy. Even so, throughout our history, democracy has been a goal of a very significant proportion of the population. Sincere and understanding democrats have undoubtedly existed in all social strata, among most or all occupational, ethnic, and other groupings in both Republican and Democratic political parties. Commitment to the values and goals of democratic ideals has been particularly evident within the community of scholars. Perhaps we associate democratic commitment most with this group because it has been so articulate in explaining and promoting democratic ideals.

This same scholarly community, primarily university professors, is now flooding the country with writing which takes a highly pessimistic view of the future of democracy in this country. Some proclaim democracy already dead; they raise questions about whether Americans generally are bored with democracy and whether they have ever understood the ramifications of democracy well enough to be committed to it in the first place. They look to the schools to remedy our flagging interest in democracy—if indeed it is flagging. Also, scholars interested in the role of education as related to democracy tend to blame the schools for not educating people to be committed to and participate in democratic decision making.

This brings us to our central point: No citizen can know what cultural tendencies to be for or what to be against if he does not understand both what a democratic culture is and the particular ways in which our culture is either democratic or not. For a teacher to encourage students to study democracy intelligently, the teacher must understand the culture. Therefore, if democracy is to have any chance of survival in the United States, we cannot afford the luxury of culturally unsophisticated school teachers. To most believers in democracy, this alone would be sufficient reason for demanding that no one be permitted to teach until he is well saturated with knowledge about the culture, and also sufficient reason for requiring prospective teachers to take at least one democraticallly oriented course in cultural/social foundations of education.

THE CONCEPT OF DEMOCRACY

After all that has been written about democracy, it may seem trite to offer another definition. However, our experience has been that most college students, even seniors, have difficulty defining democracy concretely enough to provide a usable goal; further, they tend to define democracy in ways more appropriate for life two centuries ago than today.

A General Definition of Democracy

Democracy may be best thought of as a method by which people relate and by which they make group decisions. It seems more useful to think of democracy as a method, or process, rather than as a set of institutional structures; institutions often give the appearance of being democratic, although actually they can be no more democratic than permitted by the values of those in charge. For example, it seems democratic to devise institutions which let people vote, but if the elections are rigged, or if key information is kept from the electorate, voting ceases to be a democratic practice.

As we will use democracy, it refers to a process of shared decision making whenever two or more people, seeking similar goals, have decisions to make. Democratic decision making requires that all parties concerned have full access to all pertinent available information, that they have as much opportunity as they want to discuss the information, that they be sufficiently competent to understand the implications of their knowledge, and that, once a decision is made, the surrounding social milieu will permit its implementation.

We expect leadership to arise within a democratic group. But a democratic leader tries to educate the members of the group in the art and science of leadership so that his post is always dispensable—someone else in the group will always be available to assert leadership. The idea of democratic group leadership becomes more clear when we compare a democratic group with laissez-faire and authoritarian groups. Laissez-faire groups are leaderless; each member is on his own and, in the thinking of proponents of laissez-faire, each member by acting in his own self-interest promotes the self-interest of all. An authoritarian group is commanded by a single leader or governing clique; the leader or leaders have full authority to make decisions for the group and they are only displaced through death or resignation.

Ever since John Dewey proposed early in this century that democratic processes be introduced into schools (an idea then and still radical) teachers have often confused laissez-faire with democratic processes. Under the name of democracy, teachers have experimented with turning students loose to do as they please. The Summerhill idea is essentially laissez-faire, not democracy. If students prove capable of becoming a self-governing group, laissez-faire may turn into a kind of student grass-roots democracy; otherwise, laissez-faire is but another word for anarchy. The introduction of anarchy into schools in the guise of democracy has given democracy in education a bad name. This is unfortunate because it has been demonstrated that democracy can be made to work in school situations if it is seriously tried.

Democracy as a Balance of Freedoms and Restraints

Many persons have naively equated democracy with freedom in the laissez-faire sense mentioned above, and as a result have concluded that democracy is impractical in such institutional settings as corporations, the military, and schools. Such people are still "hung up" on the conception of democracy held by many of the founding fathers of this nation, and on the conception of freedom presented in Adam Smith's *Wealth of Nations* —fittingly published in 1776. At that time, people could not foresee that in a highly industrialized, urbanized, interdependent culture freedom would be impossible unless accompanied by restraints. A large measure of personal freedom is possible in a frontier society, but the same freedoms which are tolerable in a nonmechanized, noncrowded rural or frontier setting are clearly impossible in the world today. Rampant freedom would permit too many persons to restrict or abolish the freedoms of those in a less strong or favored position.

Because, in an advanced industrial society, the number of restraints required may outnumber the freedoms permitted, *the chief aim of the democratic process becomes that of determining which freedoms and which restraints will prevail.* This issue does in fact appear to be the one most frequently debated at national, state, and local levels. Should the Federal Government impose effective wage and price controls so that everyone will be free from unbearable inflation? Should states impose stricter antipollution laws so their residents will be more free from pollution-caused illnesses? Should a city install more stoplights at dangerous intersections so people will feel more free from accidents? Note that when we raise questions like these, the idea of "freedom from" becomes as important as the idea of "freedom to."

Although we have stressed that the method or process of democracy is more important than its supporting institutional structures, we cannot ignore these structures. The institutions of democracy must be so designed that they facilitate the use of the democratic process. For example, it seems to this writer that of all the institutional arrangements in modern society, the schools first of all should promote the use of democratic decision making. For this to be possible it seems that considerable restructuring appears necessary (this is the main topic of Part III of this book).

The Meaning of Freedom

The question of freedom of choice (or, to use a rather old-fashioned expression which to some persons is not quite the same, "free will") is integral to any discussion of democracy. It can be argued most convincingly that there is no point even trying to discuss objectives without somehow defensibly resolving the issue of how much freedom of decision humans should have.

Freedom: An Extreme View

This writer feels that Rollo May does as well as anyone in developing a position which shows individuals having a significant amount of freedom of choice while at the same time conceding the powerful role of environmental pressures.[1] May points out that we can easily err in assuming that human beings have more freedom of choice than they do. He is talking about psychotherapy, but for our purposes readers can substitute the word, teaching, for therapy. People who assume complete freedom of choice help no one, for as May says, ". . . the 'full freedom' assumption we are describing actually separates and alienates the person from his world, removes whatever structure he had to act within or against, and leaves him with no guideposts in a lonely, worldless existence." Further, therapists (teachers) who pretend to be giving their subjects complete freedom to choose as they wish are "subtly dishonest." They smuggle in their own values, as any reasonably perceptive patient (student) soon finds out.

[1] Rollo May, *Psychology and the Human Dilemma*. New York: Van Nostrand Reinhold Company, 1967. The following discussion is adapted from this book, especially Chapter 12.

Determinism: An Extreme View

May then points out that an opposite extreme view exists in which therapists rely heavily on cultural standards as a model for the reformation of deviance—with even small amounts of deviance seen as unhealthy. May refers to this as "distrust of freedom" and the "new puritanism." Within psychiatry and psychology, May suggests, the distrust of freedom leads to an emphasis on "behavior control." [The currently "in" term is "behavior modification."] He names Carl Rogers as a leading figure in the "pro-freedom" group and B. F. Skinner as the leading figure in the "anti-freedom" group. There have been exchanges between these men, in which Rogers has referred to Skinner as a "rigid determinist." Skinner's standard rebuttal to people like Rogers, even to interactionists who take a third position, is that they are not unscientific only in their approach to the study of human beings but that their social philosophy in the long run could lead only to anarchy instead of a well-controlled society.

May inescapably gets into the question of what agency, under the view of environmental determinism, does the controlling—or, to use a Skinnerian term, the "operant conditioning." It makes no sense to say that one part of an individual controls the others, so the question resolves itself to "outer forces." It hardly makes sense, says May, to state that "society" controls individuals because society consists of individuals. Like numerous professional critics of Skinner, May feels the proponents of "anti-freedom" really have in mind that individuals be controlled by a coalition of clinical psychologists and psychotherapists who would decide how people *should* behave, and they would be conditioned to so behave by using behavior modification techniques. (Readers should here, also, translate psychologists and psychoanalysts into educationists—school administrators, consultants, counselors, and teachers.)

The Meaning of Free Choice in Today's World

We come now to the question of what freedom, freedom of choice, or freedom of decision making, can mean in the context of contemporary industrialism or post-industrialism. There is, without doubt, much determinism in modern cultures, that is, innumerable pressures on individuals to yield to outside demands. But, as May says,

> *Freedom* is . . . not the opposite of determinism. Freedom is the individual's capacity to *know that he is the determined one,* to pause between stimulus and response and thus to throw his weight, however slight it may be, on the side of one particular response among several possible ones.

What enables an individual to know how he or she is determined, to know the need for establishing an interval for thought between stimulus and response, and to decide in which way to throw his or her influence, however much or little that influence may be? May uses a term coined by Paul Tillich, the *"centered self."* One achieves a centered self "through methods relying on *internal consistency* in the individual and *significant patterning* in contrast to fragmentation."[2] If we understand the necessity of viewing the human self as holistic, and as functioning maximally only when it is aware of inconsistency and taking steps to confront it, we have the first point in May's development of the meaning of freedom.

His second point is the need for *responsibility*, which he defines in terms of its root meaning, "responding," or "response to." A person is behaving responsibly toward the deterministic pressures of environment when he asserts himself against the environment, when he fights back— provided, of course, that he does not like the environment. May, who often uses Hegelian concepts, refers to this as a *dialectical* relationship between the individual and his world.

In any transactional or dialectical relationship, freedom on both sides is limited. Individual freedom is always limited by environmental pressures; but environmental pressures in turn are always limited by the response to them of individual selves. This is all that freedom can ever mean, and it is all that determinism can ever mean. But it is enough to refer to "free choice—within limits."

Democracy and Relativism

Democracy in a modern context cannot be understood without a grasp of the concept of relativism. The idea of relativism has often come under attack by those who lean toward authoritarianism. It is charged that relativism, when applied to human thought generally, leads to nihilism—an absence of guiding values, or anomie as defined above. This argument is based upon a mistaken conception of relativism. That relativism can be a positive concept is well demonstrated by Bigge's "positive relativism."[3] His view assumes the need for "fixed points of reference"—as a commitment to democratic values. Such points of reference may be called "relatively absolute." They provide bases for asserting and testing hypotheses, and developing "working truths" to guide human endeavor.

Further, positive relativism (contrasted with the pessimism of *nihilism* and superficial *optimism*) assumes *meliorism* as a crucial guiding value. Bigge regards meliorism not as an absolute implying the human condition will necessarily improve, but rather as a valuing of persistent attempts to improve humankind's lot. Whatever the results, such attempts provide a

[2] May, p. 177; italics his.
[3] Morris L. Bigge, *Positive Relativism: An Emergent Educational Philosophy.* New York: Harper & Row, Publishers, 1971, pp. 6–7.

direction which is positive," that is, "logically affirmative" and "capable of being constructively applied"—as in "positive proposals for the betterment of society."

Below is a discussion of several issues with which relativism is concerned. There are also definitions of relativism that differ from the one we are to give and use in this book. Not many people are "pure relativists"; rather, it is a point of view which they keep gravitating toward.

a. Truth as Situational (Relational, Configurational, or Contextual)

To a relativist, truth is determined by the total situation. What he sees as true about any process or object depends on what else he is aware of at the time. We mean a building is high *compared to other buildings within our experience.* Is a twenty-story building high? Yes, if all others are only three or four stories. No, if they are skyscrapers.

Understanding the nature of relativistic truth can be aided by understanding the concept of *field*, especially as defined by the psychologist and social scientist, Kurt Lewin: A field is "a totality of coexisting facts which are conceived of as mutually interdependent. . . ."[4] The term "field," which we use in this sense, resembles the term "system."

A classroom of students has many "field characteristics." How student *A* behaves may be a consequence of—or a function of—the way other individuals behave. The achievement of student *A* will be judged by himself, the teacher, and his classmates partly in relation to how well other students achieve. (*A* may achieve a good deal, but if all other students achieve more, *A* will seem stupid; in a different class *A* might be the highest achiever, so he would seem bright.)

Only to a certain degree is a classroom itself a self-contained field of forces; it is always subject to influence by larger fields and is capable of influencing them. How noisy a classroom seems will be a function of the general noise level of the school. A classroom of students who are shouting, shoving chairs, and dropping books may seem pretty quiet if an orchestra and choir are practicing next door.

b. Truth as Tending to Change

Relativists do not regard an interpretation of a situation as forever and finally true. Assertions are called truth if they command more supporting evidence, however slight, than competing assertions. Relativists do not

[4] Kurt Lewin, "Behavior and Development as a Function of the Total Situation," in Leonard Carmichael (ed.), *Manual of Child Psychology,* 2d ed. New York: John Wiley & Sons, Inc., 1954, p. 219. Lewin's formulation is derived from a statement by Albert Einstein.

usually anticipate great longevity for their truths, as new evidence or alternatives may suddenly appear.

Because a truth changes does not mean that it was not formerly true. But with a changed situation, a different interpretation becomes the new truth. Newton's conception of the universe was true for his day, but by the early twentieth century new knowledge could not be interpreted adequately using Newton's laws. The usefulness of Newton's laws was limited to special cases in which the only data needed were those which Newton had.

Since relativistic truths are admittedly limited by changing situations, many people wonder if there is still anything solid to stand on, especially as relativistic views have invaded the humanities, including ethics. Even though they see no alternative to relativism, many people remain bothered by the feeling that their moral principles may crumble with unpredictable situational changes.

c. Relative Absolutes

A number of assertions such as, "A solid object heavier than water sinks when placed on top of water," persist unchanged. A relativist may call such tested assertions which have no known exceptions *relative absolutes*.

Why does a relativist not wish to simply call an apparently dependable rule an absolute? Not because he denies that absolutes exist (a consistent relativist concedes that anything may be possible; see Section e below). He describes even the most dependable rules as relative absolutes because he does not *know* that the situation *will never change*. In the case of the heavier-than-water object, he has no way of knowing beyond a doubt that gravity will always operate as it now does.

d. Truth as Invented, Not Discovered

A relativist prefers to say that truth—which we here equate with reality—is an invention of man. He justifies this on the ground that, given his way of defining truth, it is not something which exists somewhere out in the universe, but is rather man's perceptions of what is around him. Truth is what man sees as being true—it is his interpretation of his perceptions. Alternately, *truth, or reality, is what man makes of what comes to him through his senses.*

To a relativist, perception is not taking direct "readings" of his environment. His eyes do not "see" as a camera "sees." To him, perception must include what goes on inside the perceiver. Perception involves at least three simultaneous events: (1) a desire to perceive the environment in accordance with his goals or wants at the time, (2) interference of memories of past experiences, and (3) the existence of something "out there to see."

To be motivated to perceive, there must be some specific want to be served—some personal goal. What a person wants to perceive will alter what he does perceive. If John wants to see evil in James, he can arrange the facts he thinks he knows about James so as to make James look very bad. Someone who wants to see good in James will also arrange the facts he thinks he knows in a way to suit his purpose.

Prior experiences leave memories which may cause people to distort their perception of the environment. We call these memories *mindsets*, which result from the environment habitually looking a certain way so a person is accustomed to sensing them in a certain way. If the environmental reality is changed, because of habit a person continues trying to sense it in the familiar way. (This may explain why proofreaders sometimes overlook misspelled words.)

A great deal of empirical psychological evidence, much from controlled laboratory experiments, supports the above description of how perception works. A skilled psychologist can rig the situation to get a subject to perceive just about anything the psychologist wants him to perceive. Also, subjects in a hypnotic trance can be induced to hallucinate all manner of things—sights, sounds, smells, etc.—that are not physically present. And, of course, trial attorneys know that two witnesses rarely report events identically, because they actually perceived the events differently.

Thus perception is not only individualized but contains a large component of the creative. Human beings to a large, though variable, degree make their own environment—the only reality they will ever know. So, relativists feel truth getting should be described as invention rather than finding.

Readers may wonder at this point if what relativists say about perception is true—how any two people ever agree on what is true. People do manage to agree sufficiently well on many things so that they are able to unite in common causes and to take effective group action. This is possible because the perception of some things in the environment is neither very complicated nor very warped: people have about the same goals, the same earlier experience to bring to bear, and approximately the same sensory functioning. Consequently we can get group agreement on many things, and mass agreement on many relative absolutes.

e. Reality without Theoretical Boundaries

Relativists are attracted to the idea of an open-ended universe (or, the "concept of the open universe"). It appears that relativists themselves have not made enough of this concept or have unwittingly viewed what they label "the universe" in ways contradictory to the main tenor of their thought. Relativists often have not made all possible deductions from the open universe concept to ensure their outlook being internally harmonious.

The idea seems at first simple enough—in effect, *anything may be possible* (not necessarily in a particular situation, but sometime, some-place, under some circumstance). "Anything" is taken here to include not only what people so far have been able to conceive but also what is yet inconceivable.

A consistent relativist must concede that there may be absolutes—truths with a capital "T"—in the form of natural, divine, or some other category of law. A relativist who says, "All truth is relative," has made an absolutistic statement. He has no way of knowing absolutely that all truth is relative; it is only a *working hypothesis* which he finds more useful for him than any other at the time.

f. A Relativistic Test of Truth

Relativists do not all agree on the best tests of the accuracy of perception. A test which has been popular is that people simply decide to accept as true whatever most people think is true; or a more cautious person may prefer calling nothing true unless there is a consensus that it is. There are serious problems involved in this test of truth. If everyone agrees that an assertion is true—there may even be a consensus that it is—and if we can be sure everyone has used the best evidence available to make that judgment, then we have warrant for calling the assertion true. To most Europeans during the Dark Ages the earth was flat; this was their truth and it probably served their purposes well enough at the time. That this state of affairs could exist for several centuries suggests that available evidence considered by people of that era was very limited and also that it was limited for the wrong reasons—there was evidence all around them to suggest that the earth was not flat, but people could not perceive this evidence because of their mind-sets. These mind-sets had an authoritarian source, the church of that time.

The preferred test of truth held by many relativists today is what we might think of as an experimental approach. If one assumes that an assertion is perhaps true and deduces the consequences of acting as if it were true, then if the anticipated consequences do indeed occur there is good reason for treating the assertion with respect. If on repeated tests the anticipated consequences continue to appear, we may come to feel that we have a *good working hypothesis* which we can confidently refer to as true.

Looking at the testing process this way we can maintain a relativis-tic position and still regard a truth which is believed by only one or two persons as better than a truth believed by everyone else. In many matters only a few persons have the education or access to the needed gadgetry to test many kinds of assertions. In such cases, we still regard truth as an outcome of a consensus, but a consensus of only those having the fullest access to pertinent evidence.

Democracy and Humanism

Democracy is a humanistic social philosophy. In a modern context, humanism is usually defined as a philosophy which rejects supernaturalism and asserts that human beings, as a part of nature, have an essential worth and dignity and some freedom of choice. Humanists assume that through the use of reason and science persons are capable of achieving self-realization—that is, goals emerging from the interaction of the self and its perceived environment.

A METHOD OF CULTURAL STUDY

This section will explain the method of cultural study preferred by the author. It is not the only method; many persons might prefer another. There are a variety of methodologies through which inquiry into cultural matters may proceed. The method described here seems compatible with the major aims and themes of this book. But in order to justify our chosen method, we need first to explore a major epistemological issue as it relates to the study of man.

Inadequacy of the Inquiry Model of Physical Science

We suggest that there is no one fixed scientific method. A suitably productive method of inquiry varies with the nature of the subject matter or problem being studied. A method of inquiry can be judged only within a frame of reference, or context. We suggest that when we shift the focus of study from the nonliving to the living, at that moment we create the need for a shift in method of study. What is a proper method of inquiry in physics or chemistry is not necessarily proper when studying man. Sociologists may find the method of physics suitable for certain problems in their field, but probably not for many of them.

There is a central issue here that divides scientists, particularly in fields studying living subjects—biology, physiology, medicine, psychology, psychiatry, and the social sciences generally. Scholars in these fields who operate in the behaviorist tradition apparently feel that to merit the name "scientific," any field of inquiry must use the methods of physics and chemistry—underlying which is the assumption that behavior is predictable because it stems from the operation of dependable natural laws. A corollary assumption is that if the behavior of one's subject of study is predictable, it is predictable in some amount and thus can be stated in quantitative terms and handled statistically.

In sciences which deal strictly with the nonliving, or with the purely physical or chemical behaviors in living matter (as organic chemistry), most of the common research can be tackled under these assumptions. But in sciences which deal with the living, the application of the standard behavioristic approach rules out any possibility of freedom of choice (or free will).

What form may scholarly investigation take in studying human individuals and groups, if it is not to be governed by the investigatory model of physics? Investigation involves developing hypotheses and testing them, as in the physical sciences, but the form of both hypotheses and data may change. If one is going to study human culture without bypassing its most central interests, one must deal with values. Cultural study requires the making and testing of many hypotheses *about* values, although assertions whose meaning hinges on value-laden words (value judgments) probably cannot be tested directly. What a social scientist can do is test the usefulness of values in helping people achieve other values.

The concept of what can function as evidence or data probably has to be broadened when we try to study humans and their works. In the physical sciences acceptable data are usually confined to quantifiable facts. But in studying human culture we often find qualitative data most useful, including data from introspection or from thought processes which might best be called intuitive. Further, we probably cannot understand much worth knowing about human beings without taking into consideration their purposes or aspirations—something physicists do not have to do when studying gravitational forces, the behavior of crystals, or nuclear fusion.

In this book one of our major concerns is studying ideology (defined as highly evaluative and usually absolutistic beliefs asserted about sociopolitical matters). Assertions of ideology are usually phrased so it is very difficult to test their truth directly. We can construct testable hypotheses, however, which throw light on ideological assertions. We can thus at least understand them better, and in the end make better institutional judgments about them than we could if they were left unstudied.

In this kind of investigation, we will make no claim of either neatness or definitiveness. An investigator does the best he can—knowing that his own ideological convictions may get in the way of the objective study of other people's ideologies. Much of the time the best we can do with ideological statements show that they do not make sense—because their terms cannot be defined, they are illogical, or contradict other ideological statements made by the same person.

Methodological Role of Controversial ("Outrageous") Hypotheses

As we look back upon the history of inquiry, it appears that a large proportion of the fundamental breakthroughs in science have been a result of individuals with a creative bent originating a new interpretation which at the time of its formulation seemed to most persons a complete violation of common sense and of authoritative teaching. The "great hypotheses," which, when verified, have changed the course of human thought and history, seemed at the time thoroughly "outrageous."

Galileo, for instance, proposed a variety of "uncommonsense" notions, including supporting the theory of Copernicus that the sun is the center of the solar system, but was forced to recant on threat of excommunication or possible execution. Centuries later, Charles Darwin, as a result of his "outrageous" hypotheses, was castigated throughout the Western World and his name is still a fighting word among Americans who remain frightened by the unorthodox.

Perhaps the most fantastic hypothesis of all time is partially stated in the following quotation:

> The mass of a body is a measure of its energy-content; if the energy changes by L, the mass changes in the same sense by $L/9 \times 10^{20}$, the energy being measured in ergs, and the mass in grammes.
>
> It is not impossible that with bodies whose energy-content is variable to a high degree (e.g., with radium salts) the theory may be successfully put to test.
>
> If the theory corresponds to the fact, radiation conveys inertia between the emitting and absorbing bodies.

This quotation is the final three paragraphs of Einstein's famous 1905 paper "Does the Inertia of a Body Depend upon Its Energy-Content?" Note the humility of Einstein's proposal: he is not even sure his hypothesis can be tested. Yet, he has proposed one of the most "outrageous" hypotheses ever—namely, that matter and energy are both forms of the same thing and are interchangeable. The few other physicists who understood Einstein's paper were greatly excited by it, and after a long process of testing, it altered our whole conception of the universe.

In the physical sciences the situation now is radically different from what it once was. Now when a physicist proposes incredible theories about the world of nature, the general public not only foregoes stoning him to death but actually seems quite entranced.

"Outrageous Hypotheses" in the Social Sciences

Social science has produced few innovations on the grand scale of a Galileo, a Newton, a Darwin, or an Einstein. We think offhand of Adam Smith and Karl Marx among the historical progenitors of contemporary social science. Smith's influence is still major in the thinking of one group of conservative thinkers; Marx's dialectical materialism remains, in this country, a blasphemous notion to many.

But there appears to be a direct correlation between major breakthroughs in social science and the number of proposed hypotheses that seem to run counter to common sense. Unfortunately there have been few bold hypotheses and consequently almost no significant breakthroughs in the history of social science. It seems probable that no other branch of science has been as dead historically or remains as dead as social science.

This is not to suggest that no social scientists have seen the connection between bold, highly original, "outrageous" hypotheses and fundamental breakthroughs in their field of study. The thinking of the early twentieth-century social scientists who were the intellectual descendants of Charles Peirce and other members of the Harvard Metaphysical Club of the 1870s, such as Thorstein Veblen, Charles and Mary Beard, and particularly James Harvey Robinson, was tending in this direction.

Probably the first American social scientist in this century to write a book which grappled directly with this issue was Robert S. Lynd.[5] Lynd proposed that not only were social scientists of his time not producing anything worth bothering about, but that the only way in which social science could achieve the prominence and productiveness of the natural sciences was to borrow the most valuable tool of the natural sciences— the "outrageous hypothesis." In his book Lynd used the expression "outrageous hypothesis," and then proposed situations on which he felt social scientists should concentrate.

One of Lynd's outrageous hypotheses was:

> If democracy is to continue as the active guiding principle of our culture, it will be necessary to extend it markedly as an efficient reality in government, industry, and other areas of living; otherwise, it will be necessary to abandon it in favor of some other operating principle (p. 215).

This may not seem outrageous until one thinks about it long enough to see that implementing it would require rewriting major sections of the Constitution, the socialization of much of industry, and turning upside down many other institutions, including the public schools.

[5] Robert S. Lynd, *Knowledge for What?* Princeton, N.J.: Princeton University Press, 1939.

Since World War II, the number of persons in the social sciences who have taken Lynd and his forebears seriously can be numbered on fewer than the fingers of one hand. A decade after the war, a Columbia University sociologist, C. Wright Mills, proposed that the functioning of political power in this country could best be explained by hypothesizing a "power elite" which maintained a tight control over our culture from the top. Because Mills seemed to be saying that political democracy in this country was an illusion, many readers (including other social scientists) were angered. Quickly, there was an outpouring of literature attacking Mills, as well as some defending him. This forced people whose minds were not already made up to rethink the whole question of who really does run the country. Mills' theory, which most Americans then considered dangerously unconventional, led, therefore, to a great amount of investigation which produced much new knowledge about how power works.

To cite a more recent example, the psychologist and social philosopher, B. F. Skinner, argues in his 1971 book, *Beyond Freedom and Dignity,* that the concepts of the freedom and dignity of humans, long associated with the idea of democracy itself, are obsolete. Humans are not free, says Skinner, because all their behavior is caused by their environment, everything humans do is a result of how their environment has conditioned them. As things now stand, he says, human behavior is so misguided that it endangers the very survival of humankind. Skinner proposes a utopian society in which everyone will be conditioned to behave in a way that will not only guarantee human survival but also make all humans happier.

Skinner's ideas have pleased a lot of persons but have outraged many others. They have produced a flood of polemical literature, but also much thoughtful inquiry. As in the case of Mills, it hardly matters whether Skinner is right. What does matter is that he has aroused much interest in an important issue about which most people have been apathetic. His "outrageous" ideas will lead to much more inquiry and to an enlarged stock of useful knowledge.

The examples of Lynd and Skinner show that although social scientists cannot often make use of the full methodology of physics, they can be more effective by adopting the tool that has lifted the physical sciences to their position of prominence and influence—the "outrageous hypothesis." Perhaps even our textbooks would be more stimulating and useful if they too contained occasional forceful assertions of unorthodox ideas.

OBJECTIVES OF THIS BOOK

The author has in mind a number of objectives for this book. They should be considered in relation to the two alternative approaches to textbook writing described at the end of this section.

1. To help students get a better view of both the culture as a totality and how the culture and schools interact or can be made to interact. Culture will be defined largely in terms of ideas and the book will highlight a certain kind of idea, ideas manifested in statements of ideology.

2. To acquaint students with a particular approach to cultural study, that of marshaling data around controversial hypotheses. The writer does not expect to prove or disprove the statements of ideology contained in the book. From them we will derive hypotheses which we can illuminate with evidence, but which for the most part are too complex to be definitively supported or rejected. The emphasis of the whole book is on method, or process, rather than on subject matter to be committed to memory.

3. To acquaint students with major areas of controversy in our culture. The book stresses an understanding of both controversy and change, which the author sees as reciprocal forces. Further, it is hoped that our presentation of cultural issues will have enough intrinsic interest to develop in students a lifelong concern for cultural study.

4. To help students understand better how to study culture in relation to one prime objective: the maintenance of democracy. All the major issues dealt with will be viewed in terms of what they mean for democracy as we will define democracy.

5. To help students become accustomed to a critical approach to scholarship. The author does not think it helps anyone to write merely inspirational textbooks. This one will examine our culture from a critical view. The purpose of criticism is not just to adversely criticize, rather, it is to highlight what is wrong about things in the hope of motivating students to think about how things might be improved. The intent of the book is constructive, not destructive.

Many texts are presented as objective in the sense of their being neutral about issues. It is doubtful if any textbook is really neutral. Even compendiums of facts which at first glance seem to have no central themes or learnings are presumably motivated by values of some sort, if only in the selection of the facts (for how facts are selected provides its own bias).

Other texts are frankly presented as "position" or "point-of-view" books. As most readers by now realize, this is a position book. It takes a stand in favor of democratic process and those institutional structures of the 1970s that encourage the fullest use of this process. Conversely, it takes a stand against nondemocratic, absolutistic ways of thinking and acting. The overall view of the book is liberal, insofar as a liberal point of view seems consistent with the perpetuation of democracy.

CULTURAL FOUNDATIONS IN TEACHER EDUCATION

The four chapters of Part I are designed to provide a foundation for the rest of the book. Each chapter, however, has its own themes and could be read alone as a meaningful entity.

Chapter 1 is devoted primarily to introducing some of the major concepts which will be regularly used throughout the book: culture and subculture, the process of cultural change, cultural disorganization and disintegration, and the process of culture building. The final section raises the question of whether the United States, and perhaps other advanced industrial and post-industrial nations, are undergoing cultural change at a rate, and of a kind, to be properly called a "cultural revolution." After presenting a few specimen theories of a possible contemporary cultural revolution (not to be confused with a violent revolution to overthrow the government), the chapter ends with comments on the implications a revolution in ideological patterns has for education.

Chapter 2 attempts to describe what we see as a basic polarization in American culture—a polarization involving at one extreme commitment to liberal democratic values and at the other extreme commitment to conservative and often authoritarian values. Of course neither this nor other polarizations in American culture are simple; they also continuously change form. Many "liberal democrats" are liberal and democratic on some issues and not on others—just as conservatives not only divide into "classical" and "radical" groupings, but also show conservativism in some areas of life and liberalism in others. Chapter 2 ends by raising questions as to the role of schooling in a divided and fluid culture. We introduce the basic idea of social reconstruction as a possible long-range goal of education, present a few pro and con arguments, and leave this major issue for further development later.

Chapter 3 develops more fully the themes of cultural inconsistency and conflict, cognitive dissonance, alienation, and anomie. An attempt is made to show how our definitions of deviant behavior stem from the values of those in the highest power positions in a culture. Another section is devoted to specific belief patterns of our culture which influence the way students and teachers think. The final section develops some of the implications of pervasive cultural conflict and irrational belief patterns for educational practice.

Chapter 4 addresses itself to our youth culture. This chapter does not treat the peer cultures of young children, and treats only incidentally the secondary school peer culture. Rather, the focus is upon the "youth movement," as exemplified in the high school and university youth "counterculture" of the 1960s. Although a treatment of the youth movement from its first tentative beginnings in the late fifties is essential as background for discussing youth in the seventies, the chapter runs over this background rather briefly and focuses on what we have been able to make of the attitudes, values, and beliefs of youth of the seventies.

This chapter is not intended to inform prospective teachers of what they will need to know about children and youth between grades K and 12. (Courses in child and youth development take care of that.) The purpose of the chapter is to suggest what is likely to lie ahead for our culture because of the developing thought patterns of those older youth who in the late 1970s, 1980s, and 1990s will provide the nation's leadership. It is an attempt to tour the future insofar as we can by assessing the mental furniture of those who will be leaders in the years ahead. As such, the chapter continues the analysis of the fundamental nature of our culture, now and in the longer run, to which the first three chapters were devoted.

1

CULTURE, CULTURAL REVOLUTION, AND EDUCATION

... great ideas often enter reality in strange guises and with disgusting alliances.

Alfred North Whitehead

The culture concept, as used by social scientists and educators, is the most frequently used concept in this book. We will discuss both the culture concept and such supplementary concepts as subculture, cultural change, cultural disorganization (including the idea of "closed areas" of culture), cultural disintegration, culture building, and what numerous social analysts see as "the contemporary cultural revolution." A final section will suggest some implications for education of cultural change (including revolutionary change).

CULTURE AS A KEY CONCEPT IN THE STUDY OF PERSONS AND GROUPS

Before discussing culture as the term will be used most of the time in this text, it should prevent confusion to note that there are two fundamentally different definitions of the word. There is the layperson's or journalistic definition—also acceptable in

scholarly writing—which we will use on occasion. Many students know only this definition. It has to do with education, refinement, sophistication, knowledgeability in the arts, and a desire for continued self-learning. Thus, we refer to persons being "cultured" or "having a high level of culture" if they are highly educated ("schooled" or self-educated), if their life style is patrician, if they enjoy and understand the various fine arts, and if they have values which will lead to the lifelong pursuit of culture in this sense. This definition of culture, for our purposes, means the same as "cultivation," the term we will usually use to help readers avoid possible confusion between the layperson's and the social scientist's versions of culture.

Culture: An Anthropological Definition

In 1871, Sir Edward B. Tylor (1832-1917) published the first definition of culture, which to some degree is still usable as a scholarly, non-judgmental statement: Culture is "that complex whole which includes knowledge, belief, art, morals, law, custom, and any other capabilities and habits acquired by man as a member of society."[1] This definition has since

[1] Edward B. Tylor, *Primitive Culture*, Vol. 1. London: John Murray, 1871.

A culture of contrasts; science races ahead, social institutions lag.

been refined and clarified. The long-range trend seeks definitions that
emphasize the cognitive side of human life (i.e., thought, in contrast to
overt behaviors) and simplify understanding by stating on a more generic
level the closely related and probably overlapping concepts of "knowledge,
belief, art, morals, law, custom."

Further, the concept of culture has come to be closely related to
the concept of *field* as used in the technical vocabulary of the social
sciences and psychology. That is, culture is considered as an organic
concept—as an interdependent pattern of ideas—in contrast to some
earlier more atomistic definitions. The concept of *relativism* has also come
to play an important role in definitions of culture, especially in the sense
of the cognitive constructs of a culture being conceived as relativistic
rather than absolutistic.

Perhaps the first truly modern definition of culture was offered by
Robert Redfield (1897-1957). He believed the most promising approach
to inquiry in anthropology, inquiry into the nature of human thought and
ensuing behavior, was to study what happened when two diverse cultures
were brought together and had to accommodate each other with resulting
conflict and conflict-induced change.

How did Redfield define culture? As this writer interprets it, the heart of his definition is the assertion that culture is "an organized body of conventional understandings." By conventional, Redfield means historically influenced; by understandings, he apparently means something rather more complicated. For our present limited definitional purposes we can say that understanding requires seeing what something might be *for* in relation to achieving a desired end or goal.

To explain understanding the way Redfield apparently intends, we need to add an overall framework within which one sees the use of things in relation to one's purposes. The framework is what Redfield and others have called one's *world view.* This expression refers to a person's psychological world—the world of perceptions generated by the interaction, or transaction, between an individual and his perceived environment. A person's psychological world, says Redfield, is "the structure of things *as man is aware of them. It is the way we see ourselves in relation to all else."*[2]

Advanced students may see a close link between world view, Kurt Lewin's idea of life space, and Martin Heidegger's concept of a person as spreading over a field or region which encompasses all of the person's concerns: a person cannot be located spacially, only psychologically.

The foregoing ideas, although they may seem to some readers as unnecessarily abstract or highbrow, are essential to an understanding of how the term, culture, will be used in this book. Some of the key aspects of the culture concept can be presented in a less abstract way as follows:

1. Culture is ideational patterning, culture refers to ideas, not things. Institutions and artifacts tend to appear "after the idea" and are significant only as they tend to suggest further innovations in ideation.

2. Culture is learned. Culture consists of ideational patterns that are not biologically innate. Genetically derived or instinctive behavior, if such exists among human beings, is not a part of culture.

3. Culture is historically derived, that is, it is transmitted from generation to generation. Even cultural patterns that seem to spring overnight from nowhere (e.g., the "beat culture" of the 1950s), have historical roots, sharp—even revolutionary—breaks in cultural patterns from one generation to another notwithstanding.

4. Culture, by definition, has some kind of organization at its core, even though it may show many examples of disorganization. That is, the concept of culture is incompatible with pervasive ideological chaos; where this exists the culture has disintegrated. We could place specific cultures

[2] Robert Redfield, *The Primitive World and Its Transformations.* Ithaca, N.Y.: Cornell University Press, 1953 (paperback 1957), p. 86.

on a continuum ranging from tightly to loosely structured, with the latter being as close to disintegration as possible while still retaining a viable core.

5. An individual and his or her culture are continuous, in the sense that what a person is—his or her self-structure—is derived through interaction with other members of the culture, with each person usually making some degree of simultaneous impact on the selves of the others.

6. Virtually all known cultures of today are relatively dynamic (i.e., undergoing continuous change). Although this is the case, as was noted above, cultural patterns are not susceptible to easy obliteration.

Culture and Ideology

We have indicated that a culture is an idea system. It is an idea system of broad scope which contains a wide variety of "intellectual furniture." Most of the ideational components of a culture may be classifiable as understandings, as Redfield asserted, but the understandings exist at different levels of consciousness, take different syntactical forms when verbalized, and serve an infinite number of purposes.

What kind of labels can we attach to the understandings that comprise a culture? The following suggestion is not presented as complete; further, its individual components tend to overlap and in some contexts may mean essentially the same. However, we feel students need to be able to distinguish: attitude, value, belief, myth, presumed knowledge, and ideology.

Attitude   A relatively stable learned disposition to act either positively or negatively toward an object, person, group, or situation. As we will use this term, it will be presumed that attitudes are not susceptible to verbalization and, further, may never be translated into action if the attitude holder finds it impossible or unwise to do so. (Under this definition attitudes *cannot* be measured by attitude scales or any other testing instrument; persons who hold that an attitude, to be real, must be susceptible to verbalization are within the framework of a mechanistic behaviorism.) When attitudes are translated into behavior, probably the best label for the action is *habit*.

Value   A judgment concerning the worth of an object, person, group, or situation. The primary difference between an attitude and a value is that a value is a verbalized preference. Example: "Richard Nixon was the best President the United States has ever had." Value judgments contain evaluative or rating terms, such as good, bad, moral, immoral, beautiful, ugly.

Belief   Intellectual assent or anything which a person regards as true. The word does connote conviction, for example, a religious belief;

but to limit belief to this nongeneric usage virtually demands the frequent use of some substitute and makes writing unnecessarily complicated.

Myth   A group belief accepted uncritically, particularly in support of traditional practices and institutions. Although a myth may have some basis in fact, the word usually refers to imagined events.

Presumed knowledge   A belief stated as a hypothesis which has undergone scholarly tests and is supposedly a matter of fact. Within a relativistic framework, what is fact under one set of circumstances may not be under another.

Ideology   Except for attitudes (so long as we assume their unsusceptability to verbalization), all the above concepts may function as components within an *ideology*. An *ideological statement* was defined in the Prologue as a sociopolitical belief, evaluative in nature, and ordinarily held as an absolute. (Example: "The American system of free enterprise is the best economic system in the world.") A series of single assertions of ideology make up a national ideology, the best definition of which we have found to be:

> A system of interdependent ideas . . . held by a social group or society which reflects, rationalizes, and defends its particular social, moral, religious, political, and economic institutional interests and commitments. Ideologies serve as logical and philosophical justifications for a group's patterns of behavior, as well as its . . . [beliefs and] goals. . . . [Their elements] tend to be accepted as truth or dogma rather than as tentative philosophical or theoretical formulations. . . . [3]

Defined in the foregoing sense, a national (or cultural) ideology serves as a kind of societal glue. If most members of the society subscribe to the same ideological assertions, the society can be regarded not merely as a group of people living contiguously, but as a culture.

If we are to think of national ideologies as adhesives holding the national culture together, then we can assess the cohesiveness, integrity, or organic qualities of a culture by studying the ways its members view its ideological patterns. If they view their ideological structure favorably as holding together, making sense (providing both a common goal system and a group of criteria for judging competing national ideologies), then the culture can be regarded as viable or internally healthy. However, a culture may be considered internally healthy according to the foregoing criteria and yet be a menace to other peoples because its ideology may either call for aggression toward other nations, or contain booby traps which will blow the whole cultural structure to bits as it shifts from one epoch to another.

[3] George A. Theodorson and Achilles G. Theodorson, *A Modern Dictionary of Sociology.* New York: Thomas Y. Crowell Company, 1969, p. 195.

In the paragraph above, we mentioned "the way its members view its ideological patterns." A collection of ideological assertions to which most members of the culture assent may mean something quite different to members of the culture and to impartial bystanders such as foreign observers. For example, many opinion studies note the tendency of most Americans to think of the United States as a nation sympathetic to downtrodden unfortunates in all parts of the world, including our own. Politicians are likely to say, "We are the most compassionate country on earth." Because of this ideological belief we are often thought to be "the only truly Christian nation on earth."

However, an objective observer noting our having used violence as a means of settling disputes or vengeful punishment to maintain social control, and our history of cold and hot wars, might feel quite justified in regarding Americans as demented for regarding themselves as compassionate. But if the American public sees no conflict between the ideas of compassion and imposing punishment on weaker peoples, both foreign nations and internal minorities, then this ideological statement about compassion still makes sense to Americans as an adhesive part of their national ideology. There is then no feeling that our ideology contains contradictions.

If a national ideology is not under attack by persons who sway opinion, it will remain a slow-moving, often seemingly static belief system, such as that of China for perhaps 3000 years. A culture under attack by a number of its own articulate opinion leaders will be a culture in a state of conflict or tension. Cultural tension motivates change and may produce a healthy dynamic culture which, although problem producing, can cope adequately with its problems, and in the process demonstrate valuable innovative qualities. The United States has been such a culture since its beginning because we have always been a people with ideological disagreements.

But what happens when a people begin to question the virtue of a large part of their ideology? As this book will show clearly, many of our traditional ideological slogans have come into question since World War II, particularly since the mid-1960s. Although they may not have been questioned by a majority of the public, they have been questioned by possibly a majority of college and university youth, large numbers of educated professionals (including professors and the scholarly community in general), a large segment of the artistic community (especially writers), numerous school teachers and journalists, and a significant proportion of Congress.

When an established ideology begins to dissolve among a large number of opinion leaders, then a culture is in trouble. The writer believes, for substantial empirical reasons, that the culture of the United States is now in that kind of trouble. This topic will be developed later in the chapter.

THE MEANING OF SUBCULTURE

A *subculture* is a unit within a larger culture, sharing some of the ideology of the larger culture but identified by its own distinctive thought patterns. This extremely general definition may perhaps be sharpened by discusssing various-sized cultural units.

World Culture

The largest conceivable cultural entity (assuming, perhaps improbably, there are no humanlike creatures elsewhere in the universe) is the entire population of planet Earth. However, the world's people are split into so many thousand cultural groupings that it is difficult to find much they have in common. Anthropologists tell us that all the world's peoples have some kind of family organization and that if one can define religion broadly enough to mean no more than "commitment to a cause," then most people have a religion. Most peoples are committed to education, formal or informal, whether for an elitist few or for all. We could mention a few other kinds of "commonness" but in each case the way in which people think about such things and the way they act out their thoughts (behave) varies from one cultural group to another. If it is acceptable to talk about a world culture, we do so only as a conceptual device for explaining its subdivisions and hence subcultures.

In fact, thought and practice differ so from one culture to another that anthropologists make a good deal of the concept of *cultural relativism*. Almost every imaginable practice can be found someplace if one tries hard enough to find it. This poses a moral issue: Is one cultural practice demonstrably better than another? For example, is multiple marriage, in which children are thought of as "belonging" to *all* the adults who are cohabiting, better than our traditional nuclear family? Cultural relativism asserts that one can say neither yes or no—that whatever practice works for a given culture is right for that culture. There is no objective means of judging one set of practices superior to another. Students should note that *cultural relativism is not the same as philosophical relativism,* the latter referring to such philosophical schools of thought as American experimentalism and European existentialism.

What are the largest human units which have at least some cultural identity? Much has been written about the differences between Western and Eastern civilizations. Western, in this sense, refers to the related cultural groups that have emerged over the past 2500 years from roots in the Mediterranean area, particularly ancient Greece and Rome. The Western World has been culturally united by the Hebraic and Christian religious traditions, and by ways of thinking which we associate, primarily but not entirely, with Greece and Rome. Eastern civilization has included the peoples of most of Asia east of the Urals. It appears to date farther back—at least four millennia in the case of China and India—and to exemplify in certain areas marked differences in thought.

Although the intellectual differences between West and East are probably many, one is of especial interest to us here. Western civilization has tended to think in terms of dualisms, those which most concern us being a group of related dichotomies: body-mind, body-soul, body-spirit, material-spiritual, person-nature.

Although these dualisms appear to have originated among certain pagan religious sects of the Persian Peninsula, and to have been incorporated into Christianity during the first century A.D., it is helpful to relate them to Aristotle's "law of the excluded middle" which led to a tendency to think about virtually everything in "either-or" terms. The Romance languages have been structured around this either-or tendency— which, as we shall often remark, tends to interfere seriously with productive thinking. In contrast, one finds few tendencies toward body-spirit or person-nature dualism in Eastern thought; nor does one find as much of an either-or tendency in the Far Eastern languages.

To reduce this difference between West and East to its simplest form, Eastern philosophers would tend to speak in terms of the unity of the person-in-nature, whereas most Western thinkers (though not all schools of philosophy) have tended to think in terms of humans as consisting of a contesting body and spirit housed in a universe of contesting material and immaterial (spiritual) forces. We can think then, apparently validly, of two major world cultures, provided we strip away numerous superficial similarities and get down to basic "world views."

Within both the Western and Eastern worlds, there are multifarious regional, national, and local subcultures. The culture of India, with its valuing of democracy, is very different from that of China, most of whose people have never experienced democracy as we understand it. The culture of Europe, with its possible tendency toward commitment to long-range principles and personal cultivation, is distinctively different from the culture of the United States, with its penchant for pragmatism rather than principle, and its oft-labeled antiintellectualism rather than a commitment to cultivation. Of course, one could find among the educated, subcultures within most Western and Eastern cultures that share common values.

But Europe has its regional and national culture patterns (Italians tend to think differently from Swedes), as have the Americas (Indians of the Upper Amazon are different from most New Yorkers). And in each case, there are numerous comparatively small subcultures within the larger regional or natural culture, ranging in size down to a single classroom of students.

The foregoing brief excursion into cultural analysis is, obviously, highly oversimplified. But it will have been worth while if it has laid a foundation for discussing specific subcultures in the United States.

United States Subcultures

Although the characteristics of our subcultures change continuously, although subcultures disappear and reappear, and in virtually all cases overlap, we can point to some examples which, of this writing, seem valid.

Subcultures of Ethnic and Racial Origin

We treat "ethnic" and "racial" under the same head—not because they mean the same thing, but because many people think they do and tend to associate them. The chief error is in referring to ethnic groups as racially different, for example, calling Jews a race. The United States contains persons of the three major racial stocks—Caucasoid, Negroid, and Mongoloid. These racial stocks have been highly diluted through miscegenation, and race per se is rapidly ceasing to be a basis for subcultures. For example, there are few if any Blacks who do not have numerous White genes, mostly acquired since the beginning of the Southern "slave culture."

Conversely, if we go back far enough in history (as to the Mongol invasions of Europe and the period when the Roman Empire dominated the Mediterranean area and much of Europe), Caucasians received a major infusion of Mongoloid and Negroid genes. Since Chapter 11 is reserved for a treatment of race, we will say no more here than that there are probably few Americans who belong to a "pure race." Even if we could identify pure races in this country, it would probably not be of much importance; such groups could not be set apart as subcultures on the ground of race alone, but only on the ground of such cultural differences as they might exhibit. Blacks, whether "mixed" or "pure," would tend to separate into distinctive groups on the basis of social class membership, place of residence, ideological characteristics, and other factors.

We should make special note of one group of related subcultures: American Indians. They are probably farther outside the mainstream of American culture than any other group claiming some degree of racial identity. It is not their racial identity—now obscure at best because of the large amount of miscegenation with Whites—but their unique cultural heritage which truly sets them apart.

One other subculture is distinctive: the Mexican-Americans, or Chicanos, who reside primarily in the Southwest. They are a racial mixture of Spanish and Central American Indian. This minority finds acculturation slow, partly because their Mexican cultural heritage is quite different from that of people originating in Europe, and partly because their differences make education and occupational advancement into the middle class difficult.

We will make no attempt to treat "uniquenesses" of most of our ethnic subcultures—Jewish, Armenian, Irish, Polish, Italian, German, and so on. That attempt would lead into a kind of stereotyping which simply is not valid. Virtually all such groups, particularly if they have been in this country for as long as three generations, have become acculturated to the point where they tend to set the pattern for the dominant strands of our culture. Our ethnic minorities now outnumber what for most of our history was the ethnic majority, White, Anglo-Saxon Protestants (WASPs). It now appears that the WASPs will continue to decline proportionately, both in numbers and influence, indefinitely into the future.

Sex- and Age-Related Subcultures

Whenever their values differ significantly, particularly in matters related to sexual roles, men and women split into two groups which may be properly called subcultures. The most conspicuous female subculture is probably those women active in, or sympathetic to, the Women's Movement of the 1960s and 1970s. Male and female subcultures will be explored in Chapter 11.

In the literature of sociology dealing with subcultures, until recently not a great deal has been published about subcultures related to age. When this nation was primarily rural and agricultural and the family worked together at farming or a handicraft trade, the three generations which so often shared a single household were comparatively close to one another in their attitudes, values, beliefs, and knowledge. In an ideational sense they were often "all of one generation."

But industrialization and urbanization have changed that. The young begin identifying with peer groups as soon as they are old enough to play with other children. There seem to be distinctive subcultures for every age level from preschool to old age. Ages may be divided into clumps, so that members of a given clump may be identified by a distinctive ideational set and life style: children from prekindergarten through the primary grades; the middle elementary years; the upper elementary years running into the junior high period (but prior to puberty); youth of pubescent and post-pubescent age extending into the middle teens; the senior high school years; the college years (typically 18 to 24); the young or somewhat young adults who have settled into an occupation and are usuallly married and have children. Change in ideology and life style tends to slow down at this point, so we may have an age-related subculture extending from the middle twenties to the middle forties. After this is the period we call middle age, which we associate with male and female menopauses, the escape of children from the home, and the feeling that the best part of life is done with. Then there is old age and retirement, a span of years in which many people spend most of their time castigating the young and feeling nostalgic about the past.

Clearly, there is a link between sex- and age-related subcultures and subcultures based upon ideology. Up to the present, at least, people tend to become more conservative with age and to reassert ideological patterns similar to those of their parents. The link between sex and age divisions and ideological divisions may involve overlaps and superimpositions. Hence, we are dealing with very complex ways of categorizing people, ways which may be very useful under certain circumstances and not useful at all under others.

Regional Subcultures

Many Americans are identifiable as members of a regional subculture, that is, a subculture that appears in a particular geographical location. The geographical origin of a subculture may have little to do with its characteristics, in the sense that the facts of terrain, soil, vegetation, and climate may be largely irrelevant to ideologies and life style. Yet, geography may make a difference. It is hardly surprising that there is more outdoor nudity in California than in Maine, or that salt water fishing does not flourish in North Dakota.

Aside from the ethnic or ideological characteristics of the first settlers in a geographical region, probably the greatest significance of geography is in the kinds of industries and occupations it permits. A state or region which lends itself to, and depends on, war-related industries is likely to produce a large subculture of hawks and at times an opposing subculture of pacifists.

With respect to regionally related subcultures, we do find similarities in the way substantial proportions of the population think. However, we should not trap ourselves with the belief that all people in a regional subculture are alike. There may be a typical Texan, but for every thousand typical Texans there may be a hundred others who wouldn't be caught dead with a typical Texan. (The numbers are sheer guesses to illustrate the point.)

There is a Southern subculture, an East Coast subculture, a North Central subculture, Appalachian, Plains States, and Western subcultures, but in each of these large areas are smaller subcultures. New Englanders are not like Marylanders; the subculture of Utah varies markedly from that of California, a state which possibly houses a greater number of subcultures than any other.

Social Class Subcultures

Many groups that have passed for racial or ethnic subcultures have actually been social class subcultures. There are marked similarities between working- or subworking-class Blacks, Whites, Chicanos, Indians, and Orientals. The chief difference among these groups is that there are *proportionately* fewer working-class Whites and Orientals. Likewise, there are marked similarities among middle-class members of these various groups, as there are among upper-class members. However, it is extremely difficult for Blacks, Chicanos, and Indians to achieve upper-class status; and Orientals still suffer discrimination in their attempts toward upward mobility.

Because the term, "social class," may be one of dubious validity, and largely meaningless unless carefully defined, we need to provide some background here. Going back as far as we have a preserved written language, we find frequent references to stratification—people who are rulers or within a ruling elite, people in one or several middle strata, and manual laborers, the peons.

Probably the most prominent mid-twentieth century figures to stimulate research on social class were W. Lloyd Warner and a number of associates with somewhat similar ideas. Warner defined class as "community status," that is, how well one is thought of by his peers in a community small enough so that people know and can judge one another. In the Warner sense, class becomes pretty much the same as "prestige level." Aside from the difficulty of determining status, since one's peers may disagree on the status of any given individual, prestige may be gained quite differently in different groups.

In numerous United States communities studied from the 1930s into the 1950s, people gained status or prestige by having the "right jobs," displaying wealth, knowing the "right people," belonging to the "right clubs," living in the "right house" in the "right neighborhood," and so on.

A large majority of the population simply does not fit into any of Warner's concepts of upper class, upper- and lower-middle class, and upper- and lower-lower class. Where does one put the top figures in government (including politicians and members of the military establishment), scientists and technicians, artists, entertainers, housewives, athletes, scholars, and the like? Warner's system is meaningful for our purpose only if we limit its definition of social class to "status groups in the small community."

In summary, the social class studies done in the United States do not tell us much that is helpful in studying subcultures. For our purposes, we prefer taking some of our cues from the European sociologist, Max Weber (1864-1920). Weber suggested that prestige in a community (status) and social class membership were quite different and should be placed in different categories. Class, Weber said, referred to a grouping with equivalent "life chances." Life chances are the chances one has to improve one's position vis-á-vis the rest of society, primarily with reference to property, occupation, and income as they might translate into *power*. This view of class emphasizes economic factors, but in today's world, ownership and management of wealth are not the sole means to power: the military establishment is not based upon the personal wealth of its members nor is the top political establishment (although some members of these groups may happen to be wealthy).

In spite of its inadequacies, we will use the term, class, in this book, and in this section identify a few classes we will define as subcultures. Our *definition of class will be a grouping based on power and prestige and having common goals.* We will postulate the following groupings, recognizing that they omit large numbers of people who fall somewhere between the categories or are not explainable in terms of any category.

Upper Class

This group consists of top figures in business, government, and the military. Members of this group tend to mingle and to a considerable degree hold similar values. They are horizontally mobile, in the sense that many are in a position to switch back and forth from high military, corporate, and government positions. But this group is not monolithic; it not only has opposing conservative and moderate elements, but those whose power stems from economic privilege tend to divide into a propertied elite and a managerial group whose interests often do not coincide. Nevertheless, there is enough sharing of values among a large segment of this group that we feel it proper to designate those whose goals are similar a true subculture. The upper class may also properly be called a "power elite," and we will use these expressions interchangeably.

Middle Class

Under this broad rubric are various groupings; it would be more precise to talk about our middle classes, rather than a single middle class. There remains a small and diminishing middle class based on property ownership or professional self-employment. But salaried employees, ranging from low-income white-collar workers (e.g., bank clerks) to comparatively high-income white-collar occupations (e.g., bank presidents), constitute the *new* middle class. Its fastest growing element appears to be persons in managerial and technical positions (e.g., in the space and armaments industries, electronics, aircraft, and other high-growth post-World War II industries).

Working Class

By working class we mean blue-collar occupations which require skills ranging from minor (e.g., an assembly line worker) to major (e.g., a first-rate electrician) expertise. Members of the working class who are tightly unionized (e.g., many categories of construction workers) earn much higher wages and, if well led, have more power than lower-middle-class workers. Further, the working class elite forms a true subculture because of sharing a common conservative ideology and other values. As in the case of the middle class, it is more appropriate to speak of a number of different working classes.

The Under Class

This label has been little used, but seems apt to describe the unskilled, unemployed, or underemployed. This group includes the most impoverished members of our population, many subsisting on welfare or old-age pensions, or supported by friends or family. The under class is too fragmented, too little educated, and too nonpolitical to be a subculture in the sense in which we use the term. This is not to say the under class is not socially important but only to say that it does not have the characteristics of a cultural grouping as we have defined culture.

Middle America

This rather ambiguous term is frequently used nowadays by journalists and social commentators. At this time, there is no clear definition of Middle America. Apparently the term indicates a large group which cuts across the upper-working, lower-middle, and middle-middle classes. Such usage is not precise, and we prefer to distinguish between white-collars and blue-collars, as above, and their various sub-groupings.

Some writers use "Middle American" in a derogatory sense. They are referring to persons who have a meager formal education, especially in the liberal arts; who are not cultivated; who are fundamentally closed-minded and conservative; whose life styles include enjoyment of spectator sports (e.g., TV football, TV soap operas, and trite situation comedies); who are the chief "joiners" in the sense that they furnish the backbone of the membership of churches, lodges, and veteran's organizations; who tend toward old-culture values, particularly in the sense of being hawkish where war is concerned, prizing law and order over justice; and being patriotic in an old-fashioned flag-waving sense. Archie Bunker, of the popular television show of the early 1970s ("All in the Family") epitomizes this group. The term, "hard hat" has also come to have a generic meaning permitting it to embrace many of these included in the Middle America category.

As of this writing, research has not demonstrated that there is a Middle American group of the sort described above which is a genuine subculture. We all know people who fit—in fact, the journalist's definition of Middle American sounds very much like Warner's lower-middle class except that it includes also blue-collar workers (which Warner did end up lumping with lower white-collar workers under the head, "the common man level").

Significance of Classes as Subcultures

Provided we hew to the definition of class as a group united by a given power and prestige level, and sharing more or less common goals, then it may well be that our social classes are the most important of our subcultures. To the extent that they share common ideologies, and figure most prominently in the nation's power structure—discussed in Chapter 5 —they would seem more significant for the type of analysis intended in this book than the other subcultures described in this section.

Homogenization and Differentiation

Subcultures must be regarded as fluid—they change continuously. Some disappear as others emerge. When subcultures disappear, it is usually because of absorption into the surrounding larger subculture or through dispersion, followed by more rapid absorption into a variety of subcultures. Whether a subculture disappears from a location where it may long have thrived or whether its members leave their "home location" to fan out over a large region, the process of absorption is basically the same. Subcultures lose their identities by mingling with other subcultures. The process of mingling may lead to friendships and intermarriage within other subcultures and a consequent development of common values.

However, mingling of attitudes, values, and beliefs may result merely from different subcultures having access to the same mass media: a network television show so popular that people of many different subcultures watch it is almost certain to make its viewers more alike than they otherwise would be. Widely read books, newspapers, and magazines promote the same type of psychological mingling.

Schooling can greatly enhance mingling. Even though a school is racially or ethnically homogenous, students almost certainly learn something about other subcultures. If schools are integrated racially and ethnically, or by social class or ideological grouping, they may produce a rapid eroding effect on the integrity of the subcultures represented. Travel is another important factor in erasing subcultural differences. Every year Americans travel more either for vacations or business reasons. Hence, people of different subcultures have increasing opportunity to meet and share ideas.

Is our national culture developing in such a manner that we can expect to see all subcultures disappear sometime in the future? It seems certain in time that many specific subcultures will disappear, perhaps virtually all those with which we are now familiar. We can see the process of homogenization at work and point to numerous subcultures which have already disappeared. For all practical purposes, most of our European-based ethnic subcultures have mingled to the point of losing their identity. A considerable number of our subcultures based upon distinctive theologies have eroded or completely lost viability as increasing numbers of people have lost interest in theological issues or in deep religious commitments generally.

Although most present subcultures may disappear, new subcultures have a way of appearing. Some recent examples in the United States were the youthful counterculture of the sixties; the Women's Movement; and scientists, engineers, and technicians involved in space exploration. We may expect this process to continue.

Further, some of the old but waning subcultures are seeking a new vitality by resurrecting old beliefs and customs. This process has been labeled *cultural nationalism*. For example, some Blacks are promoting new interest in their earlier African culture. As a result, most colleges and universities now offer programs in African studies and African hair styling and clothing has proliferated. We cannot determine at this time how far cultural nationalism will go; it may be a fad or with us to stay.

CULTURAL CHANGE

One of the primary theses of this book is that, insofar as we know, cultural change—at least within any contexts now understood—is inexorable. In some cultures, change may move in like a retarded glacier. In others, change races forward so fast that people are dazzled and often hopelessly confused and frustrated. In most cultures, the pace is somewhere between these extremes. Change may be of such major import as to seem cataclysmic, such as the social and military consequences of learning to release the power congealed in atoms; or change may be so trivial that one wonders how it can be justified at all, as the invention of scented toilet paper.

Sources of Cultural Change

Basically, there is but one source of cultural change—*innovation* (invention). In common sociological parlance, invention refers to constructing a new idea, whether by accident or intent. The motive to innovate probably develops only in what we call a "problematic situation." The situation may have any of several characteristics but always appears to arise out of *purposive* behavior, behavior in which there is a more-or-less clearly defined goal which cannot be achieved immediately and directly because of psychological or physical barriers.

Although it rarely is, innovation may be internal to a particular culture—arising within a closed system. A completely isolated culture may have long since lost any former contact with other cultures but nevertheless continue to innovate. Much more common is innovation which is aided by, or derived from, contact with one or more other cultures. This process of the absorption of new thought by one culture from another is referred to as cultural diffusion.

Cultural diffusion is rarely a one-way street. A culture borrows, but in the process the lending culture is changed. The process of borrowing virtually always produces an exchange, so the borrowing process is a transaction. For example, when one culture comes into contact with another, there is almost always some degree of incompatibility between their thought patterns, incompatibility which must be reconciled to a point where both give and take become psychologically possible. In sociological writing, the word "syncretism" (attempted reconciliation of opposing ideas) is often used, but more descriptive is the expression borrowed from mathematics—"simultaneous mutual interaction" (the SMI concept).

A good example of SMI in action occurs in the first meeting of two religions. The proponents of each faith stubbornly proclaim their absolute rightness and try to inflict the tenets of their faith on each other. In spite of initial reluctance the "invaded" group usually adopts at least some new ideas. But in the transaction the ideas of the invaded group contaminate the "invaders." It is common knowledge at university divinity schools that modern Christianity is a complex blend of Judaism, various pagan religions of the Persian Peninsula, and still others of Nordic Europe, and that these invaded groups adopted some or most of the Christian ideas.

The modification of the culture of an individual or group by contact with one or more other cultural patterns is commonly called *acculturation*. The acquiring of a whole culture, as occurs when a child is born into a culture, or an already acculturated adult moves into a culture new to him and is forced to learn its ways, is often called by anthropologists *enculturation*. Enculturation, when applied to children and youth, is also called *socialization*, a term used more often by educators and sociologists than by anthropologists. However, it is becoming increasingly common to use these words interchangeably.

Reasons for Different Rates of Change

We have already suggested that innovations may come slowly or rapidly. To understand why this happens we must understand the basic nature of invention. We have seen that ordinarily it is motivated only by a "felt problem," but there is more to it than that.

According to the now largely outdated "great man" theory, it was formerly held that most innovation was the work of a small minority, the creative geniuses (the Prometheans), whose original thought was then adopted by others. Now, most invention is regarded as a process of accretion, with one step following another and large numbers of persons being involved.

Invention is putting together, in a novel way, ideas already in existence. The larger the idea base of a culture (which includes its own, plus what it can borrow elsewhere), the *more possible combinations* of ideas there are. A simple culture with a limited stock of ideas can innovate only slowly. A complex culture, where for each invention sought (or stumbled on) there are literally thousands of previously existing and potentially relevant ideas, can innovate at a much faster rate. Because both simple and complex cultures tend to add to their store of ideas, the rate of increase in innovation tends to accelerate. This acceleration tends to be more in accord with a geometric or, better, exponential, than with an arithmetic progression, that is, instead of the increase simulating a 1-2-3-4 progression, it is more like a 1-2-4-8 progression. Figure 1-1 graphically indicates the expected curves in two different cultural situations.

What we have said so far about invention refers more to potentiality than actuality; furthermore, Figure 1-1 and the above explanation make no distinction between types of inventions. There is conclusive evidence that in virtually all cultures certain types of inventions proceed at a rate faster than others, even though the potentiality of the idea base from which to operate is equal. Whether the existing idea base, or idea bank, leads to the maximum feasible number of innovations hinges largely on whether members of the culture want innovations. We will discuss this idea in the next section.

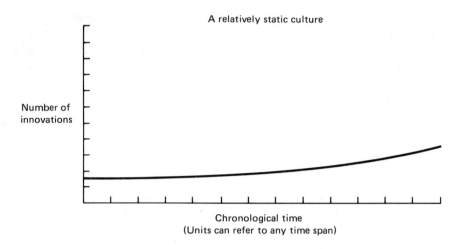

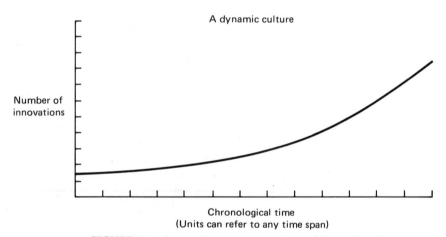

FIGURE 1-1.   Innovation rates in static and dynamic cultures.

It seems likely, barring some major catastrophe such as nuclear war or genocide, the rate of social change in all nations will become increasingly exponential. The advanced industrial nations already have such an extensive idea base from which to work, as well as the means of implementing innovations, that change is beginning to appear as a threat to survival rather than as progress. Change can occur so rapidly as to get out of hand; it can generate social problems much faster than people can solve them. Rapid change can also produce psychological anguish and breakdown in individuals—what Alvin Toffler has labeled "future shock."[4] But,

[4] Alvin Toffler, *Future Shock*. New York: Random House, 1970; Bantam, 1971.

as we will indicate in Chapter 4, there appear to be some circumstances in which a society which is forced to change may fare better if change comes with a revolutionary rush.

Uneven Rates of Cultural Change

Not all parts of a culture change at the same rate. In both its "pure" and "applied"—or technological (engineering)—aspects, science tends to spurt ahead. Other elements of culture, particularly those in which nonscientific values predominate, usually show innovation at a much slower rate.

Uneven rates of change of different parts of a culture are more obvious and dramatic in rapidly moving, dynamic industrial cultures than in slowly moving, relatively static nonindustrial cultures. Ordinarily social change is steplike and innovations appear when creative persons see a means of combining old elements into something distinctively new. Whether the steplike change in a culture is slow or fast, change in certain areas outruns change in others.

Whether public acceptance of innovation in science and technology is accepted, or even welcomed, depends on attitudes people have toward those nonscientific elements of culture directly affected by innovations in science. People may or may not fear that their vested interests will be damaged or their sacred beliefs jeopardized, or that major and unwanted changes in life style will be required. The following section will explain some situations in which science and technology is either welcomed or not.

Public Acceptance of Innovation in Pure and Applied Science

A quick distinction between "pure" and "applied" science is needed, but we need not make a major issue of it. Pure science is not distinguished by being more true, abstract, difficult to understand, or necessarily more important, than applied science. Neither can function without the other; in fact, each nourishes the other and in this sense the dichotomy of pure and applied is artificial. "Pure" refers to innovative statements about our perceptions of the fundamental "way things are" in nature. "Applied" science takes these inventive statements about "the way things are" and tries to find practical applications for them in the world of human affairs. Einstein invented a statement, largely in mathematical terms, about an assumed relationship in nature. It then required much complex scientific experimentation to verify Einstein's statement, and still more to demonstrate how an atomic bomb could be made through its use. At a somewhat lower level, applied scientists (engineers) worked out details of designing and manufacturing a practical bomb—"practical" in that it works, not that it is practical for use in future warfare.

The point of the distinction between pure and applied science just made, is simply that virtually all pure science is so highly specialized, uses such esoteric concepts, and is so far removed from what the public knows, that there is little opposition to it. Why should people oppose, in this era of history, something which bears the label of pure science and is carried on by respectable people—even if the public does not understand it?

Beginning about 1870, no less than 75 *major* inventions flooded the country before World War I. Many people were bothered by inventions they thought would affect their lives. Most opposition resulted from the insecurity naturally felt both by persons who sensed that their whole way of life might change and were not sure they would like it, and by persons who had vested interests in the old ways of doing things.

The invention of gasoline automobiles (by Benz and Daimler, 1884) probably illustrates both kinds of opposition. Some people could see far enough ahead to realize that the automobile would force profound changes in their culture and that they would not like some of these changes (for example, they may have seen how the automobile would change dating habits). But there were also the saddlemakers, harnessmakers, and buggy manufacturers who saw that sooner or later their occupations would be wiped out. Not only was their means of livelihood at stake, but also traditional handcrafts from which they derived deep personal satisfaction.

Some opposition to potentially usable inventions even had a religious base. After the 1903 demonstration of the Wright brothers' airplane, pious objections took the form of "If God had intended man to fly, He would have given him wings." However, after becoming accustomed to the inventions, most people realized that science and engineering were making life much more comfortable. The horseless carriage did get people where they wanted to go much faster than a horse and eventually about as dependably. Flush toilets were admittedly more pleasant than backyard privies. Electric lights were safer and more convenient than gas. The telephone got messages through faster than the Pony Express. By the 1920s most persons were sold on the engineers' accomplishments and eagerly waited for the next consumer item to be marketed.

So people fell in love with technology. United States culture, like that of many other nations, became "scientistic," that is, science and its products turned into objects of worship. Inventions could not be marketed too fast.

People still like to have "pure scientists" tinkering in their laboratories to see what ideas they can come up with; no one protests scientific exploration that might cure cancer, or inventions that would make life better without polluting the environment. But since the middle 1960s people in most industrialized nations have tempered their enthusiasm about uncontrolled technology. There is now a fairly widespread tendency for all sorts of people to ask about inventions, "Will its long-range consequences be good or bad for mankind?"

Despite this new caution, people will more readily accept that which comes to them labeled science and technology than they will new ideas in areas having religious or moral connotations. Culture still changes at an uneven rate; furthermore, it appears in the 1970s that stresses caused by uneven rates of change are more nearly out of hand than ever before.

Closed Areas of Culture

We will use the expression "social-moral-ideological," to cover all areas of life which do not come under science or technology/engineering. It is under this sweeping heading that we place values, beliefs, myths, ideology, and knowledge about such interests as politics, socioeconomic ideologies, race, social class, sex, courtship, marriage, male-female relations, family, religion, and so on. In these and like areas of interest people continue to hold many beliefs as *absolutes*, and to be very touchy about them. Many beliefs in these areas are held with such emotional fervor that people holding them do not want them to be examined on a reflective, that is, critically objective or scientific, level. Ideology in such areas is usually not to be touched; critical examination is taboo.

In the early 1940s a professor at Ohio State University, Alan Griffin, getting his cue from historian James Harvey Robinson, began calling any area of interest which is laden with untouchable beliefs a "closed area." The label is apt: "closed" simply means closed to impartial scrutiny or closed to reflection, closed to the use of factual evidence, closed to criticism or potential criticism.

The idea of closed areas is handy for students because it helps them understand the uneven development of culture better. If an innovation in science and technology comes along which has direct implications for a belief in the broad social-moral-ideological area, and if the belief is both closed to critical examination and incompatible with technological innovation, then immediately a cultural tension is created. The cultural tension is usually translated sooner or later to personal tensions.

Figure 1-2 is a hypothetical graphic representation of numbers of utilized innovations in open and closed areas of culture over any span of time since science and technology became important integral parts of our culture. In any span of years, at least since 1870, the rate at which innovation in science and technology has outrun innovation in the more controversial social areas is about the same.

The graph represents guesses, somewhat informed, but still guesses, about the number of utilized inventions in ideas that appeared during a time span, say, from 1900 to 1970. The only thing we can be reasonably

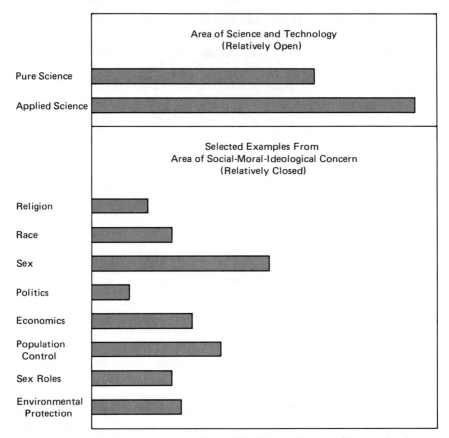

FIGURE 1-2.   Hypothetical depiction of rates of innovation in
different areas of culture.

sure about is that more utilized ideas appeared in the fields of pure and
applied science than in any of the ideological fields which contain at least
some closed areas. Conceivably, one could get data on the number of
patents granted for inventions in pure and applied science. Since it is
impossible to patent new ideas in religion, race, sex, etc., there are no
objective data available in these areas. Figure 1-2 has only one purpose:
to show hypothetically the relative disparity between the numbers of
inventions in technology and those in areas which are to some degree still
closed.

An Example of Closed Areas Blocking Solution of a Problem

Not all differential (uneven) changes produce problems. If innovations in solid-state physics outrun innovations in the game of tennis, no
problem is likely to develop because there is no direct relationship between

them. The two areas of culture are not related in the sense that a change in one necessarily has anything to do with a change in the other. If in a given year, there were several hundred inventions in solid-state physics and only three new rules for tennis, we would not say that tennis was creating a problem. Problems only occur when two or more areas of innovation are directly related, when the functioning of one depends on the functioning of another. Below is an example of how ideology in a relatively closed area does hamper solving a crucial social problem.

The Ecological Problem

In the 1950s such persons as William Vogt, Fairfield Osburn, and Harrison Brown were writing of the potential problems man could create for himself by overpopulating the planet, destroying the natural environment, and wantonly using the finite plant and mineral resources of the earth. Since the late 1960s, several hundred ecologists with respectable scientific standing have been extrapolating trends from changes in the composition of air, soil, and water which portend disaster for the human species as well as all other life. (Chapter 12 will discuss details of some of our ecological problems.) The point to make here is that even though special interest groups and part of the public have shown concern about preserving a life-supporting environment, progress has been slow.

In view of what ecologists have established as apparently true, it would seem that human beings would have begun taking more revolutionary steps before this to save the human race. Numerous steps have been taken, some of which represent solid gains, but few ecologists would say that we have done more than make a small start considering the immensity of the problem. Why do people hold back?

Ideology that Blocks Ecological Solutions

It appears fairly obvious that people hold back because of a rather complex cluster of beliefs, some a part of the ideological heritage transmitted by earlier generations and some pressed on them by organizations either unfamiliar with the ecological facts or, for one reason or another, unconcerned by them. Many of these beliefs are held as absolutes and therefore are *closed* to critical examination. Any idea that prevents man from taking serious steps toward ameliorating as best he can the thrust posed by a mutilated natural environment is an example of ideology blocking problem solution. Some ideas that make it difficult to achieve major headway in attacking ecological problems are:

"Human beings, because they are the living creatures most favored by God, have both the right and an obligation to dominate the earth and all other living creatures."

"Every married man and woman have a God-given right to have as many children as they want."

"Progress means the steadily increasing production of material goods."

"Progress can be measured by speed—the faster people can get from one place to another the more they have progressed."

"Food is not fit to eat if it is damaged by insects or diseases which affect its appearance."

"It is all right for the United States to use one-third of the world's power resources for only one-fourteenth of the world's population."

"Unless a species of animal or plant is directly and obviously useful for people, there is no reason to protect it from extermination."

"The United States must continue to be the most powerful nation in the world militarily, no matter what the cost in man power and resources."

Cultural Organization and Disorganization Defined

To understand cultural disorganization, which involves destructive conflict, it is essential first to understand cultural organization, which assumes some degree of concord and cooperation. When members of a cultural unit operate as a group, cultural organization is present. A group is any plurality of persons who through interaction over a period of time have come to understand each other's values to some degree. Group functioning is possible even though members of the group do not have the same values about all things; in fact, groups thrive on the give and take of ideas. But, by definition, a group must share some values. Central to these shared values must be rules for settling disputes amicably and for arriving at group goals when the entire group is required to take united action. In the rest of this section the writer draws heavily on the ideas of the late Arnold Rose.[5]

To present Rose's theory on social disorganization it is necessary to restate some of the above discussion of social organization. Rose begins his theorizing by making three basic assumptions: (1) individual behavior is influenced to a large degree by what the individual thinks other people expect of him, (2) a social group is a number of persons who know what to expect of other members and know what other members expect of them, and (3) the expectations which any one member of the group holds for

[5] Arnold M. Rose, *Theory and Method in the Social Sciences.* Minneapolis: University of Minnesota Press, 1954, pp. 6–12. Rose's position, like that of numerous other sociologists and social psychologists, is strongly influenced by the social psychology of George Herbert Mead, *Mind, Self and Society.* Chicago: University of Chicago Press, 1934.

another is based on his understanding of his own values—how he would act in a given situation. A culture is a group, the members of which can to a large extent anticipate the behavior of the others because each person, through knowing his own values, knows fairly well the values of the others.

Conflict develops in two ways. For any of numerous reasons the larger group ceases to have shared, long-term values or goals. As group goals become fragmented, the group itself fragments; factions develop around various goals with no faction adhering to all the original goals. For example, the faculty of a public school may operate as a team. They have common and well-understood purposes. But some disruptive factor may enter the situation, such as a new faculty member who disagrees with the previously accepted faculty goals and persuades some teachers that he is right and the rest of the faculty is wrong. This kind of fragmentation is called *interpersonal conflict*.

A second way that conflict develops is when a number of persons are in contact with one another but no one any longer really understands or shares the goals of anyone else. A person finds that he can no longer predict what other members of the group will do in a given situation. He no longer knows how they feel about him. When this kind of situation develops, an individual cannot maintain any self-identity; he cannot describe any coherent set of values or beliefs which he feels are uniquely his own because he can no longer "read" what the others think of him. He experiences *intrapersonal conflict*.

Symptoms of Disorganization

In this section, we will treat personal disorganization separately from cultural disorganization simply as a matter of convenience in organizing. Personal disorganization, if it exists on a fairly wide scale, produces a subculture, or national or regional culture, which is disorganized; and, at the same time, a cultural group, when disorganized, tends to produce personal disorganization within its members. In this context, personal and cultural amount to the same thing: they are bound by a virtually inescapable transaction, or, if one prefers a more descriptive label, a SMI relationship (simultaneous mutual interaction), as mentioned previously. The topic of personal disorganization will be developed farther in Chapter 3.

Cultural Disorganization

The term anomic, denoting people having no guiding values, can also be used for groups, cultures, subcultures, except that when an aggregation of people reach a point of sufficient anomie that they no longer have any rational goals in common, the aggregation can probably no longer be called a culture. What makes for a culture has ceased to exist.

Yet, anomic aggregations of people do seek desperately for leadership; they cannot direct themselves, and eagerly search for someone who can give them firm directions as to what to do. When a leader is found, the group, by adopting the leader's goal statements and values, may become a culture again. The culture may be temporary, especially—as has often been the case—if the leader is also highly anomic and leads by impulse, hallucinogenic visions, or presumed directions from a supernatural authority.

There is another closely related symptom of anomie. Anomic individuals not only have difficulty arriving at goals; they also have great difficulty choosing means appropriate to the goals. If their leader proclaims the goal of "peace on earth," both anomic leader and followers may try to achieve this goal by starting a world war or some lesser but violent disturbance.

Perhaps better than anyone else, James MacGregor Burns has described the predicament a nation can get in when people in positions of power and their dependent followers regularly try to follow disjunctive means-ends sequences. Such people tend to believe that "the end justifies the means," and rarely achieve their ends because the means they select lead in a quite different direction. From the Vietnam War comes the classic example of inability to see logical relations between means and ends: the officer who said "In order to save the village, we had to destroy it."[6] This discussion will be resumed in Chapter 3.

CULTURAL DISINTEGRATION

Disintegration refers to the state a society may find itself in after it has passed through a period of heightening disorganization. There comes a point where there are no longer any leaders who can lead, or if there were rational leaders, the people would not recognize them.

Up to this point in the chapter, it has been possible to illustrate such concepts as subculture, cultural change, closed areas of culture, cultural disorganization, and the like, with illustrations from United States culture. The present topic, cultural disintegration, is much harder to illustrate except hypothetically. This is because, as of the time of this writing, the United States shows symptoms of serious disintegration only here and there, not sufficiently widespread disintegration to provide concrete illustrative material concerning an entire culture during its final collapse.

[6] For an excellent treatment of the ends-means problem, see James MacGregor Burns, *Uncommon Sense*. New York: Harper & Row, Publishers, 1972.

Therefore, to a large degree the remainder of this section is a hypothetical model. This does not mean this material is pulled out of thin air; historical case studies provide examples of societies in dissolution. What we lack is any certain way of knowing, if United States culture were to disintegrate, whether what would happen here would resemble what has happened elsewhere.

Cultural disintegration occurs when a culture ceases to be functional. A culture ceases to be functional when social controls over interpersonal conflict break down. Each group is "on its own" and each tries to survive through any means. In one form of group evolution, each group becomes increasingly totalitarian, purging itself of all who dissent from group goals; each becomes a military or para-military enclave. Then, at any time, any particular group may feel gravely threatened by another. An authoritarian group which feels threatened is paranoid, tending to see threat almost everywhere. When fear reaches a critical level, the group attempts to destroy its imagined or real threats before being itself destroyed. Thus hostility between groups mounts until groups use violent means against each other with the intent to destroy. This often means armed warfare, but with little or no centralized direction. In addition to the label disintegration, we may call such a situation *cultural chaos* or *anarchy*.

We need to emphasize the "enemy complex" which a disintegrating culture is likely to adopt to shore itself up a little longer. Before use can be made of the enemy complex, the leader or leaders of the culture must still be rational enough to understand the uniting function of an external or internal enemy or both. Historically it has been rather typical for cultures in an advanced state of disorganization or in a state of developing disintegration, to create "enemies." If the leaders can convince large numbers of the people there is an enemy so dangerous that everyone's freedom or even life is at stake, then fear is likely to have a temporary uniting effect.

We are talking here, of course, about the role of imaginary enemies. If leaders and led, thinking rationally, perceive a real enemy who seriously endangers them, then trying to confine or destroy the enemy is an act of sanity. Often it is difficult to distinguish an imaginary from a real enemy, and therefore difficult to judge an "enemy-prone" people as suffering from delusions or as satisfactorily rational.

CULTURE BUILDING

Even within a dying culture, culture building can continue and apparently must take the following general form: there must be a group disassociated from the mainstream of the old culture—committed to attitudes, values, and beliefs in most instances diametrically opposed to those of the old culture. The conceptual patterns of the new, rising culture should lead to considerable synthesizing of the disparate ideas of the old culture during its period of disorganization and incipient disintegration. This tends to produce a steady reduction in the level of conflict. Even though the new value system fuses some old with the new, numerous old values must be completely discarded. Values which produced disorganization and disintegration in the old culture must be destroyed. Otherwise, the new culture will contain the same elements that destroyed the old and will therefore also be self-destructing. Examples of culture building in process can be found in the following section on cultural revolution and elsewhere in the book.

CULTURAL REVOLUTION: FACT OR FANCY?

Most scholarly observers, whether liberal or conservative, agree that the period since World War II, and particularly since the early 1960s, has been a period of cultural turbulence and accelerated cultural change. Observers' interpretations of this period in our history vary drastically. Some see it as a temporary revolt, sparked by irresponsible youthful troublemakers, not fundamentally unlike numerous other revolts in our history and certainly of lesser significance than the revolt of the South which instigated the Civil War, the reaction against Victorianism occurring in the 1920s, or the reaction of the 1930s against the establishment institutions associated with the Great Depression of that decade. Such observers see the "generation gap," about which so much has been written since the mid-1960s, as merely another of the regularly recurring breaks between the young and their elders which have been occurring throughout history. Those who adhere to the revolt thesis are mainly, but not entirely, conservatives who cannot tolerate the thought that presently occurring cultural change may cut much deeper than a mere revolt, and may not be susceptible to suppression or diversion as revolts usually are.

Scholars on the liberal to left side of the political-social spectrum are more inclined to think of the present era not as a revolt, but a revolution, centering perhaps in the United States but bringing along with it other nations as well. They disagree on the precise nature of the revolution, on how far along it is, and what its outcome may be. After studying much that has been written on the subject, including speculative works as well as the empirical studies, the present writer believes that the concept of revolution, as it will be defined in the following section, fits the situation better than the concept of revolt.

The Nature of a Cultural Revolution

One point must be emphasized strongly: *a cultural revolution is a revolution in thought*. It involves a fundamental shift in values and beliefs, a turning upside down of the ideology that held the culture together prior to the revolution. It may require many years (conceivably centuries) for an ideological shift to produce widespread and revolutionary changes in people's overt behavior or in institutional structures. The industrial revolution, for instance, began as a redirection of ideology—related in part to the growing strength of Protestantism—and is still in progress. In contrast, the ideological shift may be rapid. The Manus of New Guinea, studied by Margaret Mead in 1928 and again in 1953, have during that short span of years moved from a Stone Age to a twentieth century culture ideologically, and in much of their individual and institutional behavior.

A cultural revolution is rarely, if ever, total: no matter how far-reaching it is, at least some of the prerevolutionary ideology is retained, and often a considerable amount of it. But a cultural change can be considered revolutionary if the core values of the culture, those which have been most binding, are abandoned by a majority of people and in their place a new set of values, opposed to or contradicting the old, are firmly implanted.

Further, it seems plausible to hypothesize that a cultural revolution is more likely to succeed if the new ideological pattern is adopted by persons who are comparatively young, and whose more articulate members are likely to become leaders of thought by virtue of education, an established position in the society (such as upper-middle class), and organizational ability. However, cultural revolutions are greatly aided if the dissident youth are joined by a considerable number of sympathetic older persons already ensconced in positions of influence.

Specific Views of the Cultural Revolution

Although we could cite dozens of authorities on cultural revolution, we have selected three who are nonutopian, nonpolemical, and in personal makeup quite nonrevolutionary. These are Daniel Yankelovich (psychologist and opinion researcher), Margaret Mead (anthropologist), and William Glasser (social psychiatrist).

Daniel Yankelovich

Yankelovich is a psychology professor at New York University and head of his own opinion research organization. He reports the results of three major studies (1968, 1969, and 1971) of values held by college youth and presents his own interpretation of the emerging values of college youth in Part III of his book, *The Changing Values on Campus: Political and Personal Attitudes of Today's College Students.*[7] The gist of his thesis appeared as an article, "The New Naturalism."[8] We will present his thesis here in highly abbreviated form, since a much more deailed treatment will appear in Chapter 4, as well as a report of his 1973 survey.

Yankelovich, no starry-eyed utopian and not given to hasty interpretation, must be taken seriously. He raises the question of whether the student movement of the late 1960s through 1970 was a temporary rebellion against circumstances special to that period, or the signs of a deep-rooted long-range shift away from traditional establishment values. He notes that critics of the student movement have seen only the long hair, the strange costumes, the open sexuality, the use of illicit drugs, and the apparent revolt against authority as a pathological state boding no good for the future of human civilization; and, conversely, that those sympathetic to the movement tend to romanticize it, to accept uncritically all its manifestations, and to forecast an earthly paradise in the making. Yankelovich wonders if there may not be some truth in both outlooks: that the student movement may harbor simultaneously destructive as well as constructive values and beliefs.

[7] New York: Simon & Schuster, Inc.; Pocket Books, 1972.
[8] *Saturday Review,* April 1, 1972.

After placing such extremist views against his research data, Yankelovich appears fairly confident that imbedded within the movement is a "great idea." The central idea, which unites what at first glance seems a hodge-podge of unrelated or contradictory beliefs and practices, Yankelovich calls the "new naturalism." To quote him:

> The essence of the idea is that we must initiate a new stage in man's relatedness to nature and the natural. In the hierarchy of values that constitute man's conception of the *summum bonum*, the student-led cultural revolution elevates nature and the natural to the highest position. Whatever is natural is deemed to be good; whatever is artificial and opposed to nature is bad.[9]

Yankelovich concedes that what is natural as opposed to the unnatural is not easy to determine. He points out that his research into student values suggests that students themselves hold at least twenty different definitions of "natural." Yet, Yankelovich is convinced that there is an authentic student counterculture, the heart of which can be seen in three themes: (1) its stress on community, (2) its apparent antiintellectualism, and (3) its search for what is sacred in nature. Yankelovich uses the expression, "apparent antiintellectualism" deliberately; what is apparent may not reflect the deeper reality of a revolutionary new approach toward epistemology (the philosophy of "how one finds the truth").

The idea of community, which has apparently existed among hominids for at least half a million years, is hardly a radical idea. Nor is the idea of the closeness of human life and nature, which has been a part of most primitive cultures, was exalted by Rousseau, and still is a fundamental aspect of the outlook of American Indians. It seems radical primarily to those who feel the chief human role is the exploitative use of the natural environment to provide ever-rising material standards of living. Thus, the new naturalism is compounded of ideas that are very old and some ideas that are new: it is a mixture of conservatism and liberalism/radicalism.

In any case, Yankelovich seems convinced that even though the overt features of the student movement which have bothered conservatives so much may subside, there is in the making a shift in values which is truly revolutionary and will lead to a culture very unlike what we now know.

Margaret Mead

Margaret Mead, probably the best-known and most prestigious living anthropologist, Curator of New York's American Museum of Natural

---

[9] *Saturday Review*, April 1, 1972, p. 35.

History, author of more than twenty major books, offers an original and highly provocative interpretation of the cultural revolution in *Culture and Commitment: A Study of the Generation Gap*.[10] In this slim volume, based upon her "Man and Nature" lectures of 1969, she states in highly compacted form an interpretation which one can only hope will be expanded at length in a later volume.

To understand Mead's analysis, one must understand three technical terms, two of which she coined. These terms are *postfigurative, cofigurative*, and *prefigurative*. Figuration means forming something into a particular shape; figurative means based upon, or making use of shapes, patterns, or configurations (figurative has other meanings unrelated to our definitional needs here). These terms can refer to cultural shapes or patterns.

A *postfigurative* culture is one in which the shaping has already occurred and which is transmitted, as is, to each succeeding generation. Cultural transmission is linear—from grandparent to child.

A *cofigurative* culture is one in which the shaping is done *in the present by each generation.* However, cofigurative cultures appear only after the development of the nuclear family (i.e., a family pattern in which only parents and their children make up the family unit; grandparents are either no longer within the household or they have ceased to have influence).

Mead has chosen the term *prefigurative* to define our present technological society which is changing so rapidly that no one can see what is ahead. In this prefigurative society many youth have rejected most parental culture patterns and are hypothesizing prototypes of possible new cultural forms—they are prefiguring a new culture.

Mead suggests that prior to the twentieth century, most cultures were postfigurative. The family ordinarily consisted of three generations, and the grandparents, or elders, were regarded as models to be emulated. The wisdom of the elders was accepted by children and grandchildren as a "given" and not questioned. The generations were bound ideologically to one another and cultural change was insignificant (as, static cultures, mentioned earlier in the chapter). There were no problems of identity or commitment in such cultures.

Cofigurative cultures began to develop with the coming of the twentieth century when the nuclear family became common and the rate of cultural change was hastened by the growth of technology. Cofigurative culture appears when any of various factors cause the breakdown of the prenuclear family; since elders are no longer in a position to transmit their culture to their young, older culture patterns are no longer available as

---

[10] New York: Doubleday & Company, Inc., 1970 (published for The American Museum of Natural History).

models. Therefore, both parents and children must learn from their con-temporaries. There is the development and institutionalization of subcul-tures based upon age, *so that one's age peers become the chief source through which the culture is learned.* Within a cofigurative culture, there is the assumption that core values will continue to exist even though peripheral values are changing—"change within changelessness." Cofigura-tive culture began to break down about 1940. The coming of World War II, its consummation and aftermath, produced heightening levels of technol-ogy, faster rates of change, and a condition of anomie in which there were no longer culturewide cores of values left.

Mead sees the process of cultural transmission since World War II as increasingly prefigurative. The older cultural patterns have broken up, provoking a crisis which is better seen by adults than by youth. People are no longer sure of the future. However, even though directionless cultural change has baffled adults, there is also a contemporaneous pattern, a "now culture," in which only the young are at home. As we have seen, this is an open experimental pattern. The truly revolutionary aspect of prefigurative culture is that adults feel helpless, lonely, alienated, whereas the young, although feeling alienated from older cultural patterns, do understand their own youth culture and are weighing their hypothesized options for the future. In the movement from postfigurative to prefigurative culture, Mead sees a *probable reversal of the direction of education.* In a prefigurative culture wisdom may be expected to be in the possession of the young. In such a culture, therefore, *much of the significant education that occurs is the education of parents by their children.*

We can now see why Mead considers the present situation as one unique in all history, and a turning point perhaps as important as when Homo sapiens learned to use fire.

But a prefigurative society is highly unstable. We cannot predict how long it will last. Presumably it will last until the process of culture building has produced a new pattern viable enough to become relatively stable, that is to say, when a new core of values develops to form a basis for commitment and the building of individual identity. Mead is convinced that today's young (at least, those who are best educated) have rejected older culture patterns to the point that whatever new culture they build, it will be very different from anything human beings have ever before known.

William Glasser

Glasser is a Los Angeles psychiatrist, whose interests probably en-title him to the label, "social psychiatrist," meaning a psychiatrist who is interested in the interaction of individual persons and their perceived envi-

ronment of living and nonliving objects. Glasser is best known for a se-
quence of three widely read books: *Reality Therapy: A New Approach to
Psychiatry*, *Schools Without Failure*, and *The Identity Society*.[11] It is with
the latter that we will be concerned here. The central thesis of *The Identity
Society* appeared in an article, "The Civilized Identity Society: Mankind
Enters Phase Four."[12]

Glasser hypothesizes a cultural revolution of a kind which, on the
surface, seems quite different from the theories of Yankelovich and Mead.
His theory is equally provocative, and as we will see in summarizing this
section, there may be several important areas of thinking these three persons have in common.

Glasser goes back much farther in time to begin his analysis, based,
as he says, on speculative anthropology. He sees three stages through
which hominids have passed and another into which human beings are
entering. Each marks a fundamental turning point in the development of
human culture. The first hominids (upright-walking, humanlike creatures)
established what Glasser calls *primitive survival society*. They were *goal
oriented*—their prime aim was survival in a hostile environment. Through
natural selection they developed a need and capacity for intelligent cooperation; group life became established. When Glasser wrote, Australopith-
ecus was considered the first hominid, four million years ago. The later
discovery of an earlier, different ancestor of man does not invalidate
Glasser's thesis.

About half a million years ago, *Pithecanthropus* (a more developed
species of hominid) discovered the use of fire. From fossil evidence, it
appears that this development made it possible for hominids to move
much farther in the direction of having spare time, comparatively free of
stress, in which to enjoy social relations and to become involved in the
affairs of his companion hominids. This ushered in a stage which Glasser
calls *primitive identity society*. Fossil evidence suggests that there was a
long period of time in which survival could be taken largely for granted
and hominids could find time to love and be loved, to become involved
with others, and to develop elaborate rituals, ceremonies, and religious
beliefs. Roles came to be prized over the goals related to survival.

With increasing population, however, hominids' needs began to
outstrip the food supplies of peoples who were primarily hunters and food
gatherers. Agriculture became necessary, land became valuable, and to
gain control over land, hominids began to compete and prey upon one
another. By now, cultural development had reached a point where the
term, civilization, becomes applicable.

[11] New York: Harper & Row, Publishers, 1965, with a Foreword by O. H.
Mowrer; New York: Harper & Row, Publishers, 1969; New York: Harper & Row,
Publishers, 1972, respectively.
[12] *Saturday Review*, February 19, 1972.

The first civilizations appeared about 10,000 years ago. This ushered in the period in human development which Glasser calls *civilized survival society* (Homo sapiens had appeared on the scene much earlier—apparently about 50,000 years ago). Civilized survival society has been marked by hostility, aggression, and frequent wars. Although, in Glasser's view, the need for peaceful cooperation had become biologically imbedded in hominids at least a half million years ago, it came to be suppressed by Homo sapiens. However, humans remained entrapped in social orders in which hostile behavior was the rule until the mid-twentieth century (and for a majority of them, into the 1970s). During the period of civilized survival society, survival goals superseded the enjoyment of roles of the earlier stage.

But Glasser feels that beginning roughly about 1950, signs developed of a return to *what has been natural to man* since the first primitive identity society. This development, which Glasser feels is the wave of the future, he calls *civilized identity society*. Once again, we observe many humans becoming role, rather than goal, oriented (attachment to roles is an aspect of the achieving of identity). Along with role-orientation is the need for involvement with others—of love, cooperation, play, of a life more relaxed and less tension ridden. As in the case of primitive identity society, civilized identity society strives for a reconciliation with nature, which includes the enjoyment of people's own natural capacities, including sex, and a relaxation in general of the inhibitions which served a purpose in civilized survival society but which have no useful function in an identity society. In short, the 10,000 years of civilized survival society, which was brutish and frustrating to most human beings, is yielding to the biologically demanded happier existence which humans and their hominid precursors enjoyed for almost half a million years.

Referring to the present situation, Glasser says:

> Led by the young, the half billion people of the Western world have begun a tumultuous revolution toward a new, role-dominated society in which people concern themselves more and more with their identities and how they might express them. Of course, people still strive for goals, but increasingly these are vocational or avocational goals that their pursuers believe will reinforce the independent human role.[13]

Summary and Conclusions

The theories of Yankelovich, Mead, and Glasser are based on a rather considerable amount of empirical evidence and are carefully thought out. Mead and Glasser carefully place their interpretations within a historical

---

[13] *Saturday Review,* February 19, 1972, p. 31.

framework. Mead's postfigurative culture extends backward to the first beginnings of a family structure, which we surmise is a great many thousand years at the least, and perhaps to the first hominid societies. Glasser begins with the first hominid societies and suggests stages that provide a stronger basis than Mead's for interpreting the present scene. Mead's most unique contribution, it strikes us, is her belief that, in the new culture being born, the young will necessarily be teachers of their parents. This possibility is not ruled out either by Yankelovich or Glasser, in fact, it may be implied in their interpretations.

All three writers date the emergence of efforts to reject older cultural patterns at about the middle of this century and suggest that such efforts emerged from deeply rooted needs for new cultural patterns. As to the nature of the new patterns emerging, Yankelovich finds in his college and university student samples values and beliefs which he calls the new naturalism. There seems to be a striking similarity between the content of Yankelovich's concept of the new naturalism and Glasser's concept of the civilized identity society. Mead leaves the future open, as an unknown, but makes plain that she considers it primarily in the hands of the young. If the values of the young who have leadership potential are as Yankelovich and Glasser suggest, then even within Mead's conceptual framework, we can make inferences about the future which permit a coincidence of all three positions.

All three writers are concerned about the identity crisis produced by older cultural forms and the necessity of resolving this crisis in any new culture which is viable enough to last. All three writers see the young as primarily role- rather than goal-oriented. All three are humanistic in the sense of ignoring or rejecting any such mechanistic determinisms as that of B. F. Skinner.

This writer believes that there is enough substance in the areas of agreement shared by Yankelovich, Mead and Glasser to provide a defensible theoretical base for interpreting many contemporary cultural situations and problems, and this base will be used frequently in later chapters of this book.

STUDY QUESTIONS

1. It is sometimes said that a person and his culture are continuous. What does such a statement mean?
2. Compile a list of ideological statements which you feel would be acceptable to your grandparents; then a list acceptable to your parents; and finally, a list of your own. What trends do you see from one generation to the next?
3. In what subculture, or subcultures, would you place yourself? Why?
4. Many social observers think that not only are lower-income white-

collar workers and higher-income blue-collar workers the most conservative elements in our culture, but they are steadily becoming more so. If this is true, how would you explain it?

5. In addition to the examples given in the chapter, what new subcultures do you see arising in the United States?
6. Name all the areas of interest you can think of in which there are still enough taboos that they might properly be called "closed" or "comparatively closed." (The examples in the chapter are meant to be suggestive, not inclusive.)
7. What do you see as the most open and closed areas of culture among your student acquaintances? How would you assess your own thinking about areas of interest that were formerly largely closed?
8. Give some examples of cultural disorganization other than those mentioned in the chapter. At the present time, do you think the culture is becoming more or less disorganized?
9. What some social observers see as a cultural revolution may be no more than an acceleration of long-range trends, not a fundamental shift in ideology. How would you argue this issue?
10. Run over in your mind the values and beliefs of all the people you know fairly well. What proportion, if any, do you think have adopted ideas that your parents would consider "revolutionary"?

ANNOTATED BIBLIOGRAPHY

Bennis, Warren G., Kenneth D. Benne, and Robert Chin, The Planning of Change, 2d ed. New York: Holt, Rinehart and Winston, Inc., 1969.
    Probably the most useful book of readings about one of the central themes of the present book—how social change can be deliberately planned and implemented. The essays vary in difficulty, but the excellent Introduction should be readable for an average upperclassman or graduate student.
Burns, James MacGregor, Uncommon Sense. New York: Harper & Row, Publishers, 1972.
    Burns, author of eight books and numerous scholarly articles, and winner of many prizes (including the Pulitzer) for writing in the area of social philosophy, provides in this 196-page book one of the most astute analyses of the state of American culture that this author has found. Burns is especially good in clarifying popular confusion over the goals-means relationship.
Demerath, N. J., III, and Richard A. Peterson (eds.), System, Change, and Conflict: A Reader on Contemporary Sociological Theory and the Debate over Functionalism. New York: The Free Press, 1967.
    One of the best sociology readers, for students who would like rather advanced treatments of a variety of conflicting points of view. See particularly Andrew Hacker's essay on "Sociology and Ideology."
Henry, Jules, Culture Against Man. New York: Random House, Inc., 1963; Vintage, 1965.
    Called by Ashley Montagu "One of the most telling and creative examinations of American culture and its values written in this century." Part I is devoted to ideological and cultural analyses of Amer-

ica; Part II is about children, youth, and schools, and includes some fascinating case studies.

Inlow, Gail M., *Values in Transition: A Handbook*. New York: John Wiley & Sons, Inc., 1972.

An introduction to the study of value change (i.e., cultural change) in the United States in areas of economics, politics, science and technology, philosophy, the New Left, and the black community. Does not cut deeply, but a good starter for students. Has excellent bibliographies, reflecting all shades of opinion.

Kahn, Herman, and B. Bruce-Briggs, *Things to Come: Thinking About the Seventies and Eighties*. New York: The Macmillan Company, 1972.

The content of this book was developed by the staff of the Hudson Institute, founded in 1961 for the study of the future (a branch of inquiry called "futuristics"). The intent of such study is not to predict, but to explore possibilities and probabilities. The writers do not see a cultural revolution prior to the end of the century, but rather a synthesis of old culture and counterculture values. Particularly recommended for readers of the present book is Chapter 4.

Kammen, Michael (ed.), *The Contrapuntal Civilization: Essays Toward a New Understanding of the American Experience*. New York: Thomas Y. Crowell Company, 1971.

Kammen has put together a first-rate book of readings designed to illuminate the American experience "in terms of its paradoxes, its contradictory tendencies, its dualisms, and its polarities." Very useful for explaining cultural disorganization and disintegration.

McKee, James B., *Introduction to Sociology*. New York: Holt Rinehart and Winston, Inc., 1969.

This is the best basic sociology text presently available for reference use in connection with the present book. Invaluable for students who lack a background in basic sociological concepts and knowledge.

May, Rollo, *Psychology and the Human Dilemma*. New York: Van Nostrand Reinhold Company, 1967.

May is one of our best-known social psychologists and social philosophers—a psychiatrist who has mastered an extraordinary range of knowledge. He provides us with an understandable and defensible explanation of the consequences of alienation. Feelings of impotence lead to apathy and apathy sooner or later usually leads to violence. A provocative analysis of contemporary American culture and its effect on individuals.

Spindler, George D., *Education and Culture: Anthropological Approaches*. New York: Holt, Rinehart and Winston, Inc., 1963.

A book of readings, including seven essays by Spindler. Other authors represented include Theodore Brameld, Jules Henry, and Margaret Mead. Probably the best book on the use of anthropological insights in the study of educational problems.

Toffler, Alvin, *Future Shock*. New York: Random House, Inc., 1970; Bantam, 1971.

This generally well reviewed and runaway best seller, may be the best book available on what rapid cultural change does to people. Toffler discusses the accelerating rate of change of our times and suggests changes likely in our future. The book then moves into a discussion of how humans can cope with change which proceeds at an exponential rate without disintegrating pychologically.

White, Leslie A., *The Science of Culture: A Study of Man and Civilization.* New York: Farrar, Straus and Giroux, Inc., 1969.

An interesting book which elaborates the thesis of "cultural determinism." Culture is portrayed as autonomous and self-sustaining and all human behavior as a product of stimuli from the culture. This view is a form of behaviorism, and is contrary to the writer's view that individual and culture are interactive (or transactive) and the best focus for study is neither the individual nor an independent culture, but the transactions between persons and their cultural milieu.

2

CONSERVATISM, LIBERALISM, AND EDUCATION

No limit can be set to the power of a teacher, but this is equality true in the other direction: no career can so nearly approach zero in its effect.

Jacques Barzun

The intent of Chapter 2 is to describe what we see as the chief polarizations within the American ideology—the different degrees of conservatism vs. the different degrees of liberalism. We use the phraseology "different degrees of" above because most Americans are moderates who separate on often rather intangible grounds into positions properly called conservative and liberal. But we also have extremists: conservatives of authoritarian bent who toy more or less seriously with Fascist

values; and liberals who become authoritarian and make up a segment of the New Left and/or dabble with Communist-like values.

It appears that even in the seventies most teachers find it difficult to define such concepts as conservatism, liberalism, fascism, and communism. Because of this lack of understanding, they find it equally difficult to make confident and defensible statements about where they stand on the right-left continuum. Probably because of the inability to make sense out of such concepts as political/social/economic right and left, each year an increasing number of people declare themselves, when asked by pollsters, as "middle of the road" or independent.

Because of the now widely conceded possibility that American culture may become increasingly authoritarian, schools of education have a compelling duty to acquaint prospective teachers with what such a prospect means. Only if this occurs will the new generation of teachers be able to help their students assess issues related to right-left polarization.

Parliamentary democracies and constitutional "Presidential" governments, such as our own, seem to function best with two strong opposing political parties and often with a weaker third party to provide an impetus for reform. With the rise of apolitical values, or political centralism, democracy is gravely threatened. We *need* strong conservative and liberal parties.

CONSERVATISM, LIBERALISM, AND THEIR AUTHORITARIAN EXTREMES

In this section we will define the concepts of conservatism, liberalism, fascism, and communism. Our definitions may seem arbitrary but they will explain the way these terms are used in this book. Since they are used with considerable frequency, it is essential that readers grasp our intended meaning. Because these particular concepts have deep historical roots, defining them can best be approached by showing how they evolved historically.

Conservatism's Two Definitions

The two emphases of modern conservatism both stem from thinking which appeared during the era of the American Revolution and shortly thereafter in the divergent views of Hamilton and such persons as Madison and Jefferson.

Hamilton believed in a strong Federal Government, the chief power to be in the executive branch. He believed the people should be powerless to elect Federal officials directly; hence, participatory democracy was deemphasized except locally. This was the conservative position of the early 1800s.

As of the 1970s, we feel it best to call Hamiltonian thinkers "radical conservatives" (radical right). They believe in power being centralized largely in the Federal executive branch and related bureaucracies—as the Pentagon, FBI, and CIA. They would grant final decision making on national and international issues to the executive bureaucracy—*provided the President were a radical conservative.* Further, they tend toward an "end justifies the means" philosophy, which gives Federal power a ruthless, opportunistic cast.

In contrast to this view were those of Madison, and to a slightly lesser degree, Jefferson. They believed in comparatively weak central government, broad dispersal of powers, considerable direct participatory democracy, and maximized individual freedom. This essentially laissez-faire view was the liberal position of the early 1800s. We will call this stance the "classical conservative" position of the 1970s.

Conservatives in the Jeffersonian tradition would disband much of the Federal apparatus and let major decision making revert to state and local governments. They also argue for fewer restraints on individual freedom. These persons are conservatives in the sense that they would "turn back the clock" by ending the social welfare role played by the Federal Government since the 1930s. We will call these persons "classical conservatives"—one of the better-known examples being William F. Buckley.[1]

Many contemporary conservatives vacillate from radical to classical conservatism. Since these are opposing views, many conservatives seem muddle headed. But as we will show, liberals, too, may seem muddle headed as of the 1970s.

Contemporary Liberalism

Liberals may also be categorized in two groups—authentic or democratically committed liberals, and self-proclaimed liberals who either find liberal poses expedient or hold authoritarian values in conflict with democratic liberalism. When the latter are not under pressure they may sincerely believe in democratic values, but under stress their authoritarian antidemocratic values often take over. These "liberals" are muddle headed because like some conservatives they try to hold two incompatible positions simultaneously.

Authentic contemporary liberals follow certain of the colonial and early national liberals' guidelines—particularly the Madisonian belief in the firm protection of civil liberties by the Bill of Rights. But they reject economic laissez-faire on the ground that to achieve our intended goals there is no alternative in modern society to the power of a strong Federal Government.

They would use Federal power to guarantee social reforms. Modern-day authentic liberals tend to favor guaranteed economic security for all, elimination of extreme poverty, firmer controls over the powerful, equal rights for women and minorities, and greater freedom in nonharmful behaviors.

Perhaps the chief dilemma of these liberals is relying on Federal power to reach their ends. This works if the President happens to be an authentic liberal, but, as recent events have shown, fails utterly if the President is a conservative.

[1] For a first-rate description of classical conservatism, see William F. Buckley, ed., *Did You Ever See a Dream Walking? American Conservative Thought in the Twentieth Century.* Indianapolis: The Bobbs-Merrill Company, Inc., 1970, "Introduction."

Right-Left Authoritarian Extremes: Fascism and Communism

The terms fascism and communism also have a range of meanings: not only do individuals' views vary but no two Communist states are identical. Nevertheless they have certain features in common. One of these is their relation to conservatism and liberalism. Radical conservatives are already well along the way to becoming Fascists; self-proclaimed but nondemocratic liberals very easily turn into Communists. These changes from semi-moderate positions to authoritarian extremes have been common in the United States during such periods of social turmoil as the Great Depression of the 1930s, the Great Communist Witch Hunt of the 1950s, and possibly again in the politically and economically turbulent 1970s.

Fascism has evolved in nations which were underdeveloped and still largely feudal, semideveloped, or industrially developed (for example, largely undeveloped South Vietnam, semideveloped Chile under its present military junta, and highly developed Germany under Hitler).

Fascism tends to emerge in countries with a comparatively old ruling class—typically an amalgam of big business, the military establishment, and sometimes a landed aristocracy and a powerful fundamentalist church. A large proportion of the population is poor, uneducated, and increasingly rebellious. A revolutionary movement appears, led often by Communists (as in Chile) but sometimes by democrats (as in Republican Spain prior to Franco's 1939 takeover).

Their power and property threatened, the old ruling class stages a counterrevolutionary movement and if successful installs a Fascist dictatorship. Without apparent exception, historically *fascism has been a movement to keep the old ruling class in power.*

Fascist economic systems, a form of monopoly capitalism, are sometimes called corporate states. (When Hitler referred to German fascism as national socialism, the word "socialism" was pure propaganda.) In addition to having a militantly capitalistic economy, fascism tends to discourage mass education, promote racism and sexism, exhibit extreme natonalism with all its patriotic symbolism (see Chapter 6), and in some cases uses military adventures to distract the people from domestic problems.

So far, authoritarian communism has emerged in underdeveloped peasant nations with rampant poverty and illiteracy (except where military force imposed communism as in East Germany and Czechoslovakia). The old ruling elites, usually landed aristocracies, have been displaced through political revolution by a new ruling class with values claimed to derive from Marxism/Leninism. Historically, *the advent of communism involves a change in the ruling class.*

Communist economic systems are one form of socialism (for others see Chapter 9). Communism tends to promote mass education, industrialism, numerous built-in social welfare programs, racial and sexist equality, civilian domination of the ruling class, but also a tight political dictatorship and loss of civil liberties.

In addition to the other differences between fascism and communism, fascism lacks a philosophical rationale and many long-range plans except to keep traditional rulers in power. On the other hand communism has a gospel: its own usually distorted version of Marxism/Leninism. But as portrayed so well by the Yugoslavian writer Milovan Djilas, a central aim of communism may also become the preservation in power of the new Communist leadership and its bureaucracy.

Conservatism and Liberalism in America

Now that we have defined conservatism and liberalism in their chief versions, and indicated how each relates to the extremes of fascism and communism, we can move to the central theme of the chapter. We will offer evidence to show that ideologically American culture is highly conservative and that the trend since the middle sixties has been toward greater conservatism. This trend may change by the middle seventies, in part because of Watergate and related scandals, in part because economic problems of large proportions may force Middle America into a more liberal frame of mind.

Conservatism in American Culture

Readers may question whether Americans as a group are conservative. The concept is relative: people are thought conservative when their ideas seem more outdated than those of others. Ultraliberals regard the somewhat liberal as "conservative" and ultraconservatives regard those less so as "liberal." Also, the liberalism of one generation is the conservatism of the next. Equally confusing is that most people are conservative about some matters and liberal about others.

Among which group does one find the most conservatism? Our past gives clues, but the turmoiled sixties shook the country so severely that historical patterns no longer necessarily hold. Historically, rural people have been much more conservative than urban; but our rural population has so declined that their ideas affect the national scene little. In numerous community studies between the 1930s and 1950s, researchers agreed that in most respects the "lower middle class" was the most conservative group.

In a 1960 study based on opinion polling Lloyd A. Free and Hadley Cantril concluded that a large majority of Americans were "ideologically conservative," but "operationally liberal" in material values. Responding to statements representing ideology from left to right, most people chose statements reflecting a conservative ideology. But when asked about specific Federal programs they showed strong commitments to a welfare state—even to socialistic ideas.[2]

Such inconsistency is the theme of a book edited by Michael Kammen.[3] Kammen quotes Erik Erikson approvingly: "Thus the functioning American, as the heir of a history of extreme contrasts and abrupt changes, bases his final ego identity on some tentative combination of dynamic polarities such as . . . individualistic and standardized, competitive and cooperative, pious and freethinking, responsible and cynical, etc."[4] In the same book Robert G. McCloskey discusses "The American Ideology." After studying assertions of opinion leaders through our history, McCloskey finds contradictions are typical: " . . . it is characteristic of the American mind, insofar as this group represents it, to hold contradictory ideas simultaneously without bothering to resolve the potential conflict between them."[5]

What can we say about American conservative-liberal ideology which is reasonably meaningful and can be documented? Perhaps more than it seems at first glance. Evidence exists for the hypothesis that a degree of conservatism is developing which is unhealthy for a democratic culture and for educators who wish to reform schools in a democratic direction.

The Record on Humanitarian Reform

What do we mean by humanitarian reform? Many different things could be meant by this expression, but we mean socioeconomic reforms aimed particularly at protecting the weak or helpless against such catastrophes as hunger, malnutrition, inadequate medical care, blighted housing, poor education, and the like—protections which liberals tend to believe government should provide. Because of the inexorable cost of living increases, even middle income groups, if given no special protection, may suffer from some of these conditions, particularly inadequate or no medical care in the face of catastrophic illness. Basically, what humanitarian reform reduces itself to is some kind of guaranteed government income floor with specific programs for special emergencies, such as sickness and prolonged unemployment.

It should tell us something significant about the strength of con-

---

[2] Lloyd A. Free and Hadley Cantril, The Political Beliefs of Americans: A Study of Public Opinion. New York: Simon & Schuster, 1968.

[3] Michael Kammen (ed.), The Contrapuntal Civilization: Essays Toward a New Understanding of the American Experience. New York: Thomas Y. Crowell Company, 1971.

[4] Kammen, p. 4.

[5] Kammen, p. 230.

servative forces in the United States to compare how this country has managed humanitarian reform in comparison with other countries.

In Communist countries it is taken for granted that a basic income floor, including free medical care from cradle to grave and free education through the doctorate for students who can go that far, will be provided for all except political dissenters. Herein lies one of the major appeals of communism in impoverished, underdeveloped countries.

But what about free and democratic countries? Virtually all industrialized democracies or semi-democracies have seen fit to provide for the security of all their people long ago. Countries of western Europe (save for Spain, which is neither free nor democratic), the British Isles, and some units of the British Commonwealth have done this. New Zealand was a pioneer, in the sense that it established a guaranteed annual income for all and socialized medicine rather early in the twentieth century.

Any industrialized nation can afford to provide for the security of all its people. If it does not, it is because those who wield the power have other priorities. The United States is an interesting case study. Its stand on humanitarian reform would be quite incomprehensible unless we begin our discussion with the understanding that a majority of the American people *are* more conservative in the area of social reform than the people of most other industrial nations.

The United States has lagged behind other industrial nations in almost every aspect of humanitarian legislation. It is almost as if this nation has to be dragged, kicking and screaming, into the modern world. We would judge that in humanitarian legislation the United States is behind most industrial nations by from twenty-five to fifty or more years. Social reform occurs in this country only after long and heated political battles, and only after proposals for reform have become politically safe. Almost a fourth of our population lives in dire poverty, a state of affairs perhaps necessary to maintain the privileges of the wealthy, but which, from a humanitarian view, is inexcusable.

Harry Truman proposed a plan for nationalizing medicine shortly after the end of World War II. Congress refused to touch it. The whole idea of state-supported medicine, in the sense of a nationally uniform plan with full coverage for every person, remains a "closed area" in American culture. Although President Nixon in his first administration proposed a national income floor, the proposal was not only inadequate but was later dropped by the administration. When Senator McGovern, as Democratic candidate for President in 1972, proposed a similar but somewhat more adequate plan for an income floor, a majority of Americans rejected the idea as "pushing change too fast" (according to public opinion polls).

The reluctant and piecemeal way in which we handle humanitarian reform suggests that as a culture we are still much in the grip of the

Puritan belief that everyone can and should be sturdy enough to solve his problems without help from secular sources.

New Closed Areas as Exemplifying Conservatism

To equate conservatism with fear of openly and critically examining many areas of life is perhaps partly a matter of definition. Our definition of a radical conservative includes people who are afraid of inquiry in social-moral-ideological matters. As was suggested in Chapter 1, historically Americans have not wanted to hold up to honest scrutiny their beliefs and values in such areas as religion, sex, the so-called vices, the treatment of racial and ethnic minorities, economic ideology, the "place" of women, our form of government, extent of government services, and the like. Among these are examples of closed areas which are to some degree less closed than at any time in our history. But while some formerly closed areas are now open, some formerly open areas have tended to become closed to reflective scrutiny. Except for the 1950s, when Senator Joseph McCarthy had an apparent majority of Americans pathologically frightened of subversion, we know of no time since the beginning of our nationhood when criticism of our governmental system, and those personages who manage it, was so under attack by the Federal Government (the executive branch under former President Nixon particularly).

The use of drugs, paradoxically, appears more closed to truly open reflection than a century ago. It is an area of interest more surrounded by dogmatism, pathological emotionalism, propaganda, and generally irrational thought, than most other closed areas. Many youth, particularly by the time they have reached senior high school or college, apparently possess more factual data about illicit drugs than their teachers, parents, or the police. On the other hand, youth seems as unsophisticated as their parents about the dangers of alcohol, a proven killer when used in excess. One survey reported that, as of 1973, youth are "discovering" that they can achieve a higher "high" with alcohol than with marijuana. Parents, upon discovering their children anaesthetized with alcohol, are reported as commonly saying, "Thank God, it's not drugs!"[6] This is the type of irrationality characteristic of any closed area of culture.

Another area of life which historically has been relatively open to reflection and debate is the realm of personal privacy. In the nineteenth and the twentieth centuries, until after World War II, close surveillance of the most intimate aspects of an individual's life was not a common practice. This is not to suggest that snooping was never done, but that people generally reacted negatively to the idea. Also, the technology for

[6] *Newsweek*, March 5, 1973, p. 68ff.

highly effective snooping was not available. Beginning after World War II and particularly after the development of technology for space flight, all manner of miniaturized and highly sophisticated devices for wiretapping and bugging became available. The computer banks of Army Intelligence, the FBI, and the CIA became available for storing virtually unlimited quantities of data about the private lives of an unknown number of Americans.

Although freedom to criticize personal surveillance by either Federal or private agencies still remains and as a result of the shock of Watergate may continue, the very nature of highly industrialized and postindustrialized cultures is such that privacy is likely to become increasingly restricted. Lending, insurance, and other companies demand the right to know everything possible about prospective customers.

In connection with the issue of personal privacy, it is significant that the President of the United States, in March, 1974, advocated a plan for protecting citizens from the storing in computer banks of personal information such as lending and insurance companies have become accustomed to using, but that, at the same time, he failed to mention protection against the agencies most accused of spying on individuals—the CIA, FBI, and Army Intelligence. Further, the Bank Secrecy Act of 1970, permitting banks to make and file photostats of all personal checks processed, and under attack by the ACLU and the California Bankers Association, was upheld as constitutional by the "Nixon Supreme Court" on April 1, 1974—an appropriate date, perhaps, for playing an April fool's trick on freedoms guaranteed in the Bill of Rights.

We cannot tell as of this writing where the next clampdowns on freedom will be. We will make two guesses: After a decade of comparative openness of discussion about the merits and demerits of punishment as a means of preventing crime and rehabilitating the convicted, we may be moving into a pro-punishment psychology reminiscent of that of Puritan New England; and after a remarkable loosening of constraints against the realistic portrayal of both sex and colloquial language in motion pictures, on television, and in the press, we may be in for another Puritanical attack against such openness. This is speculation, of course, but something for readers to watch for. Readers may want to think about other areas of culture, at one time comparatively open, which may be subject to repression during the seventies.

The Growing Conservatism of Working People

By "working people" we mean here skilled or semiskilled blue-collar workers, mostly unionized, and skilled but comparatively poorly paid white-collar workers, still in the process of becoming unionized.

Space does not permit a historical review of the ideology of those who work in this middle range between the poor and upper-middle class. However, in the nineteenth and early twentieth centuries, relatively low-income working people, including those who were unionized, had a strong streak of social idealism in their thinking. They were interested in broad cultural reform of a humanitarian and pro-democratic nature, a long-range social program for the entire society.

Today it is only rarely that one can find in the statements of union leaders, or in the assertions of union (or nonunion) workers any traces of long-range goals that would benefit the whole culture. Worker ideology, particularly among the most skilled and tightly organized groups, seems now characterized mainly by concerns about short-range bread-and-butter goals: higher wages, more fringe benefits, better working conditions. If a nation at war will produce more jobs at higher wages, then today's workers quickly become jingoistic. If high tariffs will do the same, then workers become protectionist. If excluding minority groups from trade unions will, then a antiminority prejudice and outright racism surfaces.

Only recently have social psychologists tried to explain the switch of labor to a highly conservative ideology. In a recent study of 574 college undergraduates, representing a broad range of family backgrounds, hawkish attitudes toward war and the corollary beliefs and values associated with such attitudes (e.g., highly conservative views on religion and sociopolitical issues) were found to be closely associated with low family income, low social status, and poorly educated fathers. The researchers concluded that the motivation toward conservatism in this group of students was status insecurity which students felt could be best relieved by adopting highly orthodox beliefs.[7]

Conservatism and Antiintellectualism

Another indication of a basic conservative streak in the American psyche is our historical, and continuing, distrust of intellectuals, who for the most part tend toward liberalism (which is not to say there are no conservative intellectuals: William F. Buckley and those who publish in his *National Review*, for example). DeTocqueville and social observers ever since his time have commented on how most middle Americans, although liking the idea of practical intelligence, dislike the idea of intellectual cultivation.

The late Richard Hofstadter has defined antiintellectualism in the

[7] Robert A. Lewis, "Socialization into National Violence: Familial Correlates of Hawkish Attitudes Toward War," *Journal of Marriage and the Family*, November 1971, pp. 699–708.

following manner: "The common strain that binds together the attitudes and ideas which I call anti-intellectual is a resentment and suspicion of the life of the mind and of those who are considered to represent it; and a disposition constantly to minimize the value of that life."[8] This definition suffers from the ambiguity of the expression "life of the mind." Hofstadter later clarifies this when he differentiates intelligence and intellect. "Whereas *intelligence* seeks to grasp, manipulate, re-order, adjust, *intellect* examines, ponders, wonders, theorizes, criticizes, imagines" . . . [It is] ". . . . the critical, creative, and contemplative side of mind."[9]

Hofstadter's book analyzes historical reasons for the distrust of intellect by average Americans and documents the close link between anti-intellectualism as he defines it and conservatism. Those distrustful of intellectual endeavor (especially its critical functions) almost without exception are of conservative makeup, and this apparently includes a majority of Americans.

The Puritan Ethic in American Culture

This topic is closely linked to the topic of conservatism vs. liberalism. It is in a large sense an extension of the discussion above. It appears that in spite of the numerous obvious shifts away from old-fashioned Puritanism, we still have a deep streak of Puritanism in us. The many social observers who argue that the Puritan ethic has all but eroded away in America are not entirely wrong; but if a majority of noncollege youth adhere somewhat to traditional values associated with the Puritan ethic (as Yankelovich's 1973 studies seem to reveal), then we may have a long way to go before the traditional values of Puritanism are dead. It may turn out that a majority of Americans will never want these values "dead"; some of them may be useful even in the most advanced industrial society we can imagine, or in the era of post-industrialism which some writers are now talking about.

Puritan Ethic Defined

Just what is the Puritan ethic anyway? It stems from both a theology and a social philosophy; essentially it is the overall view of John Calvin (1509–1564). We will skip the theology and discuss the social philosophy.

The social philosophy of Calvinism (or the Protestant ethic—we use the terms interchangeably) focuses primarily on the world of work. We may reduce its main features to a few specific points, as follows:

---

[8] Richard Hofstadter, *Anti-Intellectualism in American Life*. New York: Random House, 1963, p. 7; Vintage paperback, 1964.

[9] Hofstadter, p. 25. Italics added.

1. People should function as individuals: self-contained, self-supporting, self-directed, competing with one another.

2. People should be impelled by a sense of duty, particularly duty to one's calling (or chosen occupation). This idea, if pursued, requires dedication to a life of hard work, and a conscientiousness that will result in work well done.

3. People should aim toward "getting ahead." This requires thrift and perseverance. Material success is a sign that one has pleased God and has been rewarded for his efforts.

4. The moral rules for living are strict and unchanging. Sin tends to be defined in Old Testament terms although people of Puritanical bent can find much more sin around than is identified in the Bible.

David Riesman gave the English language a new term when he identified the Puritan personality as "inner-directed." The post-Puritan conforming type of person, which Riesman saw as the most common personality type as of the 1950s, is "other-directed."[10] Writing a few years later, William H. Whyte, Jr., pursued the same general line of analysis, but used the term "organization man'" to refer to Riesman's "other-directed" personality type.[11]

The Puritan Ethic in Contemporary America

Both Riesman and Whyte argued that the Puritan ethic, for all practical purposes, was dead. They saw the beginning of its demise in the cultural "shaking up" produced by World War I and the finalization in the further wrenching of culture produced by World War II. Neither writer seems to have made a distinction between ideological values and operational values—what people proclaim as their faith and what they demand in practical terms.

As an ideology, the Puritan ethic seems anything but dead. One of the better statements of the Puritan ethic, perhaps, was to be found in the main emphasis of ex-President Nixon's inaugural and state of the nation speeches in early 1973. Although a rather large number of persons reacted with contrary views, these were primarily university scholars, a few disgruntled labor leaders, and from a Puritan view, a miscellany of do-gooders hooked on the idea of the welfare state. There was no mass outcry against the President's plea for a return to individualism, hard work, thrift, and morality.

[10] David Riesman, Nathan Glazer, and Reuel Denney, *The Lonely Crowd: A Study of the Changing American Character,* New Haven, Conn.: Yale University Press, 1950; Anchor, Doubleday & Company, 1954.

[11] William H. Whyte, *The Organization Man.* New York: Simon & Schuster, Inc., 1956; Anchor, Doubleday & Company, 1956.

As of this writing, no one can forecast the future of the Puritan ideology. Even those who proclaim it seem bent on violating it, as evidenced by the number of middle-aged businessmen in the audiences of theaters showing so-called pornographic movies.

The Military Mind and American Culture

At first glance, readers may wonder how the military mind fits here. We include it because there appears to be a military psychology, or way of viewing things, that has spread through the culture, particularly since World War II. The values stressed in military psychology are conservative in a fundamental sense, although their surface manifestations may appear to be more-or-less neutral on the conservative-liberal spectrum. It is always newsworthy when a career officer in the Army, Navy, or Air Force or when the American Legion or Veterans of Foreign Wars takes a liberal stand on any issue since the conservatism of the military has a long history and is common knowledge.

The aspects of military psychology discussed here can be interpreted as a way of bending many of our conservative values to the needs of large bureaucratic organizations, such as the Pentagon. But the same values may appear in the functioning of other government bureaucracies and in corporate bureaucracies. We might even be able to demonstrate that the traits characteristic of the military mind shape the functioning of a bureaucratized educational structure. In sum, the military view of things may represent some kind of integration of the Puritan ethic into large twentieth century organizations. This may,be a more sophisticated hypothesis than the dichotomies of inner- and other-directed (Riesman) or Puritan ethic vs. organization man (Whyte) which were presented as either-or alternatives.

We now have available a study of military ideology which not only seems to probe more deeply than previous studies but is impeccably documented from primary and largely official sources. Charles W. Ackley, a former Navy chaplain, has studied the text materials used at our military academies, journals published by branches of the armed services, speeches made by career officers, and opinion research designed to reveal how military men think.[12]

Space does not permit more than a superficial report of Ackley's study. We will treat several of his major theses and suggest that interested readers refer to his book.

The Will To Win

Military leaders try to implant in their men a will to win somewhat analogous to that of a football coach. The military mind cannot tolerate the idea of a draw or compromise solution. Ackley refers to what he calls an "attack psychology" which may in some cases lead to victory but can also lead to disaster, as when Napoleon tried to conquer Russia and General Douglas MacArthur led his troops toward the China border during the Korean War. Ackley quotes Lieutenant Colonel W. I. Gordon as saying in 1964 ". . . the will to win is fundamental, in the absolute or classical sense, to military operations in the field." He also cites Liddel Hart as say-

---

[12] Charles Walton Ackley, *The Modern Military in American Society: A Study in the Nature of Military Power.* Philadelphia: Westminster Press, 1972.

ing ". . . our goal in war can only be attained by the subjugation of the opposing will."[13]

Ackley suggests that the idea of the absolute necessity to subjugate the enemy, to crush his will to resist, is a dangerous madness, since often the other side has an equivalent will, which means that the only possible resolution of conflict becomes obliteration of one side by the other or mutual obliteration.

Ackley finds there is a large and growing military literature which urges restraint and opposes the "win at any cost" ideology. But the psychology of win at any cost is still there, more so in the Air Force, Ackley thinks, than in other branches of the armed forces.

The Fascination with the Concrete

Although military theory may be abstract, the military exercises power in particular and quantitative ways. By the expression, "fascination with the concrete," Ackley means a fascination for *"this Plan, this Order, this Enemy...."* Ackley continues, "[the military] ... specifies the concrete. So principles easily become dogmas, and 'contingency plans' actually promote action."[14]

Ackley then goes on to note that attachment to the concrete leads to an affection for sophisticated weaponry. There is a particular fascination, he says, for weaponry that can strike at long range with both accuracy and deadlines. Long-range weapons in general are more complicated, a source of affection in itself, but also highly impersonal. They are "something to play with where the soldier is." This is especially true of weapons like a B-52 bomber, a long-range artillery piece, or a missile.

The Tendency toward Structural Hardness

Although the military is dynamic in the sense of always seeking new weapons and strategies, organizationally it tends toward structural hardness; that is, it tries to reduce everything to order, discipline, rules, and fixed routines. This equates with a tendency toward absolutism in values and beliefs. In one study cited by Ackley, only 5 percent of Pentagon officers admitted to any liberal convictions.[15]

Ackley feels that the conservatism of the military is but a reflection of our cultural traditions. He notes "the religious and moral grounding of generations in the conviction that the struggle with evil is absolute and

[13] Ackley, pp. 153–154.
[14] Ackley, p. 179.
[15] Ackley, p. 205.

no quarter is expected nor can any be given—the 'Battle of Armageddon' syndrome."[16] This sounds very much like a view frequently expressed in the sermons of Cotton Mather and Jonathan Edwards during the early New England Colonial Period.

Ackley's research reveals that whereas once there was a preponderance of Episcopalians among professional military men, they now tend to belong increasingly to the fundamentalist denominations—Baptist, Methodist, and numerous evangelical/pentecostal groups. Ackley sees a trend toward increasingly pietistic thinking in the military as its career members come more and more from fundamentalist denominations.

The Tendency toward Reification

Linked with the military attachment to static systems is a tendency toward reification, that is, a tendency to treat ideas as if they had a material reality. One kind of reification is the tendency to reduce persons to things, or, as Paul Tillich says, to regard "thou" as "it." The enemy is regarded as unhuman (gooks or slopeheads, as soldiers were taught to call the Vietnamese). This, along with the identification of man and machine mentioned above, makes for a process of dehumanization. Ackley observes that this same process operates in nonmilitary bureaucracies.[17]

The Tendency to Excess

An "overkill" psychology exists in the military. Ackley sees the tendency of the military to overdo as related to a similar tendency in much of Western Civilization. When we turn to something new, we pursue it to extremes.

Ackley links modern-day extremism in the United States to our Puritan and frontier heritages.

> Puritan moral absolutism, self-righteousness, crusading intolerance, and our national experience of the frontier—individualistic, initiatory, and self-reliant—have created for us the image of the modern knight, the soft-spoken gunman reluctantly but devastatingly on the side of law and order.[18]

The Illusion of Omnipotence

Under this head Ackley focuses on the tendency of the military, and the large number of people who identify with it, to assume divine sanction

[16] Ackley, p. 205.
[17] Ackley, p. 230 ff.
[18] Ackley, p. 250.

for anything this nation might do militarily. The flag salute, with its expression "one nation under God," is an example of the extreme self-righteousness that pervades not only the military but most areas of life. With the firm belief that God is always on our side, we have "developed a myth of American omnipotence." The military has adopted a "God complex" in the sense that "No other institutions known among men presume to fuse and to control the ultimates of human existence and behavior."[19]

Liberalism in American Culture

Our definitions have suggested a frequent equivalence between liberal and democratic thinking. On the whole, liberals have more-or-less strong democratic commitments, with the various supporting values a belief in democracy requires (such as a relativistic way of interpreting things). We must include one caveat, however. There is a rather large group of people who might be called "professional liberals," who assert their views with such certainty that we can only think of them as rigid and absolutistic—a stance more in tune with radical conservatism than with authentic liberalism.

Although there are long-range strands of liberal thought in American culture dating from the early Colonial period, when we try to describe American liberalism in specific terms, we find that it has involved an aggregation of values and beliefs not always closely related, and that a considerable part of our liberalism has been an on-and-off phenomenon, frequently heading in divergent directions. As mentioned, the same individual may harbor both conservative and liberal views about the same or different issues. The fragmented nature of American liberalism may help explain why we have never had a major political party whose members and programs have been consistently liberal (Democrats, with their Heintz-varieties of members and outlooks, ranging from the radical right to the radical left, are not a liberal party, just as Republicans, with a rather large contingency of liberal thinkers, are not a consistently conservative party.)

Eighteenth- and Nineteenth-Century Liberalism

Liberalism, as it is understood in the modern world, began in the eighteenth century—the "century of the enlightenment." In America, such thinking probably peaked during the few decades before and after the American Revolution. The body of the Constitution is a mixture of liberal and conservative ideas, with the strongest assertion of liberalism in certain of the first ten amendments—the Bill of Rights.

Among the numerous outcroppings of liberal thought in the nineteenth century, we can include the antislavery movement and the ratifica-

[19] Ackley, p. 290.

tion of the Thirteenth, Fourteenth, and Fifteenth Amendments to the Constitution (1866, 1868, and 1870) that followed the Civil War and the freeing of the slaves. The Fourteenth Amendment, which states that "no State shall make or enforce any law which shall abridge the privileges or immunities of citizens of the United States; nor shall any State deprive any person of life, liberty, or property, without due process of law; nor deny to any person within its jurisdiction the equal protection of the laws," remains one of the most effective protections of individual liberty.

Further liberal thought can be seen in the comparatively persistent fight for women's rights throughout the century; in a relatively small group who preferred democratic over violent solutions to controversy (a few social philosophers and some minority religious groups, such as the Quakers); in the Populist movement of the 1890s, an example of grass-roots democracy at work, even though its immediate results were meager; in a kind of romantic naturalism with strong liberal overtones, as found in Emerson and Thoreau; and—probably most important for the long run— in the liberal/democratic/relativistic line of thought innovated by the Harvard Metaphysical Club in the last third of the century.

Twentieth-Century Liberalism

Early in the century the struggle for equality of women resulted in the Nineteenth Amendment to the Constitution which guaranteed women the right to vote. Another constitutional amendment of the early century (the Seventeenth, ratified in 1913) provided for the direct election of Senators, a clear step in the direction of a more representative democracy.

World War I severely jolted the culture, and marked a turning point between Victorian social and moral conservatism and what was to become the tentative establishment of more liberal sexual mores and, of more importance, the beginnings of a realistic literature of social protest (e.g., Sinclair Lewis, John Dos Passos, and Thomas Wolfe). In retrospect, we can perhaps view the 1920s, a highly conservative period politically and economically, as a time when some significant steps were taken toward opening a few formerly closed areas of culture to investigation. In this connection, we cannot ignore the influence of Sigmund Freud and other European and British writers (e.g., such British Fabian socialists as H. G. Wells, Bertrand Russell, George Bernard Shaw, and Sidney and Beatrice Webb, and the famous British sexologist, Havelock Ellis).

Probably most of the social reforms we associate with the New Deal years (1932–1940) could be construed as liberal in intent. It was during this period that a greater interest developed in the democratizing of our economic institutions (although in retrospect the New Deal appears much more an attempt at patchwork than fundamental change). But, at least,

New Deal thinking and legislation did mark the beginning of the first significant humanitarian legislation of broad scope (in a somewhat narrower
sense, freeing the slaves, adopting the Constitutional Amendments of the
1860s, and giving women the vote in 1920 were also significant humanitarian steps).

Following World War II, in spite of the radical conservative reaction instigated mainly by Senator Joseph McCarthy, highly significant
changes occurred. During this period, the Supreme Court, composed mostly
of liberals appointed by Franklin D. Roosevelt and led by Chief Justice
Earl Warren, made a serious and relatively effective attempt to implement
in practical terms the Bill of Rights and the Fourteenth Amendment which
had been all but ignored for a century and a half.

Congress shall make no law . . . abridging the freedom of
speech. . . . *(Copyright © George Ballis, all rights reserved)*

Perhaps the next significant major step toward a fuller democracy
was the renewed Women's Movement, beginning in 1963 with the publication of Betty Friedan's *Feminine Mystique*. Legislation supposedly guaranteeing women equal rights in work opportunities was passed in 1964, but
as of the 1970s had been only partially implemented. As of this writing a
Constitutional Amendment intended to guarantee equal rights for women
has yet to be ratified.

Historians may someday look back at the 1960s and in spite of the
turbulence of that decade, see the largely youthful counterculture that
arose, reached an apparent apex between 1967 and 1971, and then subsided
with a residue of what on the surface seem like radically liberal values,

as a major turning point in American history—the clearest outward manifestation of a cultural revolution in the making.

New Open Areas

It appears obvious that as of the 1970s some formerly closed areas of interest have lost their previous verboten character. The area that seems to have opened most by the early seventies is sex. Particularly among the educated upper-middle class and the comparatively young, not only is sex discussed with a candor which would have been unthinkable only a decade or two ago but sexual practices which were then typically concealed are now admitted to and even bragged about. The groups among which sex remains a highly controversial subject have been reduced to the elderly, the churchy, residents of small towns (particularly in "Bible belt" areas), and school boards, school administrators, and teachers.

We are also much more free in *talking about* such "vices" as prostitution, formerly tabooed language habits, and the use of drugs for pleasure rather than medicine. We are still not liberal enough to think rationally about such issues. We are only gradually relinquishing the idea that alcoholism, drug addiction, homosexuality, and compulsive gambling are moral failures or sicknesses to be treated. However, in many instances relabeling what was formerly sinful as sick remains a closed area kind of hangup: the word, sickness, can be used as an epithet for harmless, though perhaps unusual, behavior, by those who still find it difficult to look at the issues involved in unjaundiced fashion.

In highly closed area of comparative social-economic ideologies, there has been some opening. At least among some groups it is possible now to talk more honestly about the nature of communism, although not yet without some risk of being called a subversive. Still, our growing detente with China and Russia has made discussion of communism as a system more acceptable.

Conclusions

Although it is possible to enumerate numerous manifestations of democratic liberalism in our history, we can still ask: What proportion of the population in the mid-seventies understands and is committed to liberal values? The evidence suggests that although most Americans favor welfare legislation, their basic ideology is conservative and becoming more so. Recently, Yankelovich found that fifty-one percent of American adults view themselves as conservative—compared to twenty-five percent in the mid-sixties (UPI news release, October 28, 1974). It is probable that little we have discussed under liberalism is even understood by the large central mass of the American public—Middle America, as we now label this group. As of this time, it appears that at least a part of our New Deal-type legislation and implementing institutional structure is being dismantled; even more serious, from the view of liberals, is the apparent attempt of the "Nixon Court" (the Supreme Court of the seventies) to reverse various decisions of the Warren Court.

PRESSURES ON SCHOOLS

Now that we have provided a brief rundown of conservative and typically undemocratic elements in American culture, and contrasting liberal and typically democratic elements, we need to see how these contradictory strands in our culture affect education. The purpose of this chapter is to set the stage for the final sections of the book.

Conservatism in Education

Public schools generally remain highly conservative institutions. This assertion, when applied to the seventies, will strike many readers as untenable; they may point to the great amount of experimentation with modular scheduling, nongraded curriculums, team teaching, and other surface changes as evidence that schools have at last really turned experimental and progressive. It should be clear upon careful thought, however, that all of these highly touted changes do not necessarily involve any fundamental shift in the *content of the curriculum* or in *basic teaching methodology.*

School Board and School Administrator Conservatism

School boards are generally composed of members of the upper-middle class: professionals of one sort or another, businessmen, local politicians. Boards cater to the demands of conservative middle Americans, otherwise board members would stand little chance of reelection. Boards are subjected to liberal pressures and may reflect these pressures to some degree; but the predominant influence on boards, and their predominant constituency, are the more conservative elements in the community.

Neal Gross has described a significant study in Massachusetts of outside influences to which school boards and district superintendents are subjected. Those that might be interpreted as conservative far outran liberal requests.[20]

[20] Neal Gross, *et al., Who Runs Our Schools?* New York: John Wiley & Sons, Inc., 1958, p. 50.

Teacher Conservatism

We have less adequate data concerning teacher conservatism than we have concerning school board and administrator conservatism. If the common image of administrators has been that of the public relations expert, the common image of teachers has been closer to that of the preacher. This stereotype fits teachers of the nineteenth century and the twentieth century through World War II much better than it does the post-World War II crop of teachers. Vastly increased numbers of teachers have joined the American Federation of Teachers, an AFL-CIO affiliate which is much more liberal than the old mainline labor unions. At the same time, they have tended to pull away from their former close support of the NEA and its state affiliates, thus forcing the NEA into a much more liberal (and militant) stance in order to compete with the increasingly influential AFT. All this suggests that teachers are becoming more liberal.

It is simplistic, of course, to talk of teachers as a monolithic group. Teachers tend toward the conservative or liberal end of the conservative-liberal continuum in part according to which subjects they teach. Yankelovich's studies of the values and beliefs of college and university students throws some light on this matter. Although his studies, as reported, did not treat as a separate group students intending to become teachers, they did reveal something about conservatism and liberalism as related to the subjects students major in.

Yankelovich divided his sample into what he called "Career-Minded" and "Post-Affluent." The former were taking vocational majors. The latter were upper-middle class who were less interested in clearly vocational majors, except that Yankelovich includes in this group education majors with no designation as to the subject-matter interests of such majors (a way of classifying which does not serve our purpose well here). The post-affluent group includes, in addition to education majors, primarily majors in the humanities and social sciences. As of the years 1970 and 1971, 61 percent of Yankelovich's sample fit in the Career-Minded group and 39 percent in the Post-Affluent group. These figures change in 1973 (see Chapter 4). Of these groups, Yankelovich says:

> The Career-Minded majority represents the continuity in our society. On virtually every count, they hold the more traditional values on family, marriage, work, religion, saving for the future, morals, patriotism, authority, and property. It is [the Post-Affluent] ... who are the devotees of the new values.[21]

[21] Daniel Yankelovich Inc., *The Changing Values on Campus: Political and Personal Attitudes of Today's College Students*. New York: Washington Square Press (Pocket Books), 1972, p. 94.

Yankelovich's book reports studies over a four-year period (1968–1971). One trend appeared clear during this period: "The values held by the [Post-Affluent] . . . group *are* slowly spreading to others in the population, including the more Career-Minded majority of college students."[22] Yankelovich feels the spread of the new values is here to stay, and his 1973 study confirms the above prediction.

In long-range terms, this suggests—if Yankelovich's findings are valid—students going into teaching in the seventies will consist of a conservative majority, identified with vocational fields, and a liberal minority, concentrated in the liberal arts and social sciences; but that with the passage of time, perhaps by the 1980s, liberal teachers will increase proportionately and possibly become a majority.

The Puritan Ethic and Education

In discussing the Puritan ethic and education, we are probably doing little more than spelling out in specific terms a few selected aspects of the generally conservative temper of public education. Readers should recognize before proceeding that many schools have largely abandoned, and many others are in the process of abandoning the curricular and methodological emphases implicit in a Calvinist or Puritan orientation, such as the punishment of children in school. How far these schools may go is impossible to determine now. If there is, indeed, a conservative reaction in the 1970s it is likely that those schools now experimenting seriously with progressive practices will retrench and schools which are still fundamentally conservative will become even more so. But if the predicted conservative reaction does not develop, we can expect gradual movement away from school practices that reflect the Puritan ethic. Then the question always remains: Are certain aspects of the Puritan ethic compatible with the idea of liberal democracy and therefore essential to preserve? If so, schools embarked on a liberal course will probably retain, to some degree, some of the specific practices to be mentioned below.

Competition   The idea of competition is embedded in the Puritan ethic as an intrinsic feature of the doctrine of individualism. There seems clearly to be a strong emphasis on competition. There is the competition of one student against another as demonstrated in our use of grades to reward the winners and punish the losers. A considerable amount of school practice is centered around identifying the winners and giving them a boost toward occupational and status success; and conversely, in identifying the losers and either dropping them from the school program or shan-

---

[22] Yankelovich, p. 95. See also Daniel Yankelovich, *The New Morality: A Profile of American Youth in the 70's.* New York: McGraw-Hill Book Company, 1974, Chapter 3.

ing them up for a blue-collar trade. It should hardly need be said that the winners tend to be students of middle- or upper-middle class origin and the losers of blue-collar semiskilled or unskilled origin or of minority racial or ethnic group background.

In addition to the competitive flavor of the formal curriculum, competition plays a central role in determining who will participate in the most desirable extracurricular activities. In athletics, children and youth of the poor, and ethnic and racial minorities tend to fare much better; but this is somewhat beside the point. Who makes the team is a function of rather fierce competition and the losers, no matter what their social origins, are excluded from participation. Many school systems do have intramural athletic programs but many do not; and even when intramural programs are present there remains in most schools enough "competitive spirit" to guarantee that a large number of losing schools will end up looking bad— to themselves as well as to others.

Competing against one's own prior achievement, whether it be in coursework or extracurricular activities, seems more productive and more democratic. This kind of competition is usually accepted as good. But even in schools where self-competition is highly regarded, we are likely also to find a strong element of interpersonal competition.

Work   Schools uphold the value of hard work, which in itself does not violate liberal values, but it very often takes the form of "work for work's sake" or "busy work" which now occupies much of elementary and secondary school coursework. One of the least flattering things said about students is that they "refuse to work." Actually, these students don't refuse to work; they may spend long hours each week in out-of-school activities which seem important to them. These may range from model airplane building to scheming how to keep supplied with pot; from holding a part-time job to organizing a demonstration. What is usually meant when students are accused of laziness is that they won't give what is considered proper attention to the work-tasks assigned by teachers.

With further development of the accountability movement and its emphasis on the achievement of very concrete behavioral objectives (most of which are likely to strike students as busy work), it is not hard to imagine that the seventies will see a greater rejection by students of the Puritan work ethic even as teachers struggle ever harder to enforce it (to prove that they are accountable). This line of thought will be developed in Part III.

Although an emphasis on vocational education is not necessarily a reflection of the operation of the Puritan work ethic, if such an emphasis is allowed to override programs in the humanities and social sciences, as now happens in many school districts, students certainly are not being prepared for effective citizenship in a democracy. Quite the contrary; a strongly vocation-oriented curriculum tends to reflect what corporate vested interests or conservative labor unions want the schools to do. School boards, administrators, and teachers who push hard for a narrow vocationalism tend to show a strong conservative bias and a lack of commitment to liberal, democratic values. Perhaps because of lack of awareness of the issues, there seems to be a major move afoot to install a vocational emphasis at all grade levels during the seventies.

Censorship Censorship is but one more example of the Puritan ethic at work in our schools. Public schools still try to stress an old-fashioned, absolutistic morality. The many ways in which they do this could be described only in a book-length treatment; therefore, we mention here only one facet of the attempt to promote closed rather than open thinking where moral issues are concerned.

Historically, and today, one form censorship takes is the banning of many subjects from the school curriculum (e.g., *realistic* sex education) or the circumscribing of courses which could be controversial—from a conservative view—by banning certain kinds of teaching materials (e.g., the use of realistic fiction, poetry, or drama in literature and drama programs). In either case, what is at issue is preventing students from coming in contact with any teaching materials considered offensive by the more conservative elements in the community or schools.

An example of how religious fundamentalists, motivated by essentially Puritanical values, can belabor local administrators and their teachers is the controversy in California over the teaching of evolution in public schools. After nearly ten years of pressure on the State Board of Education, which by virtue of new appointees became increasingly fundamentalist in its own views, the Board decided that students in California schools should be taught not only the theory of evolution as accepted by virtually all biologists and the scholarly community generally, but also the Genesis story of creation. The State Curriculum Commission, which recommends state textbook adoptions, protested the rewriting of texts to convey the message that evolutionary theory has a shaky scientific grounding at best and should be studied only in conjunction with the Bible, as advocated by the Board.

Because of the highly lucrative textbook market in California, ordinarily publishers submit dozens of entries for every subject. However, only two biology texts written to meet the demands of the Board were submitted. Both were so unscholarly that the Curriculum Commission recommended against them (one removed material about the work of paleontologist L. S. B. Leakey and replaced it with Michelangelo's version of the Creation). The Board almost adopted these books, but was short one vote.[23] Just prior to this writing, the Board seems to have adopted new

[23] Ron Moskowitz, "Eden and Evolution," *Saturday Review/Science,* February 1973, pp. 58–59.

textbooks which exclude all references to religious theories of creation. However, the issue is unlikely to die in the foreseeable future, given the determination of the fundamentalists.

The list of books banned from public school use, even in senior high school, probably would fill the space occupied by this chapter. In America schools have practiced book banning and on occasion book burning (see Chapter 5). Books are not banned quite as readily now as formerly (censors had a major heyday in the 1940s and 1950s), but the practice of censoring the reading materials used in schools is still a major enterprise.

Similarly, censorship occurs when teachers and students are hassled by parents and administrators for the use of "vulgar language" on school campuses, for allowing teachers and students "immoral" grooming or dress, for minor flirting among students, and for other violations of traditional manners and morals.

The Military Mind and Education

Our "will to win," with its "attack psychology," is certainly not unknown in school affairs. It seems fairly obvious that it dominates most athletic competition. We probably can find it in the classroom as well, although it may not be as conspicuous there. Subduing the will of children and youth was one of the goals of education in the colonies, a logical accompaniment of the Puritan view of the nature of human life and the universe. It would be misleading to say that many teachers today view the young as people to be conquered as was the case in the seventeenth century. Yet, teachers even today do a great deal of "playing God" in the sense of peddling to students answers which are supposed to be absolutely right.

Public school people are known for their dislike of theory and their attachment to the practical approach. The best-known military theorists have shown much more interest in the abstract, the theoretical, the philosophical, than have educators. But the fascination with the concrete, which, according to Ackley also exemplifies the military mind, seems very similar to the fascination which the isolated fact has for teachers. Teachers also illustrate their liking for things concrete by their interest in gadgetry. They take to teaching machines and other mechanical aids in perhaps the same sense that Air Force pilots take to a "hot" new airplane.

The idea of structural hardness should certainly be familiar to school people. As school districts become larger, their administrative structures become increasingly bureaucratic and rule oriented. The routines become goals to be sought for their own sake. Whether there is more or less rigidity in the school systems of Chicago (or any other major city) than in the Pentagon will probably remain an open argument.

With increasingly large classes in increasingly large schools in increasingly large school districts, students may be treated more like things than like human beings. This tendency is likely to accelerate in the seventies because of widespread adoption of a mechanistic/totalitarian approach to education associated with behaviorist psychology. Reification is perhaps at the heart of what is happening in our public schools at present.

Whether there is the tendency to excess and the illusion of omnipotence, which Ackley finds in the military, operating within our public schools is more in question. Schools do promote the ideas of Americans being God's most favored people and of our military omnipotence. Schools do tend to ride each new idea that comes along to extremes—to the point where many useful ideas are ridden to death in a short time. This tendency may be explained, perhaps, primarily on the ground that we have never discovered any very defensible long-range goals for education and are forced to rely on panaceas.

ROLES TEACHERS PLAY

We will describe three roles which teachers have played, and which may remain viable options for a long time into the future. There are, obviously, many more conceivable roles, including an infinite number of eclectic compromises involving the three we will mention.

The Teacher as Conservator of Culture

This is the role which most teachers have played historically, and which a majority of teachers play today. Those who prefer (or are forced into) this role select content and teaching strategies designed to uphold the present or some former status quo. They tend to have a greater interest in the past than in the future. They distrust change, particularly if it is rapid to the point of producing cultural disorganization, or if it seems to disrupt the American social/economic system.

Unless teachers are forced into this role against their wishes, we may safely assume that teachers who adopt the conservative role do actually have conservative attitudes, values, and beliefs. However, most teachers are subject to numerous conservative pressures which may cause a liberally inclined teacher to choose the easiest way out, that is, conformity to conservative pressure.

Even if such conservative pressures did not exist, teaching geared to the status quo is the easiest approach to teaching. It requires only that teachers teach from textbooks designed for public school use, follow state or district curriculum guides, and/or use almost any of the prepackaged teaching materials available nowadays from dozens of publishers. Teachers who are hard pressed because of their work loads may find unavoidable the use of such teaching materials, virtually all of which can be depended upon to be sufficiently conservative to please any individuals or groups applying conservative pressures on schools.

Teachers can make lesson plans for each day of the school year and use essentially the same plans year after year. Since teaching for the status quo tends to avoid issues and focus on facts to be memorized, this approach permits the use of short-answer tests which can be used over and over again. The usual teaching techniques of teachers playing the conservative role are the question-and-answer recitation or the lecture. Obviously, this is the easiest way to teach, with respect to both time and energy input. Thus, many liberally inclined teachers may be forced into the role of cultural conservator simply because they are too overworked to do anything else.

An argument often given for a conservative approach to teaching is that it tends to give the culture continuity by preserving the best in our cultural tradition—the attitudes, values, and beliefs most worth perpetuating. This argument fails to recognize one problem: we do not have one best cultural tradition; rather, we have a number of competing traditions (e.g., Hamiltonian centralism and Madisonian laissez-faire; an ideology supportive of peaceful problem resolution and an ideology supportive of violent problem resolution; a tradition honoring intellect and a tradition distrustful of intellect). Any teacher trying to transmit the past is faced with a problem of selection and the very act of selection may make him a propagandist for one position rather than another equally defensible one. In this writer's experience, most conservative teachers throw the whole lump of tradition, contradictory though it may be, at students, as if all of our past values were equally true. Such teaching, if students pay any attention to it, is likely to produce serious anomie and contribute to cultural disorganization and disintegration.

The Teacher as a Democratic Leader in Amending the Culture

This position holds that teachers should relate democratically to students. This does not mean abdicating leadership, except in situations where one or more students in a class have more authoritative knowledge on the subject under study than the teacher—in which case, such students may temporarily assume leadership roles.

In a democratic classroom, a teacher's job is to help students reflectively study issues they are already aware of and to help them gain awareness of issues they have not previously understood. A democratic classroom is issue- or problem-oriented, since this appears to be the only emphasis which can insure that students will be sufficiently motivated to want to think seriously about topics that are often hard to grasp. A democratic classroom is one in which study is rigorous but pointed, directed toward the examination of the ideological contradictions of the culture. In the free give-and-take of a democratic classroom, it is assumed that teachers and students learn from each other. It is further assumed that, although when drawing conclusions a consensus is desirable, no student should be pressured into pretending he agrees with the majority when he doesn't; nor will any student ever be downgraded or in any other way punished for emerging with conclusions different from those of the teacher.

Since democratic teaching is issue oriented, and since the serious study of issues by students tends to lead students to reexamine old values and beliefs in the light of new evidence, then we can expect that students who emerge from such teaching will usually come to hold views different from those of adults with old-culture values. Hence, the young become different from their parents and the culture they help create will be an *amendment* of the old. Democratic teaching tends to *induce* cultural change, but tends to *reduce* cultural disorganization which is a common accompaniment of *thoughtless* change.

Many teachers who would like to play the democratic role end up not doing so because of pressures placed on them to play the conservator role. But many democratically inclined teachers revert to a conservative approach when they discover that playing a democratic role is much harder work. A democratic teacher can make his role as leader secure only by demonstrating a high level of expertise in his specialty and related specialties. His authority has to be earned. This requires continuous self-study. And because he approaches his teaching dynamically, the drain on nervous energy is heavy. The demand on students is also greater, because rather than playing the role of passive receivers of predetermined Truth they actively seek out answers to problems.

Lest all this sound discouraging to prospective teachers who like the idea of democracy in education, such teaching is vastly more exciting than conservative teaching. Further, teaching remains exciting throughout a democratic teacher's professional career, whereas the conservative teacher often becomes bored with himself, his students, and everything else in his perceived environment.

The democratic role, increasingly, can be interpreted as both goal and role oriented. It seeks goals associated with the preservation of democracy; but in so doing it must grapple with the issue of democratic vs. authoritarian personality structures. This forces attention on selfhood (or personhood) and the whole identity problem.

The Teacher as a Cultural Architect

This view of the teacher's role saw its first major development in the 1930s. The position says, in effect, that the role of teachers is to be familiar with the most thoroughgoing cultural analysis available and to derive from this both what appear to be inescapable directions of cultural movement and those potential directions that could be influenced by educators. The usual interpretation of this philosophy of education holds that the process of industrialization inevitably leads to a collectivist society characterized by massive urbanization, a highly interdependent society caused by a technology with very specialized division of labor, and consolidation of power in large bureaucratic institutions—governmental, military, or corporate.

Proponents of this view feel two options are still open: movement of culture toward a democratic collectivism, or its opposite, an authoritarian collectivism. The first option would strengthen the democratic strands of our culture and hopefully enlarge the areas of direct participatory democracy in spite of the overall collectivist framework. The second option would continue and strengthen the authoritarian (illiberal, nondemocratic) strands of our culture and lead to a society with perhaps a little token democracy, but primarily a totalitarian dictatorship, with the head of state, or a ruling elite, governing the nation by decree. There would seem to be room for an infinite number of compromises, with some sectors of the culture reserved for democratic decision making and other sectors reserved for direct rule by the top power figure or figures.

No one questions that the general direction of industrialism does lead to a society properly labeled collectivist, or collectivist generally with a few small areas of culture retaining for a long time some degree of independence and corresponding personal freedom. The chief issue is whether there are real options at this stage in history between these two potential directions of movement. Some social analysts argue there is no longer any option—that the United States and, in the long run, all other advanced industrial nations will have some type of centralized, authoritarian rule. Other analysts are sanguine about democratic methods and institutions continuing in nations where they have become well established and where people genuinely want them.

Those who talk about teachers as cultural architects have in mind the possibility that what transpires in the schools will be the key factor in determining whether social movement will be democratic or authoritarian. If teachers understand the issues, they can and must, it is argued, develop models of alternative democratic collectivisms. In this sense, teachers become cultural architects. With futuristic models available, teachers can proceed first, to acquaint students with the basic issue of democracy vs. authoritarianism; next, to familiarize themselves with democratic models that seem plausible; and finally, to study strategies for warding off authoritarian pressures and promoting the democratic path.

This general point of view places great responsibility on the schools and on classroom teachers in particular. It regards the schools as potentially the major vehicle for social change, with all the wisdom and responsibility this would entail.

The teacher-as-cultural-architect idea seems clearly a goal-oriented position and for that reason somewhat old-fashioned when considered in relation to the views of such social analysts as Margaret Mead, William Glasser, and Erik Erikson. However, it does offer students a chance to examine alternative worlds, and students who are alienated from the present culture and searching for some goal which will enable them to build a coherent, purposive value system may find their deteriorating sense of identity restored as they identify with an appealing long-range set of goals. Hence, this position can be role-, as well as goal, oriented.

The cultural architect role, with its eye on the long-range future, was originally strongly goal oriented. However, as we shall see in the next section, contemporary cultural architects, reconstructionists, have become strongly interested in the identity crisis of our age.

SOCIAL RECONSTRUCTIONISM: PRO AND CON

Because various proponents of reconstructionism have emphasized various facets of the positions at different times, we offer this brief map to facilitate our trip through the subject. With variations in individual views, reconstructionists call for thoroughgoing revolutionary change in our industrial collectivist society *from* an ideology promoting and consisting of attitudes, values, beliefs, myths, and behavior which they see as almost guaranteeing the possibility of eventual fascism in the United States and education that emphasizes the mechanistic teaching of facts and skills, *to* an ideology consisting of attitudes, values, beliefs, and behavior that would promote the goals of participatory democratic socialism—a creative collectivism—and both social and personal identity, or roles, *by means of* educational content and methodology emphasizing cultural issues. In one sense, reconstructionism can be said to have a scientific basis, in that its interests are those of interdisciplinary social sciences. In another sense, it cannot be said to have a literal scientific basis because it is based on a choice of values: it depends on a specific value judgment, that democratic socialism is better than fascism.

The idea of "reconstructionism" in philosophy was introduced by John Dewey and became part of the title of his book, *Reconstructionism in Philosophy* (1920). Some of Dewey's later works suggested that he was pondering the idea of *social* reconstructionism. In each case, the word, reconstructionism, referred to a position advocating the remaking or re-forming, in such thoroughgoing fashion as to be appropriately labeled revolutionary, both philosophy and society or culture.

Two Early Reconstructionists

It remained for certain of Dewey's colleagues at Teachers' College, Columbia University, to develop social reconstructionism into a school of thought in education. George Counts, in two books particularly, *The American Road to Culture* and *Dare the School Build a New Social Order?* presented a clear statement of reconstructionism.[24] Harold Rugg further developed the position in various books.[25]

Stated briefly, and in oversimplified fashion, Counts saw every advanced industrial nation as moving toward collectivism, by which he meant centralized control of most social functions, the development of large bureaucratic structures, a degree of division of labor which would ensure extreme interdependency of people, and an increasingly important role of the Federal Government in managing the society. He felt that within this framework of inevitable collectivism, the United States had but two op-tions: "a system of economic arrangements which increasingly partakes of the nature of industrial feudalism," (fascism, in today's terminology) and a "democratic collectivism" designed to diffuse property rights—a step that would require that ". . . natural resources and all important forms of capital will have to be collectively owned." In short, Counts saw only a two-way choice, what we would call today *fascism* and *democratic socialism*.

Counts saw the public schools as the most promising agency to lead the United States away from fascism and toward democratic socialism. He recognized that ". . . the school is but one formative agency among many, and certainly not the strongest at that" but he also felt that of all extant educational agencies the schools had fewer axes to grind, had more in-tegrity, and that as a group, teachers were better educated and more enlightened than the personnel in other educational agencies. He felt

[24] George Counts, *The American Road to Culture*, New York: The John Day Company, Inc., 1930; *Dare the School Build a New Social Order?* John Day Pamphlet No. 11, New York: The John Day Company, Inc., 1932.

[25] Harold Rugg, *The Great Technology*, New York: The John Day Company, Inc., 1933; *Now Is the Moment*, New York: Duell, Sloan & Pearce-Meredith Press, 1943; *That Men May Understand*, New York: Doubleday & Company, Inc., 1941; *The Teacher of Teachers*, New York: Harper & Row, Publishers, 1952; *Social Foundations of Education*, Englewood Cliffs, N.J.: Prentice-Hall, Inc., 1955; *Imagination*, New York: Harper & Row, Publishers, 1963. The last title was pub-lished posthumously and contains editorial comments by Kenneth D. Benne.

strongly that the influence of the schools was likely to increase, making his idea of the schools as leaders in social change more practical than it would seem at first glance. Counts did not argue that the schools should, or indeed could if they wished, approach any such educational task impartially: "My thesis is that the school must shape attitudes, develop tastes, and even impose ideas."[26]

Harold Rugg, writing during the 1930s and 1940s, urged his vision of *education-led* social change from an "exploitive tradition" to his ideal-ized version of a "great tradition." Rugg saw three alternatives for Amer-ican society: (1) a society of robots reminiscent of those in the not-yet-published *1984* by George Orwell; (2) a society of idle degenerates, whose stomachs might be full but whose minds would be empty; and (3) a demo-cratic, creative society in which the economic system would produce an abundance of goods with little menial labor (through increased mechani-zation) and leave workers spare time in which to become creative crafts-men working for pleasure, without the depressing rigors of competition for existence. Rugg's preferred creative democracy could also be construed as a kind of democratic socialism; to reach it he was convinced that nothing could be solved by mere reform—only by *reconstruction.*

In the process of reconstruction, Rugg saw the primary leadership coming from a creative minority, the scholarly community, the most im-portant members of which he thought were the "teachers of teachers." Following the lead of this group would be, first, the thinking and informed minority which Rugg thought constituted about one-fourth of the popula-tion; and following the lead of these two most educated groups would be the mass of labor, in whom Rugg had perhaps more faith than would seem warranted in the 1970s. Rugg felt that if his proposed movement toward a creative, democratic collectivism were to be fulfilled, an appropriate ideol-ogy would have to be developed around which people could rally. This ideology would have its mythical components, as do all ideologies, but central to it would be the making of a religion of democratic ideals.

Rugg advocated schools whose curriculums would be *culture-centered.* Culture-centered schools neither ignore nor emphasize past or present; they are basically *future oriented.* To function, they must be staffed by teachers who have not only been immersed in cultural study, but who combine both the science and the art of education. Rugg had a very high regard for art as the epitome of creativity, and creativity was an ever-present theme in all his writing.

In spite of his emphasis on culture-centered schools, Rugg did not ignore the needs of individuals; he urged the blending of the individual

[26] The above quotations are all from Counts, *Dare the School Build a New Social Order?*, pp. 45, 46, 24, 19.

and the collective, and the development of persons with a *social-self.* One of Rugg's contemporary interpreters says: "Visionary that Rugg was—and all reconstructionists are utopian visionaries—he was far ahead of his time in intuiting the essential problem of *our* time—helping people find *meaningful personal identity in a world which has become meaningless.*"[27]

Contemporary Reconstructionism

The leading reconstructionist since mid-century is generally conceded to be Theodore Brameld, who, as of this writing, has published seventeen books and innumerable journal articles. However, since Brameld's position has changed somewhat over the years, we will state his position as accurately as we can from his most recent major philosophical book, *Patterns of Educational Philosophy: Divergence and Convergence in Culturological Perspective*, and from certain of his recent articles, the most intriguing to this writer being "Education as Self-Fulfilling Prophecy."

Brameld's position is far too complex to describe satisfactorily in a few textbook pages, even though various writers attempt it.[28] Further, Brameld's position is not finalized; it has evolved enough so that reliance on his earlier publications could be misleading. We will not attempt a systematic summarization of Brameld's position, but rather will note what seem to us some of his more striking ideas.

Brameld can probably be understood better if readers are aware that he began his professional career as a "pure" philosopher, saw pure philosophy as sterile in relation to the problems of the times, then moved to educational philosophy, which he felt was also inadequate because of its tendency to ignore knowledge social scientists contribute to philosophy of education. In his view, the key social science discipline is anthropology. Brameld's position is thus based upon a fusion of philosophy, anthropology, and education.

Brameld sees education in the contemporary world as an arm of politics (a view which we document in Chapter 5). The major issue is whether education should do the bidding of the politically powerful, as it now typically does, or become a participating partner in political authority and power. Brameld regards ours as a "crisis-culture" because of its "intolerable" contradictions between ideology and practice. He feels that not only ours but world civilization is undergoing a cultural revolution of vast import. A central reason why so many people cannot see what is

[27] Sandford W. Reitman, "The Reconstructionism of Harold Rugg," *Educational Theory*, Winter, 1972, p. 57.

[28] For example, see George F. Kneller, "Contemporary Educational Theories," in George F. Kneller (ed.), *Foundations of Education*. New York: John Wiley & Sons, Inc., 1971, pp. 247–251.

happening culturally is that they are trapped in their narrow specialisms; philosophy remains the one area "that specializes in nonspecialization."[29]

He feels that it is impossible to understand or deal with educational or cultural problems apart from their cultural/anthropological context. Further, even the smallest local issue cannot be understood apart from its relation to larger issues of the local subculture; small subcultures cannot be understood apart from larger subcultures, and so on, with full understanding impossible without an awareness of global situations. Hence, Brameld is much involved with global value orientations and global cultural trends.

Like his predecessors, Brameld sees no end to the cultural crisis within the present framework of monopoly capitalism and other solidified traditional institutions except through reconstruction. He calls for *cultural reconstruction* on a local, regional, national, and global scale. His commitment is to a worldwide democratic collectivism.

Brameld feels that our culture is blighted by a narrow, opportunistic pragmatism which exaggerates the importance of means in relation to ends. One of our major problems is an absence of long-range social goals; so far, it has not been in the nature of Americans to be concerned with other than the immediate, the short-run, the expedient. We need, Brameld feels, long-range purposes of a compelling nature, purposes that would grip people with the force of religion. Brameld's "religion," like that of Counts and Rugg, is democracy—as participatory as possible given the inescapability of collectivist institutions.

Central in Brameld's thinking is the role of prophecy in helping to bring about that which is prophesized. He offers us numerous examples of how an appealing goal has motivated people to achieve what a majority has thought impossible. But he is not impressed with the little prophecies teachers often state regarding students, for example: "You're a rotten kid who won't amount to anything," followed by the youngster actually not amounting to anything because he took the teacher seriously. Brameld is intrigued by prophecies of "grand design." He says "Only the emotional and rational magnetism of prophecies that are unqualifiedly, not spuriously, radical (which is to say deep-cutting, planet-wide, and future-directing) can any longer be expected to provide the direction that mankind now requires."[30]

It appears that Brameld has not been much impressed by school subjects designed to lead only to the short-run personal goals of students.

[29] Theodore Brameld, *Patterns of Educational Philosophy: Divergence and Convergence in Culturological Perspective.* New York: Holt, Rinehart and Winston, Inc., 1971, p. 55.

[30] Theodore Brameld, "Education as Self-Fulfilling Prophecy," *Phi Delta Kappan,* September 1972, p. 58.

The worth of any part of a school curriculum can be judged only in relation to cultural patterns far larger than that of the individual school or
community. In referring to the positive use of self-fulfilling prophecy in
schools, as when we say students will learn more if they are encouraged
by their teachers, complimented for what they do well rather than criticized for what they do poorly, Brameld says:

> By constricting education as self-fulfilling prophecy to learning-teach-
> ing as an "interpersonal" process [i.e., between student and instruc-
> tor], and then, even more narrowly, by limiting this process in terms
> of reading and other cognitive phases of individual development . . .
> [teachers] have totally ignored the prophecy of future anticipation and
> direction for any group of citizens, young or old, who are struggling
> to achieve humane social-cultural goals."[31]

And quoting Warren Wagar,[32] Brameld adds: "The ultimate function of
prophecy is not to tell the future, but to make it."

Probably the major change in Brameld's thought in recent years is
to complement his former emphasis on the social, the group, the collective,
with a recognition that individuals do have identity problems, that *social*
fulfillment can no longer be regarded as the only goal of education. He
now uses the expression "self- and social-fulfillment." Although he still
stresses the collective, and feels that developments of the sixties validated
this interest, he states his philosophy as being "personal-social." He says,
in the *Phi Delta Kappan* article cited, that ". . . in one sense, the Rogers
and the Maslows are right, after all. Self-fulfilling prophecy is not only
reducible to cultural expectations; it can become personal expectations,
too." Thus, Brameld, like Glasser and others, now stresses helping people
find a role, as well as a goal, orientation.

Arguments Against and For Reconstructionism

Reconstructionism is not a popular position in American education. The
reasons appear simple and obvious. Reconstructionism, with teachers and
students being cultural architects, calls for personal and social reconstruction in a literal sense, not simply for tinkering with or patching up education and culture as they now exist. Although reconstructionism might not
appear so radical in some countries, our deep-seated conservatism, which,
as we have seen, embraces all levels of school personnel, could not be
expected to take kindly any call for revolutionary change. Most educators
at the public school level do not even understand the full arguments of
the reconstructionists; if they did they would be even more frightened of
the idea than they are.

---

[31] Brameld, "Education as Self-Fulfilling Prophecy," p. 11.
[32] Warren Wagar, *The City of Man.* Baltimore, Md.: Penguin Books, 1968.

But there are many persons in professional education who reject, or partially reject, reconstructionism. Kneller's critique is one of many.[33] Kneller points out that reconstructionists—and Kneller is referring specifically to Brameld—claim an empirical social science basis for their position that does not exist. There are very few widely agreed upon findings in social science concerning the best values for humans to accept or the social institutions most likely to promote any given set of values. Kneller makes a point we too have made, that an individualist ideology is at least as attractive to Americans as "the commitment to democratically determined social ideals." Kneller cannot see a culture as pluralist as ours coming to any agreement on long-range goals.

Kneller also criticizes Brameld's advocacy of teachers taking a stand for a definite set of long-range goals while maintaining a democratic classroom. He questions whether a teacher can be a persuasive advocate and democratic leader at the same time. This criticism of reconstruction is very old: the idea that a reconstructionist teacher is basically a propagandist no matter how hard he tries to maintain a democratic stance.

What most criticisms of reconstructionism boil down to is that it is a hopelessly utopian position in American culture at this time. Teachers are neither well enough informed nor liberal enough to accept the reconstructionist role of cultural architect. If they tried, their even more conservative administrators and school boards would see that they were banned from further teaching.

Let us take a look at the other side of the picture. A hoard of social scientists, philosophers, and educators believe that our culture and its schools are in serious trouble, for reasons which we have already tried to specify. Up to this point, we are not aware of any opponents of reconstructionism who have come up with a comprehensive, long-range, empirically defensible program that would get us out of the mess.

Reconstructionists are aware of the conservatism of a majority of Americans, including those who run the schools. They are also aware that it would probably take only one event of disastrous proportions to swing opinion around 180 degrees. The Great Depression of the 1930s caused millions of persons to question the basic validity of the "American system"; our involvement in Vietnam was less disrupting, but did demonstrate clearly how many citizens could do a complete about-face in a couple of years. We don't know what the seventies and eighties will hold, but any major crisis (an ecological disaster, an economic collapse like that of the thirties, or, unlikely but possible, a nuclear war) would bring a quick demand for revolutionary solutions. It may well be that only the reconstructionists will have comprehensive plans for such a contingency.

Our previous educational experience seems to demonstrate that public education, even through college, changes fundamentally the atti-

[33] Kneller, "Contemporary Educational Theories," pp. 250–251.

tudes, beliefs, and values of only a minority of persons. By any criteria, our schools seem to have failed to produce a citizenry capable of voting intelligently enough to maintain a self-governing democracy in an age beset with our economic, political, and psychological problems. The reconstructionist emphasis upon a culture-centered curriculum, which has never been tried, appears to be the only pending suggestion that might preserve or enhance the democracy we have, or resolve the critical social problems that pile up faster than we now can innovate ideas for solving them.

Much has been said about the utopianism of the reconstructionists, the basic thought being that they are impractical dreamers. This criticism deserves the most careful study. Most persons who make this criticism are little aware of the number of times in human history that an outrageous hypothesis of one generation became the accepted truth of future generations. But what they seem least aware of, and to this writer it is most incomprehensible, is that historically the conservative positions that strove to maintain the status quo, or to restore a previous status quo, have never succeeded for more than a short time. *The conservative posture has proved to be the most utopian of all because it never works except very temporarily; if we want to look for wild-eyed dreams, we should examine the programs advocated by conservatives and study their outcomes.*

STUDY QUESTIONS

1. The cultural analysis of this chapter has focused upon kinds of changes that can be evaluated in relation to the liberal versus conservative, or democratic versus authoritarian, continuum. What other kinds of changes, unrelated to this continuum, do you feel will occur in America in the 1970s?
2. How would you rate yourself on a conservative-liberal continuum? Can you identify ways in which you are conservative and other ways in which you are liberal? How does your overall position compare with that of your parents? Your grandparents?
3. As a study project which may help you better understand yourself, as well as American culture, develop a model (using verbal description, supplemented by diagrams if you choose) of what would be your "ideal" society.
4. In discussing conservative pressures likely to be operating in this country in the 1970s, we suggested that a "military psychology" may become more pervasive than before in many of our institutions. To carry this discussion farther, what do you think will be the effect on American culture of the two million plus veterans from Vietnam? Will they be a major conservative force? Will their ideology and behavior resemble that of veterans of World Wars I and II? Are they likely to adopt the traditional radical conservative view of the American Legion and the Veterans of Foreign Wars?

5. In addition to the examples of conservatism given in this chapter, what do you see as further examples, either now in evidence or likely to emerge before the seventies are over?
6. The main points of the Puritan ethic (or Puritan life style), such as individualism, dedication to work, and bettering oneself materially, sound attractive. What place do you think they will have in a society where work is largely mechanized and where scarce natural resources may make impractical the goal of an ever higher material standard of living?
7. Think back at your own previous education. Can you remember any examples of where a school, or a particular classroom, reflected at least some aspects of "military psychology"?
8. What examples would you add to those given of liberal tendencies in American culture? What new liberal tendencies do you see arising?
9. What data suggest that students majoring in physical education, industrial arts, and agriculture are far more conservative (and less broadly informed generally) than those majoring in English and the social sciences? How would you explain this? Do you see it as a problem?
10. From your prior schooling, can you cite any examples of teachers who seemed to change their educational philosophy from week to week (or day to day)? What specific inconsistencies in the thinking of your teachers can you name?
11. If they had been professional educators, would Aldous Huxley (*Brave New World*) and George Orwell (*1984*), have been social reconstructionists? What about Thomas Jefferson, Abraham Lincoln, William McKinley, Woodrow Wilson, and Calvin Coolidge?
12. Which of the following would you consider a religion (defining religion broadly)? Marxism, Free Enterprise, Worship of the Flag, Anti-communism, materialism, pacifism, praying for the return of the "good old days," social reconstructionism?
13. There are many more arguments revolving around reconstructionism than space permitted us to enumerate in this chapter. Add as many *pro and con* arguments as you can think of.

ANNOTATED BIBLIOGRAPHY

Bennis, Warren G., Kenneth D. Benne, and Robert Chin, *The Planning of Change,* 2d ed. New York: Holt, Rinehart and Winston, Inc., 1969. See Chapter 1 bibliography..

Boyer, William H., *Education for Annihilation.* Honolulu: Hogarth Press, 1972.

A very well-written, comparatively brief discussion of the influence of the "military mind' and military practice on education and American society generally. Boyer's treatment is less comprehensive than Ackley's, but the book is highly readable for both college and high school students. Recommended.

Brameld, Theodore, *The Climactic Decades: Mandate to Education.* Foreword by Kenneth D. Benne. New York: Praeger Publishers, Inc., 1970.

In this book, Brameld restates his basic position with special emphasis on seeking a synthesis of what his critics have referred to as unbridgeable polarities in his position.

Brameld, Theodore, *Education as Power*. New York: Holt, Rinehart and Winston, Inc., 1965.

Brameld states his conviction that it is through education, devoted to long-range goals, rather than short-run tinkering, that the entire global community can become a humane and satisfying society. One of the virtues of the book is that it is perhaps the easiest of Brameld's books for students to read.

Brameld, Theodore, *The Use of Explosive Ideas in Education: Culture, Class, and Evolution*. Pittsburgh: University of Pittsburgh Press, 1965.

Brameld attempts in this book to build a bridge between social science, philosophy, and education. He treats three areas in which social scientists have done major work: the culture concept, social class, and evolution. In each case he extracts some of the more potent, and controversial, hypotheses to use as "bridges." Compare the theme of this book with the present writer's idea of using "outrageous hypotheses" as integrating constructs.

Cleary, Robert E., *Political Education in the American Democracy*. Scranton, Pa.: Intext Educational Publishers, 1971.

Cleary organizes his content around the theme of political education and treats many of the topics included in Chapter 2. His overarching focus is on the ignorance and confusion of Americans about political matters, the extreme conservatism of teachers in this area, and the present ineffectiveness of schools.

Full, Harold (ed), *Controversy in American Education: An Anthology of Crucial Issues*, 2d ed. New York: The Macmillan Company, 1972.

Of the seeming ten million "readers," "anthologies," "symposiums," etc., now on the market, this is surely one of the best. The fifty-three essays in this collection are by the most familiar and illustrious names in education, social science, and social philosophy.

Phi Delta Kappan, September 1972.

The theme of this issue is "What Are Schools For?" In contrast to the article by Brameld cited earlier, articles by Robert L. Ebel and Joseph Junell attack the reconstructionist position. A further article by T. Robert Basset says in effect, "a plague on Ebel, Brameld, and Junell."

Riesman, David, "America Moves Right," *The New York Times Magazine*, October 27, 1968, p. 34.

One of our more eminent sociologists makes a strong argument that "the United States through most of its history has been a profoundly conservative country."

Schoenberger, Robert A. (ed.), *The American Right Wing: Readings in Political Behavior*, New York: Holt, Rinehart and Winston, Inc., 1969.

Very likely the best collection of readings available on the most extreme of our radical conservative groups. The readings are non-polemical and empirically based and provide an important sidelight on American conservatism not treated in Chapter 2.

The Seventies: A Look Ahead at the New Decade, Essays from The National Observer, Princeton, N.J.: Dow Jones Books, 1970.

Fifteen essays by editors of the prestigious weekly paper published by Dow Jones, *The National Observer.* A good collection of scholarly attempts at the game of futuristics. Respectably conservative and a good companion volume to the anthology edited by Harold Full.

Shostak, Arthur B., *Blue-Collar Life.* New York: Random House, Inc., 1969.

A well-balanced, reasonably thorough study of the major aspects of the life of blue-collar workers. On the basis of the best research available at the time, Shostak finds two of the major value orientations of blue-collars to be racism and authoritarianism; other dominant values are rejection of civil rights; opposition to modernizing schools, belief in censorship, imperialism, and militarism.

Smith, T. V., and Eduard C. Lindeman, *The Democratic Way of Life: An American Interpretation.* New York: Mentor Books, 1951.

The model of democracy in industrial culture developed in this book has been widely used by democratic social philosophers. The book has been popular with reconstructionists, including Brameld.

Theobald, Robert (ed.), *Social Policies for America in the Seventies: Nine Divergent Views,* New York: Doubleday & Company, Inc., 1968; Anchor, 1969.

This short collection of essays is so selected that for each view presented another is included which is almost diametrically opposite; but more important, the polarity emphasized is between fairly extreme versions of liberalism and conservatism.

Negative alienation. *(Copyright © George Ballis, all rights reserved)*

CULTURAL CONFLICT, ALIENATION, AND EDUCATION

No one can begin to think, feel or act now except from the starting point of his or her own alienation.

R. D. Laing

The present chapter is important for prospective and in-service teachers for several reasons. In Chapter 1 we discussed uneven social change and its tendency to produce conflict in the form of ideological incompatibilities in the culture and corollary value conflicts in the persons making up the culture. We sketched in and used the general concepts of alienation and anomie in both Chapters 1 and 2.

Here we will define these concepts specifically as they

Positive alienation. *(Copyright © George Ballis, all rights reserved)*

will be used in this book's sociological/anthropological analysis. We will suggest how the concepts can be used to help teachers understand both social problems, whether local, regional, national, or international, and also the personal problems of value choice among students.

It is not the intent of this book to treat personal problems except to help understand group or social problems. We should note, however, that to tallk of the personal and the social as if they were two distinct categories is virtually always misleading, since the kind of personal student problems that concern teachers are with rare exceptions inextricably linked to the student's cultural milieu. What teachers see as group problems are no more than a collection of more-or-less similar personal problems. The principle of the continuity of self and culture, as exemplified in the process of simultaneous mutual interaction (SMI), makes attempted separation of the individual and the social misleading. This is why *all* psychology is actually *social psychology*, and a social science, in spite of the

The lonely crowd. *(Copyright © George Ballis, all rights reserved)*

attempts of some psychologists to separate individuals and their perceived social environments.

IDEOLOGICAL CONFLICT AS A CAUSE OF ALIENATION

Although we have referred to the term, alienation, in the Prologue and Chapters 1 and 2, before developing the major theme of the present chapter we need to provide a more concrete and focused definition than we have heretofore done.

Alienate, as a verb, means literally "to make strange." Alienation, as a noun, means a "state of being"—a state of being estranged from something. Estranged, as we will use the concept, means being separated or cut off. To understand the nature of alienation we must be clear about who are the alienated and what they may be alienated from. The alineated are any individuals, or any groupings—as a social class, a generation of people, a culture or subculture—which feels disconnected from some entity with which it could be connected under different circumstances.

Following an interesting analysis by Walter Kaufman, we can use the symbol A in referring to the alienated.[1] To enumerate what any item

[1] Walter Kaufman, in his Introduction to Richard Schacht, *Alienation.* New York: Doubleday & Company, Inc., 1970.

under A may be alienated from becomes more complicated. Any such item Kaufman refers to as B. A may feel alienated from itself, from a group or combination of groups, from nature, God, or the universe, from its subculture or the larger cultural context (humankind in general, for example). There seems virtually no end to the different kinds of B from which A may feel estranged.

Estrangement from Oneself and One's Own Subculture

As we will use the concept of *alienation,* we usually refer to discon-nectedness from the culture the alienated person or group lives in or is concerned about, because the ideological patterns of that culture do not make sense because of dissonant values. In short, we willl focus on aliena-tion from cultural contradictions which are problem-generating and not easily resolved. The particular state of mind induced by this kind of alienation has been referred to by Kurt Lewin as "feelings of meaning-lessness."[2] Rollo May apparently means about the same thing when he describes feelings of "powerlessness" or "impotence" associated with estrangement from a culture with seemingly overwhelming inconsis-tencies.[3]

   If alienation is to be regarded as a feeling of meaninglessness result-ing from one's social environment failing to provide usable value-choices for one's ideology or the evidence needed to make necessary decisions in a rational manner, then anomie is a similar condition but in an extreme form.

   Anomie (a concept originally developed by Emile Durkheim) refers to the psychological state of a society or group in which there is relative absence or extreme confusion of values. An anomic culture is one in which such values as exist are so contradictory, ambiguous, or confused that the making of sensible value-choices becomes quite impossible for individuals. Individuals trapped in such a cultural milieu are also referred to as anomic. (It is not proper to refer to anomic *persons*—the word, per-son, personhood, or selfhood implies an individual with a substantial number of integrated values.)

   An anomic culture is one in an advanced state of disorganization, or one collapsing from disintegration. An anomic individual is so confused about goals and how to achieve them that he is incapable of acting rationally.

   For our purposes, both in this chapter and the rest of the book, of the various kinds of B from which a person may feel estranged, we will emphasize alienation from oneself and from one's culture (be it either a

   [2] Schacht, p. 155.
   [3] Rollo May, *Psychology and the Human Dilemma.* New York: Van Nos-trand Reinhold Company, 1967, Chap. 2.

subculture or the larger culture). Actually, it would be unrealistic to treat these as two separate forms of alienation: one of the chief reasons for feeling at odds with oneself is that one feels at odds with one or more cultural conflicts with which one identifies. Conversely, a person would be unlikely to feel alienated from his culture if he did not feel a sense of personal conflict. Here again it is useful to think in terms of the generic concept of the linkage of self and culture through an SMI relationship, as we have previously defined it.

Cognitive Dissonance and Alienation

Cognitive dissonance becomes a fundamental concept in our development of this chapter and others. It is a relatively sophisticated and carefully elaborated attempt to describe and support with empirical data aspects of intrapersonal conflict. The idea of cognitive dissonance, although historically ancient, was popularized in its modern form by Leon Festinger in 1957.[4]

The Theory of Cognitive Dissonance

The central idea of *cognitive dissonance* is quite simple. "The notions are that the simultaneous existence of cognitions which in one way or another do not fit together (dissonance) leads to effort on the part of the person to somehow make them fit better (dissonance reduction)."[5] We can see from this statement that the theory of cognitive dissonance is really a theory of motivation: when a person senses that his thinking is inconsistent, he tries to eliminate or reduce the inconsistency. This idea in itself is hardly new. The central thought, it strikes us, was proposed by Gestalt psychologists in Germany in the 1890's and called the "law of closure." In the United States it was proposed by John Dewey early in the century and was rather carefully developed in his book, *How We Think* (1910). As one might surmise, the idea actually dates from the ancient world: Sophocles' play, *Oedipus Rex*, forcefully illustrates cognitive dissonance and one approach (not a particularly happy one) toward resolving it.

We will not develop the various motivational aspects of the theory

[4] Leon Festinger, A Theory of Cognitive Dissonance. Evanston, Ill.: Row, Peterson & Company, 1957. For a briefer, somewhat more updated version, see Festinger and Elliot Aronson, "The Arousal and Reduction of Dissonance in Social Contexts," in Dorwin Cartwright and Alvin Zander (eds.), Group Dynamics: Research and Theory, 2d ed. Evanston, Ill.: Row, Peterson & Company, 1960.

[5] Festinger and Aronson, p. 214.

of cognitive dissonance in this chapter. Here, our primary interest is in the nature of cognitive dissonance, some of the nonproductive and productive ways people use in trying to reduce it, and the consequences of a failure to eliminate or reduce it. But first we need to expand on Festinger's definition. (Our expansion of Festinger's ideas is based partly on our own thinking and partly on empirical research of Festinger and others, not all of which has been in agreement.)

The basic units of Festinger's theory he calls "cognitive elements." To translate this to the terminology we are using in this book, these elements are attitudes, values, beliefs, myths, ideological assertions, and knowledge or pseudoknowledge. The relationship between one such element and another may be relevant or irrelevant. Relevancy requires that two or more elements be related in the sense that if one element changes it will directly influence one or more others. If elements are irrelevant, a change in one will have no affect on the others. An example of the relatedness and unrelatedness of cognitive elements was given in Chapter 1 in the section on social disorganization.

Relevant relations may be either dissonant or consonant (i.e., conflicting or harmonizing). For example, dissonance would occur if a white person, on principle, hated all Blacks, but found a black political candidate who represented his views and voted for him. In this case, the action contradicts the principle (in other cases a principle might contradict a principle, an action an action, a belief a belief, etc.). An example of consonance between two related elements would be the case of a person feeling a close identification with a political party and making regular financial donations to the party. Barring any variables which might produce inconsistency, the act of giving money to one's preferred party is clearly an example of consistent choice making.

Dissonance does not ordinarily occur simply because a person *holds* contradictory values and beliefs. Apparently everyone holds contradictory values and beliefs at some level of consciousness and in some degree of intensity; but unless the contradictions become problematic, one seldom becomes aware of them. This is the same as saying that a problem does not exist for anyone until he *feels* it as a problem. Apparently most of our dissonances remain buried at an unverbalized level; or, if not important enough to produce anxiety, they may be verbalized and even studied without producing motivation to reduce them. In sum, inconsistency per se in one's thinking may be no cause for distress.

Inconsistency, or dissonance, usually—though by no means always—produces problems, anxiety, or tension only after we try to act on the basis of the inconsistent cognitive elements. Because action is usually required to make dissonance problematic, we say that cognitive dissonance is often *expectancy oriented.* If we project actions which would logically follow from two relevant and incompatible cognitive elements then we tend to *see* the inconsistency. We may or may not consummate the action, but it is *projecting the dissonant elements that clarifies the nature of their inconsistency.*

Although this is usually the case, J. D. Jecker concluded that dissonance may develop simply as a result of a person's holding incompatible attitudes, beliefs, or knowledge of past actions. These cognitive elements, while not being decisions proper, are conceptual equivalents of decisions.[6] However, we need to stress the word *may* in connection with Jecker's findings. Some few individuals, probably only those who tend to think systematically and are exceptionally sensitive to how their own ideas jibe, may come to see for themselves (through reflection when they are away from a problem confrontation and a choice-making situation) whether their thinking holds together logically. To do this requires a well-developed capacity for self-analysis which apparently the great majority of people never achieve. If we assume people should develop this sensitivity, assistance from others may be necessary, as we will indicate later.

One question which usually emerges in connection with Festinger's theory of cognitive dissonance is "Why do people tend to feel uncomfortable when they sense their own inner inconsistencies?" It may be that many people do not, that they can live quite contentedly with full knowledge that their thinking is inharmonious. Yet, we have an abundance of research evidence, dating at least as far back as some of the early investigation of Gestalt psychologists, that most people develop anxiety states when they find that they believe in two opposites simultaneously. In fact, people often take desperate steps to erase in some way what they perceive as their own dissonances. These steps usually involve some kind of mental gymnastics through which the individual manages to persuade himself that he really isn't inconsistent after all. These psychological ploys come mainly under the head of *rationalization* (the actual process of which we will describe a little later). But for others, no amount of psychological self-manipulation makes the feeling of anxiety go away: probably most suicides are committed by people at the end of their psychological rope because they cannot free themselves from the worry of cognitive dissonance.

Although hard to prove empirically, it seems a plausible hypothesis to assume that the reason people become agitated over cognitive dissonance is because it gives them a feeling of estrangement from themselves, a mental state which a layman might understand under such a label as "split personality." A feeling of inner fragmentation, a lack of

[6] Jon D. Jecker, "Conflict and Dissonance: A Time of Decision," in Robert P. Abelson *et al.* (eds.), *Theories of Cognitive Consistency: A Sourcebook.* Chicago: Rand McNally & Company, 1968.

wholeness, is alienation turned into anomie: a state in which people have no sense of guiding values, no sense of direction, and, at the same time, an intense feeling of loneliness, helplessness, and confusion.

Whether a person who realizes his inconsistencies in areas of related beliefs becomes agitated and seeks to reduce his inconsistency depends in large degree on how important the inconsistency is to the person. If it seems of small importance, most persons are not bothered by the inconsistency. But if the unresolved issue places some highly cherished belief in jeopardy, and, if the person cannot hypothesize any way out, he usually becomes very anxious and tries to ignore the evidence that threatens him. High involvement, with no solution in sight, produces in some people tightening of the self-structure, a rigidity, which in popular terminology is best thought of as closed mindedness. It is because of the threat of new evidence that might amplify dissonance that people become closed to new ideas. This is how "closed areas of culture" are born and maintained. The closed-minded person is maintaining himself in a state of alienation with the culture and dropping ever deeper into a state of anomie.

Discomfort from Dissonance as Good and Bad

Alienation is commonly discussed as if it were invariably something to be avoided or reduced—as a prelude to anomie and personal and cultural disintegration. Alienation is often regarded in the literature as a kind of mental illness, as a negative state of being. This is a valid use of the term, but if one views alienation in only its negative sense, one is being simplistic to say the least.

Try to imagine a culture in which there is no alienation at all. Having asked what a totally nonalienated individual would be like, Kaufman raises these questions:

> Would a nonalienated person find no group of people, no individuals, nothing about the society in which he lived strange in any way at all? If so, could one really call him a person? And if one did, would one not have to add that his condition was severely pathological and bordered on idiocy?[7]

One could go farther and ask whether a person totally lacking in psychophysical tension could be described only as *dead*.

A person finds his own selfhood (identity) through a growing awareness of both what he likes and does not like. That is, by testing his own beliefs in the cultural marketplace he comes to understand them better,

[7] Schacht, p. xxiv.

to question some, and become even more dedicated to others. The process of questioning, of entertaining doubt, seems a necessary prelude to an-answering the question "What do I stand for?" (or, "Who am I?").

Alienation is a kind of engine of social change, whether the change is for better or worse. In spite of the human tendency to rationalize illogical decisions reflection *can be* instigated by the feeling that there is something wrong or alien about a situation. This can lead to puzzlement, curiosity, and activity designed to reduce the feeling of uncertainty. One of Karl Marx's mistakes was to condemn all alienation as bad, without realizing that the idea of cognitive dissonance describes not merely a discomforting state, one which *can* lead to disaster, but also one which includes within it a theory of motivation, without which it would be hard to conceive of human culture ever developing in the first place.

We may, then, postulate a state of mind which might properly be called "optimum alienation." We do not know as much as we should about what this level is; it probably varies greatly from one individual to another, and from one time in a person's life to another. Dr. Roy Menninger, presi-dent of the Menninger Foundation (established by his grandfather and father), has been quoted as saying, "A crisis is an event that challenges entrenched ways of thinking of things. A crisis produces a teachable moment—a time when a person is open to new ideas. It is an excellent learning situation."[8]

Levels of Group Alienation

Different groups in American culture show different levels of alienation and their overt behavior is a clear expression of this. As we will see in Chapter 4, in important ways college youth are less alienated now than at the start of the seventies but still alienated from much of traditional ideology and many institutional structures; noncollege youth appear more alienated than college youth from traditional ideology and institutions and from parental values as well. Groups showing the most alienation are minorities: Blacks, Chicanos, American Indians, Vietnam veterans, and the poor. Women, in spite of gains toward equality, remain alienated, particularly noncollege women, from what are becoming accepted values about women's roles.

Apparently Middle Americans of Caucasian descent, particularly adult males, are the least alienated group. This group is marked by ideologi-cal conservatism, generally considered an indication of relatively low alien-ation unless the conservatism is of a radical, quasi-fascist type. As already suggested, even if the alienation within this group seems less than among others, it is clearly there nevertheless. When "hard-hat" construction

---

[8] Patricia McCormack, "Had a Good Crisis Lately?" UPI News Service, May 15, 1973. Ms. McCormack describes an interview with Dr. Menninger.

workers lash out against youth who protest their own alienation militantly, they themselves are demonstrating one kind of Middle-American alienation from the youth culture, from the university education which may intensify the alienation of students, and from all the new and seemingly strange values of an emerging counterculture.

But Middle Americans are alienated from more than that: other sources of alienation include "the sense of being victimized by war, crime, work, insecurity, low wages, sickness, ethnic discrimination, shoddy merchandise, inert institutions, inequality." The symptoms which emerge "are found in voting behavior, work habits, absenteeism on the job, strikes, hard-hat disturbances, backlash, antagonism to students, and feelings of distrust and impotence. . . . Alienation does not touch everyone in this class, but it does seriously afflict a sizable minority."[9]

Whereas good, that is, positive, alienation may be highly constructive for both individuals and cultures, under other circumstances alienation has such negative, even dangerous, consequences that any culture that hopes to remain viable must come to grips with it. It may produce, as we have hinted, intolerable personal feelings that lead to a great variety of deviances, some of which may be very damaging to both individuals and groups. We have here an explanation for perhaps most psychosomatic illnesses, most psychotic states requiring institutionalization, and, in terms of the larger group, cultural disintegration.

If various groups of Americans show marked differences in degree of alienation, then we can expect to find operating such processes as the following:

1. Those most intensely alienated are likely to be attracted to rather extreme and unconventional values: they may gravitate toward the far left or the far right; they may become "cultural dropouts" in the sense of rejecting any serious attempt to work within the framework of the larger culture, in spite of its broad range of values from radical left, liberalism, centrism, conservatism, to radical conservatism, and more or less isolate themselves, sometimes in communes based on a variety of attachments— from B. F. Skinner's Brave New World (as described in his novel *Walden II*) to a kind of primitive Christianity (the Jesus People).

2. Those who are not deeply alienated, such as perhaps a majority of Middle Americans, are likely to be typically conservative and to cling to the old culture values related to the Puritan ethic. We would not expect

[9] Patricia Sexton and Brendan Sexton, *Blue Collars and Hard Hats: The Working Class and the Future of American Policies.* New York: Random House, Inc., 1971. Our analysis of various degrees of alienation was suggested by this book (especially Chapter 12). However, caution is due: most assertions made by the Sextons and others in this field are only partially supported by empirical evidence and contain educated guesses as well as sheer speculation.

much innovative thinking in this group—or even much serious thinking at all, except on close-to-hand bread-and-butter issues.

Dissonance and Rationalization

Most of the means people use to avoid a sense of conflict, as well as to reduce or live with it, come under the broad rubric of rationalization. Even this short section should show the interrelationships of these means.[10]

In beginning his treatment of rationalization, Aronson reviews Festinger's contention that people who become aware of their logical inconsistencies are highly motivated to reduce the conflict as easily as possible and do so by changing one or more of their conflicting cognitions so what was formerly in conflict will fit together. But, only rarely, says Aronson, does an experimental subject try the often comparatively long and hard method of rethinking the whole conflict and eliminating it through application of logic and empirical data (reflective thought). Hence, man is the "rationalizing animal."

People have been known many times in history to go to their death rather than change a belief which had the weight of all known scholarly evidence against it. In experimental situations, people will experience great inconvenience and discomfort, or even sacrifice what seem to be their firmly implanted moral (or other) values in order to maintain a logical contradiction. In simpler terms, *people will fight to remain irrational.* This assertion, which has been verified empirically so many times that we are safe in calling it fact, applies not to a few "crazy people," but to everyone —though to some much more than to others. Aronson says: ". . . one cannot divide the world into rational people on one side and dissonance reducers on the other. While people vary in their ability to tolerate dissonance, we are all capable of rational or irrational behavior, depending on the circumstances. . . ."[11] Further, as was briefly mentioned earlier, decision making which seems rational frequently ends making a person feel dissonant because he or she starts seeing defects in the preferred object or action, and virtues in the rejected object or action.

Rationalizing unwise decisions   Researchers have found that most people make inquiries and seek evidence of some sort before making major decisions. As soon as the decision is made they may immediately begin seeking reassurances from friends that they have done the right thing. If

---

[10] In this section, the writer will both follow and quote from the analysis of Elliot Aronson in "The Rationalizing Animal," *Psychology Today*, May 1973, pp. 46–52. (For fuller treatments of Aronson's views, see his book *The Social Animal.* New York: Viking Press, 1972).

[11] Aronson, p. 48.

serious doubt arises about the wisdom of the decision, they very quickly forget, or distort, the original data on which they based their decision. If the decision turns out badly, many people will increase their defense the more ruinous it seems. People who feel they have made an immoral decision tend to "minimize the negative aspects of the action . . . and change their attitudes about its immorality."

Rationalizing lost opportunities   Putting together the research data, Aronson suggests:

> I would hazard to say that the people who are most angry about "the sexual promiscuity of the young" are *not* those who have never dreamed of being promiscuous. On the contrary, they would be persons who had been seriously tempted by illicit sex, who came very close to giving in to their desires, but who finally resisted. *People who almost live in glass houses are most likely to throw stones.*[12]

In this example given by Aronson, we may presume that the conflict of the person who wanted to have illicit sex but decided not to is linked with a feeling of bitterness over "chances lost," and envy toward those who are taking advantage of their chances. Envy of someone else's action never seems to make the envious one feel kindly toward the envied. Although we cannot present firm data to support the hypothesis, it seems plausible that we can explain much of the moralizing done by the sanctimonious as a product of a "sour grapes" attitude. The love of "sinning" by many people may be exceeded only by their love of castigating those who do.

Obviously, we have here only a few examples of the virtually infinite number of ways in which people rationalize their beliefs. The practice of rationalization seems worldwide, although there may be some comparatively isolated or "backward" cultures in which little of it is done.

Rationalizing a decision to downgrade a goal   Aronson suggests a few conditions in which people tend to rationalize with great frequency. He suggests, for example, that when people strike to reach a goal but can't, they commonly tend to either downgrade the goal as unimportant, or to insist that the effort required would be unreasonable. If they have expended little effort, they tend to downgrade the goal; but if they have already worked hard to reach the goal, they play up the pointlessness of expending all that effort.

Rationalizing a decision to justify absurd behavior   People also rationalize to avoid seeming absurd. Aronson cites a college experiment

[12] Aronson. p. 49; italics added.

in which students were asked to do a task designed to be highly boring—after being told that the work would serve no useful purpose. After doing the work, the students "conned themselves" into thinking it was interesting enough to be intrinsically valuable. In another experiment, students were asked to do a piece of boring work, and only told afterward that it would be of no value. In this situation, students complained about the meaninglessness of the work. In the first experiment, doing the work, after being told that it would be worthless, would have resulted in making the students feel absurd. To reduce the feeling of absurdity, the students found justification for the work anyway on the grounds that it was worth doing for its own sake. In the second experiment, they had no such needs. Aronson suggests the possible generalization that people will go to great lengths to rationalize any belief or related action which makes them appear absurd.

It may be that most people are content to spend most of their lives rationalizing under these various circumstances because in most situations it makes life easier to live. But situations arise where rationalization may no longer seem worth the trouble. As Aronson says, "A person cannot ignore forever a leaky roof, even if that flaw is inconsistent with having spent a fortune on the house."

Rationalization and Deviance

We will report here a line of analysis which should help readers understand better much that occurs in our culture—particularly in the general area of deviant, or "unwanted," ways of thinking and acting. Our source is the work of Thio.[13]

Thio has been interested in trying to explain why people high in the power structure frequently become law violators, often at great cost to millions of individuals in the culture and cultural integrity itself, without feeling they are breaking the law, or, if they are aware of their illegalities, finding it very easy to rationalize them away as acts useful to both themselves and others. He is referring here to people in the power hierarchy of at least upper-middle to upper-class status, who seem unable to see how their own lawlessness harms themselves or others.

In order to achieve this happy state, the powerful have a way of defining deviance so that only the powerless are susceptible to deviant tendencies. But let us turn directly to Thio's analysis.

In the history of sociology there have been at least three major approaches to the interpretation and treatment of deviance. We need not get into the technicalities of these approaches, but to review Thio's analysis they must be mentioned briefly. The first generation of "scientific

[13] Alex Thio, "Class Bias in the Sociology of Deviance," *The American Sociologist,* February 1973.

sociologists," dating from about the first of this century, studied, among other things, people whom they considered deviant. These sociologists viewed culture as an organic whole, whose stability was to be sought and maintained. Any forces tending to disturb the social order were considered pathological and to be blunted or suppressed.

These early "social pathologists" saw as the most menacing kinds of deviancy: juvenile delinquency, prostitution, drug addiction, physiological defectiveness, mental illness, poverty, and any kind of crime that seemed conspicuously and immediately disturbing to social order. Their outlook boiled down to a determination to maintain the established social status quo by suppressing any disquieting behaviors. That this was a highly conservative view, loaded against any kind of social change that might bother the upper classes (with whom these sociologists identified closely), now seems obvious.

Defining Deviance as Value Judgments

By the 1950s, many sociologists began to see that the earlier approach was premised upon value judgments and had no real claim to scientific status. Sociologists now began to talk about the virtues of a "value-free" perspective. Instead of blaming deviant individuals for their problems, they began to place the blame on the social and cultural structure. They saw the cure for deviance as lying in changing the environment of the deviant. In Thio's opinion, however, they defined environment much too narrowly: they were concerned largely with the immediate environment of the bothersome deviant, primarily large urban slums. But although this was perhaps an advance over the earlier value-laden way of defining deviancy, adherents of this position still failed to take into consideration how and why certain acts were defined as deviant and others not. In short, even as late as the 1950s, differentials in power between social classes was not seen as relevant to definitions of undesirable behavior.

The third phase, and the one still in vogue, is more sophisticated in that it recognizes that in spite of the self-proclaimed objectivity of the "value-free" way of labeling deviancy, defining deviancy is still very much a matter of making value judgments. Even so, Thio argues that sociologists all too often continue to label as deviants the same categories of people so labeled by sociologists early in the century: ". . . the prevailing prejudice against the powerless indirectly leads the labeling theorists to concentrate on the types of deviance commonly committed by the powerless and thereby deflects their research efforts from the deviance typically committed by the powerful."[14]

Thus, laws against deviancy focus on those most often apprehended (because they are powerless). If under-class crime, such as armed robbery,

[14] Thio, p. 5.

for example, seems to be increasing, the usual recommendation is to pass more encompassing and severe laws against it. Contrariwise, laws against all categories of white collar crime have remained comparatively mild.

For example, in 1973, the Equity Funding Corporation of America, a financial services institution, contrived a scheme through which, during the 1960s until 1973 (when the corporation collapsed) it managed to swindle the public out of $400,000,000. Although as of this writing the case has not been settled or the culprits brought to trial, this type of

operation rarely leads to fines of more than a few thousand dollars or prison sentences of more than a year or two. But a bank robber, who gets away with $400, is likely to receive a twenty-year penitentiary sentence.

Rationalization of Upper-Class Deviance

The psychological process which makes such labeling seem logical to the powerful Thio describes as follows: on one hand, the powerless is so often labeled deviant that he comes to see himself as at least a potential deviant if not an actual one—the sinful, bad guy of society. This kind of self-image leads the powerless to perform the very acts of deviance of which the powerful accuse them—the kinds of "under-class" crime enumerated above. On the other hand, argues Thio,

the same social, cultural, and political process tends to induce a powerful person to conceive himself as a respectable citizen without any deviant potential, and thereby encourages him to commit acts of deviance (e.g., corporate price-fixing, political bribery and deception, and unconstitutionally waging wars) that he himself is *not* likely to define as deviant. Thus, insofar as one is dealing with the etiological problems of deviation, one may say that the powerless are more sinned against than ready for sinning, while the powerful are more enticed to sin than ready for sinning.[15]

The tendency of the powerful to be unable to see their own "sins" is an example of holding to inconsistent values but being unable to see

article **By RAYMOND L. DIRKS and LEONARD GROSS**

the root causes of wall street's own watergate

EQUITY Funding Corporation of America, a financial-services institution, began operations in 1960 with $10,000. Its "product" was a new way to purchase life insurance. You bought shares in a mutual fund; you borrowed against that equity to pay your life-insurance premiums. In effect, you used your money twice—and if the stock market went up in the interval, you made money on the deal.

By 1973, Equity Funding listed assets of nearly $750,000,000. It managed mutual funds and a savings and loan association worth another $320,000,000. Its record of growth in the *(continued on page 146)*

HOW THE NEW YORK STOCK EXCHANGE, THE LIFE INSURANCE INDUSTRY, THE SEC AND A HOST OF OTHER GUARDIANS OF THE PUBLIC WEAL ALLOWED THE AMERICAN PUBLIC TO BE SWINDLED OUT OF $400,000,000

A purse snatching is regarded as *serious* deviance because of its often conspicuous consequences; a $400 million white collar swindle is *minor* deviance because it gets only a headline.

them as such. The powerful are opposed to what they see as crime, but they hold a double standard they do not recognize. They have succeeded in the mental gymnastics of rationalizing away their simultaneous commitment to lawfulness and law-breaking. They are as anomic as the underclass criminal, but it is a very genteel type of anomie.

Constructive Confrontation of Dissonance

We have seen that when cognitive dissonance leads to discomfort most persons cannot easily tolerate it. They tend usually to try to keep

[15] Thio, p. 2.

their inconsistencies, but rationalize them away, as in the major example given above: the individual at a high level in the power structure who breaks the law but manages to persuade himself that the law was foolish or mistaken in the first place, or that the public well-being was best served by his breaking it. The rationalizing approach to dissonance leads only to the individual becoming more alienated against himself, more fragmented, and is not a helpful solution to cognitive dissonance.

What, then, should our approach to cognitive dissonance be? In our opinion, and in that of most writers on the subject, what is called for when a person senses his inconsistencies is honest confrontation of them.

As we have indicated, some people have little difficulty sensing their own inconsistencies through self-analysis. People who can do this may, as we have suggested, try to rationalize away the inconsistency or they may try to face the inconsistency squarely and think it through to a solution. But on the basis of all the evidence we have the great majority of people are neither capable of seeing their own inconsistencies, except when choice-making forces them to recognize their opposed beliefs; nor are they able, even when they recognize their dissonances, to do anything more constructive than engage in rationalization. In any case, it appears that most people do not manage internal inconsistency very well.

Therapy as an Aid to Dissonance Reduction

Psychotherapy usually has the purpose of helping people to: (1) verbalize inconsistencies which are anxiety producing but which the subject has not been able to put into words, and (2) think through the inconsistency with reference to both empirical evidence and logic in an effort to resolve it rationally. This approach leads to *reflective confrontation* of the conflict, the only approach we know which enables a person to get out of trouble rather than more deeply into it. Rationalization seldom pays off in the long run; the farther it is pursued, the more a person gets into a psychological bind.

Whether therapists recognize it, those who try to help their patients by unveiling their inconsistencies and thinking through them reflectively are in the intellectual tradition of Peirce, James, and Dewey. The foremost American psychotherapist in this tradition probably was the late Harry Stack Sullivan, whose influence has been widely felt among humanistically inclined psychotherapists.

Readers should understand, however, that there is an opposing school of thought among therapists which stems from the behaviorist tradition. These therapists employ Skinnerian reinforcement theory, which theoretically leads to behavior modification by rewarding wanted responses. This approach is not designed to cultivate thoughtful self-analysis, however, but only to change overt behavior.

Teaching and Dissonance Reduction

School teachers, without trying to become therapists as therapy is usually conceived (a treatment reserved for people in more psychological trouble than most school pupils), may also strive in their teaching to help students recognize their inconsistencies and explore hypotheses which, when tested with factual data and logical principles, will bring about a reduction or elimination of personal inconsistency. Such teachers are at the same time, of course, assisting in building a culture better able to cope with conflict than our present culture.

At this point, we are getting into one of the major themes of this book: how to educate students to function in a humanistic, self-governing democracy. Since this is a topic we return to repeatedly, we will say no more about it here.

ALIENATING CONFLICTS IN AMERICAN CULTURE

In this section, we plan to present readers with common specimens of logical conflicts in American culture—some of long standing, some recent. We have been suggesting examples of such conflicts beginning with the Prologue. But so far we have not tried to draw together a specific list of the kinds of logical contradictions that, *if they are sensed as such,* produce intrapersonal conflict, cognitive dissonance, or free-floating anxiety, which are unrelated to a particular conflict but rather a function of many conflicts that cannot be specifically identified.

Such conflicts, when recognized by the individual holding them, become alienating or anomie-producing. If we were to use such an expression as mental illness, then, given the themes of this book, the following contradictions would be—when recognized—the primary causes of mental illness for many people. But other people would see the "mess" and would attempt to cope somehow in order to save their own self-identities. They might do this through some one or more of the psychological processes mentioned earlier in the chapter, particularly rationalization.

Ideally, people taking up the cultural challenge would confront such conflicts squarely and try to revise their own beliefs and the culture to reduce conflict. But it appears likely that the most common approach of Americans, especially the group we have defined as Middle Americans, is to rely heavily on rationalization and, in so doing, make even the most absurd logical conflicts disappear from psychological view.

However, whether a majority of Americans avoid enough cognitive dissonance through the use of rationalization to achieve a satisfactory level of contentment, the logical contradictions of the culture remain. Even the most complacent individual is always under the risk of being forced into confronting his own concealed inconsistencies, with resulting confusion, frustration, alienation, and anomie. We may even plausibly hypothesize that sooner or later inconsistent, although seemingly contented, people, living in a paradoxical culture, run more risk of becoming seriously anomic than people who sense personal inconsistencies, see their link to conflicts of the culture, and confront the issues reflectively.

Some Perennial Value Conflicts in America

Some historical background seems essential at this point as a foundation for treatment of some of the most troublesome value conflicts of the sixties and seventies. We can trace from the Colonial Period certain contradictions which are as much with us today as ever. Most of these contradictions can be placed under the following heading in the form of contradictory couplets.

Individual Freedom versus Equality and Group Solidarity

If everyone is free to do as one pleases (a state of anarchy), then through being born of the right parents or getting lucky breaks, certain people will acquire large quantities of both power and wealth. The fortunate ones, the winners, all too often gain power and wealth by riding roughshod over others who are less lucky. We can identify, then, a logical conflict which for many becomes a psychological conflict that is personally bothersome (i.e., cognitive dissonance).

Everyone should be free to do as he pleases, short of committing serious crime, BUT

Everyone should be guaranteed equality of opportunity whatever this may require.

This particularly contradictory couplet can be restated to give it an economic twist. It is perhaps within this economic context that the greatest number of people have been bothered by it. According to our Puritan "get ahead" ethic, people are free and encouraged to accumulate as much wealth as possible. But our human and material resources, although capable of expansion up to some unreached finite limit, cannot under our system of capitalism prevent there being a great many losers for every winner. We can state the dichotomy as follows:

Everyone should be free to acquire as much wealth as he is capable of, BUT

Everyone should have a basic minimum to permit decent living.

The issue of freedom takes still another twist. Individualism has always been pitted against another value—the cherishing of order, or as we now often see it, conformity. Pressure to conform has always been with us; contrary to David Riesman's suggestion that "inner direction" characterized the nineteenth century person and "other direction" the middle-to-late twentieth century person, the demand for conformity was probably greater in colonial New England than any time since. The pressure to conform was so great, in fact, that nonconformists were called witches and executed, as at Salem in 1692. So we can state another dichotomy:

Everyone should be free to do as he pleases, short of committing a serious crime, BUT

Anyone who does not follow rigidly the mores of the group should be punished.[16]

Lynd's Specimen Conflicts

Robert S. Lynd compiled a list of *value conflicts* derived in part from his Middletown studies, which, although having deep historical roots, seem more applicable to the twentieth than to earlier centuries. We will paraphrase these loosely below.[17]

1. Individualism (including the ideas of "survival of the fittest") is the American way, BUT

People should work cooperatively to achieve common purposes.

2. Because man is a rational creature, he is capable of guiding his own behavior wisely, BUT

Every practical politician or businessman knows that people need help to make up their own minds.

3. Democracy, in which issues are decided by popular vote, is the best possible social system, BUT

No business could survive if decision making were left up to the vote of its employees [nor could any other bureaucracy, ranging from the army to a school system].

4. The goal of everyone should be to get ahead—to be successful, BUT

The kind of person you are, your character, is much more important than money or social status.

---

[16] For a concise but meaty and heavily documented treatment of the existence of the above-mentioned conflicts in American life, see Robert E. Cleary, *Political Education in the American Democracy,* Scranton, Pa.: Intext Educational Publishers, 1971, pp. 14–18.

[17] Robert S. Lynd, *Knowledge for What? The Place of Social Science in American Culture,* Princeton, N.J.: Princeton University Press, 1940, pp. 60–62.

5. The family is the most fundamental of our institutional structures, BUT

Our national welfare depends on business, and all other institutions should conform to its demands.

6. Spiritual and esthetic values are the most important goals in life, BUT

Everyone owes it to himself, and his family, to concentrate on getting ahead financially.

7. We should welcome new ideas; that is what progress is all about, BUT

Tried and true ideas are best; we must depend on the old virtues to see us through today's problems.

8. Hard work, a sense of duty, and thrift are the only values by which one gets ahead in our free enterprise system, BUT

If you want to make money, your best chance is to know the right people.

9. It always pays to be honest, BUT

A businessman would inevitably go bankrupt if he told the truth about everything.

10. America is a country of unlimited opportunity, and people can be as successful as they want to be, BUT

You can't have a general without privates (i.e., not everyone can be a boss).

11. Whether people recognize it, business and labor are really partners, BUT

A businessman would be crazy to pay higher wages than he has to.

12. Everyone should get as much education as possible, BUT

People can be overeducated, for example, most university professors are too impractical to run a business.

13. Science and technology are among man's greatest achievements and we couldn't do without them, BUT

Scientists have no business tampering with the more sacred of our institutions, such as religion, family life, patriotism, sexual mores, and the like.

14. Children are a blessing, and in addition a high birthrate keeps the economy growing, BUT

No couple should have more children than they can afford; excess children only add to the welfare rolls.

15. Women are morally superior to men, more kind and gentle—the "finest of God's creatures," BUT

Everyone knows that women are overly emotional, can't work together, can't make practical decisions, and are generally inferior to men.

16. One of man's highest callings is public service, BUT

Public service doesn't pay very well, and if a person is smart, he will head where the money is.

17. America has the finest system of justice in the world, for both rich and poor, BUT

Anyone in trouble would be out of his mind not to hire the best lawyer he can afford.

18. Poverty can and should be abolished; it is shameful for a nation as rich as ours to have millions of poor people, BUT

There will never be enough for everybody and without losers there would be no winners.

19. It demoralizes people to give them handouts which they have not earned, BUT

A Christian nation can't let the unlucky and the handicapped starve.

Lynd does not suggest that such specimen contradictions as the above are immutable. Our cultural contradictions tend to change form with the passage of time, and we can't predict what our major inconsistencies will be a decade ahead. Lynd is basically right about that fluidity of our cultural disharmonies, but, as suggested by Cleary, it seems likely that we can trace a few uniquely American contradictions which we have had with us since the beginning and which will be around for a long time to come.

Some Additional Contemporary Conflicts

The following lists of contradictory couplets were compiled by the present writer. To prove their existence in the same sense that we can prove that a certain mixture of gasoline and oxygen will explode when ignited is, of course, difficult if not impossible. Basically, the following listing was compiled from the writer's experience in listening to people talk, reading what they write, and making inferences from what they do. Many of the couplets form the theme of well-researched books read by the writer. Probably students of the writer, over a thirty-year period, have, through what they have communicated, furnished more evidence than any other source on which to base a list as this. And quite a few of the couplets are but statements of dissonances with which the writer himself has had to struggle.

None of the following couplets involves a contradiction for readers who do not see the two items as mutually incompatible. As stated here, and with no additional qualification, the items of the couplets are logically contradictory; they are psychologically contradictory *only to those who see them as such*.

We have attempted a rough two-way classification of the following couplets. The first group is intended to represent conflicts which are not only deep-seated in our culture, but cover a lot of psychological territory, and involve issues in social philosophy. The second group is intended to be less deeply rooted, narrower in scope, more transitory, and less philosophical. This kind of classification is in large part based on subjective judgment and probably many readers would shift certain items from one group to the other.

Contradictions in Social Philosophy

1. There are absolute Truths which human beings need to learn and guide their behavior by, BUT

As a practical matter, we can't live by absolutes much of the time; this is an age in which most people view ideas relativistically.

2. Old-fashioned values are often best; they are time-tested and help keep the culture stable, BUT

One thing we can be sure of is that the culture will keep changing, probably at an increasingly faster rate.

3. In bringing about the change we want, we should remember that if our ends are good, then we should use any means that work in achieving them (or, "the end justifies the means"), BUT

We can't reach our goals if our chosen means push us in the wrong direction (or, ends are subsumed within the means, or ends and means are organically related).

4. An advanced industrial culture necessarily has to mechanize and quantify its major processes, BUT

Mechanized, computerized, automated work and social institutions are dehumanizing, and lead only to alienation and anomie.

5. Trying to plan the development of a social system in relation to long-range goals can lead to loss of individualism and freedom, BUT

Institutions are too large and business too monopolized for laissez-faire to work any more; even the most conservative business managers try to plan the future of their corporations at least ten years ahead.

6. Upper-middle-class "egghead types" are overeducated, impractical, and tend to criticize and boat-rock, BUT

Any culture which has produced major innovators in the arts and sciences has been one in which intellect, including critical thinking and dreaming up unconventional ideas, has been prized.

7. Although democracy is a nice ideal to talk about, the major institutions of an industrialized nation could never really be run democratically, BUT

Democracy is the only social system we know of that does not accept the rule of tyrannical dictators and loss of personal freedom.

8. Americans have always been a spiritual, God-believing people and the American system is built on religious belief, BUT

In a world where science and technology prevail, and our basic orientation is materialistic, people don't think seriously about God anymore.

9. Every enlightened person knows that the environment determines what we think and do and that individuals are not really responsible for their behavior, BUT

We know from personal experience that to at least some degree we are free to make our own choices and therefore cannot escape all responsibility for our decisions.

10. No democracy or any other system of human relations can exist indefinitely unless almost everyone is committed to a basic sense of honesty, BUT

American society would collapse if we told other people what we really thought; not only does a system of free, competitive enterprise rest on sharp business practice, but even common courtesy requires that we not tell the truth.

Some Currently Concrete and Visible Conflicts

The following contradictory pairs of belief-statements appear to the writer as likely to include most of the major "fighting issues" of the seventies and perhaps the eighties. Their arrangement is not meant to signify order of importance, although those placed early in the list are clearly developing as of this writing (late spring 1974).

1. The President is the elected leader of all the people, and as such he should be granted all the power he needs to carry out the general will, BUT

Since the 1930s each President has seemed to demand and get more power in relation to the Congress and the Courts, and we run a grave risk of the Presidency turning into a dictatorship.

2. Our system has not worked well since it ceased to be dominated by the Puritan ethic, BUT

Other democratic countries make a welfare state work, and in this age of interdependence trying to follow Puritan values puts too much strain on people.

3. The "straight" values favored by Middle Americans are what made the United States great, BUT

The old-fashioned straight values have given us war, hypocrisy, poverty, and inability to cope with change; the ideas of the youthful counterculture are more suited for life today.

4. It is more important to grow industrially and make use of the natural resources God gave to man than to try to keep the water, air, and soil super-clean, BUT

Continued destruction of the natural environment can only lead to major ecological catastrophe and even threaten the survival of the human race.

5. Military training is the best kind of training for help in coping with life's problems; former military officers make the best business and political leaders, BUT

Military training makes most people authoritarian in outlook and unsuited to preserve democratic values.

6. The brave men who fought in Vietnam know more about real Americanism than anybody else, BUT

Too large a proportion of Vietnam veterans were brainwashed to the point where they can no longer think critically and reflectively.

7. The United States must remain the Number One nation in the world, both for our good and that of all other nations, BUT

Trying to be Number One has drained our human and natural resources to the point of making it much more difficult, if not impossible, to solve our most serious problems.

8. The United States should dominate the world economically because in the long run everyone in the world will benefit, BUT

American economic expansionism, through multinational giant corporations, has made most formerly friendly nations hostile and uncooperative and is likely to lead to more international monetary and economic crises.

9. All the men who escaped the draft during the Vietnam war by pretending to be conscientious objectors should serve long prison terms at hard labor—or be executed for treason, BUT

If this nation were the Christian nation it claims to be, it would be compassionate and grant war objectors the right to follow their consciences.

10. The best way to reduce crime, particularly the use of illegal drugs, is to imprison for life or execute anyone caught selling or using any illegal drug, BUT

The human race has always used drugs for pleasure and most people who shout against smoking pot or using cactus juice themselves use alcohol, nicotine, prescription narcotics, and innumerable other drugs.

11. The best way for America to save itself is to turn to the fundamentalist religions and find salvation through Christ, BUT

Most religious fundamentalists are authoritarian in makeup and have no use for democratic values.

12. In a free enterprise system business firms should be given free rein to advertise as they wish; if they fudge a little on the truth, then caveat emptor, BUT

Much advertising promotes the use of dangerous or useless products and results in waste of the buyers' money and general distrust of the honesty of all businessmen.

13. If we can't trust the President of the United States and those who man the Office of the Presidency (the Cabinet and other executive agencies), then we can't trust anyone, BUT

Presidents and their appointees are human, and have unusually good opportunities to practice corruption for political or personal financial reasons.

14. Any means is justified to protect what the President defines as national security, BUT

Using paramilitary measures to win an election subverts the national security more than anything else.

Theodore Brameld in a recent book also presents a list of cultural contradictions, most of which we have paraphrased in one of the above groups. He makes a particular issue of which views are absolutistic and which experimental (relativistic). He concludes that "On the whole and granting exceptions, we may say that self-interest, inequality, planlessness, and nationalism tend in our culture to be absolutist in spirit and action; whereas social interests, equality, planning, and internationalism tend in our culture to be experimentalist in spirit and action."[18]

CULTURAL CONFLICT AND EDUCATION

Since the first chapters have each been building toward an explicit and reasonably detailed treatment of our culture's logical conflicts in numerous areas of interest, of their accompanying psychological (or intrapersonal) conflicts, and of the integrally related matters of alienation, anomie, and identity crisis, obviously there are enormous implications for how we organize and operate our schools. However, since most of the content of Part III of this book is devoted to making clear and pointing out the implications for education of a culture in conflict, we will touch on only some of the most immediate implications here.

Alienated and Anomic School Personnel

Apparently not much research has been done with respect to the extent and kind of alienation, or the extent of manageable anomie, which can be found among teachers, guidance and counseling personnel, various types of educational consultants, principals, superintendents, or school boards. Nor have we been able to find research concerning identity problems

[18] Theodore Brameld, *Patterns of Educational Philosophy: Divergence and Convergence in Culturological Perspective.* New York: Holt, Rinehart and Winston, Inc., 1971, p. 29.

among such school personnel. Reverting to a term which we do not particularly like to use—mental health—we do find a brief treatment of this topic in Myron Lieberman's *Education as a Profession.*[19] Lieberman points out that good mental health for teachers has been equated with "adjustment" in the sense of conformity, passivity, obedience, and the like. Teachers who exhibited adjustment in this sense have usually been highly rated by school boards, school administrators, parents, and other concerned people. Lieberman rejects the emphasis upon adjustment as an adequate criterion for judging the effectiveness of teachers. He says "The 'well adjusted' teacher is . . . all too often the teacher who is satisfied, who is not critical, who does not make trouble for supervisors or administrators. The dissatisfied teacher is supposed to be 'poorly adjusted.' " In discussing the inadequacy of equating adjustment with good mental health, Lieberman dips briefly into the literature of psychiatry and, in addition, points out how certain passages in Dewey's *Democracy and Education* have been misinterpreted to uphold the virtues of adjustment.

In an attempt to get at the extent of mental illness among teachers, Lieberman is forced to draw from some old and highly controversial studies, which we need not describe here. He hypothesizes that "Teaching appears to be more likely than most occupations to subject the individual to conflicting pressures that undermine personality integration." Aside from this comment, Lieberman's general conclusion seems to be that "The incidence of mental illness among teachers is not definitely known, but probably it is about the same as for the population as a whole." Nothing upon which Lieberman had to draw at the time he wrote this book would have been likely to employ, in connection with teachers, the concepts of identity, alienation, or anomie.

In a more recent book, Thomas A. Ringness devotes a chapter to "The Teacher as a Person."[20] Although Ringness refers briefly to some of the older sources on the study of teacher personality (including a few of those mentioned by Lieberman), he bases his conclusions mainly on studies made in the 1950s and 1960s. The present writer considers these studies spotty in quality and value, particularly because they continue to focus on ideas of "good personality" or "good mental health"—concepts which, as of the seventies, seem rather obsolete. In particular, most of them define the personal characteristics of teachers in highly evaluative language—classic examples of those who have power over teachers asserting value judgments concerning what teachers should be like.

[19] Myron Lieberman, *Education as a Profession.* Englewood Cliffs, N.J.: Prentice-Hall, Inc., 1956, pp. 234–238.
[20] Thomas A. Ringness, *Mental Health in the Schools.* New York: Random House, Inc., 1968.

In what Ringness calls a "classic study" by David Ryans,[21] it was found that three patterns of teachers could be identified, as follows:

Pattern X—friendly, understanding, versus aloof, egocentric, restricted
Pattern Y—responsible, businesslike, systematic versus evading, unplanned, slipshod
Pattern Z—stimulating, imaginative, surgent versus dull, routine[22]

After accumulating many kinds of data, both elementary and secondary teachers who rated high on these three patterns were compared to teachers who rated low, and a number of personal characteristics of those who rated high were listed. The characteristics sound very good, but none attack directly or imply very much indirectly about teachers' understanding of the culture and its conflicts, or their own degree and type of alienation, or the characteristics of their self-concepts (Ringness does devote a chapter later in the book to the importance of self-concepts among students). What Ringness does conclude from Ryan's study is that "...the higher-rated teachers tend to be well-rounded, personally and socially adjusted, and genuinely interested in pupils."[23] Ringness also suggests that the positive characteristics evinced in Types X, Y, and Z might be used as a basis for recruiting teachers because these characteristics are "relatively stable."

Ringness cites another study intended to show relationships between personality traits and teaching.[24] In this study, the investigator classified prospective teachers according to whether their motives for wanting to teach were liking for children, liking for the subject matter, or such practical considerations as job security and working conditions. In relation to a list of what Ringness calls "desirable personality traits" it was found that those who plan to teach because of fondness for children and youth or love of subject matter have more of the desirable traits; and, conversely, those who plan to enter teaching for "practical" reasons are not only low in these traits, but "might even seem to have poorer mental health." Our intent is not to criticize this study in any major way, particularly since Mitchell included in his listing of desirable traits "imagination and unconventionality" and "adventurousness and social boldness"—both traits which readers will see harmonize with what the present writer conceives as "culturally demanded" traits of teachers. How-

[21] Reported in Ryans' book, *Characteristics of Teachers,* Washington, D.C.: American Council on Education, 1960.

[22] Ringness, p. 35.

[23] Ringness, p. 36.

[24] See J. V. Mitchell, Jr., "Personality Characteristics Associated with Motives for Entering Teaching," *Phi Delta Kappan,* Vol. 46, June 1965, p. 531.

ever, this study is also highly judgmental, with the researcher proposing the criteria by which to judge the "good guys" and the "bad guys." As people who do research about teachers are usually higher in the education power hierarchy than teachers, this might be considered as another case of the powerful defining the deviances allowed to the relatively powerless.

Ringness proposes his own set of criteria for judging what is "good mental health." Although he states them in some detail, generally they fall under the broad headings of ability to understand others, ability to communicate, ability to serve as models of good traits for students to follow, and ability to express oneself. Further, drawing upon a study by R. A. Matthews and L. W. Rowland, Ringness lists "Some Signals of Problems" (i.e., mental health problems). Several of these "signals" describe behavior that most people probably regard as bizarre, such as talking to oneself or hearing voices (nonexistent voices, we presume); but most items on the list, such as "strange losses of memory," "having peculiar tastes," "complaining of bodily ailments that are not possible," "showing big changes in behavior," and "thinking people are talking about him" would have applied to many notable intellectuals who have been creative thinkers and teachers.[25]

Such a list appears to this writer a further example of "the battle of value judgments" concerning what good mental health is. Even worse, it seems to be a complete failure to see any relevant statements a person makes about a teacher's fitness or unfitness as stemming from the quality of the culture or the interaction of individuals and their perceived cultural milieu.

We will complete this chapter with a report of studies directed by O. J. Harvey, of the University of Colorado, which seem to us to get much nearer the heart of the primary problem (the problem being, in our view, how to revise schools and teaching to promote liberal, democratic values in a fascist-tending society). One factor in the problem is how to recognize democratic-promoting and authoritarian-promoting perceptual systems (or personality structures) and to see how they function in relation to cultural issues. This factor has been one of Harvey's chief interests.

O. J. Harvey and His Four Personality Systems

O. J. Harvey and a group of associates, working under a grant by the Group Psychology Branch, Office of Naval Research, to the University of

[25] R. A. Matthews and L. W. Rowland, *How To Recognize and Handle Abnormal People,* rev. ed. New York: National Association for Mental Health, 1964. Cited by Ringness on p. 43.

Colorado, have done what this writer believes to be highly significant research in the area of comparative perceptual systems. The concept of a perceptual system may be roughly equated with the idea of personality structure, provided we view personality as a product of interaction between an individual and his perceived environment (or, to use the terminology of Kurt Lewin, as adapted in Bigge and Hunt[26]) the more stable recurring elements of one's life space. To refer to a person in terms of a perceptual system enables one to bypass the fragmentation of self implied in such categorization as cognitive domain, affective domain, and motor domain. *Perceptual system is a field concept* as used in neo-Gestalt or cognitive field psychologies (*in contrast to the atomistic view* of human beings implicit in the thinking of most behaviorists).

In seeking a conceptual schema for organizing data acquired about perceptual systems, Harvey and his associates decided that one of the most important keys to the analysis of such systems was the capacity of the system (person) to think abstractly. Harvey *et al.* envisioned a continuum, at one extreme of which is the person whose thinking tends to be highly *concrete,* and at the other extreme of which is the person whose thinking tends to be highly *abstract.* Along the continuum intermediate types can be identified and regarded as nodal points on the continuum, but there are also many persons strung along the continuum between the nodal points. The number of nodal points into which the continuum can be broken is arbitrary, but Harvey found that the most workable classification involves four systems. We will provide a brief and admittedly oversimplified description of each of the four systems, as described by Harvey.[27]

System 1 Functioning

Representatives of System 1 are highly absolutistic and tend toward closed-mindedness. They tend to be highly evaluative (i.e., moralistic in judging others with a tendency to think in black and white terms). They are high in positive dependence on institutional authority. They identify strongly with particular social roles and status positions. They tend to be strongly conventional (conservative, as we have defined this concept). They are highly ethnocentric in the sense of feeling that American values should be forced on the rest of the world. The overall syndrome characterizing System 1 persons is authoritarianism.

---

[26] Morris L. Bigge and Maurice P. Hunt, *Psychological Foundations of of Education,* 2d ed. New York: Harper & Row, Publishers, 1968, p. 399ff.

[27] O. J. Harvey (ed.), *Experience, Structure and Adaptability.* New York: Springer Publishing Company, Inc., 1966, p. 44ff.

System 2 Functioning

Persons identified with System 2 tend to be uncertain, insecure, and distrustful of authority. They tend to reject most of the generally approved social norms and other stable referents. Such persons Harvey describes as in a "psychological vacuum, guided more by rebellion against social prescriptions than by positive adherence to personally derived standards." Although System 2 persons seek autonomy and reject authority, their psychological functioning is closer to that of System 1 subjects than it would appear from their more overt characteristics. To the extent that they take a positive position, they tend toward authoritarianism, but markedly less so than System 1 persons.

System 3 Functioning

The most striking characteristic of System 3 persons is their tendency to achieve goals through the manipulation of others. Although these persons tend to find security through identification with a group, they are capable of more genuine independence than either System 1 or 2 persons. At the same time, System 3 persons find it much easier to accept common social norms than do System 2s. System 3 persons, in spite of their manipulatory tendencies, tend to socialize well. We may compare them with David Riesman's "other-directed" personality types, or William H. Whyte's "organization men." Although they tend to go along with the crowd, they are less conservative, less hidebound, less authoritarian than System 1s and 2s.

System 4 Functioning

System 4 persons can be rather quickly described: in virtually all measurable characteristics, they are the opposites of System 1 persons. They tend to be relativistic and open-minded. They are not given to moralizing about others, although this should not be construed to mean that they admire those who function at lower system levels. They are little concerned with social position. They tend to be liberal and democratic in their values. They tend to be group-minded in a broad sense (or "world minded"), rather than ethnocentric.

Other Considerations

We have condensed the above system descriptions to what seem to be the irreducible characteristics of the four systems, as measured by a variety of tests. However, there is more to be said. One of the chief interests of Harvey and his associates was to learn how to identify persons who were sufficiently resilient and flexible that they could function well under stress. The farther one proceeds along the continuum from System 1 toward System 4, the better the subjects can cope with stress. The reason appears quite clear: each higher system is more flexible than those below. System 1 persons are basically rule or routine oriented: they are lost without directions. As we move along the continuum this dependence becomes increasingly less.

We cannot ignore certain correlations because they provide strong empirical support for Harvey's contention that there is a genuine difference between persons who differ with respect to their capacity for abstract thought. System 4 persons score higher on tests of verbal intelligence and vocabulary, with System 2s a close second. On a test of "cognitive complexity," System 4s scored highest, with lower systems scoring in descending order. Systems 2 and 4 tend to be irreligious (except in a philosophical sense), while System 1s and 3s tend to be active church members. System 1s scored highest on the F-Scale (a measure of authoritarian personality), with System 3s, 2s, and 4s following in that order. On a test of dogmatism, System 1s tested highest, followed by the other three systems in descending order. In ability to role-play (a measure of imagination and creativity), System 4s were best, followed in descending order by the others.

Numerous other empirical tests were used—too many to discuss here—but they all tended to confirm the existence of the general syndrome of each system, as described above.

The Four Systems and Alienation, Anomie, Identity

In Harvey's book, from which the above data were drawn, there is no discussion per se of the four personality systems in relation to alienation, anomie, and self-concept. The implications, however, seem clear enough. System 2s almost make an occupation of alienation. System 4s tend to be alienated in a more selective and intelligent fashion because of their tendency toward critical thinking. Most System 4s would fit under our previously described concept of "optimum alienation." System 1s lapse quickly into alienation if the rules they depend on fail them and System 3s do the same if they become estranged from the group with which they identify. With respect to alienation from establishment culture, particularly its most inconsistent elements, we would expect Systems 4s, because of greater sensitivity and critical thought, to feel more alienation than the rest; we would also expect them to be capable of nonrationalizing, reflective ways of reducing alienation.

The data collected by Harvey et al. clearly suggest that System 4 functioning should be more resistant to cognitive dissonance than the other systems. In an important sense, this was what the research team set out to discover in the first place: who could hold up best under stress.

Harvey reports another study, the purpose of which was to see if system level functioning could be demonstrated to support the hypothesis that System 1 persons would show a greater tendency to "go to pieces" by "failure to ward off incongruous events." We cannot report this study in detail, except to say that subjects at each of the four main levels of abstractness (the four nodal points on the continuum) were confronted with inconsistencies which they saw as such. The most abstract System 4 persons were able to absorb more dissonant input than were System 1 persons. The most concrete System 1 persons (contrary to what one might expect at first thought) changed their opinions more readily than System 4s, particularly when dissonant input occurred in a public situation. (Readers may well think of such examples as soldiers who disapprove of murder but obey orders to shoot children.)

These findings do not disrupt Harvey's other research findings that System 1s are more closed-minded and rigid generally, just as System 4s are more open-minded and flexible generally. Although in the particular study cited here, the conclusions Harvey suggests are limited to the fact of change only under the experimental conditions as described, we might infer that System 1s changed opinion because of inability to see how to absorb contrary data through any of the coping processes described earlier in the chapter, such as rationalization (or reflective confrontation). The experiment had a follow-up period of one week and to ascertain longer-lasting effects would require much more experimentation.[28] System 4s, with their greater imagination and ability to role-play, should see many more possibilities for coping with dissonant input without major opinion revision.

With respect to self-identity, we would expect System 4s, closely followed by System 3s, to rank high for various reasons, including the apparent ability of systems high in abstractness to assimilate and manage sensed conflict better. System 1s, bcause of their attachment to the authoritarian syndrome, would tend to shift from one position to another according to the demands of authority figures above them. Persons at the concrete end of the scale find it difficult to think out for themselves "who they are"—they have to be told. System 2s are too unstable, too vacillating, to achieve a strong sense of I AM I.

Personality Systems of School Personnel

In 1971, O. J. Harvey prepared a paper summarizing research he and his group had done on the personality systems of college students,

---

[28] O. J. Harvey, "Some Situational and Cognitive Determinants of Dissonance Resolution," *Journal of Personality and Social Psychology*, April 1965, pp. 349–355.

teachers with varying amounts of experience, and school administrators.[29] Much of his data on students was from two studies done at the University of Southern California, Los Angeles, and another at the University of Texas. Findings of these studies are particularly germane to maintaining a democratic society.

System 1 teachers were found to overgeneralize, to draw sweeping conclusions from scanty evidence. They *resisted* the input of empirical data that would give them a stronger basis for generalization. They tended to stereotype their students and to expound highly conservative and ethnocentric opinions in the classroom. And as expected, they were highly rule and routine oriented, afraid of experimentation, and tended to suppress signs of unorthodoxy or creativity in students. Readers can infer other qualities we would expect in the literal-minded, unimaginative functioning associated with low capacity for abstract thought.

Harvey and associates have found virtually no System 2 types in teaching. They can be found among university students working for teaching credentials, but seem unable to get or hold teaching positions. In view of the emphasis of boards and administrators on teachers being able to socialize well and conform generally to Middle American values, it is easy to understand why the rebellious loner is a rarity in the teaching profession.

System 3 persons typically succeed and are happy as teachers. Our public schools to some degree reflect System 3 functioning. In his 1971 NCSS address. Harvey mentioned a teacher telling him, "We are trying to create a System 3 curriculum in our system because it's the fashion." Harvey went on to say "It is almost—and I don't mean to do a caricature here—as if we hold hands and dance around the flagpole and the world will be well. Certainly, there is a great emphasis here on love and affection, a great tendency toward avoiding anger." But, he went on to say, the typical method of control used by System 3 teachers, withdrawing affection, can be quite devastating for many children, more so, perhaps, than the tendency of System 1 teachers to use authoritarian means of control, including force. However, System 3 functioning probably does not represent the most common pattern, as evidence on the following pages will show.

System 4 persons, when they go into teaching, are the stimulating, exciting, creative teachers that students tend to remember the rest of their lives. System 4 teachers, alone among the four types, seem able to become highly involved with students without losing a capacity for

---

[29] O. J. Harvey, "Teacher Attitudes and Values: Effect on Students." Paper read at the annual meeting of the National Council for the Social Studies, Denver, Colorado, November 26, 1971.

approaching problems reflectively. They are the only ones who can cope easily enough with stress to operate at peak performance in situations of high involvement. But System 4 teachers are both innovative and independent and tend to be regarded as "boat rockers." School boards and administrators find them bothersome.

Proportions of System Types

Harvey reported that among the samples of college and university students studied, majors in the arts and sciences who were not planning to teach divided approximately as follows:

System 1—35 percent
System 2—15–17 percent
System 3—20–21 percent
System 4—7 percent
Unclassifiable admixtures—about 20–25 percent

Education majors break down into approximately the same kind of distribution, except that the proportion of System 1s (about 40 percent) seems to run consistently higher.

Of three thousand teachers having about five years' experience studied by the Harvey group, the distribution was as follows:

System 1—50–55 percent
System 2—less than 1 percent
System 3—20–25 percent
System 4—5 percent

The Harvey researches show that, beginning with college students, the highest proportion of System 4 persons are sophomores. *From the sophomore year, the farther a person goes in school—or, as a teacher, the longer a person has taught—the smaller the proportion of System 4s and the larger the proportion of System 1s.*

In two more studies, one in northern Colorado and one in New Mexico, principals, superintendents, and hiring officers (who, except in large school systems, are principals and superintendents) were classified on the concrete-abstract scale. The results were as follows:

System 1—90 percent or over
System 2—none
Systems 3, 4, and admixtures—10 percent or less

These same studies also sought to find what kind of teachers hiring officers try to find. They seek, and whenever possible hire, teachers with System 1 characteristics. With great consistency, they rejected applicants who have made high grades in college. In the arts and sciences, but particularly in the liberal arts or humanities, Harvey's researchers find among A-average students the highest proportion of System 4s. Harvey concludes that ". . . *hiring officers, most of whom belong in System 1, in their hiring practices, serve as a kind of filter through which the world is passed and that they exercise a tremendous influence in the overall atmosphere."* (Emphasis ours.)

CONCLUSION

We will leave it to readers to draw what conclusions they wish. We have tried to establish in this chapter certain points, the most crucial of which can be supported with a considerable mass of empirical evidence We have tried to build the chapter around the theme of the alienation of individuals and groups from a culture in an advanced state of disarray. We have tried to show the relationship between a high level of alienation and the pathological state of anomie, as well as a crisis in identity. We have tried to show that deviance in thought and action is a function of the definitions of those who hold power and apply mainly to the powerless. We have tried to identify some of the more alienating conflicts in American culture. And finally we have tried to relate all of this to the problems of education, using the most extensive research we know of in personality typing, that of O. J. Harvey and associates.

We can arrive only at the working hypothesis that school personnel, as of the 1970s, tend strongly toward authoritarian and undemocratic values; and, finally, that those who have power over students in our schools will decide, given the present system, what is and is not deviance among their students. Will students who incline toward liberal and democratic values be the deviants of the seventies and eighties? If so, what is ahead for the culture?

STUDY QUESTIONS

1. As a student, from what aspects of your perceived environment do you feel most alienated?
2. Regarding contradictions in the culture, which do you find most bothersome? What are your plans, if any, to cope with them?
3. The logical contradictions in values and beliefs listed in the chapter are only a sampler. What others can you list from your own experience (including reading), that you feel should be included as being important enough for teachers to be aware of?
4. Of your own estrangements from cultural elements, which do you interpret as desirable and to be pursued (perhaps as a "cause") and which do you feel are destructive and best reduced or eliminated if possible?

5. As a human being, it is virtually certain that you harbor in your thinking a number of logical conflicts of which you are unaware. See how many of them you can verbalize as potential cognitive dissonances (it should help to invent a number of hypothetical decisions relating to your more important life goals and role-play the decision-making process).
6. In what ways do you see your acquaintances as being alienated from some aspect or aspects of their perceived environment? Focus on such key categories of people as your grandparents and their friends, your teachers, and so on.
7. How would you evaluate your own sense of identity? Are you satisfied with your sexual identity? With your own values and beliefs? With your view of "where you are" with respect to place, time, and social environment? With your degree of control over your own life? (Suggestion: Write an essay entitled "Who Am I?")
8. Which of your own beliefs and actions do you feel would seem deviant to those who have at least some degree of power over you, such as parents, teachers, employers, or government units (local, state, or national)? Which of your deviances do you feel you could defend?
9. From your own view of what are desirable values, what do you see as the chief deviances among those who have power over you? What kinds of action, if any, do you think you should take to defend your deviances against theirs?
10. How much and what kinds of deviance do you feel should be encouraged as healthy agents of social change among your age peers? Whom might you be in a position to influence? Do you feel there is a place for deliberate violation of law to promote what you see as desired deviance from old culture, establishment values?
11. What values do you see, if any, in the kind of personality typing done by the Harvey group or other researchers trying to get at essentially the same thing?
12. Where would you place yourself on Harvey's concrete-abstract continuum? Under what circumstances do you shift from one region of the continuum to another? What important influences in your life can you identify that have made you gravitate toward one personality system (if you identify yourself with any of the four systems)?
13. How would you interpret the tendency of students and school personnel to gravitate over time in the direction of System 1 functioning? What do you think causes it?
14. If you feel you are near, or within, the System 4 region of the continuum, what kind of a "game plan" could you construct to help you stay within that framework—assuming you would like to? What strategies can you devise for staying in teaching, being reasonably effective, and advancing up the promotional hierarchy without giving up a commitment to System 4 values?

ANNOTATED BIBLIOGRAPHY

Abelson, Robert P. et al. (eds.), *Theories of Cognitive Consistency: A Sourcebook.* Skokie Ill.: Rand McNally & Company, 1968.

For readers who want in one volume a wide range of essays and research reports on the role of consistency/inconsistency (or cognitive consonance/dissonance) in human life, this may be the best available sourcebook.

Clinard, Marshall B. (ed.), *Anomie and Deviant Behavior*. New York: The Free Press, 1964; Free Press paperback, 1971.

Clinard suggests that the concept of anomie offers an explanation of deviant behavior within the context of broad social forces rather than as a product of individual biological or psychological factors. The readings present views of how anomie may be used to explain deviancy.

Erikson, Erik H., *Identity: Youth and Crisis*. New York: W. W. Norton & Company, Inc., 1968.

Erikson is one of the best-known writers on identity. He tries to integrate psychoanalytic concepts and the play of cultural forces as the root cause of identity problems. Many readers see in Erikson a streak of the John Dewey-George Mead view of self-development as a function of the interaction of a somewhat self-determining individual and his perceived social environment.

Hofstadter, Richard, *Social Darwinism in American Thought,* rev. ed. New York: George Braziller, Inc., 1959.

Generally regarded as the best treatment of the development of the idea that the idle, poor, and weak are such because of genetic defects and that, conversely, the wealthy and powerful are such because of genetic strengths; and that "nature should be allowed to take its course" by weeding out, through premature death, the lowest strata of society.

Horney, Karen, *The Neurotic Personality of Our Time*. New York: W. W. Norton Company, Inc., 1937.

Horney, as one of the first psychoanalysts to push the idea that individual personalities tend to mirror the major conflicts of the culture, saw three major debilitating conflicts in this country: competition and success vs. brotherly love and humility; the stimulation of needs vs. the incapacity of the society to fulfill them; and freedom of choice vs. limitations the culture imposes on freedom.

Kittrie, Nicholas N., *The Right to Be Different; Deviance and Enforced Therapy*. Baltimore: The Johns Hopkins Press, 1971.

An effective argument for helping deviants who require it, but not controlling or suppressing deviancy of a type that does not endanger others. A well-reviewed and highly regarded treatment of the subject.

Laing, R. D., *The Politics of Experience*. New York: Pantheon Books, Inc., 1967.

This is only one of more than half a dozen books Laing has authored or coauthored. His psychology is phenomenological and existential, and he may be charting a new path away from both Freudianism and behaviorism in interpreting and treating mental illness—which to him is a form of alienation.

Marcuse, Herbert, *One-Dimensional Man: Studies in the Ideology of Advanced Industrial Societies*. Boston: Beacon Press, 1964.

Marcuse's pessimistic analysis of American society as a stabilized form of quasi-fascism in which dissent and revolutionary impulse are all but absent. Our society is "one dimensional" because it has lost its capacity for self-criticism and self-renewal.

May, Rollo, *Psychology and the Human Dilemma*. New York: Van Nostrand Reinhold Company, 1967.

Rollo May, one of our most prominent humanist psychologists, writes in this small book of alienation and loss of identity in the modern world. The basic theme is the dilemma created by man's trying to see himself as both subject and object, as capable of self-determination but often trapped by environmental demands. One of the best treatments of the issue of freedom vs. determinism. Also related to this chapter is May's *Love and Will*, New York: W. W. Norton & Company, Inc., 1969.

Murchland, Bernard, *The Age of Alienation*. New York: Random House, Inc., 1971.

One of the better general treatments of alienation as a persistent state of humankind. Develops the theme of alienation from St. Augustine to the present. Good case studies and numerous good references for further reading in the footnotes. A well-written and readable book for those who want historical background.

Schacht, Richard, *Alienation* (with an introductory essay by Walter Kaufman). New York: Doubleday & Company, Inc., 1970.

The body of this book, by Schacht, is a historical treatment of the concept of alienation, including the views of Hegel, Marx, Fromm, and Horney, and including chapters on the sociological literature and alienation in existential philosophy. Schacht is technical and for advanced students. Kaufman's essay of about fifty pages is the best treatment this writer has seen anywhere in an easily readable form. Not only is his treatment of alienation brilliant, but his analysis of American culture is highly provocative.

Snell, Putney, and Gail J. Putney, *The Adjusted American: Normal Neurosis in the Individual and Society*. New York: Harper & Row, Publishers, 1964.

A first-rate and highly readable book on alienation in America. The authors argue that traditional American values labeled "middle" or "moderate" (status quo oriented), are so taken for granted as to be almost invisible, but are so contrary to human "self-needs" that they produce a widespread illness among those Middle Americans who think they are the most "adjusted" or "normal."

Toffler, Alvin, *Future Shock*. New York: Random House, Inc., 1970.

Toffler's analysis of the stress on individuals produced by a highly dynamic industrial civilization is generally considered one of the better treatments of this subject. He presents an interesting theory of a kind of mass psychosis which he calls "massive adaptational breakdown."

Ullman, Albert D. (ed.), *Sociocultural Foundations of Personality*. Boston: Houghton Mifflin Company, 1965.

An interesting book of readings, all of which are pertinent in one way or another to this chapter. Ullman himself, and most of the essays, reflect what now seems a rather old-fashioned functionalist approach to cultural analysis, as well as a Skinnerian-type of behaviorism. Readers wishing an interpretation sharply different from that of the present writer will find this readable book useful.

Urick, Ronald V., *Alienation: Individual or Social Problem?* Englewood Cliffs, N.J.: Prentice-Hall, Inc., 1970.

Perhaps the best primer on alienation for students without prior background. Chapter 2 is the best short, lucid treatment we have seen which is not overly simplistic. Urick identifies four types of alienation: social isolation, meaninglessness of culture, normlessness (or estrangement), and powerlessness.

Youth: The turbulent sixties. (Copyright © George Ballis, all rights reserved)

Youth: The placid seventies.

4

YOUTH CULTURE AND EDUCATION

The major points we have learned from the Manus are that change has to be across-the-board and that you must take all three generations with you; otherwise, the older people are just a dead drag.

Margaret Mead

This chapter on the young, the final chapter in Part I, is to a considerable degree a culmination of the first three chapters of the book. Its chief themes are: (1) the youth movement and development of a counterculture during the sixties; (2) the decline of activism, but the continuation of many counterculture values into the seventies; (3) some characteristics of youth outside the counterculture; (4) how the counterculture may reflect a fundamental cultural turning point in American, and perhaps world, culture; and (5) the implications of all this for education.

As these topics are developed, readers will find rather steady use made of the concept of alienation as developed in Chapter 3. We will try to show ways in which both youth and the adults who influence them, or whom they influence, are affected by both negative (unhealthy) and positive (healthy or optimum) alienation. Our assessment of the role of alienation will help us see more clearly the options that may be available for the remainder of the seventies, the eighties, and beyond.

GENERATION GAPS—OLD AND NEW

What do we mean by a generation gap? Who are the young and who are the old? A generation is defined technically as the number of years between the average age of parents and the average age of their children. A generation varies in length, depending on how early in life couples begin producing children. In some cultures reproduction begins when couples are in their middle teens; in others it may not begin until they are nearing 30. When teenagers have children, the span of their generations may be no more than twenty years. In the United States, as of this writing, the span of a generation is approaching thirty years, meaning that most grandparents died before their last grandchildren were born.

Who are the young? As a reasonable definition in relation to our purposes, we will refer to "the young," "youth," or "the younger generation" as persons in the age range of 14 through 24. This age range includes most high school and college students. At about the age of 24 most young Americans have taken on the traditional combination of adult activities. They have mostly settled into an occupation, are recently married or soon to be, and are ready to beget a new generation. The age span 14–24 is also a convenient choice because the U.S. Bureau of the Census treats this span as a population category for which to collect statistics.

To say that the young are those between 14 and 24 is to imply that the "old" are persons 25 and over. This would be a nonsensical definition, of course; Americans can't even agree on defining middle age, except that the older one gets, the older he perceives middle age to be. (The author now regards middle age as 58.) For our purposes, we will simply refer to persons over 24 as "adults"; however, we will have occasion to use the term "parents" (ages 25 to 45, perhaps?) and "grandparents" (those over 45?). Such crude definitions should serve our needs well enough.

After presenting this definition of the young, an immediate qualification is necessary. Our intent in this and other chapters is to view the young as psychological entities—that is, although chronological age pro-

vides a useful framework, the most useful definition of youth for our purposes is to include all those who "think young." The chronologically
young can fulfill the cultural role we attribute to them only if they see
themselves as psychologically different from those who are older. Most
youth in the 14-to-24-age range are little different in their values and beliefs
from their parents and grandparents. They are young in years, but they
"think old." Conversely, many people who are chronologically older,
eighty-year-old great-grandparents included, tend to "think young." Since
one of our major interests is in trying to unravel the consequences of the
interaction between those who "think young" and those who "think old,"
then for large numbers of people, a few million perhaps, chronological
age tells us little or nothing.

For the above reason, we have used and will continue to use the
expressions "new culture values" and "old culture values," or to refer
simply to new culture vs. old culture.

As suggested in Chapter 1, industrial and post-industrial cultures
tend to change rapidly; as the pool of newly invented ideas, leading to
new artifacts, builds up, the innovative capacity of the culture tends to
develop at an accelerating rate. The gap in ideas between the young and
the established generations of parents and grandparents expands until
the young and their elders find it difficult if not impossible to understand
one another, let alone tolerate the divergence in belief. Alienation becomes
conspicuous, particularly among those who feel left behind (the poor, the
racial and ethnic minorities, and often women) and among those who, by
virtue of superior education, feel themselves ahead of the old culture (the
intellectual community generally, and any upper-middle-class or upper-
class person who has come to reject some or most of the core values of
industrialism or post-industrialism).

But there is also a counterforce to estrangement between new culture and old culture ways. By the time advanced industrialism is reached
and a culture is moving into a post-industrial phase, as is the United
States, a comparatively large proportion of parents (and even grandparents) have acquired considerable education, and in the process have
become more flexible, more relativistic, in their thinking than was imaginable, say, fifty years ago. Adults may be confused about many things,
but a greater proportion of them are more open to innovation in life style.
Their own children may play an increasingly important role in their education (as we noted in Chapter 1 when explaining Margaret Mead's interpretation of cultural revolution). We would expect to find the most
relativistic adults among the educated upper-middle class and perhaps
little or no generation gap at this level. Middle Americans have been held
together by attachment of both young and old to old-culture values, but
studies of noncollege youth as of 1973 indicate that the coming seventies

will exhibit significant divergence in values and beliefs as between young and old.

If there is no major clash between upper-middle-class youth and their parents, or between middle- and lower-middle-class youth and their parents, or between middle- and lower-middle-class youth and their parents, then we may ask whether there is a genuine generation gap in this country. Apparently there is little gap within the educated sector of society, but a potentially major difference between nonschool, blue-collar youth and their elders.

Seymour Lipset does see a "gap" which may be of major significance. It stems from a clash in values between college youth, and to some extent secondary school students, and others. Only incidentally shown between young and old, it is a gap between students old enough to be influenced by campus culture and most of the nonstudent portion of the population. However, as Lipset points out, this is not a complete description. There is also a gap between the more intellectualy inclined high school teachers and the general community, and even more between college professors and the general public. The gap, then, is between liberal intellectuals (students, faculty, and a good many upper-middle-class professionals) and conservative nonintellectuals—the latter making up the great majority of the population.[1] But studies to be cited later strongly suggest that noncollege youth, including those in blue-collar jobs, are adopting counterculture values at a rapid rate.

The kind of gap Lipset describes may seem like a generation gap, however, because student intellectuals are more likely than anyone else to actively support liberal—often rather far out—causes. The nonliberal adults we call Middle America become the most agitated by liberalization of student values. In the sixties their sons and daughters may also have been bothered, but the parents were more articulate. *There may be, then, a continued tension between liberal student intellectuals and older conservative nonintellectuals.*

BACKGROUND: YOUTH IN THE SIXTIES

We will refer to the humanistic/democratic values exerted by a portion of the youth of the sixties as an authentic *counterculture*. We are aware that some social observers deny that there ever was a genuine counterculture; but the residue of the movement of the sixties, increasingly clear in 1974, supports rather conclusively the hypothesis that not only was there a real and influential counterculture of the sixties, but that, in

[1] Seymour M. Lipset, "Polls and Protests," *Foreign Affairs*, April 1971, pp. 549–555.

spite of fundamental changes in tactics and strategy, it attracts more members now than at any time.

During the sixties a sharp split occurred among 14–24-year-old youth—not only between youth and their parents and grandparents, but also between youthful subcultures. This split was based on conspicuously different attitudes, values, and beliefs in almost all areas of interest. In retrospect, it appears virtually certain that the United States' deep involvement in the ongoing Southeast Asian revolution and the interference of the draft in youths' plans greatly exacerbated a potential split which was presumably bound to come anyway. There were clear signs of a counter-culture developing before the war became a hot issue. Also, once the existence of the schism was clear, the major youth camps differed on many matters other than war. Sharp differences in values appeared in such areas as sex and sexism; religion; foreign policy; law, order, and justice; race and ethnic group relations; ecology; and even the work ethic itself.

The Dissident Subculture

Dissident youth refers to young people of both the sixties and the seventies who were generally dissatisfied with the traditional values of American life, the American system, the American way.

Any scheme for classifying the dissident subculture into further subcultures may seem as arbitrary as slicing a pie. At least the following conceptual scheme seems workable as a means of better clarifying the nature of dissidents as a total group.

Revolutionary activists During the sixties a rather miniscule group, including the Weathermen, advocated the use of violence against property or persons in efforts to affect social policies. Accurate figures on the number of youth within this category seem impossible to obtain. According to a Harris poll taken in July, 1970, 11 percent of college and university students classified themselves as "far left" and said they were "not against the use of violence." One must remember, however, that this was a year of high tension. The war had escalated and many youth faced the prospect of fighting in a war they opposed on moral grounds. Yankelovich's polling, apparently more careful than Harris or Gallup polls, supported the Harris result in that 10 percent of his sample called themselves "radicals."[2] Considering that the 1970 college and university student population was over 7 million, it is hard to believe that 700,000 (10 percent) would have resorted to violence. At that time it was popular to

[2] Daniel Yankelovich, Inc., *The Changing Values on Campus: Political and Personal Attitudes of Today's College Students.* New York: Washington Square Press, 1972, p. 59.

use the word radical. As of 1973, revolutionary activists appear to be no more than 2 percent of college and college-bound students.

Nonviolent activists These were youth, deeply alienated from and marches; gave speeches; organized gatherings like the Woodstock Festival (with attendance estimated from 300,000 to 500,000); and communicated much of their message with music. Between the early 1960s and 1970 this group made itself felt to at least some degree in almost every college and university in the country. Student strikes closed down a number of schools for varying lengths of time, the two most publicized probably being San Francisco State College and Columbia University.

Noncollege youth, comprised mainly of Blacks and other minorities, joined with college activists, as did a few adults. Although it seemed like a much larger number at the time, it is highly unlikely that at the very most, more than about $3\frac{1}{2}$ percent of the population of the country could be considered activists. This is, of course, a fairly sizeable number, about six and two-thirds million.

Nonactivist dissenters These were youth, deeply alienated from old-culture values, who held back from visible activism because of timidity, a personal philosophy antithetic to activism, lack of opportunity, or other reasons. Probably a considerable number of nonactivist dissenters were trapped in conservative peer groups or under too close parental control to do more than think or talk to sympathetic listeners. This writer got the impression that at one point in the late sixties most of his students fell within this category. We have no way of estimating the size of this grouping; possibly most of them belong within the group of six and two-thirds million *potential* activists mentioned above.

Cultural dropouts In contrast to the activists and nonactivist dissenters who tried to work within the mainstream culture to change it, the so-called hippies chose not to fight old-culture values, but to escape from them. They may have begun as activists and become discouraged, or never have identified with activist philosophy. Many were runaways who headed for the enclaves of Haight-Asbury in San Francisco, Venice in Southern California, or Greenwich Village in New York City. Some worked part or fulltime, some attended school; but when the day's job was done, they retreated to their enclave. They wrapped themselves in a cocoon of protest music, sex, drugs, and unorthodox grooming and clothing. *Newsweek* (October 26, 1970) estimated the number of runaways in this group at one million. Like other dissident youth, most dropouts were from upper-middle-class families.

Phonies There seems no question that thousands of youth who pretended to be "of the movement" were not sincere, but were either going along for kicks or trying to escape the law by blending with the authentic dissenters. It now appears that some infiltrating phonies were

Federal provocators conducting surveillance operations as part of a massive Executive Branch program which was organized in 1970 to spy on both young and old dissenters.

The Straight (Nondissident) Youth Culture

The dissident youth culture consisted of only a small minority of American youth, the liberally educated, most affluent part of the college youth population, plus ghetto Blacks and other discontented minorities. To understand their polarization during the sixties, we must look at straight youth, most of whom came from lower-middle to upper-lower homes and had little education past high school. Straight youth reflected the views of Middle America deeply rooted in our traditional Puritan ethic.

It seems likely that there was no significant generation gap between the youth of Middle America and their parents. Lipset tells us that:

> The idealism of much of non-college youth at that time was in fact reflected in a show of highly patriotic feeling, support for the war and even in a disproportionate backing for George Wallace's 1968 presidential candidacy. Furthermore, opinion polls dealing with the relationship of age to views on the Vietnam war have consistently shown that persons over 50 have been more numerous and more consistent in their opposition to the war than have all other groups. . . .
>
> However, a "gap" does exist. *But it is between persons on and off campus* rather than between the younger and the older . . . The non-college population . . . has over the last five years gradually moved in a conservative direction, until by 1970, 52 percent described themselves as conservative, as against *34 percent who thought of themselves as liberals.*[3]

Lipset apparently oversimplified here, not mentioning Blacks and other minorities who shared many values of campus dissidents and at times worked with them. Nor did he foresee the spread of counterculture values to noncollege youth.

Turning to these college dissidents, we wish to reemphasize the sharp campus polarization in the sixties—a liberal-to-left minority and a conservative majority. Only in mid-1968 did a Gallup poll show campus opposition reaching 50 percent. But by then 48 percent of the general public had come to oppose the war—showing little difference between students and the public. More interesting, among young adults 21 to 30, only 38 percent felt the United States mistaken in its war policy. Thus in the whole population, the below-30s as a group were more hawkish than those over thirty.[4]

[3] Lipset, "Polls and Protests," p. 548; italics added.
[4] Lipset, p. 548.

Lipset points out that, in 1968, on-campus student opposition to the war rose sharply because of our rapidly deepening involvement in Southeast Asia. Yankelovich also found that the traditionally conservative group on campus—the vocational/technological majors—liberalized somewhat during this period.[5] Thus, as the United States population as a whole was turning more conservative, conservative college and university students were becoming to some degree more liberal.

In spite of what seemed like slow movement of straight youth at the end of the decade toward a more liberal/democratic orientation, coupled with some acceptance of dissident ideas in most areas of life, the straights remained a highly conservative element in our society. Because, except on the war issue after 1968, the straights did not identify with the dissident youth movement and remained a kind of "silent majority," it is difficult to categorize them. We will risk the following little boxes:

College and university straights   In view of the mass of largely indigestible data, it is hazardous to say much about this group as of the end of the decade of the sixties. There is evidence that, during that decade, student straights moved faintly left toward a very bland dissidence. The in-college straights did seem to constitute a subculture among straight youth. If they were not appreciably more liberal, they did have different goals: they were determined to move into white-collar occupations, to be respectable and socially mobile after entering the world of work. They were better informed than noncollege straights, more cultivated, and more restrained about activities which would seem "unprofessional."

What was the composition of this group with respect to vocational interests? We can at least show the majors of the graduating class of 1970. In descending order of popularity, their majors were business and commerce, engineering, biology, health professions, and the physical sciences. It should not be concluded that all students enrolled in these majors were status quo oriented. A small minority belonged with the dissidents, probably more of these in mathematics and the physical sciences than in other majors.

This group as a whole could perhaps best be labeled *moderates*. They shied away from extreme positions, as well as from overt action as a modus vivendi.

But not all college conservatives were nonactivists. During the height of the campus disturbances (1967–1970), a semiactivist group was identifiable. Their view seemed to be: "I like the way things are and I'll oppose, with violence if need be, anyone who acts dissatisfied with the American way."

We must recognize the quasi-fascist character of some student

---

[5] Yankelovich, *Changing Values on Campus*, p. 95.

thinking and be aware of the possibility that there was and still apparently is a core among the militant straights who could easily be converted to a group like the various "youth for Mussolini" or "youth for Hitler" groups in Europe during the 1930s. Some students in this category formed clubs reminiscent of rightist organizations of that time.

Noncollege white-collar straights   Outside the college/university community, we could find in the youthful work force of the sixties a few million youth with only a high school, or high school plus two-year community college education who were gainfully employed. Their jobs tended to be in the lower white-collar category: stenography, general clerical, sales, civil service, and a variety of service occupations. We find no evidence that this group of young people was politically oriented (unless toward the Republican party) or would identify with any type of new-culture dissident group.

Blue-collar straights   We refer in this section to youth between about 18 and 24, a large majority of whom have finished high school, and perhaps junior college, who are trying to establish themselves in what will be their life work. Like college and university youth in the nonliberal arts majors, they are fundamentally conservative but probably susceptible to a three-way categorization.

1. *Left of center blue-collars.* As of the late sixties (and even more in the early seventies), the news media reported almost weekly that blue-collar youth are "lackadaisical about the traditional work ethic." Almost all of these youth are employed, those most publicized are in mining or manufacturing. Particularly, we read about the reaction of youth to factory assembly lines characterized by a high rate of job turnover and absenteeism as well as careless work habits.

These youth are probably not alienated from the larger culture, but rather from monotonous, dehumanizing jobs—the kind of alienation which figured so prominently in Karl Marx's sociological writings of the 1840s.

2. *Centrist or neutral blue-collars.* It seems probable, although adequate factual data are not available, that the largest group of blue-collar straights function at a comparatively low level of alienation. Their dissatisfactions are similar to those of almost everyone else—rising cost of living, low wages, air pollution, scarcity of adequate housing, unsympathetic employers, etc. Most members of this group are establishing families or planning to, getting on pretty well with parents and other adults, and retaining roots within the traditional cultural mainstream.

3. *Right of center blue-collars.* We would expect these to be the sons and daughters of skilled upper blue-collar parents who adopt the values of their parents. Their fathers, and occasionally their mothers, have had a long history of labor union membership in conservative, elitist craft unions, such as, the building trade unions.

Traditionally, this group has liked the idea of high tariffs and any sort of American imperialist ventures that might promise economic benefit. They also tend to be anti-Communist, pro-war, racist, against equal rights for women, pro-police and "law and order," and hostile toward intellectuals of any sort, but particularly dissenting college and university youth.

THE COUNTERCULTURE OF THE SIXTIES

So far in the chapter we have treated only incidentally the specific values, beliefs, and life styles of dissident youth. In this section, we will dig into what dissident youth of the sixties were like as personalities. But to understand better the counterculture that became so visible in the sixties, we need to start at the beginning, which was in the fifties.

Prelude: The "Beats" of the Fifties

During the 1950s most youth of the industrialized nations were conspicuously lethargic with respect to sociopolitical issues. In the United States, about the only stirrings were in the miniature subculture of writers who called themselves the Beat Generation. Few persons took the Beats seriously. Members of the old culture who were aware of the Beats berated them as incomprehensible bohemians, primarily because their image was not respectable—they wrote and talked in "obscenities," dressed oddly, had sex in unorthodox ways, and showed an aversion to "normal" kinds of work.[6]

A handful of serious social scientists and philosophers came to take the Beats seriously as literary harbingers of an emerging counterculture which would gain impact. Some of the expressed values of these writers can be seen in the comment by Kerouac about the term "the Beat Generation." He says this generation was a "group of new American men intent on joy ..." "... the slogan or label for a revolution in manners in America." But he also had a vision of " 'Beat' ... as being to mean beatific ..." in a religious sense.[7]

Most Americans were caught by surprise by the turn the youth movement of the 1960s took. The social milieu of this decade produced a youth culture markedly different from the Beats', although it too opposed many traditional social values.

[6] Books giving insight into the Beats include: Thomas Parkinson (ed.), *A Caseboook on the Beat.* New York: Thomas Y. Crowell Company, 1961; and Lawrence Lipton, *The Holy Barbarians,* New York: Julian Messner, 1959. Parkinson's anthology of literature and criticism includes such authors as Corso, Burroughs, Ginsberg, Kerouac, and Rexroth.

[7] Jack Kerouac, "On the Origin of the Beat Generation," in Parkinson, pp. 68–76.

Youth values of the sixties: Have they changed in the seventies?
(Copyright © George Ballis, all rights reserved)

Counterculture Values and Beliefs of the Sixties

In this section we will point out what seem to be the primary abstract goals of the counterculture of the sixties, and how these goals came to emerge. It does not pretend to be a history of the movement.

Concern for Equalitarianism

Evidence of a growing concern for equal rights for all was the promotion of the cause of civil liberties. The first significant activism related to this issue was white expansion in 1960 of the black college students' sit-in movement in the South. This effort of white activists continued to be a major concern through the 1963 Birmingham demonstrations and the 1964 Mississippi Summer Project organized by the Student Non-Violent Coordinating Coommittee (SNCC).

Concern for Free Speech

This movement was first manifested in the Free Speech Movement of 1964 on the Berkeley campus. We need not get into the steps that led to students' demands for free speech, nor to other actions having nothing to do with free speech per se. Our point here is that in 1964 free speech became a major issue in the student movement. The idea of free speech for the young was dramatized and publicized nationally. In a decade, the promotion of candor and openness has led to at least a temporary decline in censorship, remarkable gains in honesty in classroom discussions, and probably better communication generally between youth and adults.

Concern for Peaceful Resolution of Disputes

In February 1965, the Vietnam War became the major issue on college campuses when Johnson steeply escalated the war by ordering the systematic bombing of North Vietnam and making the commitment to send as many troops as needed to win for the South Vietnamese the struggle against communism. Since then, American involvement in what students considered an Indochinese civil war—in which the Communist goals seemed more representative of the Vietnamese people as a whole than those of the South Vietnamese government—provided the single greatest motivation of the student movement.

Although the war was the overriding issue, peace as an abstract ideal for all peoples and peaceful means of settling disputes instead of violent ones became important goals of the student movement.

Concern for Participatory Democracy

Perhaps the first active demand for participatory democracy was to be found in the civil rights movement beginning about 1960. Although events then focused on gaining these rights for Blacks, the events in the South had implications everywhere for the principle of participatory democracy—and the dissident youth of the nation began to feel that the young also deserved rights of participation in decision making which had always been denied them.

According to one activist report, in the student strike at Columbia University in 1968, the major aim of the students was to win the right to share in decisions concerning what the university was to stand for. Students charged Columbia was focusing much of its research capacity on developing the implements of war and had become a tool of the industrial-military complex. They did not believe a university should be under such outside control and wanted to make their voices felt in the determination of autonomous university policy.[8]

Partly because of these events, both high-school and college students the country over began demanding more say in how their schools

---

[8] Alexander Klein (ed.), *Natural Enemies??? Youth and the Clash of Generations*. Philadelphia: J. B. Lippincott Company, 1969. See Tom Hayden, "two, three, many columbias," pp. 135–137.

should be run, as well as more say in the policies governing the communities in which they lived.

Concern for Freedom in Personal Life Styles

Under the influence of the Beats of the fifties, an increasing number of young dissidents began to demand much greater freedom in living their lives according to their own values. The concern for a life style that would clearly identify youth as members of a protest movement, or a counterculture, led to new styles in grooming and dress, the use of drugs, and permissiveness in sex, communal living, the coining of a new youth cult language, and the use of music not only as a sensuous experience but also as a media for advocating counterculture values.

One of the more important aspects of the counterculture was a desire for leisure and flexibility in living routines. During much of the sixties, most dissident youth resisted typing themselves down to conventional work hours. Many did hold jobs, but commonly they were temporary—a means of acquiring enough "bread" for a few weeks of leisure on little more than a survival basis. Of course, some were supported by their families or friends.

Disdain for Traditional Political Interests

A majority of counterculture youth seemed apolitical. Most were "political independents." They tended to pass up elections, to be critical of both Democratic and Republican parties. However, a minority were political activists in the sense that they advocated fundamental changes in the American system and expressed admiration for politicians and intellectual leaders on the political left. The expression, "The New Left," which many counterculture members identified with doesn't refer so much to activist politics as to a way of life, most features of which we have described above.

Concern for the Natural Environment

Ecological interests became incorporated in the youth movement of the sixties well after the movement had developed. Like most other aspects of the movement, ecological interests received less attention than the war and the push for civil rights. Nevertheless books by Barry Commoner, Paul Ehrlich, and other prominent ecologists were widely read by youth, and courses in ecology were added to the curriculums of most colleges and universities.

Concern for Humane Values

In a broad sense, all the characteristics we have described as belonging to the counterculture come under this head. If the counterculture had one thrust which embraced all the rest and served to distinguish it most sharply from its opponents, it was the humanist values to which most of its members were committed. Humanism, as the concept is used in this volume, was defined in the Prologue as a feature of democracy. Humanism linked with positive relativism welcomes experimentation with new value systems and new roads to knowledge. The epitome of humanistic achievement seems reflected in Harvey's concept of the system 4 person; and in a much narrower sense in our concept of an optimally alienated person. The humanistic slant of counterculture values contrasts sharply with the materialism and rigidity of old-culture views.

We have deliberately presented the best side of the counterculture. Clearly, not all of its members achieved the values we have described above. From this writer's point of view, however, countercultural values (except for political passivity) that surfaced with the Beats in the fifties and evolved into a rather coherent pattern by the end of the sixties seemed at that time to represent humankind's best hope for the future.

THE SEVENTIES: A DECADE OF TRANQUILLITY

In sectioning off youth of the sixties and youth of the seventies, we do not mean that there is anything intrinsically special about 1970, the introductory year of the new decade. As a matter of fact, the year 1971 marked a crescendo in youth's developing active protest against the Indochina war, and such protest continued in a somewhat lower key through Christmas of 1972. Virtually every aspect of what seems to be the new counterculture of the seventies began in the sixties if not in the fifties. For our purposes, the decade of the seventies may be said to begin in 1971 or 1972, when overt student activism with all its fanfare and noise began to disappear from high school and college campuses. Similarly, although an apparent upsurge in conservatism among a majority of the American population, particularly the great middle mass, may characterize the 1970s, the conservative trend was clearly visible according to the polls as early as 1965. Readers should regard our using the 1970 breaking point as purely a matter of organizational convenience for this chapter.

There is much about the seventies that remains a puzzle to social analysts. With respect to the major nonwar goals of the counterculture of the sixties, which had been pushed with a good deal of determination and attendant publicity, we now hear little. *From surface appearances*, it looks as if the counterculture, on which not only youth but an increasing number of adult liberals had pinned so much hope, was by 1973 all but dead.

In the following section, we will try to enumerate what seem to us some plausible, and to a considerable degree empirically supportable, reasons for what seems like the subsidence of the youth movement and the counterculture.

The Late Sixties and Early Seventies in Retrospect

It now seems possible to refine interpretations of what actually occurred between about 1967 and 1971. Earlier we described the youth movement of the sixties as investigators then saw it. If viewed with caution, our description of this period may be about as accurate as any. But on the basis of Daniel Yankelovich's extensive 1973 survey, which included cross sections of both college and noncollege youth (the latter included only once before, in 1969), and utilized depth interviewing techniques, we can hypothesize a rather different perspective.

Yankelovich now sees the 1960s to 1971 as a time when two youth movements occurred together. First was a revolution in moral/social values which continued through the 1960s and, largely achieved among college youth by 1973, is being rapidly adopted by noncollege youth in the 1970s.

Second, there was a temporary "political revolution" induced by the Vietnam war—the cause of most of the overt activism so evident on campuses from 1967 until it seemed to youth both that their political efforts had failed and that our role in the war would soon end. Yankelovich says of this period:

> The war was like having a despised stranger living in your home at the same time that a baby was born in the family. With the departure of the stranger, the situation may at first seem to return to what it was earlier, but it soon becomes apparent that the new baby has created its own pattern of changes in the life of the family.[9]

The social revolution Yankelovich refers to as the emergence of the "New Values " resembles his "New Naturalism." (See Chapter 1.)

In order to reach conclusions about new-culture beliefs as of 1973 and the long-range trends suggested, we can compare these and earlier findings. So, in addition to Yankelovich's research, we will also draw from the longitudinal studies the American Council on Education conducted from 1966 to 1972, and continued in 1973 with the University of California at Los Angeles.[10]

[9] Daniel Yankelovich, *The New Morality: A Profile of American Youth in the 70's*. New York: McGraw-Hill Book Company, 1974, p. 9. Hereafter we will call this report Yankelovich (1974).

[10] See the annual reports from the ACE Office of Research, 1966 through 1972, and the 1973 report from the Graduate School of Education, UCLA. Individual titles are not uniform but all refer to national norms for entering college freshmen.

The ACE and ACE-UCLA studies differ from those of Yankelovich. Their questionnaire, which covered demographic as well as items designed to reveal values, was given to a large cross section of beginning freshmen (170,000 or more annually). Obviously the findings were not of college students, as such, but rather of college-bound high school graduates. They tell us primarily about the consequences of the high school years for the college bound.

Although later we will discuss findings for the same ideological categories we used to describe youth of the 1960s, we will devote this section to some of the broader conclusions it appears we may now safely draw.

Alienation of Youth

College youth, although pursuing with gusto most of the counter-culture moral/social values (excluding the political) which appeared in the sixties, seem considerably less alienated from mainline culture than as recently as 1971. About three out of four college youth feel that life is going pretty well for them and that the future is likely to yield about what they want. The proportion saying ours is a "sick society" declined in 1973 to 35 percent. Interest in maintaining family ties increased. And in 1973 college students had decided they could find both self-fulfillment and an adequate living in standard careers.

In spite of this, alienation from major old-culture norms and institutions increased since 1971. Criticism of our penal system, political parties, and big business has risen significantly. Commitment to traditional religion declined markedly since 1969, with an even more dramatic decline in the belief that patriotism is an important value. There was more worry in 1973 about maintaining personal privacy. And criticism of the whole Establishment increased between 1971 and 1973.

By 1973 the most alienated were noncollege youth, who make up about 75 percent of the youth population. Although rapidly adopting the moral/social values of college youth, noncollege youth feel particularly alienated from the world of work. A primary job goal of both noncollege and college young persons is work which will be self-fulfilling; among noncollege youth the Puritan work ethic is rapidly disappearing. The idea that "hard work always pays off" declined greatly in acceptance. But working noncollege youth wish they could have more education. When asked if they would commit six years to a combined work-study program leading to a college degree, 71 percent assented.

In 1973 the two categories of youth which showed extreme alienation were minorities and Vietnam veterans. Among black and other minority youth, 55 percent regarded ours as a "sick society" and 76 percent denied that we have democracy. Veterans, much more than youth as a whole, felt financially squeezed; twice as many felt they were "second-class" citizens; and alcohol and drug use was twice as high among veterans.[11]

Mysticism and the Occult

Interest among both young and old in mysticism and the occult has surged upward during the seventies. This phenomenon may be closely linked to alienation from old-culture beliefs; on the other hand, it may reflect a struggle toward something which will eventually prove highly constructive. It is virtually impossible to define either of these words meaningfully. Apparently, the *occult* refers to some realm beyond ordinary comprehension, a realm of knowledge sometimes considered achievable only through some sort of mystical experience. Those who proclaim themselves or others as *mystics* apparently feel certain of the existence of, and their ability to achieve contact with, some reality not accessible through ordinary perception or logical processes.

As far back as we know anything of human history, there have been some persons claiming mystical powers—persons variously called witch doctors, medicine men, shamans, spiritualists, psychics, saints, or whatever. With the coming of the scientific era, perhaps properly dated from the eighteenth century, educated people have increasingly rejected the claims of all varieties of mystics until by the middle of the twentieth century mystics of most kinds had fallen upon hard times. Persons who claimed special "psychic powers" came to be regarded generally as more than a little odd.

By the mid-seventies, persons well educated in the scientific tradition are rapidly developing a serious interest in events not susceptible to traditional explanations. The exponents of extrasensory perception seem to have demonstrated beyond little doubt that some persons can perform various kinds of thought transference not explainable by present understanding of our five-plus senses. Finally ESP has not only become respectable but a legitimate area of scientific investigation. Linked to this interest is perhaps an even stronger interest in the conscious control of autonomic bodily processes (such as body temperature, pulse and respiratory rates, oxygen need, etc.). Further, these interests in the mystical, including deliberate controls over bodily functions, tie in with certain beliefs associated with Zen Buddhism. Readers should note that such heresies were first

[11] Yankelovich (1974) Chaps. 13, 14. See also Robert Jay Lifton's *Home From the War*. New York: Simon and Schuster, 1973. Lifton offers a provocative analysis of psychological problems among veterans.

advocated by the Beats of the 1950s, and were taken much more seriously by the open-minded young than by most adults.

Rather than a temporary counterculture aberration, these new interests may involve serious experimentation with nonstandard ways of knowing. One aspect of counterculture thought has been the suspicion that the approach to knowledge commonly used in a scientistic, industrial society is arbitrarily limited.

The Switch from Goal to Role Orientation

Among college youth, the desire for a job in which to express oneself increased between 1970 and 1973 from 56 to 68 percent. The desire for a personally challenging job rose from 64 to 77 percent. Although 61 percent of noncollege youth want a job with good pay, 65 percent want a job on which they can "use their minds" and 70 percent want interesting work. The desire for work that is self-fulfilling is coming to override the desire for success (as acquiring wealth and social prestige). Youth appear ever more eager to develop themselves as persons and not settle for the traditional routines.

Liberalization of High School Students

Data from the 1960s about this group is scarce. We have some empirical evidence which suggests there was no meaningful value pattern among high school youth then; confusion was the rule (reported by Seymour Lipset, *Saturday Review*, November 1972, pp. 68–70). However, the ACE studies of college-bound high school youth indicate that something in the total high school age cultural milieu has moved high school students far toward liberal thinking, especially where personal freedom and egalitarianism are concerned. Yankelovich's noncollege samples of 1969 and 1973 indicate a similar trend among high school graduates and dropouts.

Youth Culture of the Seventies

Many persons, even social scientists, deny the presence of a counterculture in the seventies—which virtually everyone agrees did exist in the sixties. Previous overt activism has indeed yielded to youth's presenting a cool exterior. However, to insist that youth have "gone passive" simply disregards research evidence.

We will draw empirical evidence primarily from the two studies mentioned above: Yankelovich's 1973 research, particularly in relation to that of 1969; and the ACE and ACE/UCLA studies.

It now seems clear that the values of college youth, given a few years lag, tend to spread to noncollege youth and down to secondary school youth. Further, youth values tend to work upward, again with a time lag, and influence adult values —just what Margaret Mead has maintained would increasingly happen. In this section we will enumerate what we feel are significant categoires of belief, as in describing the 1960s counterculture. Comparisons will be noted.

Concern for Equalitarianism

Yankelovich (1974) found concern for our black minorities had lessened; it now focuses more on American Indians. Our tentative interpretation is that by 1973 it may have appeared clear to most youth that Blacks were gradually winning their struggle for equal opportunity and that in a national sampling most youth are unaware of the Mexican-American minority's problems.

The ACE studies are indecisive on beliefs about minorities but do suggest a fairly high level of concern. About 39 percent would give disadvantaged students preferred treatment on campus (down from 44 in 1970). About 35 percent favor an open admissions policy for colleges, down markedly from 61.4 in 1970. Assent to "The Federal government is not doing enough to promote school desegregation" dropped from 51.7 percent in 1971 to 48.6 in 1973.

The most dramatic change is in beliefs about equality for women. Not a countercultural value in the sixties, both the 1973 Yankelovich and the ACE studies indicate that among college and college-bound youth women have largely won their demand for full equality at the ideological level. The story is different among noncollege youth, where many young women themselves still cling to the old Kinder, Kirche, Küche idea.

Concern for Free Speech

Not only has the concern for free speech persisted among the young; it is now largely taken for granted as a right. Further, it now includes both content and style: any subject can be discussed using any words that communicate. The so-called "dirty word movement" began with the Beats in the fifties, was pushed by the 1969 Berkeley free speech movement, and has apparently accelerated since, abetted by the collapse of motion picture censorship.

But more important in long-range cultural impact is a continued push against censorship on high school and college campuses. For example, the ACE studies show that in 1968, 56.4 percent of the sample approved of censorship of student publications; by 1973 the figure had dropped to 30.8. In 1968, 31.7 precent felt college officials should have the right to ban extremist speakers from campus; but by 1973 the percent was 23.1. Since the ACE samples consist only of entering freshmen not yet infected by libertarian ideas of "radical" professors, it appears that the valuing of free speech now begins in high school—whether because of or in spite of the values of high school teachers.

Concern for Peaceful Resolution of Disputes

Although the proportion of college youth and noncollege minorities in the sixties who approved of violence as a means was undoubtedly exaggerated (as indicated earlier in the chapter), a segment of the youth population—never more than a few percent of the whole—in their enthusiasm for whatever cause they pursued did commit many violent acts.

Yankelovich says that college youth in 1973 had come to reject violence virtually in toto. The ACE studies offer no direct evidence of views on violence, but in 1971 (the peak year) 58.5 percent of college-bound youth said they had demonstrated during the past year. This figure dropped to 9.5 percent in 1972; no figure is given for 1973.

Concern for Participatory Democracy

We have little scientific data about democratic commitment in the 1970s. Yankelovich's earlier studies suggest a strong commitment to grass-roots democracy among college students but also much cynicism as to whether it would ever be attainable within the American system. Even so, it is common knowledge among educators that in most of our more prestigious colleges one outgrowth of the 1960s' demand for greater student participation in school affairs has been student representation on many key faculty committees.

Further, as part of the "new candor," students seem much less wary in the 1970s about criticizing openly (but now more politely) administrators, teachers, and curriculum. Students are simply no longer passive "receivers of knowledge" as was expected of them prior to the 1960s. Even though the overt activism seen as recently as 1972 seems to have disappeared from campuses, the "new" students are far more independent than their forebears.

Two items in the ACE studies are revealing. Students were asked to react to "Faculty promotions should be based in part on student evaluations" and "Students should have a major role in specifying the college curriculum." Since 1958, one or both of these assertions were among the top five to which students agreed. Student evaluation of faculty got strong assent, from 63.2 percent in 1968 to about 76 in 1971–1973.

Concern for Freedom in Personal Life Styles

This also has gained increasing support since the 1960s. Among college students, Yankelovich (1974) found: the desire for more sexual freedom jumped from 43 percent in 1969 to 61 in 1973. Acceptance of a legal ban on marijuana declined from 38 percent in 1969 to 71 in 1973.

In the general area of personal freedom the most significant changes found by Yankelovich were among noncollege youth, with desire for more sexual freedom increasing from 22 percent in 1969 to 47 in 1973. He also found that among noncollege youth premarital sex, homosexuality, and abortion all gained markedly in acceptance with an equivalent decline in the percent of students agreeing to "Living a clean moral life is a very important value."

The ACE findings may be even more significant, since they project farther into the future. Questions about sexual behavior per se were not asked, but the belief that college officials should have the right to regulate student behavior declined between 1968 and 1973 from 23.3 percent to 11.4. A more dramatic shift uncovered by ACE was in views about marijuana: the percent of entering freshmen approving legalization rose between 1968 and 1973 from 19.4 to 48.2.

Among Yankelovich's more interesting findings was that by 1973 unconventional personal behavior had become almost completely divorced from leftish political views; in the 1960s these items correlated closely. Apparently in the 1970s even conventional Republicans are likely to wear unconventional long hair and clothing, mate without marriage, and smoke pot.

Disdain for Traditional Political Interests

Through 1973 youth continued to show decreasing interest in political party affiliation and to see themselves as apolitical or independent. Collegians appear at least twice as active politically as noncollege youth. Of those who identify with a party, twice as many are Democrats as Republicans. Among the more apathetic noncollege youth who stated a preference, Democrats have a two-to-one edge. But noncollege youth are generally more conservative politically than college youth.

Political apathy and the difference in political views between college and noncollege youth were revealed in the 1972 Presidential race. About 75 percent of college students voted, favoring McGovern over Nixon by four to three. Less than half the noncollege young voted, splitting their votes about 50-50.

The ACE studies suggest that Yankelovich's findings are likely to continue among college youth. In 1973 over 50 percent of entering freshmen had no political preference, but of those with a preference 34.8 percent called themselves left of center, whereas only 14.5 chose the right.

Concern for the Natural Environment

From what scanty evidence we have, environmental interests remain strong. The ACE studies confronted students with the assertion "The Federal government is not doing enough to control pollution" in 1970. Of all the assertions students agreed with, this led with 92.9 percent assent. The figure dropped to 89.6 and 88.1 percent in 1972 and 1973. But the decline may result from adding to the questionnaire an item on women's rights, about which students felt so strongly that pollution problems were pushed to second place.

No data on this subject were obtained from Yankelovich's 1973 survey. The present writer, from personal experience, can comment on California youth: During summers they are taking to the wilderness as never before. We are not sure just what this means. One might infer, however, that this trend is linked somehow with Yankelovich's calling the counterculture a "new naturalism" (see Chapter 1).

Concern for Humane Values

Even if hard evidence is difficult to find, there is much suggestive evidence. According to the ACE studies, students planning to major in humanities have declined between 1966 and 1973 from 32.5 percent to 22.5. This is confirmed by Yankelovich (1974), who reports that the percent of students majoring in vocational, technical, and preprofessional areas increased from 55 percent in 1968 to 66 in 1973. These figures bear careful scrutiny, however. Yankelovich finds that the values of vocationally oriented students are rapidly liberalizing and also that the chief job concern of students has become interesting, challenging, and self-fulfilling careers. Students in 1973 want to get ahead and make money—but not through routine work. Career goals are conventional, but as Yankelovich says, a central idea is to find self-fulfillment in a conventional career.

Also significant is the response of entering freshmen in the ACE studies about their most prized life objective. In 1970 "helping others" was fourth from the top, with 64.9 assent. In 1971, 1972, and 1973 this goal was second (exceeded only by the desire to gain a "philosophy of life," with assent consistently above 60 percent).

Putting together all this data, we feel it is an acceptable working hypothesis to say that youth remain strongly humanistic in their leanings. As we have suggested, this may be one of the central features of the youthful counterculture and one of its chief sources of alienation from mainline materialistic and mechanistic values.

Additional Data

A number of Yankelovich's 1973 findings do not fit under any of the above categories. To us, one of the most significant is the tendency of both college and noncollege youth to move from the concept of "wants" to that of "rights." We have discussed some of these rights the young demand: greater egalitarianism, greater freedom of speech, greater participation in all sorts of decision making, and virtually unbounded freedom in life styles.

But there are more. Yankelovich's combined college and noncollege samples in 1973 regarded as rights participation in decisions about the nature of their jobs (83 percent), the best medical care for everyone from cradle to grave (54 percent), and a college education for all youth who want it (48 percent). Other rights, with lesser support but suggesting the direction of youth-culture thought, include secure retirement, the rights of everyone to a job, a guaranteed minimum income, and an interesting job.

Readers sophisticated about comparative social systems will recognize the strong trend toward democratic socialism in this kind of thinking. American youth do not use the word "socialism" much, but it seems clear that if the present youth generation could have its way, the American cultural revolution would take us in the direction of social systems such as exist in New Zealand, Scandinavia, and to a lesser degree in parts of Western Europe and in Japan.

Youth and Cultural Revolution

In Chapter 1 we introduced three investigators' interpretations of the cultural revolution: Daniel Yankelovich, Margaret Mead, and William Glasser. Yankelovich sees a fundamental shift from valuing artifice to valuing what is natural—what he calls "the new naturalism." Mead sees another shift. Her concept of prefiguration culture concerns the young superimposing new cultural patterns on the old and reversing the direction of education: as the young, adapted to the new, show a wisdom about contemporary situations which their elders lack, parents have no resort but to learn from their children. Glasser argues that we are entering a historical stage in which the goal of mere economic survival seems much less important than doing something interesting with one's life—his concept of civilized identity society.

It would appear that what evidence we have about the direction of cultural change, particularly as revealed in studies of youth values, at least partially supports each of these three interpretations. All around us we can observe youth rejecting the artificiality and hyprocrisy embodied in old-culture standards. Evidently youth see through what is occurring better than a majority of their parents and grandparents. And apparently achieving a satisfactory identity, or self-fulfillment, has come to have priority over the older notion of "work hard to get ahead."

From the beginning of this book we have made cultural revolution one of our major themes. We have also suggested that historically cultural revolutions have occurred without political revolutions and with no more than incidental violence. The direction in which the new values is taking us, however, sooner or later will require fundamental institutional change. As a people, Americans have managed basic cultural change and its attendant institutional change without violence (as in the "sexual revolution"). The one exception is the nation's inability to cope with the issues which led to the Civil War. The question now before us all is whether our economic, military, and governmental bureaucracies will acquire enough internal flexibility to revolutionize themselves peacefully. If not, we can expect only cultural disintegration without concomitant culture building—and social chaos possibly accompanied by serious violence.

Much of what we have said about the new values, and the continuing counterculture of the seventies, may be invalidated by a series of disastrous events which may have effects now wholly unseen on the values of the young. We are thinking of America's domestic problems: lack of faith in the system induced by the Watergate scandals, President Ford's pardon of Richard Nixon, and an economic system which now appears less viable with each passing month. Further, events abroad, particularly the prospect of mass starvation, will profoundly affect the thinking of American youth. Out of all this may emerge extreme cognitive dissonance: a profound disrespect for law but at the same time possibly greater concern for the unfortunate.

YOUTH AND TODAY'S SCHOOLS

We will say much less in this section than many readers will feel is pertinent to issues raised in the chapter. Certain omissions from this section are intended to avoid their overlapping topics to be developed in Parts II and III.

We assume throughout the book that social analysts who argue that the United States—and probably most of the world—is undergoing a fundamental cultural revolution are probably right. To get a balanced picture of an authentic cultural revolution we need to think in terms of decades or perhaps even a century or more.

During a period of cultural revolution, unless the revolution is irresistably pressured to run through its course in two or three decades, schisms are almost certain to appear. Primarily they will occur between those who are aware of the nature of the social change occurring, who know it cannot be stopped but perhaps can be guided; and those who see no inevitable fundamental change, who feel that basically traditional patterns can be maintained, and who regard people talking about revolutionary change as subversive.

This section should be interpreted against this backdrop: a large, old-culture, relatively conservative majority of Middle Americans; and a rapidly expanding opposing group, liberal to leftish, generally highly educated, who are aware of a cultural revolution and want to guide it in their own preferred directions, which in this country is toward liberal democracy and a more-or-less socialized economy. This opposing group is the counterculture—whether we are referring to the 1960s or 1970s. Conservative reactions of a decade or so in length will slow its motion, but, theoretically, it cannot be stopped short of installing a Fascist police state, which still would probably be only a temporary barrier to the cultural revolution.

In general terms, the most valuable role of the schools would be to: (1) serve as a brake on overly enthusiastic young radicals who want to push change faster than the culture can absorb it, and (2) liberalize the conservative majority of students, so they can take in stride the changes they will have to accept during their lifetimes. We feel that these twin roles can best be accomplished by establishing an interactive dialogue between liberal/democratic and conservative/authoritarian youth. We will now discuss some negative effects of the school system as it is today.

School-Produced Negative Alienation

As before, we use the expression *negative alienation* to refer to alienation that is unconstructive, leads to anomie, and from anomie often to apathy or to senseless violence.

In what we are about to say concerning school-produced alienation of youth, readers should understand that we are not referring to all administrations or all teachers. We are referring to what may be a majority.

School-induced alienation is of two broad types. One is conspicuous in the sense that students complain about the practices that cause it and sometimes revolt against it with student strikes, sit-ins, vandalism, and arson. We will call alienation of which students are aware *self-conscious alienation*. The second type of alienation, much more serious, is caused by school practices that students do not see as alienating because they are so accustomed to them. They take them for granted. We will call this type of alienation *unrecognized alienation*. Because it is unrecognized, and not susceptible to reduction by "blowing off steam," it may easily drive students over the brink to a state of anomie.

Self-Conscious Alienation

We will treat the first kind of alienation under three heads.

Alienation against authoritarianism   Schools have traditionally been authoritarian. Teachers seldom move up the promotion ladder if they are burdened with democratic inclinations. O. J. Harvey's research, reported at the end of Chapter 3, indicates more than 90 percent of school superintendents are System 1 personality types. Teachers are not a whole lot better. According to Harvey's research 50+ percent of his sample are also System 1 types. These data are for public schools and grade levels from K through 12. We have no statistics at hand for higher education.

Alienation against restrictive rules   As suggested previously, college and university students have won a great deal in their fight for personal freedom. The concept of "the student as nigger," no longer describes the relationship between administrators and students, or administrator/ faculty coalitions and students as well as it did in the sixties. However, much remains to be accomplished at the college level.

But secondary school students do not fare as well. They are placed in courses without their consent. They must cope with written excuses, hall passes, special permissions to make almost every move. It is the policy of most schools to try to know where every student is every minute of the school day. Students are under constant surveillance, in some schools even when they go to the toilet. Obviously not all schools are this bad, but too many are.

Alienation against pointless subjects   Questions have been raised by professional educators about useless baggage in the curriculums of almost all schools, from the primary grades through the university. Until the end of general passivity among students, that is, until the sixties, students obediently enrolled in all the required or recommended courses no matter how badly they were taught or how useless they seemed. Although there was a great deal of low-key grumbling, of course, apparently it had existed among a few students prior to the sixties. Students are no longer convinced that education should be a form of disciplining, of strengthening the will to see unpleasant tasks through to the end.

Unrecognized Alienation

We have yet to show how, unknown to most students, most contemporary curriculums are "setting up" students for critical psychological problems later on by promoting unrecognized inconsistencies. Schools do this in a variety of ways, some direct and some indirect. We will treat this question under five heads.

Avoidance of cultural study   The particular kind of alienation we are most concerned with in this book is alienation of individuals and groups from the culture in which they live—not some small segment of the culture, but the entire complex pattern of attitudes, values, beliefs, myths, and purported knowledge. We have stated that if the overall culture fails to make sense, seems contradictory and irrational, then those who are seeking a comfortable psychological environment will not find it by trying to identify with the culture.

Our first point is that public schools do not now hold teaching about the culture as a central goal. Rather, schools tend to avoid it. Students are required to take a certain minimal amount of social studies and in some schools contemporary literature. The required social studies courses are usually·American and world history and civics, with the frequent addition of a semester of "American problems" for seniors. No social studies core integrating sociology, social psychology, and anthropology aims at exposing in reasonably accurate form the culture's inconsistencies.

Falsified content   It is also a matter of common knowledge among professional educators that most teaching materials used in social studies courses, or other courses that carry social studies content, are at the very best grossly oversimplified. Typically, it is both oversimplified and to a degree falsified, if not by adding untrue material, then by selective omissions, so that readers get a highly distorted picture. Further, interspersed with what may be somewhat factual content, we commonly find in textbooks and other materials designed for any grade level below university graduate school a generous amount of editorializing—the textbook author's interpretation of what is good and bad, right and wrong, ugly and beautiful.

It is not a matter of conjecture that content dealing with the culture is largely untrue. Howard K. Beale found this to be the case in the 1920s.[12] Arthur Walworth, after comparing how the most popular American, Mexican, Spanish, British, and German textbooks described the wars in which the United States and each of these countries were antagonists, found that the books of each country presented a picture so ethnocentric that one could hardly recognize them as referring to the same wars.[13]

Since then we have had many reports on the distortions and literal untruthfulness of much content taught in school. One of the best known and highly praised of these reports is that of the late Jules Henry.[14] After much study of school practices and curriculum content, Henry's overall conclusion emerges in the following quotation:

An intellectually creative child may fail, for example, in social studies, simply because he cannot understand the stupidities he is taught

[12] Howard K. Beale, *Are American Teachers Free?* New York: Charles Scribner's Sons, 1937.

[13] Arthur Walworth, *School Histories at War.* Cambridge, Mass.: Harvard University Press, 1938.

[14] Jules Henry, *Culture Against Man.* New York: Random House, Inc., 1963. See especially Chaps. 7 and 8.

to believe as "fact." He may even end up agreeing with his teachers that he is "stupid" in social studies. Learning social studies is, to no small extent, whether in elementary school or the university, learning to be stupid. . . . What idiot believes in the "law of supply and demand," for example? But the children who do tend to *become* idiots, and learning to be an idiot is part of growing up! Or, as Camus put it, learning to be absurd.[15]

In addition to being handicapped by the falsification of content prepared expressly for student reading, teachers who would like to acquaint students with an undistorted picture of the culture are further handicapped by the censorship of much supplementary reading they might like to assign.

Contradictory content   In this writer's doctoral study of economic content in textbooks designed for grades 7 through 12, he found no more than a half dozen books (out of roughly one hundred analyzed) in which the authors did not contradict themselves by making assertions which were mutually exclusive. For example, it was apparent that many of the textbook authors did not know the difference between classical, laissez-faire economic theory, and the then new but widely mentioned Keynesian economics; nor had they even a primitive understanding of how a socialist economy functions. The writer frequently encountered a statement on one page asserting the universal truth of the assumptions behind classical economics and on the next page a statement asserting the same about a controlled economy.[16]

In studying these books for economic content, other social studies areas, such as political science and sociology, were also perused. Although the frequency of contradiction in noneconomic social studies content was not tabulated, the writer found about as much contradiction in other areas as in economics.

To understand the total extent of contradictory material that students encounter, it is necessary to consider the views of teachers—which in the classroom tend to override textbook content. Although any teacher will occasionally tell students contradictory things (after all, who is completely free of inconsistency?), many teachers this writer has watched seemed so confused about the subject they were teaching that they tended to contradict themselves several times every period.

Omission of epistemological study   Epistemology is that branch of philosophy that has to do with how one goes about finding what is true. It is a study of methods by which one can obtain the knowledge he needs to solve problems. The tendency of most teachers is to omit almost entirely

[15] Henry, p. 287.
[16] Maurice P. Hunt, *The Teaching of Economics in the American High School,* unpublished doctoral dissertation. Columbus: Ohio State University, 1948.

this kind of study. We are aware that professional educators have been arguing for most of a century that it is more important to teach students how to find out than to teach them what is so at the time. But most teachers receive no education in college in epistemology.

Teachers are able to show students how to find definitions in a dictionary, how to look up subjects in reference books or encyclopedias, and where to find materials in the school library. These are skills which can be memorized, which have a certain usefulness, but which have no bearing on epistemology, or the methodology of getting knowledge.

Educational taxonomy   Taxonomy refers to the "science of classification." Popularized first in biology, the idea of classifying behavior has invaded the field of education. Benjamin S. Bloom of the University of Chicago and a group of associates have done the spadework in educational taxonomy.[17] They classified human behavior into three broad categories: the cognitive, the affective (emotional), and the psychomotor. Under each of these heads, behavior is broken down into small segments on a scale ranging from simple to complex.

Cognitive learning is intellectual learning ranging from the memorizing of discrete facts to the understanding of principles or generalizations. Affective learning is learning how to express emotions appropriately. Psychomotor learning is skill learning, such as, how to throw a ball.

Teachers who like or are compelled to develop long lists of objectives to guide their teaching have been attracted by the seeming tidiness of the three-way classification of Bloom and associates. But classroom teachers typically treat the tridimensional taxonomy as if students were composed of three disparate parts. They devote periods to intellectual learning, other periods to inducing students to emote, and still others to requiring them to make motions. Students can become thoroughly baffled by being treated as if they were made in segments.

Guaranteed Anomie

Let us now take a look at what schools are doing to children and youth. We assume that, given the present disorganized state of the culture, students come to school already confused about the cultural milieu.

First, we perpetuate this confusion by giving students a very limited opportunity to study broad cultural patterns.

Second, we compound this confusion by telling, or requiring students to read, falsified accounts of what the broad cultural pattern is.

Third, we compound confusion to the point of hopeless perplexity by communicating to students different, and contradictory, accounts of what is happening in the culture.

[17] Benjamin S. Bloom (ed.), *Taxonomy of Educational Objectives Handbook I: Cognitive Domain*. New York: David McKay Company, Inc., 1956.

Fourth, we fragmentize them by treating them as if they came to us in three separate parts.

The only logical conclusion we can draw from this is that if students have mild symptoms of anomie when they come under the control of the school, by the time they leave school their self-structure, their sense of identity, is so fractured that, like Humpty Dumpty, no one can put them back together again. If they feel alienated from a confusing culture when they enter school, when they leave, the culture will seem far more incomprehensible. Education, *as we now practice it,* may well be the most ingenious device ever invented for producing anomie to the point of mental illness.

FUTURE DIRECTIONS: FOCUS ON MORAL VALUES

A central interest of virtually all children and youth is moral values. Because confusion over values is produced by school practices such as we have described (and the numerous conflicting value systems thrust at the young by parents, peers, church, youth groups, and other sources), children and youth wage their own battles with themselves and others to reach adulthood with some sort of guide to live by.

In addition to presenting cultural study, which helps acquaint the young with the welter of conflicting values around them, it strikes us that teachers have an obligation to acquaint students with systematic attempts that have been made to describe people according to value systems they have found both workable and unworkable, or desirable and undesirable. For example, O. J. Harvey's approach to personality typing could well be a part of the study of every high school student in some school course.

Even more useful might be the stages of moral development described by Lawrence Kohlberg of Harvard University. Kolhberg and some of his colleagues studied the development of moral thinking of a group of fifty males over a period of eighteen years. Although describing moral stages in a fashion as neat as Kohlberg has done may be as arbitrary as dividing a pie, they make a highly provocative starting point for the study of what moral growth can entail.

Kohlberg decided that his data warranted describing six stages, each merging into another until the top stage is reached. The two earliest stages he calls the *preconventional level;* the middle stages, *the conventional level;* and the two final stages, the *postconventional level.*

The Preconventional level

Stage 1 is the earliest stage in a child's life at which we can find guiding values. Few educated adults would want to see children remain at this level of maturity. Small children judge the goodness or badness of an act, almost entirely by whether it will result in reward or punishment. Hedonistic self-interest is the guide. Kohlberg refers to this outlook as a "punishment and obedience orientation."

Stage 2 reflects a somewhat broader knowledge of what the social world is like. At this level, the child has come to understand the meaning of quid pro quo or, to use Kohlberg's language, "you scratch my back and I'll scratch yours." The child has learned that he can gain benefits for himself by satisfying other people's needs. We have all observed the time when a child of four or five begins giving candy or goodies to others, expecting something in return, even if only a smile and a "thank you." Kohlberg refers to this stage as the "instrumentalist relativist orientation" —obviously not meaning the mature relativist view we described in the Prologue.

The Conventional Level

At Stage 3, a person begins to equate good behavior with that which pleases others. The young person has come to understand fairly well the expectations of others, and has become reasonably clever at knowing how to please. The person at this level tends to have stereotyped images of what others expect and he works at conforming to these images. Kohlberg refers to Stage 3 as the "interpersonal concordance or 'good boy-nice girl' orientation."

As Stage 4, the developing person becomes quite concerned with the concept of authority and rules which can be regarded as "fixed." The person has learned the concept of duty, and has come to value showing respect for authority and maintaining the social status quo for its own sake. Kohlberg refers to this stage as the " 'law and order' orientation."

We should note that many persons, possibly a majority in our culture, never get past the conventional level. We should also note that Kohlberg's Stage 4 has elements in common with Harvey's System 1 types.

The Postconventional Level

At Stage 5, a person has begun to think in terms of "general individual rights and in terms of standards that have been critically examined and agreed upon by the whole society." There is concern for what is consensually agreed upon but the person is also beginning to cherish his or her own personalized values and opinion. Stage 5 differs from Stage 4 in that although there is still concern for legalism, there is also a questioning of established rules and willingness to seek changes in them. Kohlberg suggests that this is the "official" morality espoused by the United States Government and the Constitution. In our opinion, a majority of people never reach this stage, although they might if they were educated differently. Kohlberg calls this stage the "social-contract legalistic orientation."

Stage 6, in our present culture, seems reserved for a comparatively few. The good is defined in terms of independently but carefully thought out ethical principles, which, to use Kohlberg's phrase, are "based on logical comprehensiveness, universality and consistency." Moral values at this level are abstract rather than concrete like the Ten Commandments. Here is conscience operating at its highest level. The person's fundamental guide is furthering the dignity and well-being of human beings as individuals. There is the suggestion that, in spite of the abstractness and universality of moral principles held at this level (the "golden rule" is an example), moral decisions in concrete instances are situational, that is, relativistic in a positive sense. Only at the top level can morality be considered open-ended. One notes a relationship between this stage and Harvey's System 4 types.

These stages are, of course, analytical constructs. Nevertheless, they apparently describe pretty well what the course of development is, even though it may be a very rare person who achieves and remains consistently at Stage 6. [18]

As to how teachers can best help the young mature morally, we are in general agreement with Kohlberg that, first, the school situation itself must exemplify moral justice; we would add that the testing of moral values in a democratic classroom, with students being encouraged to reflect critically, is another requirement. High school students are old enough to read Kohlberg's own writing on the subject.

STUDY QUESTIONS

1. Seymour Lipset argues that there is no generation gap of any significance in the United States, but there is a significant gap between the values and beliefs of college and university students and the rest of the population. What do you think is the basis for this contention?
2. In what sense might it be said that there is a generation gap in the United States? If such exists, is there reason to be concerned about it? Is there a "gap" between you and your parents?
3. Chapter 4 portrays college students majoring in one or more of the humanities and achieving a high academic level in a very favorable light. Do you think this is an indefensible kind of favoritism? Would you call it an "elitist" position? What category or categories of youth do you feel would be likely to make the best national leaders in the 1890s and 1990s?

[18] Lawrence Kohlberg, with Phillip Whitten, "Understanding the Hidden Curriculum," Learning, December 1972, pp. 10–14. See also Kohlberg's "Moral Development and the New Social Studies," Social Education, Vol. 37, May 1973, pp. 368–395.

4. Assume a situation—any situation—in which a drastic change in cultural values, beliefs, and actions is required. Do you think this change is most likely to be achieved by radicals who prefer to work outside the main center of the culture (the Establishment)? Or do you feel the changes can best be made by leaders of change working through the Establishment? If you chose the radical approach, do you think there is ever a situation in which violence might be justified? Does the mainstream culture regularly use violence to achieve its aims?

5. Why do you think so much more research has been done on learning the characteristics of college/university youth than on out-of-school youth? If more were known about out-of-school youth do you think it would change the picture presented in this chapter?

6. The categorization of "blue-collar straights" was based on a number of scraps of evidence, rather than any major formal research. Do you feel it is valid? Would you use a different scheme of categorization?

7. What comes to your mind when you see the expression, "counterculture"? No matter what time in history one chooses to think of, would there be a counterculture? Would a counterculture always consist mainly of secondary or college students? Where would you place dissident minority youth with little formal education?

8. For organizational purposes, the main part of the chapter was divided between the decade of the sixties and the decade of the seventies. Does this kind of organization place too much emphasis on differences between these two periods? Do you think there are significant differences?

9. Under the general head negative alienation, various examples are given. These were meant only to be examples. How many more examples can you add to the list?

10. In the section discussing whether certain counterculture beliefs that emerged in the sixties are likely to survive (both among the young and adult liberals) through the seventies and beyond, the text interpretation is based largely on short-range trends because of the difficulty in projecting current situations into the future. Which counterculture ideas that might be considered "new thinking" or "new emphases" do you think are likely to survive? Why?

11. How would you describe your personal life style? Do you consider yourself a free, or liberated, person? If so, of what kind?

12. The writer makes a distinction between self-conscious alienation and invisible alienation. Has your reading of the book so far made you become conscious of any of your own previously invisible alienation? Has it made you aware of inconsistencies you did not know before that you had?

13. It is obvious from the final section in the chapter that this writer is quite critical of certain public school practices. What other criticisms would you guess the author would have of the schools? Has any of the criticism of education so far presented made you feel the author, like Ivan Illich, would want to abolish formal schooling altogether?

ANNOTATED BIBLIOGRAPHY

Flacks, Richard W., "The Liberated Generation: An Exploration of the Roots of Student Protest," *The Journal of Social Issues*, July 1967.

One of the better articles on the characteristics of student activists and their families from a special issue of the JSI on youth. Activists come mainly from upper-middle-class professional (not business) families, with both parents well educated and usually liberal. Student protesters tend to get higher grades than nonprotesters and to form a kind of intellectual elite on campus.

Gerzon, Mark, *The Whole World Is Watching: A Young Man Looks at Youth's Dissent.* New York: Viking Press, 1969.

Gerzon was a Harvard undergraduate when he wrote this book explaining the reasons for, and the nature of, the youth movement. Written from the view of a young dissident, this book is one of the most penerating and objective available.

Goodman, Paul. *Growing Up Absurd: Problems of Youth in the Organized System.* New York: Random House, Inc., 1961.

In this classic, called by different reviewers both the worst and the best on the subject of youth growing up in American culture, Goodman assumes that there are innate needs in human beings and when the young try to fulfill them, they are blocked at every turn because the whole of American civilization, with its emphasis on conformity, institutionalized stupidity, fixation on social climbing and acquring wealth, meaningless work, etc., denies all the most fundamental of human needs.

Gottlieb, David, "Poor Youth: A Study in Forced Alienation," *The Journal of Social Issues,* Spring 1969.

This entire issue is on alienated youth, but Gottlieb's essay is something special. Instead of treating alienated upper-middle-class youth, he focuses on the kinds of alienation afflicting those at the most impoverished level and reaches an unorthodox conclusion: the very poor are not nearly as hostile toward the affluent middle class as they are envious.

Hampden-Turner, Charles, *Radical Man: The Process of Psycho-Social Development,* Cambridge, Mass.: Schenkman Publishing Company, 1970.

Hampden-Turner, drawing on his own studies of psychosocial development plus those of Lawrence Kohlberg, develops a model of the radical left personality. A humanist highly critical of behaviorist psychology and mechanistic social science, he covers a broad range of topics in this book, but his portrayal of the New Left student is especially relevant to Chapter 4.

Keniston, Kenneth, "The Agony of the Counter-Culture," in Grant S. McClellan, compiler, *American Youth in a Changing Culture.* The Reference Shelf, Vol. 44, No. 3. New York: The H. W. Wilson Company, 1972.

Keniston's article is perhaps the best in an anthology of first-rate essays. Keniston argues convincingly that there are two separate and irreconcilable cultures in the United States—the traditional old culture and a now largely demoralized but authentic counterculture.

Keniston, Kenneth, *Young Radicals: Notes on Committed Youth.* New York: Harcourt Brace Jovanovich, Inc., 1968.

Keniston reports his research on leaders in the "Vietnam Summer Project" which convinced him of the depth of commitment of these young people to community organizing and peace work as part of the more sweeping objective of cultural change.

Kornbluth, Jesse (ed.), *Notes from the New Underground*. New York: Viking Press, 1968.

One of the better means of finding out what the counterculture of the sixties was about is to read selections from the then extensive underground press of both high school and college students. The author finds both folly and wisdom in the call for social change of the kind desired by the counterculture.

Libarle, Marc, and Tom Seligson (eds.), *The High School Revolutionaries*. New York: Random House, Inc., 1970.

The editors, both teachers in New York City when they prepared this book, decided that too much had been written by ill-informed adults about high school dissenters. During the summer of 1969 they traveled throughout the country and talked to high school students and asked many students to write candid essays on how they really viewed things. They also collected other documentary material, such as newspaper clippings. This is the best book we have seen which is almost entirely written by high school students.

Luce, Phillip A., *The New Left Today: America's Trojan Horse*, Washington, D.C.: The Capitol Hill Press, 1971.

At one time a self-proclaimed active member of the New Left, Luce turned against it on the ground of its—to him—totalitarian character. Luce's writing has appeared in Buckley's *National Review* and in the *Reader's Digest*. Worthwhile reading for those interested in how persons of the authoritarian left can shift smoothly to the authoritarian right—in the name of "individualism."

Newfield, Jack, *A Prophetic Minority*, Introduction by Michael Harrington. New York: New American Library, 1966; also Signet.

One of the founders of Students for a Democratic Society (SDS) writes on the early history of the organization. He not only describes events but how divergent philosophies of various activists influenced the movement.

Yablonsky, Lewis, *Robopaths*, Indianapolis: The Bobbs-Merrill Company, Inc., 1972.

Yablonsky describes the development of pathological robots (Robopaths) so dehumanized by technology that they lack compassion and even the ability to communicate at a *human* level. He compares this group with humanistic, optimally alienated, democratically committed social critics. If the robopaths gain control, the outcome can only be automated genocide for all others. The robopaths would seem to be much of Middle America, as led by radical conservatives.

Yankelovich, Daniel, "The New Naturalism," *Saturday Review*, April 1, 1972.

In this brief article, Yankelovich, drawing upon his studies of the values of college youth, achieves a tour de force of sorts by integrating in a single coherent and plausible theme virtually all the strands of the youth movement and the broader cultural revolution he feels is occurring. (See Chapter 1 for a description of Yankelovich's interpretation of the cultural revolution.)

part

II

CULTURAL AREAS
OF SPECIAL CONCERN
TO TEACHERS

The following introduction is intended to explain the rationale of Part II in more detail than was possible in the Preface or Prologue and to discuss briefly some major shifts in the views of many social scientists, the understanding of which is essential to the cultural analysis in Part II. Each chapter in this section has basically the same purpose and general format. Part II is designed to perform several functions for prospective or in-service teachers.

First, it is designed to help them get an even more thoroughgoing picture of the attitudes, values, beliefs, knowledge, pseudoknowledge, and myths which make up American culture; but contrary to the discussion of the same subjects interspersed throughout Part I, we will link opinion patterns with *specific* areas of the culture. These problem areas are in at least some sense "closed areas of culture," as explained in Chapter 1. Therefore, the first section of each of these chapters will illuminate thought patterns where confusion and dissonance are at a comparatively high level, along with verboten or tabooed subjects of thought.

Second, the central part of each chapter will consist of the analysis of one explicit issue within the problem area to which the chapter is addressed. The issue selected for in-depth exploration obviously will not include all the important issues; it was selected because of its probable interest to readers and because of its critical implications for education. Each issue is introduced in the form of an "outrageous hypothesis," on the assumption that this is an increasingly needed way of organizing social science data (see the discussion of this in the Prologue). If readers are bothered by the expression, "outrageous," they can substitute some milder term such as "controversial," "unpopular," "unusual," or "far out."

Third, each chapter in Part II will include in a final section what this writer sees as some of the more important implications for education of the ideological and institutional structure related to the area of culture under analysis. One basis for selecting these particular chapters for Part II is that all the cultural areas represented tell us a great deal about what transpires in school and why.

The central purpose of each of the following chapters is to help students understand better the culture (and world) in which they live, and which as future teachers they dare not be ignorant of except at the peril of being isolated, "know nothing" instructors. However, we have designed these chapters with another important purpose in mind. *The chapters in Part II are intended to illustrate one demonstrably effective method of teaching students about their culture.* The first section of each chapter, on belief patterns, is intended to help prospective teachers understand the "raw material" of all effective education, that is, the kinds of foolish or contradictory ideas floating around in the culture that students bring to school with them. To do any kind of a job, teachers have to have some idea of the "mental furniture" their students have acquired from home, community adults, their peers, and the mass media.

From this usually confused and inconsistent mental furniture, teachers or students can select hypotheses for class study; or, often better, teachers can introduce assertions sharply relevant to student beliefs, *but controversial enough to produce cognitive dissonance in students and hope that motivation will arise to produce serious study.* This is a major reason for studying culture through the medium of highly controversial but testable assertions. Teachers have used this approach at least since Socrates. Sometimes it is known as "playing the devil's advocate."

In developing these chapters as in the previous ones, there is a risk this writer does not know how to eliminate. The risk is in making wrong assessments about what prevailing cultural attitudes, values, beliefs, myths, and purported knowledge are. The writer has read as much of the literature on this subject as time permitted. Some of the writing on American ideology is based on careful empirical research, using the best available testing devices (including in-depth interviewing). Some writers use a more intuitive approach; they size up popular thought patterns on the basis of long experience in studying people by listening to them, reading what they write (as in letters to newspaper editors), or inferring what kind of underlying belief must have been present to motivate a given action.

There is also evidence to be had from public opinion polls conducted by the Gallup and Harris and other less known, but perhaps equally reliable, polling organizations. However, we have reservations about public opinion polling as a means of uncovering the most cherished and stable beliefs of many respondents who, we are inclined to think, often either give the first answer that comes to mind or the answer they think the interviewer wants to hear. We have drawn on all the sources available to us at this time and hope we present a picture which is at least somewhere near correct. For the most part, we have not tried to document many of the assertions presented, although where documentation has seemed useful we have used it.

One last but highly important point: In marshaling evidence around the "outrageous hypotheses" stated in these chapters, we have made no attempt to *prove* a hypothesis true or false. In each case the evidence we have presented seems to support at least somewhat the hypothesis. *Our main interest in developing these chapters has been to illustrate a method of approach, not to collect irrefutable evidence in support of an argument.*

A MODERN APPROACH TO CULTURAL ANALYSIS

For readers to understand well the organization and thought content of Part II, they need some background in what has been apparently a fundamental shift in the outlook of many social scientists, particularly those coming into prominence in the 1960s and their proteges now being educated for the future. We have, in effect, a "new social science," which relies on a different model of cultural reality than was commonly used in the United States prior to the late fifties and early sixties.

Because sociology, in its shift from old to new patterns, has received more attention than other social sciences, we will focus on it. Readers should understand that we define sociology very broadly, however. We particularly see sociology, anthropology, and social psychology as overlapping and interacting core subjects in the social sciences, whose general methodological approach can be applied in political science, economics, history, and human geography.

The Old View: Functionalism (Static Homeostasis)

American sociology has been dominated by a school of thought usually called *functionalism* or, occasionally, *structuralism*. Functionalism is inherently concerned with equilibrium maintenance. Historically, functionalists have tended to be conservative in the sense that they have directed their analysis at change-oriented or disturbing elements of culture and sought ways of eliminating these disturbing factors in the interests of equilibrium, system maintenance, or, in more familiar language, preserving the status quo.

During the past decade or two, numerous dissenters in sociology, both young and old, have singled out Talcott Parsons as perhaps best exemplifying the functionalist approach and also as being the most conservative of all prominent sociologists. Sociologist Alvin Gouldner is usually mentioned as one of the leading persons to have vigorously pressed the attack against functionalism, particularly the Parsonian version, during the 1960s and into the 1970s. The split between these two schools, functionalists and nonfunctionalists, has developed enough intensity that annual meetings of the American Sociological Association sometimes display a major schism.

The antifunctionalists have been given various names—the sociological left, sociological radicals, and the Sociology Liberation Movement (the latter preferred by the left-wing caucus of sociologists). The nature of the two opposing outlooks can best be explained by beginning with a schematic representation (Figure 1) of two models of a national cultural pattern.

The first diagram in Figure 1 represents a societal model as viewed

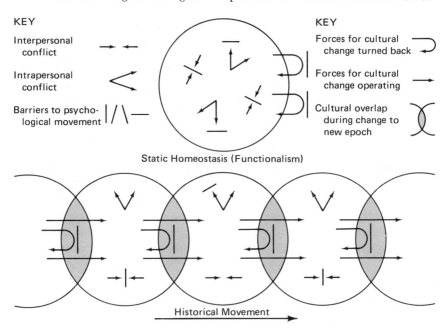

FIGURE 1. Two opposing models of a national cultural pattern.

by traditional functionalists. Functionalists conceive of society as a system of interrelated parts; no one part can be understood in isolation from the rest, and a change in one element tends to force rearrangement of all other elements if equilibrium is to be restored. Thus, functionalism is an example of field theory, which was mentioned in the Prologue in connection with relativism. However, the field concept of conservative functionalists is one of *static homeostasis*, that is, it is assumed the field can and should be managed so that major upsetting forces will be suppressed and the field will maintain a more-or-less steady state over a long time.

The single circle of the functionalist model represents a society, social order, nation, or national culture. Forces that would tend to move the society into a basically different pattern are indicated by arrows extending from the circle but curving back upon themselves. This curving back means the pressures for basic change have been blunted or redirected by barriers so they exert no lasting pull on the system exemplified by the circle. Within the system, interpersonal conflict is blunted by barriers between the opposing individuals or groups. Intrapersonal conflict is shown as being resolved by blunting or sealing off one of the opposing goals felt by individuals so as to eliminate their inner conflicts. (See Key.) The consequence is that even though there are continuous conflicts or other disturbing factors, counterforces (barriers devised by those who control the system) will keep it in a steady or status quo state, hence the model name of static homeostasis.

In traditional functionalism, an act is *functional* if it contributes to the stability of the system; it is *dysfunctional* if it produces imbalances and disorder. (One can also use the expressions, positive functions and negative functions.)

The New Sociology (Dynamic Homeostasis)

The second societal model in Figure 1 represents the views of the anti-functionalists. The overlapping circles each represent a society during a historical epoch. An epoch is a period of time in which a society is *relatively* stable, and, up to a point, can be described adequately by the single-circle functionalist model. During each epoch the society is in a *somewhat* steady state, describable in terms of *somewhat* static homeostasis. But note that not all the arrows representing forces for cultural change that extend from the circles turn back upon themselves; some do, but more push on ahead. These are the forces for change that cannot be overridden and that sooner or later will induce the breakdown of the relative stability of one epoch and push the culture into a new and very different epoch. In fact, the new epoch may be so different that the shift from one epoch to another can be described as nothing less than revolutionary. In time, however, the new epoch too will be subjected to enough disequilibrating forces to produce a new crisis and the movement to a new epoch, and so on, throughout history.

In the dynamic model, note that some internal conflicts, both inter- and intrapersonal, are resolved, as theoretically they *all* are under static homeostasis, but others are not. They remain as unresolved conflicts and produce the motivation for change that dissolves a given epoch and leads to the next. In the dynamic model, therefore, some internal social turbu- lance is considered normal even during the most stable times.

Members of the Sociology Liberation Movement are concerned about societal conflict and the evolution of one epoch into another, but *they do not oppose conflict and change per se in the interests of preserving a conservative, relatively static culture.* They see challenge in change and the possibility of building a culture with different values and ideologies, which, to them, may be a far better system for human life than those that have preceded it.

Although this explanation, including Figure 1, is an oversimplifica- tion, it should help students see the major outlines of what the argument is about. One oversimplification we should note particularly is that func- tional analysis, analysis of the system in terms of positive and negative functions, may be used effectively by liberals as well as by conservatives. The present author favors the dynamic, change-oriented model because, to him, it fits the facts better. But in the book, we will use functional, or semifunctional, analysis on occasion because it is a useful conceptual tool.[1]

The Dynamic Model and Part II

Although most sociologists, whether functionalists or members of the reform movement, make hypothesis testing central to their methodological approach, members of the Sociology Liberation Movement are most likely to employ outrageous hypotheses as primary tools simply because such hypotheses pose alternatives to our present institutional structure.

The Institutionalist View

Also highly useful to readers of Part II should be an understanding of what we will call *institutionalist social science.* This probably involves little more than a demonstration here of a modern conception of the breadth of pertinent evidence—what all should be included as proper data in soci- ological, political, and economic analyses.

[1] Among the best references on present sociological turmoil is an issue of the *American Journal of Sociology* (Vol. 78, No. 1, 1972) devoted entirely to "Varieties of Political Expression in Sociology." We call especial attention to Seymour Lipset and Everett Ladd's article, "The Politics of American Sociolo- gists." Whether functionalists or not, the vast majority of sociologists are on the liberal side of the political spectrum.

Since the beginning of the development of separate social science disciplines as school subjects, most social scientists have tried to maintain a kind of atomism, an attempt to keep more-or-less strictly separate each new subject as it developed. This began in ancient Greece with the first writing in history and political science, although the Greeks were much more interdisciplinary than social scientists came to be in the late nineteenth and first half of the twentieth century.

Particularly in the twentieth century, the claim has been made by many social scientists that to develop and preserve the "integrity" of the various social science disciplines they must be kept strictly separate. Even the nineteenth century tendency to integrate political science and economics into the single subject of political economy came to be taboo.

The line of thinking begun in the nineteenth century by Peirce, James, Dewey, and further pursued by those influenced by them (e.g., historians Charles and Mary Beard, Carl Becker, Frederic Duncalf; master of jurisprudence, Oliver Wendell Holmes II; sociologist Charles Horton Cooley; and economist Thorstein Veblen) is, if anything, an integral part of the "new social science."

It is unfortunate that institutionalism, as the label for a school of thought, has been associated largely with Thorstein Veblen and the subject of economics. What Veblen and a succession of institutionalist economists had in mind as the best way of viewing economics was virtually identical to what all the others mentioned above had in mind in connection with their own specialties.

One idea of the institutionalists is that developing a high order of technical proficiency, in connection with short-range objectives, is a misguided emphasis. Rather, much more attention should be given to long-range decision making within the context of the total social system. Wherever a long-range trend can be established, irrespective of the area of life in which it operates, it must be kept in the picture in evaluating the role of any particular subject area, such as history, political science, or economics. Institutionalists are therefore both change and future oriented.

Further, the institutionalists are always concerned with underlying assumptions whether openly stated or implied. Many of the implied assumptions of social scientists relate to the "nature of human nature." At the same time, most social scientists have lacked the background in historical and comparative philosophy and psychology to be able to defend or even understand very well their assumptions about the nature of humans. As Gruchy, writing about institutionalist economics in particular, says, institutionalist economists treat human beings as ". . . purposive individuals living in a changing social world."[2]

2 Allan G. Gruchy, *Contemporary Economic Thought: The Contribution of Neo-Institutional Economics,* Clifton, N.J.: Augustus M. Kelley, Publishers, 1972, p. vii.

The social-philosophical commitments of the institutionalists also are revealed in their commitment to humanistic, democratic, and relativistic values. Gruchy suggests that "The economics that is being fashioned today in the western world is reflective of the new era of planned participatory democracies that is unfolding."[3] Further, in discussing the difference between orthodox and institutionalist economics, Gruchy says they are "... in essence two very different ways of comprehending economic and other reality, the one evolutionary and the other static and cross-sectional."[4] Here, Gruchy is referring to the contrast between the concepts of static and dynamic homeostasis as we described them earlier in this introduction.

It will have occurred to readers before now that this writer is an institutionalist. This overall view has been reflected in the book up to this point, but will show through even more clearly in the chapters of Part II. We will handle the social and educational analysis of Part II from the assumption of an ever-changing world and will draw upon any data that seem pertinent, no matter what their subject field of origin, in an interdisciplinary fashion. And at all times our commitment to democratic, humanistic values should show through.

[3] Gruchy, p. viii.
[4] Gruchy, p. vi.

5

THE POWER STRUCTURE
AND EDUCATION

*. . . and that the government of the people, by the people, for the
people, shall not perish from the earth.*

Abraham Lincoln

Discussing the power structure and how it affects
the schools is in a large sense discussing politics. But what people see on the surface as politics is often trivial, irrelevant, and
ephemeral. Instead we prefer the word, power, as a more inclusive and useful concept in cultural analysis.

If we regard politics as a distorted, temporary expression
of power, we may reasonably assume that the functioning and
institutional structuring of power probably form the foundation

FEDERAL GOVERNMENT

Corporate Oligarchy

military establishment

Labor Unions

John Birch Society

veterans organizations

Daughters of the American Revolution

STATE GOVERNMENTS

Accrediting Agencies

Publishers

Chamber of Commerce

Universities

Foundations

National Education Assoc.

CHURCH GROUPS

Local Governments

Ku Klux Klan

Test Makers

Consultants

TAX PAYERS ASSOCIATIONS

District Superintendent

schoolboards

PTA

Principals

Parents

(Copyright © Ronald W. Hendershott, all rights reserved)

of a culture; the understanding of power is the primary requirement for understanding culture.

Further, education—both informal and formal, public and private— is an integral part of the power system. It is to a large degree molded by those who have power over it; but education, in turn, has the potential for molding the values and behavior of the powerful.

Virtually everything a teacher does is affected directly or indirectly by the power structure. Older educational sociology textbooks confined themselves to the relation between schools and their local community and to the wok of teachers within the local school bureaucracy, as if this explained all of the politics of education. It should be obvious, however, that state, regional, and national power centers have an interest in public education. Even more, the international setting affects the way national power systems view the functions of public education.

This is, therefore, a key chapter in Part II, and all the remaining chapters will draw from it.

THE IDEOLOGY OF POWER

The kinds of values and beliefs people hold about power may be called an ideology because we are referring to an evolving, supposedly cohesive body of convictions. Most of these convictions are not based on evidence but are taken on faith. However, ideological patterns may through emerging contradictions become too chaotic to describe except as patterns of conflict.

We shall discuss two aspects of our power ideology: (1) values and beliefs that we associate with the old culture, and (2) values and beliefs that we attribute to a newly developing ideology of power. We must recognize, of course, that the old culture-new culture dichotomy, when used in analyzing power, has both conceptual weaknesses and advantages. The differences between the political beliefs of middle-aged persons who are relatively satisfied with the world are more sharply different from those of the college-age counterculture than is the case in some of the other areas of cultural concern. This sharp differentiation appears in the following references which were chosen from a wide literature concerning power.

In discussing the ideology of power, we shall draw heavily from a book by Free and Cantril. Although this book is very useful, the authors create for themselves two problems; fortunately neither are serious.[1] First, their study requires frequent use of the concepts, conservative and liberal. They define today's conservative as believing in laissez-faire (the liberal ideology of the days of John Locke, Montesqieu, and Adam Smith, and in

[1] Lloyd A. Free and Hadley Cantril, *The Political Beliefs of Americans: A Study of Public Opinion.* New York: Simon & Schuster, Inc., 1968; Clarion, 1968.

America, James Madison and John Adams). They define today's liberal as a person who believes the full power of the Federal Government should be used for the general good—to eliminate poverty, racial discrimination, unemployment, and faulty education. If this requires placing much power in the Office of the Presidency, including its immense bureaucracy, then so be it. We should remind readers that such definitions are simplistic and ignore the distinction between classical and radical conservatism as we explained it in Chapter 2.

Second, Free and Cantril discuss ideology and another category of beliefs they label "operational." *Operational beliefs* are specific statements of what people want the government to do, of the action they expect. They discuss these desires as if they were nonideological and had no theoretical value-based underpinnings. This strikes us as a false dichotomy: we see operational beliefs as simply a competing ideology with its operational implications spelled out. However, these authors do imply this in describing American political beliefs as schizoid.

Americans as Ideologically Conservative

In describing *ideological beliefs* revealed by the polls, these authors find a highly conservative pattern. The following statements, paraphrased from their book, are illustrative:

> —God raised this mighty nation as the land of the free—not to flounder in the swamp of collectivism.
> —We're losing freedom all the time and heading in the direction of socialism.
> —The government wastes so much that taxation is killing us.
> —The government has gone too far in interfering with free, private enterprise.

We get a very different picture when we turn to *operational beliefs* held by many of the same people making such assertions as those above.

> —There should be more Federal aid to depressed areas.
> —The government should guarantee everyone a job.
> —The government doesn't do enough for the elderly.
> —We need a comprehensive system of state-supported medical care for everyone.

Free and Cantril conclude that while about one-half of respondents assert a conservative ideology, about two-thirds support a highly liberal (or Keynesian) operational ideology. In fact, large majorities sound like the New Left when answering certain operational questions. Table 5-1 shows the contradictory nature of American beliefs about politics and power.

Table 5-1
IDEOLOGICAL AND OPERATIONAL SPECTRUMS

	Ideological Spectrum (%)	Operational Spectrum (%)
Consistently or predominantly liberal	16%	64%
Middle of the road	34%	21%
Predominantly or consistently conservative	50%	14%

Source: Adapted from Lloyd A. Free and Hadley Cantril, *The Political Beliefs of Americans: A Study of Public Opinion.* New York: Simon & Schuster, Inc., 1968, p. 32.

Occupation is a significant variable in the United States with respect to political views. Between 50 and 60 percent of professionals, business persons, and farmers are *operationally* liberal; but 75 percent of blue-collar workers are. Education also makes a difference. In their *operational* beliefs, college-educated persons are about 50 percent liberal, whereas those with only a grade school education are 75 percent liberal. But age affects these figures: people over 50 are considerably more conservative than those under 50.

Summing up, the authors say the most operationally liberal are young, identify with the working class, and live in large or medium cities, mostly in the East. Jews and Negroes are exceptions: whatever the other variables, they are the most operationally liberal of any subgroups studied.

One of the more important conclusions from the Free and Cantril study is that *about one-fourth of Americans are both ideologically conservative and operationally liberal.* Middle-of-the-roaders are inconsistent on some issues part of the time and consistent on others. But of the ideological liberals, about 90 percent are also operational liberals. Hence, *liberals are far more consistent than nonliberals.* The authors conclude that the discrepancy between ideological and operational outlooks among conservatives and many middle-of-the-roaders "is so marked as to be almost schizoid." The least schizoid are the college educated, the well-to-do, professionals and businessmen, urbanites, Jews, and Blacks. The most schizoid are uneducated, white, poor, and southern. For our purposes, we prefer the word, anomic, to schizoid.

There has been much discussion about the political views of blue-collar workers—the so-called "hard hats." Free and Cantril place them as operationally liberal (about 75 percent) and ideologically conservative (44 percent conservative; 21 percent liberal).[2] Sar Levitan's book on blue-

[2] Free and Cantril. p. 16.

collar workers seems to substantiate considerable inconsistency and confusion among this group, but also, on certain issues, a deep conservatism.[3]

There is reason for concern about blue collars' views in certain
areas: 86 percent have favorable views toward policemen, 81 percent toward the military, 62 percent disapprove of legal marches, 61 percent would not disobey a law they considered unjust, and 83 percent
would not obstruct the government even as a last resort. These views may
seem healthy or unhealthy depending on the values of those who judge.
But they make one point clear: *blue collars are strongly in favor of authority and law-and-order.* Would blue-collar workers form a central core of
support for a military dictatorship some time in the future? Actually, the
main thing we know about the blue collars is that they are operationally
liberal on a number of welfare issues.[4]

Specimen Youth Culture Beliefs about Power

One would expect to find new-culture political beliefs in greatest concentration among the most ideologically liberal: in urban areas; among
the young more than among the old; in the Southwest, probably among
many Chicanos; and especially among college and university students,
Blacks, and Jews. But this is not necessarily the case, Yankelovich's research on college and university students seems the most comprehensive
and usable as of this writing. Yankelovich says:

> In the light of the research, the political values of students show
> themselves to be more volatile than their social values—more sub-
> ject to swings in both directions, more inconsistent, less thoughtful,
> and less thoroughly examined. This is not so at the far Left and far
> Right ends of the political spectrum, but it is for the majority.[5]

This political volatility shows up clearly in party affiliations and attitudes
toward parties. In 1969, 23 percent of students belonged to neither major
political party; by 1971 the figure had risen to 37 percent, but by 1973 had
dropped to roughly the 1969 figure.

On political parties, Yankelovich's 1973 sample would like to see
"fundamental reform or elimination of" by the following percentages:

---

[3] Sar A. Levitan (ed.), *Blue-Collar Workers: A Symposium on Middle
America.* New York: McGraw-Hill Book Company, Inc., 1971.

[4] Howard L. Reiter in Levitan, pp. 101–113.

[5] Daniel Yankelovich, Inc., *The Changing Values on Campus: Political
and Personal Attitudes of Today's College Students.* New York: Washington
Square Press, 1972, p. 49. For 1973 data, see Daniel Yankelovich, *The New
Morality: A Profile of American Youth in the 70's.* New York: McGraw-Hill Book
Company, 1974, Chap. 12.

college youth, 61; noncollege youth, 64. In his 1971 study, 54 percent of college youth agreed. When asked the best means of achieving social change, 78 percent of students (1971) felt their best chance was by working as individuals within their community. Only between one quarter and one third of students were concerned about expressing themselves through a political party. It seems clear that college students have little conception of the role of a strong two-party system in maintaining democracy.

The following assertions are paraphrased from questions Yankelovich used in his 1973 research; the first assent percentage given is for college youth; the second, for noncollege youth.

—The real power in the United States is vested in giant corporations and financial institutions. (84%; 49%)
—The real power in this country lies in the Congress. (24%, 30%)
—The President of the United States is the chief center of power (34%; 24%)
—The final power in the United States is in the hands of the general public. (11%; 12%)
—The Republican Party has the real power. (4%; 3%) The Democratic Party. (2%; 2%)
—American society is only in name democratic—society is run by special interests. (63%, 58%)
—Life in America is better than life in other countries.
—Institutions needing basic reform or elimination; political parties (61%; 64%); penal system (69%; 50%); big business (54%; 45%); the military (54%; 38%); the Congress (34%; 31%); the FBI (37%; 27%); the Supreme Court (21%; 24%).

Yankelovich is led to conclude, "While noncollege youth have adopted the social and personal value system of the college campus, they continue to be considerably less alienated from American society than their better-educated peers."[6] This opinion is based on the finding that 57 percent of noncollege youth think their values are similar to those of most Americans, whereas only 40 percent of college students think so. With regard to the nation, in response to the question of whether things are going very/fairly well or very/fairly badly, Yankelovich found almost a 50-50 split. In both college and noncollege samples, 48 percent took the optimistic view: 51 and 50 percent, respectively, the pessimistic.

That students are confused is suggested by their assent to "I am tired of hearing people attack patriotism, morality, American values" (college youth agreed, 65 percent; noncollege, 78 percent). But 94 and 92 percent, respectively, felt business is high on greed and low on responsibility; 88 percent of both samples felt our foreign policy is too self-serving; and 86 and 84 percent were worried about invasions of personal privacy.

[6] Yankelovich, p. 50.

What are the characteristics of students who regard themselves as liberal or members of the New Left? And what are the characteristics of those who claim conservatism? While Yankelovich's study omits this important information, Seymour Lipset offers us some partial answers.[7] He relies on a special study done for the *Saturday Review* which procured data on the beliefs of not only college and university students but also out-of-school youth of college age and high school students.

Of Lipset's sample of college students, 43 percent identified themselves as liberal, 31 percent as middle-of-the road, 16 percent as conservative or radical right, and 9 percent as radical left. Although these figures do not agree with Yankelovich's findings, their general tendency does not seem incompatible.

With respect to out-of-school youth of college age, we note a definite increase in conservative leaning. Only 24 percent identify themselves as liberal, whereas 47 percent call themselves middle-of-the-road. But note: almost 1 in 4 (24 percent) of out-of-school youth identify themselves as conservative or radical right. Four percent, most of whom we may presume are minority group members, call themselves radical left.

With respect to high school students, Lipset's data are sketchy, but the picture we get is of more indecision and probably confusion than among college and university students. The figures for high school students are almost identical with those of college-age out-of-school youth. Only in the liberal category, where 5 percent more high school students claim identification, is there a difference of more than 1 to 2 percentage points.

The *Saturday Review* study from which Lipset draws his figures reveals another kind of relationship which may be of key importance—the relation between students' liberality or conservatism and the grades they get. In the case of high school students there is only a mild tendency for students with A and B averages to be more liberal than students with C averages. But at the college level, the relationship between grades and political leaning becomes much more pronounced. Students with liberal to radical left views were mainly students with B to A grade point averages; students with conservative to radical right views were mainly C students. Further, liberals and leftists were found mainly among majors in the humanities and social sciences; and conservatives and radical rightists were found mainly among students with vocational majors, chiefly, agriculture, engineering, and industrial arts. Lipset states that the correlation of high grades and liberal and New Left view has been verified in repeated studies.

[7] Seymour M. Lipset, "How Education Affects the Youth Vote," *Saturday Review/Education*, Vol. 15, November 1972, pp. 68–70.

Stages of Moral Maturity and Political Orientation

Toward the end of Chapter 4, we described six stages of moral maturity as elaborated and empirically supported by Lawrence Kohlberg. After Kohlberg's work became well known, others attempted to apply his categories in interpreting social phenomena other than the direction of moral growth itself. One such research project attempted to connect Kohlberg's stages with the political leanings of persons who fit a particular stage. The research settings included the San Francisco Bay and Boston areas.[8]

The purpose of the study was to discover at which level of moral development persons at various points of the social-political spectrum might be. The subjects studied were classified in terms of a liberal-conservative continuum, with extremists of either the left or right considered radical. The results should not surprise any well-educated person, but they might seem very distasteful to the semieducated. Some interesting sidelights turned up, however, which proved enlightening even to the most sophisticated. One such sidelight was that few persons can actually comprehend behavior pitched on more than one level above their own; that is, a Stage 4 person finds a Stage 6 person quite incomprehensible, and moreover, a probable threat to social stability (the Stage 4 person prizes change highly).

Attempts to achieve Stage 6 involve in large measure a "search for self." Self in this context should not be taken to mean some kind of "absolutistic inner essence," but rather a group of harmonious, workable values which will enable a person to "know who he is" and to have a clear sense of direction in life. This is no easy task, especially in view of the fact that a person seeking Stage 6 is neither understood nor appreciated by the majority. "In any society the Stage 6 individuals, and to a lesser extent the Stage 5 ones, are the experimenters, the innovators, the dynamic segment of society."[9] The conservative majority never takes a bright view of innovators—they rock too many boats (and even swamp some).

Hampden-Turner and Whitten express well what a Stage 6 person goes through: "The quest for self may require many of the things conservative abhor: permissiveness, experimentation, incompleteness, frankness about previously taboo topics, criticism of and skepticism toward the inherited truths, and the recognition of contradictions."[10] The authors also state well how a Stage 6 person appears to those at the Stage 3 and 4 levels: "The old culture believes that the spontaneous self betrays the individual, causes trouble, impedes the installation of new technology,

---

[8] Reported by Charles Hampden-Turner and Phillip Whitten, "Morals Left and Right," *Psychology Today,* April 1971, p. 39ff.

[9] Hampden-Turner and Whitten, p. 76.

[10] Hampden-Turner and Whitten, p. 43.

weakens moral imperatives, undermines social control, and is bad for business."[11]

As one should expect, persons who regard themselves as conservatives tend to operate at Stages 3 and 4. Self-professed liberals and moderates tend to operate at Stage 5. An unexpected finding, however, is that radicals tend to operate at either Level 6 or Level 2. Radicals of the left operate more often at Level 6 than at Level 2. Radicals of the right tend to operate at Level 2. Silvan Tompkins (as mentioned in the *Psychology Today* article), has made a distinction between left-wing and right-wing ideology which this study seems to support. Tompkins suggests that the leftist thinks of man as the measure, and as an active, creative, thinking, desiring, loving force in nature. The rightist feels that man can find his full stature only when he struggles toward, participates in, and conforms to some ideal norm or essence basically independent of man.

Levels 3 and 4 persons favor law-and-order over justice, tend to approve of war, show symptoms of racism, and are turned on by such concepts as patriotism, the flag, duty, honor, loyalty, family, discipline. They tend somewhat toward being opportunists, but not nearly as much so as Level 2 persons.

This important study throws considerable light on not only the youth movement but political involvement in general. Young dissidents are mainly either at, or seeking, Stages 5 and 6 of moral maturity, but some (many of whom come under our label of "phony") never get above Level 2. Those who do not have the courage to be overt activists are more likely at Stage 5, the activists at either Stage 6 or 2, with the latter being a disrupting influence in the movement. The straight students who are not part of the movement at all, who lack any rebellious feelings, operate mainly at Levels 3 and 4.

The object of the next section of the chapter is to demonstrate on a limited scale how evidence can be marshaled around a hypothesis which would seem outrageous to many persons, but which must be confronted honestly by the public in any culture that presumes to call itself democratic.

AN "OUTRAGEOUS HYPOTHESIS" ABOUT POWER EXAMINED

There is a large literature on the power structure of the United States. Much of this was couched in very general terms until the 1950s and 1960s when the competing theories presented were able to build upon more empirical evidence than had been available before. Since the mid-sixties, particularly, we have been getting an increasing number of empirical studies as more factual data have been produced.

[11] Hampden-Turner and Whitten, p. 74.

Hypothesis: *A "power elite" determines national policy and action in all issues of major national and international concern, with the masses of people taking little or no part.*

Although various writers wrote about power prior to the 1950s, prominent among these being James Burnham and Floyd Hunter, we can pretty much date the beginning of the controversy over the comparative validity of elitist and pluralist theories of power with the publication of C. Wright Mills' *The Power Elite* in 1956. To fully understand Mills' position, however, it is necessary to study his three key books: *New Men of Power, White Collar,* and *The Power Elite.* Mills' final book, *The Marxists,* although little discussed, helps to round out his thinking.[12] *The Power Elite* has had by far the greatest impact.[13] Ralph Miliband, in an essay in Domhoff and Ballard, says that Mills' thesis in *The Power Elite* can be condensed to the four points below (which are so condensed by Miliband that understanding them fully requires prior knowledge of both social science and Mills' way of defining certain terms).

1. In America, some men have enormous power denied to everyone else.
2. These men are, increasingly, a self-perpetuating elite.
3. Their power is, increasingly, unchecked and irresponsible.
4. Their decision making, based on an increasingly "military definition of reality" and on "crackpot realism" is oriented toward immoral ends.

The last point, particularly, requires further explanation. By a "military definition of reality" apparently Mills means thinking based on the same assumptions and logic that characterize the thinking of most of our more influential admirals and generals, both active and retired.

Mills' point is that not only do career military men tend to think in a special way, but that their assumptions come to be adopted by many, if not most, persons who comprise the power elite—whether corporate executives, high-ranking political figures, or, of course, the military.

---

[12] C. Wright Mills, *New Men of Power,* New York: Augustus M. Kelley Publishers, 1948; *White Collar,* New York: Oxford University Press, 1951; Galaxy, 1956; *The Power Elite,* New York: Oxford University Press, 1956; Galaxy, 1959; *The Marxists,* New York: Dell Publishing Company, Inc., 1962.

[13] Perhaps the best book about *The Power Elite* is by G. William Domhoff and Hoyt B. Ballard, compilers, *C. Wright Mills and The Power Elite.* Boston: Beacon Press, 1968. It includes a compact description of Mills' theoretical position, reviews and essays by Mills' critics, Mills' answer to his critics, and an essay by Domhoff that seeks common elements in the criticisms, analyzes them, and presents a compromise view free of what Domhoff sees as Mills' worst mistakes. The pages to follow draw heavily from this book.

The expression, "crackpot realism," also requires explanation. In spite of its polemical tone, this term can be defined so that it has substantive meaning. Viewed in the context of Mills' other writing, it appears that he means "opportunistic pragmatism," that is, a kind of unprincipled fluidity of view that can be directed in any way to best serve selfish ends.

In "immoral ends," Mills is not using "immoral" in its usual narrow sense of pertaining to so-called vices, but rather as any goal or end that damages other people. In this sense, business monopolies, war whose chief purpose is enriching a few, or misleading advertising would all be immoral.

Mills' Three Societal Layers

Mills' conceptual model can be diagrammed as in Figure 5-1. The pyramids at the top represent the apex of three institutional structures: A is the corporate oligarchy; A^1 is the military oligarchy; and A^2 is the political directorate. A and A^1 are drawn the same height to indicate

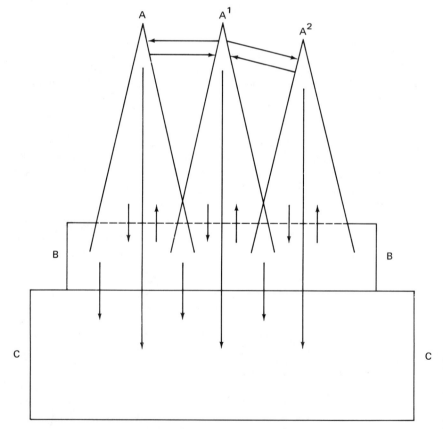

FIGURE 5-1.   Mills' conception of the power structure in the United States.

equivalent power. Mills felt the political directorate was less powerful than the corporate or military oligarchies and hence A^2 is drawn shorter. Persons who dominate decision making in these three institutional areas make up the power elite. This layer consists only of the top leaders, not their constituencies.

The three elements of the power elite interact with one another, and more often than not work cooperatively. Persons in these groups are united by what Mills called a "coincidence of interests," that is, their goals are sufficiently alike that they tend to share similar values. The ties between the three elements are indicated by arrows near the top of each pyramid.

Layer B in the pyramid represents the middle level of power. It includes both potential and actual leaders, organization leaders, and memberships. Among them are Congress, managers of corporations ranging from small to fairly large, larger labor unions, professional organizations such as the AMA and bar associations, veterans organizations, chambers of commerce, conservation organizations (particularly the Sierra Club), the farm bloc, Consumers Union, the NAACP, the Mafia (if such exists), and countless others. These groups interact in various ways; some cooperate, some oppose each other, and some go it alone.

The middle power level makes decisions in matters of less than major national or international interests; they "govern" the social structure below the central interests of the power elite. In managing national affairs at regional, state, and local levels, they find it necessary to show more concern for public opinion than does the power elite. Persons and organizations at the middle power layer sometimes move into the top pyramids—hence the broken line separating the A and B levels and the vertical arrows indicating upward and downward movement.

The bottom layer, C, consists of the "mass"—the poor and very poor, the semiskilled and low-salaried skilled workers, civil service workers, the unemployed, people on welfare, enlisted military personnel, small farmers, persons with meager education, and most racial and ethnic minorities. Within Mills' framework, the mass is not so much definable in terms of occupation, income, social origin, or group identification as in their *powerlessness*.

In Figure 5-1, the long arrows extending downward from near the apex of each pyramid into the C stratum of power indicate the direction in which power flows—downward from the top, and rarely if ever upward from the bottom. The shorter arrows extending from inside stratum B downward into stratum C indicate the direction of power flow with respect to the middle and bottom layers. Mills conceded the possibility of power flowing upward from C to B and B to A during a major social crisis; such a reversed flow would represent a revolutionary situation. We have drawn the figure to indicate the direction of power flow during normal times.

Mills never claimed that the power elite always has its way. H never said that it is always united. And he never said that the power elite always acts in its own best interests; in fact, he viewed the power elite as composed of men, and a few women, who varied in capability from brilliant and wise to dismally stupid. These qualifications are essential to give Mills' interpretation even a reasonable amount of credibility.

Mills' "Liberal" Critics

The liberals Mills referred to are New Deal type liberals who dominated much social thought from the 1930s through the 1950s. Most of these persons, by the standards of the 1970s, would be considered pretty conservative. The "liberals" whose critical essays appear in Domhoff and Ballard are: Robert A. Dahl, William Kornhauser, Talcott Parsons, Dennis Wrong and A. A. Berle, Jr. Except for Berle, a corporation lawyer when these essays were written, they were all scholars at major universities.

Although none of Mills' liberal critics leveled precisely the same criticisms at his thesis, most of them tend to accept an opposing theory: a pluralist theory of power (with no one dominant power center). Their common criticism is that it is difficult if not impossible to prove that there is a power elite. Instead of a three-layered power system, these scholars see a two-layered structure, with the division between the layers blurred by interpenetration. This pluralist view of the power structure can be diagrammed as in Figure 5-2.

The larger circles indicate individuals or groupings with more power than those exemplified by smaller circles. The top layer comprises

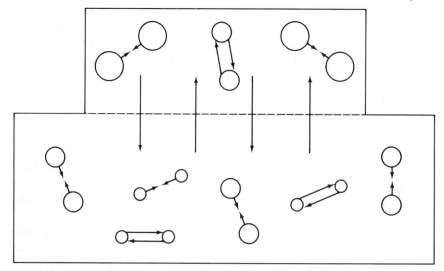

FIGURE 5-2.   A pluralist power structure.

the persons and groups which the Millsian model places in both the elite and middle power categories. This upper stratum contains no individuals or groups with significantly more power than others in the same stratum. Further, the elements in this stratum have so few common goals that they tend to cancel out each other's power. (David Riesman, a pluralist, refers to such upper-layer organizations as "veto groups"—each is in a position to "veto" any push for dominance by other individuals or organizations.)

In the two-layer model depicted in Figure 5-2, individuals and groups in the bottom layer are seen as having significant decision-making power —enough to counter any excesses achieved through cooperation among units of the upper layer to pose the threat of governance by a ruling class.

In Figure 5-2, paired arrows pointing at each other between circles indicate organizations with opposing interests, opposite-direction paired arrows indicate cooperative interaction, and vertical arrows through the broken line indicate upward and downward movement of individuals and organizations, as well as the flow of power.

Empirical Studies Attempting To Prove Elitist Theory

In his concluding essay, Domhoff searched criticisms of Mills' theory for any theoretically plausible common ground that could be factually supported. Considering later events, Domhoff found that the arguments of some critics appeared weak because their forecasts did not turn out to be true.

Since Mills' critics generally criticized him on the ground that he had not convincingly proved the existence of a power elite, Domhoff and some other social scientists in the 1960s undertook studies to see if Mills' thesis could be supported empirically. With the advantage of belonging to the upper class, E. Digby Baltzell cross-checked membership in prestigious private schools, Ivy League colleges, "gentlemen's clubs," exclusive summer resorts, and the boards of directors of large corporations and foundations. He located a distinctive group whose names appeared repeatedly in these organizations—a group of leading businessmen, lawyers, and civic leaders who interact personally and intermarry.[14]

Since Baltzell's research was not definitive, Domhoff designed his own follow-up studies. He developed criteria for upper-class membership and studied the social backgrounds of major institutional leaders, political campaign donors, and decision makers. He found that members of his sample were deeply involved as directors or partners in the nation's largest banks, law firms, foundations, boards of trustees of major universities,

---

[14] Edward Digby Baltzell, *Philadelphia Gentlemen* (originally entitled *An American Business Aristocracy*). New York: The Free Press, 1958. See also his *The Protestant Establishment: Aristocracy and Caste in America*. New York: Random House, Inc., 1964.

largest opinion forming associations, the largest of the mass media, and the executive branch of the Federal Government.[15]

Domhoff collected a mass of more recent research data which, although not as definitive as he would like, he feels effectively refutes the pluralist notion that the nation is governed by a multiplicity of power centers with opposing interests, none of which has a decisive advantage over others except perhaps very temporarily. Domhoff is convinced that there is an identifiable power elite (not to be confused with what most writers mean by an upper class). This group comprises no more than one half of 1 percent of the population (which still adds up to more than one million persons). However (on the basis of his and some dozens of other studies), this group has a central core numbering at most a few thousand persons with the hundreds of governing heads of the largest corporations being the most powerful elements within this group.[16]

Pluralist Theories

Although elitist theories of power have been popular, we cannot neglect the credentials or the arguments of a number of pluralist theorists. Perhaps the most prominent social scientist to insist that power in America is pluralist rather than elitist was the late Arnold Rose who was generally considered one of the most reputable sociologists. His book, *The Power Structure*[17] has been regarded by reviewers as the best book presenting a pluralist viewpoint.

Rose disagrees that there is a "mass" which is impotent, alienated, and manipulated. He cites numerous "lower level" organizations that speak for those Mills considered powerless—PTAs, labor unions, the NAACP, ACLU, League of Women Voters, and the American Legion to name a few. Rose also sees as significant but competing power centers the major political parties, Congress, and the state legislatures. He does qualify his pluralist position somewhat by noting that the power of the executive branch of the Federal Government is increasing relative to other power centers.

Although Rose's scholarship has been widely admired, it appears that his arguments are vulnerable in several ways. In citing groups that represent the interests of the lower power level, it strikes us as naive to include the Farm Bureau or the American Legion, both of which usually

[15] G. William Domhoff, *Who Rules America?* Englewood Cliffs, N.J.: Prentice-Hall, Inc., 1967.

[16] G. William Domhoff, *The Higher Circles: The Governing Class in America.* New York: Random House, Inc., 1970.

[17] Arnold Rose, *The Power Structure.* New York: Oxford University Press, 1967.

appear to represent the interests of large corporate groups and only rarely the "little man." Rose also tries to establish many of his points merely by asserting them, not through empirical evidence. The arguments of Rose's chief critics are described in Domhoff's *Higher Circles*.[18]

The Military-Industrial Complex

One side of the power elite thesis we should examine more carefully concerns the concept of the *military-industrial complex* which President Eisenhower made a major issue in his famous farewell address. There is no question about the prevalence of high-level military men as advisors and aids in the Federal executive branch. Equally pertinent is the number of retired military officers who hold high managerial positions (often on boards of directors) in the one hundred major corporations that accept military contracts. As of 1969 they numbered 2072.[19]

Apparently, there is enough of a link between the military and the corporations to make Eisenhower's expression, "military-industrial complex" legitimate, though its modus operandi is not reflected in statistical charts. Career officers, particularly those of high rank, have an ideology replete with supporting myths that has been frequently and clearly stated.[20] To suppose that this ideology has not affected the thinking of top civilians leaders, both corporate and governmental, would seem most unrealistic. Thus, "the military definition of reality," which Mills accused top civilian leaders of being controlled by, seems well supported by data from the late 1960s and 1970s.

Weakness of Mills' Thesis

In the light of both theoretical and empirical studies since Mills' death in 1962, it seems evident that Mills was wrong on several important points.

—In evaluating the respective amounts of power exercised by top figures in the three institutional structures analyzed by Mills (corporate, military, and political), Mills allowed the political directorate less power than the other two. In view of the steady trend toward presidential government, particularly since the Lyndon Johnson Administration, a strong argument can be made that the power structure focuses in the executive branch of the Federal Government.

[18] Domhoff, *Higher Circles*, p. 319ff.

[19] Adam Yarmolinsky, *The Military Establishment: Its Impacts on American Society*. New York: Harper & Row, Publishers, 1971, p. 61. This is probably the most useful reference for both observational and statistical data of the link between military, government, and corporate establishments.

[20] In addition to Ackley's book on the military mind (see Chap. 2), see Schiller and Joseph D. Phillips, *Super-State: Readings in the Military-Industrial Complex*. Urbana: University of Illinois Press, 1970.

—Mills' "institutional approach," that is, studying as separate entities the institutional structures of big business, the military establishment, and the Federal Government, has been generally attacked as simplistic because it does not emphasize enough their interpenetration.

—Mills undoubtedly oversimplified the nature of the power structure of his middle and lower power layers. The pluralist explanation of the power structure may actually fit pretty well the ideology and behavior of middle and lower groups. The middle group may, as pluralists say, tend to neutralize itself through the conflicting values of its different units.

The lower power layer is probably not as powerless as Mills' conception of the "mass." Talcott Parsons is likely right in suggesting that groups at this level do have a measure of internal cohesiveness, if for no other reasons than kinship and "the whole mass of associational activities and relationships."[21]

—Mills did not adequately treat the role of the judiciary and the legal profession. The Supreme Court presents a complex problem of analysis. Here, the use of historical data becomes invaluable. Although Talcott Parsons and functionalists emphasize the role of the Supreme Court as a "veto agency" in relation to the legislative and executive branches of the government, the writer does not feel that historical evidence supports this view. Rather it appears that at times the Court is a truly independent agency, as likely to rule against the interests of the top power group as not (the New Deal Court of Franklin D. Roosevelt's last administration and the Warren Court are good examples). But at other times, the Court rather consistently rules in their favor. During periods of transition from an independent to a proestablishment court, or vice versa, Court rulings may go either way. Although on some issues, such as the abortion ruling, the Nixon Court has made rulings regarded by many as liberal, the general tenor of this court seems harshly "law-and-order" and "antilibertarian."

Studies of Small and Moderate-Sized Communities

The first major study of community power structure was Robert S. and Helen Lynd's investigation of a comparatively small North Central city which they called Middletown. Their first study was published in 1929.[22] To establish a time perspective, the study was repeated in the next decade and indicated the changes that had occurred.[23] W. Lloyd Warner, in asso-

[21] Talcott Parsons, "The Distribution of Power in American Society," in Domhoff and Ballard, p. 80.

[22] Robert S. and Helen Lynd, *Middletown.* New York: Harcourt Brace Jovanovich, Inc., 1929.

[23] Robert S. and Helen Lynd, *Middletown in Transition.* New York: Harcourt Brace Jovanovich, Inc., 1937.

ciation with Robert Havighurst, Bernice Neugarten, Paul S. Lunt, Leo Srole, J. O. Low, and others, studied several communities, ranging from comparatively small rural-based towns to a moderate-sized city—Newburyport, Massachusetts—which they gave the name Yankee City. In ensuing years many community studies were made.[24]

The outcome of these studies, particularly those bearing Warner's name, was a model of small town life based upon stratification, in which each social class displayed a distinctive life style and function in the community. These descriptions of community life were simple and comparatively static. It was obvious who ran things: the upper class was the most influential when it chose to be, but let the upper middles do much of the chore work of governing the communities studied. Although the term, power elite, had not yet been popularized by Mills, these descriptions of community life were fundamentally elitist; they talked of controlling classes and ruling cliques.

Study of a City

One of the few attempts to study power in a fairly large city was that of Floyd Hunter, whose Regional City (Atlanta, Georgia), had a population of half a million at the time of his research.[25] Hunter described power as residing in a power elite composed of the top leadership in several community institutional structures. Hunter calls these structures "pyramids." They can be diagrammed roughly like Mills' three pyramids of power, except that in Regional City Hunter identifies more institutional pyramids—economic, governmental, religious, educational, professional, civic, and cultural. Above these institutional structures, however, there is also a "policy-making structure" which dominates decision making in the economic, professional, governmental, and civic institutional structures.[26] The relation between the policy-making structure and the institutional pyramids is reciprocal, in that the policy-making structure is itself drawn from the top leadership of the other pyramids.

Hunter began his empirical research by selecting over 175 persons from lists of leading civic, professional, business, and fraternal organizations, government, and "society" and "wealth" personnel suggested by directories and other sources. He then selected "judges" to name the 40

[24] Walter R. Goldschmidt's *As You Sow* (New York: Harcourt Brace Jovanovich, Inc., 1947) compared two small towns in California; August Hollinghead's *Elmstown's Youth* (New York: John Wiley & Sons, Inc., 1949) described a North Central town in one of the better studies.

[25] Floyd Hunter, *Community Power Structure: A Study of Decision Makers.* Chapel Hill, N.C.: University of North Carolina Press, 1953; Anchor, 1963.

[26] Hunter, Figures 8, 9, 10 on pp. 91, 95, 96 of the Anchor edition.

most important persons from the master list. Twenty-nine of the 40 were businessmen and Hunter concluded that the 40 did in effect function as a power elite in running Atlanta.

A Pluralist Theory of Community Power

Sociologist Richie P. Lowry conducted a study of a small, rural, northern California community fictitiously named Micro City as part of his doctoral work at the University of California. In the published version of his thesis, he emphasizes the following points.

Lowry attacks both elitist interpretations of small town government as simplistic, unprovable, and failing to explain the often fast-changing power structures, and pluralist interpretations for not explaining the unique variables nor offering generalizable theories—since each "pluralistic" community seems a law unto itself.[27]

Lowry concludes that under modern conditions community elites are short-lived; there is too much of a gap between traditional community ideologies and conditions produced by social change to retain a stable pattern of government. Most small communities today are characterized by deep internal conflicts that produce opposing groups and encourage pluralism.

Micro City exemplified the results of people returning from decaying cities to suburban communities, which become microcosms of the larger culture peopled by a variety of occupational, educational, ethnic, and political groupings. "Contemporary Micro City is a peculiar mixture of new and old, the present and the past. In many ways it is typical of other small but rapidly growing American communities and particularly of communities in the major agricultural regions of the western United States."[28]

Micro City had 30,000 people with a potential of 80,000 by 1980. A majority of its residents were Republican and deeply conservative. The one newspaper and the school board promoted this conservatism. It contained a state college of whose newcomer faculty the conservative majority was highly suspicious.

Who ran Micro City? First, there were the "old-timers" who effectively governed a generation ago. On occasion they still tried to affect major community decisions, but felt their influence had largely disappeared and that they were ignored. Second, there were the downtown businessmen and real estate interests who had managed to secure control of the City Council. But the attempted domination of this younger group was

---

[27] Ritchie P. Lowry, Who's Running This Town? Community Leadership and Social Change. New York: Harper & Row, Publishers, 1965, p. xxii.
[28] Lowry, p. 3.

largely through force of personality rather than by policies or issues. As one official put it to Lowry, "Everything in this damn town is based upon who you know, not what you know." Lowry suggests that this "cult of personality" makes democratic process almost impossible to locate or introduce.

In identifying local leaders, a useful conceptual dichotomy is to categorize them as "Local" and "Cosmopolitan." Conflict between them seemed inescapable in Micro City. Local leaders typically were "parochial and provincial" and had little formal education. They tended to pre-dominate among the elected officials of the town. Cosmopolitan leaders were "ecumenical and sophisticated," and often liberal. They were usually recent arrivals. Their role in local government was primarily one of filling appointive posts where their expertise was essential, or serving as ad-visors. Many were on the State College faculty.

Because of the conflict generated between Locals and Cosmopoli-tans and between liberals and conservatives, a type of "mediating leader" tended to rise spontaneously. Lowry found that all three types of leaders —Locals, Cosmopolitans, and Mediators might play any of the three roles.[29]

The Power Locus in a Typical Small Village

"Springdale" (a village of about 1000 in a township of about 3000)[30] is in New York 25 miles from three commercial-industrial centers where part of the population works. The community is almost exclusively WASP. The primary economic base is agriculture, for which the village is a service center.

The village board consisted of businessmen. No one was elected to the board unless he shared the community ideas of low taxes and expendi-tures. The township board was dominated by prosperous farmers. The two boards often conflicted. The village board was so apathetic that Vidich and Bensman referred to it as "government by paralysis." Nominees to the boards were selected by the machine—the Republican Committee. Occasionally a Democrat served on the township board.

On the surface Springdale appeared to have a pluralist power structure with at least some democratic features. With so many conflicting interest groups, one might wonder what held the village together. The answer, Vidich and Bensman found, was an "invisible government" of four persons (fictitiously named) running the village and surrounding township. Mr. Flint, attorney to the village council, controlled nomina-

---

[29] Lowry, pp. 130–131.

[30] Arthur J. Vidich and Joseph Bensman, *Small Town in a Mass Society: Class Power, Religion in a Rural Community.* Princeton: Princeton University Press, 1958; Anchor, 1960.

tions to the council and, through informal influence, the village government. Mr. Lee, township council clerk, controlled both the local newspaper (by virtue of holding its mortgage), and the township government (partly because no one else could interpret his financial accounts). Mr. Young, a lawyer and former judge, exerted a strong sub-rosa influence in community affairs because his county and state government contacts could procure special favors for the community.

But the central figure was Mr. Jones, who operated a feed, building supply, and hardware store. By knowing everyone in the area and by having a forceful personality, he controlled the village through Flint, and the township through Lee. His popularity made him the logical choice to intercede with Young. In effect, therefore, one man, Jones, "invisibly" governed both the township and village. In a very real sense, Springdale had an elitist power center which differed from metropolitan or national power centers mainly because its four principals, though they did not always agree, were spatially and psychologically very close to each other and to their constituency.

The Trend Toward Presidential Government

The trend toward presidential government refers to the trend (noticeable particularly about the mid-twentieth century) of the executive branch of the government to dominate the others. It also means the growth of a pattern of government in which the executive branch amasses powers undreamed of by most of the Founding Fathers—except, perhaps, by the Hamiltonians.

Some Powers Which Have Accrued to the Presidency

Roles of the Presidency which are not directly authorized in the Constitution, but assumed over the course of time are neatly stated by two students of the Presidency, Rossiter and Finer.[31] The roles have tended to include (1) control over the entire administrative personnel and operation; (2) power to act, almost regardless of statute, in any emergency; (3) power to initiate laws and exercise the power, both positive and negative, of the veto; (4) budget-making power; (5) power to conduct diplomacy and make treaties, committing the nation to agreements with other nations, disposing of American troops, etc., in such a way as to *court or avoid* war (emphasis added); (6) power as Commander-in-chief; (7) power to exercise considerable patronage; (8) access to the public by means of

[31] Herbert Finer, *The Presidency: Crisis and Regeneration.* Chicago: The University of Chicago Press, 1960, p. 118; Clinton Rossiter, *The American Presidency.* New York: Harcourt Brace Jovanovich, Inc., 1960.

press conferences, where he alone determines what he shall say and what excerpts shall be flashed on the television screens; and (9) access to television and radio to tell his side of any political story, with no equivalent right conceded by the networks to other branches of government, say, the Speaker of the House, the opposition party, or the majority leader of the Senate. Because of the glamour and prestige accorded the President as Chief of State and leader of his party, he is the most important source, and object, of newspaper stories and receives far greater than the amount of attention given Congress.

Routinization and Institutionalization of the Presidency

The terms, routinization and institutionalization, as used here, have somewhat limited meanings. Writers on the Presidency use these terms regularly in a way special to that office. A lucid explanation of the concepts and their implication is provided by Dorothy James; our treatment is largely derived from hers.[32]

Routinization refers to the idea that when a President innovates a new area of authority—not specifically granted in the Constitution—this new power becomes routine. Except for the unlikely event that the Supreme Court declares the assumption of the new power unconstitutional, the new increment of presidential authority becomes a part of the presidential system. The President who innovated it can use it repeatedly and, even more important, the Congress, Supreme Court and voting public will expect each succeeding President to use the new power.

Routinization of new presidential practice leads to institutionalization of the acts that have become routine. That is, when the President takes on new power, the means of exercising it usually requires an expansion of the presidential bureaucracy. To be executed effectively, the new power may require establishing a major new department or subdepartment of the executive branch, an advisory committee, or special aides.

Three Conceptions of Presidential Power

Although not all experts would necessarily agree that the following three models are valid, they have been presented by James MacGregor Burns, one of our most prominent political scientists.[33] Burns asserts that three distinctive notions about the role of the President developed at the

[32] Dorothy B. James, The Contemporary Presidency. New York: Pegasus, 1969, Chap. 2.

[33] James MacGregor Burns, Presidential Government: The Crucible of Leadership. Boston: Houghton Mifflin Company, 1966, see Preface, Chap. 1, and later sections.

time the nation was founded: the Madisonian, Jeffersonian, and Hamiltonian theories.

Madison's concept stressed checks and balances, negotiating among minority coalitions, the inappropriateness of the government to make major innovations except as authorized by broad popular support, and a President with strictly limited powers. Although Madison was not advocating anarchy, Burns shows that Madison was a proponent of a comparatively weak central government.

Jefferson, in contrast, felt that although a system of checks and balances was desirable, the three branches of government should function as a team under the leadership of the President. Further, Jefferson made a large issue of the need for two strong political parties playing a key role in the democratic process. The parties would serve as a means of two-way communication between the people and their government, as well as a means for nominating and promoting candidates for office.

The Hamiltonian concept called for a strong central government and allowed only minor participatory democracy. As Burns explains, Hamilton believed the successful functioning of the government would depend on "energy, resourcefulness, inventiveness, and a ruthless pragmatism in the executive office . . ." around which the whole Federal Government should revolve.[34]

Burns considers it significant that the first Presidents exemplified these three concepts of presidential function. Washington was clearly a Hamiltonian, at a time when this view was badly needed. John Adams' theoretical views of government were similar to Madison's (although certain of his presidential acts seem to negate these views). Once in office, Jefferson developed the governmental form that Burns calls "Jeffersonian."

Burns grants that different times and national moods call for different conceptions of the Presidency. In periods of crisis, we may need a Hamiltonian president. Lincoln played the Hamiltonian role in operating a virtual dictatorship during the Civil War; however, because Lincoln seems to have had strong democratic values, his administration did not endanger democracy. Still, Burns prefers the Jeffersonian model, and notes that "to some Americans . . . Hamiltonian opportunism, the rise of a powerful presidential bureaucracy, and the yearning of both intellectuals and the masses for strength in the White House—form a volatile and dangerous combination in a democracy."[35]

The Constitution is so ambiguous about the Presidency that all three models described have been regarded as constitutional. In a few instances, actions by a Hamiltonian President have been struck down by the Supreme Court; but this proves little, because, as Presidents tend to appoint jurists who reflect their own views, what is unconstitutional at

[34] Burns, p. 29.
[35] Burns, p. 121.

one time becomes constitutional at another. Particularly since World War II, Presidents have expanded their personal power and that of the entire executive bureaucracy.

National Security as a Weapon of Executive Power

Since about 1965, the President has operated under an umbrella called "national security." Whether the United States had any authentic national security problems at that time is open to debate, but since our detente with China and the Soviet Union and our "peace with honor" in Vietnam, it is difficult to imagine as of 1974 just what external or internal enemies of any consequence the nation has.

However, buttressed by the claim that our national security is at stake, we now know the executive branch can plan and execute a system of *international and domestic surveillance* similar to that performed by the secret police of certain of the most distasteful foreign dictatorships. Although the presidentially approved plan to make of the FBI a true secret police was revoked because of J. Edgar Hoover's intransigence, the executive branch was able, beginning in the summer of 1970, to harness the efforts of the CIA, the National Security Agency, and the Defense Intelligence Agency for a comprehensive system of surveillance of domestic dissenters of all sorts, including teachers, Congressmen, government workers, youth groups, black militants, and so on.

More recently, under the shield of national security, top presidential assistants conducted the most widespread and effective program of political espionage and sabotage in the nation's history, employing illegal manipulation of funds, burglary, and wiretapping. The "enemy" in this case was apparently the democratic electoral process itself, although many of the President's supporters felt it was only the Democratic party.[36]

The concept of national security—no matter how secure the nation may be—is also used in peacetime by the Office of the Presidency, with the willing assistance of the military establishment, to justify the development of costly new weapons systems and the maintenance of large fighting forces and stockpiles of war material. Without legal warrant, it was used to justify massive bombing of Cambodia during the spring of 1973.

Evaluation of Presidential Government

These developments, however, do not answer the question, "Is presidential government a good or a bad thing?" James MacGregor Burns in the mid-1960s, although voicing some reservations, seemed to be saying that

---

[36] Much of the above was not known until late spring, 1973, and the 1970 "plot" to install domestic surveillance was not fully reported until the last week of May, 1973.

presidential Government in the United States has been inevitable all along and that it offers great potential for implementing democratic values in an age of advanced industrialism. He saw the Presidency as the one possible agency through which the will of the people could be funneled, and the only agency with the power to keep the nation on a democratic path. To Burns the Presidency was potentially the directorate of the people— an office under the direct control of, and responsive to, the total citizenry.

However, in view of the American experience since 1966, Burns has raised serious questions about the workability, in a modern context, of a presidential system of government. In his latest book (as of this writing), Burns seems to feel that the American public is so confused about the relation between means and ends, as is also the executive branch of the government, that rational functioning of our political system has become all but impossible. Failure to understand that one's ends are implicit in the means one uses to achieve them leads to the doctrine that "the end justifies the means." This idea, formerly associated with authoritarian communism, appears to dominate much of both private and public life in the United States today.[37]

James sees present-day liberals as in an ironic position: after promoting the centralization of power in the Presidency (beginning with Franklin Roosevelt), they can now see that such a process is safe only if the President is a democratically committed person, and is, at the same time, extremely well informed and strong enough to break through the communication barriers the bureaucracy surrounding the office tends to erect.[38] Fisher has reached the conclusion that the balance of powers intended by the Founding Fathers has eroded away under the presidential system and the only means of avoiding an authoritarian/totalitarian state would be through drastic amendment of the Constitution.[39] In the introduction to his excellent book of readings, Hirschfield also adopts a pessimistic view, suggesting that "The executive's control over America's nuclear arsenal gives him more naked power than any man has ever possessed."[40]

Power as Conceptualized for this Book

After studying the sources noted above, plus a great many more, including the daily press, the writer feels that of the two major opposed theories

[37] James MacGregor Burns, *Un-Common Sense.* New York: Harper & Row, Publishers, 1972.

[38] James, *The Contemporary Presidency,* p. xi.

[39] Louis Fisher, *President and Congress: Power and Policy,* New York: The Free Press, 1972, pp. 236–239.

[40] Robert S. Hirschfield (ed.), *The Power of the Presidency: Concepts and Controversy.* New York: Atherton Press, Inc. 1968, pp. 9–10.

of how power functions in the United States (elitism vs. pluralism), elitist theory commands far more support than pluralist theory.

Pluralist theory is probably most applicable for interpreting the power structure in this country during much of its history prior to the 1930s; and for interpreting the exercise of power in many local communities in some areas of decision making. Even in local communities, however, power elites come and go, and some local events are quite outside the hands of locals to control—for example, the supply and pricing of petroleum products which rests with Aramco, an international petroleum cartel, in cooperation with the eight or ten largest petroleum companies in the United States.

Elitist theory was not only highly controversial, but in bad repute in the mid-1950s when Mills published *The Power Elite*. However, since the mid-1960s an increasing number of books and scholarly articles have appeared which promote some form of power-elite theory. As of the 1970s, it is difficult to find more than a handful of social scientists who care to defend a pluralist theory of power.

We therefore conclude that the hypothesis around which we have been marshaling evidence for so many pages is essentially correct. We will be more explicit, however, by spelling out in some detail our own theory of power in Figure 5–3.

In Figure 5–3, A^1 refers to the core, or innermost power center, of the power elite—the President and his top advisers, perhaps some cabinet members, the Supreme Court, boards of directors of foundations and boards of trustees of major universities, the leadership of the hundred or so largest corporations, top Pentagon figures, and military field commanders. The number of persons in this group can only be estimated, but at most it is probably no more than a thousand.

A refers to the remainder of the power elite—according to both Baltzell's and Domhoff's empirical studies. no more than one-half of 1 percent of the total population (i.e., roughly about a million persons, probably less).

Level B is the middle layer of power, whose decision making is confined to matters of less scope and importance than those of organizations at the A level. The elements of the middle layer include both leaders and members of national, regional, or state organizations such as the following: medium to rather large corporations; Congress; the Federal Court system and state supreme courts; legislatures of our largest states; political parties; larger labor unions; military or paramilitary organizations not a part of the armed forces; Federal regulatory agencies; national veterans organizations; the Committee for Economic Development (CED) and the National Association of Manufacturers (NAM); the national Chamber of Commerce; reformist and consumer organizations (e.g., Common Cause,

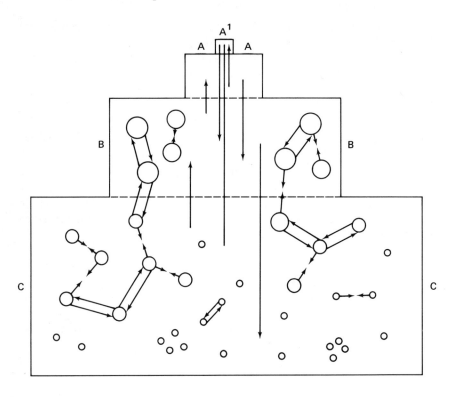

CODE

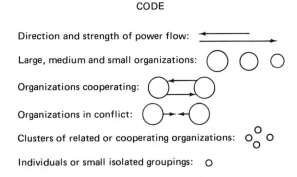

FIGURE 5-3. American power structure as assumed in this book.

the National Organization of Women; the NAACP, Zero Population Growth, the Sierra Club, and Consumers Union); and a variety of professional organizations (e.g., the AMA [which is losing power], the NEA, the American Association of University Professors (AAUP), perhaps the American Sociological Association); and much of the mass media.

Level C consists largely of regional, state, and local groupings (although a few may be national in scope) ranging all the way from kin and friendship groupings, PTAs, clubs, state and local governments, local and appellate courts, local police forces, units of the League of Women's Voters, smaller labor unions, organizations based on ethnic or race affiliations, taxpayers associations, Boy and Girl Scouts, YMs and YWCAs, churches, 4-H Clubs, local entertainment and news media, state colleges and universities, and the like.

Even though there is organization at Level C, readers should first note that, like Level B, organizations vary greatly in size and strength, some are in conflict and some pull together, but what sets level C apart from level B is: (1) Level C organizations are more dispersed, smaller, less powerful; and (2) Level C includes millions of people who belong to no formal organizations, who, if they are united at all, unite chiefly through family and friendship groups or a common feeling of alienation. This large section of persons at Level C are *essentially powerless* and correspond fairly well to Mills' concept of the *mass*.

It appears that a major defect of all the earlier elitist theories in explaining power in the United States is that they have paid too little attention to the rise of presidential government. As previously noted, it was not until the sixties, and particularly after 1965, that elitist theorists began seeing the Office of the Presidency as the coordinating agency for other major power centers, including the military and corporate oligarchies. However, the seventies may see fundamental changes with the possibility even of a dispersal of power which would make a modified pluralist model more acceptable than at any time since the 1930s. As of 1974, it seems possible that the Watergate scandal will reduce significantly the power of the President, increase the power of Congress, and cause leaders of many middle-level power centers to collaborate in the dispersal of power which, heretofore, they have been content to let the top power echelons gradually extract from them. There is perhaps even room for hope that average voters will become sufficiently interested in politics to try seriously to understand the American power system and vote in a way to strengthen such democratic forces as exist.

THE POWER STRUCTURE AND EDUCATION

Now we will suggest some of the more conspicuous implications of the American power structure for the functioning of our public schools. The topic will be resumed, in a different context, in the chapter "Who Should Control the Schools?" Here we will discuss the top power layer (the power elite), the middle power layer, and state and local power. This trichotomy is artificial, because to a considerable degree the three levels form an organic whole. Although lines drawn between them are arbitrary, it seems advantageous to treat these power levels separately.

Top Power Echelons and Education

Some writers have argued that the power elite has little concern for how the public schools operate so long as public education tends to be supportive of the present social system. This is probably true concerning details; we can hardly imagine the board of directors of ITT or General Motors becoming agitated over whether schools should have courses on sex education. Even so, the top power layer does take various steps which are at least potentially capable of having a profound influence on education at the local level.

The Federal Government

We shall begin with the executive branch. Beginning mainly in the 1960s, presidents have proposed legislation to create special education programs and to permit Federal funding for such programs, especially in the more impoverished states or impoverished school districts in wealthier states. Part of this legislation has related to equalization of education for Whites, Blacks, and minority ethnic groups.

The Department of Health, Education and Welfare (HEW) makes numerous studies of problem situations and proposes specific remedies. In addition, HEW publishes leaflets, pamphlets, and a magazine, *American Education,* devoted to educational issues. Publications of other Federal departments such as Commerce and Defense are also intended as educational and have been used by many teachers. Now that "Federal aid to education," once a highly controversial subject, has become nationally popular, we may expect the Federal Government to move increasingly toward providing funds and programs for local levels—except for temporary cutbacks when a particular President puts Federal aid to education low on his priority list.

Congress is, and will continue to be, inevitably involved with public education. Legislation proposed by the executive branch has to be approved, modified, or rejected by Congress; further, Congress controls the purse strings and can accept, increase, or trim the President's budgetary requests. Because Congressmen feel closer to their constituency than members of the executive branch, it is likely that the Congressional tendency will be to vote more money for aid to education than the President requests—which may not help if the President chooses not to spend the money authorized.

The Supreme Court can, and is likely to, play an important part in Federal policy regarding education. The Court's 1954 decision in Brown v. Board of Education declared laws requiring separate but equal schools for Blacks and Whites were unconstitutional. This led to Congress' passing the 1964 Civil Rights Bill and subsequent efforts to abolish even de facto segregation due to residential patterns. Court decisions affecting parochial education, religion in the public schools, freedom of speech, and other matters, have had, and will continue to have, major direct and indirect influence on how school affairs are conducted.

The Military Establishment

Although the military establishment is attached to and is constitutionally under the control of the executive branch, it deserves separate treatment here. The Department of Defense publishes numerous materials about the armed forces, which may or may not seem controversial to educators. Teaching materials propagated by Defense are likely to more-or-less glorify the armed forces and their functions, but perhaps even of more significance, to inject into the larger culture a military psychology and the Pentagon's own bureaucratic myths. One incident illustrates well what can happen.

During the 1960s the Department of Defense produced a film called *Why Vietnam?* It had an aura of authenticity because it quoted President Johnson, Secretary of State Rusk, and Secretary of Defense McNamara. The department called this item "one of our most popular films;" it was widely shown in colleges and high schools. It was presented as "historical fact," but one of the nation's most widely acclaimed historians has asserted that virtually all of the purportedly factual content was either patently false or seriously distorted.[41]

A film such as *Why Vietnam?* is relatively unimportant compared to the amount of enforced military education provided through the Reserve Officers Training Corps (ROTC). The basic program was originally mandatory for all male freshmen and sophomores in Land Grant Colleges. Later, it was introduced in numerous private colleges and universities. The program is operated by military professionals and uses teaching materials supplied by the Department of Defense. Students may contract for a full four-year course leading to a reserve commission in the armed forces. Although the ROTC came under sharp attack in many universities during the 1960s, and some schools dropped the program, this loss was offset to a degree by new schools applying for ROTC contracts with the government.

The Junior ROTC, designed for high schools, has also been operated

[41] Henry Steele Commager, *The Commonwealth of Learning*, New York: Harper & Row, Publishers, 1968, p. 227.

by the professional military with similar teaching materials. It, too, has come under attack, but survives in numerous schools. Many junior high schools have had a "little brother" version, the Cadets, handled by local teachers. The Civil Air Patrol program admits boys and girls between 13 and 18 years of age.[42]

The Major Corporations

In a discussion of the role of giant corporations, readers should understand that individual corporations usually tend to funnel their wishes through their trade associations. Examples of these associations are the National Association of Manufacturers, the Aerospace Industries Association of America, the Automobile Manufacturers Association, the American Iron and Steel Institute, the Mining and Metallurgical Society of America, the American Petroleum Institute, and the Association of American Railroads.

The views of corporate interests are expressed through a business-oriented press. Most of these newspapers and magazines are high quality and useful to teachers, but are also sympathetic enough to corporate aspirations that teachers wishing to be objective would want to counterbalance them with more liberal publications. Among the more important publications are The Wall Street Journal, National Observer, National Review, Business Week, and U.S. News and World Report. Less reputable because of its propagandistic character is The Nation's Business, published by the Chamber of Commerce of the U.S.A.

The general press (newspapers, magazines, books) in its editorial policies tends to support top- and middle-echelon power centers—except for small-town papers which may concern themselves only with community affairs. As previously indicated, highly conservative or radical-right publishers dominate at least 80 percent of the industry, and slant their news accordingly. However, the 20 percent of neutral or liberal papers include some of the most influential papers in the country, a few of which have national circulation, for instance, the New York Times, Washington Post, St. Louis Post Dispatch, Los Angeles Times, and Christian Science Monitor.

It appears obvious that large corporate interests have abundant opportunity to saturate the culture with a "big business ideology." Through the business-oriented press, the majority of general newspapers, the electronic media, and a few general magazines (e.g., The Readers' Digest)

---

[42] William Boyer, "War Education," Phi Delta Kappan, May 1967, pp. 418–421; also, see Boyer's recent book, Education for Annihilation, Honolulu: Hogarth Press-Hawaii, 1972. Yarmolinsky includes a sketch of ROTC programs, pp. 232–233; Ackley treats the "military mind" (which dominates the ROTC).

American minds are bombarded regularly with procorporate articles, editorials, columnists, news, and advertising.

Cultural saturation with an ideology uncritically favorable to the American business system is bound to influence the thinking of many individuals, groups, and organizations that exert direct control over the schools. Publishers of textbooks and other teaching materials may slant such materials to reflect a one-sided probusiness ideology. To the extent that public opinion influences educational practice—as it does, particularly through state legislatures, state superintendents, and local school boards— it may force on the schools a curriculum with a lopsided pro-big-business emphasis.

The large corporations also play some role in school finance. On occasion individual corporations and trade associations supply grants to school systems so the schools "favored" can develop some special program its sponsors feel will support corporate interests. However, it is likely the primary way of reaching schools financially is through foundations. For example, since its founding the Ford Foundation has shown a strong interest in education and has supplied funds for numerous experimental programs. The foundations may have no particular corporate message to propagate, but only a few foundations have been known to promote strongly liberal or leftish ideas.

Both trade associations and individual corporations publish free and low-cost educational materials intended for publicity and educational purposes. The author once sent a hundred post cards to trade associations and large corporations requesting samples of material available free in classroom quantities. He received enough to fill four file drawers. They ranged from the solidly informational to the blatantly propagandistic.

The Middle Power Echelons and Education

The middle layer of the national American power system differs from the top layer largely because it lacks unity. This layer includes many individuals and organizations that have an interest in the informal education of adults as well as the formalized education of children and youth in schools. The attempts of these groups to dictate in one way or another what should be taught, and how, may not be as effective as efforts of the top power group, or state and local groups. This is likely because at the middle-power layer there are such multitude of groups with opposing interests that the power of each may to some degree be canceled by one or more veto groups.

There are the middle-sized corporations and minor trade associations that advocate probusiness education. Veterans organizations advocate education for patriotism (as they define it) and for military preparedness. The national AFL-CIO and individual unions are interested in injecting prolabor content into school curriculums. The American Medical Association argues against "socialized medicine." The Boy and Girl Scouts of America and Campfire Girls advocate "wholesome" living, including conventional morality. Groups such as the NAACP, CORE, Urban League, and B'nai B'rith fight against racism in the schools. Church groups argue for—or against depending on the group—religious education in schools. The Daughters of the American Revolution castigate anything revolutionary. The Womens Christian Temperance Union and the Prohibition party both attack the evils of alcohol. The American Farm Bureau Association fights for large corporate agricultural interests, while the Grange and Farmer's Union fight for small farmers. The John Birch Society tries to convince the general public as well as educators that many school programs are a Communist plot. Minute Men of America urge everyone to be alert for a Communist takeover any minute. Conservation organizations manage to get their subject introduced. Ralph Nader's organization and Consumer's Union urge consumer education, while the National Safety Council wants safety education in every school.

The foregoing "veto" groups represent only a fraction of organizations that have an interest in how the schools function. Many have local affiliates, but the local subgroups rely heavily on the nationals for inspiration, money, and teaching materials.

State and Local Pressures

In most states school practice is heavily influenced by the opinions of the governor, the legislature, the state superintendent of schools, and the state board of education. No one should be misled into thinking that state governments function autonomously: many of their actions stem from pressures applied by groups higher in the power hierarchy—the national power elite and such middle-layer groups as were mentioned. But, equally, state actions are also influenced by public opinion which seems to spring from the grass roots but is in the main influenced by forces at the top and middle power layers in the culture.

Since state and local controls over education are treated in Chapter 14, we will develop this subject later.

Conclusion: A Case Study of Power at Work

One of the most frequent targets of power exercised over schools has been the content of education: pushes come from outside the schools either to include something new or to discard a subject being taught. One outcome is that teaching materials often contain much more myth than fact. Nelson and Roberts have done one of the best studies on censorship and the schools since Howard K. Beale's *Are American Teachers Free?*[43]

Nelson and Roberts describe hundreds of instances of censorship, but because it illustrates points we wish to make better than other examples, we have selected an event that received national notoriety in the early 1940s. This is the case of the Rugg social studies textbooks.

Harold Rugg (1886–1960) was an internationally known, highly reputable educator and social scientist who spent most of his professional career at Columbia University. Because public school social studies textbooks in the 1920s were primarily myth, Rugg decided a series of honest books to cover all grades from primary through junior high school were needed. With a research team of sixteen young social scientist educators, Rugg began researching and writing in the 1920s.

His intent was to produce factual, interesting books which would not ignore the large controversies of our culture. They were not biased in

[43] Jack Nelson and Gene Roberts, Jr., *The Censors and the Schools*, Boston: Little, Brown and Company, 1963.

favor of the then current WASP majority; they pointed out flaws in our capitalistic system and contradictions inherent in our Constitution. As the books appeared, they were acclaimed widely by educators and social scientists as the first honest portrayal of the United States in public school textbooks. By 1939, Rugg had completed his series. That year, school systems of the United States purchased 300,000 copies and Rugg was regarded by teachers generally as one of our most outstanding educators.

Beginning in 1939 there were a few forays by conservative pressure groups against the Rugg books, but nothing major occurred until September, 1940, when the *American Legion Magazine* attacked Rugg. It made these books one of its "patriotic causes." The Legion was ably assisted by several other organizations including the National Association of Manufacturers, the Advertising Federation of America, and the DAR. Despite a general acceptance of the Rugg books in 1939, it required only a year and a half to convince large numbers of parents and other adults that the Rugg books were not only against religion and capitalism, but were subversive, and that Rugg was a dangerous radical with Communist leanings. Everyone who knew Rugg personally knew that his first commitment was to democracy and that he had been neither a member of nor associated with any left wing organizations.

There were hundreds of hearings in 1940 concerning the Rugg books. Rugg himself attended many. When he and his supporters asked persons at the hearings why they were attacking the books, one of the most dismaying responses received was "I haven't read the books, but. . . ."

The present author was teaching in a small city high school in Ohio in the school year of 1943–1944. During the previous school year, the local American Legion had sponsored a public burning of the Rugg texts (which had been used locally for several years), replete with the staging of what the Legion apparently regarded as proper patriotic ceremonies—including the burning of a cross in the town square Ku Klux Klan style!

The affair of the Rugg textbooks illustrates much that we have tried to convey in this chapter. When the Legion and DAR acted, they were representing several elements of the power elite in the United States but primarily the interests of the military establishment and the military conception of reality. When the NAM and the Advertising Federation entered the stage, they represented large corporate interests. There was little or no protest from groups in the middle power layer or at the local level—except from teachers and school administrators. In the absence of protest, it can be said that most elements of the middle, state, and local power centers *encouraged* this act of censorship. Thus, individuals and groups at all power levels, both public and private, were about equally culpable. The case of the Rugg texts illustrates as well as any case known to this author how, in an instance where the public schools are imagined to be a threat to the American power structure, the most socially useful part of the curriculum can be excised in a span of little more than a year.

STUDY QUESTIONS

1. Do you think anyone could be elected President of this country if that person was opposed by big business and the military? Do you think big business and the military could function as major power centers if the President opposed it?

2. Develop a list of the ways in which large corporations exert control over national, state, and local governments. How much power do you think big business in the United States should have?

3. Under what circumstances, if any, do you think it is appropriate for a powerful person or group to lie to stay powerful? Could any power center remain such for long if it told the truth all the time?

4. A former president of General Motors once said that "What is good for General Motors is good for the country." Do you agree? Why or why not?

5. Most political scientists feel that there is a fascist streak in American culture. On what do you think they base their arguments? How would you define fascism in the context of American culture?

6. As of this reading, what do you think the consequences on the nation of the Watergate scandal of 1972–1973 has been? What do you think the situation would be if the Watergate episode had remained secret?

7. List all the contradictions you can find in the American Constitution.

8. Suppose you were asked to rewrite those parts of the United States Constitution relating to the functioning of power. How would you change it?

9. How could the United States Congress be reformed so it could exercise its intended powers more efficiently?

10. Many social scientists see the interest of certain powerful labor unions and their employers merging so that they are likely to form a single power bloc (the Teamsters Union and employers of teamsters are often given as an example). What is behind this movement? Do you think it is good or bad for the country?

11. As you understand the meaning of democracy, how many of your friends do you feel are committed to it? What about your parents? Your grandparents?

12. How would you describe the power system in your own home community? Is it what it seems on the surface or do there seem to be invisible forces "pulling strings"?

13. What organizations or other groupings in your community represent the interests of the national power elite? Where would you place in the power hierarchy the John Birch Society? The American Nazi Party? The Daughters of the American Revolution?

14. Have any of the schools you have attended been controlled by a power elite? If so, who composed the elite?

15. Do you think the main purpose of the schools is to serve as spokesmen for major power centers? If you don't (and no one really thought you did), what do you think could be done to rectify the situation?

16. If the public schools are now very low on the power "totem pole," what steps do you think could be taken to give them more authority and autonomy?

17. How would you evaluate your own power status with reference to your friends, family, teachers and school officials the local police?

ANNOTATED BIBLIOGRAPHY

Bogart, Leo, *Silent Politics: Polls and the Awareness of Public Opinion.* New York: John Wiley & Sons, Inc., 1972.

Bogart is a well-known specialist on public opinion polling and this book is about how polls not only report but influence what people think. He shows how polls have been used to manipulate opinion on many issues. Since the present book often relies on poll data (for want of any better), readers should dip into Bogart's book to maintain proper skepticism.

Bradshaw, Kenneth, and David Pring, *Parliament and Congress.* Austin: University of Texas Press, 1972.

Both authors have been clerks of the British House of Commons for more than twenty years. Their book is an authoritative and detailed comparison of the parliamentary and presidential systems of government.

Domhoff, G. William, *Fat Cats and Democrats: The Role of the Big Rich in the Party of the Common Man.* Englewood Cliffs, N.J.: Prentice-Hall, Inc., 1972.

Domhoff, whose conception of the power structure has caused many of his critics to view him as some kind of "radical leftist," demonstrates in this book that he is nonpartisan. A good study on how money can buy congressional votes.

Evans, M. Stanton, *The Future of Conservatism: From Taft to Reagan and Beyond.* New York: Holt, Rinehart and Winston, Inc., 1968.

Evans, editor of the *Indianapolis News* and associate editor of the *National Review*, assesses the future of conservatism in the United States. He feels the odds favor a resurgence of conservatism because much of the electorate is tired of the encroachment of centralized power upon personal autonomy.

Hofstadter, Richard, *The Paranoid Style in American Politics and Other Essays,* New York: Alfred A. Knopf, Inc., 1965.

A collection of essays on moods and beliefs underlying Americans' political actions. The essays include discussions of both the habitual American belief that the nation is always under threat by "conspirators," and the alienation from American traditions of pseudoconservatives (what we called in the Prologue *radical* conservatives).

Keogh, James, *President Nixon and the Press.* New York: Funk & Wagnalls, 1972.

Keogh reports the strenuous efforts of the Nixon Administration to combat biased news reporting about Nixon's management of domestic and foreign affairs. Keogh feels that never in recent history has the work of a dedicated President been so unfairly treated by journalists. He argues against any kind of journalistic advocacy and for straight reporting of facts only. Keogh was a former special assistant to President Nixon and is a long-time friend of the President and his family.

Lens, Sidney, *The Military-Industrial Complex*. Philadelphia: Pilgrim Press Books, 1970.

Lens is a veteran journalist and free-lance author who writes on the organic relationship between the giant corporations and the military establishment. Well documented and a good source of statistics not generally available.

Levin, Murray B., *Political Hysteria in America; the Democratic Capacity for Repression*. New York: Basic Books, Inc., 1972.

Levin argues that American ideology has always been polarized, with Adam Smith's concept of laissez-faire at one extreme and John Locke's concepts of equality and natural rights at the other (a conflict mentioned in Chapter 3 of the present book). These opposed ideas create a tension that various elites exploit by creating mass hysteria, usually "red scares." A hysterical majority then tries to destroy any dissenting minorities.

Nelson, Jack, and Gene Roberts, Jr., *The Censors and the Schools*. Little, Brown and Company, 1963.

Probably the best book since the 1930s on how national, regional, and local pressures are applied to administrators and teachers to censor the reading material of students. This book shows clearly the timidity—or lack of concern—of school boards, administrators, and teachers when confronted with pressure groups who prefer that schooling be brainwashing rather than education. The situation may have improved slightly since 1963.

Schrag, Peter, *Voices in the Classroom: Public Schools and Public Attitudes*. Boston: Beacon Press, 1965.

Schrag spent three months visiting ten communities to observe school functioning. He concluded that schools tend to be creatures of the local community and highly subject to all the prejudices and pressures one might expect. Very good material on academic freedom and pressures applied on teachers to avoid the controversial. Schrag leans toward the "open classroom" idea but feels there are no simple answers to reforming our authoritarian schools.

Sheridan, Walter, *The Fall and Rise of Jimmy Hoffa*, New York: The Saturday Review Press, 1973.

Sheridan, an investigative reporter, has written a critical biography of Hoffa and the Teamster's Union. This book is particularly significant for the 1970s because of the growing link between certain big unions (the Teamsters especially), large corporate interests, and the Federal Government.

6

UNITED STATES FOREIGN POLICY AND EDUCATION

One of the ironies of education is the extent to which some teachers believe that the practice of dishonesty is necessary to the teaching of honest patriotism.

Lawrence E. Metcalf

The most prestigious of our professional educators have become increasingly cognizant since World War II of the implications for public education of the international scene. The United States is no longer an island unto itself as isolationists have thought it should and could be. Everytime a citizen votes for a President and Vice-President, a congressman, or even elected state officials, that voter is in effect voting for or against a detente with nations formerly regarded as "enemies," continuation of the arms race, economic protectionism, economic or educational aid to Third World nations, support of vicious dictatorships we euphemistically refer to as a part of the "free world," a particular international monetary system, and so on and on.

To state the case more sharply: American citizens, by their votes, may in large measure determine whether there will be a World War III, a guerrilla-type world civil war between the have and have-not nations, or, in fact, the survival of civilization itself.

Yet, as we will make clear in the final section of this chapter, our public schools have achieved virtually nothing in educating future citizens about foreign peoples and their problems. The curriculum is largely a blank in this respect; international education is one of the major pieces of unfinished business of public education and it would be impossible for us to overstress the necessity of major corrections—and soon.

BELIEFS—OLD AND NEW—ABOUT AMERICAN FOREIGN POLICY

As the first foreign policy statements made by the young United States almost two centuries ago reflected an isolationist slant, and as isolationism has since played a prominent role in our belief patterns, we shall begin by examining ideas related to this concept.

Isolationist Beliefs

Isolationism, stated as a general position, says in effect, "Foreign nations should mind their own business, stay out of our affairs, and we should do likewise." George Washington's farewell address is a classical statement of isolationist policy: "... since history and experience prove that foreign influence is one of the most baneful foes of republican government... The great rule of conduct for us in regard to foreign nations is, in extending our commercial relations to have with them as little political connection as possible. ..."

Some other statements of belief held by isolationists might be as follows:

—The United States should confine its interests to its own affairs or, at most, to the affairs of North and South America.
—It is just as well that we don't know very much about distant nations or that other nations don't know everything about us.
—The United States should develop its economy in the direction of self-sufficiency so as to be economically independent.
—The military effort of the United States should be strictly confined to defending our own boundaries.

Since it is no longer possible for the United States to ignore the rest of the world and since other nations seem to have no intention of ignoring us, the old ideas related to self-sufficiency have undergone major changes, particularly since World War II. In the thinking of many persons, isolationism now takes the form of a "go it alone" policy in the intervention into the domestic affairs of certain other nations. Many Americans now seem to think:

—The United States should have the right, unilaterally, to dominate or interfere with, as we wish, any other country.
—The United Nations, NATO, SEATO, and other organizations are acceptable to us only if we can dominate them.
—It does not matter what other nations think about us.[1]

Expansionist and Imperialist Beliefs[2]

Under this heading we suggest examples of beliefs that have supported the varied and numerous moves to expand our own territory and to dominate other nations for religious, economic, political, or other reasons. During the long period of westward expansion on the North American continent, there was an underlying idea which came to be called "Manifest Destiny." The idea of Manifest Destiny was well stated by the editor of a New York newspaper who wrote in 1845 of "our manifest destiny to overspread and to possess the whole of the continent which Providence has given us for the development of the great experiment of liberty and federated self-government." This was obviously a highly idealized version. Manifest Destiny was a cover for a mixture of economic and political motives: gaining more land for the increasing horde of Anglos and other Europeans, more room for the expansion of slavery, and more valuable natural resources. In retrospect manifest destiny seems to have had little to do with spreading liberty or self-government except among the invaders themselves, as evidenced by such oft-repeated slogans and beliefs as:

—The only good Indian is a dead Indian.
—Mexicans are too childlike to bring civilization to the Southwest.

[1] See Lloyd A. Free and Hadley Cantril, *The Political Beliefs of Americans: A Study of Public Opinion.* New York: Simon & Schuster, Inc., 1968, Chap. 6, for majority opinion supporting isolation in the 1930s and the contrasting minority holding such views in 1964.

[2] Arthur A. Ekirch, Jr., *Ideas, Ideals, and American Diplomacy: A History of Their Growth and Interaction.* New York: Appleton-Century-Crofts, 1966, has chapters on "Manifest Destiny" and "Expansion Abroad," which discuss interacting ideology and national interests—how Americans have been motivated by them and used them to rationalize their actions.

—Fifty-four forty or fight.
—Remember the Alamo!

As our interests turned southward during the second half of the nineteenth century, Americans formulated many opinions about our Latin neighbors such as:

—Central and South American countries are not morally responsible.
—Central and South American countries are incapable of governing themselves.
—Latin America should welcome American business investment.

By the end of the nineteenth century our gaze had gone beyond our own hemisphere, the culmination of a process begun shortly past the mid-1800s but not then fulfilled. Still goaded by the idea of Manifest Destiny, our views about overseas expansion in the 1890s, although having a slightly different cast, remained fundamentally the same:

—It is the duty of the United States to help educate, civilize, and Christianize the Oriental heathens.
—The United States should be allowed to trade with any country it wishes even if we have to force the recalcitrant natives to trade with us.
—It is good for United States traders to profit as much as possible without worrying much about those they trade with.
—The United States ought to take possession of what overseas territories have not already been seized by the European powers.

In 1899, at the close of the Spanish American war, President William McKinley's thinking exemplified that of most Americans. After praying for divine guidance in deciding what to do about the Philippines, McKinley paced the floor all one night and the answer came to him, "There was nothing left for us to do but to take them all, and to educate the Filipinos, and uplift and civilize and Christianize them...." That this view did not lead the United States to become a major colonial power was due to European nations having already adopted almost everything of value in the Pacific and Far East.

In the twentieth century the picture changed. Expansionism came to mean largely economic expansionism in the only manner available to us. Its supporting ideas can be found in these newer beliefs:

—Foreign nations should be grateful for American corporate investment on their soil.
—Overseas investment is good for everybody; it stimulates our economy and raises the standard of living of the foreign nations involved.
—All foreign nations should have sense enough to adopt American capitalism as their way of life.

—Foreign nations should be willing to trade with us on terms that will guarantee a favorable balance of trade to the U.S. (i.e., trade that will put foreign nations in debt to us).
—No foreign nation has the moral or legal right to seize American-owned corporate property.

Such ideas as those above may still be widely held by some Middle Americans. But this kind of ideology is at least partially under attack, especially the notions that all other countries should adopt American-style capitalism and that foreign governments have no legal or moral right to seize U.S. property on their soil.

Beliefs about Ethnocentrism, Nationalism, Patriotism and War

Although this heading seems very broad, beliefs subsumed under it are all related to some degree.[3] They include ideas like the following:

—The United States has exerted a greater influence for good, morally and in all other ways, than any other nation.
—One's first loyalty should be to the government of the United States, or My country, right or wrong.
—Critics of United States foreign policy are guilty of treason and should be dealt with accordingly.
—When the United States is threatened by foreign powers, everyone should close ranks and support our government.
—The flag is the chief symbol of our way of life and should always be treated with respect.
—A true patriot sincerely participates in all ceremonies of a patriotic nature.
—God has always been on the side of the United States, both in peace and in war.
—The United States has never fought an unjust war.
—War is always better than peace without honor.
—Any patriot should be willing to die for his country.

Some New-Culture Beliefs

It appears obvious at this point in the 1970s that young dissidents as well as many older persons are disillusioned about our traditional beliefs regarding foreign policy, diplomacy, nationalism, and patriotism. The nature of the new ideology is not clear yet because it is still in the making. The writer hypothesizes that the merging ideology governing foreign relations, war, and patriotism may lead to the establishment of such beliefs as the following:

[3] For a good short treatment of nationalist ideology, see Arnold J. Toynbee, "The Reluctant Death of Sovereignty," in *The Establishment and All That*, Santa Barbara, Calif.: Center for the Study of Democratic Institutions, 1970.

—The United States does not necessarily represent a model culture for the rest of the world to follow.

—Americans can learn a lot about how to manage their own affairs from other countries, even countries we have defined as our enemies.

—The United States is guilty of having started enough wars; from now on we should present to the world a peaceful image and try to atone for past aggressions.

—American corporate industry should either withdraw its investments from other countries, or at least make them nonexploitive and cease interfering in internal political affairs of other countries.

—The United States should quit trying to shore up every dictator who claims to be anti-Communist; instead, this country should get on the side of popular revolutionary movements.

—Patriotism can better be thought of as the duty to be critical of one's own government and sincerely generous of others. (In Yankelovich's [1974] college sample, only 19% felt patriotism was an important value.)

—No one should regard as true, without proof, statements made about foreign relations by any branch of the Federal Government.

AN "OUTRAGEOUS HYPOTHESIS" ABOUT FOREIGN RELATIONS

We should stress the tentativeness of anything we say about foreign relations during the middle seventies. The United States, in part because of its geography, could play a basically isolationist role in the community of nations from its beginning until the 1940s—a full century and a half. There remains a considerable segment of opinion that feels the United States should avoid all political entanglements abroad and concentrate on its domestic problems. This is apparently yet a minority view, but the minority holding it has probably increased since our protracted involvement in Indochina and because of our severe domestic problems.

However, the hypothesis we have chosen to examine focuses on what in effect is largely a domestic issue, and one concerning which many pertinent facts are available. Further, it probably has as many, if not more, direct implications for education as any other assertion we could have selected.

Hypothesis: *Nationalism and patriotism are both obsolete and a threat to human survival.*

Before discussing evidence relating to this assertion we must clarify its meaning. There are serious difficulties involved in defining nationalism and patriotism; we hope readers can manage without a formal definition of "obsolete" and "threat to human survival."

It would be convenient to be able to use a dictionary definition for these terms, since Webster's Third International Unabridged Dictionary defines both nationalism and patriotism simply as devotion to one's country or nation. Unfortunately, these definitions are too simple for scholarly writing, particularly when dozens of books have been written on the subject of nationalism and the foremost experts in the field have devoted hundreds of pages struggling to define the concept.

Lest readers think we are being flippant, nationalism has varied meanings in varied places and its meanings continue to evolve. Also, some writers use nationalism and patriotism interchangeably while others try to make a sharp distinction between them. Thus, there are extra definitional burdens in trying to test this hypothesis.

Nationalism

To understand nationalism as a form of group loyalty, we need to see the concept in relation to other kinds of group loyalty. There is loyalty to family, clan, tribe, town, city-state, feudal principality, nation—and perhaps to come in the future, federations of nations (such as a "United States of Europe"), and finally international or global loyalty, which a few individuals have already achieved. Most twentieth century persons are nationalists.

Hans Kohn has defined nationalism as a state of mind in which the supreme loyalty of the individual is to his nation. Carlton J. H. Hayes (with Kohn, considered one of the two major writers on nationalism of this century) has defined nationalism as a sentiment in which patriotism is fused with nationality but also with one's final allegiance to his nation. These concepts of nationalism say in effect that a dedicated nationalist will put loyalty to his nation above that to lover, family, clan, community, or any possible unit to which a person could give his loyalty.

If nationalism refers to devotion to a nation, we have to decide what a nation is. It will not do simply to say that a nation is a parcel of inhabited land with a government. To the nationalist, the concept of nation may include any or all of the following, in any mixture: an area of land, either had or wanted; a people who to some degree share a common culture and can communicate with one another; a set of goals or aspirations for the land and its people; some reasonably stable social and economic institutions; a common sovereign state (government); a shared belief in a common history, rarely bearing much relation to fact; a preference for one's fellow nationals over those of other nations; a shared pride in past achievement, often imaginary; and a shared indifference or hostility toward at least one other nation and preferably several.

We could name more aspects, but these are the most important. To the extreme nationalist all these and other loyalties meld together into a kind of mystical feeling of awe or reverence for an abstract concept of, for want of a better name, fatherland or *patrie*.

Of these features of nationalism, shared goals or aspirations are of key importance; more than any other feature, they help us distinguish between liberal and reactionary, and early and later nationalisms.

Early Nationalism

Nationalism, as the concept is now used, did not appear until the Cromwellian revolution in England in the 1640s. The aspirations of Puritan nationalism were "liberal" in the sense that they aimed at eradicating monarchical authoritarianism and feudalism. The Revolution of 1776 in the American colonies was a further push in the same direction. Although these steps were important, Kohn regards them as peripheral to the French Revolution of 1789 which he sees as the key to the meaning of liberal nationalism. The French experience, says Kohn, taught Europe:

> The cult of liberty, the aspiration toward nationhood one and indivisible, the longing for a new national cohesion and a new national spirit, the idea of a state rooted in popular consent and enthusiasm and supported by the active participation of the people—all these concepts were eagerly learned from France.[4]

Although this may have been the initial message of the French Revolution, French aspirations changed markedly between 1789 and 1793. Now, the "... tyrant to be fought was no longer the domestic oppressor but the foreign enemy; the liberty worshipped was not so much individual freedom ... but national independence and power." French nationalism became militant and expansionist and was thus distinguished from that of the English-speaking countries. Nationalism in Europe generally developed an absolutist cast, except in some of the smaller countries with established traditions of liberty, local self-government, and limitation of power, where nationalism promoted democracy (as in Switzerland, the Netherlands, and Scandinavia).[5]

Nationalism thus took two directions, one liberal, the other reactionary and authoritarian.

Twentieth-Century Nationalism

Divergent forms of nationalism persisted into the twentieth century; in a number of countries extreme turns were taken. The nonliberal nationalisms began to take on characteristics we associate with authoritarian dictatorships. The idea of a common descent and racial purity being basic

---

[4] Hans Kohn, The Age of Nationalism: The First Era of Global History. New York: Harper & Row, Publishers, 1962, p. 3.

[5] Kohn, pp. 3–5.

factors in nationalism was implied as early as the 1850s by Count Arthur de Gobineau, whose essay on race brought him ardent German admirers. Even the composer Wagner became a follower of *gobinism* (which the count claimed distorted his views), and began pushing anti-Semitism shortly after mid-century.

In France vacillation between an authoritarian and a democratic-tending nationalism continued through the nineteenth and into the twentieth century. Russian nationalism, authoritarian during the nineteenth century, continued so in the twentieth. The outcomes of authoritarian nationalisms were a Stalinist-type communism in Russia and the development of fascism in Italy, Spain, Portugal, and Germany (under the label of Nazism). Even into World War II France exhibited an internal ideological schism, with some French still advocating authoritarian nationalism and others advocating something more democratic. The only political movement to oppose nationalism—particularly its authoritarian forms—was Social Democracy (a European expression for democratic socialism).

Kohn argues that the basic ideas of fascism were much more widespread than many historians have recognized and that fascism was a potent force in a number of countries that did not officially claim it as their national ideology. However, many social scientists might argue that Kohn's definition of fascism is oversimplified. Kohn says "Fascism . . . [is] an exaggerated self-centered form of nationalism . . . [and] prevailed almost everywhere, though sometimes in disguised form.[6]

The shift in nationalism toward the right during the late nineteenth and early twentieth centuries was either not seen or misunderstood by many people who should have known better. The foremost U.S. nationalist of that period was Theodore Roosevelt, who proclaimed a "new nationalism" that would use the power of the central government to revive and enforce "the old pioneer sense of individualism and opportunity."[7] This led to "trust busting" and other approaches to "giving the government back to the people" in this country, but, perhaps a little like France, the United States from the 1890s to the mid-twentieth century showed intermingled and confused streaks of both liberal and authoritarian nationalism.

Nationalism and God

One aspect of nationalism in a number of countries is not merely that nationalists proclaim ethnocentrically that their people and their

[6] Kohn, p. 26.

[7] Louis L. Snyder, *The New Nationalism*. Ithaca, N.Y.: Cornell University Press, 1968, p. viii. Snyder, Kohn, and others state or imply the existence of a remarkable naivety in the United States about the developing directions of nationalism in Europe and elsewhere.

nation are "better" than any other, but that God favors their nation above all others.

In discussing the evils of nationalism, Kohn sees two of its most dangerous forms as those in which nationalists claim (1) common racial descent and purity (seen in countries heading toward overt fascism), and (2) divine sanction. When nationalism is tied to God's will, nations become not only exceptionally contemptuous of all other nations—who presumedly lack God's support for good reason—but all their wars are in effect religious wars, which tend to be more protracted and bloody than nonreligious wars. In discussing nationalisms that are not tempered by identification or sympathy with the values of humanity as a whole, Kohn says:

> Such a nationalism especially when it is based upon racial or religious uniformity or exclusivity produces, if it disposes of [sic] military strength and a militant spirit, a grave threat to its neighbors, and in any case a source of spiritual decay to its own members. A nationalism which claims sanction by the will of God or History, by religion or by a semireligious ideology, leads to the dangerous assumption of the position of a "unique" people, a chosen people.[8]

If any nation in the world has experienced a problem of trying to reconcile the special support of God and need to serve God's will with secular goals inconsistent with obedience to God, it is the United States. Paul Nagel has done a remarkable study on the roles of religion and secular, humanitarian ideals in the United States during the nineteenth century. Nagel based his study on thousands of original documents—letters, diaries, sermons, speeches—as well as hundreds of published works, focusing on the period from 1798 to 1898.[9]

Nagel's primary aim was to uncover, more thoroughly than anyone else, the struggle of Americans to decide what nationhood meant for this country. Nagel feels that trying to grasp what the United States stood for was the central feature of American thought during the nineteenth century, and that by the century's end a majority of the population felt they had resolved this issue.

Nagel focuses on nationality, which he defines as "what it means to be a nation." He regards this as including nationalism but being a broader concept, since to him nationalism means a form of consciousness conveying superiority, whereas nationality ". . . encompasses both the matter of citizenship and the ideology arising from belonging to a polity . . ."[10]

[8] Kohn, *The Age of Nationalism*, p. 13.

[9] Paul C. Nagel, *This Sacred Trust: American Nationality, 1798–1898.* New York: Oxford University Press, 1971.

[10] Nagel, p. xii.

Religion was a continuing and central factor in determining what Americans thought about themselves. They regarded their nationality as a divine trust and themselves as stewards and couched most of their talk about nationality in religious terms, speaking of our physical and political settings as being God's vineyard. Nineteenth-century America was a "politicized culture chained to a theological post."

There was an almost universally felt desire to be faithful tools of a demanding God, whose demands happened to coincide very much with the theology of John Calvin; but at the same time there was an equally strong desire to establish a democratic republicanism, guided by a free citizenry. The problem of Americans was that they wanted both the authoritarianism of divine rule and the freedom of a secular democracy, ideas which obviously contradict one another.

Whereas many historians have depicted American goals as being clear and Americans as knowing where they were going and why, Nagel argues (and supports his argument with massive documentation) that Americans have been a tormented psychologically disturbed people. Partnership with God ". . . became both an awesome asset and a torment for the nation." The torment, of course, was a result of feeling that the nation's "Trust" was to establish freedom under a God who demanded not freedom but obedience.[11]

How could the nation capitulate to God's will and at the same time freely determine its destiny? Secular democracy, which puts man in the foreground and God in the background, was clearly not the answer. "America waited for God until 1898 when the suspense ended." The problem was resolved by the Spanish-American War. President McKinley was not alone in seeing how to resolve the moral conflict: the answer was religious—and, more than a little, economic imperialism. We would now go forth and Christianize, first the Filipinos, but next all the rest of the Orient. Senator Platt called each American ship in Manila harbor "a new *Mayflower.*"

The war and its mission were badly needed. With the United States largely under the control of the business trusts, and with political and business corruption rampant everywhere, it was evident that something else was required. We had not done very well with republicanism, but "The century of debate over nationality found Americans more comfortably allied with God at its close than in 1798."[12]

With God behind us each step of the way, we were now in a position to civilize the Filipinos, to Christianize and trade with the Asians, and, more important, to face the twentieth-century challenge of four wars, including the longest one in our history.

[11] Nagel, pp. 50–51.
[12] Nagel, pp. 252–253.

Nationalism after 1945

Among writers talking of a "new nationalism" since the mid-twentieth century, Snyder has done one of the better studies. Much of this section will be indebted to him. Snyder says:

> The use of the term "new nationalism" is justifiable as an arbitrary device to facilitate its study. There is no such thing as a new nationalism in the same sense that there is no "ancient, medieval, or modern history"—divisions are made merely for the sake of convenience.[13]

(United Nations)

The new nationalism is a continuation of the old with some twists that make it unique enough to deserve a separate section. Snyder feels that 1945, the end of World War II, is a convenient dividing line. In the post-war era "new and vital characteristics" are superimposed on nationalism's earlier forms.

The reactionary nationalism of the nineteenth century had brought

[13] Snyder, *The New Nationalism*, p. 5.

twentieth-century authoritarian, totalitarian states—fascist and communist. But even where nationalism did not take forms leading to military aggression and internal persecution, it had remained a strong force toward ethnocentrism and separatism, as the experience with the League of Nations had demonstrated and later the inability of the Western World to help itself through international cooperation during the economic collapse of the 1930s.

The blood bath of World War II tamed reactionary nationalism in Europe to the point where the establishment of a common market was possible and we even began to hear talk of a United States of Europe during

(Copyright © Maurice P. Hunt, all rights reserved)

our lifetimes. But the pulling together of a number of European states has produced a kind of international nationalism which may be on the way toward keeping the world fragmented with Western Europe opposing both the Communist world and the United States; with continued union it might, like the United States, regard itself as one nation and compete as an ethnocentric entity with the other major power blocs. But although this may be an aspect of the new nationalism, what Snyder focuses on is the nationalism of all the new states that have come into existence since the war.

When the United Nations was established it had fifty-two member nations; in March, 1974, it had 135. When the British, French, and Dutch lost their overseas colonies after World War II, new nation-states formed rapidly in both Africa and Asia. Further, the nationalism of most of these new states has tended toward ethnocentric self-serving ends, and has often used violent means. One part of nationalism that has never changed is the idea of complete sovereignty for each nation, no matter how disastrous the potential consequences. As each new nation has used nationalism to go its own way, Snyder feels the world is much the worse for it. *It is the intensified fragmentation of those parts of the world containing a large proportion of its people (Africa, large parts of Asia) that Snyder calls the "new nationalism."*

Older nationalisms, whether benign or malign, have usually had some kind of logic—some basis in ethnic unity, a logical economic or geographic unit, a common language and other features of a common culture. The older nationalisms, when not fascist-tending, have served a purpose in giving people something to identify with and a basis for group formation less restricting than that of the old feudal dynasty or city-state. The nationalism of Europe and the American colonies led to large free trade units, as well as the development of laws and currencies covering much larger spans of territory. Hence it made possible the development of more dynamic economic institutions and steady, if often slow, gains in economic security.

In most cases the new national states have no rhyme or reason. Peoples without a common history or language are combined; peoples with a common history and language are split. When Snyder talks pessimistically of the new nationalism, he is not suggesting that the same irrationalities have never happened before: he considers it ridiculous, if the world is going to be composed of nation-states, that Britain and what came to be the United States were ever separated, and that Canada with its differing and often incompatible traditions (French and English) should be one country. These two examples, and one could find many more, of the illogical grouping of people illustrate rather precisely what Snyder is talking about when he refers to the new African and Asian states.

Patriotism

We have seen that some writers use the concepts of nationalism and patriotism almost interchangeably and others make little use of the concept of patriotism in discussing nationalism as their main issue. Yet, patriotism can usefully be defined as a different concept from nationalism but one which helps us understand nationalism better.

Patriotism as Means

Although we have not encountered in the literature a definition of patriotism as a means or method, we see such a way of viewing patriotism as one way of cutting through the semantic fog that has so often surrounded the terms patriotism and nationalism.

Although nationalism is also a means toward certain ends, it tends to be widely regarded as an end-in-itself. If we so regard it (for our purposes here), we can make a clear distinction between patriotism and nationalism by saying that *patriotism involves a group of beliefs and ensuing actions intended to achieve the end of nationalism.* Patriotism may refer to *any* cluster of beliefs and related actions that help serve nationalism; as such, what is viewed as patriotic evolves historically and varies widely from culture to culture. There is historical warrant for treating patriotism as means. Nationalism began to appear when narrower loyalties got in the way of the commercial and industrial revolutions. It was the need for larger political units with common currencies, languages, laws regulating trade, and military establishments to prevent robbery and other disruptions to business (as well as to protect against the expansionism of other states) that brought nationalism into being. As nation-states were formed there was no immediate reason for ordinary men and women to "love" or owe allegiance to the nation in the near-religious sense implied in the concept of patriotism. Their personal allegiances were still to the smaller units—the family, clan, town, or feudal lord.

It strikes us that the most plausible hypothesis concerning the origin of patriotism is that patriotism was taught through a variety of educational agencies by the power elites interested in creating, maintaining, and expanding their nations. Patriotic feelings among the citizens of the new nations had to be created to engender the support needed for national survival.

To us, patriotism hinges on convincing people to view favorably a number of items that *symbolize* a nation, that are concrete enough for people incapable of highly abstract thought to grasp, and that people can be persuaded to rally around when the nation's rulers need dedicated support—as during any national crisis, particularly war. One of the roles of a public school system has been to teach students positive feelings toward the national symbols so that when the symbols were displayed people would as a matter of habit act in a manner to serve the national interests.

The Instruments of Patriotism

What are some common national symbols that can be used to induce patriotism? Among the foremost are the name of the country itself, flag, national anthem, the military establishment with its uniforms, anthems, styles of drill, etc., national heroes, patriotic organizations, holidays, language, expressions symbolizing prized institutions (even if they do not exist, like "free enterprise" in the United States), and, of course, the land itself. The land may be symbolized by some special feature, like Bunker Hill or Mt. Fugi.

One could, of course, go on and on, because there is no theoretical limit to the numbers of objects and actions that can be made to symbolize a nation. There are mythical figures (Uncle Sam), national sports, in some nations a national religion and in others simply *having* a religion or expressing a belief in God (crucial in the United States), shrines and museums, animals (eagles are common), national seals, famous achievements, a special architecture, and so on and on.

A person's patriotism can be judged by the amount of reverence he shows to the symbols. In the case of many symbols, lack of the demanded ceremonial treatment or a show of respect is illegal. In any case, the symbol serves its function if a citizen is criticized or ostracized for not showing some degree of devotion to it. A patriotic symbol is, in a sense, like a law: it is a device for requiring behavior supportive of the nation and its ruling elite or elites; failure to obey its signal results in punishment. A symbol is not merely like a law requiring obedience; it is like an oath of loyalty. To salute the flag respectfully is like signing such an oath.

When nationalism moves toward reactionary ethnocentric extremes (fascism), patriotic ceremonialism becomes the custom and those who hold back are severely punished. Conversely, when nationalism moves in the direction of commitment to liberal democratic values, patriotism in its traditional sense ceases to be of great interest. Patriotism in a democracy is little more than a collection of ceremonial gimmicks which we try to force on school children and which adults with few other interests may find a source of entertainment.

To illustrate the extent to which patriotic fervor is often carried to remind Americans that we are one nation, God's chosen people, and let the Devil have the rest of the world, we will report a situation described by Gray. After returning home to Connecticut from the peace march on Washington in 1969, Gray reports that a group assembled on a public green to read the names of the 40,000 American dead in Indochina. First, outraged citizens cut their loudspeaker cable. Second, an antiwar priest was banned from pastoral duties because he had prayed for the North Vietnamese as well as the American dead. Third, after citizens from eighteen adjoining small towns had planted "trees for peace," vandals uprooted sixteen of them. Gray concluded, "The division between the two Americas struck me not so much as political but as cosmological, ethical, religious. . . ."[14]

[14] Francine du Plessix Gray, "Slum Landlords in Eden," *Saturday Review,* November 18, 1972, pp. 73–78.

American Nationalism: Virtue or Evil?

After our brief exploration of nationalism as a general phenomenon, viewed by its students as serving a necessary function under some circumstances and a pernicious one under others, a short review of American nationalism may help us evaluate more realistically the initial hypothesis about the threat of nationalism.

Nationalism and Imperialism

It has been a standard Marxist/Leninist orthodoxy that an integral feature of the American system is imperialism, defined as a built-in and inescapable need for capitalist nations to dominate and exploit all other nations weak enough to submit. Yet, there is serious question as to whether American imperialism can be viewed this way or has, in fact, ever existed according to the Marxist/Leninist model.

We feel that Thornton's relatively simple definition of imperialism is much more usable to describe certain American beliefs and actions. "Imperialism is . . . the direct control of one area and its inhabitants by the government of another."[15]

In the sense in which Thornton defines it, the United States has pursued a policy of imperialism throughout its history and continues to do so. Its first form was gaining control of additional land areas. The first expansionist tasks faced by the young United States were: (1) to get the Indians "out of the way," (2) to eliminate French-controlled territory on the continent, (3) to eliminate Spanish control wherever it seemed in the way, (4) to firm up a border with Canada which would secure as much territory as possible without another war with England, and (5) to discourage Russia from pushing colonization southward along the West Coast. After achieving these aims, a lull existed in territorial expansionism until the late nineteenth century. At that time we gained possession of all land possible without serious conflict with any European power but Spain— including the Philippines, Guam, Samoa, Hawaii, and Puerto Rico.

Control of foreign nations for purposes of economic gain developed momentum only after our period of territorial expansionism was over. The twentieth century has seen the steady "corporate colonization" of all countries into which American business could gain entry. This included virtually all of Latin America, Canada, Europe and to a lesser but still significant degree Indochina and a few parts of Africa. By mid-century, the oil reserves of the Middle East were up for grabs and corporations of several nations including the United States moved in.

Although American firms have invested heavily in Europe and are

[15] A. P. Thornton, *Doctrines of Imperialism*. New York: John Wiley & Sons, Inc., 1965, p. 5.

beginning to do so in Japan, these countries have understood imperialism well enough from their own experience to prevent our firms from achieving a seriously exploitive position. Further, some other advanced industrial powers have begun, and are continuing at an accelerated rate, to develop their own international corporations (Japan, for example, is beginning to "penetrate" the U.S. with their automobile and electronics industries).

The United States and Third World Revolutions

Nations large and small are likely to consist of factions. A government may or may not have the support of a majority of the people. Our interventions in other countries often seem to have been attempts to keep in power, or place in power, a dictator, or authoritarian oligarchy, who promised to protect American business or other interests.

In virtually all the Third World countries a revolutionary ferment has been building since well before the middle of this century. The working people of these nations have long struggled to "get into the twentieth century" and have developed their own indigenous revolutionary movements. Typically these movements have come to be led by Communists, often by default because the nations of Western Europen and the United States have refused to side with the peasants and town laborers and have instead supported the ruling feudal elites. We can probably safely assume that, in at least some instances, United States foreign policy has had the effect of aiding Communist expansionism and diminishing or destroying latent or developing democratic movements. In any case, the unsavory dictators and military juntas the United States has supported, and in several cases (with the aid of CIA manipulations) actually placed in power, have rarely if ever been preferable to the Communist governments that might otherwise have taken over.[16]

It has been the consistent policy of the United States since World War II, under the banner of "containing communism," to get on the unpopular side of the numerous Third World revolutions; this may turn out to have been the worst foreign policy mistake of our entire history. Behind such policy is a distorted nationalism, fraught with authoritarian overtones.

Conclusions about the Hypothesis

We offered the proposition that "Nationalism and patriotism are both obsolete and a threat to human survival." As space has allowed only a

[16] Richard J. Barnet, *Intervention and Revolution: America's Confrontation with Insurgent Movements Around the World*, New York: The World Publishing Company, 1968. Also pertinent is the running debate between Dennis H. Wrong and Robert Heilbroner over whether communism, whatever its faults, is perhaps the only operable system for bringing Third World nations into the twentieth century. See Irving Howe (ed.), *A Dissenter's Guide to Foreign Policy*. New York: Praeger Publishers, Inc., 1968, Part III.

superficial review of limited evidence, the data presented can hardly be considered adequate, in themselves, to permit more than a few highly tentative conclusions.

Nationalism

Nationalism has served a probably necessary function in the historical development of nations. Without the rise of nation-states as the commercial and industrial revolutions proceeded, the modernization of Western Civilization would have had to proceed in a different and perhaps much slower manner, or it might not have occurred at all.

Nation-states offered a basis for identification at a time when feudal states were breaking up and people were highly uncertain about the future. These states provided security in many ways, just as they displaced some of the older sources of security. On the other hand, authoritarian and aggressive nationalism ("My country—right or wrong," "Manifest Destiny," and "God follows the Flag") was bound to be self-defeating eventually.

Nationalization, insofar as it is a barrier to international cooperation and eventually to a genuinely functioning world government, appears to have become an anachronism. Boyd Shafer speculates on what could possibly lead toward internationalism—better communications, multinational financial and industrial organizations, increased trade, and the international scientific community.[17] He concludes that the grounds for hope are not the brightest: "A new messiah is perhaps too much to hope for—and likely he would be a general." But others are not this pessimistic.

The period of imperialistically oriented nationalism may be about over in the United States—not necessarily because there are not still a number of powerful persons who would like it pursued indefinitely, but because changes in the total world situation have by now begun to block the extension of American military/economic control of foreign territories. It is not merely ironic, but very likely absurd that as of 1974 the American military establishment is planning to spend a mind-boggling trillion dollars over the next ten years getting ready for the next major American military involvement.

FOREIGN POLICY AND EDUCATION

As we suggested at the beginning of the chapter, little or no empirical evidence can be found to suggest schooling has taught average Americans much of significance about foreign affairs. One of the major problems

---

[17] Boyd C. Shafer, *Faces of Nationalism: New Realities and Old Myths.* New York: Harcourt Brace Jovanovich, Inc., 1972, p. 7.

is that school authorities simply do not consider international education important enough to allow time for it in the curriculum.

Curriculum Content on Foreign Affairs

Dorothy Westby-Gibson, drawing data from articles that appeared in the *Saturday Review* in 1966, says:

> A 1964 survey showed that less than ten percent of the students elect courses dealing with the non-Western World in those colleges which offer them. At the high-school level the gap in knowledge is even more acute. In New York State, for example, less than two percent of the high-school student's time is reported as spent in studying the areas of the world that include two-thirds of the world's population. It has even been suggested that we may soon know more about the moon's surface than we do about other peoples of this planet.[18]

If one understands how little interest professional educators have had in education about foreign peoples it is rather surprising that New York high school pupils spend any time at all studying the non-Western World. Butts has investigated the history of foreign affairs education, insofar as it is revealed in the yearbooks of the National Society for the Study of Education (NSSE). Until 1969, in more than 130 yearbook titles over 67 years, he found only two titles on this subject—one published 30 years ago, the other 10.[19]

During the 1930s and 1940s, the Progressive Education Association advocated the inclusion of foreign affairs education in the curriculum. This was done in some schools, but the focus remained on the Western World, the only part of the globe ordinarily treated in world history textbooks. Also, the theme of such education was "Let's all be good neighbors." There is no evidence that this early attempt had significant outcomes.

Between about 1947 until the mid-1950s teaching about countries other than our allies was generally forbidden in public schools in the United States. In some districts, Los Angeles being one of the more notorious, boards and superintendents even forbade the mention of the United Nations in the classroom. Here again we are forced to face up to the fact that public schools are, or at least have been, under the iron thumb of the power elite. Numerous suppressions occurred in the fifties on the order

[18] Dorothy Westby-Gibson (ed.), *Social Foundations of Education.* New York: The Free Press, 1967, p. 162.
[19] R. Freeman Butts, "America's Role in International Education: A Perspective on Thirty Years," *The United States and International Education,* Sixty-eighth Yearbook of the NSSE, Part I. Chicago: The University of Chicago Press, 1969, p. 3.

of the public burnings of the Rugg textbooks as described at the end of Chapter 5.

University Programs

Fortunately, at the graduate school level of our more prestigious universities the situation was different. During the period of major suppression at lower grade levels, a number of universities, major professional organizations in education, and several major foundations began developing a strong interest in foreign affairs education. The National Defense Education Act of 1958 provided federal funds ". . . to stimulate colleges and universities to enlarge and deepen their instruction in the languages, culture, society, and thought of the emerging countries of the non-Western World."[20]

Through the influence of the agencies mentioned above, the goal of foreign affairs education came to be defined as something quite different than only to teach neighborliness. An emphasis developed on teaching about the values, beliefs, and behavior of peoples in the Third World and to a lesser degree the Communist world also. Further, at the university graduate school level the demand for honest education developed. Such education took two forms: first, formal study in the university and second, travel of American scholars abroad.

It was hoped by foreign affairs experts, who were at the same time concerned about the weakness or nonexistence of foreign affairs education in the public schools, that this new goal and actions to implement it would gradually filter down to the elementary and secondary school levels. Very little did.

Even university scholars were seriously handicapped, both in their desire to travel and to secure the facts needed for their teaching here, by bans on travel to Communist nations. The number of authentic scholars of the Soviet Union, China, North Korea, and North Vietnam, for example, could probably have been counted on one person's fingers, and most of these scholars were dismissed from their employment or continuously harassed. Even among university graduate school professors, it now appears in retrospect that less has been known in the United States about communism, and the indigenous cultures of people in nations with Communist governments, than has been known by scholars in most other advanced industrial nations.

The Noneducation of Education Professors

As a result of various acts passed by Congress, including the potentially promising International Education Act of 1966, there has been an increas-

[20] Butts, pp. 17–18.

ing flow of students and scholars back and forth between the United States and most other countries—excluding, of course, certain Communist-controlled areas. This has been all to the good, except that our exchange scholars have been almost entirely in the humanities and the natural and social sciences. In 1967-1968, *only 8 percent of our scholars abroad were professors of education.*[21]

The paucity of education professors attempting to acquire expertise in foreign affairs bodes ill for the future. If our public schools are ever to install adequate programs for teaching our young about the rest of the world, and about the risks of reactionary, undemocratic nationalism, it will be through the aegis of our schools of education. The movement of the 1970s toward requiring mainly methods courses and field experience (observation and student teaching) and deleting basic theory and informational courses from credential programs can do nothing but worsen an already bad situation.

It appears that schools of education are even in the process of abandoning courses in comparative education to make way for teaching a narrow technology of education which means nothing apart from defensible long-range cultural goals. The present popularity of Performance Based Teacher Education (to be described in Chapter 13) has shifted the emphasis in teacher preparation to short-run behavioral objectives—a move which can only reduce what potential our schools of education now have for pushing foreign affairs education.

Even if schools of education were to wake up to global realities, firmly entrenched public school practices would be highly frustrating to internationally minded teachers. Throughout the United States ethnocentric values are taught through the daily flag salute, and frequent playing of "America the Beautiful," "God Bless America," and our favorite song glorifying war, the "National Anthem."

What Must Be Done

Americans generally forget that within global civilization, they comprise only about 8 percent of the total population. They also forget that more than half the world's population is chronically hungry and is likely to be much hungrier a few years from now. They seem quite unaware of a possible future state of global warfare between the have and have-not nations —a war in which the latter will have most of the advantages.

Yet, this need not happen. The best chance of the Third World nations for avoiding hunger and modernizing at least to the point where they can enjoy enough food, medical care, and other necessities, is through

[21] Butts, p. 23.

establishing their own systems of free public education and educating themselves to ameliorate their own problems in their own preferred way. The Third World needs American assistance, both financial and technical, in developing comprehensive educational systems. That they are now getting too little of such aid, and what they are getting all too often carries with it the demand that these nations adopt the "American system," is a result of the appalling ignorance of the vast majority of Americans about anything occurring outside their immediate neighborhoods.

Only the right kind of education can alert the American public to the not-so-long-range threat. We must begin educating every child for international allegiance rather than nationalistic chauvinism.

STUDY QUESTIONS

1. Try to verbalize your own beliefs about how the United States should relate to other nations. Make a list of belief-statements and compare them with lists made by other pupils.
2. To sample what older people in various categories think, ask your parents, grandparents, a local businessman, a clergyman, a Legionnaire, a John Birch Society member, etc., to state their beliefs about American foreign policy.
3. If you feel a strong emotional tie to the United States as an abstract entity and enjoy patriotic ceremonies, try to analyze the particular psychological satisfactions you gain thereby. Could you switch this allegiance to another country?
4. Whether or not you are traditionally religious, assume you are. How do you explain the intimate link many Americans make between God and country? Do you seriously think that God prefers the United States over North Vietnam?
5. Christianity teaches forgiveness as a prime virtue. How do you explain the refusal, to the time of this writing, of the President and apparently most members of Congress, as well as most American citizens, to accept the idea of unconditional amnesty for conscientious objectors?
6. What would be your attitude toward a person who proclaims himself a citizen of the world rather than of a particular country?
7. Why do you think the expression "under God" was added to the pledge of allegiance? If the addition was appropriate, why was it omitted when the pledge was first officially composed in 1924? Prior to the 1890s, there was no Pledge of Allegiance for school children. Explain how the nation survived for a century without one.
8. As a self-proclaimed Christian nation, dedicated to the memory of the "Prince of Peace" (Christ), how do you explain the violence aroused in Americans against those who advocate peaceful solutions to conflict?
9. The United States was founded by a band of revolutionaries. School children are taught to honor the Founding Fathers. How do you explain the general fear that the word, revolution, arouses in the minds of most Americans?
10. Do you feel that the United States is superior, according to the most

important criteria, to all other nations? What are your criteria? What would happen if most Americans came to admire some other country more than the United States?

11. Write an essay on what you learned in public school about foreign affairs. How many pages were you able to write? How much of it do you still think is true? Are you aware that your teachers ever lied to you about American foreign policy?

ANNOTATED BIBLIOGRAPHY

Barnet, Richard J., *Roots of War*. New York: Atheneum Publishers, 1972.
    Shifting from his earlier view that our almost continuous military adventures since World War II grew from the independent operations of our approximately 400 "national security managers," Barnet now feels that this group—mostly former bankers, industrialists, and corporate lawyers—is motivated primarily by the self-interests of the entire corporate oligarchy. Thus, our foreign policy has been a logical consequence of the social, political, and economic organization of our whole society. The United States will cease being a "warfare state" only when our whole institutional and ideological structures have undergone fundamental change. A highly recommended book.

Barnet, Richard J., *Intervention and Revolution: The U.S. in the Third World*. New York: The World Publishing Company, 1968.
    Barnet's stature as an analyst of U.S. foreign policy has increased steadily from the late sixties and into the seventies because his prognostications have been remarkably prescient. This is considered the best available book on the long-term global revolutionary movements and corollary civil wars in underdeveloped nations, and the persistent tendency of the United States to intervene unilaterally on the side of authoritarian, semifeudal dictatorships.

Friedman, Edward, and Mark Selden, *America's Asia: Dissenting Essays on Asian-American Relations*. New York: Pantheon Books, Inc., 1971.
    An anthology of twelve essays by a group of young scholars lacking in ethnocentrism and possessing an objectivity uncharacteristic of most earlier writers on American foreign policy. Of particular interest for teachers is Kagan's analysis of how American textbooks have falsified the story of our relations with China.

Houghton, Neal D. (ed.), *Struggle Against History: U.S. Foreign Policy in an Age of Revolution*. New York: Washington Square Press, 1968. With an Introduction by Arnold J. Toynbee.
    This anthology follows the same general theme of Barnet's book on intervention and revolutions, but presents a much wider range of views. Much worth looking at, even if only for Toynbee's provocative introduction in which he asserts that Americans seem incapable of learning from history.

Kalb, Marvin and Bernard, *Kissinger*. Boston: Little Brown and Company, 1974.
    A highly regarded book about American foreign policy since 1969. The authors regard former President Nixon as the instigator of the moves to establish detente with China and the Soviet Union and our Vietnam policy (for a combination of good and politically self-serving

reasons) and Kissinger as Nixon's instrument. The book is rather worshipful toward Kissinger and this has been seen as its major flaw: the Kalbs fail to discuss several serious failures of the Nixon-Kissinger strategy, including some serious misconceptions about several nations and actions which promoted the alienation of Japan and Western Europe and unnecessarily prolonged the Vietnam war.

Kaplan, Morton A., *Dissent and the State in Peace and War: An Essay on the Grounds of Public Morality.* New York: Dunellen Company, Inc., 1970.

One reviewer says of Kaplan's book, "the sober academic applying (of) Rand-type analysis, particularly to the problems of the arms race, intervention, and the role of the U.S. in world affairs." We include Kaplan because on every foreign policy issue he takes almost a diametrically opposite stand to that of such liberals as Barnet, Parenti, and Pusey. Kaplan has been called the University of Chicago's "Hawk conservative in residence."

McCoy, Alfred W., with Cathleen B. Read and Leonard P. Adams, II, *The Politics of Heroin in Southeast Asia.* New York: Harper & Row, Publishers, 1972.

In one of the most fascinating exposes of modern journalism, McCoy describes in detail how the CIA aided in the export of opium and heroin from Laos to the United States. McCoy describes the parts played by Laotian officials, officials of the Thieu government in Vietnam, organized crime, and the CIA. CIA attempts to suppress the book failed because CIA officials could offer no rebuttal to McCoy's facts.

Parenti, Michael, *The Anti-Communist Impulse.* New York: Random House, Inc., 1969.

In the opinion of your author, this has to be one of the best books on the seizure of the American public by a pathological fear of communism, and what this kind of psychology had led to by way of witch-hunts and its influence on foreign policy since World War II.

May, Ernest R., *"Lessons" of the Past: The Use and Misuse of History in American Foreign Policy.* New York: Oxford University Press, 1974.

May, director of the Institute of Politics at Harvard, has written a thought-provoking book on a virtually unexplored theme. He argues that Stalin was never interested in Sovietizing *all* of Eastern Europe but that an American over-response to Soviet moves in East Germany, Poland, and Bulgaria led to a fear-inspired takeover by Stalin of other countries. May's basic theme is that many foreign policy moves by the United States have been based on *misperceptions* of the intentions of foreign governments.

Pusey, Merlo John, *The U.S.A. Astride the Globe.* Boston: Houghton Mifflin Company, 1971.

Pusey is an associate editor of the *Washington Post* and his book reflects to a considerable view the editorial slant of this newspaper. Since the *Post* has been right so much of the time in recent years, Pusey has to be taken very seriously. About American foreign policy since World War II, the book gives special attention to the President's war-making powers.

Quigg, Philip W., *America the Dutiful: An Assessment of U.S. Foreign Policy Since World War II.* New York: Simon & Schuster, Inc., 1971.

This is a rather concise defense of U.S. foreign policy since World

War II. Like Kaplan's book, it is included here to present the "other side." But Quigg is less theoretical and far more readable than Kaplan. Highly recommended for readers who want a generally plausible rationale for our foreign policy.

Shafer, Boyd C., *Faces of Nationalism: New Realities and Old Myths.* New York: Harcourt Brace Jovanovich, Inc., 1972.

For student reading, this is the best book we have found on the history and ramifications of nationalism. Shafer's own leanings are antinationalist but the book is primarily explication, not advocacy. Highly readable and well within the range of bright senior high school students, but also highly valuable for college students who have read little in this field.

Rehabilitation center, American style. *(Copyright © George Ballis, all rights reserved)*

CRIME, JUSTICE, AND EDUCATION

The more laws and orders are [emphasized] . . . the more thieves and robbers there will be.

Lao-tse, 500 B.C.

The crime problem and problems related to the American system of justice are of great importance for all public school teachers. Aside from the need of teachers to have some grounding in all the major problematic areas of our culture, illegal acts or deviances of marginal legality comprise a part of the school milieu that most teachers have to face many times in a school year.

The reason should be obvious: children and youth,

beginning in the elementary grades, get in trouble with the law with great frequency. Pupils break numerous laws while on campus: laws banning smoking and profanity, failure to obey orders from their legal superiors, vandalism, assault with intent to injure, possession of dangerous weapons, and so on. When teachers apprehend students for violating a law, they have a legal obligation to report it (concealing crime is itself illegal and teachers who do so put themselves in jeopardy).

But what do teachers do when they feel the law disobeyed is itself foolish? It may be a law that community adults, including the parents of the apprehended student, disobey regularly. And what if a teacher discovers a student committing an illegal act which the teacher also commits regularly—for example, smoking marijuana?

The moral issue here is one of the knottiest that teachers have to face. If students disobey laws which are widely regarded as pointless, which may have been in the state or federal codes since the nineteenth century, and which people generally disregard and police also prefer overlooking, then what is a teacher's moral obligation? During the Prohibition Era of the 1920s, large numbers of persons continued consuming alcohol. In fact, it was continuous and flagrant disregard for the Prohibition Amendment that led to its repeal—and almost everyone felt "good riddance."

There is another moral issue which teachers cannot disregard. Harassing students for breaking anachronistic and generally stupid laws, which almost everyone else breaks, teaches students a general contempt for law. If schools try to strongly enforce a "law and order" policy, they may produce attitudes in students conducive to serious law violation when students become adults. Do we want schools to be breeding grounds for serious adult crime? Presumably not, but the question has to be raised and faced.

COMMON BELIEFS ABOUT CRIME, LAW, AND JUSTICE

Crime statistics are notoriously inaccurate, partly for technical reasons and partly because of some personal or political advantage in doctoring figures. The same may be said of reports on attitudes, values, and beliefs about crime, but for different reasons; studies in this area are simply inadequate. Of the belief patterns reported below, we have drawn primarily from opinion research conducted by the National Opinion Research Center, using a sample of about 10,000 persons, supposedly somewhat representative of national thought (hereafter called the NORC studies). We have also pulled data from an opinion study in Washington, D.C., conducted by the Bureau of Social Science Research (the BSSR study). These opinion studies were reported in 1966 and 1967, respectively. Data from Harris and Gallup opinion surveys, and some miscellaneous sources have been used, as well as our subjective impression of what people think. Most of our data on public ideology about crime was drawn from Winslow.[1]

We will break our belief statements into these categories: (1) crime, (2) the law and law enforcement, and (3) the court system and criminal justice. Responses depend largely on how questions are phrased. People will advocate punitive approaches unless at the same time presented with preventive or corrective approaches, which they usually prefer.

General Opinions about Crime

—The crime rate keeps going up year after year.

—Crime is one of the most serious problems this country faces (rated as second in several surveys).

—Juvenile delinquency is one of the most serious problems this country faces (this option is especially prominent in smaller towns).

—The highest crime rate is within the under class.

—The most serious crimes are those most likely to be committed by under class people: physical assault, rape, robbery, burglary, murder, etc.

—Women are less likely to commit crimes than men.

—Minority groups (especially Blacks, Chicanos, and Italians) commit more crime than people of British or Northern European descent.

—Organized crime is perpetrated mainly by people of Italian descent.

—Crime increase is a result of a decline in family stability and weak parental guidance (in one study, 38 percent said yes).

—Crime is the result of a generally bad environment (30 percent in same study said yes).

—Crime is a result of getting in with the wrong companions (16 percent said yes).

—Crime is an expression of sin and can be defined only on the basis of divine moral law.

—Exposure to TV and movie violence leads to crime.

—Exposure to pornography or any kind of obscene materials leads to delinquency or adult crime, especially sex crimes.

—Use of any drug for pleasure rather than medicine is sinful, hence criminal.

—The less educated people are, the more likely they are to turn to crime.

—The only real solution to the crime problem is to persuade potential criminals to turn to the Savior, Jesus Christ. (Widely held in the seventies; see Chapter 8).

Beliefs about Law and Law Enforcement

—There should be laws to prohibit every immoral act and such laws should be severely enforced. Or, you can legislate morality if you make the punishment stiff enough.

[1] Robert W. Winslow, *Crime in a Free Society.* Belmont, Calif.: Dickenson Publishing Company, Inc., 1968, pp. 15–30.

—We need more and tougher laws if we are ever to control crime.

—If we enforced stringently the laws we now have, it would largely solve the crime problem.

—Crime is best controlled by use of repressive measures (more and tougher police, more use of police dogs, tear gas, mace, etc.). (In one study, 60 percent said yes.)

—Crime is best controlled by improving the social situation (such as poverty) and teaching the young morality. (In one study, 40 percent agreed.)

—Police should spend more time trying to prevent crime than trying to catch criminals (agreed to by 61 percent of sample).

—Police are too hampered by laws and court decisions protecting criminals to do their job properly.

—People who have money for lawyers don't have to worry about conviction for crime.

—Demonstrations, if peaceful, should not be considered criminal. (Agreed to by most middle- to upper-class people; not agreed to by a large proportion of Middle Americans.)

—It is up to the police, not private citizens, to try to prevent crime or assist victims ("I am *not* my brother's keeper"). (One-third in NORC study agreed.)

—Every known approach to controlling crime should be used—preventive, corrective, and punitive. (A majority view, even if contradictory.)

—The way police (and courts) treat you depends on *who* you are.

—Laws should all be obeyed, even if they seem unjust to some people; if a law is unjust, people should work to change it, not disobey it.

—It is better for police to arrest innocent people than risk missing a guilty one (42 percent of sample agreed).

A recent study reveals much about contrasting views about law enforcement of different categories of people. A group of University of California, Los Angeles, researchers has found that, when asked how they would spend $1 million (if they had it) for the public good, a representative sample of Whites would spend it on police protection, whereas representative samples of both Blacks and Chicanos would spend it on education.

Beliefs about the Court System and Criminal Justice

—The American court system is the most just in the world.

—Judges are superior morally and in wisdom to almost everyone else.

—Most lawyers are crooks.

—The higher priced a lawyer is, the better he is likely to be.

—Most judges are too lenient with criminals.

—We could reduce the crime rate by increasing the penalities for crime (50+ percent of sample agreed).

—The courts let delinquent teenagers off much too easily.

—The fairest kind of trial is a jury trial.

Some Unorthodox "Counterculture" Beliefs

The belief-statements listed above, in so far as we can ascertain, are beliefs held by either a majority or a plurality of Americans; they are popular notions. But the academic community, university students, and many educated professionals, including criminologists, hold to beliefs which are quite different—often the opposite. Many of these could be said to be liberal beliefs about crime and its treatment. We will present a sampling below (most of which have been uncovered in the studies mentioned).

—Crime statistics are inflated because it is to the advantage of the FBI and state and local police agencies to do so.
—Crime is a symptom of much deeper problems and will never lessen much until its causes are eliminated.
—The greatest number of illegal acts, although they may not become part of crime statistics, are committed by the upper-middle and upper classes.
—Illegal acts that hurt the largest number of people are those that come under the head of "white-collar crime."
—Changes in the crime rate result from passing laws making illegal what formerly was legal or from changing reporting and statistical methods.
—There is no evidence that exposure of teenagers to pornography leads to more crime; such exposure may even have a reverse effect.
—There is no evidence that smoking pot or using hallucinogens, such as peyote, leads to the use of hard drugs or any social evil.
—Morality cannot be legislated and it is a waste of police and court effort to try.
—Stiffening punishment does not inhibit crime; its most likely effect is to increase it.
—Nothing could be harmed and much could be gained by legalizing all "non-victim crimes."
—Supreme Court decisions guaranteeing greater fairness in police and court procedures neither increase the crime rate nor seriously handicap the control of serious crime.
—Sometimes the only way a stupid law can be eliminated is through mass refusal to obey it.
—Penal institutions should be genuinely rehabilitative instead of the "schools for crime" they now are.

AN "OUTRAGEOUS HYPOTHESIS" ABOUT CRIME

The popular folklore beliefs and values related to crime may greatly exaggerate the seriousness of crime in relation to other problems this country faces. However, it does appear to be true that the homicide and violent assault rates are higher in the United States than in Britain,

Western and Northern Europe, and Japan. The streets of Tokyo are safer to walk on at night than the streets of many small towns in the United States.

The form crime takes and the amount of it are closely related to other areas of special concern treated in Part II. The crime problem is intimately related to the power structure, our religious institutions and practices, our economic institutions, and race and ethnic discrimination. Male crime may even be related to sexism because of our continued "machismo hang-up," which may encourage males to commit certain kinds of crimes for their halo effect.

Before examining our "outrageous hypothesis" on crime, we will define what we mean by crime. As reported in the literature, including the *Statistical Abstract of the United States,* we find no standard definition. Crime figures range from "number of suspected illegal acts" to "number of persons convicted in court." Figures therefore include many innocent persons. For our purposes a very general definition of crime will suffice: *crime* is an offense against the public welfare or social order.

Crime may be classified in various ways. There are crimes against persons and crimes against property (the latter, of course, frequently being injurious to persons). There are political crimes, which authorities are usually loath to admit and call them something else to avoid bad publicity. Significant classifications as of the seventies are crime with victims and victim-free crime—the latter being the subject of much heated debate (for example, is the expression "victim-free crime" itself a contradiction in terms and a violation of logic?)

Hypothesis: *No harm would result if all present non-victim crimes were legalized.*

Some persons might find it difficult to define "harm" in an assertion such as the foregoing. We plan to define harm as "any psychophysical damage" to persons other than those committing the illegal act. For example, an act generally considered illegal throughout the United States is buying and consuming alcohol prior to the age of either 18 or 21 (depending on the state law). However, if a youthful drinker *does not injure others* as a result of his action, then we define the act as victimless.

The problem of definition is not quite this simple, however. One writer states the following definition: Non-victim crime ". . . refers essentially to the willing exchange, among adults, of strongly demanded but legally proscribed goods and services." The same writer goes on to say that this definition does not include the factor of possible harm, so he refines his definition to ". . . the combination of an exchange transaction and lack of apparent harm to others."[2]

[2] Edwin M. Schur, *Crimes Without Victims.* Englewood Cliffs, N.J.: Prentice-Hall, Inc. 1965, p. 169.

Schur's definition omits one highly important category of victimless crime, namely, solitary acts that involve no "exchange" between adults. There are, in fact, many illegal solitary acts, some carrying very heavy punishments. Obviously, someone has to be an observer to the act and report it for the lawbreaker to be apprehended—but this does happen

According to the Kinsey Report and other comprehensive studies of sexual behavior, in deep rural areas sexual intercourse of farm boys and sometimes adult males with domestic animals is relatively common. (Men who grew up in a deep rural environment know that without a Kinsey Report). Such laws are seldom enforced. Who is going to arrest a five-year-old for attempting to establish a sexual relationship with a pet dog? Further, who is going to arrest a grown-up when his (or her) defense could rest on the argument that the act was between two consenting adults?[3]

For our purposes in this section of the chapter, we will define nonvictim, victimless, and victim-free crime as *any consensual or solitary illegal act which, to the actor's best knowledge, is either totally harmless or negligibly harmful to others.*

Historical Origins of Nonvictim Crime

We can only assume that there have been so-called victimless crimes since the beginnings of some sort of religion. The reason for this assumption is that the criminal nature of a victimless crime usually derives from the belief that it is *sinful* in the eyes of some supernatural power, and its commission will result either in divine punishment of the entire group to which the "sinner" belongs or, at the very least, to the sinner's damnation and incarceration in hell.

Since the above explanation seems the only conceivable grounds for declaring an act wrong which harms no one but the person committing the act, it appears to be the only explanation we have as to the origins of the concept of non-victim crime. Chapter 8, on religion, will explain more fully the rationale of the linking of sin, immorality, and crime in the thinking of the religious, particularly people who belong to the fundamentalist denominations and sects.

Examples of Nonvictim Crime

We will begin with what appear to be the types of victimless crimes most subject to controversy as of the seventies. It appears that pornography and

---

[3] See *Playboy*, August 1972, pp. 188–189, for a chart on laws regulating sex offenses in the United States, with detailed information on specific kinds of illegalities and prescribed punishments.

drugs are most controversial at this writing, but certain aspects of sex and bodily exposure are almost as much at issue.

At the time of this writing, a new fad—particularly among college youth—is running naked in a public place. This "streaking" is likely to be a short-lived phenomenon but is nevertheless causing great concern among moralists, district attorneys, and police. According to a Supreme Court decision some years back, nudity per se is not illegal, even in public places, if the nude person does not draw attention to his or her genitals for sexual purposes.

In the writer's city of residence, Fresno, California, the district attorney has been urging the City Council to make streaking a criminal offense "in order that we may better serve . . . [the public]." The D.A. sought the advice of various local persons, including a minister. The minister wrote back, "The naked that our Lord has called upon to clothe are not those on a spring lark, but those too poor to even clothe their bodies."

While the D.A. agitates against streaking, posts members of the police force at places where the next incident might occur, and in general spends much of his time and that of the police trying to apprehend marijuana users, loiterers, prostitutes, and theater owners showing X-rated movies, the rate of violent crimes in Fresno increased 29.6 percent between 1972 and 1973.[4]

Pornography

The chief problem in discussing this category of victimless crime is that no one so far has been able to define pornography to the satisfaction of more than a few people, let alone the whole population. The term is so related to highly personal values that we can quite truthfully say that what one person perceives as pornography, another may perceive as useful, desirable, or even beautiful.

The Supreme Court, under the leadership of Earl Warren, reached what its members at that time thought might be a workable definition (the Roth Case, 1957). Paraphrased, the definition said in effect that any public depiction of sexual acts, the human body, or use of language traditionally called obscene was pornographic if the total item in which it was depicted "had no redeeming social value whatsoever, including that which might be unorthodox or controversial."

What seemed at one time to be a workable Supreme Court decision has been found to have at least one serious defect—people cannot agree on what has "redeeming social value." To complicate the matter more,

[4] From the *Fresno Bee*, April 9, 1974.

attempts have been made to distinguish between garden-variety pornography and "hard-core pornography." The purpose of trying to make this distinction lay in a fairly common belief that adults could be subjected to ordinary pornography without necessarily being damaged, but that no one under any circumstances could experience *hard-core* pornography without suffering incurable damage.

In part because the Supreme Court could not really resolve the issue of pornography and in part because the Nixon Court seems to some degree committed to decentralizing legal decision making, a 1973 Court decision threw the whole problem back to local communities, thus paving the way for thousands of local court actions and the risk of censorship of not only pornography intended as pornography but of books, songs, and paintings considered classics.

Because the religious find it increasingly difficult to persuade the young and educated adults that immorality and sin equate automatically with crime, they have increasingly pitched their arguments on a "morality of consequent action," that is, if pornography per se is not criminal, then exposure to it leads to behavior which is. This argument has been pushed with especial vigor where there has been a threat of children or teenagers being exposed to what is perceived by would-be censors as pornographic.

We will now enumerate and comment on some of the most common types of pornography. It is inescapable that we will bridge the extremely fine line between pornography and sexual offense, since these two areas overlap at numerous points.

The human body The notion that the human body, or at least parts of it, are obscene, undoubtedly stems from the mind-body dualism borrowed by early-day Christians from a pagan philosophy of the Persian Peninsula, Manichaeism, which stressed the dualism of light and dark, good and evil, spirit and matter. The spirit-matter dualism became a spirit-body dualism in which the flesh was considered unclean and corrupting and the spirit pure or potentially so. This view was adopted by St. Augustine and influenced the thought of much of Western Civilization.

Americans, and some Europeans, have over the centuries given the idea of indecency of the flesh a peculiar twist: some parts of the human body are regarded as obscene, dirty, and shameful whereas other parts are not. The obscene parts are any organ or other bodily feature clearly related to reproduction. Hence the sex organs (particularly when tumescent) and pubic hair are regarded as obscene.

Bodily functions Not only are parts of the body directly related to reproduction—and parts near them—considered obscene, but the functioning of these parts may also be regarded as obscene. Sexual intercourse in the standard missionary position is authorized as a strictly private activity, but is sharply criticized as a spectator sport, which many motion pictures and night club shows have made it during the past decade. Even simulated sexual activity in public is taboo.

Intercourse in other than the standard position is regarded as immoral, as is masturbation, which may be a punishable offense depending on the views of the particular local authorities to whose attention it comes. A long list of activities referred to as perversions are legally criminal.

Language taboos   Although language taboos are increasingly difficult to enforce, they are an important part of the total behavioral pattern called pornographic. As in the case of bodily parts and functions, questionable words and expressions can be arranged on a continuum of dirtiness: from "*the* word" at one end to words at the other end which are not shocking but considered in bad taste.

Pornography as victimless crime   That pornography, when publicly depicted, is widely considered a crime is obvious because in most communities such depictions of human behavior are illegal. It is usually covered by some blanket law prohibiting public lewdness (to be defined by local authorities, most often the clergy and police officers). The question of whether anyone is actually victimized by pornography in the sense of being harmed by it will be discussed later.

Drug Use

American attitudes toward illegal drug use are analogous to those regarding pornography and sex. They stem from the same spirit-body dualism that regards "pleasures of the flesh" as evil in contrast to the higher spiritual pleasures of contemplation, worship, prayer, and the like. Any drug is suspect if it produces feelings of psychophysical pleasure: intoxication, euphoria, pleasing hallucinations, "expanded consciousness," dreamlike states, and so on. Drugs that have *only* medical value (even fake ones), in the sense of being promoted for curing disease, are looked on favorably.

We will make an attempt, which readers should regard as tentative, to classify drugs according to their likelihood of harmfulness to persons other than the user.[5]

Depressants ("downers")   With the exception of alcohol as it affects some persons, depressants tend to produce relaxation, euphoria, and sleep. Their use in moderate amounts reduces aggressiveness and promotes a calm peaceful state, hardly likely to lead users to harm others. Overdoses can lead to stupor, coma, and death; in this sense, the incau-

---

[5] Our sources include all the articles we have been able to find that appear scholarly and nonpolemical. The best source of concentrated data about drugs that we used is a chart entitled "Major Drugs: Their Uses and Effects," *Playboy*, September 1972, p. 143ff (a foldout).

tious user can be irretrievably damaged. Continued alcohol overdose also tends to lead to irretrievable damage to the liver, cardiovascular system, and other vital organs. Drugs commonly placed in this category are barbiturates, opium-derived drugs, tranquilizers, and certain inhalants.

Stimulants ("uppers") Drugs in this group, like all the rest, have differing effects on different individuals; for example, antidepressants in some cases produce depression, and caffeine relaxes many users. In general, however, their effect is to stimulate activity and increase alertness. It is increasingly the opinion among drug experts that one family of drugs in this group, the amphetamines, may be the most dangerous of all drugs in fairly widespread use, if used heavily and over a continued period.

. . . for possession of one marijuana cigarette.

Uppers include amphetamines, antidepressants, cocaine, caffeine, and nicotine.

Psychedelics This group cannot be classified either as "uppers" or "downers." Their effect is apparently highly individualized, particularly in the case of the more potent substances. Psychedelics include hallucinogens and cannabis (marijuana).

Drug Use as Victimless Crime

Making any sweeping generalizations about the relation between illicit drug use and the harm such use may cause to nonusers would be dangerous indeed. For one thing, experts don't agree, and this writer prefers to do little more than suggest hypotheses for further study.

One of the more controversial drug experts, former President Nixon's drug chief for two years, has conducted considerable research (and studied the research of others) and come up with at least one argument that seems fairly impressive and also harmonious with views of many "liberal" experts. We are referring to Jerome Jaffe, who probably knows as much about drug use (and addiction) among American troops during the Vietnam war, and what happened to army drug users after returning to the United States, as anyone else.

As we interpret it, Jaffe's most significant finding is that the kinds of drugs people take, whether addiction occurs, whether drug use harms the user or anyone else, and how easily addiction can be cured, are largely *situational*. That is, drug use and its consequences can be understood only in relation to a complex configuration of circumstances; as this configuration changes, so does the pattern of drug use and its consequences. For example, whether a person who begins using heroin (which has been considered the most addicting drug of all), then continues to use it, and becomes addicted to it, can then shake the addiction quickly, slowly, or not at all, appears to depend on the Gestalt of things. Turning to marijuana, which frightens the uneducated public almost as much as heroin, Jaffe makes the same claim: it may be totally harmless to others, or it may not—again depending upon the situation.

Where Jaffe becomes controversial, particularly compared to most other drug experts, is in his tendency to mix politics with drugs. He does this in a variety of ways. One example is his assertion that although it would be all right for the educated upper-middle class to have freer access to drugs now banned (particularly marijuana) because they are bright enough to know how to handle drug use without harming themselves or others, the—by implication—less bright blue-collar lower-middle and upper-lower classes (i.e., Middle Americans) could never learn how to use drugs without abuse.

Therefore, says Jaffe, drugs now banned should continue to be banned to everyone. After asserting that marijuana is harmless so far as anyone knows, and so are even harder drugs for people who know how to use them, he adopts a hard-line argument about keeping the present laws to prevent the unwashed masses from having access to them and abusing them.[6]

[6] T. George Harris and Jerome H. Jaffe, "As Far as Heroin Is Concerned, the Worst Is Over: A Dialogue between Harris and Jaffe," *Psychology Today*, August 1973, p. 68ff. In same magazine, see Harris's "Jaffe, Nixon and the Politics of Technology," p. 32, for an objective, very informative editorial on Jaffe and his views.

Most drug experts we have read, although sympathizing with Jaffe's contention that drug use and abuse cannot be understood except situationally, disagree with most of Jaffe's other views—particularly on the maintenance of present hard-line legislation. We can even find at the far liberal end of the spectrum at least one expert who would let Americans legally take any drug they want, without limitations imposed by educational or social prestige level.[7]

We would like now to suggest a few hypotheses of our own based on what appears to be *as good factual evidence as we can now get.*

—The only drug categorized as a depressant which seems to incite some persons to injure others is alcohol; and most alcohol users who injure others while drunk would be potentially dangerous while sober.
—Narcotic use per se does not produce victim-type crime; it is the laws that prevent users from acquiring the drug cheaply and legally that incite criminal acts now associated in the public mind with narcotics use.
—Stimulants are most unlikely to lead users to harm others, although they do tend to lead to heightened activity which conceivably might *energize* a lazy potential criminal to the point where he would do something harmful to others.
—The situation regarding psychedelics is very mixed; those that produce severe hallucination or panic might lead an otherwise peaceful person to some violent act against others. On the other hand, none of the careful research using adequate sampling techniques and control groups, indicates that marijuana use leads users to injure anyone else: if there is such a thing as a "peace drug," this appears to be it.

Sex

A variety of forms of sexual behavior that are illegal appear to belong under the head of victim-free crime. These are mainly "consensual sex offenses," that is, shared sexual behavior between two or more consenting adults.

Sex acts that generally seem to be victimless, but are illegal in at least some states and carry a wide range of penalties, include prostitution (legal only in Nevada on a local option basis); homosexuality (illegal in all states, although since the American Psychiatric Association asserted, in April, 1974, that homosexuality is not a mental sickness, we may expect to see repressive laws eased sooner or later); adultery (illegal in 40 states); cohabitation (illegal in 26 states); fornication (illegal in 23 states); "general

[7] Thomas S. Szasz, "The Ethics of Addiction," *Harpers*, April 1972, pp. 74–79. Szasz makes a powerful argument, based on factual evidence, that the war against drug use is counterproductive: there would be less use of dangerous drugs, less addiction, and less associated victim crime, if all drug control laws were repealed.

lewdness" (a catchall expression, under which are lumped all other kinds of sexual behavior disliked by your local police; illegal in 40 states); and "crimes against nature" (another catchall expression that applies mainly to sex acts not sanctioned by conservative religions, the most common being oral sexual stimulation; illegal in 41 states).

Next to unorthodox sexual relations with the living, laws are common banning sexual intercourse with a corpse. These laws are hard to enforce. If the culprit is attempting intercourse with a person who is as frigid and passive as some people, the offender could always tell the judge he had no way of determining during the act whether his partner was dead or alive.

Drunkenness

Although we included alcoholism in our discussion of drug use, since more people are arrested for public drunkenness than for any other one act, this problem deserves special attention. In 1970, well over 1 million arrests were made on this charge.[8] However, this figure is disputed by criminologist Norval Morris, who claims the actual number of arrests is 2 million. Whatever the correct number, it is misleading in the sense that a much smaller number of persons than number of arrests are involved. One report is probably not highly exceptional: Six habitual alcoholics in Washington, D.C. have been arrested over the years a total of 1409 times for public drunkenness and have served a collective 125 years in jail.[9]

Disorderly Conduct

Like general lewdness, this catchall type of charge permits police to arrest people when no specific laws cover the offense. The offense itself is often defined by the police officer on the spot, although to book the arrested person a charge covered by statute has to be made. Examples of acts that come under disorderly conduct include prostitution and soliciting (if there are no specific laws covering these acts), begging or "panhandling," loitering, refusing to identify oneself to a police officer, insulting a police officer, scuffling and restrained fighting (without intent to injure), harassing others, making unnecessary noise, and other offenses.

Some of these acts have victims in the sense that they involve annoying and irritating, others do not. Laws against loitering (which seems rather obviously a victimless offense) are vague at present because of their possible unconstitutionality.

[8] *Statistical Abstract of the United States,* 1972, p. 150.
[9] Cited by *Los Angeles Times* syndicated columnist, Clayton Fritchey, July 11, 1973.

Except perhaps for traffic offenses, disorderly conduct is the second most common cause of arrest, with slightly less than half the arrests being made for drunkenness.

Gambling

No one knows how long human beings have gambled, but dice have been found in the ruins of ancient Pompeii—some of them loaded. Although legal gambling is increasing in the United States as an important new revenue source, it is estimated that for every dollar bet legally, five to seven are bet illegally. The total amount of illegal gambling may run as much as $40 billion annually, almost half the direct budget for the military.[10]

It appears that no matter what kind of legislation is passed, a rather large proportion of the American people enjoy gambling and will continue to gamble. Further, whereas gambling was once mainly limited to the very poor or the very affluent, as of the seventies we have a new breed of gambler: the middle- and upper-middle-class suburbanite.

Vagrancy

Between eighty and ninety thousand arrests for vagrancy occurred in 1970. Wanderers who bum around and seem to have no place to go are subject to vagrancy charges, though vagrancy, like lewdness and disorderly conduct, seems to be another catchall category created to permit police to arrest people who bother them.

Comparative Amounts of Victim and Nonvictim Crime

A commonly given estimate is that *about half of all arrests and about half of all police time is spent trying to apprehend and arrest people for victimless crime,* or crime that is not more annoying to others than a host of legal activities.

This estimate can be confirmed by government statistics, to the extent that they may be approximately accurate. Arrests for the following categories of acts constitute approximately half of all arrests made in the United States in a year: Prostitution and vice, nonviolent sex, drug abuse, gambling, liquor violations, drunkenness, disorderly conduct, and vagrancy; with drunkenness, disorderly conduct, and drug violations ranking first, second, and third, respectively.[11]

[10] "Everybody Wants a Piece of the Action," *Newsweek*, April 10, 1972, p. 46ff.

[11] *Statistical Abstract*, p. 150.

Whether the cost of all attempts at crime control in the United States tend to split about 50-50 as between victim and nonvictim crime, we do not know. At the local level, it is at least plausible to assume that this is true. Whatever the proportion may be, the state of California alone, between 1960 and 1973, spent $577 million arresting and prosecuting 400,000 people on marijuana charges.

Legislating Morality

Attempting to control victimless crime by passage of laws has been a subject for dispute. The central problem, it would seem, is that victimless crime as a legal concept is a direct outgrowth of public views of what is and what is not moral; and opinions regarding morality are to a large extent religiously derived.

In a theocracy, the equating of sin and immorality, and immorality and crime, would be logical. In a secular state, such equations do not seem logical to large numbers of people. In a country like the United States, which is both highly secular and materialistic, with strong tendencies to regard morality as situational, but at the same time is also in the grip of fundamentalist religious outlooks (as Chapter 8 will demonstrate), there are bound to be opposing pressures. Many persons will continue to insist on suppressing what they perceive as immorality by law and punishment, while many other persons will object strenuously to this practice.

Circumstances under Which Control Is Possible

The chief practical problem in preventing victimless crime through legal approaches is that when there is no victim there is no plaintiff. There is no one to protest the action except possible spectators who have a moral axe to grind, the arresting officers, and prosecuting attorneys who are expected to enforce the law, even if the illegal act harms no one.

Duster makes a plausible suggestion about conditions under which any law can be enforced. He juxtaposes two variables: whether there is a plaintiff (victim) and whether the illegal act is visible, that is, to some degree public. Table 7-1 is derived from Duster's analysis.[12]

The chart is interpreted as follows: In the first example, there are not only a plaintiff but also witnesses; in the second, there is a plaintiff (who may have bruises to support the story); in the third, although the act is observed, the observers may feel sympathy and try to help the drunk rather than call the police; and in the fourth, there is neither plaintiff nor observer. Duster suggests that the possibility of enforcement order

[12] Troy Duster, The Legislation of Morality: Law, Drugs, and Moral Judgement. New York: The Free Press, 1970, p. 26.

Table 7-1

		Arena of Occurrence	
		Public	*Private*
Nature of *the Offense*	Victim as plaintiff	1. Example: A drunk hits bystander in public bar	2. Example: A drunk hits lone companion in isolated desert
	No victim as plaintiff	3. Example: A drunk falls down in crowded park	4. Example: A drunk falls down in isolated desert

is 1, 2, 3, and 4. In the first example, enforcement is easy; in the fourth, impossible.

Ethics of Attempts To Enforce Victimless Crime

Several ethical problems appear whenever a serious attempt is made to enforce laws which make acts without victims illegal. We will mention a sampling of those one regularly encounters in the writings of criminologists, jurists, and other interested students of the problem.

Police as participants   Since victimless crimes do not have a "natural plaintiff," in order to enforce laws forbidding acts which are ordinarily committed in private, law enforcement officials have to arrange an "artificial plaintiff." This is easily done by having a plainclothesman become a "consensual party." That is, a plainclothesman poses as a customer for a prostitute, buys her services, according to frequent reports makes full use of her, and then arrests her and plays the role of plaintiff in the ensuing trial. Or, to use another example very commonly practiced in the sixties and seventies, a plainclothesman scouts around to find someone who has marijuana or some other illegal drug to sell, makes the purchase, and then makes the arrest.

Serious questions have been raised about any law whose only means of enforcement is to have police pose as civilians and become participants in the illegal act in order to achieve arrests. This practice, common as it appears to be, is of dubious constitutionality aside from how it might be assessed on the basis of moral principle alone.[13]

---

[13] See the Report of the President's Commission on Law Enforcement and Administration of Justice, Washington, D.C.: Government Printing Office, 1967, section on "Crimes Without Victims." Also see Jerome H. Skolnick, *Justice Without Trial.* New York: John Wiley & Sons, Inc., 1966, p. 210.

Dishonest research   Prior to writing this chapter, we have studied the research evidence on the psychophysical consequences of marijuana use. With considerable frequency one finds, not as part of a major investigatory report, such as that of the President's Commission on the Study of Marijuana and Dangerous Drugs, but typically as a short news item in a newspaper or news magazine, a report by some unheard-of investigator with the initials M.D. or Ph.D. after his name, which purports to prove that marijuana has quite disastrous effects on both "mind and body." Upon reading such reports, one frequently finds that the research sample consisted of only three or four subjects, utilized subjects atypical of the general population (as, for example, inmates of a mental institution), and virtually without exception did not utilize a control group. These "researches" are obviously without scientific merit.

We frequently find similar researches on the dangers of drugs which, when abused, actually are dangerous, but which greatly exaggerate the unknown dangers. Barbiturates are one favorite subject of new investigations which depict dangers the medical profession has been quite unaware of even after a century of medical use of the drugs.

Why these minor but sensationally reported researches which do not follow any of the canons of adequate scholarly investigation? Publicity seeking by the researchers is one possibility. Political catering to some government, corporate, or religious power center is a more likely reason, however, because without a relatively potent reason for conducting phony research or using adequate research as a basis for conclusions which are non sequiturs, most persons would not want to risk a professional reputation (assuming they have one) merely for a single splash of publicity.

In the general area of victimless crime there are numerous vested interests—some very powerful—that want to keep the laws as they are or make them even more stringent. We think of fundamentalist religious denominations and sects and of high political figures who have similar views and run on a platform of "reforming morals" or "promoting law and order." Drug manufacturers who reap a fortune from the sale of tranquilizers and barbiturates might well oppose the decriminalization of marijuana, for example, since it performs similar functions. Liquor interests might also oppose the decriminalization of marijuana because such a move would almost certainly reduce alcoholic beverage sales.

Another example of dishonesty in reporting facts can be charged to the antipornography forces. In 1967, Denmark repealed all laws prohibiting the sale of written pornography to persons 18 and over. Although rape remained unchanged, by 1970 exhibitionism had decreased by 58 percent; peeping had decreased by 80 percent; molesting of women had decreased by 56 percent; and molesting of girls under 14 had dropped by 69 percent.

That the repeal of antipornography laws in Denmark resulted in such a marked decrease in sex crime has largely been kept from the American public. The press has paid scant attention to it, and antipornography groups refuse to make any mention of it, continuing to peddle as vigorously as ever their contention that pornography is a chief cause of sex crime.

One result of such reports is that the young, particularly college youth, know that members of the Establishment are lying to maintain some vested interest. As a consequence, Establishment authority figures lose still more of the small amount of credibility they have left.

Punishment that produces criminals   Laws prohibiting acts that do not have victims have the effect of making criminals out of people who originally showed no criminal tendencies. Hundred of thousands of people who would otherwise lead normal, productive lives are arrested and often jailed for behavior they had good reason to think was harmless. Salmon suggests that "The greatest problem of our law regarding marijuana use is that it makes criminals of a very large group of our young people." He elaborates by pointing out that arresting them and subjecting them to trial brand them as criminals, in their own thinking as well as the thinking of others.

Salmon goes on to say, "The disrespect these young people have for the marijuana laws may spread to a more generalized disrespect for the law and political processes." Those sent to jail have an even greater stigma attached, and, in addition, while jailed, associate with habitual criminals who can present all manner of arguments as to why a life of crime "pays." In the year for which Salmon presents figures (1968), in California 98 percent of juveniles arrested on marijuana charges had no previous arrest records, nor did 80 percent of adults arrested on such charges.[14]

The same argument applies to those arrested as consumers of pornography and those arrested for victimless sex offenses.

Conclusions about the Hypothesis

The available evidence appears to support almost entirely one side of the issue: both research evidence and expert opinion, with but rare exceptions, point toward the desirability of either drastically modifying or eliminating entirely laws designed to control morality when the behavior referred to is harmless to others. Further, it can be argued on philosophical grounds that if people are educated to understand the consequences of their actions upon themselves, they should be free to do with their lives what they please.

[14] Robert Salmon, "An Analysis of Public Marijuana Policy," *Social Casework,* January 1972, pp. 21–22.

CRIME, JUSTICE, AND EDUCATION

Although this chapter glances largely at only one aspect of the crime problem, we have probably confronted readers by now with enough material to make pertinent the questions: What should schools teach about law, crime, and justice? What educational goals would most help students to become thoughtfully and critically law abiding?

Public Schools and Legal Socialization[15]

Socialization, as sociologists, psychologists, and educators use the term, means the process by which an individual learns the culture of his group, including the role or roles he will play in the culture. From our view, this is an interactive or, preferably, a transactive process. Socialization should not mean "learning to conform," but a growing into the culture via a process of give-and-take. As individuals appropriate cultural norms, they examine them critically and in refusing to accept some, either induce change in the group to bring its norms more in line with what the individuals prefer, or failing that, remain to some degree individualists, nonconformists, persons exhibiting alienation which, hopefully, will be of a positive kind.

As the young grow into a culture they are socialized in a variety of ways: they must learn to cope with the cultural ideology and a variety of institutional structures and processes. In addition to family, political, economic, and religious socialization, the young are affected by "legal socialization."

The Public Schools as Microlegal Systems

A public school can be considered a microlegal system, a system where the concept of "rule," "norm," or "law," must be applied. Unless we are to prefer capricious lawlessness or anarchy, there is no way to conceive of a school as a legal entity except as an institution with specified rules or "laws." But outside pressure groups, school boards, administrators, and teachers have been considered the "lawgivers" of the school. The students have been regarded as subjects and socialization has often meant nothing more than learning to obey or suffer punishment.

In the school, legal socialization can be broadly defined as the learning by students of the numerous rules governing the school and, hopefully, the rationale or reason behind them. Legal socialization also implies

[15] In developing this final section of the chapter, the writer owes much to the *Journal of Social Issues* special issue on "Socialization, the Law, and Society," June L. Tapp (ed.), Vol. 27, No. 2, Spring 1971.

some sort of response to the rules or laws of the school, ranging from passive obedience to overt mutiny, with various possible responses falling between.

Study of Law as an Instrument of Change

Zimring and Hawkins reject the view that the law merely reflects the moral sentiments most people in a culture have, and that, as such, the law is simply another instrument for stabilizing present moral ideas to prevent or slow their change. They claim that law can be an instrument for social change, and that it should be studied in the public schools within the context of a dynamic conflict-change cultural model.

As a means of changing social custom, new laws vary in efficacy depending upon: (1) the nature of the custom to be changed, (2) the social characteristics of individuals or groups whom the new laws are intended to change, and (3) the particular manner in which the threat of punishment is carried out. (The number of variables under each of these items is so great that these authors go no further than presenting samples of them.)[16]

If a new law makes some act illegal which was not previously illegal, will it actually effect a change in people's values and lead to new kinds of behavior? The authors cite the failure of the prohibition law of the 1920s to change people's drinking habits as an example of a law designed to induce social change failing to have the intended effect. They see antimarijuana laws of the sixties and seventies as a similar type of unworkable attempt to change moral values. But these two cases, even if combined with similar examples, are not enough to make the case that passing legislation mandating new kinds of thinking and behavior is necessarily futile.

Zimring and Hawkins raise questions about the efficacy of legal punishment as a deterrent to crime. To the extent that law does succeed in restraining crime, it requires widespread supporting values, for example, if by the time they reach adulthood people have developed strong values favoring the sanctity of property, laws making burglary illegal may have an additional effect in restraining burglary—but only if the prior supporting values are there.

Although Zimring and Hawkins do not get into public school practice in connection with the use of laws to change social customs, we may infer some directions in which such a discussion might lead. *The study of law in relation to accelerating or retarding social change could be one reason for introducing constructive discussion of legal issues into the school curriculum.*

[16] Franklin Zimring and Gordon Hawkins, "The Legal Threat as an Instrument of Social Change," *Journal of Social Issues* (cited above), pp. 33–48.

Law in Relation to Moral Maturity

Tapp and Kohlberg move head-on into the relationship between moral and legal socialization and what this means for education. Of the present situation and how to improve it, they say:

> Unfortunately, many concerned with individual legal development have failed to appreciate the universality and the dynamic of either moral or legal reasoning. Instead they have frequently transmitted fixed adult cliches about moral and legal dilemmas rather than a conflict-solving approach. If societies' agents are not merely to institutionalize blind obedience, but are to stimulate principled perspectives, they must understand more entirely the process of developing and crystallizing legal values.[17]

Tapp and Kohlberg build on Kohlberg's earlier work in trying to identify and describe stages of moral development which he sees as universal in human beings, although influenced by environmental circumstance. Kohlberg developed a widely known six-stage model, but reduced this model to three more inclusive stages, which we will present very briefly.

Preconventional level   This is the "morality" as well as the "legal" orientation of small children, although some people get "stuck" at the preconventional level and never rise above it. At this level, "good" and "bad" are seen only in terms of what will lead to punishment or reward. There are no moral principles, as such.

Conventional level   This level is characterized by active support of the "fixed rules or authority" in a society. As a person approaches the top of this stage, he becomes committed to duty in the sense of obeying fixed rules, showing respect for authority, and maintaining the given social order. A majority of persons do not get above this level. At this level, people show a strong "law and order" orientation, but in the absence of deep commitments to any other moral principle we would expect to find at this level considerable "pragmatic expediency."

Postconventional level   This level is characterized by "a clear effort toward autonomous moral principles with validity apart from the authority of the groups or persons who hold them. . . ." At this level, people show an awareness of the relativism of personal values; they have a strong concern for the *procedures* involved in reaching consensus. "The stress is on the legal point of view, but with the possibility of changing law in terms of rational, social utility rather than freezing it in terms of law and order." At the highest development (the universal Ethic stage), people are

[17] June L. Tapp and Lawrence Kohlberg, "Developing Senses of Law and Legal Justice," *Journal of Social Issues* (cited above), pp. 65–91.

concerned with testing moral principle in terms of logic, consistency, and universality.

Going back to Tapp's analysis in a preceding essay, law is to be regarded as an "interactional phenomenon" which is forever dynamic and changing. This is a situational concept of law, growing from the situational morality of people who reach the postconventional level of development.[18]

Conclusions

Our own conclusions about how schools could best proceed in the legal socialization of students has been implied in the above positions of Zimring and Hawkins, and Kohlberg and Tapp. Although teachers need to help students learn about present institutional structures and behavior as they pertain to law and justice, including their seamy as well as positive aspects, what is much more important is that teaching and student activities should be designed insofar as possible to help students achieve personal moral maturity.

There is no magic formula for this. Certainly, encouraging students to participate in "student government," as it is now ordinarily practiced, doesn't cut deep enough; aside from its usual underlying phoniness (students have no real decision-making authority), it involves too few students to justify much emphasis upon it.

We feel that students should be encouraged to formally study in school the deeper philosophical issues relating to the general area of jurisprudence (with such study buttressed by observation of lawmakers, the police apparatus, and the courts). What is a law? How do laws originate? What is the function of law? What situations make people want to either obey or disobey laws? How does our whole legal system tend to preserve the interests of the power elite and help them keep those below "in their place"? Such study, if placed on the level of reflective problem solving, might move many students well along the road to moral maturity and hence genuinely constructive legal socialization.

STUDY QUESTIONS

1. The State of Delaware legally abolished public whipping as a form of punishment for crime in July, 1972. Although public whipping had not been used in the state since 1962, many persons opposed its abandonment. What is your opinion of this as a form of punishment? Why did Delaware wait so long to abolish a law passed in colonial times?
2. Which laws do you break? Presumably, you have a reason for whatever lawbreaking you do. What is your justification?

[18] June L. Tapp, "Reflections," *Journal of Social Issues* (cited above), p. 3.

3. In all opinion studies made, the American public continues to show a strong commitment toward punishment as a means of deterring crime or because "criminals deserve it." This is not true in all advanced countries, most of which abolished capital punishment and extreme prison sentences long ago. How do you explain this aspect of the American ideology?

4. Why do you think "white-collar crime" (as exemplified in shoplifting, embezzling, breaking antitrust laws, giving money illegally for political campaigns, illegal government spying, etc.) has not been considered historically as a serious problem in relation to "underclass crime"— mugging, robbery, violent assault, murder, etc.? Why do white collar criminals get short prison sentences (if any) whereas a bank robber may be imprisoned for twenty or thirty years?

5. One argument against repealing laws making victimless acts illegal is that if a person harms himself (as by the use of heroin) he cannot help but harm his loved ones. Is there really any such thing as victim-free crime?

6. What sorts of things do you think we should try to teach elementary school children about law, crime, and justice? Be explicit and defend your answer.

7. What do you think we should try to teach high school students and why?

8. Most public schools are exemplars of a "law and order" system. There are strict rules to be followed and punishments for disobeying. Do you think schools carry this too far? How permissive should a school be?

9. If you became aware that a fellow student is breaking a law, would you report him? Do you know of students who smoke marijuana? Have you ever turned them into the police? Why or why not?

10. If you think students should be punished in some way for not following school rules, what kinds of punishment would you recommend? In what order of preference would you place them? Do you think there is still justification for spanking or other corporal punishment?

ANNOTATED BIBLIOGRAPHY

Berry, Mary Frances, *Black Resistance/White Law*. New York: Appleton-Century-Crofts, 1971.

    A hard-hitting book on the history of Federal Government collusion with local governments to apply the idea of "law and order" in such a way as to discriminate against Blacks. Helps readers understand why ghetto Blacks hate police; they see them as agents of white repression.

Brecher, Edward M., and the editors of *Consumer Reports, Licit and Illicit Drugs*. Boston: Little, Brown and Company, 1972.

    This is very likely the most carefully researched, objective, and responsible book yet written on the nature and use of controversial drugs. Based on five years of research, this book is considered the definitive reference on the subject. Highly recommended.

Demaris, Ovid, *Dirty Business: The Corporate-Political-Money-Power Game*. New York: Harper's Magazine Press, 1974.

    An up-to-date book on white-collar crime and outside-the-law misdeeds within the top echelons of the giant corporate business structure. Well documented and indexed, this appears a better reference for student reading than earlier exposés.

Dorman, Michael, *Payoff: The Role of Organized Crime in American Politics.* New York: David McKay Co., Inc. 1972.

Dorman describes and documents how organized crime could exist only through the sufferance of government—how, except for its political connections, organized crime could be quickly eliminated from the American scene. The book leaves open the question of how high into government the influence of organized crime may reach.

Douglas, Jack D. (ed.), *Crime and Justice in American Society.* Indianapolis: The Bobbs-Merrill Company, Inc., 1971.

A first-rate general treatment of the crime problem in this country, with an attempt to get at its underlying causes. Good essays on the nature of law and crime, the court system, and our ways of handling convicted offenders. These readings do not paint a pretty picture of the way we go about handling crime.

Geis, Gilbert (ed.), *White-Collar Criminal: The Offender in Business and the Professions.* New York: Atherton Press, 1968.

This book contains a wealth of good material on the kind of crime which does the nation the most damage, both financially and in terms of the total number of damaged lives, that is, crime in the "upperworld." The ordinary Middle American has little conception of the amount of upper-middle and upper-class crime that exists or its cost to the nation.

Klotz, Daniel, *Ring around the White Collar: An Educator's Guide to White-Collar Crime.* Unpublished M.A. thesis, California State University, Fresno, 1973. (Available on loan from the CSUF library.)

A highly readable, fact-laden study of the amount and kinds of white-collar crime in the United States. Contains the most comprehensive and up-to-date bibliography on the subject this writer has seen.

Rawls, John, *A Theory of Justice.* Cambridge, Mass.: Harvard University Press, 1971.

A book for advanced students who have a philosophical interest in the meaning of justice. Basically, a treatise on ethical theory, but with potent implications for our system of criminal justice.

Reckless, Walter C., *American Criminology: New Directions.* New York: Appleton-Century-Crofts, 1973.

One of the country's better-known criminologists writes a general textbook in criminology, more comprehensive than most, which students should find very useful as a general reference on the subject.

The Report of the Commission on Obscenity and Pornography, the text with dissents and an Introduction by Clive Barnes. New York: Bantam Books, 1970.

This presidential commission, instigated by President Johnson, documents beyond necessity a fact which every careful student of the subject has known all along: what are popularly labeled "obscene" and "pornographic" books, pictures, motion pictures, etc., do not harm anyone and apparently teenage exposure to them promotes a healthier sex life in adulthood.

The Ripon Society and Clifford W. Brown, Jr., *Jaws of Victory: The Game-Plan Politics of 1972, the Crisis of the Republican Party, and the Future of the Constitution*. Boston: Little Brown and Company, 1974.

This first-rate book, reflecting the views of liberal eastern "Rockefeller-type" Republicans, is an attempt to explain the *why* of the Watergate scandal and its associated white-collar criminal acts. The writers blame primarily the "strategic" approach to politics of the Nixon people, dominated by a win-at-any-cost and paramilitary psychology. Because of its probing into causes, probably a better book on Watergate than Carl Bernstein and Bob Woodward's *All the President's Men* (New York: Simon and Schuster, 1974).

Schur, Edwin M., *Crimes without Victims*. Englewood Cliffs, N.J.: Prentice-Hall, Inc., 1965.

Focuses particularly on abortion, homosexuality, and drug addiction. A concise, readable book that pulls together a large amount of research evidence. Schur is critical of laws against victimless crime, but his arguments are not oversimplified.

8

RELIGION, CHURCH, AND EDUCATION

You want a trip, man? I'll give you a free trip. It's really a groovy high. It's called Jesus Christ and it will really blow your mind.
A former Hell's Angel and drug pusher
(name withheld)

Understanding the history of religious faith and practice in the United States, the religious issues surrounding the writing of the Constitution, the ongoing struggle of about 185 years to fully implement the First Amendment with respect to the separation of church and state in our public schools, and the general religious tenor of the nation of the 1970s are all important to teachers. In fact, we can scarcely imagine a teacher being fully professional without considerable sophisticated knowledge in these areas.

THE RELIGION OF THE FOUNDING FATHERS

| NAME | RELIGIOUS PREFERENCE | |
	THEIST	DEIST
George Washington		✓
John Adams		✓
Thomas Jefferson		✓
James Madison		✓
James Monroe		✓
Benjamin Franklin		✓
John Winthrop		✓
James Wilson		✓
Thomas Paine		✓
Joseph Hawley		✓
Ethan Allen		✓
Elihu Palmer		✓

Yet, it seems clear that a large majority of teachers have virtually no knowledge at all about these matters. There seems to be nothing required in college curriculums for prospective teachers, not even in colleges ·that have rather substantial humanities requirements for freshmen and sophomores. Honest teaching about religion in the United States is rarely encountered—almost never at the elementary and secondary level and only spottily in any except our most prestigious universities.

School boards, administrators, and teachers, in spite of negative Supreme Court decisions, continue to promote sectarian religion in public schools through teaching religiously derived values if not the pure theology itself. They thus open themselves to the charge of unconstitutional acts.

But at least as serious is the major topic analyzed in this chapter: teachers are continuously guilty of inflicting on students gross untruths about the religious origins and basis of the United States government and our major institutional structures.

The format of this chapter varies somewhat from that of other chapters in Part II in that more space is devoted to belief patterns, or ideology, and less to demonstrating how we might go about testing "outrageous hypotheses." This was not originally intended, but our research indicates that the religious belief patterns of the United States are probably more complex than the belief patterns underlying any of the other topics treated in the chapters of Part II, and therefore deserve the expanded coverage.

IDEOLOGICAL PATTERNS IN AMERICAN RELIGION

As with beliefs in the other areas of cultural concern treated in this section of the book, Americans demonstrate about as much inconsistency as the imagination can conjure. At the level of abstract verbalization where people assert their beliefs in general terms, almost all adults proclaim some kind of religion. At a more concrete action-oriented level, their unverbalized and often unverbalizable beliefs are often antireligious according to any meaningful concept of religion.

Despite new significant developments in the seventies, it seems probable that the basic situation is little changed from that of more than twenty years ago. In 1953, more than 9.7 million Bibles were sold in the United States; but according to one study, when a representative sampling of adults were asked to name the first four books of the New Testament, more than half could not name even one. Will Herberg, one of our foremost sociologists of religion, commented at the end of the fifties that

"America seems to be at once the most religious and the most secular of nations."[1]

Eighteenth- and Nineteenth-Century Backgrounds

In religion, as in most other areas of life, Americans have always been more or less polarized on a liberal/conservative continuum. If we look briefly at its history, we can understand better this polarization in the late twentieth century.

Theism versus Deism

In religion, the conservative/liberal dichotomy of the eighteenth century, the "Age of the Enlightenment," was between traditional theism and the religion of "science and reason"—deism. Theism insists on the existence of one God, usually conceived as anthropomorphic, who created the natural universe and laws that govern it, as well as man and moral values, and who is at the same time transcendent and immanent. This is a brief statement of the central idea of Catholicism, Lutheranism, and Calvinism as they existed then and as they exist in their fundamentalist versions today.

In contrast, deism is a humanistic religion which rejects supernaturalism in any form and regards human reason as the basis of human life, and man as the inventor of his own moral values. Deists of the eighteenth century usually accepted the existence of a God conceived as the creator of man, the universe, and its natural laws, but as one who refrained from interfering in the operation of natural law or in human affairs. The deist conception of God made of him no more than a functionary, of no particular importance after creation, and thus led rather easily to agnosticism and atheism.

Although deism was very popular among educated colonists at the time of the American Revolution and into the early nineteenth century, the nineteenth century as a whole settled into a pattern of the traditional denominations reestablishing themselves. The early century saw a resurgence of the revivalism of the early eighteenth century and was known as the "Second Great Awakening." Frontiersmen found it easy to let the problems posed by mere survival distract them from religious interests but were periodically "saved" by traveling evangelists.

Theism under Attack

A combination of influences converged in the nineteenth century, particularly after the Civil War, to shake religious orthodoxy. The impact

[1] Will Herberg, *Protestant, Catholic, Jew: An Essay in American Religious Sociology.* New York: Doubleday & Company, Inc., 1960 (Anchor Books), p. 3.

of the publication of Charles Darwin's *Origin of Species* in 1859 and *The Descent of Man* in 1871, was increased by the flowering of science during that period both in Europe and the English-speaking nations. The social sciences were also emerging in somewhat modern forms, with anthropology and psychology both offering explanations for religious behavior other than the existence of supernatural forces. The general level of education was rising, a development which has commonly jeopardized traditional religious views.

As a consequence, early in the twentieth century the "modernist movement" in religion began. This was a movement in the direction of liberalizing and democratizing religion, of viewing science as a road to truth superior to revelation. The path was now opened to controversies that would lead, step by step, to the religious developments of the post-World War II period.

Religious Belief between World War II and the Seventies

Central to understanding ideological developments in religion since 1945 is an understanding of the still largely orthodox beliefs of Middle America. What is new is attacks against a group of more-or-less standard beliefs, common to most of the major denominations. These attacks have come from ultrafundamentalists who feel that standard beliefs are too liberal; from religious liberals and leftward-tending radicals who think standard religion is much too fundamentalist; and from an assortment of newly risen cults, ranging from Christian primitivism to satan worship, and non-cultish intellectually sophisticated alternatives to the Judaic-Christian tradition, such as Zen. Before examining the attackers, we should look first at what is being attacked.

Traditional Middle American Orthodoxy

Sociologists and historians of religion have available a wealth of historical documentation as to *what* the religious beliefs of people were prior to the 1930s. However, the historical record provides no statistical data on what *proportion* of the population believed what, or the *degree of intensity* with which specific beliefs were held. Since the 1930s increasing use has been made of opinion studies. What we present in this section is an integration of a variety of opinion studies, ranging from somewhat dubious Gallup poll results to more carefully made studies involving questionnaire or interviewing techniques. With funds from the National Science Foundation and other sources and as part of the University of California's Research Program in Religion and Society, Stark and Glock have since the

1950s been sampling religious opinion, checking their findings against Gallup poll results, and publishing their findings periodically.[2]

In this section we will draw primarily from the Glock and Stark studies, the studies of Streiker and Strober, and Hudson's historical work.[3]

Beliefs about God Historical Christianity and twentieth-century fundamentalism view God in essentially the same manner as theism everywhere; some of these beliefs may be stated as follows:

—God is anthropomorphic and male (often illustrated in older Bibles as an elderly man with a white beard and an intense, fierce gaze).
—God is omnipotent, omniscient, and omnipresent.
—Although God is all-powerful, Satan, leader of the fallen angels, is powerful enough to be a threat (although in the Great Final Showdown it is assumed that God and the Saints will win and banish Satan to hell forever).
—God is both loving and stern, forgiving and vengeful (and in still other ways has human qualities).
—God's ethical edicts appear in the Ten Commandments.
—Transgressing the Commandments requires repentance in order to receive God's forgiveness.

How many Americans believe in God as described in the foregoing statements? All the opinion research data we have suggests that between 90 and 95 percent of American adults assert a belief in some version of God; *between 70 and 75 percent believe in God as portrayed in the belief-statements above.* However, the denomination or sect one belongs to has a strong influence on the proportion of believers in the traditional theistic God portrayed above. For example, 99 percent of Southern Baptists, 96 percent of the Sectaries (evangelical and pentecostal groups), 81 percent of Catholics, and 81 percent of Missouri-Synod Lutherans are convinced of the existence of a theistic God. But at the other end of the continuum, only 39 percent of Jews and 41 percent of Congregationalists are so convinced.[4]

[2] Rodney Stark and Charles Y. Glock, *American Piety: The Nature of Religious Commitment.* Berkeley: University of California Press, 1968. Previous volumes by Glock and Stark, also a part of the Research Program in Religion and Society, include *Religion and Society in Tension,* Skokie, Ill.: Rand McNally & Company, 1965; and *Christian Beliefs and Anti-Semitism,* New York: Harper & Row, Publishers, 1966. Volumes by other authors emerging from the RPRS include N. J. Demerath III, *Social Class in American Protestantism,* Skokie, Ill., Rand McNally & Company, 1965; and Donald Metz, *New Congregations: Security and Mission in Conflict,* Philadelphia: The Westminster Press, 1967.

[3] Lowell D. Streiker and Gerald S. Strober, *Religion and the New Majority: Billy Graham, Middle America, and the Politics of the 70s.* New York: Association Press, 1972; Winthrop S. Hudson, *Religion in America.* New York: Charles Scribner's Sons, 1973.

[4] Streiker and Strober, pp. 125–126. Their figures are derived from the Stark and Glock studies.

Beliefs about Jesus Christ   Streiker and Strober have pulled together the findings of Glock and Stark studies of the early 1960s concerning American beliefs about Jesus Christ. As in connection with views concerning God, the most traditional in belief are Southern Baptists, the Sectaries, Missouri Lutherans, and Roman Catholics. Also, as in the case of beliefs about God, more than half the members of all denominations except Congregationalists and Unitarians hold to the fundamentalist beliefs associated with theism. The common beliefs may be stated as follows:

—Jesus Christ was a supernatural, divine figure.
—Jesus Christ was born of a virgin.
—Jesus Christ performed miracles, such as walking on water, raising the dead, and transforming water to wine.
—Jesus Christ is the savior of mankind.
—Jesus Christ was resurrected after death and ascended to Heaven.
—Jesus Christ will return to earth (the "second coming" or "second advent").

Beliefs related to the Bible   Beliefs concerning the Bible may be stated briefly because people tend either to believe it is a divine document or they do not.

—The Bible is the Word of God and literally true in its entirety (according to a Gallup poll, believed by 79 percent of American adults; only 13 percent believe the Bible to be only a "great piece of literature").

Beliefs about heaven and hell   The following belief-statements were derived from either Gallup poll findings or the studies of Stark and Glock.

—A person's soul lives on after death (roughly 90 percent say yes).
—There is a literal place called Heaven where the righteous will live in eternal bliss (71 percent of Protestants and 80 percent of Catholics agree).
—There is a literal place called Hell where unrepentant sinners will be tormented forever (54 percent of Protestants and 70 percent of Catholics responded affirmatively).
—To get to Heaven, it is absolutely essential to believe in Jesus Christ as savior.
—To get to Heaven it is absolutely essential to accept the Bible as the literal word of God.
—To get to Heaven it is necessary to pray.
—To get to Heaven it is necessary to do good for others.

Consistent with what we would expect, a higher percentage of Americans feel that belief in Jesus Christ, in the Bible, and praying are all more important to gain entry to heaven than to "do good for others" (roughly 60 percent recommending belief in Jesus Christ to 50 percent recommmending doing good for others).

Beliefs about man and society The more likely people are to believe the series of assertions we have presented on the above pages, the more likely they are to have beliefs about man and society that are both pessimistic and ultraconservative. This connection has been observed deep into the historical past but became glaringly conspicuous after World War II. The following specimen belief-statements should give readers the idea.

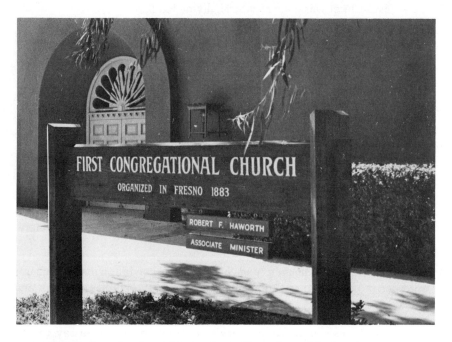

—Man is born in sin and is intrinsically evil until he has been "saved" by accepting Jesus.

—Unredeemed sinners deserve punishment, not forgiveness; the best way to reduce crime is to increase the amount of punishmnt.

—Love of Christ and country go together; a good Christian is a good patriot.

—Atheism and communism are the same thing.

—The most important social cause for Americans is to fight communism.

—The nation should not hesitate to go to war to destroy or contain communism.

—Social conditions will get worse rather than better; the Bible forecasts a time of great troubles and we have reached that time.

—Social reformers are misled; after all, "the poor ye shall always have with you."

—A love of God and capitalism go together.

—Ability to acquire material wealth is a sign of righteousness; the rich should not be condemned for their riches.

Post-War Religious Modernism

Although religious modernism developed early in the century and influenced a rather considerable minority of educated people, it was not until after World War II—not until the 1960s in fact—that modernism turned militant and became a disrupting force among both Protestants

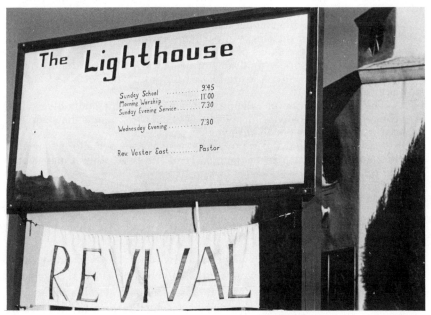

Like half a century ago, American religious beliefs are still polarized between modernism and fundamentalism. (Left and right, *Maurice P. Hunt*)

and Roman Catholics. The new militant modernism was accepted more easily by the larger Protestant denominations of the northern and western United States which had been gradually moving in a more liberal direction for decades.

We will begin with belief-statements that reflect the core of modernism and show the contrast between modernism and fundamentalism as the two movements took form in the 1920s. The basic premises of modernism have not changed since then except that since 1945 modernism has become still more of a social religion and has adopted militant tactics.

—God is a force in the universe, a kind of divine energy that pervades everything animate and inanimate.

—God does not take a personal interest in individuals, does not answer prayer, does not cause miracles; man himself, as possessor of a piece of the universal spiritual force, is one of the prime manifestations of God.

—It is ridiculous to talk about "God being on our side" during a war; the whole idea of war is irrational, as is the advocacy of violence in settling any kind of dispute.

—All that man can ever know about God and the universe is what can be learned through use of scientific method.

—Jesus Christ was born of a human mother and father and was divine only as every person is; however, he was one of the world's greatest ethical teachers.

—The Bible is neither supernaturally inspired nor factually true for the most part; but the Gospels, particularly the Sermon on the Mount, convey the main teachings of Christ.

—Man is born morally neutral, not in sin; what human beings make of themselves morally is a product of the interaction of a self and its environment.

—The chief function of religion is to make people socially aware and concerned about solving problems, particularly helping the poor and downtrodden to better themselves.

—Man is better off and more realistic to accept a meliorist view of life; continuing progress in the quality of life is possible if man works for it.

—Democracy is to be preferred over authoritarian totalitarianism, relativism over absolutism.[5]

Twists and Turns of the Seventies

Religious orthodoxy has always been authoritarian or absolutist, even when it has emphasized individualism, as Calvinism in colonial days came to do. Within most denominations it has also been totalitarian in the sense that all members were expected to accept the same theology or be cast out of the denomination.

Beginning in the fifties and continuing into the seventies new religious developments emerged on the American scene. These included:

1. A political "radical conservativism" or "radical right" appeared which shared among other beliefs a fanatical anti-communism and an equally fanatical religious fundamentalism. In one reputable study of the radical right, it was found that of its membership 81 percent were religious fundamentalists.[6]

---

[5] Most of the foregoing belief-statements are derived from or implied by material in Hudson, pp. 274–277; Streiker and Strober, pp. 88–89; and Robert N. Bellah, *Beyond Belief: Essays on Religion in a Post-Traditional World.* New York: Harper & Row, Publishers, 1970, Part III.

[6] Raymond E. Wolfinger *et al.,* "America's Radical Right: Politics and Ideology," in Robert A. Schoenberger (ed.), *The American Right Wing: Readings in Political Behavior.* New York: Holt, Rinehart and Winston, Inc., 1969.

2. The rise of new sects and cults, including youthful fundamentalists ("Jesus freaks," or more politely named, "Jesus people"), cults inspired by Far Eastern religons led by a rapidly multiplying number of gurus of one sort and another, satan worshippers, and many others.
3. A tendency among the more liberal Protestant denominations to engage in political activism, and in some cases, to form splinter groups which have identified with the New Left.
4. The most important schism of modern history in the Catholic Church, with the formation of a theologically rebellious and politically activist Catholic left.

The Jesus People   Clearly within the Christian tradition, but not the tradition adult church members are familiar with, are the "Jesus people." Their members are both young and not-so-young.

Because of its newness and fluidity, it is impossible to list the belief-statements of this group as confidently as we can those of the old denominations and sects whose beliefs have been polled by Gallup and other organizations and intensively studied by historians and sociologists of religion. As yet there are not many good books on the movement.[7] Hudson tells us:

> . . . by 1967 there were traces of a reviving interest in Jesus among the "street people," "cop-outs," and "trippers" of California. Perhaps it began with "rock music." . . . The turning of "rock" to "protest" themes seemed to lead quite quickly to "secularized" religious themes to express and convey the message of disaffection and alienation.[8]

Because, as Hudson remarks, the Jesus People are such a variegated lot, it is virtually impossible to generalize about them. The one thing the Jesus people seem to have in common is an intense alienation from not only the mainline denominations but from all the rest of the culture. We will hazard these belief-statements as seeming to characterize the thinking of at least a large number of these people:

—The best life is a simple communal one, like that of the first Christians.
—Mankind is living in its last times; Jesus will return very soon.
—Schooling, knowledge, learning are pointless goals; all one needs is Jesus.
—The authority of our commune leaders is not to be questioned; democracy and religion do not fit together.

---

[7] Generally recommended as the best book is R. M. Enroth, E. E. Ericson, Jr., and C. B. Petets, *The Jesus People,* Grand Rapids, Mich.: Wm. B. Eerdmans Publishing Company, 1972.

[8] Hudson, *Religion in America,* p. 431.

—Males must dominate; women are weak and as temptresses promote immorality.[9]
—The use of alcohol, tobacco, and drugs is sinful; also sinful are premarital sex, the wearing of makeup and seductive clothes by women, and accumulating private property.
—People should not get involved in politics or other worldly matters; political activities have done no one any good.

The new mystics The number of mystical cults pretending to draw their inspiration, ideas, and ceremonies from the Far East seems limited only by the number of gurus bearing Indian names. Their numbers grow like inspired mushrooms. It now appears that a substantial proportion of the not-so-well educated members of the youthful New Left of the sixties have given up on causes and sought mystical solace. Kopkind finds that:

> Gurus, swamis, roshis, dervishes, gods, and therapists are building impressive movements and extensive institutions while the traditional left sects contract in size and influence. Rennie Davis, once the New Leftist *par excellence*, has become a devoted organizer for the aggressive religion of the Satguru Maharaj Ji, the teenage Avatar (that is, God).[10]

AN "OUTRAGEOUS HYPOTHESIS" ABOUT RELIGION

The area of religion, particularly religious ideology, is a difficult field in which to derive testable assertions. For example, none of the belief-statements earlier in the chapter about God, Jesus Christ, the Bible, heaven and hell, miracles, and the like, is subject to any kind of scientific or reflective test because, even though they commonly have a syntax appropriate for hypotheses, much of the vocabulary used is not operationally definable and the only "supporting data" come from the scriptures or someone's personal experience with revelation.

A few of the belief-statements presented earlier, particularly under the head of "beliefs about man and society," do provide us with testable assertions. We can, for example, readily test the notion that "Communism and atheism are the same thing," or that "Crime is reduced by making punishment more severe."

Hypothesis: *The United States was not "founded under God," nor is it basically a Christian nation.*

[9] Mary White Harder *et al.*, "Jesus People," *Psychology Today*, December 1972, p. 45.
[10] Andrew Kopkind, "Mystic Politics: Refugees from the New Left," *Ramparts*, July 1973, p. 26.

School children are told repeatedly that the United States was "founded under God" and that we live in a "Christian nation." Artifacts and customs promote this impression. Our coins and paper currency bear the statement "In God we trust." The oath of allegiance contains the expression "one nation under God." When an oath is administered, the person holds one hand on the Bible.

Before we can present evidence relating to the truth or falsity of this assertion, it is necessary to define what is meant by "founded under God." We will reword the expression to mean "founded by men who believed in God, and who intended that the nation be governed, and that its citizens live in a manner consistent with God's laws."

The hypothesis can then be rephrased as follows: *The United States was not founded by men who believed in God and the validity of Divine Law, nor have most Americans since demonstrated a sincere belief in Christian ideals.* We believe that most Americans would understand such a statement and would regard it as both untrue and offensive.

The Religion of the Founding Fathers

Early in the chapter we contrasted theism and deism. We mentioned that deism was a popular religious movement among the educated during the latter part of the eighteenth century and into the early nineteenth.

The Men and Their Beliefs

Leaders of the period preceding, during, and after the Revolution did not deny a belief in God; in fact, they referred to God often and some of them prayed. But their notion of God was that of God as a spiritual force, the Creator, and quite in contrast with the anthropomorphic God of the theists.

Who among the Founding Fathers were clearly deists? Apparently most of them were, and those who did not proclaim themselves as such, showed conspicuous deist influences in their thinking. Benjamin Franklin, George Washington, John Winthrop, and Thomas Jefferson were self-proclaimed deists. John Adams, James Madison, James Wilson, and James Monroe appeared to hold the same or very similar beliefs. Thomas Paine's *Age of Reason* (published in two parts, 1794 and 1796) led to the accusation that Paine was an atheist.

Benjamin Franklin stated his view of the religious denominations of the colonies in this manner: "I found them more or less mix'd with other articles, which, without any tendency to inspire, promote or confirm morality, serv'd principally to divide us, and make us unfriendly to one another."[11] "Washington openly avoided church services and refused the

[11] Bellah, *Beyond Belief*, p. 173.

Eucharist, while Jefferson made disbelief a fashionable heresy.[12] John Adams preferred the word Providence, rather than God. Referring to the deism of the Founding Fathers, Bellah says: "Though much is selectively derived from Christianity, this religion is clearly not itself Christianity. For one thing, neither Washington nor Adams nor Jefferson mentioned Christ in his inaugural address. . . ."[13]

Morgan reminds us that Jefferson thought no tax should be levied to support religion and that "learning and religion were incompatible." Madison wrote a pamphlet condemning a bill which would have provided a tax to support teachers of Christianity. He argued that "disbelief should enjoy the same rights as belief." Madison condemned the appointment of chaplains for the House and the Senate.[14]

Religion and the Constitution

The Constitution of the United States mentions religion only three times, twice in connection with minor points. The only important statement involving religion in the body proper of the Constitution is in Article VI: ". . . but no religious Test shall ever be required as a Qualification to any Office or public Trust under the United States."

Article I of the First Amendment states that "Congress shall make no law respecting an establishment of religion, or prohibiting the free exercise thereof. . . ." Although the meaning of this statement seems clear enough, Butts shows clearly that its full implications cannot be understood without understanding the argumentation and debate in progress since 1776.[15]

Probably James Madison, more than anyone else, attempted through his speeches and writings to make clear what the Constitution should specify regarding religion. He insisted on two major points: (1) the Federal Government must not provide for an established religion or permit any infringement on the free rights of conscience or the free practice of religion, and (2) the states must also be subject to the same restrictions. The House of Representatives approved, but the Senate refused at the time to buy the second of Madison's ideas; it was not until the adoption of the Fourteenth Amendment that full Bill of Rights protections were extended to the states.

Some constitutional lawyers since have argued that Madison was

[12] Homer W. Smith, *Man and His Gods*, Foreword by Albert Einstein, New York: Grosset & Dunlap, Inc., 1952, p. 401.

[13] Bellah, *Beyond Belief*, p. 175.

[14] Richard E. Morgan, *The Supreme Court and Religion*. New York: The Free Press, 1972, pp. 17, 19.

[15] R. Freeman Butts, *The American Tradition in Religion and Education*. Boston: Beacon Press, 1950, pp. 78–79.

not really concerned about preventing cooperation between the Federal Government and religion. But Butts shows that Madison's intent was ". . . to prevent *all* forms of single or multiple establishment [of a state church] as well as prevent 'cooperation' between the states and the federal government and any or all churches."[16]

All one needs do is study carefully the writings and speeches of Madison and others to realize that the intent of the Founding Fathers was to prevent government at any level from becoming involved with religion in any manner. The nation was founded as a purely *secular* nation, with religion to be left a matter of individual conscience.

Church opposition to a democratic system It is one of the major paradoxes of American life that over the course of time the intent of the Founding Fathers was distorted or forgotten. The first five Presidents of the United States were deists. The only President since that time and until the twentieth century who did not proclaim a commitment to the Calvinist theistic tradition was Abraham Lincoln, whose religious attachment, to the extent that he had one, was Congregational-Unitarian—the only denominations which to the present time have kept largely intact the deist faith.

In the twentieth century, only two Presidents could be construed as being relatively nonreligious or at least outside the Calvinist tradition: Franklin D. Roosevelt (an Anglican) and John F. Kennedy (a liberal Catholic).[17]

Discrepancy between Abstract and Operational Beliefs

We have noted earlier that a majority of Americans in the sixties and seventies, when questioned about what they believe, express a fundamentalist theology. Although fundamentalism has never valued the ideas of brotherhood and "good works" above repentance and salvation, it would be unfair to say that they reject as a theological principle the concepts of the brotherhood of man and a loving, forgiving God. They do hold these ideas as part of their creed. The question we wish to explore in this section is the extent to which religious fundamentalists believe and act in ways quite incompatible with their Christian creed.

Support of Radical Conservative Causes

We saw in Chapter 5 that Middle Americans, who make up the core of the fundamentalist churches, accept and promote the use of force

[16] Butts, p. 80. See also Butts' excellent article, "James Madison, the Bill of Rights, and Education," *Teachers College Record,* December 1958, p. 124.

[17] Robert S. Alley, *So Help Me God: Religion and the Presidency, Wilson to Nixon.* Richmond, Va.: John Knox Press, 1972.

against those with whom they do not agree. During the student marches, assemblies, and rallies of the sixties and early seventies, on various occasions the press reported incidents where blue-collar workers attacked gatherings of rebellious youth—the most publicized incident being the beating of students in New York City by hard hat construction workers. "Police-type" methods of resolving disputes seem to have particular appeal to the upper blue-collar population.

Coupled with the fear of dissent seems to be an awe of powerful government and a tendency to support it without question. Related to this is a respect for law—any law, even the most unjust—simply because it is law. This law-and-order orientation of Middle Americans works to keep on the books outdated, inhumane laws which punish merely for the presumed virtue of punishment itself.

A policy of territorial and colonial expansionism has been supported historically by most denominations and sects that have a mission program. American-based mission programs have usually been Protestant, as evidenced by the attitude of the government in relation to our colonizing the Philippines: "We must take them and Christianize them . . ." as President McKinley said (even though the Philippines had already been Catholicized).

We must also remember the extreme anti-communism of American religious fundamentalism since the Russian Revolution, particularly since World War II. Fundamentalist religion has lent its full support to our military adventures in Korea and Indochina, and its leaders have rarely spoken out against the napalming of civilians or atrocities such as the various Mai Lai's. We can therefore observe an extreme selectiveness with respect to whom we should feel forgiveness or sympathy for: a baby born of Communist parents can be mutilated in war without qualms of conscience, whereas much is made over the needless destruction of civilians in non-Communist nations.

Organized in the late 1940s, the Christian Crusade (which publishes a magazine by that name) was founded by the Rev. Billy James Hargis, a fundamentalist evangelist whose only education was from "institutions" officially listed by the United States government as degree mills. Hargis has on many occasions publicly deprecated education and has said "I think it is the ignorant people who are going to save this country."[18]

We have no way of knowing the total extent of the Hargis following as of this writing; as of the sixties the best educated guess would be

[18] Quoted in John H. Redekop, *The American Far Right: A Case Study of Billy James Hargis and Christian Crusade.* Foreword by Senator Mark O. Hatfield, Grand Rapids, Mich.: Wm. B. Eerdmans Publishing Company, 1968. Because of its heavy documentation and balanced presentation, this is probably the best study of Hargis and his movement.

Blessed are the meek :
for they shall inherit the earth.
Matthew, 5:5

several millions. The Hargis forces have attacked foreign aid (which is always likely to get into Communist hands), proposals for disarmament, proposals for a detente with any Communist nation, and on the "positive" side, has advocated war with Communist nations. In answer to his own question, "Should we surrender to Castro or SMASH him?" Hargis says that "Honor demands the liberation of Cuba from the hands of this godless despot."

Religious fundamentalists have taken a hard line traditionally with respect to crime, justice, and the law. However, the hard-line attitude is rather selectively applied. Fundamentalists are largely responsible for the sort of public opinion that makes it politically difficult to erase from federal and state codes the laws against non-victim crimes. Most non-victim crime legislation was passed originally at the instigation of fundamentalists. Anthony Comstock, a spiritual leader of the fundamentalists, was Secretary of the Society for the Suppression of Vice between 1873 and 1915. Comstock was responsible for the federal statute forbidding the sending of "obscene material" through the mails, a law which has produced continuous litigation to this day.

More important, perhaps, than any of the matters discussed above are American views toward the treatment of those convicted of crime.

Whereas the liberal denominations have usually taken strong stands for rehabilitation as the chief emphasis in handling the convicted, fundamentalists tend to favor punishment.

Religious fundamentalism is not only compatible with extreme economic conservatism; most fundamentalists assert an economic ideology that stresses individual responsibility for economic security, competition, the accumulation of wealth, a profit motive, and the inevitability of poverty.

It would be a grave mistake, however, to link only the lower-middle working class with attempts to fuse Christianity and a highly conservative version of capitalist economics. Although there are not many, we have fundamentalists among the rich and well-born, too. Among them are some who have written books equating Christianity and laissez-faire capitalism. Howard E. Kershner has produced one of the better examples of this genre of books. He upholds the freedom of business oligarchs to do as they please, attacks organized labor, defends poverty, and attacks any type of "New Deal" economic reform—all in the name of God and Christ and, by carefully selecting and quoting out of context, makes it appear that Christ was the first ardent capitalist.[19]

Whether Christian beliefs about charity, sharing, brotherhood, and so on can ever be made compatible with our kind of capitalist economics is questionable. The young "Jesus People" in their communes may be the only group with an "economic system" consistent with traditional Christian beliefs.[20]

Historically, fundamentalists of British or northern European descent have been highly racist, with a history of defending slavery until the Civil War, and white dominance and strict segregation from the Civil War until the 1960s.

The record of the small fundamentalist sects on race has been poor and still is. Redekop's study of Billy James Hargis and the Christian Crusade demonstrates clearly an unequivocal opposition to civil liberties generally, although Redekop does not feel that Hargis himself is a rabid racist. Redekop does feel that the fundamentalist movement was ready in the late sixties for a major expansion which might have brought with it a resurgence of fundamentalist racism.[21]

Issues involved in beliefs about life and death may reveal the fundamentalist mind even more than other subjects do. Is suicide to be condoned? Church groups have promoted and succeeded in having enacted

[19] Howard E. Kershner, God, Gold, and Government. Englewood Cliffs, N.J.: Prentice-Hall, Inc., 1957.

[20] See James McEvoy III, Radicals or Conservatives? The Contemporary American Right. Skokie, Ill.: Rand McNally & Company, 1971.

[21] Redekop, The American Far Right, pp. 40, 194, 200.

legislation making suicide illegal. Suicide is of such concern to some church groups that there has been a serious proposal to spend a large sum of money "fencing" the Golden Gate Bridge so people can no longer jump off it.

Another issue is whether euthanasia should be legalized. At present, even if a person with a terminal illness requests that he be allowed to die, it is common practice to use artificial life support systems to keep the person "alive" as long as possible. Euthanasia, of course, presents different issues from that of merely withdrawing artificial life support systems, although many persons see them as basically the same issue.

In the late 1960s the first international conference on Ethics in Medicine and Technology convened at Houston, Texas. About 250 persons attended. Six major papers were presented and ardently debated. Our concern is with the final paper, prepared by a world-famous German Protestant theologian, Helmut Thielicke. It is a theological analysis of when a medical doctor would be morally justified in withdrawing an artificial life support system from a dying patient.

Thielicke argues that when man was created by God, man was at first a partner of God, but when man (i.e., Adam) sinned, the partnership was broken and forever more man will be a subject of God. As a subject, man is forced to become what God intended him to be, a creature—the only living creature—with a consciousness of self. "This consciousness of self has reference particularly to knowledge about what lies ahead, and hence also to knowledge about death." Thielicke then goes on to say that:

> Only because of self-consciousness does suffering, for example, have any meaning. For connected with the gift of self-consciousness is the duty—and also the possibility—of "reacting" to suffering. We react whether we combat it or accept it, whether we give up in the face of suffering or let it become the crucible that tempers and strengthens us, whether we resist to the point of nullifying it or proceed to integrate it into our life. Thus, for man suffering can be an ethical act; it can even become a positive duty.[22]

According to Thielicke, man's ultimate duty is to suffer; without suffering there can be no meaningful existence. When does a human being cease being human and become only a biological organism? Thielicke's answer is when the person is no longer capable of suffering, as perhaps in a deep coma prior to death. Only when a person is no longer able to suffer does a physician have a moral right to let the person die. But at this point, Thielicke adds a caveat. He argues that even though a person is in a deep

[22] Helmut Thielicke, "Ethics in Modern Medicine," in Kenneth Vaux (ed.), *Who Shall Live? Medicine, Technology, Ethics.* Philadelphia: Fortress Press, 1970, pp. 161–162.

coma, the doctor can have no sure way of knowing that the person is not still self-conscious at some level, still capable of suffering. Therefore, there is no point before natural death when it is moral to withdraw the life support system.

Perhaps Thielicke's argument gives us a key to analyzing most of the issues we have raised in connection with fundamentalist theology and humanity. Perhaps each issue can be discussed in terms of whether the best course of action is that which will produce suffering or that which will reduce or eliminate suffering.

Whether we are discussing power and its use, our relations with foreign peoples, crime and justice, the economic system, race relations, sexism, the sins of sex and vice, or the beginning and end of life itself, one can take a position which excuses or even advocates suffering on the ground that through suffering man atones for Adam's sin and thereby makes for himself a place in heaven. Or, one can take a position that minimizes human suffering as much as possible, that prefers pleasure and self-fulfillment on this earth over pain.

If one opts for suffering, one is taking the position that many religious fundamentalists tend to take. It seems obvious from their views and actions that they prefer punishment of others over compassion. If one opts against suffering as a duty, one is taking a position consistent with religious modernism, with the stands taken by the liberal churches.

In case readers have doubts about the influence of religious fundamentalism on American attitudes toward suffering, it is enlightening to note the difference between Americans and the relatively non-Puritanical British. In Great Britain, terminal cancer patients are permitted to die pain-free deaths. The means is simple: Heroin is a far more effective pain killer than morphine and its medical use, illegal for any purpose in the United States, is legal in Britain. Further, LSD is also a remarkably effective pain killer, and though legally banned for medical purposes in the United States, is used in Gritain Britain to reduce or eliminate the pain of terminal cancer patients and at the same time induce comforting phantasies.[23]

Conclusions about the Hypothesis

What have we been able to demonstrate concerning whether the nation was "founded under God" and is basically a Christian nation? Since the

[23] Stewart Alsop, as told to Dick Cavett early in 1974 and aired over ABC-TV, July 11, 1974, after Alsop's death from cancer. Taped about two months before Alsop's death, it was clear that Alsop was deeply embittered by the American ideology which mandates pain for the hopelessly ill.

hypothesis involves two different questions, we come up with two different conclusions, one clear-cut, the other more complex.

In view of the intellectual climate of the late 1700s and early 1800s, and the values of those who led the Revolution, formed a government, and wrote its Constitution, it seems quite meaningless to say the nation was "founded under God." The framers of the Constitution among other things, were trying to found a nation unlike Britain, which would have no established church; governmental and religious institutions would be entirely separated and all individuals would have freedom to worship— or not worship—as they pleased. Although much of our history as a nation has been marked by church-state struggles of some form, the intention was to avert such struggle by designing a Constitution for a secular state, not a theocracy.

As to whether the United States has been or is a Christian nation, we get into the complications of defining "Christian," and the perhaps even more difficult complication of people being logically inconsistent. It is a historical fact that most Americans have called themselves Christians, but we have had two broad categories of Christianity—at least in this century. We have had fundamentalists and modernists and their views on many issues are light-years apart. Yet each group can make a case for calling itself Christian.

As for the operational beliefs of Americans, and their overt behavior, Christian fundamentalists are particularly inconsistent in that they tend to be conservative in an extreme or radical, not a classical, sense, and support mostly causes which are antihumanitarian, antilibertarian, antidemocratic.

On the other hand, since World War II the more liberal, modernist denominations have moved into a pattern of somewhat militant support for liberal causes. If New Testament teachings imply some sort of "social gospel," then the modernist churches have moved a considerable distance toward achieving it and can be viewed as perhaps consistently Christian.

To be fair toward religious fundamentalists, we must point to a movement which has been developing for the past few years among a minority of evangelical Protestants and is led primarily by a younger generation of preachers—those who came of age in the 1960s. The movement is toward more liberal political views and generally more liberal views on many social issues. In 1972, it surfaced in an "Evangelicals for McGovern" committee; at Thanksgiving time, 1973, some fifty evangelical leaders met in Chicago and published a "Declaration of Evangelical Social Concerns," which was subsequently endorsed by more than six hundred prominent evangelicals. The document is not merely liberal, but for religious fundamentalists, radical. It denounces racism, sexism, and the maldistribution of wealth in the United States. Given enough time, we could see a major shift in the traditional blind conservatism of our fundamentalist denominations and sects.[24]

RELIGION AND EDUCATION

Following a brief review of religion as it has involved education historically in this country, we will relate some of the key court decisions about religion and education. Then we will discuss what we see as continued widespread and unconstitutional teaching of religious sectarianism.

Religion and the Schools: A Historical Review

Of the three or four ongoing controveries in education with us since the Colonial Period, the place of religion in education has been one of the most prominent, basic, and continuing. Many issues remain unresolved in the seventies but at least the issues are now clearer and the alternatives more visible. The most useful historical treatment of this theme that we have found is that of Butts, and this section is based upon his recent book.[25]

Influenced by the "Great Awakening" of the early 1700s a number of colonial churches established sectarian schools during that century: Presbyterian, Dutch Reformed, Anglican, Congregational, Lutheran, Moravian, Mennonite, Quaker, Baptist, and Methodist. But during the final fourth of the century, spurred by Jefferson's idea of compulsory secular elementary education for the common people and availability of secular higher education for students wishing it, a move gradually developed toward free, publicly supported, secular education as the only education harmonious with democratic civilization. Between the 1770s and the 1860s there was a slow but steady development of a common school for elementary students, open to all, and controlled by local and state governments.

Considered in its total aspects, this long-range move was intended to provide an alternative to sectarian education. The people recognized that if the schools taught the doctrine of a single church, they would remain sectarian. At the same time, public demand required that the schools offer religious instruction. "They found the common religious doctrines of Christianity in the Bible (i.e., the Protestant Bible). If the

---

[24] "The New Evangelicals," Newsweek, May 6, 1974, p. 86.

[25] R. Freeman Butts, The Education of the West: A Formative Chapter in the History of Civilization. New York: McGraw-Hill Book Company, 1973. Chaps. 11 and 12.

schools would teach only the nonsectarian principles of Christianity as contained in the Bible, they argued, all sects would be satisfied."[26]

But the nineteenth century saw the immigration of millions of Roman Catholics to the United States. Catholics argued that the public schools were sectarian Protestant and went about establishing their own parochial schools which the Protestant majority refused to support with public monies. It was evident by the late 1800s that most Americans had opted for an elementary education which would be nonsectarian, publicly financed, and open to all of America's children. (Later this same view came to apply to secondary education.) The expected achievement of elementary schools (and later of a *part* of secondary education) was "literary [reading and writing] wrapped in piety and moral behavior."[27]

This situation remained basically stable for more than half a century. Protestants had their public schools and Catholics had their parochial schools, the latter being separatist, religiously oriented, and supported by tuition paid by parents. But in the 1950s and 1960s, the Catholic Church mounted increasing pressure to obtain financial aid from public funds on the grounds that Catholic parents were being taxed twice to provide schooling for their children and that if parochial schools were allowed to close for lack of funds, the added cost of educating Catholic young in the public schools would greatly exceed the cost of public subsidies to Catholic education.

The issue was not limited to parochial schools however. A strong move developed in the 1940s to insert openly sectarian education into the public school curriculum, including both the sectarianism of Catholicism and the numerous Protestant denominations. The first attempt was the "released time" program, which was declared unconstitutional by the Supreme Court in the famous McCollum case (1948).

It was not until 1962 and 1963 that the Court decided that prayer, bible reading, and some other forms of religious exercise in public schools were unconstitutional. Still undecided is the status of religious holidays, baccalaureate services, and other religiously related school activities.

As might be expected, however, conservative groups are not likely to let school prayers die gracefully; according to a UPI news release of September 25, 1973, the American Legion was pushing vigorously for an amendment to the Constitution which would permit prayers to be said in school.

But if the move to rid the public schools of sectarian teaching has been largely successful, the decision of the general public by the beginning of the twentieth century that parochial education should not in any way be financed out of the public treasury began to erode by the 1930s. In

[26] Butts, The Education of the West, p. 410.
[27] Butts, The Education of the West, p. 425.

1930, the Court declared permissible the use of public monies to provide textbooks for nonreligious subjects in parochial schools. In 1947, the Court accepted the idea that parochial school students could be transported to and from school on public school buses. Still undecided is the question of whether public schools can require students to take courses the content of which parents may feel is offensive on religious grounds

Butts regards the Elementary and Secondary Education Act of 1965 the "most important new piece of federal legislation . . . since the Morrill Act of 1862." (The Morrill Act provided federal support for the establishment of "agricultural and mechanical" colleges in the states.) The significance of the ESEA lies in its being a major breakthrough—the first serious and major attempt to provide federal funding for schools. Its significance for our purposes here, however, rests on its authorization of a variety of money appropriations for parochial schools: the purchases of library resources, textbooks, and other teaching materials provided "no such aids should be used for religious instruction and all aids continue to be owned by public authorities."[28]

Actually the Act leaves the situation pretty much wide open. Federal officials are free to decide for themselves what grants to make and what grants not to make to parochial schools, in spite of the assertion in the Act that federal officials cannot exercise control over local school programs.

The ESEA could not have been passed by Congress without compromising the separation of church and state mandated in the Constitution. To get an act at all, a great deal had to be given the Catholic Church which it had not been able to get previously.

As of this writing, the situation with respect to public schools seems in an uneasy state of equilibrium. In 1968 Pennsylvania enacted a law which would provide public monies to help pay the salaries of private school teachers in certain nonreligious subjects; in 1969, Rhode Island did the same; twenty-two other states were debating whether they should follow. But in 1971, by almost unanimous decision, the Supreme Court declared the Pennsylvania and Rhode Island laws unconstitutional. However, federal funds in large quantities are still being doled out to private colleges and universities.

We may summarize the church-state issue as it has pertained to schools by saying that, until 1930, the long-range trend since the Colonial Period had been toward the secularization of public education. This trend has been reversed in rather dramatic fashion since then by the granting of public assistance, in one form or another, to parochial schools. However, since World War II, legislation and court decisions have gone far in

---

[28] Butts, The Education of the West, p. 440.

eradicating the conspicuously overt teaching and practice of sectarian religion in public schools.

What Can Public Schools Teach about Religion?

If the intent of the Supreme Court, and possibly a majority of the public, is to eliminate religious sectarian teaching in public schools the question still remains: What are public schools to do about religion? Religion, organized and unorganized, is such a basic interest of Americans that public schools would seem remiss in simply ignoring the subject completely in designing curriculum.

Apparently it is legal to teach anything one might wish *about* religion so long as what is taught is nonsectarian and nonproseletyzing. This means that courses can be taught in world history which include church history; in the history of religion and the church; in comparative religion; in the sociology and psychology of religion; in the Bible as literature and history; and perhaps in other religiously related subjects.

One religiously related subject is the general area of moral values. Many states have laws that mandate the teaching of moral values. These laws do not specify *whose* moral ideas are to be taught, and since our culture is riddled with confusion and inconsistency in this area, most public schools make no formal effort to comply.

Sectarian Values in Nonsectarian Schools

American culture is overloaded with values, beliefs, and myths that stem from religion, if not from current religion, from religion of earlier periods of history. Beliefs with a direct religious base, dating from centuries back, or even thousands of years back, still may be firmly held and cherished as Absolute Truth even though those holding them may have no idea that their source of origin was one or more religions—Christian or pagan.

In this section, we present a few examples of beliefs taught in public schools that are sectarian in the sense that they, whether school officials and teachers know it, originally derived from theology.

Oaths and Holidays

Schools still regularly require students to pledge allegiance to the flag and "one nation under God." The Supreme Court ruled in 1943 that students who had a religious basis for not saluting the flag could not be required to do so.

Considering the time (in the 1950s) when "under God" was inserted in the oath (fundamentalism was riding high), it seems most likely that

The curriculum of our secular public schools is still strongly influenced by Calvinist values.

the concept of God intended is the theistic, anthropomorphic conception of religious fundamentalists. Thus, the oath is not only a violation of the religious freedom of Jehovah's Witnesses, but probably of almost all religious modernists as well, and is almost certainly unconstitutional.

Public schools still observe ceremonies related to religious holidays that are exclusively Christian: Thanksgiving, Christmas, Good Friday, and Easter. Few students are likely to feel burdened by a school holiday, no matter what its basis; but observance of Christian holidays are not matched with observance of Jewish holidays except in communities where most parents are Jews and Buddhist holidays are apparently ignored altogether in public school practice. This is an invasion of the religious freedom of any denomination or sect which is not Christian.

Baccalaureate ceremonies and Christmas programs are in a state of limbo because the Supreme Court decisions of 1962 and 1963 (which banned Bible reading, prayer, and other religious ceremonies) appears ambiguous on certain points.

Our Economic Ideology

Certain features of the American economic ideology are sectarian in the sense that they stem originally from John Calvin's theology and were later amplified by the Puritans of England and the Massachusetts colony. The work ethic ("dedication to one's calling," thrift and accumulation of wealth) and economic individualism (leading to the competition ethic) are religiously secretarian. This would suggest that schools that *advocate* these values are probably behaving unconstitutionally.

Our Sexist Ideology

Although most people now seem to feel that they risk some censure for being self-proclaimed sexists, nevertheless it now appears a backlash may be arising from the still-sexist elements of the population. One evidence of this is that the proposed Equal Rights Amendment to the Constitution (designed to guarantee fully equal rights to women) is stalling at the level of state ratification.

Although historically most cultures have given men a higher status than women for a variety of reasons, in cultures dominated by Christian belief sexism appears to stem rather obviously from Christian beliefs (Eve was responsible for the "fall" in the Garden of Eden and women have been blamed for Eve's mistake ever since). In the Christian world, therefore, sexist beliefs are fully as religiously sectarian as is belief in capitalist ideology—perhaps even more clearly so. Not only is sexism practiced within the public school bureaucracy, but most schools still teach sexist beliefs to children and youth.

Sin and Morality

Although we do not use the word "sin" very much in public schools any more, teachers are expected to teach morality. Before getting into this subject, we would like to quote Theodore Powell:

> Some curriculum specialists and educational advisers with more temerity than good sense have set forth outlines of what should be done in the public school about the teaching of moral and spiritual values . . . it may seem unkind, if not unduly harsh, to describe the proposals as another expression of the totalitarian spirit. . . .[29]

What is sinful and what is immoral? Our cultural answers to this question are firmly rooted in Christian belief. Since Christ had nothing to say about most acts that contemporary fundamentalists call sin, our religious answers to what sin is are based, at best, on hearsay evidence.

First, there are the orthodox beliefs about sex. We have mentioned some of the more common ones earlier in the chapter. Perhaps most at issue in the seventies are what Christian fundamentalists refer to as "perversions" (i.e., any sexual practice you don't agree with) and sex out of wedlock, commonly practiced by a large proportion of both youth and adults.

Second, there are the vices. We know of no biblical injunctions against consuming alcohol in moderation, smoking pot, betting on horses, using tobacco, or loafing in the sun. Yet these, and dozens of other behaviors, are condemned by fundamentalists and are taught as being sinful, immoral, and leading to hell in many of our public schools.

STUDY QUESTIONS

1. Millions of Americans exhibit a great display of piety on Sunday, but in connection with their profession or business cheat, steal, and lie the other six days of the week. How would you explain this?
2. John Dean, prize government witness in the Watergate scandals, guilty himself of several felony offenses, said he survived the ordeal of testimony only through prayer. What do you make of this kind of psychology?
3. Do you consider the Hebraic-Christian Bible literally true, that is, factual? If so, how do you define fact? If the Bible is a narration of facts, why can't such facts be used as evidence in a court?

[29] Theodore Powell, "The Dangers of Liberty," in Theodore H. Sizer (ed.), *Religion and Public Education*. Boston: Houghton Mifflin Company, 1966.

4. Presuming you know people who disclaim any belief in religion, what do you make of them? Do you think they are sincere? Do they seem to have good mental health? What are some arguments for noncommitment to any organized religion?
5. The belief that loss of chastity prior to marriage is immoral or sinful appears to stem not from any teachings of Christ, but from St. Paul. Why, then, are our sexual mores associated with Christianity? Why are the Ten Commandments associated with Christianity?
6. What does the word, sin, mean? Has it tended to become a meaningless concept with the growing secularization of our culture? How could you prove that any act is a sin?
7. Is the Supreme Court inconsistent in not declaring unconstitutional coins bearing the words, "In God we trust"? If it is unconstitutional to have chaplains in public schools, why is it not equally so to have them in the United States Congress? To be consistent, should prayers said in Congress be declared unconstitutional?
8. Recalling your own public school experience, what kinds of values clearly of religious origin did your teachers try to foster?
9. In case you are one of those rare students who has read the New Testament, what do you think would happen to Christ if he were to return in the flesh and resume teaching what the Bible attributes to him?
10. Politicians are notorious (in this century) for belonging to and attending a church. For the most part, the aides and cabinet members of ex-President Nixon who have been convicted of felonies were faithful churchgoers. How do you explain this?
11. Many fundamentalists have demanded that public school teachers grant them "equal time" in the curriculum to refute anything taught which they don't agree with, such as the theory of evolution. Do you agree or disagree with this argument? Why or why not?

ANNOTATED BIBLIOGRAPHY

Bellah, Robert N., *Beyond Belief: Essays on Religion in a Post-Traditional World.* New York: Harper & Row, Publishers, 1970.

A very good historical and comparative treatment of world religions by a former Harvard and now University of California sociologist, with critical analysis and some tentative forecasts. Bellah feels traditional American religious *fundamentalism is behind many of our social problems* and is not optimistic about the American future so long as a majority of Americans hold the beliefs they do. A scholarly and highly thought-provoking book for better students.

Berger, Peter, *The Sacred Canopy: Elements of a Sociological Theory of Religion.* New York: Doubleday & Company, Inc., 1967.

In this book, Berger discusses reasons why traditional religions have come under attack and analyzes the phenomenon of religion from a sociological view, with a focus on the basic question, "How can any religious view of the world be made plausible to people?" One of the best books of the past decade on the sociology of religion.

Dimoch, Marshall E., *Creative Religion: As Seen by a Social Scientist.* Boston: Beacon Press, 1963.

As a contrast to the fundamentalism of Jorstad and the sympathy for Middle American values and beliefs of Streiker and Strober, this little volume, written by a leader in the Unitarian-Universalist Association, presents well one version of religious modernism.

Hudson, Winthrop S., *Religion in America: An Historical Account of the Development of American Religious Life*, 2d ed. New York: Charles Scribner's Sons, 1973.

Included here not because it is the best religious history but because, as of this writing, it is the only one which carries readers into 1972. A rather disorganized conglomeration of neutrally presented facts. Well indexed and a useful reference source.

Jorstad, Erling, *New-Time Religion: The Jesus Revival in America*. Minneapolis: Augsburg Publishing House, 1972.

Jorstad is a pious sympathizer of the *Jesus People* among the young and the *new fundamentalism* that is, in the seventies, producing schisms in the large liberal denominations. This religious tract gives "the other side" in contrast to the writings of religious historians and sociologists. Jorstad reveals the thinking, although too sympathetically to be objective, of the "new fundamentalism."

Paul, Leslie, *Alternatives to Christian Belief: A Critical Survey of the Contemporary Search for Meaning*. New York: Doubleday & Company, Inc., 1967.

Paul is a professor at The Queens College, England, and a prolific author of books on philosophy and social comment, many with a religious theme. Perhaps the best book on non-Christian belief systems that have developed wide appeal: Chardin's phenomenology, Marxism, existentialism, and certain psychological schools of thought that have been held as religion—behaviorism, Freudianism, and Jungianism.

Schoenberger, Robert A. (ed.), *The American Right Wing: Readings in Political Behavior*. New York: Holt, Rinehart and Winston, Inc., 1969.

Each reading in this book is in effect a research monograph. The writers report a series of empirical studies on various aspects of the *radical right*. Most of these researches demonstrated the integral link between the radical political right and the more extreme fundamentalist religious sects. Highly recommended because of its *research* orientation and reliance on *primary sources*.

Sizer, Theodore (ed.), *Religion and Public Education*. Boston: Houghton Mifflin Company, 1967.

A first-rate book of readings covering a wide range of topics related to the handling of religion in public schools. Particularly recommended: Lawrence Kohlberg's essay, "Moral Education, Religious Education, and the Public Schools: A Developmental View."

Streiker, Lowell D., and Gerald S. Strober, *Religion and the New Majority: Billy Graham, Middle America, and the Politics of the 70s*. New York: Association Press, 1972.

A sympathetic biography of Graham, this book is much more than that. It attempts an *analysis of the belief structure of Middle America*, and, except for a few extremists of the far right, finds it basically good. Its world view is well exemplified in the beliefs of Billy Graham.

The authors warn the liberal mainline denominations to become more fundamentalist or suffer continued losses in support.

Ziff, Larzer, *Puritanism in America: New Culture in a New World.* New York: The Viking Press, 1973.

Perhaps the best history of Puritanism, defined not primarily as a theology but as "a particular way of living." Excellent background for the twentieth-century view as expounded by such historians as Samuel E. Morison and Perry Miller that piety leads to moralism, which is transformed into bigotry, sentimental revivalism, and often humanitarian benevolence.

OUR ECONOMIC SYSTEM
AND EDUCATION

If the goal of technological civilization is merely to do more and more of the same bigger and faster, tomorrow will only be a horrendous extension of today.

René Dubos

Economists and other social observers often comment that the American public, including most businessmen and educated professionals, are "economic illiterates." One can make a case that because of its importance sheer ignorance about economic matters is America's most critical problem, one which could easily prove fatal to our culture and society. Since public school curriculums include very little economics, and what is included is superficial, uncritical, and often simply untrue, we feel that public education has not aided our society in this area, but actually has been highly damaging.

Clearly, therefore, our public schools need to do something to rectify the economic illiteracy of American citizens. The school curriculum should provide high school graduates with some basis for intelligent voting; after all, the platform of virtually every political candidate contains some program for purported economic reform. Unfortunately, most politicians are as unsophisticated economically as are their constituents.

Aside from the moral obligation schools have toward our society to educate all students about economic basics, many economic issues directly affect public education. Public schools, like other public sectors of the economy, suffer continual economic deprivation. There is no economic reason why public education could or should not be much better funded than it is. Yet, unaware teachers often promote the very economic myths that obstruct adequate school support. For this reason, much of the chapter's final section on education and economics will be devoted to just how school finance fits into the overall economic picture.

SOME COMMON ECONOMIC BELIEFS OF AMERICANS

The popular economic ideology is derived from several fairly understandable sources. Its inconsistencies appear to relate closely to the different schools of economic thought which have existed since the first economic theorizing produced two contradictory views: mercantilism vs. laissez-faire. Since then (the 1700s), we have seen the rise of several socialistic economic models, the development of the institutionalist school (since the late 1800s), Keynesian theory (first popularized in the late 1930s), and a variety of post-Keynesian outlooks which began to emerge in the sixties and are still emerging.

The late sixties saw a resurgence of interest in Marx's particular brand of socialism, and this interest is growing apace in the seventies, with many new books on the subject, and at least two scholarly journals, The Insurgent Sociologist and Telos.

The following categories of belief-statements include beliefs still widely held which are in the Adam Smith, laissez-faire tradition; beliefs opposing laissez-faire; beliefs supporting the idea of a welfare state; a miscellany of beliefs related to different issues; and what we see as some "new culture" beliefs, exemplified not only in the informal thought of liberal-to-left university students, but increasingly in the writing of prominent academic economists (e.g., John Kenneth Galbraith, in his most recent book as of this writing, Economics and the Public Purpose, proposes the outright nationalization, that is, socialization of a number of major industries).

Beliefs in the Laissez-Faire Tradition

If it is not already obvious to readers, we will make clear later that not many people believe in the doctrine of laissez-faire capitalism today. Some adherents are well-known, but very few still argue for the laissez-faire model proposed by Adam Smith and the classical economists who followed him. Our chief exponents are persons who identify themselves as classical conservatives, such as columnists James Kilpatrick and William F. Buckley, Jr. and the small University of Chicago "conservative school" of economists, most prominent of whom is probably Milton Friedman. Some of the belief-statements of this tradition are:

—One of the most important motivating forces is the search for economic self-gain.
—Government should have only minimal control over the economy. (Adam Smith felt that the main economic function of government, aside from providing a medium of exchange [money], should be preventing the rise of artificial monopolies and regulating natural monopolies.)
—Free competition, central to which is competitive pricing, is the prime regulating force.
—With free pricing and free entry of anyone who chooses into business, the law of supply and demand will keep goods and the demand for them in balance, and in addition regulate prices.
—With wages uncontrolled, each worker will rise to his maximum level of competency, and thus guarantee an economy of maximum efficiency.
—Everyone should work for what he gets; it demoralizes people to get something for nothing.
—If there are no artificial wage controls (as now enforced by unions), there will be no unemployment (except for the sick, crippled, and infirm).
—Whatever benefits business, benefits everybody.
—A laissez-faire economy is self-regulating and requires no centralized planning.
—Any business which cannot make a profit without government aid should be allowed to go bankrupt.
—Laissez-faire capitalism is the best economic system ever invented by man.

Beliefs Opposed to the Laissez-Faire Tradition

The general public still holds many beliefs harmonious with the Adam Smith laissez-faire model, but they mix these unknowingly with a number of incompatible beliefs such as the following examples which depict our system in rather opposite terms from those of the above classical conservatives.

—Business firms become fewer and larger each year.
—Small farmers and businessmen are being pushed out by the large corporations.

—Our antitrust laws are not effective in stopping the concentration of power in giant corporations.

—Through monopolistic agreements among themselves, businessmen are able to keep prices fixed at an artificially high level.

—Big business, big government, and big unions work together at the expense of the consumer.

—Because of subsidies, tax breaks, and other favors, the rich get richer and the poor get poorer.

—Most businessmen are as dishonest as they can get away with.

—Big business can get almost any favor it wants from government by bribing key congressmen and other top government officials.

Beliefs Concerning "Welfare Capitalism"

As commonly defined, welfare capitalism came into existence in the United States with Franklin D. Roosevelt's administrations in the 1930s. The basic ideas associated with it have prevailed and been developed still further in step-by-step fashion ever since. We will list a small sampling of beliefs supportive of this development.

—Capitalism can be made to work much better for the average person if it is reformed to provide greater individual security and fewer shady business practices.

—There should and can be guaranteed economic security from the cradle to the grave (through social security, medical plans, unemployment insurance, and a floor under income).

—Labor should have the right to organize, bargain collectively, and strike if necessary.

—The Federal Government should regulate business to prevent dishonest advertising, selling worthless or dangerous products, serious price inflation, pollution, unsafe working conditions, etc.

—Major efforts should be made to eliminate poverty and keep unemployment to a minimum.

—The government should use fiscal or other controls to eliminate the recession-boom cycle.

—It is the responsibility of the Federal Government to keep the economy growing at a steady rate.

—When some product or service that is badly needed is not being or could not be profitably provided by private business, the government should put that business under public ownership and subsidize it if necessary.

—There should be considerable long-range planning of economic development.

Miscellaneous Beliefs of the General Public

Below are a few specimens of the kinds of beliefs frequently expressed by laymen that do not appear to fit well under any of the foregoing categories. We include them because some are good illustrations of why professional economists regard the masses as economically ignorant. Nevertheless, some of them may have some slight merit.

—Sales and excise taxes are better than income tax.
—High tariffs increase employment and wages.
—We have to have a high level of military expenditures to keep the economy prosperous.
—Most people on welfare could be self-supporting if they wanted to be.
—People living on inherited wealth are not a burden on the economy.
—Progress is best defined as steadily increasing per capita income.
—A guaranteed minimum income for everyone would not only bankrupt the nation but would cause most people to quit work.
—Very few people would work unless they had to to keep from starving.
—The national debt will have to be paid back sometime.
—To have continued prosperity, it is necessary to have an expanding population.
—There is no reason why America's present rate of economic growth cannot continue indefinitely.
—Almost all business executives are competent men, especially those who run big corporations.
—Capitalism and democracy mean the same thing.
—The antitrust laws have slowed the growth of monopolies.
—When the government wastes money it is the taxpayers' money; when private corporations waste money, at least it is their own money.[1]

Some Counterculture Beliefs about Economics

We will state below a few beliefs apparently rather widely held by people who do not identify with the establishment culture. As previously suggested, this group consists mainly of university students majoring in humanities (primarily social science majors) and a considerable number of professional economists associated with universities and certain foundations.

—American style capitalism will never eliminate poverty or unemployment because both perform positive functions in maintaining the system.
—We are heading into some kind of economic collectivism and our only alternatives seem to be democratic socialism or an authoritarian collectivism governed by the large corporations with military support.
—The real power in the country is vested in big business and giant

[1] Readers interested in one of the best books on American economic ideology should see Thurman Arnold, The Folklore of Capitalism. New Haven, Conn.: Yale University Press, 1937. Little of the folklore of the 1930s has changed. Among more recent writers whose books convey a great deal about economic myths held by the public, see Richard Hofstadter, Robert Heilbroner, John Kenneth Galbraith, and Michael Harrington.

financial institutions (in Yankelovich's most recent sampling, 58 percent of university students agreed).
—Progress in the affluent nations can no longer be defined as increasing GNP; we have to face up to the prospect of a "steady state" or "zero growth" economy.
—The continuous seeking of greater affluence may damage, rather than improve, the quality of life for most Americans.
—The Puritan work ethic has been outdated ever since the development of automated methods of production.
—Handicraft labor, done at one's own preferred speed, is much more satisfying than office or factory jobs.

In line with our analysis in Chapter 4—indicating that in spite of the cessation of the counterculture noise of the 1960s, the new-culture beliefs which took hold then are still alive and flourishing in the 1970s— we should note a marked shift in noncollege working youth beliefs since 1969. According to Yankelovich's most recent polling (cited in Chapter 4), the percent of working class youth agreeing that "hard work always pays off" dropped from 79 in 1969 to 56 in 1973; further, the percent agreeing that they would "welcome less emphasis on money" rose from 54 to 74.

AN "OUTRAGEOUS HYPOTHESIS" ABOUT ECONOMICS

Although most beliefs about economics held by the general public, and those educated enough to know better, are outrageous, we have chosen one which is likely to seem outrageous to almost all Americans, including most professional economists. This hypothesis should be of special concern to teachers, however, because it runs directly counter to what most teachers would assert; further, its broad scope permits us to say a good deal about our economic system as a whole.

Hypothesis: *Because capitalism is rapidly ceasing to be a viable system, our major economic problems could be more easily solved under a socialist system.*

The first problem in connection with working with this assertion is defining "capitalism" (we will define "socialism" later). Since this is an exceedingly slippery term and most people have their own highly personalized definitions that most others would not accept, we feel the best approach toward definition is to offer a historical treatment of how the expression originated.

The Theory of Capitalism

Capitalism is based on a body of theory which, beginning with Adam Smith and extended by J. B. Say and David Ricardo, was well established and widely accepted by the 1830s. This body of theory was known as *classical economics* and is so called today. Classical economics was soon exported to the United States, where it became the gospel of economists for a century until the Great Depression of the 1930s and the introduction of the nonclassical economics of John Maynard Keynes.

The beliefs of classical conservatives or, as we shall call them, the proponents of the theory of capitalism, have never been tried in their entirety. England came the closest to trying "pure capitalism" in the early 1800s when the nation exercised no government control over the economy, not even protective tariffs. Even though the theory of capitalism has never been tried except for that brief period (when pressures against complete laissez-faire built so rapidly that it soon had to be abandoned), the argument has never ceased that it is a good theory and that any country adopting it consistently over a sufficiently long period of time would have as nearly a perfect economy as the mind of man could conceive.

The theory of capitalism includes two crucial assumptions about human nature: human beings, by their inborn nature, will compete with each other and will each attempt to better themselves economically. The theory also assumes that the act of producing goods provides exactly the right amount of purchasing power to buy them. Overproduction (or underconsumption) is impossible, since purchasing power always equates with the value of the product. The balance between supply and demand will keep prices relatively stable and prevent either a major depression or harmful inflation. It is assumed that there will always be a large enough group of sellers and buyers so that monopolistic agreements can not be made to hold for either side. If competition is functioning as it must, no individual seller will ever be able to affect the market price of his product nor will any coalition of buyers be able to affect it.

We thus get to the function of price competition in the theory of capitalism. If a product is scarce in relation to demand, its price goes up; with an increase in price, production of the product goes up and purchases decline until supply and demand are in balance. Conversely, if a product is plentiful in relation to demand its price will fall; the declining price will discourage producers from making as much of the product and will encourage buyers to buy more of it, thus again bringing supply and demand into balance.

Under capitalist theory, competition always refers to price competition. Without completely free pricing, according to the dictates of the supply and demand situation, one does not have capitalism in its classical sense. Prices include wages, because under the theory of capitalism labor is a commodity like everything else; if there is a surplus of labor, wages fall and as wages fall the demand for labor increases, thus making unemployment theoretically impossible.

If one views the theory of capitalism in its purest form, as we have described it, it is evident that as a theory it is masterfully put together. It is neat, symmetrical, parsimonious, and if one accepts all its assumptions, has no loose ends. It is little wonder that capitalism was presented as the ideal economic system in college courses in economics in the nineteenth century and up to World War II.[2]

The Necessity of a Free Market

The theory of capitalism is based on the theory that a free market exists. According to the theory of a free market,

> every element of industry is regarded as having been produced for sale, as then and only then will it be subject to the supply and demand mechanism interacting with price. In practice this means that there must be markets for every element of industry; that in these markets each of these elements is organized into a supply and demand group; and that each element has a price, which interacts with demand and supply.[3]

We have quoted this statement of Edwards *et al.* because of its implications. As they point out, labor, land, and money are necessary elements of industry and to have a true market economy, these elements must be organized in markets subject to the free operation of the law of supply and demand. They must have been produced for sale. Unless labor, land, and money can be demonstrated to have been commodities produced for sale, and are actually bought and sold in a free market, the whole structure of capitalist theory collapses.

Some Innate Problems in Capitalism

Are people willing to be treated as commodities? If they seem reluctant to play this role, is it because they are too stubborn to want to help make capitalist theory work? Whatever their motives, it seems to be a clearly established fact that rather than wanting to be commodities in a wholly competitive free market, humans tend to band together, at great sacrifice if necessary, to prevent this from happening.

Workers band together in unions. Employers band together to fix

[2] Perhaps the best book offering a highly sympathetic treatment of the theory of capitalism published in this century is F. A. Hayek, *The Road to Serfdom* (Chicago: University of Chicago Press, 1944). The title of Hayek's book derives from his belief that if government controls over the economy were continued after World War II, we would be "on the road to serfdom."

[3] Richard C. Edwards, Michael Reich, and Thomas E. Weisskopf, *The Capitalist System*. Englewood Cliffs, N.J.: Prentice-Hall, Inc., 1972, p. 95.

prices; their trade associations function as unions. But more than this, humans tend to band together in numerous other ways, in families, clans, tribes, professions, and all sorts of organizations of creed and friendship. To induce them to function as commodities in the market, they have to be torn from their moorings so that every person is only an individual.

Polanyi, in a book now considered a classic, draws heavily not only from the study of modern industrial cultures but also from anthropological research, to demonstrate that in no human culture known will people willingly allow themselves to be treated as commodities. He traces in detail the development of political economics from the first British attempts to establish a free market economy, and shows how, step by step, the free market economy was abolished. It was abolished because human beings refuse to behave atomistically—not only laborers, but their employers as well.

Typically, in the history of Europe and the United States, employers were the first to abolish free market practice by forming trusts. Much of American big business was organized as monopolies or semimonopolies between the Civil War and 1900. And the very businessmen who refused themselves to act like commodities, crushed virtually every attempt by labor to form unions to prevent their being treated as commodities.[4]

The nineteenth-century classical economists shrewdly recognized that unless human beings are considered "naturally competitive" their whole body of theory would collapse. Therefore, a naturally (i.e., instinctively) competitive human nature was posited by the economists, as they continued perfecting the theory of capitalism from their tenured university jobs (post-competitive).

When people apparently refused to obey this assumed instinct for competition, the economic theorists regarded them as perverse—they violated their own God-given natures. If the theory of capitalism did not work as well in practice as it looked on paper, the blame was placed on human stubbornness.

Cooperation versus Competition

One of the tasks undertaken by Polanyi was to introduce evidence from anthropology showing that no culture studied up to that time had a free market economy, nor was there any historical record of a free market economy ever having existed. Margaret Mead has thrown important light on the conditions under which humans will compete.[5] First, there is no

[4] Karl Polanyi, The Great Transformation. San Francisco: Rinehart Press, 1944. The example of union busting is ours, not Polanyi's, but it harmonizes with his analysis.

[5] Margaret Mead, Cooperation and Competition Among Primitive Peoples, rev. ed., paperback. Boston: Beacon Press, 1961.

anthropological evidence that human beings have an "instinct" to compete economically or otherwise. Competition is a cultural invention. In some cultures competition, as Americans understand the concept, does not exist. In others a particular kind of competition may exist, such as in the playing of games having winners and losers. In still other cultures, competition may take the form of seeing who can do the most intricate wood carving. But the form competition takes is always culturally defined. Further, there are forms of competition human beings will not voluntarily undertake. *People will not compete for a livelihood unless a ruling elite forces them to;* and if people are forced to compete for a livelihood, they continuously seek ways to end the competition or reduce it to the point where the losers cannot lose very much.

But what about competition in American culture? Classical economic theory prescribes competition among all elements of the market, including human beings. But when the new nation was founded, one of the first steps taken was to place a protective tariff on eighty-one different commodities. Although the duties were not high (ranging from 5 to 15 percent), they were designed both for producing revenue and discouraging imports of goods that would compete with the nation's young manufacturing industries. Protective tariffs are a means of eliminating or reducing the competition of foreign-made goods.

One purpose of unions is to reduce competition among workers. With the introduction of factory methods of production and a demand for wage labor, workers began organizing craft unions, or guilds, as early as the 1780s. In the period following the Civil War, a group of notable tycoons managed to form monopolies in a number of indispensable industries. To promote corporate solidarity against the rising "threat" of organized labor, the major corporations founded the National Association of Manufacturers in 1895.

Operating under the myth that businessmen should want to compete, but if they are stubborn about facing the risks of competition should be *forced* to compete, the loophole-filled Sherman Antitrust Act was passed in 1890. The Sherman Act was ineffective in preventing business monopolies; further, as its wording made it applicable to labor organizations, it was potentially a "union busting" act. Some of the Sherman Act's weaknesses were corrected by the Clayton Act of 1914. However, most people have been mislead about the actual purposes served by antitrust legislation; they have been led to believe that the purpose of antitrust legislation is to prevent business monopolies. As Thurmon Arnold points out in a rather devastating analysis,

> it became necessary to develop a procedure which constantly attacked bigness on rational legal and economic grounds, and at the same time never really interfered with combinations. Such pressures gave rise to

the antitrust laws which appeared to be a complete prohibition of large combinations. The same pressures made the enforcement of the antitrust laws a pure ritual.[6]

Arnold goes on to say:

The effect of this statement of the ideal and its lack of actual enforcement was to convince reformers either that large combinations did not actually exist, or they were about to be done away with just as soon as right-thinking men were elected to office.[7]

Noting that prostitution tends to flourish best where public outcry against it is greatest and legislation banning it is most publicized, Arnold compares our laws against prostitution to the antitrust laws.

Perhaps their lack of inhibiting effect can be seen in the enlargement of business firms. In the late nineteenth century a multi-million dollar corporation frightened people. In the 1970s a multi-billion dollar firm with branches around the world is taken for granted—and so is the decreased competition.

On what terms will Americans accept competition? So far as we have evidence no people will subject themselves except under great duress to the kind of competition in which the loser *loses everything*. But, obviously, Americans accept competition in almost any area where *losing will not be disastrous*. We have competition in amateur sports (but if the stakes seem high enough, even little people cheat, as in the Great Soapbox Derby Scandal of 1973). Competition in most professional athletics shows that even losing is profitable—the loser earns, though the winner earns more.

Do Americans accept competition in the economic area? Is there any authentic *price* competition left? This is the final test of whether any capitalism, in its classical sense, remains. In any industry where there is no producer or coalition of producers large enough to influence the price of the product, and in which labor is unorganized and the government neither directly nor indirectly influences pricing, then we have a free market and authentic capitalism.

Since most farm prices are influenced by some kind of government control, only a small part of agriculture exhibits true price competition. Another example of classical capitalism at work would be among American Indians or other individual craftsworkers who sell their products—provided there are no pricing agreements among the producers. It is possible to identify a handful of other relatively insignificant industries where pricing is still free. This is about the entire extent of capitalism, in the classical tradition, in the United States today.

[6] Arnold, *The Folklore of Capitalism*, pp. 207–208.
[7] Arnold, p. 208.

Critical Problems of American-Style Capitalism

Critics of the American economic system insist that the system has certain innate deficiencies that will force a shift to a fundamentally different system. We will describe a few of these inherent problems but readers should understand that these examples in no sense exhaust the list of problems unsolvable under our kind of capitalism.

Economic Concentration and Price Inflation

This problem, like the others we will mention, is probably an unavoidable outcome of the capitalist's erroneous interpretation of human nature. To avoid competition, corporate industry has moved more or less steadily toward cooperative (i.e., monopolistic) arrangements that permit them to administer prices (i.e., set prices, without regard to the so-called "law of supply and demand"). This enables industry to pass all increased costs on to the consumer.

Labor, also to avoid competition, has become largely unionized. Unions have in most instances become powerful enough to enforce wage demands that exceed the percentage gain in labor productivity. This increases business costs, but such costs are a part of those transmitted to the consumer.

Thus, apart from shortages of raw materials or other temporary cost-increasing factors, American capitalism contains a built-in prescription for continuous inflation. There are reasons for inflation other than the above, but the hard fact is that nobody knows how to control inflation in the American or most other capitalist economies.

Economic Priorities Irrationally Determined

Without a free market system, corporate oligarchs with some help from the Federal Government decide what goods and how many they will produce on the basis of what will promote corporate power and profits. Here again, powerful unions often influence these decisions by their aversion to changes that might reduce the number of jobs. The result of this is that the corporate/union combination, with some but not much government interference, decide our short- and long-range economic goals quite apart from the needs of the people. Many goods and services produced are unnecessary, wasteful, and dangerous.

The American economy, in spite of its still high productivity per capita, is probably the world's most wasteful. One example: According to the best estimates, we waste between 30 and 50 percent of all our energy resources annually. When the determination of economic priorities is based on personal profit seeking, the end results are disastrous, ecologically and otherwise.

Poverty and Unemployment as Necessities

If poverty and unemployment did not serve some necessary function under our system we would have neither. Scandinavian countries have no poverty and usually manage to keep unemployment rates under 1 percent. Gans has identified fifteen functions that poverty serves in this country.[8] He then shows that a number of these functions, were they to be eliminated, would produce dysfunctions for the affluent and powerful; therefore, as a practical matter, poverty cannot be eliminated under our form of capitalism no matter how high the per capita GNP might become or how urgent the demands to eliminate it among reformers who are not members of the important power elites. Our brief review of Gans' analysis is an oversimplification; interested readers should refer to his original article.

According to Gans, poverty performs the following functions:

1. Poverty ensures that the "dirty work" (a certain amount of which exists in any economy) gets done, since taking care of the dirty work is the only means of survival for most of the poor.

[8] Herbert J. Gans, "The Positive Functions of Poverty," *American Journal of Sociology,* Vol. 78, No. 2, September 1972, pp. 275–289.

The most economical means of transporting people is by railroad,
but railroad passenger service became so bad in the United States
that most people prefer the luxury of airlines. Would this occur
in a planned economy? (Left, *Maurice P. Hunt;* above,
United Airlines)

2. The poor subsidize numerous activities that benefit the affluent by, among other things, working for extremely low wages. Gans uses "subsidize" here in the sense of providing economic aid to others by forgoing it yourself.
3. Poverty creates jobs for a number of occupations and professions whose function it is to serve the poor (e.g., social workers).
4. The poor take goods off the market that the affluent refuse to buy (e.g., obsolete, defective, and second-hand goods and substandard food).
5. The poor can be identified and punished as alleged or real deviants in order to uphold the preferred moral norms of the affluent (see, for example, Thio's analysis of deviance described in Chaps. 3 and 7).
6. The poor provide psychological catharsis for those of the affluent who may feel guilty; their being made recipients of charity convinces the affluent of their own altruism and morality.
7. The poor, who tend to engage rather openly in violations of Puritanical moral standards, provide vicarious satisfactions to those affluents who would like to do the same but feel they cannot because they must maintain a posture of moral rectitude.

8. The poor provide a measuring rod for status, especially the status of skilled blue-collar workers who need someone to look down upon.

9. The poor, if prevented from bettering themselves, assist in the upward mobility of the nonpoor who can always find ways of exploiting the poor to their advantage.

10. The poor provide a function for the upper-uppers, the aristocracy by birth, who spend a great deal of time and some money in charitable endeavors.

11. The poor help make possible "high culture" (what we have called cultivation). They provided the labor, for example, that built the pyramids and medieval churches; and they make possible surplus capital to support artists and intellectuals.

12. The "low" culture of the poor produces forms of expression and customs that can be adopted by the affluent for their own pleasure (e.g., jazz, spiritual, and country music); they also provide subjects for writers whose books the affluent find recreational.

13. The poor serve as symbolic constituencies or opponents of political groups. For example, the liberals need the poor as a "cause" and conservatives need them as "welfare chiselers."

14. Since the poor are powerless, they can be made to absorb the economic and political costs of change and growth in American society. Only the powerless can be successfully moved around to make room for freeways, urban redevelopment, or creation of urban open space (we would add also that the poor are ideal subjects for medical experimentation).

15. Because the poor are not in a position to be politically active, they make politics more "centrist" and therefore more stable; if the poor were permitted enough upward mobility to participate in the political process, they might become a radical political element intolerable in our capitalist system.

Gans points out that some of these functions can be performed in other ways and therefore do not require an impoverished class, for example, automation could take care of much of the dirty work now done by the poor. Nor is it necessary to have a group paid only survival wages to subsidize activities prized by the affluent; these activities would be paid for without the poor, *but at a higher cost to the affluent.* And some groups whose livelihood now hinges on the poor could employ their talents in other ways, for example, social workers could serve the rich. Gans comes up with substitutes for poverty to perform a number of the other fifteen functions listed, however, usually only at higher cost to the powerful and therefore not practical.

But Gans raises serious questions as to whether there is any substitute for the poor in providing such functions as serving the status and mobility needs of the nonpoor (particularly the blue-collar working class), the philanthropic needs of the guilty affluent, and the needs of Democrats and Republicans to have objects of sympathy and hatred. Also they are the chief constituency of our more fundamentalist churches. Gans feels

(Maurice P. Hunt)

Urban development: often it succeeds only in moving the poor from inner city to periphery.

that the really irreplaceable role of the poor is their political stabilizing role—"since no other group is willing to be disenfranchised or likely enough to remain apathetic—" to preserve the system.

The implied conclusion in Gans' analysis is that anyone who argues seriously in favor of eliminating the poverty of the bottom 15 percent or so of our population must, to be consistent, also argue in favor of fundamental changes in our whole socioeconomic system to eliminate the "loser" characteristic of the poor and the attendant benefits to society.

As a matter of cold fact, the gap between rich and poor has been increasing since the early 1970s. The gap is in disposable, after-taxes income, and a result of an increasingly regressive tax system. Price inflation also hurts the poor much more than the rich because the poor have to spend *all* their income to survive.

Functions of Other Persistent "Problems"

One could apply the same functional analysis to any other kind of so-called "problem" which has existed for a long time and refuses to go away in spite of all the talk and legislative efforts of social reformers. Long-standing problems that continue to appear unsolvable are almost certainly no more than activities which are more functional than dysfunctional, in that they contribute more to our particular socioeconomic system than they subtract from it. Among these persistent "problems" are unemployment, prostitution, gambling, pornography, illicit drugs, economic wastefulness, dishonest advertising, planned obsolescence, shoddy workmanship, and on and on. If people really want to eliminate such phenomena, and at the same time want to be honest with themselves, they must also advocate widespread system changes.

Economic Dependence on the Military

Because of discrepancies in the so-called savings-investment cycle (too technical to explain here), under our economic system it is necessary for the government to spend on the average more money than it collects through taxes and otherwise. Deficit spending is unavoidable if the rate of unemployment is kept within politically manageable levels (often regarded as 5 percent of the work force). Deficit spending provides the stimulus that enables us to prevent business recessions from developing into the type of economic collapse we experienced in the 1930s.

Obviously, there are innumerable ways in which the Federal Government can spend enough money to accumulate a deficit each year. One would be to provide everyone with a guaranteed minimum income and thus eliminate poverty. But this is not acceptable because the rich need the poor.

The one type of expenditure psychologically acceptable, even to the poor, is expenditure for the military establishment. Aside from the fact that so many people profit from defense spending that it could not be stopped, people demand it on the grounds of national security.

This requires that the nation always have an "enemy" with a major military potential; so far there has been no difficulty in arranging this. The Soviet Union also needs an enemy to distract its people's attention from domestic problems. Maintaining enemy status is a form of cooperation between the United States and Russia that benefits both nations.

Continuous deficit spending by the Federal Government also makes inflation inevitable, thereby adding a second reason for inflation in addition to the one mentioned above.

There are other problems which under our economy no one knows how to solve, such as the tendency of any profit system to promote increasing corruption in both business and government. But we have mentioned enough problems already to indicate why many serious and responsible social scientists feel alternatives to capitalism must be examined sympathetically if also critically.

The Socialist Alternative

Socialism is often no more than a symbol, the generic name for a large variety of idealized socioeconomic models that have little more in common than a preference for cooperation over competition (if even that); but it is also a reality existing in greater or lesser degree in every country (though taking a great many different forms). It appears almost certain that very few Americans outside a minority within the intellectual community have any clear idea of what socialism has meant historically or as a working reality might mean today.

Socialism: Historical Meanings

As actual movements, proposed movements, or theoretical systems, most of the numerous socialisms of history can be categorized under four main heads.[9]

Utopian Socialisms

Utopian socialisms have in the past been conceived as any of hundreds of plans for uniting the most oppressed elements of stratified socie-

---

[9] This categorization is one followed by Harry W. Laidler, in *Social-Economic Movements*. New York: Thomas Y. Crowell Company, 1946. It is adequate for treating socialism up to the World War II period.

ties into a revolutionary force to bring about opportunity, equality, and social justice for the oppressed. Within Judeo-Christian civilization, we can go back to some of the prophets depicted in the Old Testament: Amos, Hosea, Isaiah, Jeremiah, and Ezekiel. These prophets lashed out at the rich and prophesied a day when people would live in peace and cooperation in an equalitarian social order to be established with God's aid—a Kingdom of Heaven on earth.

Some centuries later the most revolutionary of them all appeared, the Christ of the New Testament. Until Christ came to be interpreted as an ally of the wealthy men of finance and industry—after the commercial and industrial revolutions—he was generally portrayed as a leader of the impoverished whose teachings would bring about the equalitarian and just kingdom (whether in heaven or on earth is a matter of interpretation) foreseen by the Old Testament prophets.

Not only the poor and oppressed in the ancient world developed dreams of an ideal society. Plato's *Republic* embodied in its laws and institutions "the fundamental unity of the moral individual with the socialized state."[10] Among Romans, Virgil, Horace, Tacitus, Juvenal, and Josephus wrote of utopian societies; Seneca wrote admiringly of the communism of man in his "natural state."

Sir Thomas More (1478–1535) and Erasmus (1466?–1536) wrote influential works on close-to-nature communism. Francis Bacon (1561–1626) in his *New Atlantis* took a different approach by describing a utopian society based upon applied science. Out of these backgrounds, and later writings of European social theorists, came a modernized version of utopian socialism. The eighteenth century produced a covey of them in France, Henri de Saint-Simon being one of the most famous.

Charles Fourier's (1772-1837) specific model of a utopian socialism gained wide enough appeal to lead to the establishment of a number of experimental communities both in Europe and the United States (34 in America). Probably Brook Farm is the best known. The Britisher, Robert Owen experimented with a somewhat different ideal community in his New Harmony, Indiana.

Such experiments still go on; how long the commune movement of the sixties and seventies will last no one can say. As people became increasingly frustrated with high pressure urban living, it seems at least possible that communes will continue to multiply (see Chapter 8 on the "Jesus People").

We can perhaps define utopian socialism well enough for our purposes by saying that it involves communal living, the common ownership of most kinds of property, close cooperation, and the enstatement of such

[10] Laidler, p. 10.

values as brotherly love, peace, humility, helpfulness to others, and the simple life.

Marxism

Karl Marx (1818–1883), it now seems clear, was the most influential social theorist of the nineteenth century, perhaps of the entire historical period of the human race. More than half of the world's population resides in nations whose governments proclaim Marxism as the official faith or whose governments seem about to fall into Communist hands (e.g., the rest of Southeast Asia and perhaps a considerable part of Africa).

Unfortunately, there is a great deal of misunderstanding about Marx. Just as the scriptural teachings of Jesus Christ are ignored by almost all self-proclaimed Christians, so Marx's social theory is ignored by almost all self-proclaimed Communists. As we have indicated previously, there is a resurgence of interest in Marx in many of today's non-Communist countries, including the United States. This new interest, at least on the part of many contemporary Marxist students, seems to be motivated by a determination to reexamine Marx's writings—particularly his less well-known publications, his letters, and his assertions as recorded by his contemporaries.

Among today's writers on Marx, it may be that Michael Harrington has done the best job of extracting from Marx's original analysis both what is most authentically Marx and what is most relevant to social conditions as they exist in the latter part of the twentieth century. Our treatment here will be based on Harrington unless otherwise noted.[11]

One misinterpretation of Marx comes from failing to understand that his theory of when a truly socialist society could develop included certain necessary preconditions, two of the more important being that (1) a society must already be industrialized to the point where relative abundance is possible and where economic hardship can be eliminated for everyone, and (2) most people in that society must be employees and self-consciously so.

In countries that have undergone Communist revolutions neither of these conditions has preexisted. Communism has been enstated only in countries still semifeudal, where poverty was rampant, and also where there was no large group with an "employee psychology" (with the exceptions of Czechoslovakia and East Germany where communism was forced upon industrialized nations).

Communism as it exists today conforms to what Marx envisioned as "anti-socialist socialism." Marx was a socialist, not a Communist, except

---

[11] Michael Harrington, *Socialism*. New York: Saturday Review Press, 1972.

for one very brief period and even then he did not advocate any presently known system of communism.

This leads us to another major mistake made by most of Marx's interpreters. Even those of noted scholarship have focused too much attention on one period in Marx's life—from 1848 to 1850—when, for a variety of reasons, Marx bitterly though temporarily rejected the commitment to democratic processes which he had earlier developed and was to return to even more strongly later. Beginning with the publication of *The Communist Manifesto* (1847), a contradictory document which combined revolutionary polemics with some astute insights about human society, he asserted until 1850 a doctrine which seemed authoritarian. It led to wide dissemination of the idea of the "dictatorship of the proletariat," in which, it could be construed, he meant that members of the radical left intelligentsia would rule over the working class until a time when the uneducated workers could be educated to govern themselves in a "classless society" where the state would eventually "wither away."

Harrington presents a rather convincing argument that even during Marx's period of bitterness and seeming disregard for democracy, he did not really mean what he has been taken to mean, particularly in his highly personalized and paradoxical use of the word "dictatorship," by which he meant "state" or "government" without the necessary implications of strong-man rule.[12]

Many writers have noted the apparent modernity of Marx's views concerning alienation. His view of the nature of man was also remarkably prescient. He saw human nature as arising from a self/environment transactionalism, and he was quite clear on the integral relationship of means and ends—"what begins as a means becomes an end."[13] Thus Marx rejected an idea dear to the "pragmatic politics" of both contemporary communism and capitalism—that "the end justifies the means." This seminal thinking, coming as it did considerably prior to the exposition of John Dewey's transactionalist theory, enables one to understand one of the motives for the renewed interest in Marx by scholars of the late 1960s and 1970s.

Many persons, even self-proclaimed students of Marx, seem unaware that Marx (and his associate, Engels) changed his mind on certain key issues at least three times. Marx did not finalize his views until the period between 1850 and his death in 1883. He ended up finally with a view of socialism which was

reformist with a revolutionary purpose, in that it saw an alliance with trade-union gradualism as a step toward the abolition of classes. It

---

[12] Harrington, Chaps. 3 and 4, esp. pp. 43–52 and 57–64.
[13] Harrington, p. 40.

advocated the democratic ownership and control of large-scale means of production, not the distribution of wealth or decentralized production. But it was fearful that bureaucracy would usurp democratic power, and therefore fought tenaciously against the equation of socialism with state ownership pure and simple.[14]

To make the picture more complete, we should add that Marx foresaw the possibility that trade unionism might turn conservative and non-reformist—as apparently it has as of this writing—and that his version of socialism might be a long time in coming.

Communism

We will use this label to designate what most nations which are now professedly Communist have in common. There may be more than a bit of semantic murder in doing this; it seems clear that no two Communist countries are alike. While most of them may proclaim allegiance to a political and socioeconomic theory that they attribute to Marx, as revised by Lenin, their practices differ. Yugoslavia may be the only Communist country that approaches the democratic socialism advocated by Marx in his later years; yet, even here, Marshal Josip Tito has vacillated from an authoritarian "big brother" to a slightly democratic father figure. Even so, workers in Yugoslavia's industrial plants may have more say in how the firms operate than workers in any other country in the world.

In Communist countries the central government owns all heavy industry (mining, manufacturing, and transport), the mass media, and communications. The degree to which land is under government ownership and farmed by collectives varies greatly. Economic planning tends to be in units of five years but the general direction of the economy is planned in terms of much longer spans of time.

The buildup of capital goods is pushed at the expense of consumer goods. Except for a floor under incomes which prevents poverty of the depth that exists in many non-Communist countries, the income range between the lowest paid workers and the highest paid managers, scientists, and artists appears to be about as great as in the United States.

Probably Communist countries have about as many economic problems as capitalist countries. Yet, the presence of a government funded and controlled medical system that offers a respectable amount of medical care for all, and government funded education all the way through the doctorate for those who choose and are capable of attaining it would seem to be important pluses. Also, the apparent ability of Communist governments to prevent critical food shortages that could lead to famine, make those

[14] Harrington, p. 70.

who were impoverished and without security prior to the advent of communism feel that they are vastly better off.

Communist economies are viable even in those countries where the average standard of living remains very low. The ability of the central government under a system of extensive government ownership to control both savings and investments and to direct investment into those industries most crucial to economic survival and growth contributes to this viability. The ability of the government to control pricing and thus maintain price stability, and hence cost-of-living stability, is obviously advantageous. Cyclical ups and downs in Communist economies similar to those in capitalist economies are theoretically impossible and apparently so in practice. The economic "downs" under Communist rule are caused not by overproduction (or underconsumption), as is typically the case in capitalist countries, but by shortages.

Whether the economies of the Communist countries are properly called socialist is a matter of definition. According to Marxian theory, as developed between 1850 and the death of Engels in 1895, communism is "anti-socialist socialism," in the sense that the people do not democratically control either the economy or the state. And this leads us naturally to our last topic under socialism, democratic socialism as conceived in the twentieth century.

Democratic Socialism

Democratic socialists draw a great deal from "The Unknown Karl Marx," to use the title of a chapter in Harrington's book. A good example is Erich Fromm, who apparently feels that not only are Marx's concepts in psychology highly relevant to the contemporary historical epoch, but also that another Marxian concept is essentially correct, that is, that participatory democracy as a basis for ownership and control of economic institutions is the only way to avoid intolerable worker alienation under advanced industrialism.[15]

Likewise written from a foundation of Marxist theory is Lerner's blistering attack on the Communist countries, particularly the Soviet Union.[16] Lerner sounds somewhat utopian and simplistic at times, but probably most democratic socialists would largely agree with his definitions. "Socialism," says Lerner, "is radical democracy extended to every area of our collective lives." He extends this a little later with the asser-

[15] Erich Fromm (ed.), *Socialist Humanism.* New York: Doubleday & Company, Inc., 1965. Also see Fromm's *Marx's Concept of Man.* New York: Frederick Ungar Publishing Company, 1966.
[16] Michael P. Lerner, *The New Socialist Revolution.* New York: Dell Publishing Company, Inc., 1973.

tion, "Socialism means ownership and control of the means of production, democratically by the people, rather than by a government bureaucracy. The critical element in our understanding of socialism is the democratization of the economy and of all areas of political and social life."[17] Lerner does credit the Soviet Union for its ability to provide medical care, food, clothing, housing, and education for all, even though he despises the system's authoritarian nature.

Harrington, who is as much in love with the idea of socialism as any socialist, tempers his enthusiasm by recognizing that some convincing arguments against socialism have been advanced by such respected social scientists as Kenneth Boulding, Robert Heilbroner, and Daniel Bell.

Except for the orthodox economists, who still dream of a laissez-faire utopia, it appears that most social scientists like the *idea* of socialism but simply do not think that the kind of socialism proposed by its more romantic advocates is ever likely to come about. They are willing, rather, to settle for almost any kind of welfare state that is not fascist. But Harrington makes a more interesting argument, it seems to us, than anyone else. In his last chapter, he begins by stating his conception of a wholly fulfilled socialism:

> It is the idea of an utterly new society in which some of the fundamental limitations of human existence have been transcended. Its most basic premise is that man's battle with nature has been completely won and there is therefore more than enough of material goods for everyone. As a result of this unprecedented change in the environment, a psychic mutation takes place: invidious competition is no longer programmed into life by the necessity of a struggle for scarce resources; cooperation, fraternity and equality become natural. In such a world man's social productivity will reach such heights that compulsory work will no longer be necessary. And as more and more things are provided free, money, that universal equivalent by means of which necessities are rationed, will disappear.
>
> That, in very brief outline, is what socialism ultimately is. It will never come to pass in its ideal form, yet it is important to detail the dream in order to better design each approximation of it.[18]

Harrington concedes that there are potent arguments against the possibility of the human race ever reaching the economic abundance necessary for socialism and also against the idea that a large enough number of people would ever want socialism to push hard politically for it. But he is also convinced that some approximation of socialism should not be ruled out as being completely impossible.

Conceding that the ecologists make convincing arguments about

---

[17] Lerner, pp. 287, 292–293.
[18] Harrington, *Socialism*, p. 344.

abundance (and that they do will be detailed in Chapter 12), Harrington thinks that there are three possibilities to explore. First, he argues that it should be possible to change our power technology so that there could be an abundance of power which would be nonpolluting and would not produce disastrous climatic changes; he suggests, for example, that humankind has never really tried to develop a technology for making maximal use of solar and geothermal power. He combines this argument with the notion that population growth may be controllable, that indeed eventually it will be out of sheer necessity. Finally, he argues that humans can, and will have to, change their consumption habits away from their present excessively wasteful habits to life styles much more abstemious but still quite comfortable. He feels that counterculture youth have already shown leanings in this direction.

As to the political question—whether a majority of Americans would want socialism even if it were to become feasible—Harrington pins his hopes on gradual shifts in attitude of the employee class which now embraces almost all of those who are gainfully employed. Harrington feels that even the "old working class"—now turned conservative—still has, and may come to see more clearly, a vested interest in the "democratization of power." He also sees a "new" working class coming into existence, the sons and daughters of the old working class who feel more alienated and are perhaps somewhat more liberal than their parents.

Further, Harrington feels that a large segment of the educated, upper-middle-class population is likely to become increasingly liberal, indeed perhaps radical. This possibility seems to have been demonstrated by the student movement of the 1960s and even though a militant counterculture seems no longer to exist, any interpretation suggesting that the educated will ever return to pre-1960 values is likely wrong.

Conclusions about the Hypothesis

With respect to the failures of capitalism, we have apparently entered into a period of major confusion, not merely among a disillusioned public, but among orthodox economists as well. Economic orthodoxy at present includes commitment by a few to the classical laissez-faire model, and commitment by a large majority of economists to post-Keynesian economics (a position not described here).

There is another school of thought in economics, historically called institutionalism, which allows for much more flexibility because it assumes the basic validity of a change/conflict societal model. The modern institutionalists, of whom Galbraith and Swedish Gunnar Myrdal are perhaps the best known and most articulate, seem increasingly doubtful that capitalism in any form we have known will last very long. Robert Heilbroner, whom we would also designate an institutionalist, in his most recent book seems to think the demise will come relatively soon.[19]

If one is to accept the definition of socialism offered by our most dedicated socialist writers, socialism could not really come into being until the major economic goal of most people (excluding the orthodox economists and most of those now comprising the top power centers)—that is, *abundance for all*—had already become a reality. Although Harrington's definition of socialism may be as good as any, if we let it go at that we would have nothing to say about the hypothesis. To stay within Harrington's framework, for example, makes the resolving of ecological problems of central importance, but no more important than resolving the political problem of creating a "self-conscious" employee class with a vision of a better life under socialism.

But suppose we think of socialism both as an extension of the welfare state idea (basically New Dealism further implemented) coupled with an extension of the already large amount of government ownership and control over industry, and this combination further coupled with a more responsibly democratic government.

This kind of definition of socialism may be internally contradictory, in the sense that more responsibly democratic government may be quite impossible without democratization of our two authoritarian institutional structures, large corporate industry and the military establishment. Democratization of these structures may never happen, in part because it would be too unpopular among those who now make up the top and the lesser power elites, and in part because no one has yet demonstrated how it is possible to debureaucratize any powerful bureaucratic institution. Is it even worth one's time to talk of installing on a large-scale participatory democracy either in big business or the military?

That the long-range drift in the United States and other advanced industrial nations (apart from the Communist nations) is toward more government ownership, or, if not outright ownership, more centralized control of economic institutions, seems a fact beyond dispute. That this drift, whether or not accompanied by political shifts to left or right, is likely to lead to more firmly established welfare statism, also seems beyond dispute.

Lest anyone should think that either democratic or authoritarian socialism would somehow introduce a new paradise on earth (as Harrington sometimes seems to imply), we should point out that certain annoying problems of present-day monopoly capitalism would be almost certain to persist.

One such problem relates to institutional structure, the fact that

[19] Robert Heilbroner, *An Inquiry into the Human Prospect.* New York: W. W. Norton & Company, Inc., 1974.

under any system where controls are highly centralized large bureaucratic structures develop. We have such bureaucracies now and undoubtedly they will multiply and become larger and more complex under any form of future collectivism we can envision.

In the matter of economic efficiency, as measured by productivity per man-hour of labor, we find little reason to suppose that further collectivism would contribute much. Already, our giant corporate conglomerates have become all but ungovernable, and almost everyone agrees that one could hardly think of the U.S. Postal Department or the army as paradigms of high efficiency.

However, even in a no-growth economy, presumably manufacturing processes would be continuously brought under automation, which to a degree would offset the prospective declines in efficiency due to increasing scarcities of natural resources now either in short supply or soon to be. On balance, the evidence suggests to us that whatever kind of system we move into, material standards of living may well have "peaked out," and industrial nations will have to face up to the more simple life.

THE AMERICAN ECONOMY AND EDUCATION

Our type of economic system has so many implications for education that we can treat only a few and urge those interested to pursue the question further. One significant aspect of the financing of education in this country is that it does not operate under any long-range plan; the most common practice is to plan only through the next fiscal year. No central authority determines national priorities, as in many nations. The total national budget in any year is largely a matter of a compromise settlement growing out of contesting multitudinous pressure groups claiming portions of our total national product. We will take a brief look at the outcome in the following section.

The Financing of Education

First, what political units bear the dollar cost of education and how much does the dollar cost amount to? Any available figures are obsolete since expenditures tend to go up each year and the comparative amount contributed by the different political units tends to shift. Figures in this section are from the *Statistical Abstract of the United States, 1973.*

Table 9-1 has several significant things to say. We find, for example, that public education receives support from all sources of about $74 billion a year. (We will show later what this figure tells us about spending priorities in this country.) Local school districts have to come up with

Table 9-1
SCHOOL EXPENDITURES BY SOURCE OF FUNDS, 1973
(IN BILLIONS OF DOLLARS, EXCEPT AS PERCENTS)

Source	Expenditures ($)	Percent of Total (estimated)
Public Schools		
Federal	8.3	11.2
State	29.2	39.4
Local	27.5	37.1
All other	9.1	12.3
Total	74.1	100.0
Private Schools		
Federal	1.9	11.8
State	0.2	1.3
Local	0.1	0.6
All other	13.9	86.3
Total	16.1	100.0
Total—all schools	90.2	100.0

more funds for public education than do state governments. Less than 12 percent of the funding of education comes from the Federal Government. These figures are all significant—for various reasons as we will try to show.

Questions about Priorities

If public education is the most important enterprise in which this nation can be engaged (which this writer believes), then in relation to other expenditures public education receives penurious treatment.

The federal military budget for 1975, as passed by Congress, is approximately $82 billion. Since President Ford wants more than this, the official budget may end up several billion higher. But this figure is highly misleading: it does not include such items as interest on the portion of the national debt accrued for military spending, veterans' programs, research and development not labeled military but actually intended to have primarily military value, or monies spent for foreign economic aid which is actually intended by the Pentagon to have military value. Estimates on the *actual* amount spent on the military vary greatly, but tend to run from $110 billion upward. It may well be that the nation spends almost twice as much on its military establishment as on public education.

Between 1965 and 1972, the officially announced expenditure on the space program (from the *Statistical Abstract*, 1972) was about $37 billion. It seems fairly obvious that one outcome of the program, communications satellites, has potential value in bringing the nations of the world closer together through reduction of nationalism. We can even imagine their major use as an educational tool in assisting underdeveloped nations in building their own systems of public education; imagine, for example, an international educational television network.

However, it is difficult for us to see space exploration (which is conducted largely to find out more about the solar system) as being as valuable as public education, particularly if public education were to focus on what the Founding Fathers intended: to make possible and preserve and enhance the ability of citizens to run a self-governing democracy.

Questions about the Need for School Funding

The Coleman Report, discussed elsewhere in this book, as interpreted by Harvard's "conservative sociologist in residence," Daniel Moynihan, suggests that it would do little or no good to spend more on public education because what students will learn through formal schooling is determined before they begin school by their early home environment. The Report has been interpreted to prove that better school plants and better-paid teachers are irrelevant.

It strikes us that there is much garbled logic in the Coleman/Moynihan thesis. Their arguments assume that the nature of public education, for example, the curriculum, the strategy of teaching, remains fixed. It assumes that if the pessimistic findings were valid for the early sixties, they would be valid within a humanistically and democratically oriented public school system, where education focuses on reflective problem solving. However, we did not have that kind of public school system then and do not have it yet, but we could have it if enough people were to become concerned about it. And people may before the seventies are finished.

If teaching were what it should be, it seems difficult to argue that increased funding would not help—average class size could thereby be cut in half, libraries well stocked, and school rooms made bright, cheerful places. Although our opinion remains in the realm of speculation, it seems to us that given the right kinds of improvements in schooling we could well use double the $70 billion now spent annually on public education. This would particularly be the case if we were to equalize financial support from one school district to another.

Inequality of School Funding

As long as our local school districts bear more of the cost of public schooling than do state governments, the per pupil annual expenditure will fluctuate wildly from one district to another. The reason should be obvious:

local school funds come almost entirely from real estate taxes. Some school districts have a strong tax base per pupil, others have a very weak tax base. Consequently, several million pupils attend impoverished schools staffed by impoverished teachers, whereas a few million more lucky pupils attend schools with abundant funds. The latter very likely have better teachers (though this is not guaranteed); certainly they have better libraries and other teaching materials and opportunities to take field trips.

The Serrano and Rodriguez Cases

When, in the Serrano case, the Supreme Court of California ruled that inequality in per pupil financial support was unconstitutional under the Sixteenth Amendment, educators the country over hailed the decision as a major breakthrough. Numerous study groups, including education committees in state legislatures, began planning means for rectifying present inequities. A commonly advocated move was to turn all public school funding over to state governments who would return it to school districts divided equally on a per pupil basis.

Then in the spring of 1974 the United States Supreme Court, in the Rodriguez case, ruled that nothing in the federal Constitution implied that financial support per pupil should be equalized. Although this overturned the Serrano decision, in states, such as California, whose state constitutions contain phraseology equivalent to that of the Sixteenth Amendment, educators could still look to the courts for equalization in funding on grounds that their state constitutions mandated it. This has happened in California and presumably will in other places.

But not all states have constitutions with articles equivalent to the Sixteenth Amendment of the federal Constitution. Amending state constitutions is a laborious and usually slow job. In a society in which all social benefits have a dollars-and-cents price tag attached, local and state power elites are almost certain to use all the political clout at their command to fight state constitutional amendments if they fear the outcome could reduce the per pupil financial support in districts now populated by the wealthy. Theoretically, this type of problem would be far more amenable to solution under a democratic socialist economy.

Is Federal Funding the Answer?

Some educators feel that we should move in the direction of increased federal funding, a matter within the domain of Congress. As Table 9-1 indicated, although the amount of current federal funding is not breathtaking, it would help a great deal if parceled out to reduce the kind of inequity we are talking about. Many federal programs have particularly been designed to help impoverished school districts, but all too often federal monies earmarked for public school support are disbursed on a "no-strings-attached" basis and end up in school districts least in need.

It would require a major act of Congress to obligate the Federal Government to take the steps the Serrano decision mandated. Even if the Congress could be so persuaded, there might be a presidential veto to contend with. At present, nothing has really been solved and no solutions seem near.

All this is very unfortunate because the intent of Jefferson and others who were concerned with the role of public education in a democracy was to provide not only free, compulsory public schooling for all, but also "equal access" to it by all. An impoverished school district cannot provide equal access. This appears to violate the whole rationale of a democratic, self-governing nation, since the uninformed vote of adults who did not have equal access to education counts just as heavily as the vote of an adult who attended well-funded schools.

How Approach Economic Education?

One innovation in public education that appears highly necessary is the addition to the curriculum of solid course work in economics—not orthodox economics which now marks available textbooks—but an economics course focused on issues of the type we have tried to illustrate in part in this chapter. Until teaching materials suitable for such a course are prepared, teachers will have to scrounge for materials from scholarly journals, magazines, the press, and such field resources as their community can provide. A full year of economic study at the senior high level would seem minimal.

But we can think of an additional way of approaching the problem of providing all secondary students with some realistic and highly problem-centered teaching in economics. Why not let students themselves become involved in the business management of the school? We are not suggesting that students be asked to take over this function, but rather to work out simulations and models. Students could study and debate the amount of money needed by the school, how it should be distributed and used, and where the money will come from.

This would require students to get into such matters as how we determine our national priorities, issues of federal vs. state vs. local funding, the comparative merits of different kinds of taxes, accountability for how the money is finally spent, the role of power centers in making such decisions, and even the question of whether increased school funding would significantly improve education.

If students were to do this, they should learn in a hurry that many of the obstacles to rational school financial support are implicit in the

American system of capitalism. At this point, students could be encouraged to study school finance in nations that operate differently and to invent alternative models designed to meet the requirements of problems indigenous to the United States.

STUDY QUESTIONS

1. Define the expression "free enterprise." How does the meaning of free enterprise (if it has any) differ from profit system, private ownership, democracy, capitalism? Do any of these words have a clear meaning in today's world?
2. What forms of competition other than price competition can you identify? Are any of them worth having? Is competition the best basis for any economic system? Is there any kind of competition which would be a sufficient substitute for price competition?
3. Name the items you buy which you are sure are priced solely according to supply and demand factors. Would any of the following be priced according to genuinely free pricing: gasoline, automobiles, clothing, processed foods, wine, medical care?
4. If you are a commodity, as the theory of capitalism holds, what is your value? What dollar figure would you place on it? Some people say a price cannot be put on a human life; could such people logically believe in capitalism?
5. Does the prospect of steady price inflation during your lifetime bother you? If price inflation has become an inescapable part of modern capitalism, can you think of any reforms in the system that would make inflation hurt less? Does inflation hurt business profits?
6. Do privately owned corporations levy taxes on their customers? What is the difference between a price that yields an excessive profit and a tax?
7. Much merchandising includes the use of such sales pitches as "Buy one for the regular price, get the second free," or "Thirty-five cents off with coupon." Is the customer getting a bargain in such cases? Someone must pay for these items: do the company's stockholders dig it out of their pockets? Or the company manager?
8. Private owners are supposed to be able to operate a business more efficiently than the government. How would you compare the efficiency of hydroelectric plants operated by the Army Corps of Engineers and Lockheed Aircraft or Penn Central Railway?
9. Public schools are examples of socialized enterprise. How would you compare the overall efficiency of operation of a public and a private school?
10. People who damn socialism the most fiercely include retired generals and admirals, conservative tenured university economists, members of many religious orders, and retired presidents of the United States. How do you explain the hostility toward socialism of people who live under it?
11. How would you analyze the Watergate and related scandals in relation to our type of economic system? How do you explain that all the per-

sons convicted of crimes in connection with Watergate are conservatives who seem to hate any member of the New Left?

ANNOTATED BIBLIOGRAPHY

Finn, David, *The Corporate Oligarch*. New York: Simon & Schuster, Inc., 1969.

The best book we have found on the ideology, hangups, and overall character of America's top business executives. Finn, head of one of the country's larger public relations firms, writes of people he knows personally. Readable and highly objective.

Galbraith, John Kenneth, *Economics and the Public Purpose*. Boston: Houghton Mifflin Company, 1973.

Galbraith's views are slightly more leftish in this book than in *The New Industrial State,* indicating that he is able to do something extremely rare for an economist—change his mind.

Goodwin, Leonard, *Do the Poor Want to Work? A Social-Psychological Study of Work Orientations*. Washington, D.C.: Brookings Institution, 1972.

Reports an extensive piece of research on the attitudes of welfare recipients. The conclusion is that the unemployed have the same attitudes toward work as the employed but a lower level of self-confidence. Demolishes the belief that most people on welfare want to be supported that way.

Harrington, Michael, *The Other America: Poverty in the United States*. New York: The Macmillan Company, 1963.

Generally considered the best book on poverty in the United States, this book has had a very wide readership. Extremely well written, as are all of Harrington's books, this volume explains how most of our poverty is "invisible" in the sense that middle-class persons don't go where it exists.

Hayek, Friedrich, A., *The Road to Serfdom*. Chicago: University of Chicago Press, 1944.

By general agreement, probably the best book defending classical economic theory. Hayek is a "classical conservative," who manages to remain remarkably consistent. Few economists share his views today, but he presents them with force and clarity.

Heilbroner, Robert L., *An Inquiry into the Human Prospect*. New York: W. W. Norton & Company, Inc., 1974.

One of our most prolific writers on economics and social affairs has changed his mind since he wrote in *Between Capitalism and Socialism: Essays in Political Economics* (Random House, 1970) that "capitalism would last a long time." This small, pessimistic book is Heilbroner's latest thoughts.

Heilbroner, Robert L., *The Worldly Philosophers: The Lives, Times and Ideas of the Great Economic Thinkers*. New York: Simon & Schuster, Inc., 1953.

For the initiate in economics this book provides first-rate background for understanding the numerous contradictory ideas about economics we are confronted with.

Heilbroner, Robert L., et al., In the Name of Profit: Profiles in Corporate Irresponsibility. New York: Doubleday & Company, Inc., 1972.

Probably the best book up to 1974 on corporate dishonesty. The book details six case studies and tells of the handful of employees who lost their jobs for reporting corporate "atrocities."

Myrdal, Gunnar, Challenge to Affluence. New York: Pantheon Books, 1963.

Myrdal's second book about the United States. As probably the most internationally renowned social scientist, he analyzes what he sees as fundamental weaknesses in the American economy. Very interesting because what he forecast for the decade ahead has turned out to be largely accurate.

Passell, Peter, and Leonard Ross, The Retreat from Riches: Affluence and Its Enemies. Foreword by Paul A. Samuelson. New York: The Viking Press, Inc., 1973.

A sharp and reasonably effective criticism of the new generation of "no-growth" economists. Passel argues that the only way our most pressing problems, including poverty, can be solved is through continuous economic growth.

Schumpeter, Joseph H., Capitalism, Socialism, and Democracy, 3d ed. New York: Harper & Row, Publishers, 1950.

Considered, with John Maynard Keynes, one of the two major economists of the twentieth century, Schumpeter writes very provocatively on why capitalism is doomed and describes a model for a workable socialist alternative. The first section is one of the better critical treatments of Karl Marx. Schumpeter's own commitment was to laissez-faire capitalism.

Silk, Leonard S., Nixonomics: How the Dismal Science of Free Enterprise Became the Black Art of Controls. New York: Praeger Publishers, Inc., 1972.

Silk, former economics editor of Business Week and later financial columnist for The New York Times, writes an amusing book about Richard Nixon's economic beliefs. Reveals well the contradictions in American economic ideology.

350

10

RACE, ETHNIC GROUPS, AND EDUCATION

... the Negro problem is intertwined with all other social, economic, political, and cultural problems, and its study affords a perspective on the American nation as a whole.

Gunnar Myrdal

One of the most persistent and emotion-arousing issues in public education since the founding of the nation has been what "to do about Negroes." During the antebellum period, it was taken for granted that if slaves were to be educated at all their education was the responsibility of their owners. After the abolition of slavery, the education of Blacks became a major issue in the South. Should they be educated, and if so how much? The outcome was the development of two public school

351

systems—the already existing schools for Whites and a new separate and highly unequal system for Blacks.

Blacks who migrated to the North were accepted with more or less grace into the established public schools, so in the North integrated schools could be found in the late nineteenth century. Racial integration in the North was not entirely popular, however; and as urban centers enlarged and Blacks tended to settle into their own neighborhoods, de facto segregation came to be a common pattern, as it still is today.

Since the Supreme Court decision in 1954 ordering desegregation throughout the nation, the issue has been fraught with emotional barrages of pro and con arguments not noted for their rationality. As desegregation requires the bussing of pupils in many communities, bussing has been an integral part of the whole desegregation issue, although upon close examination bussing seems to be more of a smoke screen. It has been established factually that in a large proportion of school districts it requires more bussing to continue de facto segregation than integration would require.

So we have in this chapter one of the hottest current school issues. And since parents and politicians in large numbers have loudly exploited the issue, it remains continually before us.

AMERICAN BELIEF PATTERNS WITH RESPECT TO MINORITIES

Who are the minorities in the United States? Most conspicuous are those who are clearly identifiable because of surface characteristics: Afro-Americans, Mexican-Americans, American Indians, and Asians. But the very poor, including not only a disproportionate number having black or brown skins but also several million Whites, constitute another minority category, as do Caucasian ethnic groups from Southeastern Europe and the Mediterranean area. Least discriminated against among racial minorities, apparently, are Asian-Americans who have tended to do well economically and whose children and youth tend to be high achievers in school.

Old-Culture Beliefs about Minorities

Much of our material on old-culture beliefs is drawn from or suggested by Gunnar Myrdal.[1] His study will be discussed later in the chapter. Here we present only belief patterns.

—Differences between human groupings are mainly genetic rather than learned; hence, we cannot expect racial and ethnic minorities ever to change much.
—Negroes, as descendants of Noah's son Ham who sinned against God, were meant to be cursed by God and doomed to servant status.

[1] Gunnar Myrdal et al., An American Dilemma: The Negro Problem and Modern Democracy, 2d ed. New York: Harper & Row, Publishers, 1962.

—Not all people are equal, either in genetic endowment or in the right to equal opportunity.

—Anyone with Negro ancestors, no matter how few, or how light his skin, is a Negro.

—Any Anglo-Saxon or North European blond who mates with a dark-skinned person, will produce children who resemble the dark-skinned person in mental, physical, and moral characteristics.

—Hybridized persons are inferior in all respects to people of a pure race, especially if the pure race is Caucasian.

—In relation to Caucasians of Northern European or British ancestry, Negroes, American Indians, Mexican-Americans, and people of Southern or Southeastern European ancestry are less intelligent, less responsible, less moral, more cowardly, and more lazy.

—Dark-skinned peoples (Negroes particularly, but also American Indians) have no cultural past: no written language, no art or music, no architecture (this assertion is offered as proof of their inferiority to Caucasians).

—It is acceptable for a white man to have sexual relations with a dark-skinned woman; but it is immoral, disgusting, and intolerable for a dark-skinned man to have sexual relations with a white woman.

—Dark-skinned people have more criminal tendencies than white-skinned people (e.g., Blacks commit more crimes of violence, as do Mexican-Americans; American Indians are drunkards and thieves; the Mafia consists of dark-skinned Italians).

Old-Culture Beliefs as Affected by Education Social Class, and Religion

Because the expression, old culture, includes a great variety of people whose views do not coincide, the belief-assertions listed above are rejected by many older persons, especially the educated.

A qualification often stated to help offset these negative characteristics is that dark-skinned people have special qualities that help compensate for their weaknesses. For example, Blacks have a better feel for music than Whites, or black males have a special talent for athletics. Mexican-Americans make better agricultural workers than Whites, especially in unpleasant field work. American Indians have more patience; some have more artistic talent than most Whites. Dark-skinned Europeans make better factory workers.

Social class membership is apparently an important determinant in beliefs held about people with dark skins. Upper-class Whites think better of dark-skinned minorities than do blue-collar workers; this is probably the case because upper-class people feel no threat from dark-skinned minorities and also tend to see a great many defects in lower-class Whites. The most bigoted Whites appear to be blue-collar workers. The skilled, upper blue-collar group has been notorious for keeping Blacks and other dark-skinned minorities out of their unions and apprenticeship programs.

Among religious denominations and sects, the liberal denominations have pushed strongly for better treatment of minorities, although they did not become activitist in this respect until about 1960. Fundamentalist denominations and sects have tended toward strong prejudices against minorities.

The Rank Order of Discrimination

One frequently mentioned aspect of Myrdal's monumental study is the research team's attempt to determine what Whites fear most about granting Negroes full equality. Although this data was based upon impressionistic evidence rather than carefully controlled empirical research, the conclusions seem plausible to any perceptive American who has lived among prejudiced Whites for a few years. The following items are listed in decreasing order of importance to Whites:

1. Intermarriage
2. Social mingling
3. Desegregation (of public facilities, schools, churches)
4. Equal political rights
5. Equality before the law
6. Equality of economic opportunity

The Myrdal investigatory team found, when more-or-less representative samplings of Blacks were asked about what they *wanted* the most, and in what order, their preferences tended to be the *reverse* of what White's most feared. In other words, Blacks wanted economic equality more than anything else and intermarriage less than anything else. This suggests that the fears of Whites bear no relationship to reality: what Whites fear most Blacks don't want. Probably a substantially similar situation would be the case with respect to Indian and Asiatic racial minorities.

New-Culture Beliefs about Minorities

Arnold Rose, in his introduction to the 1962 edition of *An American Dilemma,* in commenting about the changes that had occurred since 1944 when it was first published, says "Prejudice as an attitude was still common, but racism as a comprehensive ideology was maintained by only a few."[2]

Myrdal's entire book is organized largely around the theme of the contradictoriness of American thought. He asserts that deeply rooted within the American belief system is a commitment to what he calls "The American Creed." The American Creed originated in the thinking of the eighteenth century—the "century of the enlightenment"—and was expressed in Jefferson's assertions in the Declaration of Independence about equality and natural rights—"the pursuit of life, liberty, and happiness."

[2]Myrdal, p. xliv.

It was also expressed in the French revolutionary slogan, "liberty, equality, fraternity." These ideas were reinforced by the development of a liberal branch within Protestantism (as exemplified in the rise of Unitarianism and Congregationalism, reinforced by the original liberalism of Quakerism) and supported in part by certain features of the English Common Law.

The basically equalitarian American Creed has existed since the period of the Revolution, but always alongside it has been a diametrically opposite ideology that supports the ideals of inequality, prejudice, injustice, and suppression of dissent. In the seventies, the American Creed is being expanded by the best educated of the upper-middle class, many university students (particularly those with majors in humanities), and many university professors. What are some of these new-culture beliefs?

—Everyone, including women, is entitled to equality of opportunity.
—Intellectual and personality differences between racial and ethnic groups are a result of interaction between genetic and environmental factors, in which even genetic factors end up being modified by environmental pressures (i.e., all such differences can best be explained as a matter of learning).
—Hybridization, as produced by interracial mating, is more likely than not to result in progeny of greater psychophysical strength than either parent.
—There is no biological reason, and no longer any valid social reason, why different races and ethnic groups should not intermarry freely; in fact, free intermarriage is probably the only way of eliminating discrimination permanently.
—Segregation of races or ethnic groups is indefensible in any situation; free mingling should be a cherished goal.
—Blacks, Indians, and Asians all have a long and admirable cultural tradition—in many respects a tradition more admirable than that of Caucasians.
—Because of centuries of discrimination, minorities deserve something more than mere equality of opportunity; if anything, they deserve a head start.
—Because of special features of their cultural tradition, most minorities have something unique to offer and should be encouraged to do so.
—All groups have an equal right to personal self-fulfillment or self-actualization and should be aided in developing along the lines they wish.

AN "OUTRAGEOUS HYPOTHESIS" ABOUT RACIAL AND ETHNIC MINORITIES

It is probably more difficult to think of assertions treatable as hypotheses in the general area of majority-minority group relations than in most of the other areas of concern treated in Part II. There remain areas of controversy, however, and in certain of these areas the controversy may be hotter than it was a decade ago.

Hypothesis: *If all intelligence testing were outlawed, it would help significantly in reducing racism in the United States.*

There seems to be a new form of racism developing in the United States. It is unlike earlier racist movements because it claims a "modern" kind of scientific support—the support of a small group of psychologists hooked on tests and other so-called objective measurements as a means of learning all we will ever need to know about human beings. The present controversy surrounding IQ and race relates primarily to Whites and Blacks; however, most of the pro and con arguments could apply to other groups as well.

The New Hereditarians

The argument as to whether inheritance or learning is the more important in making people what they are goes back at least to ancient Greece. Largely shelved for 2000 years, it became an issue again in the eighteenth century with the development of the idea that all human beings are equal in potential at birth and become what their environment makes them (John Locke's *tabula rasa* theory). This equalitarian view, as we have seen, was dominant in the American colonies by 1776, where it was pushed with particular vigor by Thomas Jefferson.

The role of genetic inheritance came back on the scene in the nineteenth century, particularly after the acceptance among many intellectuals of Darwinism. Herbert Spencer's theories about humans being as subject to the law of the "survival of the fittest" as a herd of deer competing for food, which led to Spencer's concept of "social Darwinism," also emphasized the importance of heredity.

But such behaviorists as John Watson had reinvigorated the *tabula rasa* idea by World War I. By the time interactionist theory came to be felt—the 1920s and after—it appeared that the long-standing nature/nurture controversy had given way to the belief that since there was then no way of knowing what part of a person's thought and action was attributable to genetics and what part to learning, the nature/nurture issue had become irrelevant. The generally accepted assumption of geneticists was that phenotype (that which emerges when environment has done its work on whatever genetic tendencies may exist) is all that students of behavior had to study.

However, certain psychologists rejected this new way of viewing persons and sought ways of discovering through tests the quality of neurological structures, which it was felt could be done through the use of IQ tests. After thirty years of popularity, serious questions began to be raised about IQ tests, particularly the pencil-and-paper group tests widely used in schools. It was found that these tests had considerable predictive value in indicating the future success of students in middle-class schools and in occupations for which middle-class schools tried to prepare their students. It was also found that a simple vocabulary test had about the same predictive value. Because students who lacked a middle-class home background tended to score poorly on these tests, it gradually came to be assumed that IQ tests were "culturally biased." In spite of attempts to make "culture fair" tests, by the 1960s almost all psychologists had decided that a truly impartial test could not be made. This is where things stood in 1969.

Arthur Jensen

In early 1969, the *Harvard Educational Review* published an article by psychologist Arthur Jensen of the University of California at Berkeley. Jensen claimed that on the basis of the most careful research possible, it appeared that IQ scores were not only meaningful as a measure of basic intelligence, but that 80 percent of what an IQ test measured was a direct result of genetic endowment and only 20 percent a result of environmental learning. Further, Jensen pointed out that any representative population of Blacks tended to score about 15 points lower than any representative population of Whites. Jensen had exploded a bomb by renewing the nature/nurture controversy in a way to make Blacks appear genetically defective so far as intelligence was concerned.

Jensen's evidence was derived almost entirely from IQ test data from supposedly representative samplings of Whites, Blacks, Mexican-Americans, American Indians, and Asians. Rather than reporting its details, we will report his conclusions. Jensen emphasized that his data were based on averages for populations and provided no base for judging individuals.

With respect to Whites vs. Blacks, where the real fighting issue lay, Jensen argued that Blacks can range in IQ all the way up to the maximum testable IQ using the best present tests just as can members of white populations. He asserted he was talking only of group averages and that virtually all studies showed an IQ deficit of 15 points for black populations taken as a whole in relation to white populations taken as a whole.

In Jensen's most recently published article as of this writing, he insists (as he has repeatedly) that he is not a racist, asserting that to him racism means

> discrimination among persons on the basis of their racial origins in granting or denying social, civil or political rights. Racism means the

denial of equal opportunity in education or employment on the basis of color or national origin. Racism encourages the judging of persons not each according to his own qualities and abilities, but according to common stereotypes. . . . The scientific theory that there are genetically conditioned mental or behavioral differences between races cannot be called racist.[3]

As to the quality of his evidence, Jensen insists that "many scientists have re-examined the environmentalist explanations of the black IQ deficit and found them to be inadequate." He says that Blacks in this country score on the average about one standard deviation below Whites. Thus, approximately only 16 percent of Blacks score above the *average* white person. This difference, says Jensen, holds true for the eighty standardized mental tests for which there is any published data. The significance of such a difference, says Jensen, cannot "be wished away because of a belief in equality."

Jensen then introduces the caveat that an "individual's success and self-fulfillment depends upon many characteristics *besides* intelligence. . . ." However, Jensen does consider IQ scores a crucial measure of an individual's ability to compete in a culture such as ours. Jensen brings this point home by asserting that IQs below 70 (what he claims as the breaking point between normalcy and retardation) occur seven times more frequently among Blacks than among Whites.

After complaining about the contention of environmentalists that an IQ differential of 15 or so points is basically meaningless, Jensen says that it always remains a *possibility* that environmental circumstances could explain away part of the black IQ defict; but that this appears highly improbable as an explanation of all or even most of the deficit.

Environmentalist theory has failed in its most important predictions, says Jensen, but aside from that he finds it quite plausible to hypothesize a racial difference in the genetic basis for IQ scores when all other other differences we associate with race are clearly and provably genetic (such as body shape and proportion, cranial shape and size, pigmentation, hair form and extent, distribution of blood types, color blindness, taste, etc., etc.). It would really be surprising, Jensen insists, if genetic factors failed to apply also to neurological functioning and hence to mental traits. In fact, Jensen maintains, intelligence, as measured by tests such as the Stanford-Binet, shows a strong hereditary basis among European and North American Caucasian populations (according to family lines), and Jensen doesn't know of "any geneticists today who have viewed the evidence and who dispute this conclusion." Although their results vary in minor ways one from another, all studies add up to the irrefutable con-

[3]Arthur Jensen, "The Differences Are Real," *Psychology Today*, Vol. 7, No. 7, December 1973, p. 80ff.

clusion that genetic factors are about twice as important as environmental factors in producing a given intelligence level.

Jensen concedes that many IQ tests are culturally biased, but that many others (most others, Jensen seems to imply) are culture-fair in the sense that they use "nonverbal, simple symbolic material common to a great many different cultures." Of these culture-fair tests, Jensen says, we can obtain dependably accurate measures of ability to generalize, distinguish similarities and differences, see relationships, and solve problems. That is, they do not just test specific bits of knowledge, but rather the capacity for abstract reasoning.

Jensen feels that one of the heaviest guns in his arsenal is the fact that on tests that include both culture-fair and culture-loaded items, Blacks actually do better on the culture-loaded items than on the nonverbal, problem-oriented, culture-fair items. Among all groups tested, Blacks are unique in this respect, says Jensen. He cites widespread experimentation with the Wechsler Intelligence Scale with its eleven different subtests that range from culture-loaded to culture-fair to support his contention. When the WIS is given to samples of Puerto Ricans, American Indians, Mexican-Americans, and Asians, the results are opposite: these non-black groups not only do better than Whites on the culture-fair portion of the test, but do as well as Whites, and this includes even groups as remote from our cultural mainstream as Arctic Eskimos. In fact, Asians, even recent immigrants who know little or no English, score higher on the culture-fair portion of the WIS than do Whites. Jensen argues that because he willingly concedes intellectual superiority to Orientals, he could not be a white racist.

Jensen refutes one by one a number of specific arguments against the validity of using IQ tests as a measure of intelligence. He cites what he sees as clear evidence that the race of the test-giver has no bearing on results, nor such factors as verbal deprivation, low motivation, or teacher expectations. No matter to what extent these factors operate, Blacks still average out with a 15 point IQ deficit.

In referring to what he calls the "sociological fallacy," Jensen tries to refute the argument of many sociologists that when different racial groups are matched in terms of socioeconomic level, differences in IQ scores tend to be erased. To achieve any socioeconomic level one can identify, says Jensen, requires a selecting out of nonrepresentative Blacks; since to achieve even a lower-middle-class level a Black must be superior in relation to other Blacks. Further, says Jensen, Blacks who do achieve upper-blue-collar or middle-class white-collar status, tend on the average to be lighter in color, indicating that they have a greater proportion of "white genes" than the average Black.

Another of the sociologists' fallacies is that malnutrition and other health problems lower IQ test performance; Jensen counters this argument by asserting that although this may be to some extent true in some other parts of the world, there is no evidence that any segment of the American population suffers enough malnutrition or other health disability to affect IQ scores. He cites American Indians as people who are less well nourished and generally less healthy than Blacks, but who, on the average, do much better on IQ tests than Blacks.

In stating his recommendations, Jensen says that the intelligence deficit of Blacks underscores their need to have full equality of opportunity, as should every other group. He maintains that his own social philosophy is both equalitarian and democratic.

Richard Herrnstein and Hans J. Eysenck

In September 1971, Harvard psychologist Richard Herrnstein published an article on IQ and heredity in *The Atlantic Monthly*. He reports Jensen's thesis (by then widely known as Jensenism), agrees in substance with Jensen's contention that IQ is largely hereditary but unlike Jensen, does not push the hypothesis that the deficiency in IQ is largely a Negro problem. Rather, Herrnstein argues that IQ is a determiner of social status within a stratified system. He argues that in a society like ours, the ideology of which stresses an open class system, any attempts to equalize educational opportunity can only lead to those having the highest IQ rising to the top and those of lowest IQ forever remaining at the bottom. This, Herrnstein argues, would create a highly stratified system—a meritocracy based upon hereditary castes.

To Herrnstein, to the extent that we reduce environmental differences, we increase the importance of hereditary differences. Tendencies to succeed or fail in an open class system could, in the absence of counteracting environmental influences, lead to family lines whose genes virtually guaranteed either success or failure, just as genes within a family line may produce a generation-after-generation tendency toward diabetes, hypertension, blond hair, or tall stature.

The implication of Herrnstein's position seems to be that we should not tamper with environmental factors but should leave them as uneven as they now are. Since Blacks tend to be born and reared in environments detrimental to achievement, they and sympathizers with their desire for equality of environmental opportunity see Herrnstein's argument as also being anti-Negro.

England has a counterpart to Jensen, Professor Hans J. Eysenck. At one time Jensen studied under Eysenck, and their views about the importance of the hereditary component in determining IQ scores are roughly parallel. Critics of this general position tend to lump Jensen, Herrnstein, and Eysenck together.

The Special Case of William Shockley

William B. Shockley, a Stanford University physicist, was co-winner of a Nobel prize for the invention of the transistor. No one questions Shockley's expertise in physics, but for reasons still unclear, he chose to enter the arena and pose as an expert on IQ, intelligence, and race. Shockley accepted Jensen's hypothesis that 80 percent of any individual's intelligence is hereditary, that Blacks have an intelligence deficit unknown among any other races or racial mixes, and launched a crusade to warn the nation of the danger of dysgenics.

Shockley defines *dysgenics* as "retrogressive evolution through the disproportionate reproduction of the genetically disadvantaged." Shockley's proposed antidote for the disaster of dysgenics is to sterilize all low IQ people, black or white, under a "bonus plan" which would provide cash incentives for voluntary sterilization. Since Shockley's plan for sterilization would primarily affect Blacks, it is understandable that Blacks and their sympathizers became highly agitated.

Shockley was at a disadvantage from the beginning in his advocacy of sterilization of all people with low IQs. With no formal education or noticeable self-education in genetics, psychology, or testing, Shockley has been singularly given to making assertions which cause geneticists and testing experts to cringe. Nor has Shockley helped himself by his tendency toward absolutistic thinking, in contrast to the carefully qualified hypotheses of Jensen and Eysenck. The Department of Genetics at Stanford has referred to Shockley's "research" as "hackneyed pseudoscientific justification for class and race prejudice," and several members of the National Academy of Sciences signed a letter describing Shockley's ideas as "such simplistic notions of race, intelligence and 'human quality' as to be unworthy of serious consideration by a body of scientists."

Arguments Against the Hereditarian Position

The purpose of this chapter would not be served by a detailed treatment of the storm of criticism aroused by Jensen, Herrnstein, Eysenck, and Shockley. However, a few things need to be said.[4]

As might be expected, the theories of the new hereditarians have been very upsetting to Blacks and liberals generally. The charge commonly leveled at these men is that if they, themselves, are not racists, their theories lend themselves ideally to use by racists of all descriptions, in the United States and abroad. Strong pressures have been exerted to

[4] This topic, and part of the above, was drawn largely from Berkeley Rice, "The High Cost of Thinking the Unthinkable," *Psychology Today*, December 1973, p. 89ff.

prevent these men from having a platform on which to air their views. Much of the criticism has been highly emotional and not scientifically based. Further, many of the critics can be charged with not having read carefully the writings of the hereditarians and not really knowing what their hypotheses are.

Even so, the critics can be divided roughly into two categories: first, those with or without scholarly credentials who have castigated the hereditarians with emotional rhetoric and few facts, and, second, critics with scholarly credentials who have framed careful arguments based on the best factual data available and have stated their cases without polemics in the best traditions of scholarly debate.

Since, in our opinion, the most effective critiques of the hereditarians emerge from genetic knowledge, it seems appropriate to report the analysis and supporting data of Theodosius Dobzhansky who is generally regarded as, if not the world's foremost, at least among the three or four leading experts in this field.

Dobzhansky begins his analysis by pointing out that no two human beings in the world are identical biologically; even "identical twins" are not identical in an absolutistic sense. "Human equality and inequality are sociological designs, not biological phenomena. Human equality consists of equality before the law, political equality and equality of opportunity. These are human rights that come from religious, ethical or philosophical premises."[5] Issues concerning human equality must not be confused with biological diversity, which has no known exceptions.

What enables a person to achieve a given IQ score, Dobzhansky asserts, is some interactive combination of genetic and environmental factors; but any claims that it is possible to determine what proportion of each factor produces the final outcome go far beyond any known evidence. Dobzhansky questions Jensen's contention that 80 percent of a person's IQ score comes from heredity, in part on the grounds that hereditability does not count for anywhere near this much in very many of the genetically influenced traits that we can measure in either animals or plants.

This is not the main argument against the Jensen hypothesis, however. "Genes *determine* the intelligence (or stature or weight) of a person only in his particular environment. The trait that actually develops is *conditioned* by the interplay of the genes with the environment." Even though identical twins have identical genes, no two identical twins are really identical because even if raised in the same family they are not both subject to an identical environment. The effect of environment on the development of identical twins is clearly shown in studies of identical

---

[5] Theodosius Dobzhansky, "Differences Are Not Deficits," *Psychology Today*, December 1973, p. 97ff. Dobzhansky, as of this writing professor of genetics at the University of California, Davis, has won virtually every honor available for his work in human genetics.

twins separated at birth and reared in very different environments (the more different the environment, the more divergent their IQ scores).

According to Dobzhansky, it is indefensible to say that genes can determine anyone's upper or lower limits of intelligence "since existing environments are endlessly variable and we constantly add new ones, to test the reactions of a given gene constellation in all environments is obviously impossible." This fact, and it is a fact insofar as it is possible to establish facts in an area as complex and little understood as genetic inheritance, should in itself pretty much demolish the position of Jensen and those who argue like him.

But Dobzhansky is not content to stop there. He describes a phenomenon often referred to as "regression toward the mean." The nature of this phenomenon can be illustrated by the results of a broad program of IQ testing in England. By pulling together the data from some 40,000 tested inviduals, including all age ranges and all socioeconomic levels, it was found that among adults the upper professional level had an average IQ of about 140; on the other hand, among unskilled laborers, the average adult had an IQ of 85. But the crucial finding was that children of the upper professional group had an average IQ of about 121, approximately 20 points lower than their parents; also, that the children of the unskilled laborers had an average IQ of 93, 8 points *higher* than their parents.

Would the third generation of each of these two categories (upper professional and unskilled laborers) have an IQ averaging in the neighborhood of 100—the average for large populations on which the IQ test used has been stardardized (a "built-in" average; i.e., scoring formulas are designed so the average must be 100)? Perhaps, but within each generation there will be those who rise much higher than their parents and those who sink considerably lower. We are referring here to both socioeconomic achievement and IQ.

But herein lies a rather crucial question: does IQ cause the socioeconomic achievement or does socioeconomic achievement cause the IQ achievement that goes with it? There is evidence now from numerous studies that a stimulating environment, including stimulating parents, schooling, and jobs tends to increase IQ—as much as 30 or more points for a single individual in many cases. In the absence of a stimulating environment, IQ achievement tends to sink.

Dobzhansky asserts that this same phenomenon (regression toward the mean) applies equally in cross-racial studies. He recognizes that Jensen deals with the environmental influences on IQ and does in fact appeal to studies that try to equate black and white environments, particularly of given social class levels. Because Whites and Blacks of the same socioeconomic level still, when tested, reveal an IQ deficit for Blacks, Jensen concludes that the IQ deficit of Blacks can be attributed only to genetic differences. But belonging to the same socioeconomic class proves little

about similarity of environmental influences. There are a great many more environmental variables (undoubtedly including hundreds that no one has yet thought of) than could ever be explained simply by membership in the same social class. Dobzhansky says, "After psychologist Arthur Jensen explicitly recognizes that heritability of individual differences in IQ cannot be used as a measure of average heritability across populations, he tries to do just that." And of Jensen's general conclusions, Dobzhansky says, "I remain unconvinced."

Dobzhansky gets into, but does not develop fully, what we see as a more crucial issue than any so far mentioned. He reminds us that IQ is not a result of a unitary trait determined by a single gene. Rather there are many other human traits, governed by interacting constellations of genes, that relate to "mental" functioning. One would have to understand how all of these traits interact to produce functional intelligence (i.e., ability to solve with reasonable efficiency the kinds of problems that a particular individual most wants to solve in his own life situation). That is to say, before we could even begin to get at the heritability of functional intelligence, we would have to know far more than we now do about all the traits that produce it. Capacity to do well on IQ tests may be the least important of this unknown number of relevant traits.

White Racism: Some Interpretations

We could hardly let the matter rest at this point. Even if we grant that Jensen and Herrnstein are not themselves racist in their deeper and unverbalized attitudes, the fact of white racism remains. Were it not for the widespread existence of white racism in the United States and elsewhere, Jensen's and Herrnstein's theses would have caused hardly a flutter. Many people were bothered by these men's arguments because they saw in them ammunition for bringing to the surface an underlying racist attitude that most Americans hold. Therefore, we will devote this section to an attempt to explain what is behind white racism.

A Proposed Definition of Racism

Racism is an "ism," that is to say, like communism, fascism, socialism, capitalism, and Calvinism, it is an ideological pattern. Ideologies may have something to say about reality beyond the nature of the people who assert them, but usually not much. Typically, ideologies tell us quite a bit about those holding them but little of significance about anybody else.

Most definitions of racism are overly simple because they refer mainly to its symptoms and outward manifestations, and only superficially to the deeper values and motivations of those who can properly be called racists. The following definition of racism is overly simple, but it may give us a base from which to expand. Racism is "An ideological orientation and form of ethnocentrism, in which it is maintained that one's own group is a distinct race that is inherently superior to other races."[6]

Margaret Mead on Race

In August 1970, Margaret Mead and James Baldwin spent about seven and a half hours discussing race. The book reproducing their talk

---

[6] George A. and Achilles G. Theodorson, *Modern Dictionary of Sociology.* New York: Thomas Y. Crowell Company, 1969; Apollo ed., 1970, p. 329.

is one of the most readable sources of Mead's thinking on race as of 1970.[7] This section summarizes and paraphrases what strike us as Mead's major points. Our treatment is very much boiled down. In cases where Baldwin said something with which Mead fully agreed, we have paraphrased Baldwin without making the distinction; we assume his statement paralleled Mead's thinking.

What is central to white racism irrespective of the minority toward which it is directed? A combination, Mead says, of power and fear. The dominant white majority (or minority, in the case of South Africa) senses differences between it and the minority, differences which are not always in favor of the white majority. Cultural groups the world over have tended to show fear of other cultures markedly different from their own.

Fear alone can be translated into persecution only when one group is enough stronger than another to have power over it. In the United States, large numbers of Whites do not understand Negro culture and because it is different, it is feared. And in the United States, the Whites are dominant. With the power of dominance resides the power to suppress and persecute.

This is only a surface explanation, however. There are questions to be answered as to why both Whites and Negroes see each other as being so different from one another. At one time, Mead was all in favor of assimilation; but as of 1970 she saw the "black power" movement as in part an attempt by Negroes to preserve and assert very real cultural differences which were of deep historical origin. Whites, too, have sensed a cultural difference. But neither Whites nor Negroes have understood very well all that might lie behind the differences.

Mead sees one difference as being not so much a matter of the respective cultural traditions as of symbolism relating to lightness and darkness. Mead has found in all her anthropological studies that darkness, even among dark-skinned people, elicits fear. Fear of darkness is not merely a holdover from childhood. Night has produced more dangers for most peoples than has day. In premodern cultures, people liked having a fire burning at night, and they have often engaged in moon worship. In modern cultures, most people prefer having some lights burning at night. Mead considers as ridiculous attempts to equate darkness with dirtiness; but to equate darkness with danger has made eminently good sense for most of the world's peoples.

It is a rather easy transition to relate what is safe to goodness, and what is dangerous to badness. African languages make sharp distinctions between light and dark and place value on lightness. Early Mediterranean Caucasoids (even though relatively dark skinned) adopted a light-dark

---

[7] Margaret Mead and James Baldwin, A Rap on Race. New York: J. B. Lippincott Company, 1971.

American Indian life.

Mexican-American life.

symbolism in connection with their religions, both pre-Christian and Christian. Hence, angels were depicted as white.

As Christianity worked northward to the fair-skinned Teutonic peoples, the idea of angelic forces being white was deeply cherished. People who were white—like angels—found it easy to adopt notions of biological superiority. People tend to behave very badly, Mead suggests, if they think they are the color of angels.

Whites not accustomed to close daily association with black-skinned people probably have found blackness of skin worrisome if not downright fearsome. No sweeping generalizations should be asserted from this, however, because it is obvious that some cultures of light-skinned people have been quite color blind with respect to race (Scandinavians. for example). Education, Mead feels, may offer a pretty good clue as to how particular white cultures react to dark-skinned people; further, the whole light-dark symbolism is probably disappearing from the thinking of people, if for no other reason than that darkness may pose fewer dangers to modern humans than to their ancestors.

Of much greater significance than light-dark symbolism in explaining modern white racism (and its counterpart, black racism) is the very real cultural differences mentioned above, but not explained. Mead feels that the most significant difference between Mediterranean- and African-based cultures is that historically the Mediterranean cultures had a written language whereas African cultures did not.

Each of these two cultural bases conferred both advantages and disadvantages. Cultures with a written language, although they have the potential for developing science, mathematics, and modern technology, also have a tendency to become wedded to the written word, including their own written histories. What is captured in writing tends to become regarded as Absolute Truth, leading to lack of flexibility. Africans developed large kingdoms and intricate cultures which were transmitted from one generation to another by word of mouth. This was possible only through the development of a major talent for remembering. For example, they kept in mind genealogies extending backward hundreds of years. They were "orally verbal" in orientation; because their history was word-of-mouth, it was easily revised as conditions demanded revision. This produced a flexibility conducive to innovative thought, and helps explain the originality of African art forms.

Mead also thinks that people with a written-language orientation could never have survived the stress of being uprooted, torn from their native culture, and kept in slavery for more than two centuries. People with thousands of years of orally verbal culture behind them are unlikely to lose the particular traits conferred by such a culture in a mere two or three hundred years. Thus, African Americans are still culturally distinctive. They depend less on the written word and more on memory and body language.

Mead sees white racism as declining and likely to continue declining. It is harbored primarily by lower white-collar and upper blue-collar workers, who remain edgy about the real cultural differences between Whites and Blacks, which their education has not helped them understand.

The Myrdal-Rose Theory of White Racism

In evaluating the factual findings and conclusions of the famous Myrdal study, we must remember that it was done a rather long time ago.

The idea of the study was conceived by the late Newton D. Baker, son of a Confederate Civil War officer and a newcomer to the Carnegie Corporation Board of Directors in 1931. Through his urging the Carnegie Corporation funded a major study of the "Negro problem" in the United States.

The Board decided that the best director for the study would be a foreigner from a nation without racial problems. The person should have an international reputation as a scholar and the best possible kind of educational and experiential background. After narrowing the search to Switzerland and Scandinavia, Swedish social scientist Gunnar Myrdal was selected. Myrdal chose as his chief assistant the late American sociologist Arnold Rose.

Myrdal, as it turned out, fulfilled all expectations as a person fully qualified to study the most critical problems of American culture. Probably no one since Alexis de Tocqueville, who published his famous two-volume *Democracy in America,* in 1835 and 1840, had such outstanding credentials for the task of "sizing up" American culture, and probably *An American Dilemma* comes nearer than any other book to reflecting the same acuteness, accuracy of analysis, and futuristic accuracy found in *Democracy in America.*

Myrdal began his study in 1938 and finished it in 1942. The 1483-page volume, *An American Dilemma,* was published in 1944. A 324-page condensation, *The Negro in America* by Arnold Rose, was published in 1956.[8]

The methodology of the American dilemma study Myrdal approached his study from a social psychological orientation. The study is empirical, but empirical in the manner of an institutionalist social scientist. Only occasionally did Myrdal have much use for data which could be neatly quantified. A great deal of in-depth interviewing was done, and data from every source available was utilized—all other major studies, statistics published by the government and private agencies, etc.

The Negro problem as a problem of Whites One overall conclusion was that the "Negro problem" is not caused by Negroes but by Whites; the problem of race relations in the United States has little to do with Blacks, and everything to do with the psychological problems of Whites of both sexes. "Although the Negro problem is a moral issue both to Negroes and to whites in America, we shall in this book have to give primary attention to what goes on in the minds of white Americans,"[9] "The race question involves the saving of black America's body and white America's soul. . . . The real problem is not the Negro but the white man's attitude toward the Negro."[10]

[8] Arnold Rose, *The Negro in America.* New York: Harper & Row, Publishers, 1956; Boston: Beacon Press, 1956.
[9] Myrdal, *An American Dilemma,* p. xlvii.
[10] Myrdal, p. 43.

Inner-personal White conflict about race Myrdal uses the expression, "inner-personal," which appeared in Kurt Lewin's psychological writing of the 1930s. The term refers to the tensional area of the self, and is highly appropriate to Myrdal's concept of the race problem as being primarily a product of cognitive dissonance.

Myrdal suggests that the "Negro problem" in America would take a different character, and would be easier to handle scientifically, if it involved mainly conflicts in values between Whites and Blacks. That is, if the conflicts arising from white-black relations took the form of interpersonal conflict, it would be more overt and susceptible to objective description and prescription. But Myrdal sees the conflict also as intrapersonal:

> We shall find that even a poor and uneducated white person in some isolated and backward rural region in the Deep South, who is violently prejudiced against the Negro and intent upon depriving him of civic rights and human independence, has also a whole compartment in his valuation sphere housing the entire American Creed.[11]

When we place against the American creed of equalitarianism some of the more potent beliefs held by Whites about Blacks, it is easy to see the specific nature of the dissonance in which many Whites are enveloped. Historically, it appears that the major concern of Whites has been to maintain Negroes in the situation of a caste rather than a social class. By caste, we mean a division similar to the caste system of India. To secure caste status for Blacks has required a set of beliefs relating to the presumed, but as we now know highly distorted, biological differences between races.

To rationalize and defend a caste system, it is essential for Whites to hold such beliefs as the following:

—The Negro people belongs to a separate race of mankind.
—The Negro race has an entirely different ancestry.
—The Negro race is inferior in as many capacities as imaginable.
—The Negro race has a place in the biological hierarchy somewhere between the white man and the anthropoid.
—The Negro race is so different both in ancestry and in characteristics that all white peoples in America, in contradistinction to Negroes, can be considered a homogeneous race.
—The individuals in the Negro race are comparatively similar to one another and, in any case, all of them are definitely more akin to one another than to any white man.[12]

[11] Myrdal, p. xliv.
[12] Myrdal, pp. 103–104.

Myrdal and his research team concluded that large numbers of Whites, particularly the uneducated or semieducated, did in fact hold beliefs such as the above when the study was made.

The Black condition as a vicious circle Since Myrdal sees the Negro problem in America as essentially one in which Whites suffer mental ill health because of extreme cognitive dissonance and become authoritarian and aggressive as a result of their own frustrations, it is necessary to note that Negroes have problems, too, and in many respects do not meet what Whites have defined as adequate norms for human behavior. Myrdal's massive book contains more than twenty chapters on the plight of the Negro: inability to get ahead economically and politically, discrimination in the courts, lack of social acceptance, relatively poor health and high crime rate, difficulty with schooling, and so on. But Myrdal ascribes these Negro problems to the problem of white inner conflict which prevents Whites from facing up to what Negroes need to better themselves.

Conclusions Concerning the Hypothesis

Although we have drawn the above rebuttal of Jensen's position largely from Dobzhansky, it should be noted that he is only one representative of a community of prestigious geneticists virtually all of whom think that the Jensen argument cannot be supported. Further, virtually all anthropologists apparently agree that the Jensen hypothesis is highly suspect. Anthropologists have at their command different categories of evidence, among which is a wealth of information about how people of different racial composition confront and solve (or fail to solve) their own unique problems.

It is not irrelevant to note that Negroid peoples, as well as others, have demonstrated historically a capacity to survive in natural environments so hostile that one can only wonder what remarkable level of functional intelligence must have been operating. One of the better examples, perhaps, is the Australian Aborigines, which are racially unique, showing residues of Negroid, Caucasoid, and other genes. Not only did the Aborigines learn to survive as hunters and food-gatherers in a climate almost devoid of rainfall, but they developed an intricate culture as well. People do not conquer an environment as unfriendly as theirs without being first-rate problems solvers which requires a high capacity for abstract thought.

Readers should also note that some of the few followers of Jensen claim racial history as a support for the Jensen thesis. They point to the Caucasoid-invented civilizations of India, Babylonia, Egypt, Greece, Rome, and Europe generally. They also point to the innovativeness and "high culture" of ancient China and Japan. In contrast, they note the paucity of cultural achievement among Negroid populations. This kind of analysis shows great ignorance of cultural history, an ignorance which could in part be rectified by reading the studies of Herskovitz.[13]

In our opinion, the most basic weakness of all psychologists who place great faith in IQ test results is their failure to recognize that not only are all definitions of intelligence highly arbitrary, but that they also involve value judgments. In essence, *they define intelligence as that which IQ tests measure.* This definition strikes us as being logically equivalent to the famous Coolidgism, "When prices rise, inflation occurs." Psychologists hooked on testing often trap themselves in this kind of circular reasoning. A psychologist can label any of numerous ill-understood human traits or asserted traits (introversion, extroversion, conformism, passivity, creativeness, homosexuality, courage, schizophrenia, accident proneness, quantitative reasoning, qualitative reasoning, emotiveness, etc., etc.), define them in a general and usually normative way, develop a test that purports to measure them quantitatively, and then, when pressed for more specific and nonevaluative definitions, come back at the critic by asserting that "the trait is what the test measures."

Unfortunately, some Blacks and white liberals who have been among the most vociferous critics of Jensen, Eysenck, and Herrnstein seem to think IQ scores are fully as important as Jensen, *et al.* do. Their chief criticism has been that the difference in IQ (which the critics also equate with intelligence) is a result of environmental inequities. Even geneticists of the stature of Dobzhansky phrase critiques along this line. In a recent news item, we read that Bobby Seale of the Black Panthers is urging geneticists to administer IQ tests to a broad spectrum of ethnic groups so comparisons can be made between Northern Italians and Southern Italians, Chinese Americans and Japanese Americans, Appalachian Whites and social register Whites, and so on—all on the assumption that IQ deficits equivalent to the black IQ deficit would turn up and thus clear Blacks of the stigma of the "15-point IQ deficit."[14]

Our own hypothesis is that the central issue has no bearing on "IQ deficits," but rather involves the definition of intelligence. IQ tests are constructed by testmakers who want intelligence to mean something which they can test for and depend on the tests to place the testmakers in a favorable light. Mssrs. Jensen, Eysenck, and Herrnstein, we presume, all test high on the Stanford-Binet, Wechsler, and other widely used IQ tests, particularly the subsections on reasoning.

[13] Melville J. Herskovitz, *The Myth of the Negro Past.* Boston: Beacon Press, 1958.
[14] AP news release, December 16, 1973.

Although intelligence testing may serve a few legitimate functions other than providing employment for several thousand psychologists, it has a number of negative aspects as well. One negative aspect of IQ tests is that their scores can be used as weapons to enforce many kinds of social controls: they enable the powerful to more effectively keep the powerless in their place. But the issue here is the use of IQ scores to keep Blacks in a position of inferiority, and in this connection we can only conclude that the hypothesis is essentially true. Just how much racism might be reduced by legally banning all use of IQ tests we have no way of knowing; after all, white racism is complex and has many other grounds than comparative IQ scores. But in the final analysis, the current furor over IQ and race strikes us as an unsuccessful exercise in mental masturbation by a group of people who, in the main, are intellectually impotent.

RACE, ETHNIC GROUP, AND EDUCATION

Historically, liberal thinkers in the United States have liked the "melting pot" idea and have promoted the virtue of assimilation of racial and ethnic minorities into the cultural mainstream. Most professional sociologists have also been in favor of assimilation as a long-range answer to the tensions produced by intergroup hostilities and discrimination. L. Paul Metzger has made an interesting though sketchy study of the views of American sociologists since the 1920s and of Gunnar Myrdal, *which assume assimilation as an eventual outcome of diverse ethnic/racial groups living in close proximity.*[15]

However, the Negro activist movement, which began in the late 1950s, and the high level of tension reached in the 1960s, dissuaded this sociological community from their previous belief that assimilation would come automatically, by slow increments, and without any particular turmoil. Further, the "black power" movement, with its seeming demand for separatism, and the support or partial support of this movement by many black and white intellectuals, was a further blow to the conventional wisdom of the older sociological community.

The sociologists discussed by Metzger have, among other things, placed a great deal of faith in the public schools as instruments for equalizing educational opportunity, reducing intergroup tensions, and in general guiding the process of assimilation. As of the first half of the

[15] L. Paul Metzger, "American Sociology and Black Assimilation: Conflicting Perspectives," *American Journal of Sociology,* Vol. 76, No. 4, January 1971, p. 627ff.

1970s, we are now in the midst of a major dialogue as to whether the schools have demonstrated that they could perform this function.

Desegregation and the Coleman Report

In the 1950s, the Supreme Court ordered the desegregation of public schools throughout the United States "with all due haste." A study of the effectiveness of integration as a means of improving the academic achievement of Negro children and youth was commissioned in the early 1960s. The report, *Equality of Educational Opportunity*, published in 1966, became known as the Coleman Report, as the study team was directed by James S. Coleman of Johns Hopkins University. This massive study involved

testing 470,000 school pupils, 60,000 teachers, and gathering data on some 4000 schools.[16]

It is unnecessary here to get into the Coleman study at length. However, the most significant purported findings to be derived from it are the following:

1. As judged by quality of plant, estimated quality of teachers, modernity and quantity of teaching materials, and class size, all-Negro schools were not very much poorer than schools attended by all Whites.
2. To the extent that some schools were poorer than others, the quality of the school seemed to have no significant bearing on achievement of students.
3. The difference in quality between Negro and white schools in the South is less great than the national average.

Although these findings were contrary to expectations, some other findings from the study gave even more cause for thought, at least among traditionally minded school people. Per pupil monetary expenditure did not seem to be a major factor in pupil achievement. Home background seemed to be much more important in influencing a child's school achievement than any other single factor. Racial integration in itself had little effect on academic achievement.

Aftermath of the Coleman Report

One consequence of the Coleman Report was to lend ammunition to taxpayer associations that have argued all along that too much money is spent on schools in view of the educational outcome. Opponents of bussing, who typically are opposed to the whole idea of racial desegregation, have also used the Coleman Report as a "factual" argument to attack bussing.

More important for our analysis here is that the late 1960s and early 1970s have seen the emergence of a school of "revisionist" historians and other critics of public education, who argue that public education cannot be demonstrated to have reduced poverty, erased class lines, or provided the poor, Blacks in particular, with economic opportunity equal to Whites.

Greer, for example, has claimed that from colonial times the chief function of the schools, in spite of the rhetoric of equalitarians, has been to assist in the upward economic mobility of children already middle class

[16] For student reading, we recommend Frederick Mosteller and Daniel P. Moynihan (eds.), *On Equality of Educational Opportunity; Papers Deriving from the Harvard University Faculty Seminar on the Coleman Report.* New York: Vintage Books, 1972.

and to train, in contrast to educate, the poor to be compliant laborers and stay in their place.[17]

Greer's revisionist history may contain a large element of truth, but this does not necessarily make it relevant to what should be our chief concerns. Christopher Jencks and others have also attacked public schools on the grounds that "Neither family background, cognitive skill, educational attainment, nor occupational status explain much of the variation in men's incomes."[18] To us, not only the Coleman Report but most of the revisionist literature following it has missed the mark. The Coleman studies were intended primarily to determine whether black-white school integration enabled Blacks to better themselves significantly in an economic sense—better jobs, higher incomes. Those influenced by the Coleman findings also seem to have been almost entirely concerned with the effectiveness of the public schools historically, or their effectiveness after integration, in improving the condition of the poor, a disproportionate number of which are black, and ameliorating the harshness of our social class system.

There are now at least two major matters at issue: (1) Were the Coleman studies valid in a factual sense, as well as such later studies as those of Jencks and associates, in their conclusion that schooling does little or nothing to improve the condition of the poor? and (2) if public schooling has not improved the lot of the poor, should this be a basis for damning public education?

A variety of critics have come to the fore during the past few years who dispute the criticism of public education as we have sketched it above. Levine, for example, questions whether performance on achievement tests tells us much worth knowing about the economic goals of education. Citing studies of Jacob Mincer, Levine points out that if one looks at the whole population, black and white, poor and middle-class, a complete secondary education does add 10 percent to the lifetime earnings of people.[19]

In the same article, Levine cites evidence indicating that the Coleman/Moynihan conclusion that class size made no difference in achievement is at best open to very serious question. In schools where the quality of teachers appears exceptionally high, class size does seem to make a significant difference in achievement.

[17] Colin Greer, The Great School Legend: A Revisionist Interpretation of American Public Education. Foreword by Herbert J. Gans. New York: The Viking Press, Inc., 1972.

[18] Christopher Jencks et al., Inequality: A Reassessment of the Effect of Family and Schooling in America. New York: Basic Books, 1972, p. 226.

[19] Donald M. Levine, "Educational Policy After Inequality," Teachers College Record, December 1973, p. 171.

Greene raises questions as to the validity of any criticism of public education based on the sole criterion of its contribution to economic success. Greene tells us:

> It is my impression that the intention behind school reform in the last decade was to make distinctions (through compensatory and remedial education, for example) on the basis of differences in achievements due in large measure to previous neglect, segregation, humiliation, and the ravages of poverty. Hobbled by lack of support, never adequately tested, reform has not been proven to be a failure *unless* one insists on income equality as the criterion.[20]

In the same article, Greene raises basic questions about the "be all-end all" of education. She feels that all pupils cannot be treated the same, and that we should not expect the same results for all pupils. What we should do is enable "diverse individuals to learn how to learn." She argues for justice as a primary goal of education—"a matter of equal and universal human rights," to quote Lawrence Kohlberg. Or, drawing from John Rawls, the criterion should be fairness, meaning that the weakest pupils deserve the most help.

Conclusions

It should be obvious that Blacks and other ethnic/racial minorities (except for most Asians) have not been treated fairly in our public schools—neither historically nor presently. But our view of what the schools *should* be doing for minorities may differ from that of most other writers on the subject.

We are convinced, for one thing, that public education not only should not, but by its nature cannot, provide the kind of direct boost to minorities and the poor in general that will enable them to achieve middle-class status. It is our opinion that poverty serves too many positive functions for the rich for the schools to make any direct change in the situation.

What the schools can and must do is provide for minorities a heavy enough dose of cultural study so they will understand well the kind of civilization in which they live and especially the dominant power structure. Further, the schools must somehow provide the motivation and skill to assist minorities in becoming politically effective. Since the ethnic/racial minorities and the poor in general constitute well over 15 percent of our adult population, potential voters all, they could provide the necessary "swing vote" to put in high office the officials who would

[20] Maxine Greene, "The Matter of Justice," *Teachers College Record,* December 1973, p. 181.

be most likely to instigate the radical economic reforms necessary to redistribute wealth and eliminate poverty by placing an adequate floor under all incomes.

STUDY QUESTIONS

1. What is your opinion of integration of minorities through intermarriage with majorities? (That this can happen with apparently positive results is demonstrated in one of our best sociological laboratories: Hawaii.)
2. How would you define intelligence? Are you satisfied that intelligence is "that which IQ tests measure?" If not, what is it? How would you rate your own intelligence?
3. The case of Professor Shockley is not unusual, in that scientists, both pure and applied, often speak outside their fields of expertise. Both Edward Teller ("father of the hydrogen bomb") and Admiral Hyman Rickover ("father of the atomic-powered submarine") have posed as experts in education. Was it proper for them to do so?
4. Margaret Mead is only one social scientist among several who attribute white racism in part to the impact of black-white symbolism. American advertisers play up the virtues of whiteness—in bread, laundry, teeth, and numerous other items. Do you think this feeds white racism?
5. How do you react to Myrdal's view that white racism is a problem of Whites, not of Blacks? Why?
6. If the primary function of public schools should be for citizenship, and not economic equalization, what is your opinion of the present major emphasis on vocational education in public education?
7. In many communities studied, it has been found that it required more bussing to maintain segregation than to introduce desegregation. In such communities what logical arguments could be made against bussing?
8. If races are essentially equal, how do you explain the exceptional creativity and performing ability of Blacks in the arts, especially music, and in athletics?
9. How do you explain the ideology in the United States that says that anyone with a single black ancestor should be classified as Negro? Does this means that all Americans are Negroes?
10. Would you like to see a Black, Chicano, American Indian, or woman as President of the United States? Why or why not?

ANNOTATED BIBLIOGRAPHY

Benedict, Ruth, *Race: Science and Politics,* including Ruth Benedict and Gene Weltfish, "The Races of Mankind," Foreword by Margaret Mead. New York: Viking Press, Inc., 1945; also in Compass paperback, 1959.

One of the better basic books on the meaning of race, the history and politics of racism. A good companion volume to Tannenbaum and Herskovitz. Very readable and considered something of a classic.

Berry, Brewton, *Almost White*. New York: The Macmillan Company, 1963; also in Collier paperback, 1969.

This book focuses on the results of miscegenation: the large population in the United States of people who are mixes of Negro, Indian, and Caucasian. Berry, professor of sociology and anthropology at Ohio State University, is a leading authority on mestizos and American Indians. Very good reading.

Grier, William H., and Price M. Cobbs, *Black Rage*, Foreword by U.S. Senator Fred R. Harris. New York: Basic Books, Inc., 1968; Bantam paperback, 1969.

Subject to rave reviews and for a considerable time on the best seller list, this book, authored by two Negro psychiatrists, is probably the best treatment available of what it "feels like" to be a Black in a white racist culture. Highly recommended.

Griffin, John Howard, *Black Like Me*. Boston: Houghton Mifflin Company, 1960; also New York: Signet, paperback, 1969.

The fascinating if rather horrifying story of a white novelist who blackened his skin chemically and shaved his hair so he could pass as a Negro. He then toured the South extensively to find out what it was like, as of about 1960, to be a Negro in the South. An extremely readable book about experiences which could only be called incredible.

Herskovits, Melville J., *The Myth of the Negro Past*. New York: Harper & Brothers, Publishers, 1941; Boston: Beacon Press, 1958.

Herskovits produced a badly needed book at a strategic time; this volume deals with the history of African cultures and should dispel the myth that Africans were incapable of developing complex cultures, in their own way fully as "advanced" as any other cultures in the historical past. We are shown how a highly cultivated people were uprooted, torn loose from its historical roots, and reduced to chattel slavery.

Kuttner, Robert E. (ed.), *Race and Modern Science*. New York: Social Science Press, 1967.

This collection of first-rate essays by biologists, anthropologists, sociologists, and psychologists is one of the better collections of readings on how scientists view race and problems growing from race relations. Some essays are rather technical, but the book is a very good reference source for upper division and graduate students.

Montagu, Ashley, *Man's Most Dangerous Myth: The Fallacy of Race*, 5th ed. New York: Oxford University Press, 1974.

Montagu probably shares with Margaret Mead the reputation of being one of the two most seasoned and intellectually prolific cultural anthropologists in the United States. This book, now updated for the 1970s, is rated by most critics as the best book on race written by an American. Montagu combines science and humane wisdom—as does Mead—in an extraordinary manner, and is always worth reading. His thesis is that the concept of race is both fallacious and highly damaging to the future of humankind.

Nash, Gary B., and Richard Weiss (eds.), *The Great Fear: Race in the Mind of America*. New York: Holt, Rinehart and Winston, Inc., 1970.

This first-rate book of readings contains nine analytical essays on the origins and nature of white racism. In addition to white racism directed toward Negroes, the book also treats white discrimination toward Indians, Mexican-Americans, and European and Asian immigrants.

Silberman, Charles E., *Crisis in Black and White*. New York: Random House, Inc., 1964; also Vintage, 1964.

One of the better books about white racism in the United States. Particularly useful for busy students because Silberman, well-known for his *Crisis in the Classroom* (1970), has managed to condense more of the history of racism and its impact on American culture in recent times in 370 pages than anyone else seems to have done.

Tannenbaum, Frank, *Slave and Citizen: The Negro in the Americas*. New York: Alfred A. Knopf, Inc., 1946; also Vintage, n.d.

Tannenbaum shows vividly why there is a "Negro problem" in the United States and none in most of Latin America. The author draws on the history of slavery and shows why slaves came to be regarded as chattel and something less than human in the United States, but were never so regarded in Latin America. A book of fundamental importance to any study of white racism in the United States.

Fascinating womanhood. *(Copyright © George Ballis, all rights reserved)*

11

SEXISM AND EDUCATION
F. A. GUERARD

> *For the full-time housewife and mother is a recent phenomenon, a by-product of technological unemployment; and symbiosis long preceded parasitism as the economic relation between the sexes. Therefore in response to Freud's question, "What do the women want?" the answer is they want to function as insiders. And when it is asked why they seek to crash a man's world, the answer is they are not trying to enter a man's world, they only wish to re-enter the world: there is no other.*
>
> Nancy Reeves

Public school teachers need to be informed on how attitudes, values, and beliefs related to sexism, that is, categorical discrimination because of one's sex, affect all Americans. Their understanding of sexist ideology just could help enable students to be active citizens of the world.

This chapter will consider sexism as the social expression of men's traditional discrimination against women. We do not mean that all men discriminate, nor that they are never discriminated against. But the chapter concerns one kind of sexism, the preponderant male American opinion: "I don't mind women if they keep in their place—and we will define their place." It also concerns women's opposition to this viewpoint in ways that affect both teachers and students.

Modern research in psychology, medicine, and anthropology are now affecting ideology about women. But even before this research appeared, some women, with the collaboration of some men, tried to change the ideology through the "Women's Movement."

Although women have made a few notable gains in legal equality, the right to an education, and very recently a few bread and butter issues, feminists are still working to repeal sexism and achieve humanist goals for both men and women.

THE IDEOLOGY OF "WOMAN'S PLACE"

How men and women relate depends on their ethnic background, social class, rural or urban orientation, age, religion, philosophy, and other obvious factors. But, people's thoughts about their roles are sufficiently similar throughout the United States that, allowing for exceptions, general statements seem dependable. This is possible because of our common history of attitudes, values, and beliefs extending far back in Western Civilization. Still, some of the historical background will seem preposterous to many modern Americans.

Traditional Ideological Pattern

Since ancient times, tribal taboos about women's biological makeup have affected women's privileges. Primitive peoples feared the supernatural forces connected with menstrual blood, so women were sequestered during their periods to avoid polluting the good spiritual forces of both people and nature. One African tribe even forbade all women to walk on the pastures, for fear the ground be affected and the cattle die.[1] Similar categorical logic lingered in protective legislation which has denied modern women access to various activities.

Greek Wisdom to Western Church Dogma

Greek philosophers have also influenced the ideology concerning women. Plato was pretty much a feminist in assessing the roles of men

[1] The general background of this subject is discussed in Sir James G. Frazer, The Golden Bough: A Study in Magic and Religion. New York: The Macmillan Company, 1951, pp. 12, 13, 260.

and women. In his *Republic* he asserts that "the woman is naturally fitted for sharing in all offices . . ." So he prescribes the same education for both.[2]

Aristotle disagreed because ". . . the male is by nature superior, and the female inferior; and the one rules, and the other is ruled . . . the inequality is permanent."[3] He believed that only men should be educated, a privilege extended to certain male slaves, but not women—who should obey. Although Aristotle was long regarded as the first scientific student of nature, most of his assertions about nature seem absurd in a modern light.

Still, Aristotle's ideas overshadowed Plato's, because St. Thomas Aquinas combined them with St. Augustine's mysticism in *Summa Theologiae*. Until recently this book was the foundation of Roman Catholic theology. Moreover, when the Protestant Reformation rejected certain Catholic tenets, they did not reject Aristotle's ideas about the inferiority of women and children or their role as objects to be used by adult males. Hence in Western Civilization the main Christian churches have propagated male dominance on no better evidence than Aristotle's "science."

No wonder colonial New England, begun as a theocracy, saw the adult white male ruling in an authoritarian manner. Slaves and women "did not exist officially under the law; both had few rights and little education; . . . both had to breed on command."[4]

Although married women fared better than widows and spinsters, they had no legal rights over money or property. New England Blue Laws subjected women to severe punishments, including wearing the scarlet letter for adultery, which with fornication was considered a primary offense.

Despite these implications about women's inferiority, men of the Middle Ages as well as Victorians considered women as morally superior. Nice girls who became respectable women, especially in the upper-middle and upper classes, accepted the responsibility of keeping public morality on a high level. People felt it was easier for women to be virtuous because they had no sexual desires.

The traditional ideology of woman's place appears to include only male definitions of what woman is, what her roles should be, and how her deviances should be handled. One basic premise looks suspiciously like:

---

[2] *The Republic of Plato,* trans. by H. Spens. London: J. M. Dent & Sons, Ltd., 1906, pp. 146–153. However, other quotations speculate on possible serious female weaknesses.

[3] *Aristotle's Politics,* trans. by Benjamin Jowett. New York: The Modern Library, 1943, pp. 58–59, 85.

[4] Andrew Sinclair, *The Better Half: The Emancipation of the American Woman.* New York: Harper & Row, Publishers, 1965, p. 4; paperback title, *The Emancipation of the American Woman,* 1965.

woman was made to be inferior, so man must make many of her personal and all her social decisions.

Contemporary Ideological Pattern

The ensuing sections will show present reflections of historic and church-related attitudes, values, and beliefs concerning the relative capabilities and proper roles of men and women, and ways in which U.S. culture has rejected or is in the process of rejecting traditional beliefs. Sometimes old-culture and new-culture views cannot be sharply delineated.

The following beliefs about men and women refer to capabilities and roles. *Capabilities* refer to *what is possible* for each sex, whether grounded on genetic factors, learning, or, more often, their interaction. References to "physical" and "mental" capabilities are convenient, but entail a false dichotomy. What is possible physically is so only because of the "right" psychology and what is possible psychologically is so only because of how neurons, glands, and other organs function. So the writer favors the term psychophysical, which implies the total organism and avoids the mind-body dualism. *Roles* refer to *what people do* because the culture expects it, because they rebel against expectations, or for any other reasons.

Some Popular Views on Psychophysical Capabilities

Discovering and accurately expressing what men and women think about their capacities and roles is anything but easy. Depth interviews are promising, but few have been conducted. Clinical reports are useful, if we remember that psychologists too have prejudices and that "expert" contradictions appear for almost every expert assertion on what the sexes think. Actual and reported conversations provide another source, as does studying the historical evolution of belief patterns (touched on in the preceding section). These varied sources have contributed to the following statements of beliefs and the treatment of the hypothesis through which we will look at this facet of U.S. culture and how it affects education.

Old-Culture Views on Physical Capabilities

—Menstrual cycles prevent women from being suitable as employees in men's occupations.
—Women have less sexual drive than men, so they should be able to remain virgins in order to be marriageable.

Old-Culture Views on Psychological Capabilities

—There have been few female geniuses because women are inferior intellectually.

—Women surpass men at intricate and meticulous tasks.
—Only women are satisfactory at "mothering."
—Woman's "wisdom" results from her better insight.

New-Culture Views on Physical Capabilities

—Muscle power may now be the least important kind of strength in comparing men and women.
—Both men and women have psychophysical cyclical behavioral problems.
—As men and women may have equal sexual drives, they should be equally entitled to sexual pleasure; consequently only sexual acts that inflict psychophysical harm should remain in the area of morality.

New-Culture Views on Psychological Capabilities

—Sex does not determine intellectual capacity.
—If men are interested in roles that require it, they can develop the delicate coordination required.
—"Mothering" can be done as well by men as by women.
—Special insights are no more the province of women than of men.

A Contemporary Sexist Ideological Pattern

Traditionally women have usually been seen through Aristotelian glasses as weaker, less sexual, unstable emotionally and ethically, and intellectually inferior. Except for small muscle coordination, insightfulness, and the "mothering" ability, man is superior. Such a collection of opinions is disturbing—not merely as contemporary stereotyping of a biological class of beings which carries over primitive and classical beliefs, but as examples of sexism, even (indeed especially) if accepted by women.

As the term "sexism" has yet to appear in major dictionaries, we will deduce a definition from "racism." Racism is an ideology maintaining that one's own group is inherently superior to others, an ethnocentric judging of other cultures by one's own. "It expresses an unwillingness or inability to see a common humanity, condition, and problem facing all men in all societies. . . ."[5] Sexism, then, we see as an ideology maintaining that one's sex is superior to the other, and an inability or unwillingness to see a common humanity, condition, and problem facing both sexes. With this definition, we can proceed to test a hypothesis about men and women.

AN OUTRAGEOUS HYPOTHESIS ABOUT WOMEN

So far, we have suggested how ideologies relating to men and women arose and what some current beliefs appear to be. Now we need to see whether

---

[5] George A. and Achilles G. Theodorson, Modern Dictionary of Sociology. New York: Thomas Y. Crowell Company, 1969; Apollo ed., 1970, p. 135.

parts of the ideology, particularly that to which the old culture clings, is demonstrably false. Relying on what scientific evidence we have, the new culture, to the extent that its ideology can be translated into testable assertions (i.e., hypotheses susceptible to factual verification), fares much better than the old. However, in many ways the new culture oversimplifies a number of issues.

Hypothesis: *Sexist ideology in the United States obscures the often superior capabilities of women and forces their retention of a parasitic dependence on men.*

The foregoing hypothesis requires some clarification before we begin to review data. Its main thrust is intended to be that, in spite of already enacted legislation, patriarchal sexism remains a major force supported not only by men but by hordes of Middle American women. Because many persons doubt that this is still true, our main task here is to present an array of facts pertinent to the actual extent of sexist discrimination. Is it still a major factor in American life, or not?

But notice that the hypothesis also suggests that women have a number of superior capabilities—superiorities compared to men in relation to certain clear-cut criteria which we will offer. That women do exhibit—or have the potential for exhibiting—psychophysical strengths which men lack is highly controversial and would probably be rejected by a majority of both men and women. Hard evidence on this subject is scarce but new psychological/medical knowledge has been accumulating in the past few years. As a secondary task we will review a few samples of such evidence and see where they seem to lead.

The Language of Equals?

In various ways people's language implies their attitudes. The very term *humanity*, to many, connotes a lesser status for women by deleting her from the accepted generic word covering both sexes. In addition, men have used a special kind of language as an aid to keeping women in their place.

Sexist Language

Since *man* and *men* are used to indicate humans generally, as well as males, much of our communication about people leaves out women entirely, either specifically or by implication. Burr, Dunn, and Farquhar believe the use of these "subsuming" masculine terms leads not only children but adults to have distorted concepts of our society. Also, references to women as

. . . wives (Mrs.), daughters (Miss), or mothers of males who are clearly identified by name and occupation . . . deliver the implicit message that in and of themselves females are of no particular interest or importance and reflect the assumption that marital status is *the* crucial fact of life for women.[6]

On the other hand, unqualified generic terms such as peasant and pioneer are seldom seen in captions for pictures of only women. Thus women are not allowed to represent people, while men are. The authors suggest dropping the term housewife because it implies attitudes that are "inconsistent with the ideal of equal educational and vocational opportunities." They also plead for using neutral occupational terms applicable to both sexes rather than words with the suffixes "ress," or "man."

Strainchamps pursues this complaint further by taking H. W. Fowler to task for advocating in *Modern English Usage* the word *female* to refer to women, while admitting that he considers it impolite and that they resent it (though men do not find the same discourtesy evident in *male*).[7] Fowler recommended increasing the words with feminine endings to include singeress, danceress, and teacheress.

What might be a definitive test for sexist language comes from the woman's caucus set up by the National Organization for Women in connection with the 1970 White House Conference on Children. In criticizing the wording of various reports, NOW objected to the use of "he" whenever "person" was meant:

We advocate you read every report, all literature, and all written material for the rest of your life in the following way: When person is the reference, simply substitute she and her for he, his, and him, and [we] guarantee you'll shortly worry about the exclusion of the male from thought and language, let alone the behavioral reality.[8]

Obscenity In assessing the influence of both Calvinism and the industrial revolution on words having to do with sexuality, Ludovici comes up with a theory about the entrenchment of beliefs concerning the use of obscenity as it relates to women. Briefly, Victorian capitalists believed workers reading pornography would rape upper-class women, so they tried to reserve "artistic" pornography for upper-class men. They also

[6] Elizabeth Burr, Susan Dunn, and Norma Farquhar. "The Semantics of Sexism," *Social Education*. December 1972, pp. 841–845.

[7] Ethel Strainchamps, "Our Sexist Language," in Vivian Gornick and Barbara K. Moran (eds.), *Woman in Sexist Society: Studies in Power and Powerlessness*. New York: Basic Books, Inc., Publishers, 1971, pp. 240–250.

[8] Carol Burris and Wilma Scott Heide, "Critique of Reports—White House Conference on Children: Cluster on Individuality, December 1970"; quoted in Judith Hole and Ellen Levine, *Rebirth of Feminism*. New York: Quadrangle Books, Inc., 1971, p. 314.

attached a neurotic significance to so-called obscene words expressing sexuality and promoted taboos concerning them.[9] Victorian society assumed both that nice women had no natural sexual desires, and that men's passions were roused by obscenities; therefore, to remain pure and innocent women should not hear obscenities any more than should the clergy. Hence the strict taboo against profane and obscene words before women. Naturally, the taboo also applied to women's using the words. But society expected men to use obscenities at least to a certain degree to properly fulfill the masculine role.

Apparently this view toward artistic pornography and lower-class obscenity is similar to Thio's argument that the powerful members of society define deviance in such a way as to portray their own acts as normal and acts of the powerless (women and lower-class men) as deviant.

Many young women see the hold men maintain over them by the language taboo. This may explain much of the seemingly pointless use of obscenities by college women protesters in the sixties with a frequency scarcely demanded by either communication or catharsis.

Although these taboos will doubtless remain within the old culture, the new culture not only permits but encourages single standard language. In addition, former legal bans against language labeled obscene or pornographic, for some of its meanings, may be on the verge of collapse due to a June 7, 1971 Supreme Court ruling (unless a backlash disregards it, or subsequent rulings confuse it). The ruling followed the conviction of a young man offensively appearing in a courthouse in a jacket printed with the phrase "F--- the draft." In the majority opinion, Justice Harlan dismissed the claim that the word might have "violated the sensibilities of women and children present," with the comment that "the state has no right to cleanse public debate to the point where it is grammatically palatable to the most squeamish among us. While the particular four-letter word being litigated here is perhaps more distasteful than most others of its genre, it is nevertheless often true that one man's vulgarity is another's lyric."[10]

It is conceivable that this Supreme Court decision may do more for women's rights than woman suffrage once its effect has percolated into the cultural mores. Its key point in relation to discrimination against women appears to be that as women should not and will not be protected by law against hearing four-letter words because of their so-called sensibilities, it should eventually be possible for them to enter occupations and social situations formerly denied them mainly because of the possibility of hearing "another's lyrics."

[9] L. J. Ludovici, *The Final Inequality: A Critical Assessment of Woman's Sexual Role in Society.* New York: W. W. Norton & Company, Inc., 1965, p. 137.
[10] UPI and AP releases of June 7 and 8, 1971.

Male and Female Intelligence

As suggested earlier in the chapter, one of the oldest folklore beliefs in Western Civilization perpetuated by Christian theologians is that in important areas of decision making women are less capable than men. It has been held not only that a woman's general intelligence tends to be lower, but that she has numerous "special weaknesses"—as in mathematics.

We now realize that intelligence is best defined not as a characteristic measured on an IQ test, but as the ability to adequately solve the kinds of problems one confronts in life. (See Chapter 10.) There is also abundant evidence that intelligence is not "fixed" in the case of any individual, but is subject to wide variations—of motivation, sensory acuity, certain kinds of health problems, the materials one has to work with, and so on.

There is no evidence at present that the human male and female differ in potential for intelligence as we have defined intelligence. Ausubel cites studies comparing the general intellectual capacity of males and females. "Until more definitive evidence is available, it is impossible to decide to what extent," he concludes, the variations between the test scores made by males and females "are attributable to such *genuine* determinants as genic (genetic) and relevant environmental factors on the one hand, and to purely extraneous considerations, on the other."[11] Ausubel is referring to studies described by Terman and Tyler using such general intelligence tests as the Revised Stanford Binet Scale and the Wechsler Intelligence Scale. Although these are the best tests we have, the present writer still questions how well such tests measure practical intelligence— that is, ability to apply imaginative solutions to real life problems. Probably our best evidence on comparative differences between the sexes comes from anthropologists' cultural studies; none report what they consider significant differences between men and women in solving the kinds of problems they must solve to maintain a viable culture.

Although the relationship betwen verbal ability and general functional intelligence remains hazy, every teacher knows (or should), that at least until the late teen years, on the average, girls' language skills exceed those of boys. It has now been pretty well established that the average superiority of women in language capability extends through the college years. Moreover, reports of recent research—too scattered and tentative to try to document—suggest that throughout life women may have verbal capabilities exceeding those of men. If so, although this may prove nothing about comparative functional intelligence, it is of major importance

[11] David P. Ausubel, *Educational Psychology: A Cognitive View*. New York: Holt, Rinehart and Winston, Inc., 1968, p. 242.

in assessing women's ability to perform in the creative arts, top managerial positions, and politics.

Ausubel does point out that both the tests and numerous other sources indicate that the rate of genetic feeblemindedness is markedly higher among boys, as is the proportion of geniuses. If we had no other information, this would leave us hanging: what does it prove to say we have fewer subnormal girls, but also fewer notably brilliant girls? Ausubel is correct, of course, in suggesting that when one studies a roster of historical figures regarded by consensus as geniuses, men outnumber women many times over.

The present writer compiled a list of eighty-two women, beginning in the ancient world, whom a majority of students of genius would put in this category; however, the number of men who have performed at a comparable level would number several hundred. In literate historical cultures, although one can list a few women geniuses, their achievements are mainly in the creative or performing arts rather than in science or mathematics. Even if evidence shows various cultural pressures to have prevented women from developing their potential, there is no evidence that the potential for genius is not as prevalent among women as among men. Matthew Besdine, a New York psychiatrist, sees the determining factor as "Jocasta" mothering—a peculiar nurturing relationship showing high degrees of emotion, time spent on and capacity for interacting with the child's cues.[12] While dedicated, or Jewish, mothering, produces extraordinary achievement, Besdine believes Jocasta mothering (by either parent) is needed to produce genius.

When we compare men and women with special talents, it immediately becomes obvious that in the Western world of the past century or so, the greatest number of women geniuses were novelists and poets; the second greatest number were musicians, particularly singers; and the third were actresses. Men have predominated in mathematics and science, medicine, politics, and philosophy. There are strong cultural pressures operating to prevent women from expressing themselves in these latter fields, though a few have done so. Contrariwise, even in male-dominated cultures, it is difficult to prevent a woman from distinguishing herself as a writer.

In assessing woman's potential for contributions at the genius level, we prefer evidence from anthropology over the Freudian-tinged studies of a psychiatrist such as Besdine. Through their field studies numerous anthropologists have found that in many tribal cultures which were not severely patriarchal women showed a capacity for both innovation and fine craftsmanship which equaled, and in some cases exceeded, that of

[12] Matthew Besdine, "Mrs. Oedipus Has Daughters, Too," *Psychology Today*, March 1971, pp. 62ff and 110 for his bibliography.

men in the same culture. Anthropologist Melville Jacobs is one of the more interesting writers on this subject.

After suggesting that artistry can be judged by two criteria—*craftsmanship*, or skill in performance, and *creativity*, or ability to make imaginative leaps from anything that has ever been done before—Jacobs selects as an illustration the extraordinary basketry of California's Pomo Indian women prior to the destruction of Pomo tribal culture. Basketry is an art form which permits both an exceptional degree of craftsmanship and as much creativity as the mind can imagine. It is an extraordinarily rich medium for artistic expression because of the variety of materials which can be used, the range of potential forms, and the possibility of great novelty. It may even be a richer medium than other arts we are familiar with. Jacobs describes the achievements of Pomo women in this field as follows:

> the frequency of innovators in this single form of expression . . . from which men were customarily excluded, may be unparalleled in any specialized craft or intellectual specialty in western civilization. It as as if 10 to 50 or more percent of the women, for example, in northern California's Pomo Indian groups were geniuses, if the term which Euro-Americans like to employ may be permitted to equate with valued innovators. No concentration of so-called geniuses, comparable to that found among Pomo basketmakers, seems to have been reported from another sociocultural system, *not even from the free citizens of Periclean Athens.*[13]

It seems impossible to defend the folklore notion that men are "brighter" or "more talented" than women; or that in areas of special talent there is any genetic reason why men should excel in some fields and women in others. Modern evidence seems to bolster Plato's view rather than Aristotle's.

Women and Sex

To many people the very fact that a woman's body is designed to bear children automatically makes her not only different but unequal to men. Nature's menstrual signal that she is not bearing a child has been regarded as shamefully unclean, literally and figuratively. Nature's shapely signal that she is bearing a child has been regarded as shameful outside of marriage. Even within marriage, the condition was to be controlled by patriarchal decrees about conditions of employment. And how she did or did

---

[13] Melville Jacobs, *Pattern in Cultural Anthropology.* Homewood, Ill.: The Dorsey Press, 1964, p. 301; italics added.

not get into that condition also tended to reinforce attitudes concerning a woman's unequal status.

Cyclical Psychophysical Problems

Most sexist explanations of menstruation have been written by men. The subject is not trivial; it is a leading ground for male arguments that women are unequal to the demands of innumerable occupations and recreations. Men have assumed that once a month women undergo a crisis which cripples their psychophysical functioning. Actually, menstrual effects vary from an inconvenience to depression and discomfort.

Perhaps most important to teachers is a general disregard of the probable roles of cultural factors. A girl's knowledge of physiology and attitudes toward her bodily functions may determine at puberty whether her menstruation will be free of distress. Her mother's and her peer group's attitudes can also be influential. Nor can one ignore the entire cultural milieu. An important factor is whether the community is dominated by religious fundamentalism emphasizing a dualism of body and soul—communities with negative attitudes toward normal bodily functions would be debilitating. Finally, there is the recent factor of varieties of the "pill"—some eliminate the cycle, others mitigate its effects.

Dr. Karen E. Paige, University of California, Davis, social psychologist, studied a group of women taking the pill to see if distress might not be a "social response to menstruation."[14] It appeared that if a pill reduced menstrual bleeding "the universal symbol of female inferiority," emotional distress was reduced. Overall it appeared that it was the *traditionally feminine* women who tended to be distressed. She concluded the problem should be seen in relation to woman's subordinate place and the ideology defining both behavior and emotions acceptable as feminine. "Menstruation, pregnancy and childbirth . . . are the woman's primary avenues of achievement and self-expression. Her reproductive abilities define her femininity; other routes to success are only second-best in this society." She also concluded that men used taboos about menstruation to assert their claims of superiority to women and their children.

The whole argument about cyclical psychophysical problems seems unreal if confined to women—as if males were never affected by their own "ups and downs." Males may well have cycles related to hormonal changes that produce depression and psychosomatic disorders. The fact is, not much reliable investigation appears to have been done of male rhythms, except to establish that most, if not all, males have them. There is an

[14] "Beyond the Raging Hormone: Women Learn To Sing the Menstrual Blues," *Psychology Today*, September 1973, pp. 41–45.

important point to be made in this connection: from what we know, male "ups-and-downs" are much harder to predict than the relatively dependable women's "lunar cycle." In many areas of performance, this would appear to give women a distinct advantage. Those women who do suffer considerable psychophysical distress during their periods can usually plan ahead to avoid tasks requiring top performance at that time. On the other hand, men may plan a crucial activity only to find that when the time comes they are too depressed or otherwise uncomfortable to function well.

Unequal Sexual Liberation

Though conservative fundamentalists disapprove, most people might now believe women have complete parity with men in sexual relations. Men are likely to claim that because women can use the pill, venereal disease can be cured; liaisons, including living together unmarried, are possible; and the stigma attached to premarital experience is disappearing except for conspicuously promiscuous women. Surely women cannot say that they are not liberated sexually.

But the conclusion is wrong. It begs the underlying question—the implication that because men are satisfied in heterosexual experience, women should feel equally "complete" and "fulfilled" (one goal of the women's liberation movement). However, in spite of a greater orgasm capability, a large majority of women apparently do not achieve orgasm through intercourse, nor even experience much sensual pleasure. (Studies conducted with scientifically approved methodology seem to support this assertion.)[15] These women may experience tension and psychosomatic disturbances because of lack of sexual expression without knowing why. At the present time, we assume this problem begins with adolescence.

Teenage sexuality: girls versus boys The old-culture expectation is that teenage boys will begin assuming a dominant, aggressive, male sexual role. Girls are expected to look and act seductive but resist advances.

As suggested, new-culture belief patterns have been more equalitarian. At least theoretically the new culture considers it acceptable for the girl to join in frank discussions, suggest a date, or initiate lovemaking. For persons interested in abolishing double standards and achieving male-female sexual parity, this sounds helpful. The trouble is that what was said about women and sexual liberation applies during the teen years.

A girl's first heterosexual experience is fairly likely to be unpleasant

[15] One such study is Edmund Bergler and William S. Kroger, *Kinsey's Myth of Female Sexuality: The Medical Facts.* New York: Grune & Stratton, Inc., 1954.

rather than pleasant. There is little evidence that teenage boys in the United States know much about lovemaking that is likely to satisfy a girl physically and psychologically. If the girl is left feeling happy, it may be because she feels she has been kind or because the boy made her feel wanted. This reward is especially important for girls who have felt unloved by their parents. But this may be offset by a hunch that she has been "used," that she is an object, not a person.

Adult sexuality: woman versus man   Probably traditional inegalitarian views color the sex lives of most adults. The dominant man still feels that he has the right to use the body of his wife or companion on demand. Women do not formulate any rules of the game, yet they are often expected to countermand nature's rules. Though men may recognize this, many resent it and blame the woman both for cyclical interest and the interference of menstruation.

Another game some men use to dominate women is to make the woman wholly responsible for contraception, and then to be enraged at her for accidental pregnancy. Still, it was a male Supreme Court that ruled on the unconstitutionality of state abortion laws that provided another step toward making concrete the abstract idea of women determining how their bodies were to be used.

Sexual Capabilities

As suggested in the section on ideology, the old culture did not usually regard women as having sexual capabilities equal to men. Rather, they believed men desire sexual pleasure frequently and are able to achieve it; children do not enjoy sex at all; women enjoy sex only through the satisfaction accompanying giving pleasure to the man they love. In addition, they considered women who enjoyed sex abnormal; and implied that this deviation led women to become immoral.

In contrast, the ideology of the new culture is virtually the opposite; a woman who does not enjoy sex is considered either abnormal or the victim of inept lovemaking. Men of the new culture have accepted as part of their ideology concerning women the idea that women have the "right" to enjoy sex as frequently and as thoroughly as men; hence the modern man feels a responsibility to be a good lover.

Reasons for such divergent views on the psychophysical aspects of sex depend on some central facts. There is much evidence to support and apparently none to negate the notions that both males and females vary in their appetites and capacities for sexual release, but that typical, or "normal," males and females have approximately equal sexual needs.

The issue here is that female frigidity or partial frigidity still remains a problem in our culture. Women who cannot perform sexually feel guilty; men who feel inadequate in relation to these women also feel guilty. However, Masters and Johnson's findings have made possible, for all who wish it, full female sexual parity with males.

Unfortunately, the Freudian "myth of the vaginal orgasm" can afflict members of the liberal new-culture as well as their elders. As we now know, a "neurological imperative" seems to dictate that females achieve orgasm only through the nerves centered in the clitoris, so probably for the first time in human history we have information somewhat guaranteeing a means for females to avoid frigidity and males to avoid the guilt of inadequacy. This new knowledge should help dispel some mythology about the inequality of the sexes.

Further, contemporary facts should dispel myths and hangups about masturbation and place it in perspective. The old culture considered this practice at best childish or degrading, if not seriously damaging. Now it can be considered normal and in many circumstances a healthful means of keeping the sexual tensions of either sex from becoming uncomfortably distracting.

Grossman brings out another infrequently mentioned point about women's sexual liberation.[16] He sees part of women's anguish on the subject being caused by the preoccupation beginning in the 1960s with female orgasm. "What is new with us is the religious conviction that it must happen every time, or else something is wrong—someone is sabotaging the democracy of sex." His implication is that women might be better off in their relationships to forget equality of response and leave the "inevitable" performance to men.

WOMEN IN THE POWER STRUCTURE

Women in the past have been allowed some direct power in certain family roles and indirect power as appendages to men. Few have exerted much decisive power in their own right.

Much literature of the women's movements has concerned how women shall share in power—seen as the "ability of an individual or group to carry out its wishes or policies, and to control, manipulate, or influence the behavior of others, whether they wish to cooperate or not."[17] The resources to force decisions on others sometimes stem from one's social relationships and social position.

[16] Edward Grossman, "In Pursuit of the American Woman," *Harper's Magazine*, February 1970, pp. 47–69.
[17] Theodorson and Theodorson, *Modern Dictionary of Sociology*, pp. 307ff.

How much indirect power women exert through influencing the decisions of men in power positions we do not know. The hope that the influence will be unseen and supportive turns up in the stereotype, "behind every successful man is a woman."

Women's Representation in Governmental Power

The literature of the Women's Movement has been interested in women not merely as appendages to men. One inquirer is Kirsten Amundsen, a professor of government. Believing that "there is a politically significant relationship between the proportion of representative positions a group can claim for itself and the degree to which the needs and interests of that group are articulated and acted upon in political institutions," she reviewed the history of women in government offices and positions.[18] Checking the numbers of women members of Congress against women citizens, she found they had only 4 percent of the proportional representation due them as a group in the House; 2 percent in the Senate in 1970.

In contrast "black citizens have by now achieved 30 percent of the representatives they are entitled to in the House and 10 percent in the Senate."[19] The systematic hierarchy of social positions suggested seems to be: white males, black males, white women, black women. (This ranking will show up later as we look at women's earnings.)

Over the years, of ten women members of the Senate, only five have been elected; seven served less than one year. Only twenty-two Congresswomen held office long enough to obtain influential committee assignments having bona fide power. In the federal civil service in 1968, of all women employed only 0.02 were in grades where decision making occurred.[20] Amundsen concludes "In terms of formal political power, in terms of their proportionate share of representation on decision-making levels in federal, state, and local governments, . . .[the presumed] power of the American woman turns out to be a myth. . . ."[21]

Women have gained some since this 1971 study showed that two women had been appointed cabinet members, three governors, seventy-five appointed or elected to Congress. Tentative returns on the 1974 elections show no senators, but new representatives make their total seventeen or eighteen (under the 1962 record, but over last year). Nationwide elected women increased by 27 percent. Firsts for women included a mayor in a city of over a half million, a state Supreme Court chief justice, and an elected governor.

[18] Kirsten Amundsen, *The Silenced Majority: Women and American Democracy.* Englewood Cliffs, N.J.: Prentice-Hall, Inc., 1971, p. 66.

[19] Amundsen, p. 68.

[20] Amundsen, p. 70.

[21] Amundsen, p. 80.

Have women been equally represented among lawyers and judges who affect lawmaking and interpretations of power? In the United States only about 3.5 percent of attorneys and 1 to 2 percent of judges are women.

Although the situation could change, during and since the investigation of the Watergate scandals various writers on politics have pointed out that, among women who have achieved high position in government, few if any have been tainted by charges of corruption. We are not suggesting that women are innately more honest than men (after all, they greatly exceed men in amount of shoplifting), but rather that cultural pressures bear rather heavily on high-status women to be more honest in responsible positions than men. As pointed out elsewhere, the male machismo syndrome seems to lead a disproportionate number of men to act aggressively and this aggressive impulse often takes the form of crime.

Women in Nongovernmental Power Positions

Of course, politicians, attorneys, and judges are not the only persons who make powerful legal decisions. If we think of rules that have the effect of governing people's behavior, such as de facto laws, then the major corporations probably do more "legislating" than the national, state, and local governments combined. In addition to many enacted laws being dictated by major corporations, the rules of large business firms bind people even more decisively than statutes. If women were an influential force in making such corporate decisions, then we could indeed say that women wielded great power in this country. But they do not. With some regularity women get on corporate boards of directors. Occasionally we hear of a woman president of a relatively minor corporation. But Dr. Margaret Hennig's research had to cover both Canada and the United States to come up with one hundred woman corporate presidents and senior vice-presidents of firms having gross sales in excess of $10 million.[22]

Despite token representatives in many fields, we can hardly consider that women are treated as equals in being chosen as members of the power structure. They have the potential, but they have not made it yet.

Women in the World of Work

The proportion of women of all ages in the United States who work outside their homes for pay is steadily increasing. By 1970 over 40 percent of all women were gainfully employed or only temporarily employed—up from 27.4 in 1940. Many writers anticipate that if present trends continue,

---

[22] Margaret Hennig, *Career Development for Women Executives*, doctoral dissertation. Cambridge, Mass., Harvard Business School, 1971.

50 percent or more of American women will be members of the labor force within a decade. Increasingly, married women enter the labor force: from only 16.7 percent in 1940, this figure had risen to 40.4 percent in 1969.[23]

Although women have achieved the right to work for pay outside the home, the quality of their jobs is perhaps more significant than the number. Most of the jobs they obtain do not require a high level of educational attainment, creativity, leadership, or organizing ability. Despite the increase in the proportion of women in white-collar jobs (from 50.4 percent of women workers in 1950 to 61 percent in 1972), their jobs are usually among the lowest paid, least prestigious, most routine, and least creative kinds.

Women raise houses, too. *(Copyright © George Ballis, all rights reserved)*

In percentage gain over 1950 women *seem* to have done best in the "professional and technical" category. However, Women's Bureau statistics indicate this gain represents the entry of women into the lowest paid, least desirable jobs classified as professional and technical. The gain for men is primarily into the most desirable jobs.

Women's gains as "craftsmen and foremen" were in traditional women's work, such as sewing. (In clothing factories "seamstresses" are

[23] Unless otherwise noted, all figures in this section are from tables in the *Statistical Abstract of the United States.* Washington, D.C.: U.S. Bureau of, the Census, 1964 and 1972. Net and percentage gains must be considered as approximations because of undefined occupation category shifts.

usually women, "foremen" may be mostly men.) These "women's crafts" may be very poorly paid, while male craft jobs may require no more skill but pay $5 to $10 per hour. To what extent have women moved into jobs at this level? Four times more women than men have gone into factory work, and twenty-five times more into non-farm labor.

Other sources of labor statistics emphasize the comparative earnings of women. The evaluative title of a Women's Bureau shows its sympathetic approach. In *The Underutilization of Women Workers*, statistics report *women are more disadvantaged occupationally than they were twenty years ago.*[24]

Striking contrasts are seen in a report from a President's task force. Table 11-1 gives rankings similar to those seen in governmental positions and political offices.

Table 11-1
MEDIAN EARNINGS FOR FULL-TIME WORKERS
EMPLOYED YEAR ROUND

	1969[a]		1968[b]
White men	$7,396		
Negro men	4,777	All men	$7,664
White women	4,279		
Negro women	3,194	All women	4,457

   [a] *A Matter of Simple Justice,* The Report of the President's Task Force on Women's Rights and Responsibilities, April, 1970, p. 18.
   [b] *Underutilization of Women,* p. 7.

If white and Negro men's wages and women's wages are averaged, then the averaged women's wages were still, in 1970, 61 percent of the averaged men's wages. Negro women earned an average of 66 percent of Negro men's wages. *But white women only earned 57 percent of white men's wages.*

Figure 11-1 reveals proportional changes in numbers of men and women having professional and technical jobs. The figures are derived from *Underutilization of Women.* The figures show how the proportion of women in professional and technical jobs has declined. Adding injury to the insulting decline is the fact that the educational level of women has increased steadily during this century. Of women with five or more years of college, 7 percent are working in low-skilled, relatively menial occupa-

[24] Women's Bureau, *The Underutilization of Women Workers,* rev. report. Washington, D.C.: U.S. Department of Labor, 1971.

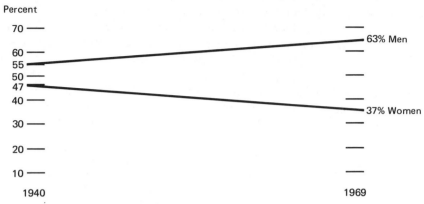

FIGURE 11-1.   Comparative changes in the proportion of men
and women workers in professional and technical
jobs between 1940 and 1969. (Percent of all people
in professional and technical jobs.)

tions. Of those with four years of college, 19 percent are in occupations of
this type. And of those with from one to three years of college, 69 percent
are in low-skilled, low-paid jobs![25]

Although these figures are not current, there is no evidence as of
this writing that the situation has changed significantly. If the nation experiences economic recession, in spite of antidiscrimination laws, it is very
likely that women will suffer more than men economically.

Equal Working Rights Benefit All

The chief gains in women's employment have been equality with
men with respect to safety standards, hours of work, and overall working
conditions in similar occupations. In spite of the Federal Equal Pay Act of
1963 and Title VII of the Federal Civil Rights Act of 1964 (which outlaws
job discrimination based on sex), major problems remaining for women are
barriers to equal occupational education, entry into numerous occupations
for which women are as well or better suited than men, promotion and
recognition of achievement, and inferior pay for equal work.

The 1963 and 1964 acts simply have not been universally complied
with, nor do they cover all workers in all jobs. Although many women
have benefited from the acts, the fact that suits are still being filed to obtain
their benefits shows the need for them, and very likely also for the Equal
Rights Amendment, which would supersede outdated, discriminatory state
laws on women's legal status nationwide. For a view of the goals and

[25] *Underutilization of Women*, p. 16.

complexity of the subject see Leo Kanowitz.[26] As he shows in excerpts from speeches made at hearings on the Equal Rights Amendment, apparently the desired effect of rescinding the so-called protective restrictions on their employment is not to give women themselves an advantage, but to better working conditions for both sexes. Equal rights work both ways and men increasingly enter jobs formerly devoted mainly to women. Women have broadened their areas of competition, but beyond these legal gains lie the specters of social attitudes working against women.

Patriarchy Still At Work

So far, we have reviewed several kinds of discrimination still afflicting women and incidental to this a few important ways in which women may have the advantages over men. This section is intended to illustrate points of view hostile toward reducing male-female role differentiation, views hostile toward the whole feminist movement.

We now present the gist of a book by a woman and one by a man. These particular books were selected because their emotionalism, conservatism, and the religious orientation of the first would be expected to appeal widely to semi-educated Middle Americans. The two books utilize quite different arguments, but each is intended as a major attack on the very idea of sexual equality. Both are on the side of parasitism.

Patriarchy in the Emotional Realm[27]

Andelin's goal is to teach every woman to be "The Ideal Woman" from a man's point of view. The ideal is named "Angela Human." Her angelic qualities include having inner happiness and a "worthy character" and being a "Domestic Goddess." Her human side is feminine, radiantly happy, and has "childlikeness."

Up to now for all time, Andelin says, man's role has been recognized as the provider, woman's as the childbearer—according to their commandments, their duties were set. Hence, among her six rules relating to his superiority in his role are: ". . . do not excel him in anything which requires masculine strength or ability, demonstrate your dependency if

[26] Leo Kanowitz, *Sex Roles in Law and Society*. Albuquerque: University of New Mexico Press, 1973. See also "The Geography of Inequality: Women's Rights in 50 States," *McCall's*, February 1971, pp. 90–95; and the *Women's Rights Almanac*, 1974. Bethesda, Maryland: Elizabeth Cady Stanton Publishing Company, 1973.

[27] Helen B. Andelin, *Fascinating Womanhood*. 16th printing. Santa Barbara, Calif.: Pacific Press, 1970. See also her *The Fascinating Girl*. Santa Barbara, Calif.: Pacific Press, 1970.

you are called upon to take masculine responsibility; have a girlish trust in him. . . ."[28]

"The Lord assigned you this responsibility (to be the Domestic Goddess) . . ." "To be a successful mother is greater than to be a successful opera singer, or writer or artist. One is universal and eternal greatness and the other merely phenomenal." Women who have *not* achieved Domestic Goddess status (the role of the mature woman), are self-centered, are not following God's sense of order, and lack character; so among Andelin's Angelic admonishments are: "Earn a place on a pedestal by building a noble character." "Revere your husband and honor his right to rule you and his children." "Don't stand in the way of his decisions, or his law." "Don't have a lot of pre-conceived ideas of what you want out of life."[29]

On the human side Andelin includes these rules: "Don't increase the family income by working." "Don't be efficient in men's affairs, such as leadership, making major decisions, providing a living, (etc.)." "Learn to express yourself when your husband mistreats you by childlike sauciness." "Develop feminine dependency." And, finally, "don't act, look, or think like men."[30]

Mrs. Andelin dropped out of a home economics college major to marry another Mormon student, have eight children, and finally to speak out against women's liberation through revising some booklets of the 1920s into her accolade for the silent majority staying in the home.[31] Through the Fascinating Womanhood Foundation, she promotes church-sponsored courses which in the 1970s are still proclaiming this message in widespread areas. One advertisement in a church section listed the men's course as covering "Man of Steel & Velvet," while the topic of the last women's lecture was "Finding Freedom Through Submission."[32]

Patriarchy in the Realm of Thought and Action

The second approach to faulting women in man's world of work is seen in the writing of Steven Goldberg. He upholds the traditional belief that women's place is the home and explains it with his "theory of limits": "The three institutions of patriarchy, male dominance, and male attainment of high-status suprafamilial roles and positions are universal, possibly manifestations of biological sexual differentiation."[33]

---

[28] Andelin, p. 116.

[29] Andelin, pp. 146–148.

[30] Andelin, p. 219.

[31] "Womanhood Is In the Home," *The Fresno Bee*, October 18, 1970.

[32] *The Fresno Bee*, September 22, 1973, A5. Two church advertisements including the phrase "Proclaiming the FOURSQUARE Gospel."

[33] Steven Goldberg, *The Inevitability of Patriarchy*, New York: William Morrow and Company, Inc., 1973, p. 73.

Patriarchy is an organized system (including politics and economics) in which males exhibit, and have the majority of positions connected with, authority and leadership. Male dominance is the term used for such characteristics within the family. Both, Goldberg says, are inevitable.

In discussing roles, he refers to Margaret Mead's finding that societies give high status to occupations considered appropriate for men; ". . . when the same occupations are performed by women they are regarded as less important." Men fill both most roles in high-status areas and the high-status roles in low-status areas. Goldberg's thesis is that there is a male "hormonal factor [testosterone] which gives males a greater capacity for aggression . . . [which] can be invoked in any area for which it will lead to success."[34] This accounts for their leadership and authority.

Goldberg believes that socialization should be geared to this biological reality. If girls had innate aggressive tendencies and were not socialized away from competition, in political and economic areas (where aggressiveness means success), girls would develop their masculine abilities and their adult self-images would be "based not on suceeding in areas for which biology has left them better prepared than men, but on competitions that most women could not win. . . ."[35] Women would have to act as aggressively as men. But this will not happen, says Goldberg, because both men and women will prevent values developing which ignore biological differences and ". . . because even if such values could develop, they would make life intolerable for the vast majority of males."[36]

Society's universal view of women is based on an observable lack of aggression in women. "All that is inevitable on a suprafamilial level is that biology requires that certain aggressive roles be associated with the male and that the leadership and high-status roles for which the woman is not biologically better equipped [than the man] be attained by men."[37] Since women do have aggression, they must therefore be socialized away from using it to achieve their ends.

Goldberg waxes wroth about feminists railing against inevitable patriarchy and male dominance and their disregarding what he sees as the universal feelings of both men and women that support them. " . . . the emotional manifestations of our biologies and the emotional prerequisites of political power . . . prescribe the limits of sexual roles and social possibilities. As long as societies are composed of human beings these feelings will be inevitable. To judge them is not merely stupid, it is blasphemous."[38]

Goldberg feels that women have great power in their role of caring for society's emotional resources, and gathers that the majority of women

[34] Goldberg, p. 45.
[35] Goldberg, p. 109.
[36] Goldberg, p. 109.
[37] Goldberg, p. 117.
[38] Goldberg, p. 227.

join him in not imagining why any woman would want to destroy her own nature by accepting the male's concept that power concerns actions, not feelings.

Women are seen as having greater duties than action. They are to provide "gentleness, kindness, and love, refuge from a world of pain and force, and safety from [men's] excesses."[39] In return they will be aided by the male motivation of wishing to protect women and children. If the feminist "wishes to sacrifice all this, all that she will get in return is the right to meet men on male terms. She will lose."[40]

The above quotations give Goldberg's overall view. He also makes scattered comments on women's working. Various women's legal rights are not relevant to his book because they do not bear on patriarchy.

Goldberg believes laws which differentiate between the sexes do not cause the difference between the numbers of men and women having positions of power. Nor does he see such laws as the primary focus of feminist literature.

"Biology can never justify refusing any particular woman any option, but it does explain universal sexual differences in behavior and institutions. . . ."[41] To women who "strive for equal pay for equal work . . . the question of patriarchy and dominance is unimportant. . . ."[42] But even though he finds economic discrimination abhorrent, Goldberg believes men are going to win, not because they are trying to oppress women, or discriminate against them economically or educationally, but because they have the hormonal aggressive advantage which both men and women feel is their due. Women will lose.

Conclusions about the Hypothesis

We have found that the language patterns still generally present among English-speaking people strongly support patriarchal sexism. We have found that although, as matter of fact, there are no demonstrable differences in intelligence between the sexes, many men and women fault women's intelligence in such areas as mathematics, science, mechanical ability, and decision making. Some of the denigration of women's intellect was presented in the section on ideology preceding the hypothesis. Some may be easily inferred from specific patterns of discrimination in schools and the world of work.

In the area of sex, we found that men, and many women, continue to defend many discriminatory practices on the basis of woman's biology,

---

[39] Goldberg, p. 234.
[40] Goldberg, p. 234.
[41] Goldberg, p. 116.
[42] Goldberg, p. 116.

as shown in her alleged incapacitation during menstruation and her career interruptions caused by pregnancy. It can be argued persuasively that both these factors have been greatly exaggerated as reasons why women should not enjoy equality to men in all areas of life. A related issue, which we did not develop, has to do with women's *overall* psychophysical toughness. We will discuss this later in the present section.

We showed that women still have an uphill road in politics, government and business employment, and the world of work generally. Thus, we find that women are highly disadvantaged in the nation's power structure—a fact which produces a kind of vicious circle: women can't get much power without having it first.

Finally, we presented some more-or-less typical arguments advanced by antifeminists—arguments which not only seem to be widely accepted by Middle American men and women but which, as of the mid-seventies, may be gaining strength.

We can only conclude that there not only remains a potent sexist ideology in this country but that millions of women who might have much to offer the culture continue a parasitical existence. This conclusion is hardly news: we presume that every educated adult except Norman Mailer already knows it. Where people disagree is on *whether* it should be so—not *if* it is so.

As stated the hypothesis includes another issue when it includes the words "superior capabilities of women." Given time and space, we could have devoted an entire chapter to this theme. It was mentioned that women appear to have greater verbal capabilities than men and that up to this time at least women seem remarkably resistant to corruption when hold political office or other positions of high responsibility.

But there is another issue which readers may want to pick up on their own and explore. On the basis of considerable data in this writer's possession, we can hypothesize that women do have a kind of general psychophysical strength, stamina, or toughness which men in American culture lack. We are not prepared to suggest whether this is physiologically innate or a product of cultural forces. More likely, to the extent that this toughness may exist, it is an outcome of the interaction of biology and culture. We will list several facts and a few hypotheses which so far command significant support, and let readers carry on from there.

—In the United States, and in most, although not all, other industrial countries for which we have data, women live longer than men. In this country, the differential is about seven and a half years. Further, the death rate of males is higher at every age from the fetal stage on.
—Women appear to be more resistant to most kinds of serious disease; further, they appear able to withstand physical deprivation better than

males (in general, women seem to survive hunger, thirst, cold, heat, and pain better than men).

—What women lack in "brute strength" they seem able to compensate for by greater stamina.

—There has appeared in the seventies a "new breed" of woman athlete. This group is setting new women's world records in the demanding sports at a faster rate than male athletes are breaking male records. In some sports, it appears we are nearing the time when men and women will be competing against each other.

—Where aggressive behavior is desirable, women seem to be demonstrating both ability and taste for it—as in politics.

—Conversely, where aggression serves no useful purpose, women seem able to adopt attitudes leading to peaceful behavior, including nonviolent resolution of conflict, more easily than men.

This writer suggests that probably the best working hypothesis for now is that excepting their reproductive specializations, men and women can do anything equally well, that one should at least be open to the idea that women may have superiorities that will be of critical value in the world ahead, and finally that these superiorities cannot be fully utilized if women are parasites.

SEXIST EDUCATION AND ITS ALTERNATIVES

Past and present informal and formal education have traditionally shown sexist characteristics. After pointing these out, we will propose some alternative ways of educating the young to reduce or eliminate the sexist emphasis. A number of pressures on the young promote the virtue of the old-fashioned, tried-and-true sex roles. They begin in the home.

Sexist Education in the Home

Parents committed to traditional sex roles not only serve as models for their children, but may either urge or force their children to conform to the roles they see as good and true—the active father earning a living outside the home and the more passive mother centering her activities around housework. Conforming begins early. Even infants are treated according to their sex.

After early infancy, toys acquire a sexist specialization. Starting with mother-in-the-home toys, girls are given dolls including those that can wet, so they can practice baby rearing by the time they are three. Doll clothes make girls conscious of the meaning of "feminine attire." Ordinary dolls (except for miniature adult dolls for older girls) are made without sexually identifying features. This sexlessness of dolls, exemplify-

Dick and Jane forever?

ing old-fashioned Puritan ideas that children should be kept innocent about sex until the age of 21, very likely plays a highly negative function in later female development. Asexual dolls are apparently assumed to arouse less curiosity and desire to experiment, and thus help to keep girls innocent regarding sex. That this may end up producing sexually maladjusted adult women bothers only the most enlightened parents.

The next category of homemaker toys for girls includes household appliances, utensils, and table service to teach a game known as "how to cook and feed guests." Other essential games are "how to clean house," and "how to decorate yourself and home." So far, the toy industry has not introduced a line of juvenile games which would teach little girls the game of "how to relate to a husband" (only adult versions as yet).

What about toys for boys? Those who want dolls (as many do), are discouraged. They learn that big little boys do not play with the same things that little girls play with. Boys are given balls, building toys, transportation toys, wrecking toys, and war toys—soldiers, guns (all potent masculine symbols), and military hardware from tanks to ICBMs. (So far, no manufacturers have been permitted to market toy Napalm.)

Sexual differences in emotional expression are stressed by parents in rearing girls and boys. It is all right for girls to cry. On the contrary, little boys are "shamed" and told that men don't cry. The stiff-upper-lip injunction comes early for boys. By the time a boy is five or six and involved with neighborhood playmates, the chances are strong that father has taught him "to take nothing off anyone." When arguments come up boys do not quietly retire. (We can visualize millions of fathers kneeling to exchange punches with their small sons.) That fathers do commonly teach boys about fighting to win, whatever the means, is too well known among students of child rearing to require documentation.

Dr. Willard Gaylin, a researcher in sex role identification sees this stereotyping as destructive in our society. Tying "strength and success, performance and action, to maleness, and weakness and passivity—even failure—to femaleness" makes both sexes suffer in adulthood as well as in childhood.[43]

Sexist Education Within the Peer Group

By the time children are able to walk with reasonable dexterity, they enter playgroups where much parental sexist teaching is reinforced by their age peers. Little girls may want to play ball and climb trees, a practice parents usually discourage, but if they are teased for doing so by their age peers, they take the injunction more seriously. Girls are traditionally supposed to play quiet "ladylike" games: hopscotch, skipping rope, jacks, croquet, etc. But little boys are supposed to play "mannish" games: building roads for their toy trucks, playing baseball, football, and "shooting baskets," and playing toy war games. Little boys are also encouraged to play with toy airplanes, including the shatteringly noisy models with real gasoline motors. Girls' conditioned lack of mechanical aptitude limits them to sewing doll clothes, crocheting, or knitting.

It would be inaccurate to say that all children's games demand very specific sexual roles, but even when they are permitted to do the same things, sexist distinctions remain. Long after most girls were allowed to play in jeans rather than dresses (a breakthrough in itself), girl's bicycles continued to allow for skirts by having no horizontal brace on the frame. Woe betide the girl caught riding a boy's bike ("that's unladylike") or a boy riding a girl's bike ("only sissies do that").

Sexist Education in Kindergarten and Primary Grades

Schooling from kindergarten through university graduate school has historically had a strong sexist emphasis which is only now being ques-

[43] Quoted in Ann Eliasberg, "Are You Harming Your Son Without Knowing it?" *Family Circle*, April 1972, pp. 44, 114–116.

tioned. In kindergarten, the school does little more than reinforce the teaching of parents and peer group about proper roles. Status also comes into play: if a child is to be designated for some kind of special responsibility (like toy caretaker or aquarium supervisor), the child selected is usually a boy (even at the age of five, it has been thought that boys could "manage things" better than girls).

In the primary grades teachers continue to stress sexist roles. Teachers expect litle boys to fight on the playground—but not little girls. They expect little boys to use naughty words, although duty requires teachers to castigate them for it. But if a little girl uses naughty words, teachers show deep trauma—a state of agitation that can hardly be lost on either boys or girls. So, like parents, teachers foster the idea of protecting girls from sin; but tolerating it, even if not gracefully, among boys who, according to cultural mandate, will all have to go through stages of vulgarity in order to develop properly.

Teaching materials used in the primary grades have been notoriously sexist. The decreasingly popular "Dick and Jane" readers portrayed girls at girls' play and boys at boys' play, girls helping their mothers be housewives and boys helping their fathers repair things. It was not until the early seventies that numerous magazine articles began to appear pointing out just how sexist teaching materials are. Ms. and other women's movement magazines have played an important role in exposing the sexism of teaching materials, but even the journals in education have recently published some articles on this subject.

Sexist Education from Middle Elementary to Twelfth Grade

By junior high school, the sexist orientation of education has been glaring. The curriculum began to split, with girls encouraged or required to take home economics and boys strongly discouraged from taking the course, if not outrightly denied the right to do so. Boys were encouraged or required to take a course or two in "shop."

The athletic program too was split according to traditional cultural sex roles. Boys went out for baseball, football, basketball, or track. Girls took up volley ball, softball, tennis, or archery. However, in view of the likely enforcement of federal legislation mandating nondiscrimination in schools receiving federal grants, this situation may change radically in the future.

The part of the physical education program which may have the deepest psychological effect on students, however, is the common use of "gang showers" for boys where they get used to seeing each other nude, and stall showers for girls so their sensibilities will not be offended by having to be seen nude by other girls. This inconsistent practice may have much to do with lack of normal sexual adjustment later. Along with this, women physical education teachers are often notably prudish and ignorant about sex, whereas men physical education teachers are more inclined to be earthy and "one of the boys."

School courses which both boys and girls are required to take emphasize the difference between males and females, with most of the kudos going to males. In history courses, students learn that all the great achievers were males. (Since the resurgence of the Women's Movement, and courses in women's studies, continuing efforts are being made to show great female achievers in American history courses and textbooks.)[44] In English courses, students rarely study women writers. Girls are taught, by implication if not directly, that "females can't do math or physical science." Conversely, boys are usually taught directly or indirectly that they can't learn sewing, cooking, typewriting, shorthand, or other subjects reserved primarily for girls.

At the high school level, schools have another way of teaching each sex its place through grooming and dress codes. Although many urban high schools have all but abandoned dress codes, many suburban and most rural high schools still retain them. The chief function of the dress codes has been to teach the young that it is highly improper, even immoral, for girls to dress like boys and boys to dress like girls. The most obvious effects are to deny girls the right to wear jeans or other male-type clothing, and to deny boys the right to wear long hair, beads, and earrings.

In addition to a steady diet of sexist teaching in formal courses and on the athletic fields, students can hardly fail to be impressed by the judgment of school boards of which sex is competent in school management. Although over 40 percent of all professional women are teachers, and in secondary schools 47 percent of teachers are women, only 5 percent of women were school principals in 1969, and there is no reason to suppose the situation has changed significantly since then. Further, of the 13,000 district superintendencies in the United States, only two were then held by women.[45]

Sexism in College and Professional Schools

Some of the same sexist patterns persist in higher education. Women are counseled into "women's jobs" (teaching and secretarial work are popular). Men are counseled into "higher professions"—law, medicine,

[44] Sheila Tobian, "Finding Women's History," *Ms.*, November 1972, pp. 49–50.

[45] Judith Hole and Ellen Levine, *Rebirth of Feminism*. Chicago: Quadrangle Books, Inc., 1971, p. 317.

business management. Few girls major in mathematics or the physical sciences; few men major in home economics or related subjects.

An old platitude, containing a great deal if not complete truth, says that for a woman to be admitted as part of the female quotas to medical or law school she has to be twice as good as the average man admitted.

Sexist hiring and promotion practices in higher education is no more likely to be lost on college and university students than it is on secondary students. Of college and university teachers holding the rank of full professor, only 9.4 percent are women. In the case of men with doctorates and twenty years experience in higher education, 90 percent are full professors; of women with identical qualifications, scarcely half are full professors.[46] This lesson is especially not likely to be lost on women who may aspire toward a career in higher education.

Conclusions about Sexism and Education

The issues of sexism and education seem simply and polemically stated to be: Have Women minds? If they have, are they capable of any thoughts unconnected with motherhood? By what authority shall they be allowed to use either their minds or bodies, and for what purposes? Must their sexual anatomy determine how their minds be allowed to function? Shall they be allowed any participation in decisions affecting their use of their minds or bodies? How much exploitation of women's bodies will society allow for the purposes of shoring up the sales of cosmetics, automobiles, clothing, or titillating entertainment; or likewise for the purpose of shoring up (through bartering in marriage) men's physical comfort by service, both domestic and sexual? How much exploitation of women's minds will society allow for the purpose of reinforcing age-old paternalistic authoritarianism (accepted, granted, by centuries of docile women), to the continued waste of their potential accomplishments?

Is U.S. education to continue to train children to expect this exploitation through stereotyped assignments of status by sex and unquestioned roles for men and women, and the fundamentalist belief that symbolically and actually woman's greatest role is to bear a man-child?

Setting these questions as some of the basic issues of education does not denigrate the obvious facts. Education can point out that: Girls the same as boys are required to attend school up to a certain age; women as well as men are allowed to pursue higher education; women are increasingly permitted to engage in occupations formerly reserved to men; and political gains have been made for women's legal rights regarding ownership of property, relationship to their children, obtaining credit,

---

[46] Hole and Levine, p. 317.

divorces, and birth control. But education must also point out the sometimes not so obvious facts of its continuing role in fostering values, attitudes, and beliefs that keep women, for all their gains, second class in many ways.

Society has not consistently helped solve the problem of caring for the children of working mothers during their working hours. Working women are paid less than men for equal work by some employers who think they can get away with it, until they are sued by individuals or governmental agencies. Women generally do find it more difficult to rise to top positions in most fields, particularly commercial, political, and professional fields.

In subtle ways, depending on the attitudes brought to school by students and teachers, women are still set apart. It is as though taboos had been placed on their minds as well as their bodies. Only if these efforts at segregation are resisted and if women are not brainwashed into accepting an image of themselves as inferior are they likely to think of themselves merely as human beings who happen to be female, just as men are human beings who happen to be male. And if they so think of themselves as humans who are sometimes concerned with anatomy, *just as men are,* during the times when they are not concerned with specific aspects of their sexuality, they will find it uncomprehensible that they should not be considered completely human persons capable of and interested in partaking of all sorts of physical and intellectual activities that the world needs to accomplish.

Women will see the world not as "man's world" with a "woman's place," but as the world with places for all humans.

Humanists, both men and women, see as a legitimate educational goal the desexing of education. This includes adding the accomplishments of women to our history texts, deleting role-programming illustrations in teaching materials, avoiding the counseling of girls out of professional fields, teaching all students to recognize the social and philosophical issues involved in governmental acts relating to women, and basically encouraging female students as much as males to take part in contributing more than warm bodies to the record of human life.

Alternatives to Traditional Sexist Education

If we grant that traditionally the schools have been political institutions that teach students to fit into the establishment, and that they have considered as important the question "Who shall be educated to fill what prescribed roles?", then in seeking alternatives to sexist education, we must ask: (1) What is the purpose of education? (2) For what roles should women be educated? and (3) Who will decide the roles?

As background for our inquiry, we need remember that although many gains have been made in legal changes concerning the rights of women to receive an education, as well as to use their education in later work or in the academic world, legal changes alone do not accomplish all that women have been seeking. The barriers remaining are attitudes, values, myths, and beliefs—the components of the sexist approach to women. We will categorically assume that women are potentially as capable of contributing to society as men, and are as entitled to earn money for their work—variations in accomplishment will occur between individual women just as between individual men.

Varied Roles Are Needed for Women

The President's Commission on the Status of Women concluded in 1965 that women must be given choices, backed by fair laws, "fair play," and social acceptance of differing patterns of life.[47] That many different and often opposing roles are desired by women is obvious from both feminist and antifeminist writings.

The traditional mother's role The Commission's report emphasized that it felt that "marriage and parenthood are fundamental human rights and no sacrifice should be made of them, nor should sacrifice be made to them. . . ."[48] Women who want to be mothers and housewives only should not be forced by opinion to work. Because of this attitude, many educators believe that girls' education should stress, or at least include, courses that are relevant to being a good home manager and a good child raiser. Traditionally these courses are restricted to girls only. The antisexist view prefers that both girls and boys should learn how to share household tasks and child care, so boys should also have such courses. Then, if the mother did not wish to work outside of her traditional role, at least she would have made her choice without the handicap of sexist treatment.

The unmarried woman Mead points out in the epilogue of the report that the Commission believed that typical women would marry, so single women, divorcees, and widows were not considered "normal." In contrast, many people, while not considering these statuses desirable. would prefer to call them acceptable.

The purposely childless marriage Because Mead believes that sexual relations are important in everyone's life, she suggests that we look at the kinds of relationships that are built up among adolescents to

[47] Margaret Mead and Frances Balgley Kaplan (eds.), *American Women: The Report of the President's Commission on the Status of Women and Other Publications of the Commission.* New York: Charles Scribner's Sons, 1965.

[48] Mead and Kaplan (eds.), p. 184.

see how they prepare for two kinds of possible marriage. There should not merely be marriage that presumes the woman's contribution is the role of bearing and rearing of children, but another kind based on a choice now possible because society no longer needs so many women bearing children (because deathrates are down). Now there can be marriage based on an intimate responsible relationship with both persons contributing individually to society.[49]

In one way, this is a return to preindustrial society's view that women had a lifelong role of contributing to society in more than her child-rearing capacity. Before industry took work out of the home, wives shared with husbands in crafts, agriculture, and businesses conducted in the home. The woman was never a full-time mother, but was expected to contribute to society as well as to her family. But there is still another view of combining women's roles.

Lifetime contributor to society as a person Alice Rossi sees the combination role of mother-worker as an ideal toward which society could well afford to work. It is ironic when approximately half the population of women is in the work force, that poor women are expected to have to support children by working outside the home, but educated women are discouraged from pursuing not only jobs but careers.

If city planning shifted the present pattern of suburban homes and central city work areas, so people worked near their homes and schools, Rossi proposes, then men, women, and even children could have greater shares in the total society of work, schooling and so-called cultural activities. With society-planned care for small children during their working or studying hours, women could keep up with their chosen fields and be more likely to reach top positions, instead of occupying only low-paying jobs.

Rossi is among numerous writers who see the specialization of housework as wasteful, particularly because it destroys the possibility of concentrating enough on a field of intellectual or creative activity to be able to contribute outstanding work to society. She points out that because studies show mentally retarded girls can be trained to be efficient housekeepers and child careers, it seems hardly logical to waste talented women for the same purpose.[50]

Given the opportunity to be a life-long contributor, women would be better mothers for not concentrating all their attention on their children,

[49] Margaret Mead, "Sexual Freedom and Culture Change," in Jhan and June Robbins, *An Analysis of Human Sexual Inadequacy.* New York: New American Library, 1970, pp. 181 ff.

[50] Alice Rossi, "Equality Between the Sexes: An Immodest Proposal," in Robert Jay Lifton (ed.), *Woman in America,* Boston: Houghton Mifflin Company, 1965.

and being able to avoid "momism" which has been detrimental not only to adolescent but to later relationships as well.

Who Will Decide Woman's Roles?

One thing men and women in the revived feminist movement are working for is the right of a woman to decide her own roles. Assuming that most people will want some sort of sexual life, a woman may, wish first to determine for herself which combination of sexual and working roles she may follow and, then, to be accepted as a person, no matter which role she chooses.

With this in mind feminists also want each woman to be able to choose the kind and amount of education she wishes and not to be told only certain subjects are suitable for females—because females only work in the fields which men in the power elite believe they should be allowed to enter.

Nonsexist Teachers

Unless teachers are aware of the number of combinations of roles now possible for women as sexual-working beings, they are likely to continue promoting, even though unconsciously, the traditional feminine stereotypes that make the public school political institutions geared only to fit women into the conservative establishment pattern of men skimming off all the top positions and women catering to their home needs. But if teachers can see the possibility of women continuing to contribute to society in many fields besides the home, they will be able to counsel girls into taking courses fitted to their individual abilities. There will be some point to motivating girls to think of lifetime, professional interests.

They may draw from William Glasser's views that each person has a set of basic needs that do not change according to sex—one of which is the need to achieve something worthwhile and is accomplished in part by the specific ego function of aggressiveness.[51] With an understanding of the new possibilities, teachers can increasingly regard girls as whole persons wanting to function in the world as insiders.

STUDY QUESTIONS

1. Male and female sexist views seem most strongly held by Middle Americans, and particularly those affiliated with fundamentalist Protestantism and orthodox Roman Catholicism. How do you explain this?

[51] William Glasser, *Mental Health or Mental Illness? Psychiatry for Practical Action.* New York: Harper & Row, Publishers, Perennial Library, 1970. pp. 3–13.

2. What logic—if any—upholds the notion that women are *generally* inferior to men yet they were also designated by God to demonstrate irreproachable "moral standards"? Are women as a group more moral than men? First, define morality.

3. When women from areas where the average human is relatively small migrate to areas where people are on the average much larger (as when Asians immigrate to the U.S.), in two or three generations they gradually become larger than average males in their homeland. How do you explain this? Would it be a good idea through selective breeding to "breed" women as big and powerful as men—or bigger? Would it help decrease male chauvinism?

4. Ms. Shulamith Firestone argues (see bibliography) that women are a separate social class and will remain a repressed class until they are no longer handicapped by their biology (size, menstruation, child bearing). She would use genetic engineering to overcome these biological inequities—including producing most babies in "test tubes." How do you react to such a "radical" proposal?

5. Firestone also argues that as adults women on the average *seem* less interested in sexual gratification and more likely to be frigid than men, because of the sexual repression of little girls. She advocates girls and boys being taught sexual play as small children and encouraged to practice it, so there would be no adult differences. How do you react to this idea?

6. One male objection to letting women into construction and police work is: women will be forced to hear too much "rough language." Is this a good argument for excluding women from any occupation for which they are competent?

7. Can you think of *any* occupation, except those requiring extreme muscular strength, for which there are no mechanical aids, which women could not do as well as men? Or any now permitted only to women which men could not do as well (except wet nursing)?

8. In some nations, a relatively large proportion of physicians, attorneys, judges, engineers, etc., are women. It is argued that such countries waste less good "brain power" than does the U.S., where it is considered quite appropriate for women of high potential to be "just housewives." Evaluate this argument.

9. Do you think public education might improve if at least half of administrative staffs, including superintendents, were women? Give reasons for your answer.

10. Can you offer any reasons which liberal humanists would accept why women as a class or category should not have the right to decide for themselves their individual goals and activities?

ANNOTATED BIBLIOGRAPHY

Bullough, Vern L., with the assistance of Bonnie Bullough, *The Subordinate Sex: A History of Attitudes Toward Women.* Urbana, Ill.: University of Illinois Press, 1973.

The story behind attitudes toward women explains their continuity and changes and their economic and social causes. Includes an excellent annotated bibliography. The authors advantageously combine their scholarly fields of history and nursing. Recommended as an absorbing introduction to understanding present views.

Cisler, Lucinda, comp., *Women: A Bibliography,* edition 6, July–October 1970. New York: published by the compiler, Box 240, New York 10024, 1970.

This pamphlet lists a broad variety of books, periodicals and bibliographies about women. Many of these categorized listings are annotated, some descriptively, some critically. Worthwhile, even if this were to be the last edition.

de Beauvoir, Simone, *The Second Sex.* New York: Alfred A. Knopf, Inc., 1953; Bantam, 1961.

In a book regarded as a classic, de Beauvoir's thesis is that men have forced women into a secondary role, comparable to racial minorities. The imposed environment, not some innate "feminine" characteristics, have resulted in women's plight. She would have women adopt most masculine values and would educate them to this end. De Beauvoir, together with Betty Friedan (*The Feminine Mystique,* 1963, which defined the frustrating "religion" of housewifery), initiated today's feminist movement.

Firestone, Shulamith, *The Dialectic of Sex: The Case for Feminist Revolution.* New York: William Morrow and Company, Inc., 1970; Bantam, 1971.

Firestone, writing from a background of Marxist philosophy, is almost certainly the most controversial of the feminist writers. She adapts class struggle theory to the two sexes and sees women as an oppressed social class, who will achieve full equality only after overcoming their biology through genetic engineering and otherwise. Reviewers see her analysis as ranging from reasonable to absurd, but in any case highly provocative.

Frazier, Nancy, and Myra Sadker, *Sexism in School and Society.* New York: Harper & Row, Publishers, 1973.

This highly readable little book discusses sexual discrimination and its roots and then turns to sexism as it operates within the school hierarchy and as it is insidiously taught to the young from kindergarten on. Excellent illustrative material and a first-rate annotated bibliography.

Greer, Germaine, *The Female Eunuch,* New York: McGraw-Hill Book Company, 1971.

Greer's title suggests her theme: she sees women as having been desexed by traditionally mandated sex roles, and therefore something less than whole. Her criticisms of marriage, the nuclear family, and the sexual repression of women are forceful, but her recommendation that women can achieve freedom solely by changing themselves seems rather pallid after such potent criticism of our whole institutional structure. Greer's writing style mixes literary and gutter prose in a fascinating way; very interesting reading.

The New Women's Survival Catalog. New York: Coward, McCann & Geoghegan, Inc., 1973.

This book "documents a massive trend among American women . . . toward self-assertion and an end to dependency." Some subjects covered are: communications (presses, publications); art and artists;

self-health; sexism in education and literature and "liberating" literature; learning; working; justice, discrimination, and rights; and building the movement. The purposes of many women's groups are stated, and sources are given for literature on many phases of feminism.

Reeves, Nancy, *Womankind: Beyond the Stereotype.* Chicago: Aldine Publishing Company, 1971.

Reeves pleads the case against women being brainwashed into being culturally adjusted to "feminine" cultures—marriage should not be regarded as a profession. Instead, she recommends education toward professional competency and keeping active in "the world" throughout life in order to lead a better life for one's self and also to help one's children to lead a better life.

Roszak, Betty and Theodore (eds.), *Masculine/Feminine: Readings in Sexual Mythology and the Liberation of Women.* Harper Colophon, New York: Harper & Row, Publishers, 1969.

The selections cover several views of women's subjugation: male chauvinism, male allies of feminism (including Gunnar Myrdal and Theodore Roszak); "toward liberation" (de Beauvoir); and the new feminism of the late 1960s (including militant manifestos for "sisterhood"). The Roszaks see a need to recognize the masculine and feminine elements in the psychology of both sexes and to end the dichotomizing roles. The selected bibliography includes not only nonfiction, but fiction and drama pointing up woman's search for equality.

Yorburg, Betty. *Sexual Identity: Sex Roles and Social Change.* New York: Wiley-Interscience, 1973.

This book questions traditional sex roles, asking why there has been so much variety in the ideals of masculinity and femininity from one place to another and in different times. It discusses sex roles in various types of societies and places, some showing few distinctions between the sexes, and others many. It also asks if there is a biological inevitability to sex roles.

Caption canceled due to smog. *(Copyright © George Ballis, all rights reserved)*

THE ECOLOGICAL DILEMMA
AND EDUCATION

. . . And God said unto them [Man], Be fruitful and multiply, and replenish the earth, and subdue it, and have dominion over the fish of the sea, and over the fowl of the air, and over every living thing that moveth upon the earth.

Genesis, 1:28

Apparently, school boards, administrators, and teachers think ecology is an important subject in view of the amount of talk and writing produced about inserting units or courses in ecology in the curriculum. Much less has been done than has been talked about, however; and when one peruses the literature it appears that school people are not overly clear as to what an ecological problem is. For example, they often equate removing litter and beautifying schoolgrounds as in some way related to ecology. These are actually aesthetic issues having nothing to do with ecology as defined by ecologists.

Such misinterpretations suggest that the present generation of teachers—and prospective teachers—don't understand well what the really critical ecological issues are. Although we cannot review in a single chapter the "critical issues of ecology," we can suggest a few and in our chapter-end bibliography point out a number more. Ecology should be of fundamental importance to educators: without confronting its most serious issues, there may be only empty school buildings in half a century.

SPECIMEN BELIEFS AND VALUES ABOUT ECOLOGY

Ecology is too new a field for much of an ideology about the subject to have developed. There seem to have been no systematic studies of beliefs and values in this area as there have been in several other problematical areas of culture treated in Part II. We will therefore rely largely on hypothesizing beliefs from experience of how people behave, and from putting together a rather vast number of bits and pieces encountered in letters to editors, speeches, conversations, magazine articles, and news stories. We are not entirely without empirical data on ecological ideology; there may be an ancient belief system which supports our older beliefs about "man in nature." Also, we have some data from the ACE studies.

Old-Culture Beliefs

Probably the general tenor of most old-culture beliefs—those of people approaching middle age or over and of conservatives generally, young or old—is "Let's continue as we are, the earth was made for people to use and we would be foolish to let nature lovers scare us."

We must remember that old-culture beliefs have a history in the Western World that extends back as far as the beginning of the Judeo-Christian tradition, which established a hierarchy with God at the top and then Man—whose explicit instructions were to "subdue and have dominion over the earth." The idea of conquest has always been a central part of this tradition, not only the conquest of nature by Man, but also of women and all foreign peoples, and finally, ironically, man by machines. This tradition has not existed among Asiatics or American Indians.[1]

---

[1] Barry Weisberg, *Beyond Repair: The Ecology of Capitalism.* Boston: Beacon Press, 1971, pp. 13–18. Weisberg makes a plausible though perhaps biased case for the belief that most of the history of the Western World can be explained by Western man's taking seriously the divine injunctions of the first chapter of Genesis.

There is evidence that concern for ecological problems does not run very deep. Bernarde, for example, cites the Princeton Opinion Research Corporation as reporting, "When the public nationwide is asked what they would be willing to pay per year in added taxes for a substantial improvement in air and water pollution control, about 2 in 3 say—nothing.[2]

As for corporation management, which we assume is usually conservative enough to be properly labeled old culture, we have more recent clues to common viewpoints. Jack Anderson has reported the extent to which corporations defy the policy recommendations of the federal Environmental Protection Agency by continuing illegal pollution practices, which they find easily possible by making sufficiently large political contributions to the political party of the executive branch of the Federal Government.[3] We have also seen in 1974 how a power shortage—whether fictitious or real—can quickly induce Americans, including the Congress, to turn against environmental protection legislation.

We feel the following represent plausible specimens of old-culture beliefs:

—Natural resources were placed on this earth for man to use and they should be used as wanted.
—People should be permitted freedom in their life style, no matter how opulent it may be, if they have money to pay for it.
—The only valid goals of an economic system are growth and greater efficiency in producing and distributing goods.
—Steady population growth is the best guarantee we have of continuing prosperity.
—We should concentrate on taking care of our own problems and let the rest of the world manage as best it can.
—Our chief problems are caused by conservationists who fight such constructive projects as the Alaska pipeline and strip mining of coal.
—The automobile is still the best means of transportation yet invented and there should be no restrictions on its use.
—If an animal species is not obviously useful to man, we should not be spending our money trying to prevent its extinction.

New-Culture Beliefs

One striking aspect of what seem to be new-culture beliefs is their frequent inconsistency and irrelevancy to real ecological problems. A good example of this was what occurred on the first Earth Day (1970). School administrators and teachers sent school children by the thousands out to

[2] Melvin A. Bernarde, *Our Precious Habitat.* New York: W. W. Norton & Company, Inc., 1970, p. 308.
[3] Jack Anderson, syndicated column, "Washington Merry-Go-Round." November 12, 1973.

gather up rubbish. It does not upset the balance of nature to litter the ground with used bottles, cans, aluminum foil, paper, and so on—although for the aesthetically conscious it mars the natural scene. Below is a scattering of specimen belief-statements held by large numbers of the young and quite a few of their elders:

—Humans should be very concerned about protecting their natural environment (among the top five concerns of youth in the 1973 ACE studies).
—The simpler our life style is, the more rewarding.
—Owning high quality stereophonic sound systems, first-rate photographic equipment, and sporty little automobiles is great fun.
—The most important thing is to live for today, neither past nor future should concern us.[4]
—Married couples should not have more than two or three children; marriage may be even happier if there are no children.
—Every attempt should be made to preserve all endangered species of animals.
—Hungry people in Africa and Asia should concern us as much as hungry people in the United States.
—To save fuel, only small economy cars should be permitted.
—Such sports as dune buggying and visiting the wilderness with trail bikes and jeeps are great fun.
—The louder music is (and many other sounds), the more satisfying.
—Everyone should back Ralph Nader and such conservationist organizations as the Sierra Club and Friends of the Earth.

Emerging Beliefs within the Intellectual Community

By intellectual community we are thinking of broadly educated professionals, including many college and university professors. The beliefs they state in their writings, even though they may not have any particular expertise in ecology, seem to reflect a pretty high level of sophistication. Below are a few such assertions:

—Ecological problems cannot be solved by one nation alone; these are global problems solvable only by close international cooperation.
—The most critical ecological problems will not be solved at all unless a large majority of the population, and corporation management, become far more concerned than they are now.
—Ecological problems are complex and interrelated and often it is difficult to see the most dangerous consequences of a given act (e.g., strip mining in the West would destroy natural beauty, but its major

[4] The culture of the young has been called a "now" culture. Perhaps no one has expressed this idea and its limitations better than Kenneth E. F. Watt, "Planning—So There Will Be a Future," in Clifton Fadiman and Jean White (eds.), Ecocide—And Thoughts toward Suvival, New York: Interbook, Inc., 1971, pp. 103–104.

ecological consequences would be destruction of agricultural land and, still worse, watershed capabilities in an area which already lacks enough water for present needs).

—There is grave danger that panic induced by a resource shortage (such as a shortage of petroleum) will result in major use of such highly polluting fuels as to cause an ecological catastrophe.

—In the long-run, basic ecological problems (such as overpopulation) are much more threatening to human life than the temporary inconvenience caused by remedial resources shortages (e.g., as a switch from fossil fuels to geothermal or solar power).

—Homo sapiens evolved in an environment of hardship and challenge; humans are basically "foul weather" animals and can live a "soft life" only at great cost to psychophysical health and perhaps survival itself.

—If a world famine of major proportions is to be averted, the affluent nations will have to move increasingly toward the predominant use of plant protein sources.

AN "OUTRAGEOUS HYPOTHESIS" ABOUT ECOLOGY

Although a great flurry of interest about ecological problems developed in the 1960s, concern may well have peaked in 1970 or 1971. As soon as business interests and the government began to see that, not only would eliminating those problems which are a menace to health and life cost much more than most interested people had thought in the sixties, but that it would also be much more inconvenient, then the whole issue of ecology became bogged in empty rhetoric.

The "heroes" of the sixties who had tried to alert us had perhaps at least overstated the immediacy of the problem. Paul Ehrlich, Barry Commoner, Kenneth Watt and many other investigators had sounded as if doomsday were fast approaching. Most people felt what they had to say was unnecessarily unpleasant; they were being told that they would have to make fundamental changes in their way of life and who except the poor wanted to do that?

Hypothesis: *Overpopulation in large parts of the world is bound to lead to mass disease, starvation, and revolutionary movements OR Malthus was essentially right except in his timing.*

Thomas Robert Malthus (1766–1834), later to be the Reverend Malthus, was considered a gifted child. His father, Daniel, was a friend of David Hume and an emotionally dedicated admirer of Jean Jacques Rousseau, with whom he enjoyed a close friendship. Daniel was an optimist about the future of the human race, something of a "back-to-nature" utopian socialist. Sons are often contrary, and young Thomas began exhibiting a more pessimistic view while still comparatively young. He may also have been influenced by his study for the ministry, which at that time (as often today) produced in students a rather gloomy view of human- kind's future in its "earthly prison."

In 1798, an anonymous published work of 50,000 words appeared under the title *Principle of Population as It Affects the Future Improve- ment of Society.* To quote Heilbroner, "In a few pages young Malthus pulled the carpet from under the feet of the complacent thinkers of the times and what he offered them in place of progress was a prospect meager, dreary, and chilling."[5]

The book, quickly identified with Malthus, was widely read and highly influential. The optimism about a glorious economic future, inspired in part by Adam Smith's *Wealth of Nations,* published in 1776, evaporated almost overnight. After reading Malthus, Thomas Carlyle labeled eco- nomics a "dismal science," a label which was to stand for at least a century. Malthus later became, in his own right, one of the more prominent economists of his day, and one could make the argument that, more than any other single person, Malthus turned the attention of the educated members of the Western World to overpopulation as a possible serious cause of future trouble.

The Malthusian Argument

Malthus's thesis is comparatively simple and more easily understood and appreciated today than in his own time, even though we are much more aware today than were his contemporaries of flaws in his reasoning. Al- though it has flaws, the basic Malthusian proposition has been thought by many to represent a flash of genius, particularly in view of when it ap- peared historically.

The Ratio between Population and Resource Increase

Malthus proposed that population growth tends to show a doubling effect, if not every generation at least with regularity, and can be pro- jected into the future only by thinking in terms of a geometric (expo- nential) curve. In contrast, the rate at which human beings can increase their supply of natural resources, particularly food, does not show such a doubling tendency and is best represented by an arithmetic (linear) curve. To illustrate with numbers a geometric progression, we would write 1-2-4-8-16-32, etc. To illustrate an arithmetic progression, we would write 1-2-3-4-5-6-7-8, etc. Figure 12-1 shows how such curves differ.

The obvious consequence of such disparity in rates of change of

[5] Robert L. Heilbroner, *The Worldly Philosophers: The Lives, Times and Ideas of the Great Economic Thinkers.* New York: Simon & Schuster, Inc., 1953, p. 70.

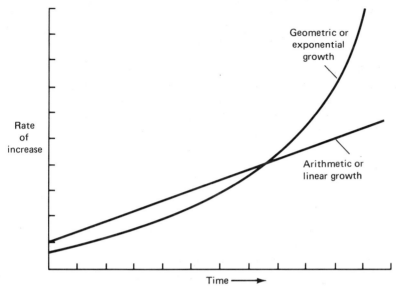

FIGURE 12-1. Linear and exponential curves illustrated.

these two crucial variables is that at some time in the future people will exist in too large numbers to be supported by their natural environment, probably by the late 1800s, Malthus thought.

Checks on Population Growth

Under the Malthusian hypothesis, obviously population growth has to be forced to slow down to match the growth at which food supply and other essential resources can be produced. Malthus, deploring the high birthrate but convinced that it was in man's nature to breed up to capacity, saw no real hope in this direction (although, we will show, he did make a suggestion in the revised edition of *Principles of Population*). All Malthus could see as a means of bringing the two growth curves into convergence were what he called "natural checks" on population growth. These natural checks were war, poverty, disease, and famine. The world of the future, as Malthus envisioned it, would be one in which these natural checks would operate on a massive scale.

Reaction to Malthusian Theory

According to James Bonar, author of a biography of Malthus,

he was the best abused man of his age. . . . Here was a man who defended small-pox, slavery, and child murder—a man who denounced soup-kitchens, early marriages, and parish allowances—a man who had the impudence to marry after preaching against the evils of a family. . . . From the first, Malthus was not ignored. For thirty years it rained refutations.[6]

Malthus, very much in the Smithian laissez-faire tradition, did not believe in government intervention in the economy or other aspects of social life. He rejected all aid to the poor, recognizing, and at that time probably correctly, that free soup kitchens or medical assistance would have no major effect other than to increase the birthrate and thus make necessary a steady multiplication of the number of soup kitchens with no end in sight.

Malthus and the Idea of "Moral Restraint"

Although the idea of contraception had been understood in the ancient world, Parson Malthus regarded it as too sinful to contemplate. Much better, he thought, to let the multiplying hordes be subjected to some or all of his natural restraints. Malthus was not hardhearted. He regretted the situation as much as anyone; but he could not escape his own logic. Not everyone agreed with Malthus, of course.

After two years of abuse, Malthus saw fit to publish a second edition of his book on population. In it, he attempted to document with case study material from that and earlier times how overpopulation and natural restraints had already come into play. He quit pushing the idea of arithmetic and geometric ratios as being necessarily the way growth rates of human beings and resources would forever continue. He advanced the idea that the birthrate could be controlled in another way if people could only see the light and so choose. This was his idea of "moral restraint." The idea involved marrying late and practicing sexual continence in marriage. Malthus's idea of moral restraint raised about as much protest as his ideas about natural restraints. Many critics thought it was a very impractical idea and Malthus did not have much confidence in it himself (although he practiced the idea, at least by marrying comparatively late in life).

The Modern Malthusians

Most ecologists or others who have shown great concern over the pressure of growing populations upon scarce resources could be regarded as modern Malthusians. Most such persons feel there was more than a half truth in Malthusian population theory and that Malthus's chief error was in his time schedule. Malthus could hardly have been expected to

[6] Quoted in Heilbroner, p. 76.

anticipate modern technology, and he misjudged particularly what technological innovation in agriculture could do to increase food supplies. On the other hand, he had no way of foreseeing what modern sanitation and small amounts of modern medicine (e.g., DDT to kill malaria-bearing mosquitoes and antibiotic drugs) could do to increase rates of population growth.

In discussing the "population problem" in the context of the seventies and eighties, we will draw upon facts and opinions presented by a number of modern Malthusians. First, we quote one self-labeled modern Malthusian, Black:

> Seen in this perspective (i.e., the time perspective of 250 to 500 years hence), the spectre of the Malthusian situation begins to haunt us again. Given the increase in world population implied by a time scale of these dimensions, the possibility of sufficient food and water being made available cannot but be once more in doubt, unless we are prepared to proceed in the blind faith that "science will provide" . . . the blunt fact remains that man can only increase in population to the numbers for which food can be available, even assuming perfect control of technology and distribution. To believe otherwise is to live in a fool's paradise.[7]

Present World Population Patterns

Using the most recent figures available to us on population growth trends and population density by areas, we will investigate what parts of the world might be considered overpopulated and what parts (if any) under-populated. Actually, raw statistics mean little; to get at what can be defined as "overpopulation" requires combining several variables; even then such a concept is likely to rest to a considerable degree on value judgments.

But we will use present data as best we can and hope that material presented here will lead readers to continue study of population problems. In connection with all this, we should observe that there are persons who argue that there are no population problems anywhere, that the very concept of overpopulation is nonsensical. However, persons who push such an argument bear the burden of explaining widespread famine as of 1973 and 1974 in both Africa and India and the presently clear prospect of a worsening of the situation in 1975 and after.

Growth Rates

The world's population grew only gradually until after the middle of the nineteenth century. It is thought there were probably from 200 to

[7] John Black, *The Dominion of Man: The Search for Ecological Responsibility.* Edinburg: Edinburg University Press, 1970, p. 131. Black is a Professor of Natural Resources at the University of Edinburgh.

300 million people on earth in the year A.D. 1 (such estimates are, of course, subject to an unknown amount of error). By 1650, the estimate was 500 million, and in 1850, 1 billion.

To the extent that these estimates are reasonable approximations, it required more than eighteen centuries for world population to grow from 300 million or less to 1 billion. It took only eighty years, however, for world population to double after 1850 (by this time, estimates had become relatively dependable). Between 1930 and 1975, the world population will have doubled again—this time in forty-five years. The next doubling is expected to occur in less than thirty-five years.[8]

What accounts for the extreme acceleration in population growth? It is not the birthrate alone, which in many parts of the world is lower in the seventies than at any previous time we know of. The main cause of acceleration in population growth is the decline in deathrates due to improvements in modern sanitation and medicine. In most underdeveloped nations, the birthrates (annual number of births per 1000 population) remain between 40 and 52—the latter figure being considered near the biological maximum.

However, even in some countries considered "backward" the death-rate (the annual number of deaths per 1000 population) has sunk to a comparatively low figure. The deathrate can be as low as 5, as in Singapore, Taiwan, Hong Kong, and the Fiji and Ryukyu Islands. At least thirty-eight nations or independent cities have deathrates lower than the United State's 9.3. A deathrate of 5 is approaching the biological minimum given the present development of medicine.

The rate of population growth is based on the difference between birth- and deathrates (but not simply by subtracting deathrates from birth-rates). Except for an occasional highly exceptional situation, short-term growth figures do not mean a great deal since they may reflect the operation of equally short-term and unrepeatable developments.

For example, the application of modern sanitation and medicine may result in a rather quick and sharp decline in deathrate and a corresponding increase in growth rate, just as an unexpected famine may reverse this situation.

Population Growth

A population growth rate of 3 percent is considered intolerable except for a very short period. It produces a doubling of the total population in 23.3 years. But given the economic conditions that prevail in underdevel-

[8] Statistics presented in this section, unless otherwise indicated, are from Philip Nobile and John Deedy (eds.), *The Complete Ecology Fact Book.* New York: Doubleday & Company, Inc., 1972. Chap. 1.

oped nations, a growth rate of 2.5 percent is probably too large to maintain for long except under very special circumstances. The areas of the world having growth rates in excess of 2.5 are:

Middle (Central) America	3.4
North Africa	3.1
Tropical S. America	3.0
Southwest Asia	2.9
Southeast Asia	2.8
Middle South Asia	2.7
West Africa	2.6
East Africa	2.6

The estimated population of these parts of the world for 1975 total about 1.7 billion, or approximately 44 percent of the estimated world population as of that year (estimates are based on extrapolations of growth trends through 1971 and are probably quite accurate enough for our purposes). If we add those additional regions of the world that have a population growth rate between 2.2 and 2.4 percent annually, then we have accounted for well over 46 percent of the total world population. We can conclude, therefore, that almost half the world's population is increasing at a rate which will double that proportion of the world's population in a time span ranging from less than twenty-six to less than thirty-two years. And these are the very regions of the world in which hunger is already endemic and in which the chief famines of recent years have occurred.

The country with the lowest growth rate is East Germany with 0.1 percent, which is for all practical purposes that which many ecologists consider ideal for most developed nations. (Paul and Anne Ehrlich advocate a growth rate of 0.0 for such countries—hence their conservationist organization, "Zero Population Growth.") North and West Europe, with a growth rate of 0.6 would be considered as coping very well so far as population is concerned. The growth rate of the United States is descending toward that figure. Population growth is lowest in the most industrialized, urbanized, and educated nations.

The population growth rate for the world as a whole, depending on the source of the estimate and the recent year in which it was made, is given variously as 2.0 or 2.1. If such a rate should remain unchanged, it would double the world's population in from thirty-three to thirty-five years.

Wealth in Relation to Population Density

There is a folklore belief to the effect that there is a positive correlation between poverty and crowding. People who hold this belief may be thinking of such places as urban ghettoes in the United States or major cities elsewhere where there is both intense poverty and crowding (e.g., Calcutta or Hong Kong). Actually, this belief does not furnish grounds for generalizing because highly crowded nations (or cities) can at the same time be among the highest in the world in per capita income.

The following figures (like the previous ones, derived from Nobile and Deedy) show the range in population density and per capita GNP for various countries. The eleven countries listed below, based on 1970–1971 statistics, are the world's wealthiest. They are the nations whose per capita GNP is $2000 or over. These figures would require correction as of the mid-seventies because of the changing value of the dollar; as of 1974, for example, the per capita GNP of West Germany in dollars would be considerably higher because of the loss of value of the dollar in relation to the mark. For the same reason, Japan would have to be included well up within this group because of depreciation of dollars in relation to yen.

Except for Switzerland, West Germany, and Denmark, it is obvious that these eleven wealthiest nations are in the low population density bracket; however, if we were to look at only the most settled parts of these low population density countries then population density figures would, of course, be far higher.

But to get a more balanced picture, we need to look at nations which are regarded as wealthy and at the same time have among the highest population density figures in the world for nations that combine both urban and fairly large rural areas. The dollar income figures for these countries are also misleading, because in all of them the dollar has lost at least some value in relation to local currency, at least as of 1974.

By any standard, nations that still have rather considerable rural areas and an average population in excess of 200 persons per square

Nation	Per capita GNP (in U.S. dollars)	Population density per square kilometer
United States	3,980	22
Kuwait	3,540	36
Sweden	2,620	18
Switzerland	2,490	151
Canada	2,460	2
West Germany	2,170	237
France	2,130	92
Denmark	2,070	114
Australia	2,070	2
Norway	2,000	12
New Zealand	2,000	10

Nation	Per capita GNP (in U.S. dollars)	Population density per square kilometer
Belgium	1,810	316
England & Wales	1,790	323
Netherlands	1,610	315
Israel	1,360	136
Japan	1,190	277

kilometer, must be considered densely populated. This is particularly true in nations in which a significant part of the rural area is too mountainous for human habitation (which among the examples given above would be primarily West Germany and Japan).

Conversely, nations with a very low population density may be among the most impoverished. There are too many such nations to be listed here; but to illustrate the point we list a few, all of which have an annual per capita GNP of $100 or less.

There are many other nations with per capita GNPs of $100 or less, but with higher population densities. We selected the group below simply to show that extreme poverty may be accompanied by extremely sparse population.

The statistics, even if not precise, at least seem to demonstrate clearly that there is no necessary correlation between crowding and poverty. If crowding is to be condemned (and there are reasons for its condemnation), it must be on grounds other than the production of economic misery.

The Meaning of Overpopulation

It is clear that different writers hold quite different meanings for the expression, "overpopulation." Writers we regard as relatively unsophisti-

Nation	Per capital GNP (in U.S. dollars)	Population density per square kilometer
Sudan	100	6
Guinea	90	16
Afghanistan	80	26
Ethiopia	70	20
Niger	70	3
Somalia	60	4

cated tend to define overpopulation only in terms of population density. But this definition is simplistic; we will use the meaning of overpopulation suggested by two recognized experts in this area, Paul and Anne Ehrlich.

The Ehrlichs approach their definition of overpopulation by developing the concept of "optimum population size." Any population in excess of this is overpopulation. The Ehrlichs feel that it is impossible to get at any meaningful concept of optimum population without taking seriously such abstract and subjective ideas as "quality of life" or "the pursuit of happiness." Yet, these ideas cannot be dealt with in quantitative terms or defined without getting involved in endless arguments. They, therefore, prefer to rely on such matters as "resource depletion, photosynthetic efficiency, human nutrition, and thermodynamic limits." This emphasis should not necessarily produce an unbridgeable dualism, however, because "questions about the *quality* of life are inextricably bound to those about the *quantities* of human beings on Earth."[9]

The Ehrlichs begin by pointing out that, at present, density of population is one of the poorest criteria for measuring optimum population. Western Europe, like Japan, has a high material standard of living partly because of the existence of much poorer nations who sell their own mineral stores to wealthy nations to get the foreign exchange necessary to survive. The only reason we do not consider Western and Northern Europe overpopulated is because these countries can drain resources from nations which, in a sense, are underpopulated or at least forced to live at a relatively low economic level. Therefore, we cannot relate optimum population at the present stage in history to a one-to-one ratio between numbers of people and the amount of natural resources provided by their own land space. We have thus eliminated two criteria as relevant: population density and possession of natural resources.

But these criteria can only be eliminated if they continue to be irrelevant over the long-run. Unless resources are renewable on a perpetual basis, a time must come when wealthy nations which import heavily will be no longer able to find other nations able and willing to export raw materials to them.

The Ehrlichs approach the general problem of determining optimum population levels by relating population size to environmental impact. They begin with the simple equation, $I = P \times F$, where I stands for total environmental impact, P for population size, and F for impact per capita. An increase in I can result from an increase in either P or F, in both simul-

[9] Paul R. and Anne H. Ehrlich, *Population, Resources, Environment: Issues in Human Ecology*, edition 2. San Francisco: W. H. Freeman and Company, Publishers, 1972, Chap. 8, pp. 199, 200.

taneously, or in P or F declining at a rate slower than the other is increasing. Rather than go through the mathematical ramifications of these relations here we refer readers to pages 260–261 of the Ehrlich book in which they illustrate the effects of a buildup in energy use.

The important point is that if population and per capita impact increase simultaneously, then I increases at a rate greater than either P or F. Their mathematics show that if population is increasing, the ensuing use of energy increases by a percent greater than the combined percentage growth of population and the growth per capita of energy use (between 1940 and 1969, world population increased by 53 percent, per capita energy use by 57 percent, but total energy use increased by 140 percent.)

If one uses the best estimates available of the quantity left of earth's nonrenewable resources, keeps in mind the explosive effects of exponential rates of growth or depletion, makes the best guesses possible about future sources of power when fossil fuels are gone, *then it is possible to estimate what size population the earth could support in comfort for an indefinite length of time.* There are hazards, of course, in any such estimates. Among other reasons, if sources of abundant, permanent, and low-cost power can be harnessed (e.g., the use of solar power, or the development of controlled thermonuclear power [controlled hydrogen fusion]), then it might become possible both to "mine" the oceans of their mineral content and also to utilize ores which are so low grade that they take far more power to extract than their present value. Even with such a development, however, we are still dealing with nonrenewable resources.

Disregarding for the moment the whole "quality of life" argument, the Ehrlichs tell us that given the present state of technology, usable raw materials, and rates of pollution, the earth is already much overpopulated. "An area must be considered overpopulated if it can only be supported by the rapid consumption of nonrenewable resources. It must also be considered overpopulated if the activities of the population are leading to a steady deterioration of the environment." Citing calculations made by biochemist H. R. Hulett of Stanford University Medical Center, given a continuation of the present agricultural and industrial system, *earth could support about one billion people at a level of affluence approximating that of the average person in the United States.*[10] (The earth will have more than 3.7 billion people in 1975.)

Regional Overpopulation in Affluent Nations

Americans who live in the northeastern seaboard area, the Great Lakes area, California's Bay area, or the coastal fringe from the Tehachapis

[10] Ehrlich and Ehrlich, p. 258.

southward to San Diego must feel their living areas are overcrowded. At least the way hundreds of thousands of Californians in these areas drive desperately to open desert or relatively uncrowded mountain areas every weekend suggests that, for many, their life circumstance borders on the intolerable.

Yet, many large urban complexes in the world have a greater density of population per unit of land space than many of the urban areas of the United States (the Japanese, for example, are considerably more crowded in the Tokyo and Osaka urban complexes; the same can be said for city dwellers in Europe and the high-density cities of Asia).

After suggesting that a world optimum population may be about one billion people, the Ehrlichs become much more cagey in discussing problems that may ensue from crowding per se. About all we can say about regional crowding is that, at least in the United States, many persons, whatever their reasons, do not like it. This introduces the whole question of value judgments as they enter into any discussion of optimum population. The Ehrlichs suggest that an urban area is overpopulated if considerable numbers of people *feel* they have too little living space; and that this is particularly the case if such people have no uncrowded places to escape to for weekends or vacations.

The Club of Rome's Studies

No treatment of the world's population problem, and its numerous ramifications for resource shortages, waste disposal, and pollution would be acceptable without including a description of the now famous studies of the Club of Rome. Readers should not be confused by its name; the Club of Rome is not connected with the Roman Catholic Church. Its name derives from the fact that this unofficial, loosely structured international organization of scientists and other scholars met first in Rome at the instigation of Dr. Aurelio Peccei, an Italian industrial manager and economist. The first meeting, attended by thirty persons, was held in April, 1968 and stimulated the research which led to a preliminary report.[11]

Design of the Preliminary Study

The design of the first study began with a subgroup of the Club first research to be completed, as published in The Limits to Growth, was established to study a variety of interrelated human problems, all of which

[11] Donella H. Meadows, et al., The Limits to Growth: The Club of Rome's Project on The Predicament of Mankind. Washington, D.C.: Potomac Associates, 1972; also New York: Signet, 1972.

had been studied singly but not as they interact with one another. Phase One of the Project was outlined during meetings at Bern, Switzerland, in the summer of 1970.

A global model, which incorporated many components not previously studied in connection with one another, was developed at the Massachusetts Institute of Technology, where Phase One was initiated (among other reasons, because of MIT's excellent computer facilities). The team, international in composition, was directed by Professor Dennis Meadows (now at Dartmouth) with financial support from the Volkswagen Foundation.

The group examined what they considered to be the five basic factors which theoretically limit growth, that is, growth of humankind and its works. These five factors are: (1) population, (2) agricultural production, (3) natural resources, (4) industrial production, and (5) pollution. The first research to be completed, as published in *The Limits to Growth*, was to be regarded as tentative, a preliminary report of an ongoing study, released for what good it might do to stimulate thought about human problems and alert people to the risks in humankind's future.

It does not require a talented study group or the use of computer science to tell any reasonably well-educated person that world population is growing, that industrial production is growing, that the rate of pollution is growing, that agricultural production is growing but not necessarily on a per capita basis, and that the amount and quality of natural resources are declining. What the Project's study team wanted to find out were the rates of growth and decline, how the five basic factors relate to one another, and what, if anything, would terminate growth and when.

The Exponential Factor

In connection with our previous discussion of Malthusian doctrine, we introduced the concepts of growth at an arithmetical or linear rate, and growth at a geometric or exponential rate. We did nothing more than introduce these concepts, and more needs to be said here about growth at exponential rates. The reason for this is that growth rates may tend toward exponentiality but be somewhat slower or faster than the doubling at each step of the previous amount as in the progression 1-2-4-8-16-32-64, etc. The analogy here is that of compound interest and the difference in length of time it would take one's bank account to double if it drew compound interest at an annual rate of 6 percent, 8 percent, 10 percent, or some other figure. This matter is important because the Project on the Predicament of Mankind found that the relationship between the five factors became meaningful only after careful calculations of the degree of exponential-tending growth where such growth existed.

In evaluating the growth of different factors in an ecological system, it is useful to know how long it requires for a unit to double in size if subjected to a particular rate of growth. A close enough approximation of the doubling time can very easily be calculated by dividing the annual growth rate into 70. The following demonstration will show how this works.

It is important to understand the consequences in long-range growth of a given rate of growth, because a growth rate that does not seem very high in the short run becomes quite explosive in the long run. For example, an interest rate of 7 percent does not seem particularly high; but it does double one's money in ten years.

Four of the five factors that limit growth have tended to show exponential change. Agricultural production is omitted here because to date its changes are linear, not exponential.

To understand what follows, it is important for readers to keep in mind that world population growth is estimated at about 2.1 percent which produces a doubling in thirty-three years, and that it requires only a small percentage increase to greatly reduce the doubling time: For example, if population increase is 2.5 percent, as it is in India and many other countries, the doubling time is twenty-eight years. If the increase is 3 percent, as in some other countries, the doubling time is reduced to twenty-three and a third years. Also, since capital expansion in some countries may be as high as 10 percent, and without improved pollution control will cause pollution to increase at the rate of 10 percent, then we get a doubling of pollution in only seven years.

Further, the closer we come to using up the entire supply of a non-renewable resource, the greater percentage of the resource we use in a given year; in this case we get an opposite effect—diminution of the resource increases at an exponential rate. If we reach a point where in a

Growth rate (% per year)	Doubling time (years)
0.5	140
1.0	70
2.0	35
3.0	23.3
4.0	18
5.0	14
6.0	11.5
7.0	10
8.0	8.7
10.0	7

year we use up 10 percent of the resource, and we continue using up the same *quantity* (not percent) a year, then the supply will last only seven years. If we increase the quantity of use, we reduce still further the life span of the resource.

Problems in Building Global Models

The Club of Rome's study team was first confronted with building a global model that would incorporate trend projections of the five factors mentioned above. However, trends reflecting growth, stability, or retraction do not proceed in synchrony. Some operate at an arithmetic or linear progression, others at some exponential rate. The exponential rate varies, according to which trend one is talking about. Further, the factors all influence one another, so a change in rate of growth or retraction in one trend affects other trends.

Models which involve as many as five continuously changing factors, all interrelated, become very complicated. An MIT team has for years been evolving new methods of understanding such complicated interactive processes; this work has led to a method called *system dynamics*. Of system dynamics, Meadows says,

> The basis of the method is the recognition that the *structure* of any system—the many circular, interlocking, sometimes time-delayed relationships among its components—is often just as important in determining its behavior as the individual components themselves. The world model described in this book is a System Dynamics model.[12]

The main object of system dynamics is to avoid the rather obvious pitfalls of the relatively static cultural models of the sociological functional analysts, to break through the limitations of conservative tendencies to want to study everything in terms of how to maintain a status quo.

Another complication encountered by the study group was what is called a "vicious circle," an example of which can occur in efforts at population control. Sometimes a backward nation has been able to increase food supplies, but this has only produced an equivalent or even greater population increase—the people have ended up more malnourished than before. Ecologists commony believe (though it is probably impossible to prove definitively) that in India, despite increased food supplies, people on the average are more malnourished now than a century ago.

The academic jargon for a vicious circle is a "positive feedback loop." This terminology, unnecessarily technical as it seems, is advan-

---

[12] Meadows *et al.*, p. 38.

tageous in the sense that it does not convey a value judgment as the term "vicious" does. Besides, some feedback loops are neutral or beneficial in long-range effect. The idea of a positive feedback loop simply is that two tendencies bear an integral relationship to one another and the significant outcome to watch is not either of the tendencies by itself but the product of their interaction. For example, population gain can only be calculated by combining two trends: birthrate and deathrate. This may involve major complexities, because birth- and deathrates tend to change at different exponential rates.

We have presented the above explanation so readers will have some idea of the problems involved in creating dynamic models. The Club of Rome study ended up with a first tentative model which could only be described through highly complicated mathematical equations and could be worked with only by using the most advanced computer science.

The Significance of Capital Growth and Population Growth

Capital growth refers to growth in the accumulation of the goods with which to produce goods, that is, new mines, transportation facilities, factories, machinery, and communications facilities. The rate of capital growth is probably the best, if not the only, index for determining the rate of economic expansion. Of course, capital growth rate means nothing if there are no longer the necessary raw materials to work with. But assuming the availability of raw materials, capital growth rate becomes a key figure in any attempts to calculate the future of humankind.

Population growth is likewise a key figure. If the developing nations are going to grow industrially to a point where their populations will be able to enjoy such basics as adequate housing, schooling, and medical care, their population growth dare not exceed the industrial growth necessary to provide these things. Their ability to feed their populations adequately also hinges on population growth being complemented by industrial growth: if they are going to develop their own agricultural productivity, they need machinery, chemical fertilizers, and agricultural research facilities. If their arable land space cannot enable them to be agriculturally self-sufficient, then they need a surplus of manufactured goods to sell on the world market to get the foreign currency needed to buy food products from those nations that produce a surplus.

Because the world's supply of natural resources is finite, it becomes imperative that population growth and capital growth be stopped long before critical shortages of nonrenewable resources develop. If a steady-state (i.e., zero-growth state) world economy is to be achieved, then it becomes imperative to know *when* population and capital growth must cease. If population and capital growth continue for too long into the future, then even the ecological optimists have to concede that a major global disaster will occur, not a disaster that would necessarily wipe out all human life, but one which would wipe out a large part of the world's population and force humankind to revert to a very primitive struggle for existence with little chance of conditions being bettered for centuries.

One of the primary aims of the Club of Rome study group was therefore to determine when population and capital growth rates would have to level off to permit a future stabilization of the world's economy which would provide the necessities of life, and perhaps even a few luxuries, for all human beings on earth.

About the only persons who disagree that a relatively stable-state economy will one day be necessary are those anticonservationists whose plans include: permanently supplementing earth's nonrenewable resources by transporting millions of tons of raw materials from the moon or other planets back to earth, dumping our wastes there in exchange, and exporting millions of surplus people to live on the more hospitable of the solar bodies. This picture has been apparently seriously painted by the Australian economist, Colin Clark, which might warrant his being included among the most radical utopians in existence.

Risks of Technical Optimism

Numerous persons are less extreme than the outer space utopians, but place perhaps unwarranted faith in the ability of pure and applied science to resolve such problems as stabilizing population growth, coming up indefinitely with new food sources (a big thing now is the idea of the world's oceans supplying unlimited amounts of food), finding substitutes for all essential nonrenewable resources, providing all the energy sources needed if the impoverished of the earth are to achieve dependable economic security, and finding a way of disposing of all the human, animal, and industrial wastes produced so that they will not be seriously polluting.

Technological optimism, to make any sense, also has to be combined with optimism about the rationality of the human animal; human beings have often—since the beginning of the scientific age—had at their disposal vast stores of scientific and technological knowledge which they have either failed to use or not used to any constructive advantage.

This has in part been because of poor communications and education, for example, the more advanced nations have understood certain sanitation practices that add immeasurably to health and longevity, which backward peoples could have applied but did not know about for decades or even centuries. The communications problem may be solved to the point where this particular kind of occurrence is not likely to be repeated.

However, even in countries as supposedly well educated as the

United States the same thing may happen, for example, the basic technology for converting coal and shale oil to cleaner synthetic fuels has long been known; but only a few university ecologists recognized that there was any reason for a crash program to make the process economical.

Findings of the Club of Rome's Studies

The outcome of this first study was embodied in two computer runs, a "standard run" and a second arbitrarily doubling the world's estimated finite resources. The first run suggested that world economic order would collapse in seventy years or so from mass starvation. The second suggested a collapse in less than a century due to pollution. The general conclusion was that humankind could save itself only by moving immediately to a no-growth policy both in population and industrialization.[13]

Although the first study was offered as only a tentative extrapolation of humankind's future, with more refined research to follow, response to it was widely polarized, emotional, and generally hostile. Knowledgeable ecologists said the model used was seriously flawed by omission of critical variables, although many said the conclusions were probably right even if for the wrong reasons.

A second Club of Rome study group immediately set about reassessing the first study and concluded that it did indeed have a major flaw—it assumed that growth tends to be undifferentiated, i.e., takes basically the same form in all parts of the world. This group developed a new dynamic world model which was "region specific," dividing the world into regions, each with its own postulated growth pattern. The group came up with an "organic growth model" in which, if the world social and economic order were seen as holistic—an interrelated totality—growth could proceed at a gradual pace indefinitely. This study included more variables, even necessary changes in human values.[14]

One interesting aspect of the organic growth model is its analogy to a living animal or plant. Growth not only takes different forms in different parts, but is faster in some. There may even be a retrenchment or recession in the growth of one part, with the whole remaining viable. In fact, retrenchment may be needed in some parts if the whole is to continue to grow (as in the case of a plant with an inadequate root system which can be saved by trimming back the top).

The second study focuses on present and future differentials be-

[13] Meadows et al., p. 29.
[14] Mihajlo Mesarovic and Eduard Pestel, *Mankind at the Turning Point: The Second Report to the Club of Rome.* New York: E. P. Dutton & Co., Inc./ Readers Digest Press, 1974, Chap. 1.

tween industrialized and underdeveloped or developing regions. If present growth patterns continue fifty years, comparative per capita income of the developed and underdeveloped world will be as 20 to 1—a gap which the investigators see as politically intolerable and by then unbridgeable. From this finding, the main thrust of the study becomes juggling those variables which humans can change until a model emerges which will permit slow but significant growth in a comparatively stabilized world.

The investigators' proposed solution is the goal of stabilizing world order by 2025 A.D. through massive aid from the developed regions to make the underdeveloped regions self-sufficient. Needed aid would be less if started in 1975; even so the required total given in fifty years would be $7,200 billion. Delaying a start till 2000 A.D. would require over $10 billion over twenty-five years—a figure too astronomical to consider. The earlier per capita cost to the developed nations would be $3,000, the latter five times greater.

The study group concludes that a solution to the global crisis is possible, but only if there is an immediate world cultural revolution—a revolution in values and beliefs. Basically such a revolution most requires a commitment among the industrialized peoples to cut back their material standards drastically for the sake of helping the less fortunate.

There seems little question that the Club of Rome's second study is far more sophisticated than the first, and is unlikely to be subject to the same kinds of criticism. Without action beginning immediately, Mesarovic and Pestel can see only mass starvation ahead for many of the peoples of South Asia and Africa—500 million children alone before 2025 A.D. With any underdeveloped nation possessing atomic power plants now able to build atom bombs (as India has demonstrated), these authors try to alert readers to reality. "Ten or twenty years from today it will probably be too late, and then even a hundred Kissingers . . . could not prevent the world from falling into the abyss of a nuclear holocaust."[15]

Conclusions about the Hypothesis

There are many ways in which original Malthusian theory seems shortsighted and overly simple today. Yet, Malthus' ideas about the exponential rate of population growth still apply to most of the world's peoples and to about two-thirds of the human race in a way Malthus probably never dreamed of.

Malthus was right in assuming that people would tend to breed up to their biological capacity, but he did not anticipate that the combination

[15] Mesarovic and Pestel, p. 69.

of industrialization, urbanization, and education would lead people to want to reduce their own fertility to the extent of changing their minds radically about what constitutes vice. To Malthus, any means of reducing fertility except sexual abstinence was a vice to be condemned and punished. In

According to Barry Commoner, writing in 1974, it requires five times as much diesel fuel to transport freight by long-haul truck as by railroad; yet, we encourage long-distance trucking and truckers fight the "piggyback" ideas. *(Above, copyright © Maurice P. Hunt, all rights reserved; right, Atchison, Topeka and Santa Fe Railway Company)*

today's world the "vices" of contraception and abortion are generally accepted as virtues—except by more than half the world's population who are either unaware of their need, do not know enough about, or cannot afford them. These people consequently use no artificial fertility checks.

Malthus also could not anticipate genetic improvement of both vegetable and animal food products and the development of pesticides which would make possible vastly higher yields from the same amount of land space; he was equally oblivious of the possibilities of multiplying the amount of arable land through irrigation and heavy use of chemical fertilizers, or the potential of the oceans as food sources. Hence, he was completely unaware that the "carrying capacity" of the earth (if we focus primarily on food supply) could be very high—just how high no one seems to know since almost every "expert" suggests a different figure.

However, population statistics look worse year by year. Let us review some potential population increases briefly. Africa, with a total of

about 354 million people, has a birthrate of 47 and a deathrate of 20 (averages for the continent). By present world standards, this is a very high deathrate. But it would require only the fairly widespread use of DDT to kill malaria-bearing mosquitoes, somewhat modern sanitation, and fairly widespread use of antibiotics to reduce the deathrate dramatically (that this can be done rather quickly has been demonstrated in Latin America, which has an average deathrate of 9—lower than the United States).

Africa is an almost certain population time bomb. With no reason to expect its birthrate to drop much, the continent presents the possibility of population growth in the 5 to 6 percent category, or a doubling in fourteen or fifteen years.

Asia is in a somewhat better situation, but not enough better to give us reason for joy. The continent's birthrate is 38, its deathrate 15—and the continent already harbors well over 2 billion people. The chief hope for Asian population growth's not being as explosive as Africa's within several years is that the Chinese government is pushing birth control for its approximately 800 million people.

Latin America, with roughly 300 million people is unlikely to increase its growth rate, although the continent still has the potential for further reducing its deathrate, since thirty various other nations have already reduced theirs to below 9, a few to 5. This potential is unlikely to be realized for some time in South America, largely because of the general poverty in all of Latin America and its generally unindustrialized and uneducated state. For these same reasons, plus church opposition to birth control, Latin America is unlikely to reduce its birthrate much for a long time. We can therefore expect a doubling of the population in twenty-three to twenty-four years.

Although it may not occur, the *probability* exists that more than half the world's population is on the verge of a rate of growth so far unknown except in Kuwait. Will it be possible to increase the earth's food supply, to feed, even minimally, the population of underdeveloped countries within the next twenty to thirty years? If the community of nations, taken as a whole, had the potential for large food surpluses—as they may, due to falling birthrates and the prospect of virtually stable populations— would these surpluses be even close to sufficient? And would the food exporting nations, chief of which is the United States, be willing to give its food surpluses to nations whose people are starving but lack the wherewithal to buy food from abroad? Americans are likely to face their greatest test of charity during the next two or three decades.

What about other Malthusian "natural checks" on population growth —war and disease? At some time far back in history, warfare may have provided a significant deterrent to population growth. But not until the development of atomic weaponry has the human race had the weapons to decimate large populations. The chance that atomic weaponry will ever be used appears more slight each passing year, although, of course, it cannot be ruled out as a possibility.

Quite likely, diseases associated with malnutrition will continue to afflict hundreds of millions of people. However, history seems to have demonstrated that these diseases do not necessarily reduce the birthrate much. They undoubtedly shorten life expectancy, but a population with an average life expectancy of 45 can maintain a birthrate of over 40—it is only necessary that enough girls survive fifteen or twenty years past puberty. But the big killers of the young and those within the fertility range of adulthood have been contagious diseases. In underdeveloped countries malaria, cholera, typhoid, dysentary, tuberculosis, and other contagions keep the deathrate in the 20s unless, with the aid of more affluent nations, modern sanitation and medicine is introduced. Such improvements can occur on a large scale in a very few years and decrease the deathrate to 10, or 11, or below. This is the prospect we now face in Africa and large parts of Asia.

We find it difficult to accept the arguments of certain ecological optimists that in less than thirty years the underdeveloped nations will have achieved high enough levels of industrialization and education to reduce their population growth rates and increase their food production rates to anything like the required level. These nations have too much working against them, particularly illiteracy. In Africa, about 44 percent of the people can neither read nor write; in Asia, 54 percent (although mass education in China will steadily reduce that figure); in Latin America, 34 percent. Since a person who may do no more than write his name is classed as literate in most of these countries, almost the entire populations remain *functionally* illiterate. This can hardly be remedied much in less two or three generations. So the combination of factors which has been shown to effect a decrease in population growth—urbanization + industrialization + education—probably cannot be installed soon in underdeveloped countries.

Unless we accept the ultraoptimists' views, despite Malthus's being wrong in relation to unforeseen factors of shifting psychology and improved technology for production, we must acknowledge that *he was apparently right in predicting that population growth (but not worldwide) would outrun food production growth. We are only now seeing the possibility of this happening a century later than Malthus's prediction.* We cannot leave our conclusions hanging, however, simply with an assertion that Malthus was essentially correct even though a century and a half off in his time schedule. There are inescapable questions as to what all of this means.

It appears increasingly likely that what our analysis means is mass hunger and starvation in enough of the world to encompass from half to two-thirds of its population. This view has surged to the front in 1974 as the "experts" who were formerly complacent have had to face the stark reality that the world's present food margin is the most critical it has been in memory. The number of articles being published on this subject has mushroomed in 1974. A recent feature article in one of the major news magazines is only typical of dozens of others.

> Even now, food shortages affect the entire world. In the last two years, famine has threatened India and visited widespread misery upon the sub-Sahara nations of Africa where an estimated quarter million people have died.
> Scarcely less shocking, more than half of the world's 3.7 billion people live in perpetual hunger. The industrial nations are swiftly buying up the dwindling supplies of food and driving up food prices so high that poorer nations cannot afford to pay them.[16]

[16] "Running Out of Food?" *Newsweek,* April 1, 1974, pp. 40–41.

There is grave danger that within less than a decade mass starvation in the underdeveloped nations may affect hundreds of millions a year. If this prospect, even though exaggerated, *comes to be believed* by the more than half of the world's population now hungry, will they simply sit back and obediently starve? Such a posture runs against the whole of history. People will usually fight in every way they know to stay alive.

We see as a strong possibility, therefore, global warfare developing between the have and have-not people. We can't be sure it would take the form of warfare the United States used against Vietnam where we employed the most sophisticated military hardware and half a million troops trying to control an internal revolution. The warfare we have in mind seems more likely to take the form of a guerrilla war of attrition, with teams of terrorists from starving countries infiltrating the still food-wealthy nations and committing large-scale assassinations, kidnappings, and massive destruction of property through arson or explosives. Armed forces of industrial nations do not know well how to combat this sort of situation, and the starving nations are likely to coordinate their efforts for the first time out of desperation. This appears a dismal prospect, but to be realistic we have to recognize its possibility.

ECOLOGICAL ISSUES AND EDUCATION

If one takes quick stock and does not probe, it would appear that public education has taken ecological problems seriously. The schools made a big thing of Earth Day when it was instigated in 1970. Administrators and teachers, with the blessing of school boards and parents, put students to work cleaning up litter. About the only other "activist" program encouraged by schools has been helping to organize student cadres to assist in collecting and transporting recyclable materials—bottles, cans, and paper. But what of the nature of present curriculum materials on ecology. At best, they treat fairly well issues in such areas as resource scarcity and pollution, but it is our impression they ignore the really fundamental issues.

A Needed Curriculum in Ecology

In view of the present paucity of honest, hard-hitting ecological content in the curriculums of most public schools, curriculum revision that permits the addition of such material seems to be the first step needed to strengthen public school programs. Such material is available in abundance. Not only are there books, magazine articles, and guest speakers, but even a few good motion pictures with ecological themes.

Whether there should be a separate course, or courses, in ecology is something of an open question. Certainly, most school courses lend themselves to the insertion of ecological content—the social studies, biology and chemistry, business subjects, home economics, industrial arts, agriculture, and so on. The advantage of having separate courses is that this provides a guarantee that ecological content—good or bad—will be there. If left to teachers of other subjects to insert a unit now and then where they think it might fit, there is always the risk that the job may not be done at all.

Studying the Community as an Ecosystem

It strikes us that it might be worth more educationally to combine formal in-school study with community study in the teaching of ecological principles. What we propose may strike most readers as impractical, but then so has every innovation in education which might offend someone (as have such innovations in any other field). Such study would be worthless if done haphazardly. We will therefore suggest the rough outlines of a plan with which it might be well worth experimenting.

Constructing a Model

The first step would be for students, after acquiring the needed background from books and other teaching materials, to draw up on paper (with the use of diagrams or charts as needed) a plan for a community that would assure its ecological viability. Since ecological problems are tied in with many other kinds of problems, a model sufficiently comprehensive to be useful as a guide would have to include a large number of community variables, some of the more important of which we will suggest below.

In devising such a model, teachers and students must remain aware that there are few communities left that are self-contained microcosms. Their own community will not be a closed system to be regarded like "spaceship earth." It will be involved in a continuous interplay with forces outside the community. For purposes of investigation, however, these outside forces can in some cases be ignored because their importance is not crucial; but if they have to be reckoned with, the model must include them. Any such model as teachers and students draw up will be highly oversimplified; even so, it is well to remember that much has been learned through human history from oversimplified conceptualizations (particularly if facts of central importance get included in the final design).

With a model in hand, a study of the students' actual community can then be done which assesses their community in relation to the model. Much good might come to a community from this kind of study, although for reasons we will mention some citizens are bound to find student investigations of this type distasteful.

Below are specimens of some types of variables which would need to be included in the model and studied in the community insofar as it is possible to do so.

The community ideology   There are various ways to find out how community citizens think about matters pertinent to the community's ecology. Students can study speeches made by leaders of opinion in the community, letters to the local newspaper editor, advertisements in the local paper, or other documentary sources. This is the easy and safe way to go about it, but may not produce well-balanced evidence.

To be more thorough, students could select a sample of random citizens (a sample small enough to be manageable) and interview these people personally or even ask them to fill out some kind of a checklist of beliefs. Our own experience with this kind of thing is that some people won't cooperate but many are glad to do so and, in fact, talk the interviewer half to death.

What are some of the features of the community ideology students would need both to include in their model and to investigate? We will suggest a few.

—Beliefs about community growth. Are people "booster types" who want to bring into the community more industry and more people? Or are they satisfied to maintain a more-or-less steady-state community?
—Beliefs about the most appropriate industries for the community.
—Beliefs about various forms of pollution. Are people concerned or not concerned about industrial waste? About human waste? About the quality of air? About water quality? About noise levels?
—Beliefs about birth control. How many children do young marrieds say they would like? How many children do people actually have?

Students and teachers would undoubtedly come up with other kinds of questions, but the above is a sample.

The community power structure   We are under no illusions that this is an easy matter for students to determine. Often adults who have lived in a community all their lives don't really know who makes the decisions in crucial matters.

One simple approach, suggested by the community studies of W. Lloyd Warner and associates in the 1930s to 1950s, is to ask a sampling of long-time residents to list the dozen or so people they consider "most important" in the community.

What does one need to find out about the power structure? If it can be ascertained who does have the final decision-making power in connection with various issues, it may be possible to infer what kinds of decisions are most likely to be made. If a local VIP owns or manages a factory that pollutes the town's water supply, it would be likely that such pollution would be difficult to eradicate. The community might have to use relatively expensive methods to purify the water and cross the cost off to community harmony.

Or, to use one more example, if the chief power figures are members of a fundamentalist religious group that opposes birth control, it might tell investigators quite a bit about probable future birthrates.

The economic base of the community This kind of information should be fairly readily available. Chambers of Commerce usually publish figures on a community's economic base.

What kinds of information would be needed about a community's economy? One kind, rather obviously, would be whether the economic base of the community is temporary, as, for example, in the case of a mining town whose mines are approaching exhaustion. It would also be significant to know if the community economy is based on a dependable, long-run source of income but not necessarily one permitting much community growth. Agricultural communities exemplify this kind of economy. But a community with industrial plants with a high growth potential (e.g., plants that produce devices to control pollution) would suggest a quite different future.

Other institutions The types of churches and their influence might well be significant. Do the churches tend toward modernism or fundamentalism or a mixture of both? Knowledge of this would tell us something about the kinds of decisions people might make about a variety of matters of ecological significance—not only birthrates, but basic attitudes toward resource use, race relations, politics, and other matters.

Does the community contain a college or university? The presence of a school of higher education seems always to have some impact on the way many community members think about important issues.

Sizing up the influence of the public schools would also be of significance. Are the schools respected in the community? Do parents have enough confidence in teachers that they are willing to entertain new ideas transmitted from the school through their children? A public school with a strong program in ecology could influence community opinion considerably, but, depending on the community, the influence might be positive or negative.

Out of a community study such as we have described (all too sketchily), students might be able to make tentative projections about whether the quality of life is likely to improve, remain about the same, or get worse. They might even be able to hypothesize whether the community is on an uphill or downhill road or likely to remain comparatively stable. Whatever they discover, they will be better prepared to be ecologically knowledgeable citizens wherever they live in the future.

STUDY QUESTIONS

1. Ecologists and other persons who worry about the future of human and other life all seem to assume that it would be a catastrophe if life forms did not survive indefinitely. What logic is there in this view? What would it really matter if human life came to an end? (Hominids have probably been around for almost 5 million years already. Isn't that long enough?)
2. During the next decade or so, Americans (and people in some other industrial nations) are likely to be confronted with the choice of trying to maintain a high material standard of living which necessitates the use of dangerous polluting fuels *or* a much simpler life with clean air to breathe. Which would be your choice? Why?
3. When a nation chooses the least economical way to carry on some economic activity (as in using large automobiles rather than trains for long-distance travel), there are usually vested interests being served. How do you explain the fact that of all the industrial nations in the world, the United States is the most anti-train and pro-auto?
4. It seems typical for Americans to think they can lead the kind of life they prefer without regard for the wishes and needs of the rest of the world. (This is a definition of nationalism.) What do you think might be the origin of this sort of ethnocentrism?
5. It appears that at this point in history, Americans of European descent could learn a lot that would be of vital importance to them from American Indians. What do you think they could learn? Why would it be important?
6. Population growth in relation to food supply and other resources presently seems quite out of control in South America, Africa, and parts of Asia. What do you think the United States could and should do about it?
7. Many cultures have historically practiced infanticide as a means of population control. Do you see any significant moral difference between this and abortion? Or use of the "morning after" pill? Explain your reasoning.
8. What is your opinion about the population size of the United States? Do you think it is optimum, or below or above optimum? Explain.
9. We are not alone in suggesting the possibility within the next decade or two of a global conflict between the havenots and the haves, the poor and the affluent. What do you think of this prognostication? If it developed, what outcome would you predict?
10. Draw up a hypothetical program of ecologic education for a public school (at the elementary level if you are an elementary major; at the secondary level, if a secondary major). Present it to the class for study and debate. If the class likes it, ask your district superintendent of schools his opinion.

ANNOTATED BIBLIOGRAPHY

Beckerman, Wilfred, *In Defence of Economic Growth.* London: Jonathan Cape, Ltd., 1974.

    Beckerman, a professor of political economy at the University of

London, writes a book-length rebuttal of ecologists, economists, and social philosophers who take a pessimistic view—particularly in connection with population growth. Referring to them as "eco-doomsters," Beckerman places his faith in technological breakthroughs which he views as making easily possible a world population of 20 billion. Interesting to read alongside Ehrlich or Meadows.

Black, John, *The Dominion of Man: The Search for Ecological Responsibility*. Edinburgh: The Edinburgh University Press, 1970.

The only book we have found addressed to the origins of human attitudes toward the world of nature. Focusing on the Western World, Black shows how the Judeo-Christian tradition has steadily found theological basis for ecologically exploitive societies and is likely to continue to do so until the tradition expires—if human life can survive that long. Highly recommended reading.

Commoner, Barry, *The Closing Circle: Nature, Man, and Technology*. New York: Alfred A. Knopf, Inc., 1971.

This extremely readable book stresses what Commoner sees as the major ecological problem: human beings poisoning themselves to death with their own pollution. Although prominent as a biologist, Commoner weaves philosophy and social science into his writing more skillfully than any other ecologist we know of and offers a more penetrating analysis of American culture. Should be read in conjunction with the recent Ehrlich book, below, for a contrast in views which are perhaps not so much contradictory as complementary.

Ehrlich, Paul R., Anne H. Ehrlich, and John P. Holdren, *Human Ecology: Problems and Solutions*. San Francisco: W. H. Freeman and Company, 1973.

One of the best recent books for student reading, this paperback presents very effectively the chief Ehrlich pitch: that the most critical ecological problem is overpopulation and the risk of a major appearance of the Malthusian "natural checks" on population growth —famine and disease in the underdeveloped countries. The authors' analysis is more qualified and cautious than in previous works and introduces students to political and economic barriers to solving economic problems. An excellent book for high school as well as college use.

Lineberry, William P. (ed.), *Priorities for Survival*. New York: The H. W. Wilson Company, 1973.

Another first-rate book of essays by a variety of authors. Many of the essays in this volume are introductions to different facets of major ecological problems. This book is particularly good for students who need basic background; should also be useful for high school student reading.

Longgood, William, *The Darkening Land*. New York: Simon & Schuster, Inc., 1972.

This interesting book focuses on pollution. Contains a report on the observations of ocean pollution by world-famous French oceanographer, Jacques-Yves Cousteau. Book also contains useful statistics on the much greater amount of illness among persons forced to breathe polluted air. The author tries to link the increasing rate of cardiovascular failure among relatively young people to pollution.

Nobile, Philip, and John Deedy (ed.), *The Complete Ecology Fact Book*. New York: Doubleday & Company, Inc., 1972.

The most useful compendium of facts to date and an excellent reference book. The 1971 World Population Data Sheet and population density chart combine statistics in a way we have found nowhere else. The excellent charts, graphs, figures and tables depict graphically a wealth of detailed factual material and are gotten up in a manner very easy to use.

Pirages, Dennis C., and Paul R. Ehrlich, *Ark II: Social Responses to Environmental Imperatives.* New York: The Viking Press, 1974.

The emphasis in this most recent book to which Ehrlich's name is attached is frugality of consumption—to be achieved by abandoning the production of luxuries and all other kinds of unnecessary consumer items and building necessary items well enough to last.

Ridgeway, James, *The Politics of Ecology.* New York: E. P. Dutton & Company, Inc., 1970.

This is one of comparatively few books devoted to the root of where the ecological problem really lies: in the manipulation of public opinion (often through falsification of statistics) by major corporations. Ridgeway gets into the monopoly aspects of the petroleum and other energy industries and the tendency of the Federal Government to team up with the corporations.

Singer, S. Fred (ed.), *Is There an Optimum Level of Population?* New York: McGraw-Hill Book Company, Inc., 1971.

A first-rate collection of essays by a variety of authorities. Well organized, with sections on optimum population as related to the natural resource base, education, health, and welfare services, and life styles and human values. In the epilogue, Singer concludes that there are ways of getting at a definition of "optimum" although we have not yet perfected them.

Weisberg, Barry, *Beyond Repair: The Ecology of Capitalism.* Boston: Beacon Press, 1971.

Weisberg sees no possibility of ameliorating ecologic problems under a capitalist economy and social system. He attempts to explain why, in his opinion, socialism of some type is the only path to salvation, and if present Communist countries have ecological problems (as several do) it is not an inherent feature of the system but merely growing pains. Perhaps biased and superficial, Weisberg is nevertheless provocative and worth reading.

part
III

EDUCATION IN
THE SEVENTIES

In Part III, we will return to two major areas of controversy in education, for which the previous parts of the book have laid the groundwork.

Chapter 13 treats the long-range goals of public education as we construe them to be if public education is to serve the purpose intended for it by the Founding Fathers: the purpose of educating people to make a self-governing, humanistic democracy work. Since it is difficult to find hard evidence that public education has been very effective at its assigned task, our first job in Chapter 13 will be to raise questions about the way educators have gone about stating goals. If the necessary goals of public education are not stated in a clear and concrete way, teachers will flounder.

We will first review and criticize traditional approaches to stating long-range goals and try to show that these earlier approaches have involved so much ambiguity as well as lack of concrete focus that they said both too much and too little. The evidence of their effectiveness seems virtually nil.

453

We will next address ourselves to the current reaction to the overly broad long-range goals of the past and the intense emphasis on short-range goals, or objectives, stated as overt behavioral outcomes, with which we have become infested in the 1970s. Although, as we will show, this approach is hardly new, it does give education a quite different cast from what we experienced between the early 1930s and the mid-1970s. We feel that the answer to our educational problems does not lie in behavioral objectives or the "accountability movement" to which they are related.

The last half of the chapter is devoted, therefore, to our suggested manner of developing goal-statements, and a discussion of a series of cultural problem areas which can serve as the basis for producing long-range goals that are both pertinent and concrete enough to serve as realistic guides.

Chapter 14 is our attempt to show how it might be possible to implement the admittedly rather utopian-sounding goals proposed in Chapter 13 and implied, of course, throughout the entire book. Chapter 14 tries to show how public education can truly be "reconstructed" by analyzing some obstacles which in the past have made the reconstructionist position something less than practical and pointing out how these obstacles are already in the process of being reduced and how they can be reduced still further.

The Epilogue is the largely subjective musings of the writer about what education can and should be in the future. The Epilogue is in a sense, perhaps, a benediction, but hopefully a foreward looking one.

13

EDUCATIONAL GOALS
IN A DEMOCRACY

*. . . since in reality there is nothing to which growth is relative save
more growth, there is nothing to which education is subordinate save
more education . . .*

John Dewey

The central purpose of this chapter is to suggest how
we might go about ascertaining long-range goals for education
which will serve the purpose—hopefully—of helping educators
redirect education to serve better both democratic and humanistic ends. To us the most important end is human survival
itself. But not this exclusively because without some hope for
"the good life" even the goal of survival begins to pale.

To help readers understand how our proposals differ

What do educators want—programmed sheep or critical thinkers?
(Both photos, Maurice P. Hunt)

radically from some earlier attempts at long-range goal setting, particularly from the confusion of the seventies about the function of short-range goals (more often called objectives), we will need to get into the *behavioral objective movement*, an integral part of broader movements of the seventies going under such generic labels as *performance based education* or the *accountability movement*.

THE PROBLEM OF GOAL MAKING

Although, as we will review later, attempts at stating long-range social goals of education have a long history, in our opinion, too much emphasis has been placed on short-range goals—for a year, semester, month, week, or class period. These sorts of goals are commonly referred to as "objectives," though some writers, such as Benjamin Bloom, at times use the terms goal, purpose, and objective interchangeably.

Meaning of Long Range in Relation to Goals

While it is impossible to draw a line between short- and long-range goals because, properly defined, short-range goals are instruments for achieving long-range goals, yet used in one sense, long-range goals may refer to goals for a single school year which employ daily or weekly objectives as steps along the way. However, it seems hardly possible to limit educational goal making to a single school year. Goals of a single or even several years (e.g., the primary, elementary, junior high school, or senior high school years) should be regarded as serving goals that extend into adulthood, even throughout a person's entire life.

But even this is limiting: since we have future generations to be concerned about, can we say that educational planning should extend no further than the life spans of pupils now in school? We feel that this should not be so. Humankind might well have saved itself many of its most dire predicaments had people's goals involved a century or more. This is especially important now, when for the first time in history, ecological problems exist which could easily extinguish human civilization within a century or less.

457

Although we may be getting into unnecessary abstractions, we hope readers will bear with our trying to distinguish between what can legitimately be called a long-range goal in contrast to a short-range goal (which we will henceforth refer to as an "objective").

What Is a Long-Range Goal?

No one tries very hard to define "long range." The late John Maynard Keynes said that the long range, or long run, refers to that period of time when all those who talk about it will be dead. This witticism really doesn't help define an ubiquitous expression which requires definition if it is to remain in the language of scholarly literature.

To have utility, a definition of long-range must specify a beginning and an end. Our definition may be arbitrary, but it should help make our discussion more intelligible: any concept of the "long range" (or "long run") begins *now*. What-is-currently-in-progress is always a part of the long range because it includes trends or tendencies which will extend to the end-point of the long range. The end-point of long range is when our forecasts, projections, interpolations, or anticipations can no longer be visualized with enough concreteness to be meaningful.

What is considered likely to happen in the future is always largely a matter of faith even in the most exact sciences, but here faith makes allowance for variables that might throw forecasts off, and then assumes that certain crucial trends we can now identify *may*, or in some cases *are likely to*, continue for some approximate length of time. When we reach a point in our extrapolation where we can say "X trend may, or probably will, terminate in about Y years," then we are talking about an end-point.

For example, when we review John Dewey's assertion about the central aim of education (quoted at the beginning of the chapter), to the effect that the only object of growth is a capacity for continued growth, we see a long-range goal-statement which has no terminal point unless it be the life span of the persons involved. Dewey's goal-statement, of course, does not exclude an infinite number of terminations of specific goals along the way: within Dewey's broad framework, it is legitimate to say, for example, that "To help students evaluate, and be ready to later reevaluate, their beliefs about the energy crisis for twenty years ahead," is a legitimate long-range goal. This would be an example of how students might learn to evaluate current data and be able to reevaluate from new data later, each evaluation setting a new specific goal within a long-range goal.

To this writer, a defensible long-range goal-statement would involve a description of an area of culture in which students are likely to have at least some values and beliefs, and which is also judged an area likely to be problematic as far into the future as we can make informed guesses.

Such personal-cultural problem areas can be described with a great deal of concreteness. Most will be areas of high irrationality (or high negative alienation or clear signs of anomie)—what we have often called "closed areas of culture."

Further, if educators were ever to see the point in it, these areas could also be described in terms of concrete values and beliefs that are embedded in the culture to the point where students, at least by the time they are in high school, are virtually certain to have some rather specific values and beliefs in the area. Or, even more useful, the *interaction* between individual and cultural ideology could be the focal point of goal-statements. Obviously, it is more difficult to determine and then state long-range goals this way than as they are commonly stated, but the ways in which such goals have been stated in the past are largely useless, as we will try to demonstrate in the next section.

Vagueness of Most Long-Range Goal-Statements

Curriculum makers have promulgated numerous long-range and relatively general goals for American education in the twentieth century. The most prominent efforts have come from the U.S. Office of Education or the National Education Association, although special presidential study commissions have also played a part. As one looks back at these goal-statements, one of their more obvious characteristics is that they are sufficiently ambiguous as to offend no one, to offer everyone something, and to permit education to go on as before with every teacher claiming allegiance to whichever set of goals are the "in goals" of the moment.

In 1918, the National Education Association advanced what it called the "Cardinal Principles of Education." These principles were supposed to reflect what people actually needed to know about life, as judged by cultural study aimed at uncovering what people actually did.[1] These Principles, which came to be known to all school personnel, were called "The Seven Cardinal Principles of Education" and were considered appropriate for all grade levels. They were:

1. Health
2. Command of fundamental processes
3. Vocation
4. Worthy home membership
5. Citizenship
6. Worthy use of leisure
7. Ethical character

[1] Committee on the Reorganization of Secondary Education, *Cardinal Principles of Secondary Education*, U.S. Office of Education, Bulletin No. 35. Washington, D.C.: National Education Association, 1918, pp. 10ff.

Obviously, such a list taken by itself is totally meaningless because it does not define the words or expressions. The bulletin did, of course, write up each of the above principles in some detail. For example, in connection with the first principle, it is *good* health which was intended. The N.E.A. asserted its own value judgments about what good health would be. Fundamental processes referred to reading, writing, and arithmetic. The N.E.A. was also suitably vague as to precisely how much and what kinds of fundamental processes were needed. "Worthy" home membership seems to have meant, among other things, knowing the importance of the home as a social institution and understanding one's place and duties in the home.

In the case of all the Cardinal Principles, specifics tend to express the values of the writers, a first-rate example of those who have power (school authorities) deciding what is deviant behavior for those who lack power (students). This writer finds that by the time he reaches "Citizenship" and reads that "Civic education should develop in the individual those qualities whereby *he will act well* his part as a member of neighborhood, town, city, state and nation . . ." (emphasis added), that he has had quite enough vagueness. Unqualified comments about acting *well* in relation to one's community could logically be used to justify the part played by prostitution (considered by many people to be a needed community service) as well as bribery (an often efficient way to get action out of public officials).

The National Education Association made another one of its better-known tries at setting long-range goals for education in 1938.[2] The NEA created a group known as the Educational Policies Commission, which came up with four main heads of goals, as follows:

1. The objectives of self-realization.
2. The objectives of human relationship.
3. The objectives of economic efficiency.
4. The objectives of civic responsibility.

The elaboration of these objectives, or goals, is more concrete, less naive, than that of the Cardinal Principles of 1918. At least, in addition to the fundamental skills, some specifics under self-realization are the development of "an inquiring mind and "intellectual and aesthetic" interests." This set of goal-statements does reflect one common view of the thirties: it seems to focus mainly on student needs with little reference to cultural needs.

[2] Educational Policies Commission, "The Purposes of Education in American Democracy," Washington, D.C.: National Education Association, 1938.

In the 1950s life adjustment education became a movement of sorts, spurred by the voluminous writing of Harl H. Douglass of the University of Colorado.[3] This movement can probably be interpreted as simply an additional step in the direction implied by the Seven Cardinal Principles and a variety of other reports issued by the Office of Education, the NEA, or special study commissions. It was a move toward making the schools "child and youth centered" in the sense of trying to assess the needs of young people in our culture, both their immediate needs as children and youth and their future needs as adults. The term "life adjustment" was apt: the whole thrust of the movement was to *adjust* students to cope with the cultural status quo. Little is implied, even this late in time, about the possible goal of education contributing to the health of the culture.

During this period, as in the 1970s, preparing students for adult work was emphasized. One pre-1950 publication of the Office of Education asserted that "Labor is the lot of man . . ." and that "The ability to work steadily for 8 hours is not a natural possession; it has to be acquired." After making these points, the publication urges that youth be provided work opportunities while in school for which they would be paid.[4]

One more example of the attempt of a special study commission to decide the proper goals for American education: in 1955 the Executive Branch of the Federal Government sponsored the White House Conference on Education. Attended by about 1800 citizens and educationists, the Conference addressed itself chiefly to the question, "What Should Our Schools Accomplish?"[5] The report to the President listed fourteen aims. Readers will see their flavor from these specimens:

1. Appreciation of our democratic heritage.
2. Ability to think and evaluate constructively and creatively.
3. Ethical behavior based on a sense of moral and spiritual values.
4. Wise use of time, including constructive leisure pursuits.
5. An awareness of our relationships with the world community.

This particular list is of interest (although scarcely mind boggling), because it illustrates again the ambiguity of such lists. What does it mean to "appreciate our democratic heritage"? The nation has many contradic-

---

[3] Harl H. Douglass (ed.), *Education for Life Adjustment,* New York: The Ronald Press Company, 1950. Douglass edited a series of widely used books with a life adjustment theme.

[4] Federal Security Agency, "Life Adjustment Education for Every Youth," Washington, D.C.: Office of Education, 1948. Another publication with the same title was authored by the Commission on Life Adjustment Education for Youth and published as U.S. Office of Education, Bulletin No. 22, 1951.

[5] *White House Conference on Education,* Washington, D.C.: Government Printing Office, 1956.

tory heritages. Are teachers supposed to teach all our heritages? Or conceal some of them? In the case of the second item, what does it mean to "think and evaluate constructively and creatively"? The report did not define thinking or the process of value testing. Even more puzzling is "Ethical behavior based on a sense of moral and spiritual values." Whose moral and spiritual values? Those pushed by some particular authoritarian church? If so, which church? What does the word "spiritual" mean? The conference certainly made no attempt to come to grips with issues in ethical theory or any other issue which would have introduced more specificity into its goal-statements.

As we look over these lists we can only see them as a kind of sloganeering approach to formulating educational goals conducted by people who, although they may have had doctorates in education, or been prominent university graduates, had no basic understanding of issues related to how one might go about inventing defensible goals for education. Such lists reveal little or no understanding of the nature of either students or American culture. They are carefully put together in only one respect: they will offend no one.

After all the conferences, the hundreds of thousands of dollars spent in studies, and the lists of long-range goals for education, what do we now have? Apparently we have a population which in the main is ill-informed about the culture and themselves. Above all both individuals and culture patterns are riddled with logical inconsistencies which, to the most sensitive individuals, become a basis for negative alienation. Earlier attempts at long-range goal setting have largely been exercises in futility.

AN "ENGINEERING" APPROACH TO GOALS

In part as a reaction to the ambiguity of previous attempts to formulate broad long-range goals, on two occasions in this century educators have reacted by turning to short-range goals stated as behavioral outcomes. A behavioral goal—or objective—describes the desired result of teaching as students' acquiring new *overt responses*.

An overt response may be verbal, as in learning to say something, or actional in the sense of a changed bodily motion, as learning to write or bat a pitched ball. Under this concept of objectives, changes of insight play no part. They are disregarded on the grounds that they are not "scientifically measurable."

The First Time Around

In the 1920s a group of American educators led by Charles H. Judd (1873–1946), W. W. Charters (1875–1962), and Franklin Bobbitt (1876–1956) attempted to develop a "scientific education" which would produce more socially useful results than earlier ways of educating.[6] These men got many of their cues from early-century behaviorist psychologists who believed that most or all of human behavior is environmentally determined. If human behavior can be explained on the basis of environmental determinism, then behavior can be modified by changing the environment.

Judd, Charters, and Bobbitt felt that by studying the kinds of behavior needed by adults to live successfully in American culture, it would be possible to develop lists of appropriate behavioral objectives. These objectives, in the form of behavioral responses of pupils, could be programmed into students by properly arranging the school environment.

Much of the work of these men was devoted to studying the social environment to find what kinds of responses produced well-functioning adults, describing these responses as specific behaviors (the objectives of education), and then planning a curriculum and teaching methods which would guarantee that students had acquired the right responses by the time they finished school.

After a major flurry of objective formulation, the "scientific education" movement of the 1920s subsided. The Great Depression of the 1930s with its accompanying social turmoil, caused a shift of interest among educators to a more issue-centered, humanistic education. The Progressive Education Association by this time had gained considerable influence and its purposes included the use of education to change the social order—an aim almost diametrically opposed to the conservative, status quo-oriented "scientific education" of the behaviorists.

Rebirth of "Scientific Education" in the 1970s

We are seeing in the seventies what seems to be a replay of the movement of the twenties. Short-range objectives, defined as changes in overt behavior, are again much in vogue. The rebirth of this approach to education can be explained only by a theory of multiple causation. Probably most teachers who are sold on so-called scientific education (although the expression "scientific" is not used much any more in this connection) honestly feel it helps them be more effective teachers. Undoubtedly many administrators also see a potential in the movement for producing demonstrable results which will make parents, taxpayers associations, and politicians happier about the cost of education.

However, in the eyes of many state legislators (who in most states have mandated the use of behavioral objectives in state legal codes), and

[6] For a lively account of this group, see John P. Wynne, *Theories of Education.* New York: Harper & Row, Publishers, 1963.

administrators as well, cheapening education has probably seemed fully as important as improving its quality. Once the hundreds of behavioral objectives get written for each school subject, the related teaching materials acquired, the teaching routines established, and the short-answer behavioral tests constructed, then teaching can be done by technicians with minimal training. Training, not education, is all teachers need under this general approach. The concept of professionalism becomes moot: most teaching can be handled by low-grade technicians, community members with spare time who will work in the classroom for the minimum legal hourly wage.

In addition to the apparent belief that widespread use of behavioral objectives may produce more output in relation to input, and will at the same time cut the cost of education, it seems clear that this whole approach harmonizes with the zeitgeist of the post-World War II period. We are living in an age dominated by advanced technology and large-scale assembly-line production, automated to reduce the need for human labor. Business corporations operate on the basis of carefully detailed routines, uniformity of method and product, and an ability to sell the product, whatever it may be, by the modern science of advertising.

Education, like mining, transport, and manufacturing, has also become a mass production industry. It seems only logical to many educators that public schools adopt basically the same procedures as other industries which have demonstrated beyond a doubt that they can achieve a tremendous quantitative output.

The Behavioral Objective Movement Evaluated

The current tendency to substitute short-range, specific behavioral objectives for broader, more flexible goal-statements has been sharply criticized by educators well grounded in philosophy, psychology, and social science. We will point out what seem to us fundamental dangers in the movement.

Short-Range Objectives Become Final Goals

In spite of denials by many educators who have written in defense of behavioral objectives, it strikes us that—at least as they are now being implemented in the classroom—they cause teachers to lose all sight of long-range goals pertinent to the maintenance of a humanistic, democratic society. The thousands upon thousands of specific objectives written to guide teaching for a semester or a school year, tend to become the only goals schools seek to achieve. We have read a dozen or so books on how to implement the use of behavioral objectives and although most authors do distinguish between highly specific behavioral objectives and longer-range general goals, the more general goals remain confined to the learning of specialties. They seem to bear little or no relation to the critical problems of the culture.

If teaching according to objectives limited only to the production of overt responses could be defended, it could be defended only as a means to some defensible long-range socially valuable end. But the essential character of an ends-means relationship becomes forgotten in the shuffle. Means become *final ends*, not ends which will serve as means to still other ends.

If the specific objectives of teachers focused on "learning how to learn," critical thinking, the testing of important human values, the study of major contradictions in the culture, and the like, the story would be different. But these are not objectives which can be described in terms of short-range behavioral responses, so they are not included.

The kinds of specific objectives being stressed are well illustrated by one writer's examples of *terminal objectives*, that is "what the learner is to *do* at the end of instruction." One such terminal behavioral objective (intended to illustrate what is appropriate for the social studies) is "The learner is to know the names of the fifty states so that he can list them (from memory) in any order."[7] So here we have it, clearly spelled out: If pupils can memorize the names of all fifty states so they can recite them back in any order, one purpose of the social studies has been fulfilled —period.

Behavioral Objectives Promote Authoritarian Totalitarianism

To a large degree, public education has always had an authoritarian/totalitarian cast in this and probably most other countries. It is authoritarian in the sense that one of the teacher's prescribed roles is always to be right or pretend to be right—to play God. By the same token, the teaching materials used contain nothing but Truth and should be memorized by students with no questions asked. It is totalitarian in the sense that all students are supposed to learn the same facts and to adopt the same values. We have tried to hold students to both authoritarian and totalitarian ends by demanding of them that they all take and pass the same tests at the same time on the same material.

Whether education under this pattern always produces authoritarian/totalitarian people is another matter. The overall cultural milieu may override the attempt of the schools to produce blind sameness. That this can and has sometimes happened is a matter we will comment on in the Epilogue.

[7] Richard W. Burns, *New Approaches to Behavioral Objectives*. Dubuque, Iowa: Wm. C. Brown Company, Publishers, 1972, p. 5.

Our main point here is that if our schools have been entirely too authoritarian and totalitarian in the past, the behavioral objectives movement can only have the effect of making them more so. Because by law *all* teachers are bound to teach by such objectives, so long as the movement remains influential we are unlikely to see much teaching that is either issue centered or thought provoking.

The occasional gifted teacher whose imagination makes his classroom efforts so exciting that his students will never again be willing to settle for anything less than full freedom of thought and a life of self-actualization, and who in the past provided our public schools with enough spark to make them defensible, cannot work under the demands of behavioral objectives.

Personality Fragmentation and Alienation

Virtually all the directives we have seen for writing behavioral objectives advocate using as an organizational base the objectives taxonomy originated by Benjamin S. Bloom and a group of his associates. We referred briefly to this taxonomy near the end of Chapter 4 and to the three books in which the entire taxonomy appears.[8]

Readers will recall that the Bloom taxonomy is triadic: it refers to objectives as cognitive, affective, and psychomotor. Cognitive objectives refer to intellectual skills; affective to emotive skills; and psychomotor to muscular skills. Whether Bloom and associates intended to portray human beings as consisting of three separate components or whether cognitive, affective, and psychomotor are intended to refer to different dimensions of a single entity, cannot be determined by reading these books or Bloom's other writing. Bloom's position seems based on such thoroughly confused premises that it is impossible for a reader to know what is really intended.[9]

Our point here is that whatever Bloom and associates may have intended, the dozens of writers who have produced books on how to write behavioral objectives do treat the cognitive, affective, and psychomotor

[8] Benjamin S. Bloom (ed.), *Taxonomy of Educational Objectives Handbook I: Cognitive Domain.* New York: David McKay Company, Inc., 1956; David R. Krathwohl, Benjamin S. Bloom, and Bertram B. Masia, *Taxonomy of Educational Objectives Handbook II: Affective Domain.* New York: David McKay Company, Inc., 1956; Anita J. Harrow, *A Taxonomy of the Psychomotor Domain: A Guide for Developing Behavioral Objectives.* New York: David McKay Company, Inc., 1972.

[9] See Maurice P. Hunt, "Taxonomizing Educational Objectives: Some Questions About the Approach of Benjamin Bloom and Associates," *Proceedings,* Twenty-Second Annual Meeting of the Far Western Philosophy of Education Society. Tempe, Ariz.: Arizona State University, 1974, pp. 127 ff.

separately. It has been our observation that classroom teachers, when confronted with the job of writing their own behavioral objectives, do likewise.

Since we have already commented on the virtual certainty that this kind of compartmentalization of objectives can only lead to the further fragmentation of pupils whose selves have already been shattered by a fragmented culture, we will develop the point no further here. Summerfield has made some pertinent comments on the now prevalent tendency to split individual selves into separate parts. In reviewing a book by George Isaac Brown, which does just that, Summerfield writes:

> I question the curiously naked notion of "techniques for teaching in the affective domain." My quarrel is with the use of one's emotions or feelings as the explicit subject matter of the teaching-learning situation. . . . In life, feelings are intricately and complicatedly embedded in reflection, problem-solving, and action.[10]

As people live their lives, do they allocate a part of each day to intellectual endeavor, another and quite separate part to emotional expression, and another equally separate part to muscular action? Yet, the thrust of the whole behavioral objectives movement is to induce teachers to teach one day for cognitive learning, another day for emoting, and another day for whatever movements are prescribed in their objectives. There must be a better way to approach the formulation of objectives and long-range goals than this.

GOALS AS FUNCTIONS OF PERSONAL AND CULTURAL NEED

Is this section we will describe our concept of need and show how it relates to individuals and a subculture or culture. Our concept of individual needs as situational has been described elsewhere at more length.[11]

Needs: Individual and Cultural

"Individual" and "cultural" represent artificial dichotomies, that is, they cannot be considered out of relationship to one another. We separate them in writing as a matter of organizational convenience only. (The reasons

[10] Geoffrey Summerfield, review of George Isaac Brown's *Human Teaching for Human Learning.* (New York: The Viking Press, 1971), in *Harvard Educational Review*, May 1972, p. 294.

[11] Morris L. Bigge and Maurice P. Hunt, *Psychological Foundations of Education*, 2d ed. New York: Harper & Row, Publishers, 1968, Chap. 10. Basically the same view of needs is developed at still more length in Arthur W. Combs and Donald Snygg, *Individual Behavior,* rev. ed. New York: Harper & Row. Publishers. 1959.

why individual and cultural must be regarded as different aspects of the same process were advanced in Chapter 1.)

Individual Needs

Historically there has been a tendency to think of individual needs as either emerging from an individual self and sensed by that self or as dictated by the cultural environment. Needs have been construed as either "inner" or "outer." Some writers have written of needs as if they were both, in a kind of alternating manner.

If one views individual needs as emerging from the self as if they were born there, then one is presumably implying, if not overtly saying, that needs which individuals feel are somehow instinctive. Early behaviorists developed lists of organically based drives that led to specific behavioral responses. There was at least a hint of instinct theory in these lists, but it was psychologists whom we do not associate with the behaviorist tradition who developed the most elaborate instinct theories to explain human thought and action—for example, William McDougall (1871–1938). Instinct theory per se is now generally considered obsolete.

If one sees needs of individuals as dictated by the environment, then an individual may or may not be aware of them. It may be a majority opinion within the culture, for example, that everyone who is not genetically defective should learn to be functionally literate, as we have defined that term. But many individuals may be unaware that there is any such cultural expectation. When we develop goals for education, one customary approach is to ask, "In view of what a person needs to know to function as an adult in our society, what must a person be taught while in school?" This approach to goal setting is based upon environmental determinism: what is, is what should be, because it harmonizes with environmental demand.

Individual needs can also be thought of as situational, a third position which bypasses the problems inherent in the inner-outer controversy. If needs are situation centered, they are not centered in a person or that person's environment, but in a person-environment interaction. Since needs arise from the interaction of a person and his perceived environment, they are as unique and individualized as the number of possible kinds of interactive (or transactive) situations. Further, they keep changing continuously. It follows that there are no universal basic needs that apply to all, except that many situationally oriented writers do talk about "maintenance and enhancement of the self" as a general need in a nonabsolutistic sense. We say "nonabsolutistic" because maintenance and enhancement of the self probably takes a different form for each person and keeps changing throughout each person's life.

Cultural Needs

Cultural needs can be defined in more than one way, depending in large part on how one defines culture itself. As in the case of individuals, we see three approaches: one growing from the premise of complete freedom from deterministic forces, another from the premise of an extreme degree of determinism, and a third from the view of culture as an interactive process.

A culture can be viewed as a group of psychologically contiguous attitudes, values, beliefs, myths, knowledge, etc. which are so divergent, so potentially if not actually conflict generating, that they form a very loose guide for cultural action—so loose, in fact, that they are really no guides at all. Individuals are placed almost entirely on their own to think and act as they please. This is cultural anarchy which might be a matter of design, as exemplified in the various anarchical movements, notably in the writings of William Godwin (1756–1836); or a matter of unintended cultural anomie growing out of cultural disorganization (as defined in Chapter 1). If such a cultural pattern is to exist, its chief need probably would be enough individual responsibility to prevent it from flying apart.

Culture can also be viewed as organic in a rather extreme sense: a culture in which a large core of ideas is shared by all members of the culture, and in which this core of ideas is comparatively stable over time, changing drastically only during periods of cultural revolution associated with the fall of old and the rise of new cultural patterns (as when a civilization declines, disintegrates, and is replaced by a new kind of civilization —the kinds of cultural swings assumed in considering such a period as a major turning point in human history). Again, see Chapter 1 on cultural revolution.

Thus, if one views a culture as tightly organic, as an entity in itself, then cultural patterns become highly deterministic. They tend to dictate future cultural patterns and to produce a relatively static culture. They tend to dictate the lives of individuals and to provide the framework for a deterministic view such as that of B. F. Skinner, and a deterministic conception of education as exemplified in most traditional (essentialist or perennialist) views of education. The chief needs of such a culture would seem to be a competent ruling elite and a passive obedient citizenry.

The third view of culture parallels the interactionist, or transactionalist, view of the individual self. A culture can be said to have situational needs; they vary greatly according to time and place. However, we may think in terms of some cultural needs as having more centrality than others. Just as individuals need to maintain a viable self, a culture also needs to maintain a core of values that do not fluctuate wildly as in the anarchic model or remain rigid as in the deterministic model. Nevertheless, it is a core of values with *relatively* high stability.

This core may include as a relatively stable aspect more than one value set or value cluster, each mutually contradictory to the rest but at the same time providing a kind of dialectic by which the culture maintains a balance. In the United States our twin traditions of conservatism/authoritarianism and liberalism/democracy exemplify a culture whose main strength has perhaps lain in continuous and intellectually productive dialogue between liberals and conservatives. We may even extrapolate further and suggest that the idea of a two-party political system (with parties of equal strength, but one being liberal, the other conservative) is a rather elegant model of one aspect of the institutional structure of a culture which is potentially highly viable, but which could lapse over into either an anarchic pattern (if each party loses sight of its own distinctive goals) or a deterministic, authoritarian one (if one party ceases to be effective so that the culture is *dominated* by the values of one party only, the results of which we can easily see in any one-party system, as in contemporary fascism or communism).

To keep a culture within a pattern that produces freedom, the balance of influence between parties has to be maintained within a somewhat narrow range: a tight-wire walker can sway some but not very much if he is to continue on his way. The chief need of such a culture is a citizenry educated to understand the culture, resolve disputes, and conduct elections in a democratic manner.

Difficulties Inherent in Set Lists of Goals

It has been a common practice within our culture—seen more sharply perhaps in our educational institutions than elsewhere—to work regularly at devising *lists* of objectives, or goals, which are presented as a kind of fixed guide. We saw earlier in the chapter how far educational taxonomists have gone in trying to detail such goal lists. In the present era of "accountability movements" in education, the lists of specific objectives as well as longer-range goals number in the hundreds of thousands if we consider all levels of education.

Why Lists of Fixed Goals Have Limited Usefulness

Readers could hardly have failed to sense before this that this writer has certain reservations about fixed lists of goals. By now the reason should be fairly obvious: if self, culture, and the concept of goal making itself are all regarded as *situational*, then how is it possible ever to construct lists of goals prior to the time of the actual teaching/learning process? There is a very important sense in which it is true (within the context of our own preferred models) that all attempts to write out a priori lists of educational objectives are not only foolish but a waste of time.

This leaves us with the question of when can the objective- or goal-making process in education begin? It can begin when teachers, with the assistance of students, begin to get a strong feel for the thought patterns of the students, and combine this category of information with their own stock of knowledge about cultural value and belief patterns. Without a knowledge of both simultaneously, neither teachers nor students can begin thinking about objectives. Goals emerge when students and teachers, working in an interactive relationship, begin analyzing inconsistencies in the area where student values and beliefs *overlap* with values and beliefs in the relatively stable core of the culture. Psychologically and culturally valid aims can emerge only at this point.

Conditions Under Which A Priori Goals May Be Stated

Those responsible for education can study the values and beliefs of young people prior to the time of classroom action (if readers did not see its significance when they read Chapter 4 on youth, they should now see the reason for the attempt to set forth trends in the ideology of youth). Such study must be ongoing because the culture of the young changes continuously; but dominant patterns of values and beliefs among the young can to a considerable degree be anticipated as much as a year ahead, and certain of their core commitments are probably susceptible to extrapolation several years ahead.

Any list of the values of the young must be held very tentatively; the young even more than their elders seem likely to adopt faddish values and beliefs and thus create temporary shifts in pattern. The importance of trying to find out what their longer-range values and beliefs, especially their more permanent commitments, are then becomes critical. But it can be done in a way to give us something a priori to work with.

Likewise, we can look at the values and beliefs of a group—subcultures and larger cultural patterns—and attempt to assess the more-or-less continuous, ongoing, stable values and beliefs. This is the motive of a certain amount of the public opinion polling done by Gallup, Harris, Yankelovich, and other organizations. But educators need to keep abreast of ideological developments in the culture through studies that involve in-depth empirical research as well as studies that are relatively subjective, philosophical, and introspective—what European sociologists have referred to as studies in the *Verstehen* mode.

Teachers can do this. If, in their college programs leading to a teaching credential, we gave them an idea of what they need to do and the supporting cultural background via formal coursework or some other approach, they would be able to keep abreast of what is transpiring within the culture. They would know what to read and to look for in television newscasts, documentaries, and dramatic presentations, as well as what to listen for in the verbalizations of others.

If teachers get a feel for what their students think and also a feel for group patterns of thinking, they can then focus their attention on where these patterns overlap. The overlap is likely to be rather great in that much of the student value and belief pattern can be seen in the overall cultural pattern and vice versa. Once this area of overlap is identified, a teacher can then look for those particular values and beliefs that reflect inconsistencies (dissonances) and are therefore likely to be problematic for both individuals and the larger culture.

Figure 13-1 is designed to show diagrammatically the area in which we locate "problem areas," that is, areas from which we can derive broad long-range goals. The large circle, A, represents a group sharing enough ideas to be regarded as a subculture or culture (the group's size could be that of a local community, region, nation, or the community of nations). The three overlapping smaller circles (B^1, B^2, B^3) represent students—any size group up to that which could no longer engage in shared thought and discussion. The area in which students have common concerns (not necessarily agreements), and in which these same concerns are found in the subculture or culture represented by the large circle, is the area from which we derive goals. However, unless this area of common concern contains inconsistent, illogical, or confused viewpoints, it is not a problematic area and therefore not a source of educational goals (our assumption all along,

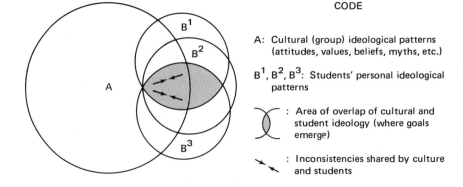

CODE

A: Cultural (group) ideological patterns (attitudes, values, beliefs, myths, etc.)

B^1, B^2, B^3: Students' personal ideological patterns

: Area of overlap of cultural and student ideology (where goals emerge)

: Inconsistencies shared by culture and students

FIGURE 13-1.   Area of interaction from which goals emerge.

of course, is that unless there are *problems* to be resolved, it is impossible to formulate any meaningful goals for education).

How We Go About Goal Listing in This Book

We will devote most of the rest of the chapter to talking about what we see as defensible long-range goals for education in American culture.

Our goal-statements will simultaneously involve both individuals and the culture. When we think in terms of the learning of individual students, the expression, "long-range goal," will imply learning which will affect that individual for life. It will change how he thinks, and in many instances although not necessarily every, how he acts overtly as he lives out his life.

When we think in terms of the learning of groups which make up the multifarious subcultures of our broader American culture, or learning which might be projected for Americans generally and therefore involve the total American culture, "long-range" should not be taken as having any foreseeable terminal point; its terminal point would be when the goal specified ceased to play a role in keeping the culture viable as a culture (not unchanged, but able to guide its own processes of change, able to avert a degree of negative alienation and anomie which would cause a general disintegration of any kind of identifiable "culture pattern"). Our own goal-statements obviously will not involve a span of time longer than that in which we can make some kind of projection, based upon the working out of what now appear as cultural tendencies which may have a comparatively long lifespan.

SOME PROPOSED LONG-RANGE GOALS FOR AMERICAN EDUCATION

For organizational purposes, we have divided this section into two parts: (1) cultural/personal goals, in which the emphasis is on group learning but in which no attempt is made to push the artificial distinction between cultural and individual; (2) personal/cultural goals, in which the emphasis is on individual need but again with no attempt to separate individual and cultural.

A goal area, as we will present it, is a description of an area of cultural/personal or personal/cultural interaction in which debilitating inconsistencies exist. The discussion to follow will therefore not be a list or classification (taxonomy). It will be a succession of descriptions of what we might broadly label problematic areas (goal areas) in which both individuals and the group have concerns. A specific goal, a number of which we propose, is a statement concerning what individuals and the group would have to know to reduce inconsistencies and conflicts in a goal area and to move toward agreement on the nature of, and potential means of solving, the most critical individual and cultural problems of the goal area under discussion.

Some Cultural/Personal Goals of Education

The following discussion does not purport to be a complete listing of major cultural goals (an inconceivable accomplishment if one regards cultural/personal tensions as situational). The goals are offered as being of major importance for readers to debate. They can be added to or deleted. The ensuing goals are not discussed in order of importance. We assume their ranking would keep changing.

The Goal of Human Survival

To pose this as a long-range cultural or societal goal would probably have seemed ridiculous prior to July 16, 1945, when the first uranium fission bomb was exploded near Alamogordo, New Mexico. Since then there has been much speculation about whether human beings as a species can survive—not with only an atomic holocaust in mind, but for other reasons as well. Let us look at a few situations which those concerned with survival have pointed to as menacing.

Teaching about the possibility of ecocide The subject of ecocide was developed at length in Chapter 12 and we will only remind readers here of the most salient points. We concluded as a result of the analysis that to some degree the general public, and even some prominent ecologists, may have been overconcerned about some matters and underconcerned about others. Starvation is likely to be endemic in large areas; indeed, present evidence points to a large loss of life in the next decade from starvation.

But, tragic as this is for the victims, the starvation of several hundred million people would enhance, rather than reduce, survival capability for the survivors. Malnutrition, however, poses an entirely different problem. At least half of the world's population is on a protein-deficient diet and there is some evidence that neurological and other biological damage is commonly suffered by fetuses of malnourished mothers and infants who are on a protein-deficient diet during the first few years of life. We cannot foresee the end result if more than half of all children born in the foreseeable future are mentally crippled through early malnutrition.

Nor do we know the result on the earth's ecosystem of the prospective destruction of all marine life, or the extent to which the human race is being damaged by its enormous intake of chemicals, many of known toxicity. So long as human beings continue to equate industrialism and rising per capita GNP with "progress," the poisoning of the natural environment will continue.

World aspirations are for affluence, which so far we do not know how to create without critical ecological damage. Not all our time bombs are necessarily related to overpopulation per se, although overpopulation (as defined in Chapter 12) will remain a severe problem in most underdeveloped countries.

Specific objectives would be studying the most salient literature on ecocide and gathering information from any available source on the risks of ecocide. Although Paul Ehrlich and Barry Commoner do not agree on all issues, all secondary school students should know their arguments and debate and evaluate them.

Teaching about the possibility of nuclear war To destroy all human life would require only a small fraction of existing nuclear weapons. Present leaders of the nations with an atomic-weapon capability are, of course, well aware of this. The danger to human life lies in the possibility of a head of state being sufficiently irrational to push the buttons releasing his nation's missiles.

The most cursory study of history reveals that in the past some heads of state have seemed incapable of thinking in terms of consequences. Adolf Hitler is but one example. Is there any assurance that this will not happen again? If there is another world war it may well be fought primarily for ideological reasons—a religious war, as it were—and participants of such wars have not historically exhibited much rationality.

With respect to specific objectives, we would suggest that students read the best of the literature on the destructiveness of atomic weaponry.[12] Students should also study what literature there is on biological and chemical warfare.

Teaching about the possibility of economic catastrophe Without getting deep into the implications, we tried in Chapter 9 to demonstrate that the economic fate in some major industrial nations in the world community is likely to be a worsening of poverty and unemployment among the bottom half or third of the population, even as the upper third or fourth become more affluent. However, if the world's impoverished become convinced, even though it may not be true, that affluence is had only at the expense of increasing poverty, world revolutionary tendencies of the period from the fifties through the seventies may seem very minor indeed.

---

[12] A good start would be Ralph E. Lapp, *Kill and Overkill*. New York: Basic Books, Inc., Publishers, 1962.

The Goal of Planning Ahead

Although not necessarily different from a number of other cultures, including the advanced cultures of Western Europe, American culture is not planning oriented. We still have too much of a streak of laissez-faire in us, too strong beliefs that, if left alone, most problems work themselves out automatically. This belief in the governing capacity of God or Nature blocks planning in most areas of life. There are exceptions, but often the exceptions end up demonstrating even more conclusively that Americans in top positions of leadership resist planning for very far into the future.

The way we approach economic problems furnishes a good example. If inflation becomes seriously disturbing, the measures taken by the Federal Government are often "temporary," as if inflationary pressures were not a long-range problem but only momentary. The same approach is used in trying to eliminate unemployment and poverty (although, as we showed in Chapter 9 on economic problems, much that is said about these problems is pretense). The United States now has a power crisis and an urban transportation crisis because of steadfast refusal to plan ahead in these areas. And in the general area of land-use planning the American record is nothing short of disgraceful.

Like other social science specialties, there is a body of theory on reasons for planning, areas of life in which planning is indicated, and how successful planning is achieved. As with the other broad goals described, a necessary means to achievement is to know the most important comparative theories. As starters in this area, teachers are likely to find beneficial such books on planning theory as Donald Michael's *The Unprepared Society*.[13]

The Goal of Peaceful Social Change

Everyone favors any social change regarded as promoting progress. In the United States, most people have equated progress with higher material standards of living and gains in social prestige. If social change strikes people as leading in some other direction, change immediately becomes controversial. Americans are especially dubious about *rapid* or *major* change unless it appears to point toward additional increments of progress as defined above. The idea of *revolutionary* change is as frightening to us as it was to British Tories in 1776.

Yet, change does tend to accelerate and to take unexpected turns. If there is occurring in the United States and many other parts of the world a cultural transition which can only be described as revolutionary,

[13] Donald Michael, *The Unprepared Society*, New York: Basic Books, Inc., Publishers, 1968.

and which is likely to occur even though a majority take a negative view toward it, then it would appear that people should be prepared to cope with it. It is our view that even massive change, largely propelled by forces so long embedded in the culture that cultural movements seem relatively determined, is susceptible to shifts in direction if people respond to the pressures of change in the most effective ways open to them.

Theories of social change It is probably an understatement to say that most people (including teachers) do not understand the process of social change very well. We could hardly expect them to, since even experts on change have competing theories about how change operates.

To get a feel for the divergence of opinion with regard to social change theory, readers may want to look at Warren G. Bennis, *et al., The Planning of Change.*[14] There are, of course, numerous other books on social change and it is our opinion that no student should leave high school without some sophistication in social change theory. Teaching about social change, like teaching about social planning, can begin in the middle and upper elementary grades, focusing in the beginning, perhaps, on the planning of one's own life, family planning, school planning, and general planning in the local community.

History of social change in the United States It is hard to conceive of any school treatment of the subject of change which does not describe major social changes that have occurred, and are now occurring, in the United States. Recent social changes of major significance would include the rise of a counterculture in the sixties, the conservative reaction to counterculture ideas, and the liberal-conservative dissonance of the seventies. Nor would a treatment of social change in the United States ignore political and economic change generally, changes in foreign policy, in religion, in the status of minorities, and the other topics treated in the chapters of Part II of this book.

Teaching about alternative social systems Now virtually ignored in the public school curriculum, the study of alternative social systems must come to have a much greater place in the education of our young. There is a special attractiveness to the idea of teaching about alternatives to everything we do of any significance. A person becomes free in large part to the extent that he is aware of alternatives to the deterministic pressures of his own culture; he can fight back at destructive cultural pressures more effectively if he can make sensible counterproposals.

Teaching about nonviolent revolution To understand the significance of nonviolent tactics and strategies for social change, it is helpful to study changes that have produced a great amount of violence. There is

---

[14] Warren G. Bennis, *et al.* (eds.), *The Planning of Change.* New York: Holt, Rinehart and Winston, Inc., 1969.

good reason to study the history of revolutions, both social/economic revolutions such as the commercial and industrial revolutions, and political revolutions such as have occurred in numerous countries: the Cromwellian revolution in Britain, the American and French revolutions, the Russian and Chinese revolutions, to name but a few. Many people have written extensively about revolution, and some of their books can be read by senior high school students. All of them are translatable by teachers to a level students can grasp. Writers on this subject include Hannah Arendt, Crane Brinton, Edward Hallett Carr, Barbara Ward Jackson, George S. Pettee, and Robert Shaplen.[15]

The concept of *cultural* revolution is not adequately treated in any of these sources; for some specimen references about cultural revolution, as seen by certain social analysts of the sixties and early seventies, see Chapters 1 and 4.

The study of social change should focus upon peaceful modes of change, exploring particularly various alternatives for guiding revolutionary social change with a minimum of violence. Americans generally do not appear to understand well how a major cultural transition could occur without violence; as we have seen in earlier chapters, violence has played a major role in our history, although perhaps no more so than in that of numerous other nations. Nonviolent change, perhaps the kind advocated and successfully practiced by Ghandi, should be required study for all students.

The Goal of Understanding Democratic Values

This goal has long been popular, appearing in almost all lists of broad, long-range goals for American education. Such goal-statements, unfortunately, are usually so ambiguous that they offer little guidance on how they might be implemented.

Teaching about the history and present state of democracy The concept of democracy probably cannot be well understood apart from a study of its history and its alternatives. As some of the better examples of participatory democracy can be found in preliterate tribal cultures, anthropology has much to offer in helping us understand the method of democracy. We can also trace the course of democratic ideas in Western Civilization from Athenian Greece onward.

Students should be helped to understand the different meanings of

---

[15] To see how a unit on revolution could be taught, students might be interested in the unit described in Maurice P. Hunt and Lawrence E. Metcalf, *Teaching High School Social Studies: Problems in Reflective Thinking and Social Understanding*, 2d ed. New York: Harper & Row, Publishers, 1968, pp. 1–20.

democracy as the concept has evolved. The late Colonial Period in America and the first three decades or so of our national government provide an excellent setting for comparing different views about democracy and contrasting our early ideas about democracy with the elitism of a number of our early leaders.

Teaching about political activism   It appears that, as of the 1970s, one of the more critical problems facing the nation is general apathy in the realm of politics. That this apathy seems even more apparent among the young than among their parents and grandparents does not augur well for the future of democracy.

Teachers somehow need to get across to students that if our presidential government is to continue functioning we cannot dispense with a two-party system with parties roughly equal in political power. The present move toward "political independence" and away from major party affiliation is a move away from a two-party system. If a majority of Americans should refuse to align with and actively support one or the other of our two major parties, all we could anticipate for the long run would be a one-party system in which the "independents" became a kind of loosely knit, volatile "party" either easily dominated by a nonpartisan strong man, or, given the right circumstances, potentially in a position to throw so much weight on the side of either Democrats or Republicans as to give one party overwhelming strength over the other.

A strong two-party system can only be maintained by activism. By activism in politics, we mean affiliation with a party, trying to reshape the party to the extent that it needs reshaping (e.g., making the Republican party a genuinely conservative party and the Democratic party genuinely liberal, but without such polarization that the victory of either party would be regarded as a disaster by the other), and supporting the party actively by giving both time and money.

Teaching about alternatives to democracy   One of the essential ways of coming to understand any concept is to seek for opposing concepts so that contrasts can be studied. The broad concept which may be most useful to study in conjunction with democracy is authoritarianism, or, because of their integral link, authoritarianism/totalitarianism. The place closest at hand to study authoritarian/totalitarian practices is often one's own school and community. This may be impractical, however, in which case alternatives to democracy which are farther from home can be studied, those in an adjoining state, for example. Or, just as one can learn as much about the horrors of war by studying the Peloponnesian War as the war in Vietnam, teachers can use historical examples or can encourage students to study decision making in a Communist or Fascist country.

Teaching about democracy in education   Since most schools operate according to authoritarian/totalitarian principles, only occasionally does a school offer much chance for students to observe and participate in democratic decision making. But some schools do and teachers should exploit these opportunities as much as possible. Teachers who want to teach about this subject could hardly do better than read one famous explanation, John Dewey's *Democracy and Education*. Although too difficult for secondary students, teachers could present the ideas to students in simplified form for discussion.

The Goal of International Cooperation

After the fiasco of the League of Nations, the limited effectiveness of the United Nations, and apparently strong nationalistic movements in many countries (particularly some Third World nations, but as of 1974, also France and possibly the United States), readers may wonder if closer international cooperation is an idle goal—something to talk about, which could not be furthered by public education.

There seems to be a developing view both in the United States and abroad that such major risks as nuclear war and ecocide can be averted only by international action and not by the unilateral action of individual nations. But if this is to occur, it is incumbent on the public schools of all nations to emphasize heavily education about other countries—the characteristics of their cultures, their potential contributions, and their problems.

Some of our most prominent educators for many years have been urging schools to strengthen their programs of foreign education. For example, Freeman Butts wrote in 1960:

> In social studies, I believe that much more attention should be given to international and world affairs at the senior high school level. This is extremely important for the years ahead and should be required of all students. I would recommend that at least an entire year or semester in social studies be devoted to foreign relations and the peoples and problems of the world.[16]

Theodore Brameld has also made more adequate teaching about world affairs one of his primary causes. He asserts:

> The pity is that, to an alarming extent, the means and ends of a viable community of nations are neglected by most educators. One hears, to be sure, occasional lip service paid to the United Nations. But what is actually required is vastly more than this: It is that the problems and expectations of mankind as a whole should become nothing less

[16] R. Freeman Butts, "Scholarship and Education in a Free Society," *Teachers College Record*, March 1960, p. 286.

than the core of *every* curriculum, beginning in its own terms of maturation at the kindergarten level and extending all the way to the college and adult levels.[17]

Teaching about Comparative Cultural Patterns

This subject overlaps the study of socioeconomic systems included in a goal area above but we state it again for emphasis. A study of comparative cultural patterns would involve study of the values, beliefs, myths, etc., of foreign peoples. The present book emphasizes the study of American cultural patterns, since this has been so neglected. But in the years ahead it may be quite as important for Americans to study foreign cultures as to study their own in order to understand alternative cultural patterns.

Teaching about world revolutionary movements As we described in Chapter 6 on foreign policy, Americans generally, including their foreign policy "experts," have found it difficult to understand that undeveloped and most partially developed nations have been the scene of internal revolutions since mid-century or before. Revolutions in the Third World nations may be rather low-key, extending over many years, with the guerrilla fighting pursued sporadically.

The revolutionary model is not everywhere the same, but if we visualize a rather loose model which roughly fits many contemporary revolutionary situations, with proper qualifications it can be used as a starting point.

Teaching about the "free world" myth This topic is closely related to that developed above, but has a different emphasis. The American government, since World War II, has kept reiterating that the world is divided into two kinds of nations: Communist nations and "free" nations. Presumably the American public is supposed to believe that a free nation allows its people freedom, or even that every free nation is happily copying the best from American capitalism. Since many countries of the "free world" have dictatorial, fascist-type governments, and the common man is not free to dissent or in many ways direct his own life, a monstrous and trouble-making myth has been perpetuated in the United States. It is imperative that students learn that the expression "free nation" as used by the U.S. government, is a euphemism for *any* country whose government publicly condemns communism and proclaims its friendship for the United States, and that the expression has nothing to do with freedom of the people.

Education in third world nations In a developing nation which is

[17] Brameld, *The Climactic Decades*. New York: Praeger Publishers, 1970, pp. 70–71.

not already either a Communist or a Fascist dictatorship, the quality of public education is probably the key to the nation's avoiding communism or fascism, coping with its problems, and gradually improving living conditions. Most underdeveloped nations cannot afford an adequate system of public schools; they also lack the needed expertise. It is urgent not only for the benefit of backward nations but for its own long-range benefit that the United States supply money and experts in education to help the backward nations develop first-rate systems of public education.[18]

Some Personal/Cultural Goals of Education

Just as the cultural/personal objectives have all been of a type to promote the personal growth of learners, our personal/cultural objectives will all be of a type to promote the health of the culture. The difference is a shift in emphasis.

The Goal of Personal Growth

We could justify placing all the items in this section under the foregoing head. However, to facilitate reading we will arbitrarily present our personal/cultural goals under three main heads, with subgoals under each.

Reducing alienation/identity problems Chapter 3, on alienation and anomie (with a section on identity), provides a guide to the kind of content we feel students should have an opportunity to examine beginning in kindergarten and continuing through high school. The concepts of identity, alienation, and anomie are not too abstract for young children to understand, and with early understanding of these processes children should have a better chance of building and maintaining an adequate sense of identity and a better chance of avoiding negative alienation.

Helpful here is Glasser's definition of healthy identity.[19] Glasser emphasizes first helping the young establish sexual identity. This involves both acceptance of one's sexuality and a clear idea as to the sex roles one wants to adopt. This suggests that all students, at various points in their physiological development, need an opportunity to learn what acceptance of one's body means, as well as the unlimited number of roles suitable for both sexes. This also suggests a rather different slant for sex education than is now common. It suggests that every school system must have a

---

[18] R. Freeman Butts, with a Foreword by Arthur G. Wirth, *American Education in International Development.* New York: Harper & Row, Publishers, 1963.

[19] William Glasser, *Mental Health or Mental Illness?* New York: Harper & Row, Publishers, 1970, pp. 13–17.

firmly implanted, permanent program of sex education, taught with a view to helping students understand the benefits of sexual expression (no Puritanical teachers, please!) and also that there are no fixed roles for either sex, except that of childbearing.

Glasser's second point is that to manage the identity problem, everyone needs a set of well-established values (or ideals) which provide a sense of direction throughout life. Since people often don't know what their most cherished values are until they are confronted with a choice-making situation which puts two or more of their values in conflict, education must provide students numerous opportunities to make choices that will bring contradictory values to light so that they can be tested.

As a third point, Glasser suggests that people need to know who they are "in respect to time, place, and social environment."[20] We do not see how this can be accomplished without immersing students in some combination of relevant history, geography, anthropology, social psychology, sociology, and perhaps other subjects taught in interdisciplinary fashion and deliberately focused on the problem of helping students understand where they are chronologically and comparatively in the history of human thought, at least the thought of their particular stream of culture (although location within a global perspective seems increasingly necessary).

Teaching for General Cultivation Like other goals discussed in this chapter, as we define it, this goal is not an end in itself. The goal of cultivation is defensible only when viewed as leading to a more satisfying personal life and a more viable culture.

Cultivation has been defined as "acquaintance with and taste in fine arts, humanities, and broad aspects of science as distinguished from vocational, technical, and professional skill and knowledge" (Webster's Third International Unabridged Dictionary). One problem with this definition is that it establishes an artificial dichotomy between humanities or liberal arts and the vocational and technical.

For purposes of this book, we prefer the approach to defining cultivation suggested by anthropologist Melville Jacobs.[21] Jacobs refers to a cultured, or cultivated, person as one who shares relatively fully in the attitudes, values, beliefs, myths, and knowledge of the culture in which that person resides and interacts. With reference to the person's own culture, he or she is cultivated if learned in all that can be learned within that culture. Using Jacob's definition, the idea of the "well-rounded" person is central to the idea of cultivation.

[20] Glasser, p. 15.
[21] Melville Jacobs, *Pattern in Cultural Anthropology*. Homewood, Ill.: The Dorsey Press, 1964, Chap. 12.

If we use this definition, the task of pursuing cultivation varies in difficulty with variations in the complexity of cultures. The fewer and simpler the thought patterns of a culture, the more chance a person has of becoming cultivated. "Advanced" industrial societies have developed such an enormous store of specialized knowledge that no individual can know more than a tiny proportion of the total culture. Persons whose interests incline toward "generalism," as with concentration on the humanities (liberal arts), are likely to achieve a comparatively high level of cultivation compared with narrow specialists.

Jacobs points out, consistent with his definition of cultivation, that at least earlier in this century such groups as the Australian Blackfellows, Bushmen, Andamanese, Veddas, Eskimos, and an array of American Indians and Palaeasiatics, were in a very advantageous position to become highly cultivated relative to their own culture; in contrast, residents of the United States, Europe, Britain and its Commonwealth, and Japan, to name some conspicuous examples, have found it difficult to achieve any effective degree of cultivation.

A person who is educated broadly and liberally and who consequently understands American cultural patterns is much more likely to see both cultural inconsistencies and inconsistencies in his own thinking than a person who is educated only in a specialty. A person who sees things broadly is much better able to cope with alienating forces in the culture and to maintain a healthy sense of identity. Individuals who have achieved as much freedom as possible in their own lives benefit the culture by providing feedback into the culture which reduces tendencies toward cultural anomie.

Teaching for lifelong learning John Dewey, in the quotation beginning this chapter, is saying that the most important goal of education is the goal of wanting to continue learning after one is exposed to content which is interesting and useful. The primary thing to be learned becomes a lifelong wish to continue learning (combined, obviously with the knowledge of how one learns to learn). Although the goal of "wanting to learn more" seems specific enough for us, critics have raised the question, "Wanting to learn more *about what?*" A person could dedicate his life to learning how to be a better burglar or heroin pusher.

We feel that such criticism misses the point. If schooling implants in students a determination to learn as little as possible, for example, a determination never to read another book after receiving the diploma or degree the student is working on, then schooling has failed in what must be its primary purpose. Before we can begin thinking about specific goals, we have to resolve the first one—how to develop in students a desire to keep learning. Unless schools can do this, they might as well close down.

Teaching the tools of learning Schooling as now practiced places little emphasis on the *process* of learning. Rather, it stresses prepackaged facts and principles to be learned. We do not wish to suggest that students *should not* learn facts and principles, but rather that if students know how to find data pertinent to the problems they will confront in living, they will learn the facts and principles when the time comes for their use.

First, students need to learn how to read, not to pick their way literally through a reading assignment, pronouncing words correctly, but to mine the process of reading for all it is worth. This calls for functional reading, which we prefer to define more broadly than many reading experts do. When we talk of students' functional reading, we mean not only their comprehending literally what is said on the printed page, but also their being able to perform two further operations: (1) analyzing a piece of writing for slants, distortions, and propaganda intent; and (2) recognizing when a piece of writing contains data useful to problems they are concerned with and using this data in furthering their own thinking processes.

The U.S. Office of Education and other agencies and individuals who report on the ability of Americans to read confine their studies and reports to literal reading. They tend to define "functional reading" as ability to read the numerous kinds of forms which people in our society have to fill out.

The U.S. Bureau of the Census reported the rate of illiteracy in the United States in 1969 at 1 percent. This figure represents the percentage of people 25 and over who have never attended school. The government defines a functionally illiterate person as one 25 or over who has had less than 5 years of schooling. Of the population 25 or older, 8.3 percent fall into this category. Both figures are meaningless because they do not use as a criterion any sophisticated reading tests which would measure one's desire to read and one's ability to read critically and meaningfully.

David Harman states that ". . . lack of testing, reliance upon grade-completion criteria, and inadequate definitions of functional literacy combine to produce serious official underestimates of the extent of illiteracy in the United States."[22]

In studies other than those reported officially by the government, the percentage of functional illiterates rises dramatically. According to a 1970 Harris poll almost 25 percent of the U.S. population cannot read well enough to fill out forms as complicated as applications for medicaid.

Harman (a reading specialist at Harvard in 1970), surveying all available data, is convinced that the percent of illiterates as judged by any meaningful functional criteria is far higher than can be found in any government reports. He estimates that the 8.3 percent of "functional" illiterates

[22] David Harman, "Illiteracy: An Overview," *Harvard Educational Review.* May 1970, p. 230.

reported by the government is more likely to be 50 percent. He bases this estimate on a study conducted in one section of Chicago which revealed that, according to reading achievement tests, 50.7 percent of the population was functionally illiterate in the sense that they could not cope with the reading requirements of everyday living.[23]

Most present definitions of functional literacy (excluding our own) refer to ability to fill out forms: applications for welfare, social security, a driver's license, bank loan, employment, etc. This definition is grossly inadequate because it ignores completely what the *culture* requires to remain viable in this age of industrialism.

The Goal of Democratic/Reflective Decision Making

American schools do not give students much opportunity for authentic democratic/reflective decision making. Many teachers, although not necessarily a majority, have some feel for democracy and its own unique method of individual and group decision making—reflective inquiry. We have already discussed what is involved in the democratic method. We have seen that its heart is the SMI concept, involving students, teachers, and guidance counselors.

"Inquiry teaching," which has been widely promoted during the past decade, may or may not lead to reflective inquiry as described by Dewey or more recently by Hullfish and Smith.[24] What poses as inquiry teaching is not always reflective teaching as the word, reflective, has been used in this century. It is not reflective when teachers enter the classroom with an a priori list of specific objectives that includes not only the "problems" for students to work on but also the answers students are supposed to get. When this occurs, as it often does, the opportunity for authentic reflection by students is greatly curtailed.

Democratic versus authoritarian decision making It seems fairly well established that people can be categorized according to personality type, with those who function democratically most of the time at one end of a continuum and those who function as authoritarians most of the time at the other end, with a probable large majority vacillating from one mode to the other. Erich Fromm made the definition of democratic and authoritarian types the subject of his first influential book, *Escape from Freedom,*[25] and has written on this subject in most of his later books.

[23] Harman, p. 230.

[24] John Dewey, *How We Think: A Restatement of the Relation of Reflective Thinking to the Educative Process.* New York: D. C. Heath & Company, 1933; H. Gordon Hullfish and Philip G. Smith, *Reflective Thinking: The Method of Education.* New York: Dodd, Mead & Company, Inc., 1961.

[25] Eric Fromm, *Escape from Freedom.* New York: Holt, Rinehart and Winston, Inc., 1941.

Reflection versus rationalization Reflective problem solving involves the use of scholarly inquiry within the general framework of scientific-humanism—a sequence of steps making a "complete act of thought." The point to emphasize here is that authentic reflection is never a process by which the thinker tries to defend what he had decided, a priori, he wanted to believe. Reflection is always characterized by elements of doubt and tentativeness.

Rationalization, to restate briefly the definition developed in Chapter 3, is the practice of selecting data in such a way as to support what the "thinker" had decided ahead of time he intended to believe. Rationalization is an exercise in deduction only: a person begins with a belief he is committed to and deduces what kinds of data would furnish support and what kinds would demolish the belief. The person then selects only the supportive data to use in arguing his position. It is most likely that a very large percent of what passes for reflection is rationalization, usually not recognized by those who rationalize.

Teaching about man's irrationality Philosophers of the Age of Reason (the eighteenth century) appear in retrospect to have interpreted poorly what human beings tend to be like in almost all cultural settings we know about. As of the twentieth century, we probably know much more than any except the nineteenth-century existentialists about man's potential for irrationality. We can now document with virtually unlimited evidence that most of what passes for serious thought is rationalization; but further, we know that much decision making is too impulsive and thoughtless, even to warrant the label of rationalization.

If we are to expect success in teaching students about reflection and its advantages, we must see that students know how little of the time we can expect people to be reflective. Probably the best writing on this subject is that of the existentialists. Teachers should be familiar with the main existentialist lines of thought so they can present them in language students can understand.[26]

What we would hope students would learn from this is that human beings can be rational, as scientists usually are when working within their specialty; but that humans also slip very easily into patterns of irrationality, as scientists often do when making pronouncements outside their specialty.

[26] Teachers lacking a background in philosophy can begin with something easy, such as William Barett's *Irrational Man: A Study in Existential Philosophy.* New York: Doubleday & Company, Inc., 1958. Perhaps the best single chapter on the origins and contributions of existential thinking is Chapter 1 of Rollo May et al., *Existence: A New Dimension in Psychiatry and Psychology.* New York: Basic Books, Inc., 1958. A recently published book reflecting a strongly existentialist view, which should be quite readable for teachers, is Maxine Greene's *Teacher As Stranger: Educational Philosophy for the Modern Age.* Belmont, Calif.: Wadsworth Publishing Company, Inc., 1973.

Some Additional Personal/Cultural Goals

We have stressed to the best of our ability what we see as some of the major personal/cultural goals that educators must accept if students are to develop as persons in their own right and as persons who can contribute to peaceful and orderly cultural transition from old-culture values to new. There are obviously an indefinite number of goals of less urgency than these—second-priority goals as it were—which are still of great importance. These goals deserve all the attention possible after first priority goals have been met to some reasonable degree. We will treat our second priority goals lightly in this chapter, recognizing that they deserve more attention than our space permits.

Education for the world of work   Although we reject vocationalism as a first-priority goal and even feel that a case can be made against much vocational education in the curriculum of the first twelve grades of school, we have not yet reached a stage where all secondary students will go on even to a two-year community college. This stage in our educational development may end within a decade or two; by the 1990s virtually all youth may complete at least two years of college.

Until that stage high schools still need to offer vocational studies that will lead to saleable work skills for their 19-year-old graduates. To expect high schools to educate students to high-level work skills is unrealistic; but high schools can give students who plan to terminate formal education at the twelfth grade minimal work skills which will enable them to be self-supporting.

Education for leisure time   If it is safe to assume that American civilization will continue to be technological in focus (even in spite of a cultural revolution which promises to devalue some old-culture dedication to materialism), then it follows that industry will become increasingly automated and the average work week will continue its historic tendency to shrink from the 66–72 hour week of a century ago to the 35–40 hour week of today to the probable 25 or less hour week of the not too distant future.

We have no original ideas to offer about what is "worthy use of leisure," but we would like to see increasing numbers of people develop at least some commitment to self-cultivation. Marshall McLuhan has not yet convinced this writer that the reading of books is obsolete. Aside from books, there is the whole world of the arts and their applications. Probably everyone has the potential to develop an appreciation of and to become a creative practitioner in some aesthetic pursuit.

Consumer education   Requiring consumer education in the school curriculum can be defended on the ground that it is likely to be a long time before we so organize our economy that distributing goods will cease to be a predatory operation. Although much is now being said about consumer protection, little more than minor protections are provided. Nor is more likely while the present power structure exists. We would be unrealistic to expect comprehensive consumer protection against dishonest business practices as long as dishonest practices are profitable.

The chief task of consumer education, therefore, falls upon the schools. Consumer education in our public schools has had a kind of Pollyanna character in the past. It has involved small issues such as "Bayer aspirin is identical to the cheapest USP aspirin on the market." It could be considerably strengthened by introducing fundamental economic issues, such as just how can a regulatory agency operate to protect consumers when its members represent the very industries being regulated?

SUMMARY AND CONCLUSIONS

We introduced the body of this chapter by raising questions about past and present approaches to educational goal determination. We reviewed the history of long-range goal writing and tried to demonstrate that the lists of goals produced by the U.S. Office of Education, the NEA, or other groups, have been too ambiguous and too dedicated to preservation of the status quo to be of much use. We concluded that long-range goals of a sufficiently concrete nature are a necessity if education is to serve either the needs of individuals or the larger culture.

Exploring how long- and short-range goals differ, we suggested that short-range goals can be defended only if they are instrumental in achieving legitimate long-range goals. We illustrated some risks involved in short-range goal making by referring to the behavioral objective movement and the taxonomy of objectives emerging from the work of Benjamin Bloom, et al.

As an introduction to the broad long-range goals proposed later in the chapter, a section was devoted to needs—individual and cultural. Needs were described as being neither determined by environment nor emerging from some inner force, but as situational, that is, arising out of the interaction of an individual and his perceived environment. Cultural needs were also defined as emerging from a concept of culture in which conflict-induced change and change-induced conflict are central, and the chief cultural need is maintenance of a core of stable enough values to provide direction and coherence; but "stable" is a relative term and cultural needs also must be regarded as situational rather than eternal. If one accepts the situationality of both persons and cultures, it becomes futile to write a priori lists of objectives for education.

Long-range goals can be derived only from consideration of problem areas that result from the interaction of persons and their cultural surroundings. Such goals cannot be written ahead of time except insofar as one can locate problem areas likely to exist for a decade or more ahead and which will permit us to anticipate conflicts in values and beliefs likely to continue in the future.

A group of interrelated cultural/personal and personal/cultural goals was based on what we see as long-range problems. We broke these goal areas into specific items to make the broad goals more concrete than older goal lists did.

Readers familiar with the social reconstructionist position (introduced at the end of Chapter 2) will recognize a reconstructionist flavor in this chapter, particularly in the long-range goals advocated.

STUDY QUESTIONS

1. To what extent do you feel you have freedom of choice in determining your own goals in life? What aspect of your environment do you feel you cannot change? What aspects do you feel at least some control over?
2. Through much of this book, and again in Chapter 13, the writer stresses the value of criticism (implied in the expression "critical thinking"). Do you agree that constructive criticism is a better habit than continuous praise and support—or passivity? Why or why not?
3. To what extent have you been able to identify the goals of previous teachers as short-range and long-range? To what extent have short-range goals assisted you in achieving long-range ones? Did weekly spelling quizzes help you learn to spell?
4. Most contemporary lists of educational goals include the goal of teaching students about drug abuse. As usually stated, this goal is too ambiguous to give teachers any clear directives. How would you state such a goal *concretely*?
5. Do you feel a taxonomy of objectives, such as that of Bloom and associates, would ever lead students to think independently and creatively? Do you see any way in which the taxonomic approach could be so used? If you have had any teachers who worked from the Bloom taxonomy, how did you react to their teaching?
6. What does it mean to say that in objective-making individual and cultural needs must be considered simultaneously? What is an individual need? What is a cultural need?
7. The goal or problems areas described in the last section of the chapter obviously do not mention specifically a number of subgoals or objectives which could have been included with equal justification. State as many of these specifics as you can.
8. The goal or problem areas described are intended to focus on the subject of cultural/personal or personal/cultural needs of a crucial sort, related to maintaining a going culture and healthy personalities. We consider them crucial because in one way or another they relate to survival or at least the quality of life. We have deliberately ignored

a number of other legitimate goals of education which, although of second or third priority, still need to be served. Describe as many of these as you can (avoid simply making ambiguous lists).

9. On what basis would you defend the goal of "human survival"? Is there a better defense for this goal than merely saying that almost everyone would agree to it?

10. Can you think of examples of the United States government planning ahead over a relatively long period of time solutions or partial solutions to major social problems (e.g., racism, crime, poverty, sexism, corporate monopoly, etc.)? If so, in what areas have long-range plans been laid? How "long-range" were the plans? How well do they seem to have worked?

ANNOTATED BIBLIOGRAPHY

Adams, Don, and Gerald M. Reagan (eds.), *School and Social Change in Modern America.* New York: David McKay Company, Inc., 1972.

A better-than-ordinary book of readings on many of the issues and areas of confusion besetting education. The book is heavy in empirical detail and has a number of useful tables and figures.

Benello, C. George, and Dimitrious Roussopoulos (eds.), *The Case for Participatory Democracy: Some Prospects for a Radical Society.* New York: Grossman Publishers, Inc., 1971.

Twenty-three essays by writer/scholars who identify with the New Left but feel that it has spent a decade fumbling and needs to begin projecting specific institutional goals. Although they all express a strong belief in participatory democracy, their proposals are quite varied.

Boulding, Kenneth E., *The Image.* Ann Arbor: The University of Michigan Press, 1961.

The "image," in Boulding's terminology, is essentially the same as "perception" as defined in the Prologue of the present book. This short and highly readable book by one of America's major economists and social philosophers is about our perceptions (often so warped as to be dangerous) in a number of cultural areas.

Brameld, Theodore, *The Climactic Decades: Mandate to Education.* New York: Praeger Publishers, Inc., 1970.

Some reviewers, including this writer, regard this as probably Brameld's best book up to its time. The essays present in a lucid and forceful way his ideas about the need in education for future-centeredness, issue-focused curriculums, teaching for sociopolitical involvement and activism, and assistance in the search for selfhood.

Bronowski, Jacob, *The Identity of Man.* New York: The Natural History Press, 1966.

Probably the most readable short treatment of how the self-identity of human beings derives from a fusion of knowledge about the outer world (perceived environment) and inner world (perceived self). Also highly recommended is Bronowski's *Science and Human Values,* New York: Julian Messner, Inc., 1956.

Butts, R. Freeman, Foreword by Arthur G. Wirth, *American Education in International Development*. New York: Harper & Row, Publishers, 1963.

This small volume is a first-rate treatment of the role education can play in underdeveloped nations and how the United States can assist in developing quality education in these nations. An effective statement about the importance of education in any country and a plea for more attention to international studies in American schools.

Coleman, James S., et al., *Youth: Transition to Adulthood: Report of the Panel on Youth of the President's Science Advisory Committee*. Chicago: University of Chicago Press, 1974.

This report attempts to describe some of the more pressing personal/cultural needs of youth in today's world. In addition to discussing the need to attain self-centered skills and knowledge, the Report stresses teaching youth how to become responsible citizens in our type of society. From this writer's view, the Report is insufficient in handling the question of what is most needed to prepare people to make a self-governing society work, but there still seems considerable useful content to this volume. We have come by 1975 to view reports associated with Mr. Coleman as rather conservative in a revolutionary world.

Derr, Richard L., *A Taxonomy of Social Purposes of Public Schools: A Handbook*. New York: David McKay Company, Inc., 1973.

Taking his cues from the taxonomies of the Bloom group, Derr tries to make a taxonomy of the *social purposes* of schools (in contrast to the focus on individual students in the Bloom taxonomies). Derr's book has a certain usefulness in helping to identify the philosopies of a few selected educators. But like Bloom, Derr fails to state his underlying assumptions, which appear to be behavioristic. He can see outcomes of education only in quantitative and behavioral terms.

Hess, Robert D., and Judith V. Torney, *The Development of Political Attitudes in Children*. Chicago: Aldine Publishing Company, 1967.

A book on the beginning of interest in politics by children (by age 7), and what kinds of views they express. The book has one very useful section describing the kinds of beliefs children hold (in Chapter 10). The evidence reveals that most small children uncritically *worship* the President.

Kaufman, Arnold S., *The Radical Liberal; The New Politics: Theory and Practice*. New York: Simon & Schuster, Inc., 1968. Foreword by Hans J. Morganthau.

Whether readers agree with Kaufman's own politics, which could be labeled New Left (although he prefers radical liberal), this book is a provocative call for political activism, within the establishment and through a political party, if democratic government is to survive. Pertinent to our suggested long-range goal of political activism.

Mills, C. Wright, *The Sociological Imagination*, New York: Oxford University Press, Inc., 1959; Evergreen, 1961.

Mills would not use sociology to preserve any status quo, but to analyze contradictions and project from them future directions of movement. Comparatively short and readable, it is one of the best introductions for students to the "new sociology."

Mumford, Lewis, *The Myth of the Machine: The Pentagon of Power.* New York: Harcourt Brace Jovanovich, Inc., 1970.

This is the second volume in Mumford's "myth of the machine" series. Mumford is one of this country's foremost and most productive (24 books to the present time) social philosophers. Although this book is not an attack on mechanized, industrial society per se, it is a plea for recognizing that we must humanize our industrial machine or it will end up destroying us all.

Robinson, James Harvey, *The Mind in the Making: The Relation of Intelligence to Social Reform.* New York: Harper & Row, Publishers, 1921.

Robinson, a noted historian, philosopher, and educator, was a contemporary of John Dewey and thought within the same general frame of reference. This 1921 classic is much more modern and has more to say about appropriate goals of education in the seventies than any but a few books written during the past few decades.

Rugg, Harold, *Imagination.* New York: Harper & Row, Publishers, 1963. Foreword and editorial comments by Kenneth D. Benne.

This is Rugg's last book, published posthumously. Imagination, and the creativity which emerges from it, was a lifelong interest of Rugg. He draws on the wisdom of both Eastern and Western civilizations and synthesizes a wealth of information into an original theory of creativity. Rugg's thinking is highly relevant to Chapter 13 because of our emphasis on creative thought as a high-priority goal of schooling.

Stanley, William O., *Education and Social Integration.* New York: Teachers College Press, Columbia University, 1953.

Stanley's book is even more relevant in the seventies than when it was published. This classic develops the theme that American culture contains so many contradictions, worsening by mid-century, that it is foolish to talk about one goal of education being "passing on the cultural heritage." Yet, Stanley thinks our democratic tradition has enough vitality to offer a basis for educational goals: the schools must devote major efforts to clarifying and promoting democratic values.

Van Til, William, *Curriculum: Quest for Relevance.* New York: Houghton Mifflin Company, 1971.

Probably the best book of readings on curriculum, with references selected from writers who have a distinctive philosophical position. Readers may find particularly useful in connection with Chapter 13, item 20, "Relevance and the Curriculum," by Lawrence E. Metcalf and the present writer.

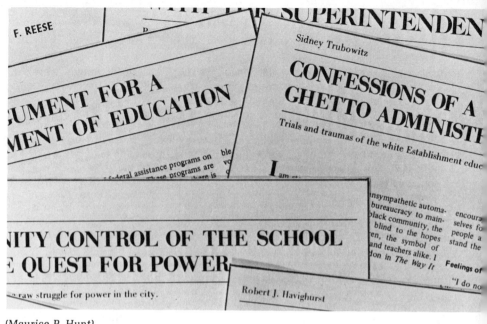

F. REESE

...UMENT FOR A
...MENT OF EDUCATION

...federal assistance programs on ble...
...programs are v...

SUPERINTENDEN...

Sidney Trubowitz

CONFESSIONS OF A
GHETTO ADMINISTI...

Trials and traumas of the white Establishment educ...

I am ...

...insympathetic automa-
bureaucracy to main-
black community, the
blind to the hopes
...en, the symbol of
and teachers alike. I
...ion in *The Way It*

encoura...
selves fo...
people a...
stand the...

Feelings of...

"I do no...

...ITY CONTROL OF THE SCHOOL
...E QUEST FOR POWER

...raw struggle for power in the city.

Robert J. Havighurst

(Maurice P. Hunt)

14

THE GOVERNANCE OF EDUCATION

In a hierarchy every employee tends to rise to his level of incompetence.

Lawrence J. Peter

The governance of education refers to control, to the power structure of our educational bureaucracy. In this chapter we will be talking as much about politics, the politics of education, as about teaching, although how well the latter is done depends a great deal on the former.

Until the mid-twentieth century the governance of education was not a major issue. It was discussed, primarily with respect to the faults of school boards and administrators, but

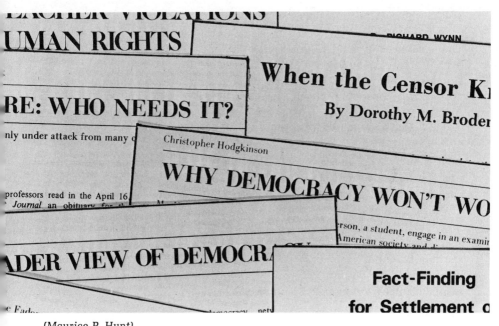

TEACHER VIOLATIONS
UMAN RIGHTS

RICHARD WYNN

When the Censor K₁

By Dorothy M. Broder

RE: WHO NEEDS IT?

nly under attack from many

Christopher Hodgkinson

professors read in the April 16
Journal an obituary for the

WHY DEMOCRACY WON'T WO

rson, a student, engage in an examin
American society and i

DER VIEW OF DEMOCR

Fact-Finding
for Settlement o

(Maurice P. Hunt)

also with respect to the role that state governments and their
agencies should play in public education.

Such discussion, however, did not raise fundamental
questions about local vs. nonlocal control or even much debate
about the proper role of teachers in the educational power
hierarchy. Local control was taken for granted. The role of
teacher as servant to the community, as a person to do his job
quietly and not talk back, was also taken for granted. Although
some books raised penetrating questions, they were read primarily by professional educators and did little to change the
view of politicians and the general public that the general political structure of education was sound.

Since World War II, particularly since the late fifties,
a literature has emerged questioning local control, advocating
a larger role for classroom teachers in making educational
decisions, and calling for involvement of the Federal Government. However, most books on the subject have ignored certain
issues which, as of the seventies, seem of marked importance.

One weakness of most of these books is that they isolate the problem of school control out of its cultural context and discuss it as if its existing problems were solvable without major changes in the total cultural pattern.

Books on school governance also tend to bypass the knotty questions of personal competence. Governance is discussed in terms of organizational charts without raising the issue that perhaps any of a variety of systems would be of equal worth if the key positions could all be staffed with genuinely competent people. And, third, most books on school governance ignore behind-the-scenes, informal controls (sub rosa, in many cases) which may be of far more importance than any shown on a formal organizational chart.

In this chapter, we will discuss a few items commonly ignored in textbooks. We will also try to support a thesis: school governance as of the mid-seventies is in precarious shape, and traditional systems show signs of such serious erosion that we should not be surprised to see fundamental changes within a decade or two.

OFFICIAL GOVERNANCE OF THE MID-SEVENTIES

By "official" we mean that which is not sub rosa, that which appears on the public flow charts, that which is written into the law. Before beginning this discussion we should warn readers that the formal structure of school governance is complicated, often confused, and anything one might say would have exceptions.

Local Governance

Local governance in the United States rests ultimately in the hands of locally elected school boards who hire administrative staffs to implement their wishes. When we talk about local control of education, therefore, we are talking about school boards and the administrative personnel they hire.

School Boards

School boards historically have taken a good deal of abuse, even though scarcely any of their severest critics advocate their abolition. Robert Bendiner, in one of the better books we have seen on school governance, says of school boards:

Of all the agencies devised by Americans for the guiding of their public affairs, few are as vague in function as the school board, fewer still take office in such resounding apathy—and none other, ironically, is capable of stirring up the passions of a community to so fine a froth.[1]

The composition of school boards tells us something about their political leanings. In 1965, the composition was as follows: businessmen, 35 percent; lawyers, 24 percent; housewives, 17 percent; doctors, 7 percent; clergymen, 5 percent. The remainder consisted of a miscellany of people, with those least represented being labor union members, who made up only 2 percent of total board membership.

The composition of boards suggests that they tend to be highly conservative about almost all social issues, including innovations in the schools they endeavor to rule. It should surprise no one that boards try to hire administrative staffs and classroom teachers who will have a similarly conservative outlook.

Aside from hiring and firing administrative staff and teachers, and making up rules to guide the operation of schools in the district, just what powers do school boards have? Boards often hire, mistakenly we presume, district superintendents who are such clever manipulators that the boards find themselves dominated by the superintendent. Unruly superintendents, however, are a very minor limiting force. What school boards can do is restricted by state governments—by the governor, legislature, state departments of education, state boards of education, and the state superintendent. Bendiner cites one superintendent, Lester B. Ball of Oak Park, Illinois, as saying that school boards control no more than 5 percent of the content of the curriculum.[2]

California has often been mentioned as the state in which the political arms of the state (governor and legislature) have been most active in legislating even minor details of public school functioning. This was perhaps true up to the seventies, but apparently politicians in many other states are finding that educational issues are close to the hearts of voters and that a governor or state legislator can win points by catering to whatever ideas please the voters. And in school affairs the wishes of voters are particularly mercurial; they move almost every year from one amateurish panacea to another.

School boards are not limited in function only by their state government. Court decisions of one sort and another must be obeyed or, if not, boards must spend most of their time figuring out how to break the law

---

[1] Robert Bendiner, The Politics of Schools: A Crisis in Self-Government. New York: Harper & Row, Publishers, 1969, p. 3.
[2] Bendiner, p. 26.

legally. Local voters more often than not refuse to pass the bond issues requested by their school boards.

Local pressure groups and prominent citizens also apply pressure on boards. To compound this problem, as we will show later in more detail, many of the pressures put on boards by such individuals and groups is to deny the constitutional rights of both teachers and students, thus raising grave questions of serious illegalities as a part of school governance.

In addition, boards are confronted with experimental programs proposed by foundations and the Federal Government, experiments often of dubious virtue, but which bring money with them and cannot be ignored.

In addition to all of these limitations, teachers are becoming better organized and more militant. Teachers demand salary increases, fringe benefits, and changes in working conditions (such as smaller classes) that boards often find impossible to meet. And now that teacher strikes have become comparatively common, boards are often caught between striking teachers and irate parents, the latter assuming that the board is responsible for ending a strike and can do so if it wants.

Administrative Staffs

It is difficult to write about the subject of administrative staffs and remain fair. Superintendents and principals and their staffs occupy rather unenviable positions. In the local educational power hierarchy, whether administrators have more to say than school boards or teachers (if teachers are effectively organized) is an open question and probably varies from system to system. But one thing can be said about the position of the local administrator: persons who fill this post are caught between school boards (which if they have virtually no other powers can at least fire their administrators) and parents and teachers who can gang up on an administrator and make the board-assigned tasks almost impossible to carry out.

The personal and professional inadequacies of school administrators have long been noted in the literature and shouted about by classroom teachers. Although this problem may be exaggerated, at least two factors have operated historically to produce weak administrators. Historically, the royal road to a principalship or superintendency was to major in physical education, demonstrate success as an athletic coach and handler of boys, move from there to a position of school counselor (often Dean of Boys), and finally to an assistant principalship, principalship, assistant superintendency, and at last superintendent. This situation no longer holds, but it was generally the case for long enough that many of our middle-aged or older administrators are little more than washed-up coaches.

Further, for reasons less easy to explain, the quality of people choosing administration as a goal has been lower than that of people choosing to remain classroom teachers. It is common knowledge that would-be administrators have lower average grades as students, get lower scores on virtually all kinds of aptitude tests, and have more difficulty than other graduate students qualifying for a master's degree or doctorate. In 1966, in a study prepared for the University Council on Educational Administration, McIntyre felt impelled to say:

> Although we have been fortunate in attracting into our field a few people who would undoubtedly compare favorably with the best in any other fields, the average student of educational administration is so far below the average student in most other fields, in mental ability and in general academic performance, that the situation is little short of being a national scandal.[3]

Readers who wish to review O. J. Harvey's studies of personality types in relation to their positions in the public school hierarchy, will remember that System 1 types are characterized by high literal-mindedness, rule orientation, lack of creativity, authoritarianism, and other unfavorable characteristics. Harvey found that 90 percent of district superintendents fit rather neatly into the System 1 category.

Later in the chapter, we will show that there are, as of 1974, some good reasons to hope for considerable improvement in the quality of school administrators over time. And as of now, administrators in general are less narrowly educated than many of their critics have led us to believe. A look at the undergraduate majors of the present generation of school administrators is instructive (see list, page 500).[4]

However, an undergraduate academic beginning may be neutralized by the graduate education of most administrators: 88 percent do their graduate work in education and rarely include any other kind of coursework. But here again, there is good reason to believe as of 1975 that this, too, is likely to change.

The Metropolitan "Community School" Issue

The issue of whether local control of education is any longer workable has recently taken a new form. In several large urban areas, notably New York City and environs, a considerable number of persons have

[3] Kenneth McIntyre, *Selection of Educational Administrators*. Columbus, Ohio: University Council for Education Administration, 1966, p. 17.

[4] Roald F. Campbell, *et al.*, *The Organization and Control of American Schools*, 2d ed. Columbus, O.: Charles E. Merrill Publishing Company, 1970, p. 209.

Behavioral science	18%
Education	17%
Physical and biological sciences	15%
History and political science	15%
Mathematics	11%
English	9%
Business	4%
Physical education and health	3%
Other	8%

charged that the school district is simply too large for one central administration. The administrative personnel are too remote from the neighborhoods the schools serve. This criticism has been raised particularly by Blacks, who feel that their children will never get fair treatment unless the black communities have their own school boards, hire and fire their own administrative and teaching staffs, and have local autonomy over spending allotted monies.

The issue boils down to the demand by Blacks and some other minorities that large metropolitan school districts should create intrinsic subdistricts that will be comparatively small and almost fully self-governing, and the counterclaim by present metropolitan administrators that trying to reestablish local control within big city environs is unworkable.

The critics of the community school movement in large cities charge that small school districts, under local control, are not functioning well anywhere in the nation. These same critics point particularly to the seemingly insoluble problems that school boards everywhere face, and question any attempt to reverse the trend toward larger districts and fewer school boards. Everything we have said above about the weaknesses of school boards would perhaps apply in connection with community schools in metropolitan areas.

Proponents of the metropolitan community school can raise some potent arguments. They conclude that the community school movement grew out of "clumsy and insensitive administration demonstrated by city-wide school authorities." The charge is made that individual schools are so enveloped by bureaucractic district regulations that they cannot innovate in even minor ways without permission from the central administration—which may take at least a year to get. Individual schools cannot choose their own teaching materials; an English teacher cannot even select a book, play, or poem for class use unless it is on a citywide "approved list."[5]

Apparently, the participants of a conference sponsored by the

[5] Henry M. Levin (ed.), *Community Control of Schools.* Washington, D.C.: The Brookings Institution, 1970. Ten papers delivered at a conference sponsored by Brookings.

Brookings Institution, whose conclusions we reviewed in the foregoing paragraph, were not aware that throughout the country, no matter what size the district, local control of education is not functioning. There is no reason to believe that school boards or administrators of metropolitan community schools could do a better job than is generally being done.

Bendiner, in a chapter entitled "The Desperate Throwback," derides the champions of metro community schools. If local control has failed under the best of conditions, he asks, how could we expect it to work under the worst of conditions? Metro community schools would increase de facto racial and social class segregation and be contrary in spirit (and perhaps legally) to Supreme and federal court decisions. In addition, "It might be remarked . . . that the domination of schools by the parents of the community is not automatically and necessarily an educational blessing." Bendiner quotes John R. Everett, president of the New School for Social Research, as saying that parents often want their children ". . . taught the same prejudices they hold and insist that the school reinforce the ideas and values they cherish. . ."[6]

State Governance

The legal control of public education, with some exceptions deriving from federal law and court decisions, rests with state governments. State governments have the authority to district their states as they wish, to consolidate, bypass, or eliminate local boards of education, and otherwise do what they please so long as it does not violate federal law. In 1968, James B. Conant advocated full state control of education. Others have advocated a compromise: leave local policy decisions in the hands of local school boards but turn the entire burden of school finance over to state governments. Any proposal which leaves a major share of school control in the hands of state governments raises serious questions.

Governors and Legislatures

Most people do not associate governors and state legislatures with the governance of education. It is difficult, perhaps impossible, to prove how much power these elected officials have in the control of school affairs—as compared, say, with some of the unofficial and sub rosa influences we will mention later. The power of state elected officials is probably to a large extent just about what they want it to be.

The United States Constitution itself says nothing about education, leaving a legal vacuum within which individuals and groups can compete

[6] Bendiner, *The Politics of Schools*, p. 192.

for control over public education. But the legal vacuum exists at the level of state government because the Tenth Amendment to the Constitution leaves to the states or people all powers not delegated in the Constitution to the Federal Government.

Further, a Supreme Court decision in 1948 asserted that federal courts can interfere with local control (under state auspices) only if such control should violate the Constitution. This decision apparently has not impressed either local school boards or state governments, since if we but care to dig them out we can undoubtedly find thousands of cases where the First and Fourteenth Amendment rights of teachers have been flagrantly interfered with. However, state governments have probably violated these rights much less than have local school boards and local administrators.

Every state has constitutional provisions of some sort for a system of public schools. They range from a general authorization to a rather detailed spelling out of how the schools will be organized and operated. But much more important than state constitutional provisions (which tend to be general enough to allow as much leeway to legislatures as anyone is likely to want them to have), is the body of law governing education enacted by state legislatures. In most states the Education Code has become a thick document, containing laws which are at least debatably unconstitutional (particularly in denial of First Amendment rights to both teachers and students) and such trivia that one wonders if state legislatures have anything to do but dream up petty regulations for their own sake.

With respect to mandating curriculum, a few states, such as California, Iowa, and Indiana, have more than thirty "curriculum prescriptions." But half the states have fewer than ten.[7] Such figures quickly become outdated, especially in view of the large amount of prescriptive legislation of the 1970s relating, among other things, to the "accountability" movement.

The question of chief importance to us in this chapter is whether state governors and legislatures (we mention both because they tend to function as a unit) are competent to exert the amount of governance over education that they now do. Governors often propose legislation relating to education; if the proposals come from legislators themselves they have to be tempered with a view to what bills the governor will sign. The question of the competence of this particular combination of laymen—amateurs is perhaps a better word—is a matter of opinion, but persons who should

---

[7] George D. Marconnit, "State Legislatures and the School Curriculum," *Phi Delta Kappan,* January 1968, pp. 269–272.

be experts on the subject tend to take a very negative view of the competence of state governments to dabble in educational affairs.

Bendiner asserts "The truth is that in the field of education little confidence is reposed in state government, and on the record little is warranted." Bendiner then quotes several persons in support of this conclusion. Roald F. Campbell says, "I think most states are grinding along and doing only those things they *have* to do." And a former governor and expert on education says, "... the states are indecisive ... antiquated ... timid and ineffective" and given their rurally dominated legislatures, "not interested in cities." Bendiner devotes the rest of his analysis to showing how state governments, by the very nature of their organization and the knowledge of their officials and legislatures, are not in a position to take part in the governance of education.[8]

State Boards, Superintendents, and Departments

Other agencies that control public education—the state boards, state superintendents, and state departments of education—operate with delegated authority. As Koerner points out, not only is there great variation in how these agencies are selected, but also in what their duties are.

State boards and superintendents may be appointed by the governor or elected by direct popular vote. There is no evidence that one means of selection is better than another. It is extremely rare that members of state boards are other than nonentities, often with no professional knowledge of education and with political axes to grind. The same can be said of many, though not all, state superintendents.

They perform a legislative function in the sense that state legislatures typically grant them authority to make legally binding decisions in certain areas. State boards may establish requirements for licensing teachers and administrators, selecting textbooks, acting as a court of appeals, being responsible for implementing desegregation, determining the school calendar, creating statewide testing programs, preparing statewide courses of study, and so on.[9]

There is such a paucity of literature on state departments of education that, short of doing a major piece of research, writers have no choice but to be extremely sketchy. State departments of education carry out policies of the legislature and the board, supply educational leadership for the state, keep the legislature informed, inspect schools, license teachers, and supply advice to individual districts. Referring to state departments,

---

[8] Bendiner, *The Politics of Schools*, pp. 168–171.
[9] James D. Koerner, *Who Controls American Education? A Guide for Laymen.* Boston: Beacon Press, 1968, pp. 84–85.

Koerner says ". . . whatever their size and powers, almost without exception they are ill-equipped to carry out their duties, and they command no great respect from the school systems of their states."[10] Koerner supports this opinion by drawing from opinions of Ewald B. Nyquist, Deputy Commissioner of Education, New York State, and James B. Conant.

Richard A. Gibboney, Commissioner of Education of the State of Vermont, presents a much more optimistic view. After saying that state departments used to be ". . . guardians of the school subsidy accounts, blind enforcers of outmoded regulations, and keepers of the archives," he argues that increasingly these departments are assuming roles of leadership in "curriculum research, teacher education, vocational-technical education, and in the complex process of facilitating educational change in basic and higher education." Immediately after this assertion, however, Gibboney says that "Trustworthy evidence is not available to document or refute this viewpoint," except for one particular federal program.[11]

Because of the place of state departments in the organizational structure of state governments, it is impossible to believe that highly imaginative leadership would emerge from such departments, or, if it did, that it alone would have any basic effect on the quality of public education in general.

The Federal Government

The first legislation relating to education passed by Congress was the Land Ordinance Act of 1785, which stipulated that one section out of each 36-section township was to be reserved for the establishment of public schools. The next move of Congress was the Morrill Land Grant Act of 1862, which granted lands to each state for a college of agriculture and "mechanic arts." Several other acts having to do with education were passed by Congress prior to the 1960s, and approximately thirty items were passed between 1962 and 1967. It was thought that the Federal Government was about to move into the field of public education in a major way, both in the areas of program innovation and financial support.

However, as often happens in a nation's political history, with a change in Federal Government administration (in this case, moving from the Johnson to the Nixon Presidency), new views came to predominate at the federal level. During the seventies, and particularly since early 1973, there has been a shift from direct federal grants to school districts and states for explicit educational purposes to federal revenue sharing with

---

[10] Koerner, p. 91.

[11] Richard A. Gibboney, "The Role of the State Education Department in Educational Change," in Richard I. Miller (ed.), *Perspectives on Educational Change*. New York: Appleton-Century-Crofts, 1967, p. 118.

no strings attached, which again has put back in the laps of state governments most of the authority for deciding just how federal funds should be spent. As the amount of available federal monies kicked back to the states is less now than before general revenue sharing was adopted, we can expect many individual school districts to be more pressed for funds than before.

It can be argued in relation to the issue of racial desegregation, that beginning with the Supreme Court's initial outlawing of segregation in 1954, the federal judiciary has had more impact on public education in the United States than any act of Congress. One can also argue that the Supreme Court decisions mandating "one citizen, one vote" also are of potentially great educational significance because of their intent to give urban interests a degree of power in legislatures and Congress equal to that of rural interests. However, implementation of these court decisions has been slow and no one knows whether the Nixon Court will reverse decisions of the Warren Court. Hence, federal court decisions may have impact primarily in providing journalists with copy.

Conclusions about Governmental Control of Education

It is scarcely a matter of debate at this point that local control of education is anachronistic; first, there is no effective local control, only the illusion of it, and what shreds are left seem destined to disappear within a decade or so leaving a legal power vacuum at the local level and the serious risk of schools being influenced locally primarily by citizens' groups, or local extensions of national or state pressure groups. Attempts to retain local control may well lead to what is in fact vigilante control.

State control of education involves major policy shifts each time there is a change in view toward education, which seems to be whenever there is a shift in dominance from one political party to the other in the legislature or the governorship. There is little long-range planning at the state level, and what little there is tends to become reversed with a change in political administration.

Federal leadership with respect to education seems as ephemeral as state leadership. Philosophy with respect to what the relationship of the Federal Government to public education should be changes with each shift in political composition of the Executive Branch or Congress. Although the Federal Government has spent some money in support of public education, the amount spent would certainly never have put a man on the moon or paid for more than a few months of B-52 raids over Indochina. There is no evidence as of the mid-seventies that local teachers and administrators can expect much effective leadership from the Federal Government, or much funding except on an unpredictable and sporadic basis.

Where then does this leave the official governance of education?

Given our form of government, and the continued hold of a conservative laissez-faire ideology among Middle Americans, we see no major changes likely soon. At present, neither local, state, nor federal governments are capable of governing education in a way to make it possible for teachers to take even the first steps toward implementing the long-range goals necessary to preserve democracy. In relation to need, American schools have probably never expended as much futile effort as in the past couple of decades.

Official control by governmental units is not the only form of educational control that exists, however. As we will show in the next section, some governmental agencies exercise a kind of unofficial control and many private agencies exert various degrees of unofficial, informal, and sub rosa control, all of which tend to have an impact more authoritarian than democratic.

UNOFFICIAL, INFORMAL, AND SUB ROSA CONTROLS

The kinds of controls over teachers and their teaching which we will discuss in this section are so numerous, so complex with respect to consequences, so often of uncertain legality, that it would require much more research than has been done, and dozens of long books, to untangle the entire web. We will mention a few specimens out of the thousands that could be mentioned.

Controls at the Local Level

Two kinds of controls greatly concern teachers and make for ineffective teaching. Perhaps even worse, they keep thousands of talented young people who would like to teach from entering the occupation. One control is over the personal lives of teachers and the other is over the manner in which a teacher can conduct a class. These controls interact in that a teacher's out-of-school life affects his classroom performance and vice versa.

Teachers' Personal Lives

We refer here to such matters as freedom of speech, political activity, membership in controversial organizations, dress and grooming, relations with the opposite (or same) sex, religious belief and practice, and the like.

Does a teacher have the same right to freedom of speech as other members of a community? The answer seems to be that occasionally and under certain circumstances a teacher does; but very often a teacher does not. This is the gist of a review of court cases undertaken by two university professors.[12]

Particularly in small towns and cities, but also in suburban sections of large cities, teachers are watched over by a variety of interested individuals and groups. The individuals may be ordinary community citizens, although usually community individuals who try to ride herd over the private lives of teachers are habitual moralists, self-proclaimed patriots, conservative businessmen and professionals, and the extremely pious. Teachers may come under fire for using slang or vulgar language; for saying or writing things critical of the community "sacred cows," such as churches, veterans groups, business organizations (e.g., the Chamber of Commerce), lodges, and the PTA; for speaking out in favor of a political candidate or party; or for criticizing a prominent citizen.

Teachers may get into serious trouble, or lose their jobs, for participating actively in a political campaign or running for office. Teachers have been chastised or dismissed for not living in the community or buying from merchants in the community where they teach. Except in large urban centers, the sex lives of teachers seem as fascinating and susceptible to criticism as the sex lives of preachers.

Teachers have gotten into trouble for wearing the wrong kinds of clothes or not enough of them or for their grooming (hair styles being a major issue in the sixties and seventies). They have been censured, and often fired, for holding part-time jobs as cocktail waitresses, bartenders, or any kind of work which seems to conservative citizens as somehow not fully respectable. Teachers are more likely than other citizens to be harassed and fired for breaking laws, such as those about sex or smoking pot.

We have described the situation as it is, not as it could be. A number of court decisions have established that teachers are about as well protected in their personal lives, under the First and Fourteenth Amendments to the Constitution, as are any other citizens. Unfortunately, most teachers do not know that they have this protection, or they prefer to avoid involvement in court action to secure their legal rights. Equally unfortunate is the fact that many school officials deny that rights guaranteed in the Constitution apply to teachers. Fischer and Schimmel describe a brief exchange that one of them had with the associate superintendent of public instruction for the State of California in 1969:

Superintendent: Teaching is a privilege, not a right. If one wants this privilege, he has to give up some of his rights.

[12] Louis Fischer and David Schimmel, The Civil Rights of Teachers. New York: Harper & Row, Publishers, 1973.

Author: Just what constitutional rights does one have to give up in order to enter teaching?

Superintendent: Any right his community wants him to give up.[13]

Although this conversation was rather special in that it transpired between one of the authors and a high state official, the present writer and his colleagues have heard similar assertions from more dozens of local superintendents and principals than they care to remember.

Teachers' and Administrators' Professional Lives

The same categories of individuals and groups mentioned in the foregoing section also take a keen interest in what transpires within district schools. School boards that like to play "big brother" to teachers and administrators, often find that individuals and groups want to play "big brother" to the school board. Like school personnel lower in the educational power structure, school boards have to be extraordinarily conservative not to receive criticism from groups such as the John Birch Society, the American Legion, and the Daughters of the American Revolution. Criticism from such groups are often accompanied by demands that schools either initiate or stop some practice. Boards are often subjected to demands by local businessmen that school materials or supplies be purchased locally, or that schools not carry on any activity which might compete with a community merchant. And, of course, board members receive advice and demands from numerous parents who have some special axe to grind.

School administrators are subject to pretty much the same pressures by the same groups and individuals. Disgruntled parents are more likely to call a principal or superintendent to register their complaint than they are to call school board members, although many parents call both.

From the standpoint of classroom teachers, community pressures which most disrupt the educational process are those that reduce or eliminate academic freedom. Academic freedom has been variously defined, but a general and widely accepted definition is the right of a teacher to use any teaching materials or make any assertions which the teacher feels would accomplish a legitimate educational objective.

Teachers have been disciplined, suspended, or fired for using teaching materials or making personal comments, which seemed to parents, community organizations, or local chapters of national organizations in any way critical of their beliefs. We have never heard of a public school teacher getting in trouble for being critical of communism, socialism, athe-

[13] Fischer and Schimmel, p. 6.

ism, sexual immorality, gambling, strip shows, or X-rated movies; but a teacher who defends any of these is almost automatically in trouble, even though the teacher may see as moral what community conservatives see as immoral. Even permitting mention in the classroom of subjects which community conservatives see as subversive, has cost many teachers their jobs.

An issue which has arisen in the sixties and seventies is whether teachers have a right, as a part of their academic freedom, to use any language they wish in front of students (or permit students to use any language they wish in the classroom). This issue has always existed but several decades ago it involved such words as "darn" and "heck." With the breakdown of censorship in the sixties and the development of the "new candor," magazines and books freely available to anyone are often studded with common Anglo-Saxon monosyllables, as well as some risque polysyllables. The same is the case with X-rated motion pictures, which any high school student who looks eighteen can attend. These words are used freely by teachers outside the classroom and even more freely by students, from kindergarten through Harvard Graduate School. Language usage was bound to become a school issue by the late sixties.

Ordinarily, in smallish schools in conservative communities, even the use of the mild expletive, "shit!," is cause for censure and the possible firing of a teacher. In a large urban school, language of this genre would probably not raise many eyebrows.

Fischer and Schimmel describe a case in Ipswich, Massachusetts, where a high school English teacher assigned a class an article from *The Atlantic* on the subject of dissent, protest radicalism, and revolt. One part of the article was a scholarly treatment of the origins and connotative meanings of the word, "motherfucker." Students were not bothered by the assignment, but most of their parents exploded in shock and anger. The teacher, Robert Keefe, was suspended and proceedings were begun to fire him.

Keefe took the matter to court and won. The court ruling, in effect, was that the use (and discussion) of *any* word is permissible in a senior high school classroom if it is an essential part of a legitimate teaching assignment. The court *did not* rule that any use of any word under any circumstances would be protected by law, but only if there were a defensible educational use of the word.[14]

The significant aspect of this particular case for us is that the teacher would have been summarily fired (and possibly blackballed so he could not find work elsewhere), if he had not taken the case to court. Going to court was no guarantee that the teacher could keep his job, be-

[14] Fischer and Schimmel, pp. 30–33.

cause in some similar cases the court did not find in favor of the teacher. Fischer and Schimmel point out that much of a teacher's protection in court hinges on the attitudes of the particular judge who hears the case. The authors cite cases teachers lost at the local and appellate level but won in the Supreme Court.

Fischer and Schimmel, as a result of their careful investigations, conclude that most community adults, school boards, administrators, and even teachers do not know what is in the First, Fourth, or Fourteenth Amendments to the Constitution. As a consequence, teachers the country over are daily denied rights guaranteed by the Constitution. And, not incidentally, high school students are also regularly denied such guaranteed rights. So far as schools are concerned, we can hardly be said to have a government based on law. Even though it is of no help to most teachers, Fischer and Schimmel do demonstrate that the courts have moved steadily toward enforcing that part of the Constitution having to do with civil liberties. Those few teachers who have the nerve and money to take their cases to court are much more likely to win now than thirty years ago.

Controls by Middle- and Upper-Power Echelons

In the final section of Chapter 5, we treated briefly and rather generally some ways in which the top power elite and, more important, power at the middle layer influence school practice. We treated the influences and controls exerted by the Executive Branch of the Federal Government, large corporations and their trade associations, labor unions, the military establishment, universities and foundations, and the like. There is no need to repeat that material here.

WHO SHOULD CONTROL PUBLIC EDUCATION?

We cannot discuss possible answers to this question without keeping firmly in mind the goals we feel education should serve. This book is not concerned with all the possible legitimate goals of education, but rather with first-priority, long-range goals related to serving the well-being of both individuals and the culture. The discussion in this section should be interpreted by readers as a follow-up of the discussion of goals in Chapter 13; our intent here is to explore the kind of governance in education which would appear most likely to make it possible for schools to achieve to some degree the major long-range goals described in the last section of the previous chapter.

Local versus Nonlocal Control

The unsatisfactory nature of present patterns of school control was described earlier in the chapter. In beginning our treatment of how schools could better be governed, we will contrast local and national control.

The Fiction of Local Control

We noted earlier that local school districts have little important decision-making power. They have little control over money matters, are dominated in curriculum decisions by state governments, and are bound by state-mandated testing programs, the demands of accrediting organizations and college entrance requirements, and a variety of unofficial and sub rosa pressure groups ranging from the national power elite to local American Legion chapters. Because local control is now a fiction—a part of the great American home rule myth—we will turn in this section to alternatives.

Nationalization of Public Education

Myron Lieberman is probably the best-known educator to have not only forecast the coming of a nationalized system of public education but to have advocated moving in the direction of nationalization. After discussing the inadequacies of local control, and among them stressing the authoritarianism and totalitarianism of education in most local school districts, Lieberman says

> Because a national system of controls is more likely to broaden the purposes of education and to preserve the professional autonomy of teachers, it is much more likely to provide a truly liberal education than a multitude of totalitarian systems under local control.[15]

Amplifying this comparison Lieberman adds

> it should be obvious that one cannot assume that a centralized system per se is more likely to be totalitarian than our own. England, France, and the Scandinavian countries all have national systems. In all of these, there is less political interference with teachers than there is in the United States.[16]

Lieberman makes no attempt to detail how nationalized education in the United States would work. He suggests that a national system of

[15] Myron Lieberman, *The Future of Public Education.* Chicago: The University of Chicago Press, 1960, p. 41.
[16] Lieberman, p. 52.

education is not necessarily the same as a federal system. A federal system "would be one in which the schools would be operated by the Federal Government." If we interpret Lieberman correctly, one important aspect of a national system would be that all schools would be dominated by the same long-range goals and that these goals would correspond to the long-range goals that a majority of Americans have in mind for the culture. In this sense, schools could be nationalized and at the same time be the legal responsibility of state and local governments.

Perhaps naively, Lieberman feels that American culture does have some rather specific long-range goals that are largely taken for granted. The fact that people do not shout about them does not disprove their existence. These goals are those related to the preservation and expansion of democracy:

> The development of critical thinking, of an understanding and appreciation of our democratic heritage, of dedication to the truth wherever it may lead—these purposes take precedence over any particular political, economic, racial, religious, or social point of view.[17]

Although Lieberman refuses to spell out specific features of nationalization, we can infer from comments scattered through *The Future of Public Education* some of what he apparently has in mind. He comments that teachers in schools operated by the Federal Government usually have more academic freedom than teachers in schools dominated by a local school board. This suggests that he may feel that federalism, tempered by some degree of decision making by officials at state and local levels, would not be a bad thing. Although he does not recommend it, he suggests that Congress could probably do a better job of stating the long-range goals of the American people than any state or local agency.

We interpret Lieberman to be suggesting that the Federal Government should provide all the financing for public education and that the amount of money spent per student would be the same the country over. Because Lieberman makes less than flattering remarks about the competence of most officials now having a hand in the control of education (the staff of the U.S. Office of Education, state departments and boards of education, state superintendents, local school boards, and local administrators) it is perhaps not unreasonable to infer that he has in mind some major nonpolitical national agency (such as the ministries of education in the democratic countries of Europe, perhaps?) supplemented by state and possibly local agencies staffed with high caliber professionals.

It does seem clear that Lieberman would relegate few decisions to locally elected school boards, if indeed he advocates retaining local boards.

[17] Lieberman, p. 64.

He does state explicitly that if local boards are to exist their functions should be primarily ceremonial. They should not control matters that boards have traditionally controlled.

We do not now intend to argue for nationalization. Our own proposal, which we will get to shortly, has a considerable amount in common with certain of Lieberman's proposals, but we doubt if many people would call it nationalization. In spite of the apparent bankruptcy of traditional local control, most people, including professional educators, still argue for it (with abundant federal funding, of course) and readers who want to review these arguments need only turn to almost any book on school governance.

Regional Control

Regional control means expanding greatly the size of school districts according to the logic of population distribution, economics, geography, or some combination of these or other factors. There seem to be two types of ideas concerning regional control of education (and infinite variations on a continuum including these types). The first type has not been played up in the literature and remains largely hypothetical. We consider it to be a model which may become a matter of serious debate within a decade or two.

Control by Large Regions

When we talk of control by large regions, we mean school districts larger than any which now exist. Such districts would cut across city, county, and perhaps even state boundaries. A district might be primarily urban, as would be the case if the Northeastern Seaboard area were made into a single district; or a district might include urban and rural areas, as would be the case if the Great Lakes urban-rural complex were consolidated.

Large regional districts might provide some of the advantages claimed for national systems of education, such as pointing schools toward more significant goals than those often saddled on schools in small provincial districts. There also is abundant evidence that the larger a school district the more personal and academic freedom teachers have.

Although initial investments might be large, our previous experience in districting suggests that, at least up to a point, the larger a district the more economically it can be operated through shared facilities and administrative staff, large-scale buying of equipment and materials, and the like. In a large regional district, there would be money to hire the best professionals available to serve full time on the regional governing board.

Metropolitan Regional Districts

The idea of metropolitan regional districts has been widely debated and the possibility of its being implemented seems much greater than that of implementing the larger urban-rural regions described in the section above. The idea of the so-called metro district grew naturally from the combined problems created by inner-city decay plus suburban sprawl, the concentration of racial minorities in the inner-city ghettoes with the middle and upper-middle class in the suburban areas, court mandates to integrate schools racially, and citizen mandates to improve the quality of education.

The metro district boundaries would be drawn to include roughly an equal proportion of Whites and minority races (when there is a balance between the two; if one group exceeds the other in size in the entire metropolitan area, individual districts would be so drawn that the proportions of minorities and Whites would be representative of the entire urban conglomerate). The districts would also be drawn to include the whole socioeconomic spectrum. Since racial mixing would not always provide adequate socioeconomic mixing, compromises would usually be necessary in drawing district boundaries. Schools would be located in the general area where the inner city melds into suburbia; and the school facility most often proposed is that of the "educational park."

An educational park is a large single campus, on which is located several high schools and more elementary schools, each an autonomous unit, except that certain facilities could be shared by all schools in the park—a central library, gymnasium and athletic fields, eating hall, and student union, for example.

Figure 14-1 shows in unrealistically neat fashion how a large metropolitan area could be districted and where the educational parks would be located. The inner circle, delineated with a broken line, marks the boundary between the inner city and suburbia. The area between the inner and outer circles is suburbia. The metropolitan area is divided into four districts, as indicated by the lines that divide the whole figure into four pie-shaped pieces. The small circles located on the broken line represent the best location for educational parks. The idea of pie-shaped school districts is logical, in that the pointed end extending into the inner city is an area of high population density in relation to the larger suburban end of the "pie."

There are some fairly impressive arguments in favor of the metropolitan regional district combined with the educational park concept. Because of the strategic locations of the parks, bussing would be simplified and relatively less expensive. Bus routes would extend outward from each park like spokes from the hub of a wheel. Racial integration would occur automatically, thus solving the festering problem of courts vs. school districts. Although evidence concerning the learning gains achieved through

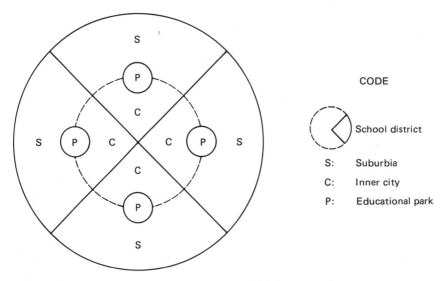

FIGURE 14-1. Metro districting for educational parks.

racial integration is contradictory, it may be no longer a matter of dispute as to the virtues of mixing together students representing the whole socio-economic spectrum.

There appear to be other advantages in metro regional districts such as we have described. Regional districts provide a large and diverse political arena. Parents in such districts hold political views from ultra left to ultra right. They also hold a great variety of opinions on economic issues, social welfare, religion, race, sexism, and all the other "closed areas" of American culture. Bigoted teachers would pretty much have to keep their views under cover. Conversely, teachers who want to introduce relevant and controversial issues in their classes would not need to worry about harassment from irate parents. There would always be parents eager to support such teachers.

Bendiner cites the famous Paradise Case in which a teacher in the small town of Paradise, California, was accused by local vigilantes of un-Americanism, subversion, and a variety of assorted immoralities (all charges being false), and points out how such persecution ordinarily occurs only in small towns. In a metro district such an event simply could not happen.

The initial cost of building educational parks would be enormous, but once built, both major economies and better education should be possible. Thomas Pettigrew, in the mid-sixties, estimated that it would cost from $40 to $50 million to build a park for 15,000 students (revise this figure to $100 million or more as of the mid-seventies). Pettigrew, a professor of social psychology at Harvard, was convinced in the sixties that, once the United States got extricated from Indochina, the nation's military budget would be so reduced that the Federal Government could and would fund educational parks in all our major metropolitan areas. (It seems rather incredible to this writer that a Harvard professor could be so ignorant of the nature of the American power structure as to think ending a war would lead to a reduced military budget.)[18]

Critique of Regional School Control

Although regional school districts would ease or resolve certain problems of school governance discussed earlier in the chapter, regional districts would not reach the heart of our problems of school governance. They would permit freer teaching, but they would in no sense guarantee that schools would significantly improve in serving such personal and social goals as we elaborated in Chapter 13. For several reasons, merely combining regional districts with the educational park idea would not help much. However, as we will try to show, *in combination with certain other moves*, the regional district idea may prove very useful. What have most of the proponents of regional districting missed?

Omission of the problem of goals Writers in education, except for those whose main background is in philosophy and a combination of the social sciences including psychology, tend to make proposals which initially may sometimes seem earthshaking but which are unrelated to the problem of ascertaining first-priority cultural and personal goals. One reason Myron Lieberman's "radical" proposals are attractive is he begins his analysis with clearly stated, long-range goals and makes no proposals unrelated to serving his stated goals.

Perhaps any writer whose conception of first-priority national goals includes "critical thinking" and "commitment to democratic values," and who hews faithfully to these goals throughout all discussion of school governance, curriculum, and methodology is bound to seem radical. Our point is that no manner of school redistricting—no manner of locating schools or mixing students to produce maximum learning—is of any consequence apart from looking *first* at goals and *second* at the most practical means of implementing them.

Omission of the problem of state governance Another serious omission in most discussions of educational reform is the now deeply institu-

---

[18] Thomas F. Pettigrew, "Urban Integration: The Metropolitan Educational Park Concept," in Arthur M. Knoll (ed.), *Issues in American Education: Commentary on the Current Scene.* New York: Oxford University Press, 1970. Pettigrew's essay is a good compact reference on the educational park idea.

tionalized tendency of state legislators, state governors, state departments and boards of education, and state superintendents of education, to mandate irrational certification requirements for teachers, curriculum content, teaching materials, and even methodology. American schools can never be improved so long as such groups continue to force their oft naive ideas on teachers.

Omission of concern for power elites Such writers as Bendiner are highly concerned about providing full academic freedom for teachers, and see the expanded school district as a step in that direction. We see the expanded district, taken by itself, as a useful way of freeing teachers of harassment by local pressure groups and individual citizen/vigilantes. We do not see expanded districts as a means of freeing schools from pressures exerted from those much higher in the power hierarchy. For example, expanded districts are hardly an answer to the partially successful attempt of the executive branch of the Federal Government to establish surveillance over political dissenters in 1970; nor are they an answer to a new issue that arose in the summer of 1973, that is, the Supreme Court decision to turn back to states and local governments the right to censor literary materials however they might please.

Omission of problems of professionalism Teaching is not a genuine profession; it is an occupation better referred to as paraprofessional. We will discuss why this is so and how teaching could be professionalized later in the chapter. Our point here is that this is a major problem in relation to improving the quality of education, and that to discuss other remedies for educational failure without considering this key issue is to miss the boat. Bendiner, who has written one of the better books on school control, does not make an issue of this.

Omission of problems of teacher organization As we will try to demonstrate later, achieving true professionalism, as well as dependable academic freedom, requires far stronger organization among teachers than they have ever had. Almost alone among educational writers, Lieberman recognizes this problem and tries to deal with it.

Control of Education by Teachers

Readers may consider the rest of this chapter as another "outrageous hypothesis" if they so choose. These proposals for school governance will seem absurd to many, but they are proposed as a hypothesis for serious study. We are under no illusions that what we have in mind will come to pass in five, ten, or twenty years. However, there are some very good reasons, evident in present trends, to think that within twenty years or so we will be well along the road to a national public school system which in the main will be governed by teachers themselves. We do not intend to

Different philosophies of governance, different teaching styles.

present a blueprint of how the system will function. It is much too early for that. We intend only to show, insofar as possible, *why* teachers should be the chief governors of the schools in which they teach, and the nature of the trends which may well make teacher governance a reality.

Communities of Scholars

When we talk about the possibility of teaching faculties becoming self-governing, many readers are likely to think that this is some new idea introduced in the 1970s by the American Federation of Teachers. The idea of self-governing faculties is more than seven centuries old. The Latin word, *universitas*, originally meant a group of people—any people—who were organized for a common purpose. But in time *universitas* came to refer to universities of faculties and students.

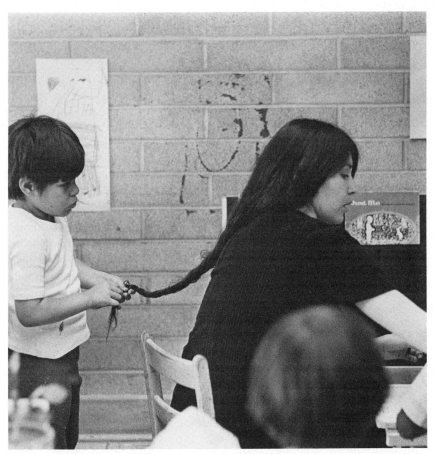

In the twelfth century teachers began to organize themselves into *universitas* and in this manner the first medieval universities were formed. Butts tells us that "The university of teachers was designed to protect their rights against the chancellor, the bishop, the king, the town, or anyone else who tried to bring them under control." Butts adds that "Likewise, the students often organized themselves into guilds for protection against the teachers, the townspeople, and each other."[19]

It would be erroneous to say that medieval university faculties were fully self-governing. They functioned within the framework of Christian orthodoxy and the Greco-Roman tradition. Further, the church prescribed the curriculum, or tried to. Even so, against church opposition Aristotelian science was gradually introduced and reconciled with church doctrine.

[19] R. Freeman Butts, *The Education of the West: A Formative Chapter in the History of Civilization.* New York: McGraw-Hill Book Company, Inc., 1973, p. 177.

The medieval universities prescribed a curriculum that stemmed from the authority of the church. Students' reading matter was limited to that which the church permitted. In this respect, many public schools today and many colleges still function within the medieval tradition.

We are not proposing that the medieval universities should be a model for today. We do feel, however, that readers should be aware that the organization of teachers for purposes of self-government, even if within a restricted framework, is hardly new; nor is the practice of teaching faculties introducing new materials into the curriculum against the wishes of the most powerful pressure group in existence.

Prerequisites of Teacher Control

To suggest that teacher control of such matters as personnel, goals, curriculum, methodology, communication with parents, and so on, is either possible or desirable in the seventies would indeed be unrealistic. Teacher control over most curriculum matters, the selection of teaching materials, and methodological issues, could be carried rather far, and perhaps to the benefit of all, before this decade is over. But it is highly unlikely that this will happen, the main reason perhaps being that the power structure of education-in-the-culture now relegates teachers largely to the role of servant to those more powerful in the hierarchy. There are signs that this situation is changing, but change in education tends to be extremely slow (except for the annual deluge of ideas for minor tinkering) and we find it hard to visualize teachers gaining much more power by 1980. By 1990, the situation may well be radically different.

We see two major prerequisites before significant teacher control can become a reality. These are achieving greater professionalism and more effective organization.

Professionalism and teachers Is teaching a profession and can teachers properly be called professional? Most school people think so; only occasionally does a teacher grumble about lack of professionalism in his occupation. The educational bureaucracy above the teacher level especially insists upon its "professionalism." Staffs of the U.S. Office of Education, state departments and boards of education, state superintendents of schools, education professors, superintendents and their central office staffs of "experts," and individual school principals all refer to themselves as "professional educators."

Have people in educational occupations tried to boost their own self-respect and improve their public image (and power) by claiming a professionalism that does not exist? Though we may accept the attempts of janitors who clean toilets to change their self-image and perhaps their social status by claiming the title of "sanitary engineers," we expect less self-serving rationalization from teachers.

There is a paucity of literature that grapples seriously with the subject of the professional status of teachers. Much of the literature seems to skirt around the problem and has the effect mainly of stroking teachers' egos.

One fairly recent book on the subject of professionalism is edited by Ronald Gross. Its thirteen essays by fairly well-known persons address the general theme of "the new professionalism."[20] The first thing we note about this book is that no precise definition is given of "professional" or "professionalism." This leaves open the question in each essay of what the writer is really talking about. Traditional professions are criticized for failing to serve a large segment of their presumed clientele—the urban poor, particularly. A plea is made for "client-centered" professions and there is much discussion of a new breed of young professionals urging social change, client control, and a relaxation of licensing requirements. We do not feel inclined to make a blanket indictment of this book because it does contain a number of refreshing ideas. But it might be best characterized not as a book on the nature of professionalism, but as a young adults' book on vocational guidance.

With respect to the question of what professionalism really means, and the further question of whether teachers are professionals, in our opinion no one yet has given us as good an answer as Myron Lieberman.[21] Lieberman points out that there is no such thing as an authoritative definition of a profession. One can, however, study occupations which traditionally have been regarded as professions and from them extract a "complex of characteristics." In each profession many individual practitioners would lack one or more of these characteristics (which may be regarded as criteria for defining a profession), but this does not invalidate the approach. At least Lieberman's criteria are not ambiguous.

Each of his items is followed in the book by concrete description, including definition of terms. He lists eight criteria for a profession, as follows:[22]

1. A unique, definite, and essential social service.
2. An emphasis upon intellectual techniques in performing its service.
3. A long period of specialized training.

[20] Ronald Gross and Paul Osterman (eds.), *The New Professionals*. New York: Simon & Schuster, Inc., 1972.

[21] Myron Lieberman, *Education as a Profession*, Englewood Cliffs, N.J.: Prentice-Hall, Inc., 1956.

[22] Lieberman, *Education as a Profession*, pp. 2–6.

4. A broad range of autonomy for both the individual practitioners and for the occupational group as a whole.
5. An acceptance by the practitioners of broad personal responsibility for judgments made and acts performed within the scope of professional autonomy.
6. An emphasis upon the service to be rendered, rather than the economic gain to the practitioners, as the basis for the organization and performance of the social service delegated to the occupational group.
7. A comprehensive self-governing organization of practitioners.
8. A code of ethics which has been clarified and interpreted at ambiguous and doubtful points by concrete cases.

The remainder of Lieberman's book analyzes the occupation of teaching in relation to the applicability of each criterion. No purpose would be served by a detailed reviewing of Lieberman's conclusions because portions of the material are outdated and teachers are different now than in the 1950s in important ways. We will comment on each criterion with reference to teachers rather briefly, mixing some of our own comments with Lieberman's conclusions.

It probably can be sustained that most teachers do perform a unique, definite, and essential social service. However, any such assertion requires qualification. It seems legitimate to raise questions as to whether all public school teachers render an essential social service for the simple reason that many of the courses taught in our schools may not be essential in the sense of societal welfare. For example, recent evidence has shown that taking driver education has no statistically significant relation to the number of accidents drivers have. Yet, we continue teaching it and probably will for a long time to come because schools have a vested interest in this course of dubious value.

With respect to the use of intellectual techniques, again all we can give is a qualified answer. Some school subjects such as mathematics, physical science, and literature obviously require "intellectual techniques." But some other subjects, with equal obviousness, require very minimal intellectual techniques. We give teaching licenses every year to numerous college graduates who are clearly not functionally literate, and most of them get teaching positions in fields where literacy is apparently not required.

A long period of specialized training (we would ourselves prefer the word, education, rather than training) is required of teachers in the sense that many states require five years of higher education for a life credential. However, educational requirements for teaching are in the process of being slackened in the mid-seventies. There is increasing talk about staffing schools with paraprofessionals analogous to paramedics widely used in the armed forces. Certain essays in Gross and Osterman recommend this as a direction in which to move. Further, there is a move away from requiring the kind of broad, liberalizing college courses which would contribute to intellectualism and a move toward emphasizing narrow vocational specialisms.

With respect to the issue of autonomy, in no sense can it be said teachers have the kind of autonomy we associate with true professionals. A typical skilled craftsman has more autonomy to do his work as he sees fit than does a teacher (persons who want a considerable amount of freedom in decision making would do better to become a carpenter, electrician, or plumber, than a teacher). With respect to autonomy, the situation is getting worse rather than better, primarily because of the "accountability movement" with its requirement of behavioral objectives.

Although an attempt is being made in the seventies to "hold teachers responsible for the outcome of their teaching," teachers do not at this time work in a situation where they can be held responsible. The reason is fairly obvious: because of the way education is governed, teachers are given formulas to follow by state governments, local governments, school boards, administrators, and various pressure groups, as reviewed earlier in the chapter. Until teachers are given an opportunity *to make their own decisions* about curriculum, teaching materials, and methods, there is little they can be held responsible for. It is unfortunate that the groups and individuals who keep teachers in straightjackets cannot at present be held responsible for *their* actions. As of the seventies, we cannot realistically talk about holding pawns responsible for their actions.

As to the service orientation of professionals, no persons in their right minds would go into teaching for the purpose of enriching themselves. Even so, teachers, perhaps because they are paid so poorly compared to professionals in other occupations, find it easy to become obsessed with matters of salary and fringe benefits. This is especially understandable during eras when the cost of living increases each year at a rate faster than teachers' salaries.

We would like to point out an issue connected with service orientation which did not exist when Lieberman wrote. We are now confronted with the argument (pushed with vigor in Gross and Osterman) that a profession should be *client-controlled*. In practical terms, this would mean that the work of teachers would be defined by students (and their parents who also often seem to think of themselves as clients of the public schools). By analogy, under the concept of the '"new professionalism," medical doctors would provide only the treatment their patients dictated (which would mean that fully licensed physicians would be unnecessary and we would make-do with minimally educated paramedics). Readers should be concerned about the difference between service or client orientation and client-control; the difference is crucial.

Teachers cannot yet qualify as professionals with respect to the criterion of having a self-governing organization. (We will comment on this in the following section.)

Codes of ethics which have been developed for teachers belong in the "literature of the absurd." Anyone who has studied such codes with an unjaundiced eye is aware that they are ambiguous and riddled with meaningless value judgments. They are susceptible to any interpretation one wants to place on them—for practical purposes teaching is an occupation which is not governed by a code of ethics.

It is our opinion (and Lieberman's) that the occupation of teaching has a long way to go before it can claim full professional status. We can probably say that teaching is partially professionalized. There have been periods when teaching appeared to be at least on the road to becoming a full-fledged profession; the seventies may yet see teachers move further toward professionalism, but only if steps are made toward correcting the deficiencies mentioned above. Lieberman's criteria of a profession are, of course, not the last word; the concept of a profession, like other concepts, is an evolving one. We should be on guard, however, against the definition of professionalism so changing that no one could use the term meaningfully—the occupation of flagging down traffic during road repair could be just as much a "profession" as teaching. If this happens, teachers will have no basis for demanding more pay or better working conditions than the road worker.

Finally, our conclusion is that unless teachers become professionalized according to criteria at least somewhat like those presented by Lieberman, school governance will regress more and more into the hands of persons who know little or nothing about education, such as state legislators.

Organization of teachers If teachers are ever to become even slightly self-governing, their organization will need to be much tighter and have different purposes than the NEA, its affiliates, or the AFT. Organization and professionalization have a close reciprocal relationship. Without a different kind of organization teachers cannot hope to become fully professional; conversely, without keeping their sights on the goal of full professionalism, teachers are unlikely to form an organization that will promote professionalism.

The forming of a teachers' organization adequate for the purposes we have in mind should be guided by clearly stated criteria. Exactly what these should be is debatable, hence our suggestions are presented to further discussion.

1. The organization should be democratic. We have seen enough examples of NEA affiliates which were not responsive to the wishes of

members, and which were so organized that it was virtually impossible to remove a leadership which had become old, crusty, and lazy, so that one of our deep concerns is the ease with which both elected and appointed top officials can be removed. Likewise, the AFT at both national and state levels can take on the worst features of any bureaucracy, including entrenchment of leadership.

2. The organization should have a widely inclusive membership. Unless virtually all classroom teachers belong and actively support the organization, it will be ineffective. We have mixed feelings about applying a "union shop" idea to any professional organization, remembering that there was a time when it was virtually impossible for a medical doctor to be licensed and practice without joining the AMA. Nevertheless, some means must be found to make the organization so attractive that almost all teachers will join voluntarily.

3. The organization should be exclusively for teachers. A professional organization of teachers, intended to help teachers become self-governing professionals, should exclude all other categories of educators. A century's experience with the NEA seems to demonstrate that an organization open to administrators and other categories of officials ends up being run primarily for the benefit of the administrators and officials and only peripherally for teachers. In recent years, however, local NEA affiliates in many places have achieved, and are exploiting, a union-type status.

4. The organization should have a strong professional emphasis. This could mean a variety of things, particularly in view of the widespread ambivalence about what professionalism means. Professional meetings should have a strong intellectual tone. Another valuable kind of professional orientation would be the publication of truly scholarly journals and books. We have suffered too long the journals of state NEA affiliates which historically have been filled with inspirational drivel or simple-minded recipes for doing this or that around a school. Nor have we been particularly enamored with the "call to arms" which is sounded in almost every issue of the various AFT journals. Why should it not be possible, for example, for a teachers organization to publish journals of the quality of the *Journal of Social Issues,* published by The Society for the Psychological Study of Social Issues (a division of The American Psychological Association)?

5. The organization should be cautious about tying itself to other organizations. This idea is suggested by issues which have grown out of the affiliation of the AFT with the AFL-CIO. That tie has undoubtedly kept many teachers who would like to join a union from joining the AFT. On the other hand, the link has given the AFT a certain leverage which it otherwise would not have.

We feel that a new professional organization for teachers should avoid any formal links with the AFL-CIO, not so much because of any past occurrences as because the AFL-CIO appears destined to become highly conservative on most social issues, to become even more of an integral part of the corporate establishment than it now is, and to continue to promote protectionism, a hawkish foreign policy, and antiintellectualism. (Obviously, such harsh assertions do not fit all AFL-CIO unions; they apply primarily to the construction worker unions and others designated generally as hard-hat.)

To readers who do not already know what is occurring, the establishment of a teachers' organization along the lines of the foregoing criteria may seem like an idle dream. As a matter of fact, the development of such an organization appears almost certain if trends now operating continue another ten years. Consider such developments as the following:

1. The AFT has grown steadily if slowly; but in some communities and states its growth has been rather dramatic, to the point that old-line NEA organizations feel seriously threatened by the loss of members moving into the AFT. Also, the AFT shows some signs of becoming more of a professional organization than a labor union.

2. Since the NEA has been losing members, it has been forced to act more like a union. In a number of states, the NEA state affiliate has promoted collective bargaining, sanctioned strikes, and in general taken a militant stance quite unlike the old NEA. Perhaps of more importance, the quality of the publications has greatly improved in NEA subject-field groups such as the NEA special organizations for teachers of social studies, English, mathematics, etc. An impressive example is *Social Education,* the journal of the National Council for the Social Studies. During the past decade it has grown from a dull, staid, unimaginative journal that skirted controversial issues, into a sprightly, interesting publication that seeks out controversial articles.

3. The NEA and AFT will almost certainly merge within ten years. In 1972, the New York State Teachers Association (an NEA affiliate) merged with the United Teachers of New York (an AFT affiliate). Similar mergers in some other states are in process and are being seriously discussed in most remaining states.

The implications of a nationwide merger of these two organizations is rather mind-boggling. Myron Lieberman states the probability nicely:

> What seems to be less doubtful (than the willingness of teachers to accept affiliation with the AFL-CIO) is that there will be a single national organization of teachers in the 1970s, perhaps within a few years. This organization will enroll two to two and one-half million members in its beginning stages and could increase to as many as three million members within five to ten years, depending upon

economic and political developments. The total of teacher dues will reach three to five hundred million dollars annually during this period, and teachers nationally will emerge as a major political force for the first time.[23]

Lieberman does not anticipate that such a development will result in a "teacher takeover" of school systems, unless poor school management forces it. However, his sympathy with the idea of classroom teachers playing a greater role in school governance is well known.

In our opinion, school management, or governance, is already in such poor shape as to create a critical problem, with the chance of a governance crisis occurring no later than the 1980s. It seems, therefore, that the merger of NEA and AFT which Lieberman forecasts may well provide the foundation for the kind of teachers' organization which could best serve the needs of the self-governance of teachers.

The Future of Present Systems of Governance

If the time comes when most public schools are governed primarily by classroom teachers, or at least when classroom teachers have the power to control whatever governing agencies they deem necessary, what is likely to happen to the present hodge-podge of overlapping and conflicting agencies that attempt to govern education? Perhaps to answer this question one should first ascertain what powers should be reserved to teachers, must be, in fact, if education is to have any deep impact on the thinking of students in problematic areas of culture and on the quality of their own lives.

Teacher determination of long-range social goals   Lieberman argues that in a democracy teachers should not be permitted to determine long-range social goals. The work of teachers involves mainly implementing the long-range goals of the broad national culture, which one ascertains by studying the culture. As we have indicated, Lieberman feels that careful study would reveal that the majority of Americans want their young to learn to think critically, to understand and appreciate our democratic heritage, and to be dedicated to truth seeking in all areas of interest. This is a sanguine view, which we wish could be supported with scientific evidence. We question, however, whether Americans are committed to these values unless it is at a very abstract level which most people do not relate to everyday life.

We feel that current evidence indicates that the values of Ameri-

[23] Myron Lieberman, "NEA-AFT Merger: Breakthrough in New York," *Phi Delta Kappan*, June 1972, p. 625.

cans are best described as inconsistent and incoherent. We find it possible to view the culture only as highly disorganized—another way of saying it is characterized by incompatible values and beliefs. If clear-cut long-range goals cannot be found by studying cultural ideological patterns, how do we arrive at goals?

One way, which has been practiced by humanists and behaviorists alike, is to ascertain what both individuals and the social group need in order to continue functioning. This is what we did in Chapter 13. We stressed the tentative nature of this kind of inquiry because stating social goals of education is not a proper task for one person, a small group, or even teachers collectively. Any individual or group pretending to have final answers about what Americans' goals *should be* is behaving in a highly elitist fashion.

Yet, there has to be some way of long-range goal determination or education will continue to drift. We have no very satisfying answers. Given the money for research, enough is known about how to uncover values so we could undoubtedly discover Americans' deeper values. Conceivably, we might be able to find out that when people have to make really crucial decisions, most would opt for critical thought, democratic methods of decision making, and searching for truth in areas of social controversy, as Lieberman appears to think. On the other hand, we might find that a fairly substantial minority would opt for these values and the majority would be too ambivalent to choose any intelligible long-range social goals. In any case, our need to know more concerning the American psyche suggests much further research by disinterested social scientists.

Even though teachers are not morally free to assert goals which may or may not reflect the thinking of a majority, they have to derive goal-statements from somewhere. Teachers are probably justified in assuming that a considerable minority of Americans, at least, have a commitment to the democratic method and since democracy is the only social system which permits continued rethinking of goals, we see no other course than for education to promote a study of democratic values, particularly the process of democratic decision making.

Simply to keep all avenues of investigation open, it strikes us that no matter how ambivalent and confused the general public may be about the meaning and desirability of democracy, our schools have a deep and abiding obligation to try to keep democratic decision making alive until such time as the general public is less confused, and, hopefully, able to use the democratic method to determine whether they want to expand the areas of democratic decision making in our culture, reduce them, or abolish them.

Where teachers must be free If teachers are not free, without the charge of elitism, to make long-range goals for the entire culture, they should be free to decide what means schools should use to equip students with the values and skills necessary to implement cultural goals. In short, the *ends* are not the teachers' problem, but the *means* are very much the affair of teachers. This is so because teachers, if adequately professionalized, are the only category of people with the ability to develop effective means.

For example, adults in a community might accept the teaching of critical thinking as an abstract but highly important goal. But laymen have had no education or experience in just how a teacher, in a classroom setting (or even an out-of-class setting) can teach critical thinking. Community adults, amateurs with respect to the technicalities of education, are not in a position to know which school courses, which kinds of teaching materials, or which kinds of teaching strategies, are most likely to achieve the end of critical thinking. As Lieberman points out, "You cannot develop thinking if the students and teachers cannot criticize anything. Teachers who are serious about developing critical thinking must have the freedom to be critical of points of view learned at home, in the community, at church, and so on."[24]

School curriculum in its broadest sense can be regarded only as a means toward broad cultural goals. The methodology of teaching, likewise, is a means toward the pursuit of broad cultural goals. One of the most serious mistakes made by public and professional educators alike is to regard the school curriculum and the way in which teachers teach as *ends* in themselves, and not *means*. At present, those in charge of school governance act as if they assumed curriculum and methodology were ends in themselves and therefore properly to be decided upon by amateurs— such as state legislatures, and local school boards. Neither of these groups know much about the best educational means of achieving legitimate social goals. But since they seem unable to distinguish ends from means, they are forever trying to dictate means.

Because only classroom teachers (and an occasional administrator who was once an effective classroom teacher) are educated to cope with means, *classroom teachers should have full control over both curriculum and methodology*. This does not mean that teachers should ignore suggestions from others, or take a "public be damned" attitude. Teachers should be receptive to suggestions, but only they should make final decisions about means.

A perennial problem teachers have in this regard is in the area of curriculum materials. To quote Lieberman again:

> If teachers should decide what subjects should be taught, then clearly they should decide what instructional materials should be used in teaching these subjects. The power to determine the choice of instruc-

[24] Lieberman, *The Future of Public Education,* p. 64.

tional materials is in fact the power to determine the subjects. Nevertheless, some people persist in the view that the school board should decide on teaching materials.[25]

Our suggestions concerning the role of classroom teachers in the control of education reduces itself to the following specific points:

1. Teachers should determine the curriculum, that is to say, the specific courses to be offered and the teaching materials to be used in these courses.

2. Teachers should determine the methodology of instruction, since no real distinction can be made between method and content (they are simply different aspects of the same thing).

3. Teachers, once fully professionalized, should set the standards for admission to the profession; that is, teachers, through their organization, should develop criteria for licensing.

4. Teachers should have the primary say in deciding who should be ejected from the profession for incompetence or other reasons.

5. Teachers should, through their organization, develop a code of ethics for the profession.

6. Teachers should have the authority to allocate that part of school money designated for the teaching function (only teachers can know whether the school needs a new set of encyclopedias or more motion picture projectors).

7. Teachers should share in deciding what kind of education they should have, particularly the "professional" (or education) courses. But to share is not to control. In the area of general education (i.e., liberal arts or humanities), teachers might resist the rigorous education they need. This is a matter of such critical concern to the interests of the culture at large that the final say probably should rest with legislatures and perhaps eventually with Congress.

8. Teachers should share in deciding what kind of education superintendents, principals, and "central office experts" should have. Administrators and consultants are *to serve* teachers; teachers logically should have a decisive say in how their servants are to be educated.

9. Teachers should have the authority to decide, or share equally in deciding, any other matters which directly affect their teaching. Although architects will continue to design school buildings, teachers know more than architects about what kind of interior arrangement most facilitates the teaching process. Teachers also know more than anyone else about what class size is workable for a given subject. Teachers should have more

[25] Lieberman, *The Future of Public Education*, p. 65.

control than they do over the amount of routine chore work which is now so frustrating to most teachers. They should have major say over the school rules pertaining to student behavior. (E.g., in many schools, teaching is seriously interfered with every day by pointless and basically unenforceable dress codes dreamed up by school boards with nothing more important to do; this should be a matter for teachers, not school boards, to decide.) These are only a few examples of what would be a rather long list.

Governance roles of nonteachers   To turn over to teachers as much authority for governance as we have suggested, would necessitate either the elimination of or change in authority traditionally exercised by others who make up the vast educational establishment. We will confine our discussion, as above, to the governance of public schools, from grades K through 12. We will not try to go into detail because this would require a book in itself. We will omit discussion of desirable future roles of federal and state governments, except to reiterate our earlier contention that state governors, legislators, departments of education and boards already go far beyond their areas of competence in making decisions about how schooling should operate at the classroom level. We will devote the rest of this section to a category of school people who could provide invaluable leadership in *ideas*: the administrators.

Although we need a category of administrators to perform the complex technical managerial functions of a school system, this category should have no control over what we have already suggested should be within the domain of teacher decision. But we need also a quite different kind of educational leader who would not even carry the label of administrator.

We are thinking of people with a broad education in the humanities, who are students of the culture, and at the same time have a solid grasp of the basic foundational areas of education: philosophy, psychology, and social/cultural foundations of education. Their work would consist primarily of *thinking* with a view to proposing innovations which teachers could reflect upon and experiment with. Such leaders would maintain a close alliance with university scholars in a variety of disciplines and would themselves be selected in part because of high potential for scholarly endeavor.

Important innovative work in the education of administrators has occurred at Teachers College, Columbia University, and at other universities. However, as of the mid-seventies many persons consider the school administration staff at Ohio State University to be the avant garde of such thinking. Campbell points out that the education of administrators has gone through various stages in this century, from "scientific management" to "democratic administration," and in the 1960s some graduate schools of education are attempting "to develop a theory of administrative behavior within a *social science framework.*"[26] Gradually stress is being placed on producing educational theorists, rather than "how to" technicians.

We should not ignore here work being done by the National Institute of Education (NIE) to upgrade school administration. The NIE was established by the Federal Government in 1972 as a separate agency within the Department of Health, Education and Welfare. Under a broad legislative mandate "to seek to improve education . . . in the United States" NIE developed a broad spectrum of goals, certain of which relate to improving administration. The NIE's projected budget for 1975 is $130 million.

Upon studying the published goals of the NIE programs, however, it appears that interest in improving the quality of school administration is peripheral and subsumed under the Teaching and Curriculum unit. The actual research has been relegated to several regional organizations. Although one of the broad goals asserted—"Principals need a chance to become educational leaders rather than disciplinarians and building administrators . . .—" is laudable, the main thrust of these programs appears to be to develop means of assisting in-service administrators to do better what their local communities want done, such as—in the case of one regional project—adoption of a "Planning, Programming, and Budget System (PPBS)."[27]

It is too early to know whether the NIE programs will improve the overall quality of school administration. We can find nothing in the programs about revamping the initial education of new administrators. In our opinion, administrators will remain uninterested in, and unable to help implement, broad, long-range social goals until there has been a revolution in the way they are educated in the first place. This suggests that the proposal of individual universities, such as Ohio State, to educate prospective administrators as social scientists and educational philosophers first and technicians (insofar as they need be) later, is the most promising step now in sight.

If the education of "administrators" continues to move along these lines, we can see the emergence of a new class of educational leaders, whether called superintendents or something more appropriate, who will be able to assist teachers in their own professionalization and organization. They will be able to perform a role which teachers, because of limited time cannot, that is, to reflect penetratingly on how best to educate our young.

[26] Campbell *et al., The Organization and Control of American Schools,* p. 214; italics added.

[27] For a statement of the NIE's general goals, see *NIE: Its History and Programs.* Washington, D.C.: Department of Health, Education and Welfare, 1974, pp. 47, 51.

RECONSTRUCTION REVISITED

In this section, we will briefly examine two major points. First, we will comment on why, under the circumstances of the mid-seventies, reconstructionism as promoted by, say, Theodore Brameld and his followers seems utopian to so many of their critics. Second, we will suggest why there is good reason to believe that present circumstances will change to make some form of reconstructionism practical, perhaps within a decade or two. (See last section of Chapter 2.)

Present School Governance and Reconstructionism

The present chapter began by showing some salient features of school governance at local, state, and federal levels. Under that section, we treated the official, legal, on-the-surface aspects of governance. A following major section of the chapter treated some unofficial, informal, and often sub rosa pressures which are a part of school governance. The material presented indicated that present systems of official governance are not merely functioning poorly, but seem in the process of collapse. In connection with unofficial pressures, we presented facts indicating that such pressures are intolerable if public education is ever to serve the broad goals necessary for human survival and maintaining or improving the quality of life.

Present school governance, whatever its organization, has the effect of shoring up the status quo. But the cultural status quo, as we tried to demonstrate in both Parts I and II of this book, is riddled with contesting interests, inconsistency, dissonance, and a general state of disorganization leading to anomie. Trying to bolster the status quo by ignoring cultural conflicts is no more than a holding action which cannot continue indefinitely.

Public schools may be analogous to a kind of dike holding back the forces of cultural change. But they are a dike with numerous cracks, and, try as they may, school boards, administrators, and teachers cannot prevent the dike from collapsing. The problem with dikes is that they are built to be rigid—they either remain stiffly in place, or they collapse quickly and totally.

It is proper that our schools preserve a part of our cultural heritage, particularly the method and institutions of democracy (fundamental to which, we are now finding, are the Bill of Rights and the Fourteenth Amendment of the Constitution of the United States). But it is equally necessary that our schools promote change by presenting students with alternatives to all that is now wrong with both our own and the world's other civilizations. An analogy better than a dike is a sieve, which preserves part of our heritage by holding it back, but lets many of the forces of change pour through.

Through a process of elimination, classroom teachers seem to be the only group left who can develop the skill and authority to encourage social change and guide it along the lines of the broad goals of the culture. But teachers in general are not ready to perform this task. Even if teachers were free to teach as they liked, their professional deficiencies would probably prevent them from effectively doing the job they must do. Most teachers are not educated to be professionals—a fault of our colleges and universities, which must be shared by liberal arts and education professors alike. In addition, teachers have little organization befitting true professionalism. Therefore, partly because they lack both the education needed to teach reflectively about cultural issues and a proper organizational base from which to work, teachers are foggy about the goals of teaching and spend much of their time in busy work, thus making reconstructionism seem quite utopian.

Future Possibilities

It is essential that public schools play a leading role in helping the young, and through them also the adults, to reexamine key aspects of the American value and belief system. Needing reexamination the most are the great areas of controversy filled with touchy or verboten issues. The public schools are the only cultural agency that can provide this reexamination steadily and systematically. Other agencies tend to pull against one another; when they undertake education, they only add to present inconsistency and dissonance.

For the first time in our history, the next two or three decades seem to offer the possibility of public schools becoming agencies that do not simply mirror the culture, but lead in the process of rethinking old outworn values and reducing dissonance to a manageable level. If the humanist push of the sixties and seventies succeeds in confining the pressures exerted by the behaviorist world view, we can anticipate teachers being educated to be much broader than mere technicians in a vocational specialty. A teacher without a background that includes substantial work in the humanities generally is like a medical doctor who has never studied anatomy or organic chemistry. The basis for intelligent practice is lacking. We anticipate that increasing numbers of teachers, and hopefully increasing numbers of university professors, will see this comparison.

If teachers can be educated to be professionals, then it seems to us that only two major steps are needed for them to function as professionals. One step is a fundamental change in school governance, the chief element of which will be to give teachers virtually complete control over the *means* chosen to serve the broad, long-range goals—the ends—of students and culture. There is considerable reason for thinking that this will happen; if there were no other reasons, the erosion of the present system of governance will compel adoption of a different system. Another step is the organization of teachers so they can protect for themselves certain essential rights, one of the most important being academic freedom. Such organization appears to be in the first stages of materializing.

Although advocating that basically teachers should function as a "community of scholars" and operate their own profession with considerable autonomy, we doubt that to place the entire burden of this on teachers is practical or even desirable.

In connection with our discussion of potential major improvement in the quality of educational leaders, whom we now call superintendents, principals, and consultants, we see a necessary role for such personnel. That these leaders would have to be of much higher caliber than most individuals who now carry the title "superintendent" goes without saying. This group, whatever the title of individual practitioners may be, needs desperately to be selected from among the top intellectual leaders in the nation.

Hopefully, their role in the future would include directing research into the nature of authentic long-range goals of Americans. Although in the last analysis, elected political bodies may have priority in this enterprise, educational leaders should not let it go by default. They should have at their disposal substantial research budgets for the purpose of tapping the public mind and proposing long-range educational goals.

Their role would also include scrutinizing critically the credential programs of schools of education without overlapping the very important stake that classroom teachers themselves have in helping design their own college preparation. The role of the top-bracket educational leader will necessarily be an advisory one, but if that advice is based upon in-depth scholarly study of a kind which few administrators engage in today, it should be extremely useful both to teachers and to legislative bodies still tempted to try to run school affairs.

Also, the role of educational leaders should include the planning of in-service educational programs for teachers—although not apart from a close give-and-take with teachers themselves who, to some degree but not entirely, may know more about what kinds of additional education they need than anyone else. Although in-service education (unfortunately, often called training) has been in practice for a long time and continues with more or less vigor depending in part on the availability of funding, its effectiveness cannot at present be adequately assessed. We are of the opinion that much of present in-service education is in the form of work-shops, sometimes of only a day's duration, in which buzz-groups hash over old solutions to old problems.

A really defensible in-service education would plunge deeply into the foundational subjects of education in which most classroom teachers are now so weak: psychology, philosophy, and clearly, extensive and penetrating cultural studies, so that no teacher who remains a cultural ignoramus could continue in the teaching occupation. It seems not to have occurred to many of our present generation of "educational leaders" that much in-service education should be in the *humanities* and *not* simply in the accumulation of additional units in mickey-mouse education courses in curriculum and methods.

Although we cannot hope for immediate major improvement in the quality of our educational leaders, new outlooks and new programs—such as we mentioned earlier—do give us hope that within a decade or two we could have a very different sort of person in top leadership posts.

To close on a rather optimistic note, there is evidence that public secondary schools already are achieving more along the lines suggested in the present chapter than they were in the 1960s—as was indicated in Chapter 4. Readers may recall that studies of Yankelovich and the American Council on Education were cited there—studies indicating that entering freshmen seem to be becoming both more sophisticated and liberal about a variety of important cultural issues. Although these changes may reflect more a "filtering down" effect of the continued spread among college students of the values of the youth culture of the 1960s, they are likely to reflect at least in part improved cultural study in the public schools.

Summary

This, then, is our proposal for the "reconstruction of education." We do not feel it is an idle dream nor do we feel it would be unimportant to the culture. With a new generation of leaders and a new type of highly professionalized and organized, and unprecedently autonomous, teachers, we can visualize our public schools exerting the kind of leadership for cultural change which the early Teachers College thinkers felt was possible.

We cannot ignore all the other forces making for social change, many of which may under the best of circumstances be able to override the influence of the public schools, but we agree in at least one respect with the early reconstructionists that, by a process of default, public school leaders and teachers are *potentially* more competent to do this than anyone else and are in a highly strategic position to do so.

With a combination of professionalism and organization working for them, teachers will be in a position to demand and acquire substantial rights of self-governance, as other professionals have. Once teachers have rid themselves of all the foolish kinds of dictation which now stem from legislatures, state educational agencies, local school boards and administrators, and all the ex officio pressure groups, they will at last be free to think seriously in terms of an issue- and future-oriented kind of teaching, designed to promote such goals as were suggested in the previous chapter. This will be reconstructionism of a healthy and practical sort. We may have no more than twenty years to wait for it.

STUDY QUESTIONS

1. How would you explain the historical tendency for "people incapable of doing anything else becoming school administrators"? (You will recognize, of course, that there have been many exceptions to this.)
2. In reviewing your own schooling, from kindergarten on, what impressions did you form of principals, deans, counselors, and other administrative staff? Do you remember any who became "hero figures" to you? If you sensed weaknesses in some of these persons, what were they?
3. What do you think the role of the Federal Government should be in relation to public education? Should all public education be financed by the central government, as it is in many countries? What controls, if any, should the Federal Government have over public education?
4. What can you think of that might make state legislatures less concerned about legislating curriculum and methods and numerous other matters which now seem outside their realm of competence?
5. Just what say do you think parents should have over the education of their children? If parents want schools to teach authoritarian/totalitarian values, should the schools cater to such parental wishes?
6. Lieberman suggests that local school boards should be retained to perform primarily "ceremonial functions." If you agree, what would these functions be?
7. Teachers and students are a kind of class set apart in that they have been denied by state and local officials various civil rights guaranteed all American citizens in the American Constitution. What are your suggestions for remedying this situation, that is, if you are bothered by it?
8. The "educational park idea" would already be a reality in many large cities if not for the initial expense, even though over the long run this appears to be the most economical approach to urban education. How do you explain the very widespread tendency in the United States to spend additional money later in order to spend less now?
9. Would teaching have more appeal to you if public school practices were to move in the directions suggested in this chapter? Why or why not?
10. Since there are no study questions after the Epilogue, this might be a

good time for student readers to write a critical review of this entire book. What errors of fact or interpretation can you find? If you were going to write a second edition, how would you revise it?

ANNOTATED BIBLIOGRAPHY

Campbell, Roald F., et al., The Organization and Control of American Schools, 2d. ed. Columbus, O.: Charles E. Merrill Publishing Company, 1970.

   Written as a basic text, this is probably one of the best surveys of the nature and problems of school governance. Unlike many books in the field, this volume gives relatively adequate play to the whole constellation of cultural forces which affect the way in which schools are managed. Excellent as a reference.

Corwin, Ronald G., Militant Professionalism: A Study of Organizational Conflict in High Schools. New York: Appleton-Century-Crofts, 1970.

   Corwin reports his research into the extent of militancy among school personnel, who the militants are, the issues in conflict, and other matters. Although reluctant to draw conclusions, the author suggests among other things that the most professionally oriented teachers are the most militant, something we would expect. Corwin is limited in his command of sociology, but the book is recommended reading anyway.

Cronin, Joseph M., The Control of Urban Schools, New York: The Free Press, 1973.

   If one is willing to discount the influence of controlling forces outside the local community—such as the top or subsidiary power elites—this is very likely the best book on how the intracity power structure dominates urban educational decisions. Cronin pulls no punches, and his book should be read by all prospective urban teachers.

Hack, Walter G., et al., Educational Futurism 1985, Berkeley, Calif.: McCutchan Publishing Corporation, 1971.

   Seven essays in which the writers try to project the future of public education. Essays include content about the "science of futurism" itself, but the chief focus of the book is on the future of school governance. Short, readable, and provocative.

Lieberman, Myron, The Future of Public Education, Chicago: University of Chicago Press, 1960.

   As in his other writings, Lieberman demonstrates that he is one of the sharpest and most provocative thinkers around, and never runs short of situations to criticize. Although rather extensively quoted in this chapter, students will profit by reading all of Lieberman's book and thinking about it.

Lutz, Frank W. (ed.), Toward Improved Urban Education. Worthington, O.: Charles A. Jones, 1970.

   A rather spotty book of readings that contains enough first-rate essays to make it worth looking into. Recommended are Cronin's chapter on the school superintendency and urban politics and Hartley's philosophical chapter on humanistic existentialism.

Milstein, Mike M., and James A. Belasco (eds.), *Educational Administration and the Behavioral Sciences: A Systems Perspective*, Boston: Allyn and Bacon, Inc., 1973.

A collection of twenty-five readings that are probably the best on school administration available. Its items are held together by a systems or field approach, with the emphasis on interrelatedness of all the forces that play upon our schools.

National Society for the Study of Education, *Behavioral Science and Educational Administration*, Sixty-third Yearbook, Part II. Chicago: University of Chicago Press, 1964.

This yearbook, with its more or less interesting variety of papers on the use of psychology and social science as a basis for building theories of administration, may illustrate the direction the education of future educational leaders will take.

Silberman, Charles E., *Crisis in the Classroom: The Remaking of American Education*, New York: Random House, Inc., 1970.

Of the flood of books critical of public education appearing during the past twelve to fifteen years, Silberman is one of the most scholarly and balanced writers. This lengthy but hard-hitting book is recommended primarily for its Chapter 11, "The Education of Educators," in which the author explores how we could further professionalize teaching.

Task Force on Urban Education, Wilson C. Riles, Chairman, *The Urban Education Task Force Report*. New York: Praeger Publishers, Inc., 1970.

Known as the "Riles Report," this study was kept under wraps in the U.S. Office of Education because of the unpopularity of its recommendations with President Nixon. The report got published only because an alert Congressman saw it and inserted it in the Congressional Record. The report's conclusion: without massive federal funding, there is no hope for public education in the big cities.

Epilogue

WHERE DO WE GO FROM HERE?

God takes care of drunkards, of little children, and of the United States.
M. Ostrogorski

I have tried to write a book to lead students into an examination of a number of the most critical issues of American culture as of the last half of the 70s—issues which are likely to remain central to our civilization for most if not the rest of the century—and to show some forceful implications of these issues for our public schools' work at all grade levels from K through 14.

Although this Epilogue draws supporting ideas from

other persons, it is personalized and speculative (or philosophical, if you prefer) in that it represents primarily the writer's thinking. I have presented a few "hard facts," but in the final conclusions, I found most useful my more than thirty years of experience as a teacher and social observer. My claim to expertise as a social observer rests to some degree upon a broadly based major in social science as an undergraduate, and upon a master's degree and doctorate which included at least as much social science as educational philosophy, psychology, curriculum, and methods.

However, as I look back over the years, my formal education was no more than a foundation upon which to build. My chief claim to competence as a social observer comes from extensive reading over the years and continuous learning from all sorts of persons: professional colleagues, students, lay persons in the community ranging from top-level professionals to those whose menial occupations did not prevent their having interesting and sometimes startlingly acute insights into the nature of our cultural dilemmas.

THE PIVOTAL ISSUE

As I view the polarization of the various ideological patterns that exist in this heterogeneous nation, I see ahead three alternative directions of movement. The first seems reasonably certain for the short run, and the other two as the most plausible for the long run.

The "Muddle-Through" Hypothesis

First, there is the possibility that the nation will continue muddling along with its present major institutional structures and general confusion and inconsistency in values and beliefs. This is not to suggest that institutional structures will not change: since World War II they have changed at dizzying speed, are continuing to do so in the seventies, and seem certain to thus continue for some time. But the change we have been experiencing, and according to our first scenario will persist for perhaps a few more decades, is change in which clear-cut, long-range goals are absent. It is change based largely upon accident, impulse, or the continuation of diverse and frequently contradictory trends now operating.

To the extent that long-range planning exists at all, we find it mainly in the military-industrial area. Corporate industry plans maximize profit and power as their central motives. The military establishment attempts to plan ahead in its persistent search for new weapons systems to keep the United States the most militarily powerful nation. It matters not that our military already possesses enough atomic weaponry to destroy all human life on earth many times over: the generals and admirals apparently seek a weapons capability for some imagined science fiction interplanetary war. A social critic can hardly escape wondering why the United States *has* to be more militarily powerful than the U.S.S.R. or any combination of nations, when both the United States and the U.S.S.R. already have the capability of planetary overkill some hundreds of times over.

The Federal Government sometimes claims to plan, as when it comes up regularly with schemes to end poverty, racial and sexual discrimination, urban decay, unemployment, pollution, ruinous inflation, private and public corruption, war and the like. But actions of the Federal Government all too often belie its well-publicized plans. One fairly obvious reason for this is inattention to what scholars, in contrast to most politicians, know about present and imminent social problems. For example, our most knowledgeable ecologists forecast the fuel shortages of 1973 and 1974 as much as thirty years ago. Only recently, after producing a belated variety of somewhat coordinated plans to ease our most pressing ecological problems, particularly pollution, the government suddenly discovered that a temporary but critical shortage of easily obtained fossil fuels could be dealt with only by eliminating or neutralizing most of its plans for ecological salvation. Our top political leaders ignored warnings until the crisis struck, and later weakened their own solutions. There is no good reason to suppose this situation will change much in the next few decades.

Our national distaste for long-range planning, though quite harmonious with our widely held belief that laissez-faire and advanced industrialism are compatible, suggests the very strong likelihood that the nation will continue as long as it can in a course of drift and muddle, using a band-aid approach to solving the most pressing social problems of any particular year. How long can this fumbling approach to social management continue? We get different answers, depending upon who does the answering.

Much of the writing produced by social scientists takes on an increasingly pessimistic tone. As previously noted, Robert Heilbroner has moved from a rather uncertain but neutral opinion about our future to one of deep pessimism. He sees ahead "convulsive change," forced upon us by breakdown and catastrophe, and the yielding of democracy to police state rule.[1] Other social scientists cited in previous chapters hold positions somewhere between those of many of today's more optimistic politicians and news commentators—presently euphoric because the smooth

---

[1] Robert L. Heilbroner, *An Inquiry into the Human Prospect.* W. W. Norton & Company, Inc., 1974.

succession of Gerald Ford to the Presidency seemed to prove that the American system works—and Heilbroner, but clearly much nearer Heilbroner's.

The Fascist State Hypothesis

Although the muddle-through hypothesis strikes us as the most plausible forecast for now, this hypothesis appears useful only for a limited period. Whether muddling can prevent a general collapse of culture and society for ten, twenty, or fifty years, a time seems certain to come when cultural disorganization will advance so far toward disintegration, that something will have to give. So one longer-range scenario for the future is a general demand for a strong-man, a man on horseback, who can grip the reins firmly, dig in spurs as necessary, and through force of personality —and the assistance of the corporate-military establishment—lead the nation from chaos to order. This is what a rapidly increasing number of social observers see ahead.

That the man on horseback might rally the popular imagination to the cause of democracy runs counter to the lessons of history. That he might lead the nation toward some kind of economic socialism (or communism) runs counter to the American psyche. All the evidence we have, and it seems enough, suggests that if a military dictatorship comes to the United States, its form will be fascist. When capitalist institutions are in intolerable disarray, the historical outcome has so far always been a fascist state. Communism has only emerged as a viable social movement in nations primarily rural and socially backward, except in such instances as Czechoslovakia and East Germany where communism was imposed through outside force.

Although American values have changed since the 1930s, most noticeably during the turbulent sixties when the youthful counterculture demonstrated that it could, if it raised sufficient hell, move the nation a little closer toward equalization of opportunity for minority groups, toward a questioning of America's long history of military intervention in foreign civil wars, toward a concern for protecting the natural environment upon which the future existence of the human race depends, and other matters, it still remains uncertain as to how much the deeper value structure may have changed. The greatest potential for fundamental change in a democratic direction may well lie in the Women's Movement, which although not an integral part of the counterculture of the sixties, developed parallel to it, and continues to enlarge its foundation in the seventies. Also, as we have indicated elsewhere, college youth continues to move toward more liberal and democratic values, even in the "conservative seventies." But here again, are such movements too little and too late?

If the most deeply held values of a majority of Americans remain what they were during the "red scare" following both world wars when democratic values seemed largely forgotten or shelved, or what they were during the economic collapse of the 1930s, then it would seem that fascist values surface rather easily in this country during periods of crisis. I am of the opinion that every student interested in the future cannot escape concern about what our own history has to say about *possible futures*. In this connection it is most informative to review how many Americans in the 1920s and 1930s reacted to Mussolini's own brand of fascism, his concept of the "corporate state."

John Diggins, historian at the University of California, quotes the peripatetic Emil Ludwig as saying to Mussolini in an interview, "Curiously enough, in the course of my travels I have found you more popular in America than anywhere else."[2] By intensively studying the literature of the 1920s and 1930s, Diggins found that numerous books, as well as hundreds of magazine articles, expressed hysterically fearful views of communism, mixed views of Hitler after his rise to power and generally laudatory views toward Mussolini—at least until his conquest of Ethiopia. In 1932, *Fortune* magazine was praising Mussolini, and even the liberal *Nation* published a pro-Mussolini article. At the time this was hardly surprising, since the controversial head of the Marine Corps, General Smedley Butler, was threatened with being court-martialed in 1931 because he made derogatory public statements about Mussolini.[3]

If fascism is in America's future, as numerous social analysts of the mid-seventies fear, it will not be called such. Whatever patriotic-sounding label may be used, the system itself will be indigenous to the United States just as American capitalism and imperialism have had uniquely American features. American fascism might be less harsh than that of Hitler's Germany—paternalistic even. But it seems most improbable that it will respect civil liberties or any other aspect of what we have known as democracy.

Collectivist Democracy Hypothesis

That continued industrialization, whether privately or publicly controlled, leads inexorably to increased interdependence and concentration of power, few social scientists would try to rebut. Under any industrial system

[2] John P. Diggins, *Mussolini and Fascism: The View from America*. Princeton, N.J.: Princeton University Press, 1972, pp. 22–23.

[3] Diggins, pp. 24–25, 36, 37–38.

predicated upon a continuous growth ethic, the development of irreplaceable resource scarcities creates one crisis after another. If, through a technological miracle, nuclear fusion were harnessed as a source of cheap and inexhaustible energy, it seems likely that this would serve only to accelerate the depletion of nonrenewable mineral resources and an incessant search for substitute and inevitably more expensive materials. William Ophuls, a Yale ecologist, sees 1973 as "a year dividing one age from another." He sees the new age as one of scarcity in relation to what the industrialized people of the earth are accustomed to and what the Third World nations want. He therefore labels the human society of the future a "scarcity society." The past three centuries, he feels, have been centuries of "abnormal abundance" in which the natural resources most essential to an industrial high-growth society have been easy to get at and process.

Many of these essential resources, as we observed in Chapter 12, are either already virtually exhausted or remain in abundance only in places where recovery will be so expensive—even given the assumption of abundant power—that products made from them will be perpetually scarce except for the most affluent members of society. Ophuls does not stress the point, but mass starvation in the Third World nations within the next few years is being forecast by too many experts to be ignored.

Although Ophuls is convinced that "our political future will inevitably be much less libertarian and much more authoritarian, much more communalistic than our present," he also feels that if human values could be changed so that a "steady state" or "no-growth" economic ethic were generally accepted, the future "could bring us a life of simple sufficiency that would yet allow the full expression of the human potential."[4]

Students will note that the view of Ophuls, Paul and Anne Ehrlich, Barry Commoner, and most other ecologists rules out the future of abundance for everyone on earth that Michael Harrington places his hopes on for a someday democratic socialist utopia (see Chap. 9). My own view is that the ecologists, in spite of misfiring now and then, have been sufficiently accurate in their forecasts that we disregard them only at our direst peril.

Although any imaginable democracy of the future seems bound to demand a great many more restraints on most kinds of freedom than we have been accustomed to, so long as everyone affected by such restraints has a share in deciding what they will be and how they will be applied, democracy remains a viable possibility for the future. Further, as

[4] William Ophuls, "The Scarcity Society," *Harper's Magazine*, April 1974, pp. 47–52.

more areas of culture now closed to free inquiry open—and there has been a strong trend in that direction since the early sixties—certain freedoms which are truly enriching to human life may become more abundant. I am thinking particularly of the traditional "closed areas" of culture, several of which have already been opened past any likely reinstatement. Among these are how the sexes relate, greater equality for women, a probable decline of racism, firmer establishment of freedom of expression, and similar developments long fought for by libertarians.

Of these three scenarios for the American future—continued irrational muddling, the repression of a fascist state, and a necessarily more collectivized but in some respects more free democracy than has previously existed—my own stand is, of course, for the latter. Otherwise, this book would never have been written.

EDUCATION FOR DEMOCRACY IN THE WORLD OF THE FUTURE

If we opt for exerting all influence possible to maintain such democracy as we now have and gradually expand areas of democratic decision making, the public schools must play a crucial role. Instead of denying the public schools an acknowledged political role, as many professional educators and perhaps most of the adult public would prefer, we must come to see our schools as the Founding Fathers saw them: namely, the primary instrument for keeping alive the democratic idea and making it work as a practical social arrangement. Jefferson's plan for mandatory, universal, free public schooling was not conceived as a device to teach students narrow technical skills for vocational purposes, to prepare a miniscule number of students for college entrance exams, to provide a baby-sitting service, or to keep troublesome youth off the streets. Rather, it was conceived as a means of assuring that every citizen could read, a qualification Jefferson felt necessary for adult voting citizens. Unless voters could read, comprehensively and critically, and thus inform themselves about issues and candidates, the idea of a self-governing nation seemed a farce.

To my way of thinking, mandatory free public education designed not merely to teach students to read, but also to study in depth our increasingly complex social problems and the qualifications and platforms of the politicians who present themselves for election, is even more essential in the latter twentieth century than in Jefferson's day. In the late eighteenth and early nineteenth centuries voters could learn through word of mouth a good deal about the issues of the day and the people running for office. Today, not only is a high level of literacy necessary, but also a broad background of knowledge about cultural issues. Without this, we all might as well hush up about democracy, freedom, liberty, justice, or any of the other ideals held by the Founding Fathers and all those who, formerly or presently, proclaim the virtues of democracy.

Erosion of the Original Purpose of Public Education

The views of the Founding Fathers concerning the necessity for, and proper role of, universal, free, compulsory public education have been questioned in recent years by several "revisionist" historians of education. For example, Katz argues that if our colonial and early national political leaders ever did dream of a system of education designed to foster democratic values and informed political activism, the dream was held by a small minority and soon subverted. Katz argues that actually the Founding Fathers wanted free, compulsory, universal education primarily to promote "law and order" among the urban poor. The ruling elite wanted a large passive working class, easily amenable to manipulation, and saw mandatory, state-controlled schooling as a device for brainwashing the children of immigrants to be trouble-free members of a working force serving the financial and political interests of the elite.[5]

Katz also criticizes the virtue of public education on the grounds that, in addition to its role in preserving a tight class structure, it has for a century operated through impersonal bureaucracies in the cities and has persistently promoted racism. Besides Katz, Colin Greer, Joel H. Spring, Clarence J. Karrier, and Paul Violas have argued in their own revisionist histories that American public schools have always played a chief role in keeping classes separate and the working class in its place.

R. Freeman Butts, whose books and numerous articles on the history of education have been noted for their balanced nonpolemical treatment, questions the tenability of the views of the revisionists. He does not say there is no truth in the new interpretations but rather that they focus unduly on class conflict and economic factors. To bolster his argument, Butts draws heavily on writings and public speeches by many opinion leaders of the late 1700s and early 1800s.[6]

My own feeling is that however true they may be, the historical reinterpretations of what public education has been are not to the point. What is to the point is what public education *must* become if the United States is to have a fighting chance to maintain democratic institutions into the long-range future.

[5] Michael B. Katz, *Class, Bureaucracy, and Schools: The Illusion of Educational Change in America.* New York: Praeger Publishers, Inc., 1971.

[6] R. Freeman Butts, "The Public Purpose of the Public School," *Teachers College Record,* December 1973, pp. 207–221. See also Butts' excellent article, "Assaults on a Great Idea," *The Nation,* April 30, 1973, pp. 553–560.

In addition to the denigration of public education found in the books and articles by historical revisionists, there has been a mounting wave of criticism of our public schools which began in the late 1950s and persists to the present time. This criticism has come from sincere and often very knowledgeable persons and focuses on the state of the schools in the twentieth century.

Purpose Bent to Science's Needs

The first major wave of such criticism appeared after the Soviet Union orbited its first Sputnick in 1958. The loudest critics were unconnected with public education. Most were old-school academicians who damned public education for not teaching adequately "fundamental" reading, writing, and arithmetic, and for neglecting higher mathematics and the physical sciences in secondary school. The schools were charged with lack of concern for the hard academic subjects. Critical books by Mortimer Smith, Mortimer Adler, Robert Hutchins, Arthur Bestor, and Admiral Hyman Rickover were widely read and, yielding to their pressure, most public schools "tightened up standards" and went to extremes in demands for academic excellence. This line of criticism began to fade by the mid-1960s when it became obvious that the new programs were contributing heavily to the dropout rate and producing a generation of youngsters whose attitude toward schooling in general was extremely hostile.

Purpose Geared toward Students' Needs

As so often happens, in the sixties a backlash occurred and a new group of writers appeared who criticized public education for its formalistic, academic emphasis. These writers dwelt on discrimination against minorities, alienation of students (and teachers) increased by harsh cold school environments, and the widespread apparent inability of schools to teach for self-fulfillment and other humane goals. Sunny Decker, Jim Haskins, Nat Hentoff, James Herdon, Herbert Kohl, and Jonathan Kozol were concerned primarily with the plight of ghetto youth; John Holt dealt primarily with the dilemmas of suburban youth and the inadequacies of their schools. The sociological basis of our flawed schooling was explored by Paul Goodman, Jules Henry, and Edgar Friedenberg. George Leonard proposed reforms according to the gospel of a rather naive existentialism. Ivan Illich and Everett Reimer advocated the deschooling of society altogether, a line of argument which Holt and some of the others, in their more recent writings, appear sympathetic to. This group of critics came to bear such labels as "neo-progressivists" and "neo-romantic radicals." I prefer to call this group of critics *romantic humanists* to distinguish their arguments from my own position which I like to call *scientific humanism.*

In retrospect, it may be that the criticisms and proposals of the romantic humanists did some good in spotlighting attention on the frustrations of children and youth induced by many of our commonly encountered school practices. On the other hand, many readers have construed the position of the romantics as "anti-public school" and have become deeply involved in exploring a variety of alternatives to public schooling, particularly the so-called *free school movement,* and to a lesser degree, the *non-school alternatives* posed by Illich and Reimer.

It strikes me, however, that the total number of people interested in school problems, including administrators and teachers, who have been deeply influenced by the romantic humanists remains relatively small. The free school movement has not made much headway. Public schools that have adopted their own versions of romantic humanism in the form of "free classrooms" have rarely adopted anything more innovative than cosmetic changes which, in long-range effect, are not changes at all.

There have been various developments, beginning as far back as the early twentieth century, which have jeopardized the ideal of universal public, free, compulsory, and secular education. I will next examine briefly some threats to the original ideal of public education as the primary instrument for perpetuating a democratic society.

The Curriculum Explosion

In the late nineteenth century, after the idea of free, compulsory secondary education had been established both legally and within the American value structure, in general all except the largest high schools offered but one pattern of courses: a college preparatory curriculum. But early in the twentieth century virtually all larger secondary schools and many smaller ones, began offering competing curriculums with a homemaking or vocational emphasis: home economics, secretarial/business, and various kinds of shop courses for boys. With the passage of time, the secondary curriculum began to proliferate with electives and elementary school curriculums began to add new topics and subjects also.

I need but mention a few of these proliferations to make the point. Physical and health education have become universally required (although in the seventies questions are being raised about the validity of making these subjects requirements for graduation). In connection with physical education, an emphasis on spectator sports developed to the point where many high schools are much better known for their athletic teams than for anything else, and special assemblies and rallies related to interschool athletics take up a significant part of the time of students. Enrollment in health and physical education includes approximately 120 percent of total enrollment between grades 7 and 12. (Percentages may exceed 100 percent when some students take more than one class in a subject simultaneously.)[7]

Numerous vocational subjects, intended to give students saleable job skills upon receipt of a high school diploma, have been added. The steady drift of secondary education toward a largely vocational emphasis that began early in the century has shown no signs of abating, and as of 1974 pressures to vocationalize the curriculum from the early elementary grades on through senior high school seem greater than ever. Vocational subjects tend to be taught as narrow specialisms, as straight technology, with no concern for study about the cultural milieu in which the vocations operate.

The general vocational area which pulls the largest enrollment is business education. Between grades 7 and 12, about 40 percent of all students are taking some course in business. Second in popularity among vocational subjects is industrial arts; enrollment in this area includes about 29 percent of all students between grades 7 and 12. Agriculture, distributive education, and what the U.S. Office of Education calls "vocational trade and industrial education" account for another 12+ percent of enrollment. Thus, more than 80 percent of students between grades 7 and 12 are enrolled in one or more narrow vocational subjects.

Other subjects which are rarely taught in a way to promote an understanding of critical social issues and help prepare students for democratic citizenship include mathematics, the natural sciences, music, foreign languages, and a variety of other courses in which total national enrollment is not high enough to be of much significance.

In an important sense, health and physical education, the vocational subjects, much math and science, foreign languages, and much music and art could be regarded as "curriculum clutter" since their subject matter does not address itself to the central role of public education. Our public schools could afford a great deal of curriculum clutter if they were doing anything approaching an adequate job of teaching the kind of critical thinking and providing the knowledgable background necessary for intelligent citizenship in a complex industrial democracy.

Since signs of intelligent voting are so difficult to locate in American culture—the Presidential election of 1972 being a truly classical example—the question immediately arises as to whether as a nation we can afford public schools in which such a large proportion of students' time is devoted to studies that have no bearing on effective citizenship. If the

[7] Figures from Kenneth A. Simon and W. Vance Grant, *Digest of Educational Statistics,* Washington, D.C.: U.S. Department of Health, Education, and Welfare, 1972, p. 42.

most pressing need of a nation that calls itself a self-governing republic is an adult public knowledgable enough to vote intelligently, then until our public schools have achieved this goal probably the most crucial question to ask is, Is there room in the curriculum for anything else except cultural studies which are both penetrating and honest?

What Subjects Are of First Priority in a Democracy?

Until democracy is solidly enough established in the United States so that some form of fascism will not continue to be an ever-present threat, it would seem logical that cultural studies could best be pursued through reading and field/laboratory programs which have something more significant to say about the culture than the mythical world of Dick and Jane. The general subject areas most indicated would seem to be the social studies and literature in all its forms (fiction, nonfiction, drama, and poetry). If taught with such an object in mind, both art and music could also be valuable agents for teaching about cultural issues, as could certain courses in business, home economics, and the natural sciences.

However, the foregoing paragraph talks only about what could be. As it now stands, the heaviest public school student enrollment is in classes called by the U.S. Office of Education "English language arts." According to the most recently available statistics, more than 140 percent of students between grades 7 and 12 are enrolled in one or more courses in this general category. This suggests that with respect to money and teacher and student time spent, this area receives the greatest emphasis. Yet, as indicated previously, the Office of Education itself now concedes that at least 18 percent of American adults are functionally illiterate and other studies indicate that in at least one large urban center (Chicago) the figure is as high as 50 percent. It is evident that the large effort we put into English has not so far paid off for large numbers of students. Hopefully, it has paid off for a minority.

But failure to teach basic reading skills to a large proportion of students is only one aspect of the whole English/language arts dilemma. Literature courses and drama programs could be first-rate media for teaching about cultural issues, honestly and in depth. But are they? There is little evidence that this is the case except in a minority of schools and for a minority of students. Otherwise, it would be impossible to explain the dismal ignorance of the adult population with high school diplomas who have little or no understanding of the kinds of issues we have a right to assume would be the focus of literature and drama study.

Third in overall student enrollment (after English and health/physical education) are the social studies. Of all students between grades 7 and 12, about 107 percent are enrolled in one or more social studies courses.

Although the Office of Education has ceased publishing statistics on enrollment in specific subjects within a general category, we can safely assume that more pupils are enrolled in history, both United States and world, than any other social studies subject. Second to history is probably civics or government. Pupils are being dosed with enough social studies, as with literature and drama, for us to expect some positive results. However, as in the case of literature and drama, no competent student of culture would be likely to claim that secondary school social studies has made many adults function adequately as self-governing citizens. In fact, there is abundant research evidence (some cited earlier in the book) indicating that pupils possess more wrong information about cultural issues when they are seniors than when they were freshmen.

The only conclusion we can draw at this point is that the public school curriculum has been overloaded with courses which in no way serve the fundamental purposes of public education as the Founding Fathers envisioned them, and that those courses which should serve these purposes have no useful long-range impact on a majority of pupils who take them. Clearly we need most to improve the quality of teaching in subjects that lend themselves most readily to cultural study and to this writer it seems obvious that we need a crash program, particularly in the literary and social studies areas, to revamp both the content of the curriculum and the effectiveness of instruction.

The Blunting of a Humanistic Emphasis

I have defined what I mean by humanism elsewhere and will say here only that the present discussion refers not to the various utopian or romantic humanisms that some educators have promoted, but to the scientific humanism which is but another name for the position that emerged from the integration of the Peirce-James-Dewey version of experimentalism with the Gestalt field psychology of Kurt Lewin and his followers.

In my opinion, education that does not carry a strong humanistic emphasis can never prepare people to function as they must to maintain a self-governing democracy. Mechanical approaches to teaching and learning produce training, not education; conditioned robots, not critical thinkers.

Mechanical teaching in the past American public schools have always suffered from teaching which was authoritarian, totalitarian, and routinized, the short-run results of which were rote memorization of facts or performance of skills. This was the case in the American colonies, whose educational practices did little more than ape those then prevalent in Europe. It remained the case after the coming of nationhood, through the nineteenth century, and is still the case in the mid-seventies.

This aspect of our educational history is so well known that we would not bring it up here, except to make a point which we rarely see made elsewhere. *The effect on students of a given approach to teaching may vary tremendously with variations in the total cultural setting.* Rote teaching and learning in some situations may translate into an education with strong humanistic overtones, whereas in other situations this would not be the case. Perhaps we can make the point with an example.

The present author was privileged to have had his first eight grades of schooling in a traditional, one-room red brick schoolhouse, located in a strictly rural setting (the nearest farmhouse was almost half a mile distant). Students in all eight grades sat in the same room, each at a desk wide enough for two students—a situation which made it possible for students to study together by pairs when the teacher gave permission. We had a different teacher each year, each one inexperienced in teaching, with only a high school diploma and one summer of normal school training as preparation. Only one of the eight teachers knew much subject matter.

The teaching materials were county-adopted textbooks, poorly written and often factually inaccurate. The curriculum included reading, writing, arithmetic, geography, civics, and history, with the addition in the eighth grade of health education. There was the traditional daily flag salute and group recitation of the Lord's Prayer. All we can remember learning from the formal curriculum was a slight increment in reading and arithmetic, which we had learned primarily from our parents, and a smattering of largely irrelevant geography—mostly promptly forgotten.

But the amount of life-related learning was tremendous. The younger children learned about sex from the seventh and eighth graders. We learned a considerable amount of biology: a nearby stream provided frogs and many creepy crawly things to slip into the teacher's desk. Birds, small animals, and vegetation were abundant. We played and fought together, loved and hated one another. We talked incessantly about all manner of subjects. The teachers shared in much of our play. Teachers could not hide their humanness: when one of my nineteen-year-old teachers took up with a twenty-three-year-old eighth-grade boy everyone knew about it and took it quite in stride.

So we learned a great deal about people and nature and their interdependence. We had abundant opportunity to test ourselves in our games, our fighting, our making up, and our loving. Above all, we learned to function as a community, in which participatory democracy developed naturally. Our education was humanistic in the best sense of the term. The erroneous textbooks were too incidental to damage us. The canned problems in arithmetic did not make robots of us nor did the teachers' flash card drills, because every day was devoted to problem solving for humanistic ends.

This kind of education is considered hopelessly old-fashioned now. Even if contemporary educators considered it meritorious, they would regard it as highly inefficient and expensive compared with modern consolidated schools where students on a single campus number hundreds or thousands.

Mechanical teaching in the seventies Although school boards, administrators, some teachers, and other apologists for education as it is might deny it, there is every reason to believe that public education of the seventies is not only even more mechanical than that of the nineteenth and earlier twentieth centuries, but that it has taken on a much heavier complexion of authoritarianism/totalitarianism than in earlier times. This is in part because the cultural milieu has itself become, in some important respects, more authoritarian and totalitarian; but perhaps even more, because the more immediate environmental setting and in-school situations themselves no longer contain those factors mentioned above, in the discussion of my schooling, which added a strong humanistic element to education in spite of what teachers and teaching materials were like.

Teaching today involves processing large numbers of students. The easiest way to do this is to imitate the assembly line methods developed by Henry Ford and updated by Norbert Wiener's cybernetics. While the psychology of our teachers in the little brick schoolhouse was learned intuitively by "feel," today's dominant educational psychology is either the programmed learning of B. F. Skinner translated into the ghastly expression, "behavior mod," or, perhaps even worse, the confused eclecticism of a Benjamin S. Bloom or a Robert M. Gagné. Every student is expected to learn the behavioral responses demanded by long lists of behavioral objectives: everyone is expected to learn the same thing, even if paced at his or her own speed. Teaching materials are mainly prepackaged. This is all very authoritarian and totalitarian and students are expected to take it seriously, and hence themselves become authoritarian and totalitarian. My childhood schoolbooks were also prepackaged, but the chief subject matter was the world of nature and other human beings, known intimately. The talisman of much modern education is PBE, performance based education, memorized and automated responses—learning how to make socially acceptable wiggles. If a student rebels, the principal may call the police.

Contemporary education is innovative The newer schools have large open spaces, moveable walls, modular scheduling, team teaching, teaching machines, teachers' aides, closed circuit television, and all the rest. We have innovation except for one item: in the social studies and literature, the *content* is scarcely more modern than when I was in school. The books students would like most to read and which would inform the most about the sleazy features of our culture, its ideological conflicts and its other problems are still banned from all but the most adventuresome big-city high schools. Social studies textbooks and other teaching materials tell the same lies, except in a smoother, and perhaps more convincing way.

Although the environmental pressures of an advanced industrial culture, in which economic, military, and other major institutional structures seem to their present managers to require an authoritarian/totalitarian framework is all very real and cannot help but influence public school practice, it seems to me clearly a copout for professional educators to insist that the kind of mass education we are now stuck with demands the same type of institutional structure, the same managerial techniques, the same uniformity of subject matter and method, as the rest of our society has moved into.

Although it smacks of the unthinkable to suggest that the main thing public schools are doing in the mid-seventies is preparing the new generation for adjustment to a fascist police state, many of us can draw no other conclusion than that this outcome is implicit in current educational practices, whether or not recognized by those who now control our schools. Nothing in the present educational scene, except education in the humanities at our more prestigious universities and liberal arts colleges, seems designed to help pupils—as adults—resist the blandishments of authoritarian political demagogues and their at least figuratively black-shirted followers.

The Illich's and Reimer's can indeed make a case that the culture would be on safer ground if the kind of formal schooling which now exists were abolished. But their argument has at least one fatal flaw which is forcefully and clearly stated by Butts when he says,

> We would still need the public schools [even if most of their present functions could be performed as well by other agencies] for the prime public purpose of learning those things that the whole people can only learn together: how to run a democratic society. And I agree with the Revolutionary generation that for the safety of the Republic this cannot be left to chance.[8]

Future Potential

Is it really all as bad as I have asserted? In some school systems, very likely yes; in others, very likely no. Further, the opportunities for making education both exciting and meaningful are probably as great as ever, if not more so.

I have tried to describe the kinds of problem areas on which teaching must center, and the study of which must have first priority in the thinking of anyone who cares about the preservation of democracy. Some

[8] Butts, "The Public Purpose of the Public School," p. 220.

of these problem areas were discussed in Chapter 13 on long-range goals. But, as I suggested in that chapter and elsewhere, it is meaningless to discuss such goals if there is no practical means in sight of implementing them.

Hence, it was necessary to conclude with a chapter (14) on how the control of public education appears to be shifting from the authoritarian and incompetent to the professional and democratic. I tried to demonstrate that in one area of major lag, the education of administrators, there is good reason now to hope for considerable improvement during the next decade. I also tried to show that teachers, through both better education and better organization, can achieve much more control over their own teaching than they now have, and that our younger teachers and university students now working in credential programs represent a quite different breed than the typical teacher who entered the profession fifteen or twenty years ago.

I have also given over much space to presenting specimen types of subject matter, the highly problematic, more-or-less closed areas of culture with which schools must deal directly and honestly if any significant improvement in the curriculum is to be had. This was the purpose of Part II of the book. In connection with Part II, I also tried to demonstrate, in the way we handled our materials, a great deal about the *how* of problem-centered teaching. I tried to show the advantages, as well as the cautions required, in using as an organizational basis for content controversial assertions of the type I have called "outrageous hypotheses." At the ends of the chapters in Part II, I tried to include comprehensive annotated bibliographies which would help teachers and students test many more hypotheses in each closed area than the one sample hypothesis we had to content ourselves with.

Along with several themes described in the Preface, and obvious to those who have read the book, I have also intended to suggest that there is much hope to be found in the developing values of the American youth culture—primarily the college population subculture, but increasingly also the out-of-school working youth subculture. Although the apathy of the young toward political activism bothers me, it seems clear that young people of high school and college age, including adults who were that age in the 1960s, harbor increasingly liberal and democratic views about most issues. If this view is correct—and what opinion survey data we have suggests it is—we need to take very seriously indeed Margaret Mead's "outrageous hypothesis," stated in Chapter 1, that we are moving into an era when we must rely ever more heavily on the young educating their elders.

Reflective Thinking as the Preferred Method of Instruction

Although I have tried consistently to demonstrate a type of analysis which can properly be labeled reflective. a bit more needs to be said about this mode of instruction. Harry Broudy, of the University of Illinois, has suggested that approaches to classroom teaching can be classified as belonging to one of three modes: (1) didactic teaching, (2) heuristic teaching, and (3) philetic teaching.

The basic principle of didactic teaching is that the teacher, using whatever techniques may be personally congenial, transmits knowledge to students. Such knowledge is chosen and organized by the teacher and offered to students on the basis that it is important for them to know.

The basic principle of philetic teaching is the creation of a closely empathetic or loving relationship between teacher and students. It is relatively unstructured, permissive, and student-guided. An example is the sensitivity group in which participants establish an intimacy that permits candid exchange of intimate ideas.

The basic principle of heuristic teaching is that students, or students and teacher working together, select problems for study which have an a priori meaningfulness for students because they relate in some clear way to the students' own lives. Heuristic teaching may utilize hypothesis testing in the manner I have tried to illustrate in Part II of this book.

I tend to identify the heuristic mode of teaching with reflective thinking. Reflective thinking is critical thinking, scientific thinking broadly defined. Its essence lies in testing hypotheses that simultaneously relate to student interests and involve matters important to cultural survival. But it would be a mistake to try to delineate sharply these three modes of teaching. A teacher whose primary leaning is toward the study of problems meaningful to students and the larger culture is almost certain at times to transmit background knowledge, through lecture or some other technique, because it is needed to pursue further study of the problem at hand. Further, it seems likely that teaching is generally more effective if there is warmth in the situation, such as we used to mean by the much overused cliche, rapport. Thus, all three modes of teaching may be present in the style of any particular teacher, including teachers committed to reflective study of problems.

This book is intended primarily as an aid to teachers with a heuristic leaning, who at the same time need a tool to provide structure. Students are so accustomed to structure that problem-centered teaching often bogs down without some kind of carefully devised guide. Hopefully, this book will have stimulated much reflection on the part of students, but within a framework that has prevented intolerable frustration. It may well be that students learn best when they are provoked to think to a point just short of the level of frustration that leads to psychological withdrawal. If the book has helped students do this, the effort that has gone into its writing will have been well worthwhile.

NAME INDEX

SUBJECT INDEX